Best Wishes to
my "cover stars"
LR Willson & Sons

Sam Clark
12.7.07

FREEDOM
IN THE
WORKPLACE

FREEDOM IN THE WORKPLACE

THE UNTOLD STORY OF MERIT SHOP CONSTRUCTION'S CRUSADE AGAINST COMPULSORY TRADE UNIONISM

BY SAMUEL COOK

Since 1947
REGNERY PUBLISHING, INC.
An Eagle Publishing Company • Washington, DC

Library of Congress Cataloging-in-Publication Data

Cook, A. Samuel, 1921-
Freedom in the workplace : the untold story of merit shop construction's crusade
against compulsory trade unionism / by A. Samuel Cook.
p. cm.
Includes bibliographical references and index.
ISBN 0-89526-035-2
1. Associated Builders & Contractors (U.S.)—History. 2. Construction industry—
United States—Management—History. 3. Building trades—United States—
Management—History. 4. Open and closed shop—United States—History.
5. Construction workers—Labor unions—United States--History. I. Title.

HD9715.U52C595 2005
331.88'124'0973--dc22

2 0 0 5 0 0 0 6 5 5

The front cover photograph is by Bo Rader of the *Baltimore Sun*, Feb. 1, 1990,
on the site of a contruction trade union strike at the Veterans Administration Hospital
located in downtown Baltimore City, Maryland.

*In memory of my college classmates and other dear friends
who gave their lives in World War II to keep America free.*

*This book is also dedicated to my beloved wife, "Bernie,"
who believes in the cause.*

ABC'S FORTY-SEVEN NATIONAL PRESIDENTS
WHO REPRESENT A PROUD TRADITION
OF MERIT SHOP LEADERSHIP

1950
CHARLES MULLAN
Mullan Contracting Co.
General Contractor
Baltimore, MD

1951
CHARLES KNOTT
Henry A. Knott, Inc.
General Contractor
Baltimore, MD

1952–1953
EDWARD COLWILL
Colwill Construction Co.
General Contractor
Baltimore, MD

1954
CHARLES FEIHE
Mullan Contracting Co.
General Contractor
Baltimore, MD

1955
WILLIAM WILDBERGER
Wildberger-Best
Construction Co.
General Contractor
Baltimore, MD

1956
ROLAND STOLZENBACH
Roland Electrical Co.
Electrical Contractor
Baltimore, MD

1957
JAMES CAMPBELL
Harry T. Campbell Sons Corp.
Concrete Contractor
Towson, MD

1958–1959
LARRY BEST
Best Construction Co.
General Contractor
Baltimore, MD

1960
JOHN KNOTT
Henry A. Knott, Inc.
General Contractor
Baltimore, MD

1961–1962
CHARLES MARSH
Elevator Engineer Co.
Elevator Contractor
Baltimore, MD

1963–1964
TRACY COLEMAN
Coleman & Woods, Inc.
General Contractor
Silver Spring, MD

1965–1966
JAMES LONG
Miller & Long, Inc.
Concrete Contractor
Bethesda, MD

1967–1968
FRED SCHNABEL
Andrichyn & Schnabel, Inc.
General Contractor
Landsdale, PA

1969–1970
JOHN LOCHARY
Property Construction Co.
General Contractor
Baltimore, MD

1971–1972
JOSEPH LAMONACA
Joseph LaMonaca, Inc.
General Contractor
Lancaster, PA

1973–1974
MICHAEL CALLAS
Callas Contractors, Inc.
General Contractor
Hagerstown, MD

1975
PHILIP ABRAMS
Abreen Corporation
General Contractor
Needham Heights, MA

1976
JOE M. RODGERS
Joe M. Rodgers & Associates
General Contractor
Nashville, TN

1977
GERALD OLIVER
Zimmerman Construction Co.
General Contractor
Traverse City, MI

1978
JOSEPH BURTON
Joseph J. Hock, Inc.
General Contractor
Baltimore, MD

1979
ROBERT TURNER
Paisan Construction Co.
General Contractor
Houston, TX

1980
TED KENNEDY
BE&K, Inc.
General Contractor
Birmingham, AL

1981
FRANZ JUNE
Gulf States, Inc.
General Contractor
Freeport, TX

1982
JOHN FIELDER
South Coast Electric, Inc.
Electrical Contractor
Santa Ana, CA

1983
ED FROHLING
Mountain States Mineral, Inc.
Mining Contractor
Tucson, AZ

1984
PAT ALIBRANDI
Interstate Electrical, Inc.
Electrical Contractor
Burlington, MA

1985
WILLIAM GENTRY
Chantilly Construction Co.
General Contractor
Chantilly, VA

1986
JEAN HAILS
Hails Construction Co.
General Contractor
Rosewell, GA

1987
JOHNNY JONES
Stanley Jones Corporation
Mechanical Contractor
South Fulton, TN

1988
MIKE PERKINS
Perkins Construction Co.
General Contractor
Dayton, OH

1989
ROBERT TURNER
R.L. Turner Corporation
General Contractor
Zionsville, OH

1990
JOHN CHAPIN
Willmar Electric Co.
Electrical Contractor
Willmar, MN

1991
JOHN SMITH
Lake Mechanical Co.
Mechanical Contractor
Eustis, FL

1992
STEVE WESTRA
Westra Construction Co.
General Contractor
Waupun, WI

1993
JOE IVEY
Ivey Mechanical, Inc.
Mechanical Contractor
Kosciusko, MS

1994
LEO ANHALT
SSI, Inc.
Metal Building Contractor
Ft. Smith, AR

1995
GARY VOS
Dan Vos Construction Co.
General Contractor
Ada, MI

1996
GARY HESS
Hess Mechanical, Inc.
Mechanical Contractor
Upper Marlboro, MD

1997
JOHN JENNINGS
Jack Jennings & Sons
General Contractor
Orlando, FL

1998
BEN HOUSTON
TD Industries, Inc.
Mechanical Contractor
Dallas, TX

1999
DAVID M. BUSH
Adena Corporation
General Contractor
Mansfield, OH

2000
W. THOMAS MUSSER
Tri-M Corporation
Electrical Contractor
Kennett Square, PA

2001
*HENRY G. KELLY
Austin Industrial, Inc.
General Contractor
Houston, TX

2002
*KEN ADAMS
Pace Electric, Inc.
Electrical Contractor
Wilmington, DE

2003
*EDWARD L. RISPONE
Industrial Specialty
Contractors
Baton Rouge, LA

2004
*CAROLE L. BIONDA
Nova Group, Inc.
Heavy Contractor
Napa, CA

2005
*GARY D. RODEN
AGUIRREcorporation
Design and Construction
Dallas, TX

* Title changed from "President" to "Chairman of the Board" effective January 1, 2001.

VERITAS

"No part of the world of human action or ideas lies closer to the central issues of our times than do the problems involved in labor relations. One may say that the heart of the matter lies in the conflict between individual freedom and the increasing activity of the state; or in the struggle between limited government and totalitarianism; or in subordination of the rule of law to executive authority... Regardless of the manner of statement, labor relations are the world of today in capsule."

DR. SYLVESTER PETRO
THE LABOR POLICY OF THE FREE SOCIETY
FORMER PROFESSOR, N.Y. UNIVERSITY SCHOOL OF LAW
AND WAKE FOREST UNIVERSITY;
ASSOCIATED WITH THE FOUNDATION FOR ECONOMIC FREEDOM;
AND ONE-TIME UNION ORGANIZER

CONTENTS

PART THREE: ABC Counter-Attacks

On June 2, 2000, at the 50th anniversary convention of the Associated Builders and Contractors ("ABC") held in Baltimore, Maryland, the author, Samuel Cook, was presented an award as one of its nine "leaders of the twentieth century who significantly influenced and strengthened the merit shop construction industry throughout the United States." Upon receiving this honor, Mr. Cook told the 1,900 contractors assembled there who represented ABC chapters located throughout the United States:

> *"For over forty years ABC has been much more to me than just another client. Merit shop construction is a noble cause, a crusade to protect and defend what I hold near and dear to my heart: American free enterprise!"*

PROLOGUE

ONE OF THE MEANINGS OF THE WORD **"CRUSADE"** is "a vigorous, concerted action for some cause or idea, or against some abuse."[1] In that sense, here is the untold story of the merit shop crusade to protect workplace freedom from compulsory trade unionism in the American construction industry. I participated in this movement as a labor lawyer during its formative years. Many critical excursions into modern times are also reported.

The documented narrative is based upon crises in the building and construction industry that have been caused by the ruthless goal of the AFL-CIO's affiliated building and construction trades unions to monopolize it. Equally documented here is the heroic response from a unique organization of free enterprise "merit shoppers" known as the *Associated Builders and Contractors, Inc.,* or *"ABC."* They and their employees have been the target of this union warfare for over half a century.

The term "merit shop" means that construction projects will be awarded on the basis of merit in open competition to the lowest qualified and responsible bidders working together in harmony, regardless of whether they or their employees choose—of their own volition and without coercion from any source—to work on a non-union or unionized basis.

This basic principle revolutionized the building and construction industry. It reflects the American heritage of liberty and the inalienable right to pursue a livelihood, with roots in the Declaration of Independence and the Constitution of the United States. It also assures construction owners, users, consumers, and taxpayers the best possible services and products for their dollars.

One writes out of one thing only—one's own experience. Everything depends on how relentlessly one forces from this experience the last drop, sweet or bitter, it can possibly give.

JAMES BALDWIN
HISTORIAN

The epic tale falls into three separate and distinct categories. **Part One** is called "Heart of the Merit Shop." It establishes the construction environment in which ABC was created in 1950; the origin of the label "merit shop"; and the factual and legal foundations necessary to understand the rest of the story. **Part Two** is about "Mobocracy on the Picket Lines." It describes the nationwide conspiracy of coercion and terrorism perpetrated by the building trades unions against the rapidly expanding ABC and its non-union members in the 1960s and 1970s. **Part Three** reports an "ABC Counter-attack" during the remainder of the twentieth century through economic, political, and legal victories over compulsory trade unionism, against all odds. The story ends with a synopsis of ABC as a remarkable free enterprise institution and some of its leading members as they enter the twenty-first century by defending America's inevitable cycle of liberty from new schemes of the building trades unions to destroy the *merit shop crusade*.

A Unique Industry

The construction business in America is unlike any other kind of enterprise. It's a world of its own. One out of every six workers in our country earns a living directly or indirectly from this industry and it accounts for over 7 percent of the gross national product.[2] Annual total revenue of the top 400 American contractors exceeds $200 billion[3] and total construction in 2004 is estimated at $885 billion.[4] But the inner workings of this singular calling are ignored by most of the news media and seldom understood by the general public.

Construction is performed in a special theatre with two distinct casts: *non-union firms and unionized firms*.

In the ideal entrepreneurial setting, open and competitive job bidding and timely completion of quality work within budgetary commitments are the measures of success or failure. These factors in turn create a speculative business characterized by fluctuations in product demand and prone to economic casualties. Fortunes have been made and lost in a financier's suite, an estimator's computer, a politician's office, or at a collective bargaining table, a union-struck project site, a government agency, in a court of law.

Property developers and owners control this dynamic field of endeavor. They solicit bids from general contractors or professional construction managers for made-to-order building projects. Assignments also include additions, alterations, reconstruction, maintenance, and repair to existing structures.

The general contractor or construction manager who is awarded the job becomes responsible for its coordination and satisfactory completion. Although they may perform a portion of the work with their own crews, they assign much of the actual building to specialty subcontractors who bid successfully for it and frequently perform in only one trade. These projects range widely in size. There are millions of small jobs performed by self-employed individuals and firms with just a few workers. At the other extreme, there are dozens of national and international construction giants who build complex structures costing billions of dollars and involving thousands of employees.

The industry also is divided into three general categories, based on type of project and the skills, materials and equipment needed. About one-third are generals and their subs who create buildings for business, industry, and philanthropic institutions. Another third are "heavy construction" contractors who build highways, bridges, tunnels, and other infrastructure. The remaining third are residential homebuilders. Governments employ all three categories.[5]

On the surface, construction is one of the most visible of all businesses. At one time or another, everybody watches the unfolding drama. "Hard hats" frequently carry out their daily tasks in plain view of the public. And construction is a hazardous way to make a living. The nature of the work involves handling huge weights, cumbersome materials, dangerous tools, and powerful machines. Job assignments can be on crowded highways, around heat, cold, noise, toxicity and explosives, in foul weather, or at great heights and depths. Physical stamina is essential and the list of precarious situations is endless. Protective clothing and special devices are worn to shield eyes, mouths, ears, and bodies. Safety is both a minute-to-minute and long-range concern.

Manpower Problems

Employment often is uncertain. It may be seasonal, on a project-by-project basis, or continuous. It is cyclical with the state of the economy and the vagaries of local labor markets. It can require overtime work at night or on

> **When I want to understand what is happening today and try to anticipate what will happen tomorrow, I look back. A page of history is worth a volume of logic.**
>
> OLIVER WENDELL HOLMES
> SUPREME COURT JUSTICE

Treat a man as he is, and he will remain so. Treat a man as he can be and ought to be, and he will become as he can and ought to be.

GOETHE
DRAMATIST

weekends to finish a job on schedule or there can be a sudden business cutback and layoff of workers.

Today a shortage of construction personnel exists at all levels. Trained craftsmen are independent, mobile, aging, and difficult to obtain and retain. Recent statistics show that through the year 2010, males age fifty-five and over will constitute 70 percent of the country's skilled labor.[6] Technicians, engineers, foremen, managers, and many other job classifications also are in great demand.

A conservative estimate places the annual shortfall of competent construction manpower at 250,000. Good workers must be sought out and enticed because construction's negative public image of sporadic, perilous, and arduous work in all climes does not entice young people away from today's soft society in spite of financial rewards. About 20 percent of those who join the American work force from now until 2012 will be immigrants, mostly Hispanic and Asian.[7]

Many of the labor crafts in building and construction—even in this age of technology and product innovation—do not lend themselves to electronics or push-button robotics. The base of the industry's *non-union workforce* consists of employees performing various levels of manual, semi-skilled, and skilled work. They gain on-the-job experience and classroom training as laborers or helpers and advance on their individual merit to become multiskilled mechanics. The alternative "blue collar" workforce—controlled by the *trade unions*—endures a long and formal progression from indentured apprentice to journeyman status in rigid, antiquated crafts founded originally on medieval nepotism.

All of these artisans—recruited from both the non-union and union training programs—are employed by general contractors and specialty subcontractors to perform in their own disciplines. They must work side by side with other types of craftspersons as teammates for mutual achievement at the project under construction.

Unfortunately, the necessary harmony does not always exist. Professional expertise, dedicated work habits, integrity, and cooperation share the human relations stage with incompetence, autocracy, greed, apathy, corruption, and violence. The underlying scenario features a physical, political, legal, and economic collision of two ideologies: *free enterprise vs. compulsory unionism.*

The Birth of ABC's Merit Shop

Because of this historic impasse, a half-century ago the city of Baltimore, Maryland, became the birthplace of the Associated Builders and Contractors. Today ABC is the largest coalition of contractors and subcontractors in America. It unites and services not only thousands of commercial, industrial, institutional, and public works contractors and specialty subcontractors of all types and sizes but also their business associates in every supporting arm of the construction industry.[8]

This ABC phenomenon was created in 1950 by three non-union general contractors, one unionized subcontractor, one non-union subcontractor, one non-union homebuilder, and an architect-developer. They were all doing business in the metropolitan Baltimore area and they all believed in the same entrepreneurial concept. It was born in the fires of a monopolistic marketplace and forged in the battles over forced union membership.

The seven pioneers christened their mission "the open shop" but it eventually became known as the "**merit shop**." During the last half of the twentieth century, many contractors began to reject the obligatory unionism demanded by building trades labor organizations because it strangled their businesses. They were handicapped by collective bargaining agreements that mandated exclusive union representation of all craft workers and their foremen. These labor contracts contained inflated wage and benefits increases, restrictive work rules, and job "featherbedding" practices that reduced profit margins, inhibited operational efficiency, and created jurisdictional grievances, slowdowns, and strikes. Big Labor, in effect, was performing a hysterectomy on the goose that lays the golden eggs.

In dramatic contrast, ABC's merit shop initiative created multi-skilled job training programs and team-coordinated work practices. Employees cross traditional craft lines and readily adapt to the new tools, materials, and job assignments required by ever-advancing technology. They receive fair wages and employee benefits with year-round job security, which increase worker morale and productivity. The anchor is cost-effective but fair and firm management in control of its employees and its business decisions.

These endowments result in a high-quality product, reasonably priced, delivered on schedule, within budget, with a minimum of people problems.

The test of a first-rate intelligence is to hold two opposed ideas in the mind at the same time and still retain the ability to function.

F. SCOTT
FITZGERALD
NOVELIST

They are also some of the reasons why the building and construction trades unions—like their industrial and commercial union counterparts—have seen a devastating decline in their share of America's workforce since 1950. Over those same years ABC's membership has grown to more than *23,000* construction and construction-related firms in *84* chapters located across the United States. And the *non-union* portion of the construction industry today builds over *85 percent* of its total national market.[9] (Craft union sources claim that this percentage ratio is lower.)[10]

Although national census figures track a million little "mom and pop" handy-crafters, the average ABC member employs fifteen to twenty-five people. Many of America's construction giants—with thousands of employees and gross volumes of business in the billions of dollars who perform on both a national and international basis—are members too.[11]

Terrorism in the Workplace

Organized labor's uncompromising objective is to monopolize all building and construction work under its archaic but sacrosanct craft traditions through mandatory union membership *at any price*. This end has justified every means from political power, legal ploys, and economic leverage to coercion, sabotage, and brute force. The notorious International Brotherhood of Teamsters[12] is an affiliated ally and supports building trades union objectives.

For more than half a century, the business and personal lives of ABC member-contractors, their employees, and their families have been invaded by this nationwide union conspiracy of evil. Broken bones, torn bodies, death threats, and the devastation of property are not philosophic differences of opinion.

The building trades also intimidate neutral parties such as construction owners, developers and users, material and equipment suppliers, architects, engineers, lenders, and creditors.

All the while—masked under a legitimate labor license to "organize the unorganized"—there is a long record of union favoritism by the executive, legislative, and judicial branches of government at all levels. Biased bureaucrats downplay or ignore strong-arm union tactics involving construction projects where non-union employees are exercising their constitutional right to work. Uncivil public servants also prosecute frivolous union charges involving non-union construction management's alleged violations of workplace laws and regulations.

Big Labor's goal never changes: compelling all contractors and subcontractors in the United States to employ outmoded trade union labor exclusively on all building projects or go out of business.

That agenda made the seven founders of the Associated Builders and Contractors and its thousands of subsequent members evermore resolute. They responded with bravery, integrity, and dignity—in this merit shop crusade for freedom in the construction workplace.

Samuel Cook
May 2005

O wad some power the giftie gie us To see oursel's as ithers see us.

ROBERT BURNS
POET

PART ONE

HEART OF THE MERIT SHOP

"The longer you look back, the further you can see forward."

CHAPTER 1

CONSTRUCTION TRADE UNION CORNERSTONES

A BARRAGE OF BULLETS RIPPED through an office doorway of the Upthegrove family's marine construction business in Opa-Locka, Florida. "Oh my god, don't move, anybody!" screamed Yvonne Upthegrove.

The targets were Yvonne's husband, Lingo, and his brother, Howard. A few days later the brakes of a huge crane were sabotaged. Its three-thousand-pound boom suddenly dropped thirty feet, fracturing Lingo's skull. He was unconscious for a week and almost died.

Within a month the crane boom fell again. Someone had poured acid on the brake bands. Luckily nobody was hurt that time, but expensive and time-consuming restoration was required and the Upthegroves had to rent a used crane. Next, a grinding compound was poured into its engine and the tires were cut. Repairs cost $3,600. Similar sabotage was performed on the firm's floating pile driver. Then an $85,000 rented crane was firebombed and a security guard's car was burned from top to bottom. Threatening anonymous telephone messages came night after night into the homes of the Upthegroves and their employees.

Why?... It all began because the little Marine Construction Company was established in 1971 on a *non-union basis* by Lingo Upthegrove, a former trade union pile driver. His wife, Yvonne, was the firm's secretary-treasurer and office manager, her brother-in-law, Howard, was vice president, and Lingo was the president.

Over the next twelve months, there was union thunder in the Sunshine State. This tiny new firm was victimized by a campaign of intimidation and brutality that began when the Upthegrove family refused to sign a labor contract that would force all of their pile-driver employees to join a local branch of the International Union of Operating Engineers. Labor officials promised "to keep bothering the company" until it capitulated. They were not interested in using the secret ballot voting procedure that is available in a federal government–supervised election to determine the personal desires of workers either to "go union" or remain "non-union." (That was because the union knew it would lose.)

In desperation, the Upthegroves sought legal protection. Unfortunately for them, the local police force was unionized and proved to be ineffective safeguards for the lives and property of the town of Opa-Locka's corporate citizenry during a "labor dispute." Next the Federal Bureau of Investigation was called for help but these bureaucrats decided that the onslaught was "outside of their jurisdiction."

"I feel like I'm living on borrowed time, but we're not giving in," Yvonne Upthegrove told the *Miami News*. "We just work hard and pray that we'll survive."[1]

That workplace terrorism against the Upthegrove family business in 1972 was just another typical occurrence in the building and construction industry. Everybody survived, union-free, in spite of the vicious assault. But no one was ever arrested . . .

At the same time, up north in Philadelphia, Pennsylvania, the Roofers Local Union No. 30's constant use of violence and corruption to promote compulsory unionism became the subject of feature articles in conservative news media. Law enforcement officials procrastinated while this greatly feared and politically connected trade union ignored unfair labor practice decisions, disregarded court injunctions, and evaded criminal indictments against the barbarous activities of its hostile officers and members. The Philadelphia Building Trades Council's labor attorney (who also represented Local 30) boasted "we lost our lawsuit virginity a long time ago."[2]

This Roofers Union was so overconfident of its nefarious tactics that on one occasion some of its members visited a non-union construction site and mauled five workers with baseball bats emblazoned with the "Local 30" insignia. The ruffians drove off but they left the bats behind in their haste, along with five victims who were a mass of bloody flesh and broken bones—one of them nearly blinded. Two less-wounded workers managed to scratch auto license plate numbers of the villains into the dirt. Soon after, positive identification of three of these union assailants occurred. The result was all too predictable. At the preliminary court hearing held some months later, non-union victims who could identify the bullies clammed up. They said they "couldn't remember anything." And the union "suspects" were freed. . . . [3]

The Early Years of Craft Unionism

Those Opa-Locka and Philadelphia brawls were selected at random from hundreds of similar assaults by organized labor over the years. They all lead to one conclusion: The building and construction trades unions in the United States have guarded fanatically what they claim is their "exclusive" jurisdiction over all construction work other than building houses. A primary source of this union power has been its control of a continuous ebb and flow of construction workers from employer to employer and from job to job. Unionized tradesmen of diverse crafts may work together for a dozen different contractors over a short period of time or they may perform together on a large project for several years and then never see each other again.

Economic conditions cause this itinerant existence. The unionized side of the construction industry workforce consists of a local pool of artisans and trainees from which all contractors and subcontractors operating in the same crafts in the same geographical area are required to draw their labor. After a construction job is completed, the laid-off apprentices and journeymen re-register and wait for prospective reemployment through future job referral from the local craft union "hiring hall."

Samuel Gompers: American Statesman

The trade unions that administer this manpower bank became a major factor in the volatile construction business after the Civil War and at the beginning of the industrial revolution. They were firmly established in many major urban centers by the 1890s under the leadership of Samuel Gompers, founder and first president of the American Federation of Labor ("AFL").

This dedicated man was an immigrant cigar-maker's apprentice who crossed the Atlantic Ocean in 1863 to become a journeyman in his craft at the

Attitudes toward unions, pro and con, are emphatic enough. But of serious thinking about unions— what kind of institutions they are, and why, and to what purpose—there is precious little.

IRVING KRISTOL
SYNDICATED COLUMNIST

5

age of fifteen. He rose to create and preside over the AFL from 1881 until his death in 1924. Trade union ranks grew to more than half a million members during his presidency.

Gompers championed the employment of master craftsmen in dozens of separate and autonomous trades. They all were required to progress at the same pace and identical wage rate within their own craft through extensive apprentice training programs drawn from traditions of the nepotistic medieval European guilds. Each craft had exclusive jurisdiction over all work performed in its field of expertise.

The blunt goal that Sam Gompers set for his trade union members was simply "more." He meant more wages, more benefits, more members, more economic leverage, and more political influence. He also believed "pure and simple" in "a fair day's work for a fair day's pay" and in the fundamental rights of "individual business ownership." He contended that "private property is the basis of personal freedom and that employers operating private enterprises are a bulwark of strength to workers in maintaining free unions." His faith in the workers' ability and need to become "property owners" was unwavering.[4]

Most significantly—but politically incorrect to mention in liberal labor relations circles today—Gompers created the construction trade union movement on the principle of "voluntarism" as opposed to any form of "compulsion." Here is one of his oft-quoted statements that formed part of the "Gompers Creed":

> . . . Guided by voluntary principles, our Federation has grown from a weakling into the strongest, best-organized labor movement of all the world. So long as we have held fast to voluntary principles and have been actuated and inspired by the spirit of service, we have sustained our forward progress and we have made our labor movement something to be respected and accorded a place in the councils of our Republic . . . No lasting gain has ever come from compulsion.[5]

Florence Calvert Thorne, who worked with Sam Gompers for many years and wrote his life story in a book entitled *Samuel Gompers, American Statesman*, included this tribute:

Intellectually, he was honest and undeviating... His constituency were the lowly, the makers and users of tools, the more recent immigrants in the process of induction into American citizenship—the most numerous single national group. The future of the nation was conditioned by whether they adopted American ways of life or whether they shifted directions.

That America was his vision and ideal, that he modeled the constitution and procedures of the American labor movement after those of the U.S.A., that he made freedom the compass guiding the progress of this numerically major national group, that he taught them to revere and help strengthen institutions rooted in personal freedom and private property and to honor responsibilities accompanying personal rights, entitles him to rank among the founders of our nation.... and places him high among American statesmen.[6]

During Gompers's tenure as president of the AFL there was a significant increase in organized labor's political involvement in government. Examples of major legislative achievements included the first workers' compensation laws, elemental safety regulations, and protective child labor statutes. Especially noteworthy, the Clayton Act of 1914 exempted unions from antitrust laws when they were not "conspiring" in concert with employers.

Most of the construction work in Sam Gompers's time was performed by specialty subcontractors who united in employers associations to bargain with local unions representing each craft in their community. These local unions were affiliated with a national or international union (i.e., U.S.A. plus Canada) that represented the same craft.

Today their hierarchical umbrella, called the Building and Construction Trades Department of the united AFL-CIO, is located in Washington, D.C. Each of the Department's fifteen or more international craft union affiliates in turn has developed general guidelines and provides technical staff assistance to dozens of local district union councils and their hundreds of local trade unions all over America. Administration and control, in turn, is vested in full-time local union representatives originally called

When I want to understand what is happening today and try to anticipate what will happen tomorrow, I look back. A page of history is worth a volume of logic.

OLIVER WENDELL HOLMES
SUPREME COURT JUSTICE

Samuel Gompers, founder and first president of the American Federation of Labor from 1881 to 1924.

7

"walking delegates." They were elected by the membership to protect each local craft union's interests in its own territory.

Union Business Agents

The AFL regarded these delegates—currently known as "business agents" or "business managers"—as its local leaders. Their reward has been power and financial remuneration, including generous expense accounts. Collectively, they and their local trade unions set the tone and established the norms for work assignments, pay and benefits, the establishment of workers' rights and duties, training and skill development, and other aspects of personnel administration.

To this day these business agents or another union official—such as the president, secretary, or treasurer—act as the chief representatives of their local union within the trade union hierarchy as well as the sole source of manpower supplied to unionized contractors and subcontractors through the union-controlled hiring halls. And these union leaders continue to regulate the work of their trade along strict craft jurisdictional lines, mediate inter-craft jurisdictional disputes, and restrict the workplace ratio of young apprentices to veteran journeymen in order to protect the job security of senior craftsmen.

Union officers also are the chief negotiators and enforcers of the local area-wide collective bargaining agreements applicable to their craft. That function has given them the power to call work slowdowns or stoppages and influence the settlement of labor-management disputes at any construction site at any time. This power to strike is considered imperative in a business climate where contractors can go bankrupt overnight and where peaceful solution through a lengthy step-by-step workers' contractual grievance procedure appealed upward through layers of management is impractical. Union representatives know that even a walkout of a few days can wreak havoc with a binding construction schedule. The threat of a slowdown or "quickie" strike thus became—and still remains—a potent economic weapon.

All of these factors made craft union business agents and other officials a force to be reckoned with by construction managers and construction users alike. For further economic leverage, local union leaders affiliate with city or area-wide building trades councils that represent all the crafts. The influence of these multi-trade councils has varied over the years, depending on the terms of their constitutions and by-laws, the extent of unionization in the geographical area, the personalities of their leaders, and the local political and economic climates. The councils frequently assume control of collective bargaining negotiations and attempts at organizing non-union firms.

The Plight of Unionized Contractors

Coping with this structured trade union pyramid over the years has caused unionized general contractors and subcontractors to operate under substantial disadvantages. Unlike their non-union competitors, they were—and still are—vulnerable to excessive wages-and-benefits payments and inefficient work rules contained in area-wide labor agreements that inhibit productivity. And these contractors need to perform at a profit under committed deadlines that leave them vulnerable to heavy penalties by their customers if their projects are not finished on time. Therefore they frequently capitulate to unreasonable union demands rather than provoke a strike. Trade union officials also have been known to extort under-the-table "strike insurance" and other cash favors from powerless contractors in return for a promise of "labor peace."

In spite of this autocratic union power, the relationship between the building trades and their unionized employers is seldom hostile. Since construction firms are required by their collective bargaining agreements to depend on the craft unions to supply skilled manpower from their hiring halls, all of these captive contractors want the best-qualified journeymen assigned to them. And labor peace is a "must." Friendly relationships with the union agents become a necessity.

This guarded closeness that has existed between professional labor leaders and construction firm executives who deal with them makes the unionized sector of the building industry in many respects a closed community. Although inevitable economic clashes between labor and management occur from time to time, there is also an understanding of and need for an amicable long-term relationship for mutual survival.

An Unholy Quadrumvirate

In 1924—the year of the death of AFL founder and president Samuel Gompers—there was minimal non-union competition, and human greed began to

"The Capitalism Stage Coach"

prevail. The great labor statesman's credo of voluntarism, personal responsibility, and a fair day's work for a fair day's pay was being ignored. Job padding, time-and-material corner cutting, and other quality-of-work deficiencies became rampant. Wage increases were soaring. The syndicated structure of the industry also tended to make dishonesty an easy and profitable indulgence. There always were contractors devious or desperate enough to proffer bribes and union representatives powerful and corrupt enough to extort them.

This absence of any serious non-union competitive challenge in the marketplace permitted monopolistic practices among an immoral trio of labor organizations, unionized contractors, and their construction users. So-called "sweetheart" collective bargaining agreements, compulsory union membership and dues, collusive wage and price-fixing deals, and rigging of project bids became common occurrences. Embezzlement, pay-offs to government inspectors, evasion of building code requirements, kickbacks to administrators of union health and welfare fund plans, and other payoffs "for labor harmony" were commonplace. Contractors and construction users wrote off these malpractices as the normal costs of doing business. Then the three conspirators passed along the burden of inflated construction costs to the consuming public.[7]

It was not surprising that Judge Kenesaw Mountain Landis wrote, "the building industry is a thing diseased," and Historian Harold Seidman concurred:

> The seasonal character of the work, the possibility of causing great damage by stoppages and strikes, and the conflicting interests of contractors, subcontractors, and supply dealers have made it a most fertile breeding ground for union corruption.... Labor czars come and labor czars go, but racketeering in the building trades goes on forever. It is truly a case of "The King is dead, long live the King!"[8]

Author John Hutchinson also described this unsavory construction industry in the *Imperfect Union*, and named a fourth conspirator that was enjoying the spoils: "Government in the United States during the latter half of the nineteenth century and the beginning of the twentieth century was not noted for its honesty." Then he amplified:

An appeaser is one who feeds the crocodile, hoping it will eat him last.

WINSTON CHURCHILL
BRITISH PRIME
MINISTER

Those were the great days of the party bosses, of corrupt political machines, of partisan and pecuniary law enforcement, of an organized sacking of the public purse. Public contracts were an especially lucrative source of graft, when the absence of effective control permitted the erection and maintenance of public facilities at grossly inflated prices, to the financial benefit of employers, union officials and political incumbents. In private building, tolerance for inferior standards was not hard to purchase.

The law was often a party to systems of bribery and extortion. Political corruption, if it did not cause industrial corruption, was scarcely a hindrance to it. The construction industry, therefore, was governed from time to time and place to place by a quadrumvirate of grafters, rich in power and resources.[9]

This disastrous state of affairs confirmed the prophetic words of a renowned British philosopher, Edmund Burke: "The only thing necessary for evil to triumph is for good people to do nothing."

"How do I stand on labor and management?"

AL HIRSCHFELD IN THE *NEW YORKER*

CHAPTER 2

BIRTH OF THE OPEN SHOP MOVEMENT

THE BUILDING AND CONSTRUCTION STAGE WAS SET for the entrance of a protagonist and World War II provided the theatre. That great conflict also helped to create the star of this drama: an unprecedented employers' association that would offer the construction industry a free market policy. Called the "open shop" and later renamed the "merit shop," this method of operation was a logical and profitable alternative to the scurrilous quartet of autocratic trade unions, devious unionized contractors, their unsavory construction users' monopoly, and crooked government officials. The hero on this stage would become known throughout the United States as the Associated Builders and Contractors, or more familiarly, "ABC."

ABC was nurtured in the historic metropolis of Baltimore, Maryland, which gained fame for its great seaport on the Chesapeake Bay and for Fort McHenry, the site of Francis Scott Key's "The Star-Spangled Banner." This same great city also is known for ethnic neighborhoods featuring white marble steps, for the homes of baseball immortal Babe Ruth, caustic journalist H. L. Mencken, and the tomb of that master of the macabre, Edgar Allan Poe. "Bawlmer"—as we natives call our beloved home town—is the domicile of the internationally famous Johns Hopkins Medical and University Institutions, the (sometimes) world-champion Baltimore Orioles and Baltimore Colts (now Ravens), a beautiful inner harbor featuring America's last sailing warship, the *Constellation*, launched in 1797 with 36 guns and a crew of 340, and the largest aquarium ever built.

Bawlmer is also the home of the world's greatest crab cakes.

Life is a great big canvas; throw all the paint on it you can.

DANNY KAYE
ENTERTAINER

Big Labor Controls Baltimore Construction

Insofar as commercial, industrial, institutional, and public construction were concerned, Baltimore in its early years was recognized as a "union town." The combination of a need for skilled artisans and a group of under-capitalized open shop contractors gave organized labor an early foothold. The staffing requirements of these non-union builders varied unpredictably according to the number of projects under contract, and they were hard-pressed to maintain and finance a stable team of crafts-

Baltimore's famous inner harbor, with the World Trade Center building in the foreground.

men. The little firms had no formal job training programs and no expertise or financial resources to withstand union mass picketing, boycotts, and other forms of harassment.

Since the building trades unions controlled worker training (through their apprenticeship programs) and supplied qualified craftsmen (through their exclusive hiring halls), non-union contractors desperate for manpower were forced to accept trade union recognition and mandatory union membership of their employees plus excessive wages and burdensome work rules. But they knew they could pass on the inflated costs to their customers since all competitors had the same labor expenses. In exchange, the contractors gained the ability to operate their projects more efficiently by alternately obtaining and laying off craftsmen via the hiring hall as business needs dictated.

The building trades unions thus emerged as a vital part of the construction field in Baltimore in the 1880s. By the turn of the century it was common knowledge that "a craftsman without a union card was a man without a trade." Compulsory "closed shop" union membership gained further support from President Franklin D. Roosevelt's New Deal legislation in the 1930s and early 1940s. Nepotism—fathers, sons, brothers, nephews, uncles, and other relatives—controlled union apprenticeship training programs so that few workers could enter the building trades without familial approval. Local union council leaders and business agents reigned over 80 percent or more of the non-residential building and construction work within Maryland and throughout the nation.[1]

They believed that 100 percent of it belonged to them.

By the start of World War II, this industry in the metropolitan Baltimore area was booming. It was due primarily to the fact that the seaport city was the location of armaments produced by manufacturing giants such as General Electric, Bethlehem Steel, General Motors, Westinghouse Electric, and Glenn L. Martin Aircraft. Related feeder businesses sprang up around these plants. There also was a need for new military facilities. Jobs were plentiful and the prospect of better wages and steady work lured thousands of workers from nearby states to Maryland's wartime construction boom.

Unions Start to Fear "Open Shop" Competitors

Non-union general contractors and developers who were engaged in home-building, low-rise apartments, and light commercial work in the metropolitan Baltimore area saw their customary job opportunities sapped by federal controls on building materials and equipment. In order to survive, they turned their skills toward war-related construction. They also continued to follow their open shop practice of using both union and non-union subcontractors as needed, working side-by-side as a harmonious team on their job sites.

Their customers—construction users—made a final award of a project based on five factors: (1) previous experience on jobs of similar size and scope; (2) compliance with plans and specifications from the architect; (3) financial stability and bonding capacity; (4) verifiable history of satisfactory performance with regard to both quality and timely completion; and (5) low bid price—regardless of union or non-union affiliation. More often than not, the successful bidder operated on a non-union basis.

When World War II ended in 1945, rationed building materials were released and opportunities increased for all open shop contractors to become available for major building work in and around Baltimore. Manufacturers and merchants needed new facilities to meet the expectations of a nation hungry for consumer goods. State office buildings had fallen into disrepair during the war and there was a demand for new or refurbished ones. Because

Repression is the seed of revolution.

DANIEL WEBSTER
POLITICAL LEADER
AND DIPLOMAT

Small opportunities are often the beginning of great enterprises.

DEMOSTHENES
ORATOR AND
STATESMAN

both the private sector and Maryland government accepted bids from all qualified bidders, non-union general contractors and subcontractors with greater workforce versatility and lower labor costs began to win an increasing share of the market.

There also was a new solution to the skilled manpower shortage. Thousands of young men who had served their country in the military branches such as Navy Seabees or the Army's Civil Engineering Corps or had received comparable technical and mechanical training in the armed services needed civilian jobs. Despite these obvious qualifications, they were rejected by the building trades unions under their self-preservation policy of nepotism. That fatal discrimination caused ambitious youngsters to join non-union construction firms, injecting their enthusiasm and discipline as they became craftsmen, supervisors, and project managers. Some even became owners of their own building businesses.

These "renegade" open shoppers were observed by Baltimore chieftains of the building trades unions with jealousy and insecurity. They never forgot that it took hard bargaining, costly work stoppages, and other economic, political, and corporeal pressures to "convince" local contractors to unionize and accept control by specialty craft unions. They also had won what they bragged were "advantageous" wages and working conditions through monopolistic labor agreements negotiated on an area-wide basis and by enacting pro-union workplace legislation.

It was understandable that organized labor became uneasy when its proprietary claim to every substantial construction project within the metropolitan Baltimore area was challenged by what it labeled "a bunch of goddamn bush-league union-bustin' scabs."

CHAPTER 3

THE "KINGFISH" DEFENDS HIS UNION TERRITORY

SINCE THE PRIMARY OBJECTIVE of the building trades unions in Baltimore was to form and perpetuate their monopoly of the construction marketplace, anything that threatened that goal was forbidden. Union members could not work for non-union employers. Collective bargaining agreements with employers specified what jobs would be performed by which journeymen in each craft and protected this senior coterie of inbred specialists by restricting the number of young apprentices who could be trained and progress to journeyman status.

Pampered union tradesmen—the beneficiaries of this familial manpower monopoly—soon learned that normal profit-driven responsibilities such as reporting for work at the project site on time, performing quality work, limiting the length of coffee breaks and lunch periods, working until quitting time, and a good attendance record were not absolute requirements to earn their paychecks. Once the bad habit of breaking standard work rules was overlooked, human nature made them difficult to correct.

The unionized contractors, without serious open shop competition, also had become lax and incompetent. Labor and material costs were not controlled, jobs were not managed efficiently, favored "pets" and other unqualified employees were promoted, productivity was poor, and project completion deadlines were ignored. This construction industry honeymoon existed in Baltimore because the trade union hiring halls were able to control the competition for manpower.

The same syndicated work ethic that stifled non-union competition also created an opposing economic force that eventually would become organized

**No fist is big
enough to
hide the sky.**

GEORGE SANTAYANA
PHILOSOPHER-WRITER

labor's Achilles' heel. The growth of an open shop movement with lower labor costs, quality work performance, steady employment, and good employee morale caught the union leaders off guard. By 1950, in the opinion of Clark Ellis, the powerful president of Baltimore's Building & Construction Trades Council, this non-union invasion of industrial, commercial, institutional, and public construction had reached intolerable proportions.

A Union Boss Fights for His Territory

Since the "Kingfish," as Clark Ellis was nicknamed, considered the open shop method of doing business a serious threat to his union shop monopoly, he was determined to stop it. He regarded all non-union firms as "no-good fly-by-night bastards" who were trespassing on his hard-won turf. Even so, to induce them to come under his craft union representation and control, first he tried the path of friendly persuasion. A few of the largest open shoppers received tempting promises of sweetheart labor agreements including operational "concessions" and the pick of top-notch skilled manpower from apprentice training programs and journeyman hiring halls.

One of the first non-union leaders that the Kingfish decided to court was a general contractor named Charles Mullan. His father, Thomas Mullan, had started the family business by buying two dump carts and two mules to haul debris away from the Great Baltimore Fire of 1904. With that humble beginning, the senior Mullan progressed into heavier construction work, always on a non-union basis. He soon owned the first road-building steam shovel ever operated in the state of Maryland.

Son Charlie was an aggressive and high-spirited pacesetter who graduated from McDonogh School (a military academy) in 1938. In 1940 he and his brother, Thomas Mullan, Jr., took over the family business. During the next ten years they expanded the parental open shop enterprise—called Mullan Contracting Company—into a highly successful general construction firm.

When the Kingfish affably approached Charlie in the spring of 1950 about the advantages of "going union," he answered frankly that he "wasn't that hungry." In those memorable words, Mullan was voicing the sentiment of open shop contractors throughout the area—and a portent of the future.

ABC Contractor

TOP: At the first construction equipment road show, held in 1909, this road scraper, which could operate on or off a set track, was considered the elite in road equipment. With the exception of steam-operated equipment, this piece was considered the most advanced machinery to date.

BOTTOM: During the early 1900s, steam shovels and steam rollers were the only available self-propelled pieces of construction equipment. The roller shown is compacting a macadam road while the bottom dump wagon is hauling in stone.

The "Top-Down" Strike-Boycott

This blunt rebuff caused Kingfish Ellis to regroup and invoke the traditional trade union method of eliminating "unfair" competition: an attack on non-union construction by what is known in labor parlance as the "top-down" method. That strategy meant bringing economic pressure to bear at the summit "where the money and control is," namely, the targeted company's management and ownership, along with its customers and suppliers. (The Kingfish knew it would be futile to try to organize Mullan's well-treated and loyal construction workers democratically from the "bottom up" by winning a majority of their votes cast in a secret ballot election supervised by the National Labor Relations Board.)

For this top-down tactic by Ellis to be successful, the strike had always been the most effective tactic in labor's arsenal of weapons. An aggressor union simply provoked a work stoppage to force the non-union contractor to capitulate to labor demands or go bankrupt. This was accomplished by picketing a common construction job site where both the "targeted" non-union general contractor and the unionized subcontractors employing various crafts were working together. At that point, the labor movement's unbreakable rule came into play: All union members must respect every union picket line anywhere at any time by refusing to cross it or be expelled from their union (and worse) as "SOB low-life scabs."

The "AGC" Supports Compulsory Unions

Kingfish Ellis believed that such a top-down scheme would be successful because in Baltimore the non-union generals frequently employed unionized subs to perform specialty craft assignments on their "open shop" projects. It was work that non-union subs either were not available or qualified to perform. Ellis assumed that his picket line surrounding such a common work situs would immediately create a hostile labor environment followed by a stoppage of all work.

The Kingfish and his Trades Council also decided to enlist the cooperation of a powerful rival construction employers' association—the Baltimore Chapter of the Associated General Contractors ("AGC"). Since the work forces of all members of AGC were unionized and controlled by the Baltimore Building Trades Council through their local craft hiring halls and since AGC members faced increasing non-union competition for important building and construction work, they willingly supported the contemplated strike.

To the dismay of the Kingfish and the unionized corporate AGCers, however, it soon became apparent that many unionized subcontractors who performed a large portion of their work for non-union general contractors voiced their reluctance to cooperate. And it didn't take long for these "disloyal" union subs to warn their favorite non-union generals of the Kingfish's strategy.

When word of this internal dissension leaked out, there was a stormy session within the leadership of the Baltimore Building Trades Council. The Kingfish predictably won that wrangle and cut off the supply of tradesmen to the recalcitrant unionized subs. It soon became known that he was targeting three prominent open shop general contractors—Charles Mullan, Charles Knott, and Edward Colwill—for the main thrust of his work stoppage.

There's an old truism that people can be divided into three groups: those who **make** *things happen; those who* **watch** *things happen; and those who* **wonder** *what happened. The Kingfish would soon discover that he was about to tangle with three charter members of the first category.*

History is the record of an encounter between character and circumstance.

Donald Creighton
Canadian historian

CHAPTER 4

CHARLIE MULLAN HOLDS A MEETING

IN **MARCH OF THE YEAR** **1950**, the Kingfish decided to contact Charlie Mullan again. This time there would be no sweet-talk. The brief conversation went something like this:

Clark "Kingfish" Ellis: "Ya got two choices, Mullan—sign uh union contract or I'll shut down yuses jobs and put youse outa business."

Mullan: "Sorry, Clark, as I told you before, I'm not interested in your offer and neither are my employees. But as you know, I do use qualified union subcontractors from time to time."

The Kingfish: "That's parta da problum youse is causin' us. It's a goddamn shame ya can't see it my way. And youse betta take good care of da wife and kids!"

Mullan: "Threats won't change my decision."

A few days later, dozens of furious union tradesmen swarmed around Charlie Mullan's construction project at the Mount Wilson Hospice on Reisterstown Road in Baltimore County, shouting curses as they picketed the main entrance. When Mullan's craftsmen began their lunch break, they raced to the job site's front gate (of their own volition) yelling, "NO UNION HERE" and stronger messages at the mob.

The Kingfish's union bullies left and never returned.

That episode was enough for Charlie Mullan. His own life had been threatened on several occasions and he arranged a security escort for his wife and his two daughters' daily trips to and from school. The time had come for

There are times when all of us have to decide which side we are going to be on, not for an evening's argument, but for the long haul.

DAVID HENNINGER
COLUMNIST

a meeting with fellow open shop contractors Charles Knott and Ed Colwill, who were on the same "hit list" of Kingfish Ellis.

This Mullan-Knott-Colwill trio of targeted open shop builders convened promptly in the living room of Mullan's house at 5212 Spring Lake Way in the Homeland section of northern Baltimore City. Their mission was to explore ways and means to defeat the impending union work stoppage against them.

An Historic Contractors' Meeting

Memories are somewhat hazy as to who else attended that first fateful meeting in Charlie Mullan's house in the Baltimore suburbs. Ernest Schultz probably was there. Edward Dickinson, Philip Cloyes, and Clifford Wells, Jr. attended the second (if not the first) get-together.

The business diversity of these seven pioneers was significant. Three of them (Mullan, Knott, and Colwill) were non-union general contractors; the fourth (Cloyes) was a unionized tile and terrazzo subcontractor; the fifth (Schultz) was a non-union sheet metal subcontractor; the sixth (Dickinson) was primarily a non-union homebuilder; and the seventh (Wells) was an architect-developer.

The Charles Mullan home at 5212 Spring Lake Way in Homeland, Baltimore—"birthplace" of ABC.

There was an understandable air of apprehension among this rebellious group of confederates due to the potentially dangerous effect of hostile picket lines and union strikers on the safety of employees and their families, plus project completion deadlines. Several of the angry businessmen favored eliminating the use of craft union labor altogether and forming a totally non-union sector of the local construction industry.

At the third meeting a more reasonable entrepreneurial spirit prevailed. It took the precedential form of a voluntary association for the mutual aid and protection of all Maryland general contractors and specialty sub-contractors working together, in harmony, regardless of their union or non-union affiliation. Charlie Mullan, a man who believed that actions speak louder than

Four of ABC's founders: (left to right) Edward Colwill, Philip Cloyes, Charles Mullan, and Charles Knott.

If we take the generally accepted definition of bravery as a quality which knows no fear, I have never seen a brave man. All men are frightened. The courageous man is the one who forces himself, in spite of his fear, to carry on.

George S. Patton
World War II
General

words, summed up the crisis this way: "The unions decided they were going to put the three of us and our open shops out of business. None of us wanted that to happen so—even though we were competitors—we decided to form a group and fight."

A new non-profit organization was incorporated and appropriate bylaws were drafted, with the able assistance of attorney Herbert R. O'Conor, Jr. The seven businessmen became the founders, the first officers, and the first board of directors of the Associated Builders and Contractors of Maryland, Inc., familiarly called "ABC." Mullan's blunt explanation was: "We could have stayed open shop and fought without forming the ABC, but by joining hands it made everybody stronger."

The original certificate of incorporation of this unique organization was dated April 11, 1950, and recorded in Liber 325, folio 266, of the Charter Records of the State Tax Commission located in Baltimore City. The three official signatory incorporators were Francis Rouchard (a staff employee of Mullan Construction Co.), Orville Wright (a lumber supplier), and Edwin Eberly (Knott Co.'s chief accountant).

The first board of directors meeting of ABC was held on April 14, 1950, at 8:30 p.m. in ABC's tiny "home-office" located at 428 Dunkirk Road in Baltimore. All seven of the founders attended and designated themselves as ABC's "charter members." On the same evening at the same place one hour later, these founder-charter-board-members elected Charles Knott as chairman of the board of directors, Charles Mullan as president, Philip Cloyes as vice president, Ernest Schultz as treasurer, and Clifford Wells as secretary. Several months later, eight new board members were added: Allen Feeser, Charles Feihe, Bruce Campbell, J. R. Gerwig, Roland Dashiell, John Sands, Roland Stolzenbach, and M. L. Robertson.

The ABC "Open Shop" Movement Becomes Official

The first official general membership meeting of the ABC of Maryland took place at 20 East Fayette Street in Baltimore City on the evening of June 1, 1950. There were fifty-one persons present.[1] Mullan, Colwill, and Bruce Campbell, president of a non-union concrete manufacturer called Harry T. Campbell & Sons, subsidized most of the initial operating expenses. The phrase "merit shop" had not yet been coined but the dedicated group's statement of intent read as follows:

> Resolved, that the members of the Associated Builders and Contractors of Maryland, Inc., believing that it is the right and prerogative of every American employer to hire whomever it desires, hereby expresses approval of an open shop policy throughout the industry.[2]

Another item of business at that meeting was the selection of a membership committee. The chosen contractors represented eleven different craft groups that worked in a broad cross-section of the industry. They included general contractors who employed carpenters and laborers and subcontractors engaged in insulation, electrical, ironwork, plumbing, sheet metal, plastering, heating, painting, and bricklaying work.

Under this committee's leadership, when a unionized firm balked against erecting steel on one of Charlie Mullan's open shop prospects, he went into the steel erection business:

I told the firm to deliver my steel to the project entrance and I would unload it. The next morning I went out and bought a mobile crane, put it on my job site, and taught my employees how to set up steel. From that day on, for about five years, I erected the steel for all open shop contractors in the State of Maryland.

When a unionized masonry subcontractor reacted negatively in the same way, several ABC general contractors set up their own bricklaying operations. If Teamsters Union truck drivers refused to make deliveries to open shop construction projects, ABCers used their own vans or cultivated the services of non-union trucking firms. And so from the beginning, every effort was made to come to the aid of any contractor or subcontractor whose business was adversely affected by trade union intimidation.

"Survival," admitted Mullan, "was almost a daily experience."

The Building Trades Picket Knott's Firm

On June 15th of the year 1950, the economic "top-down" pressure threatened by Kingfish Ellis became a reality. Co-founder Charlie Knott, ABC's 2nd president, reported at a special meeting of the little association's board of directors that the Baltimore Building Trades Council had placed pickets on six of his job sites with signs claiming that his company "PAYS SUB-STANDARD WAGES." All work stopped at these project locations because tradesmen working for unionized subcontractors dutifully refused to cross building trades picket lines.

A discussion of legal remedies that might be available to Knott to remove the pickets followed immediately. William McMillan, a renowned Baltimore trial attorney, was retained by ABC to meet and parley with Kingfish Ellis and his attorney, an equally prominent Baltimore lawyer by the name of Simon Sobeloff (who eventually became solicitor general of the United States and concluded his career as a federal appellate judge).

After several unsuccessful meetings, the Kingfish and Attorney Sobeloff were warned by McMillan that a deadline of July 3rd had been set. If the Building Trades Council failed to remove its picket lines by that date, action would be taken against what ABC contended was an illegal boycott. When the pickets

> **Take the obvious, add three cupfuls of brain, a generous pinch of imagination, a bucketful of courage, and bring it to a boil.**
>
> BERNARD BARUCH
> FINANCIER-STATESMAN

did not leave by the designated date, ABC prepared to file an unfair labor practice charge at the local Baltimore office of the National Labor Relations Board (hereafter sometimes called the "Board" or "Labor Board" or "NLRB") to test the new so-called "secondary boycott" provisions of the Labor-Management Relations Act of 1947 (also known as the "Taft-Hartley Act").

To the surprise and relief of the ABCers, Kingfish Ellis surrendered at the last hour. On the advice of Attorney Simon Sobeloff, the Baltimore Building Trades Council reluctantly removed its pickets from all targeted job sites just as ABC's unfair labor practice charge was about to be delivered to the Labor Board's regional office in Baltimore for processing.

This capitulation by Big Labor on Independence Day in 1950 was a major victory for the "open shop" cause. It united forever the small but brave band of free enterprisers who called themselves the Associated Builders and Contractors of Maryland.

CHAPTER 5

Maryland's "Little Davis-Bacon Act" Ruled Unconstitutional

NURSING A BRUISED EGO from the humiliating setback to his strike-boycott ploy, Kingfish Ellis decided to turn the Baltimore Building Trades Council's attack on ABC toward another front: the millions of dollars in Maryland state government construction projects. His craft unions had been facing severe open shop competition in that arena, too.

Firms operating under Ellis-controlled labor contracts frequently were underbid by non-union contractors for the building program of the state of Maryland. Influential persons both in and out of government had become impressed with the high quality work of these open shoppers and the cost savings they achieved for taxpayers at a time when construction needs of state government were burgeoning and its budget was parsimonious.

The Kingfish was spoiled by the fact that all federal construction work in Maryland—unlike state and local public construction—had to be performed at wage rates predetermined by the U.S. Department of Labor under an archaic "prevailing wage law" passed by Congress in 1931 and known as the Davis-Bacon Act.[1] This farcical and maladministered statute usually adopted the inflated building trades collective bargaining contract scale wages designated in the three traditional union job classifications of journeyman mechanic, apprentice, and laborer. Their rigid union-negotiated rates ignored and defied free market practices that included variable but lower-averaging non-union construction labor rates in the locality involved and the use of multi-skilled craftsmen plus more semi-skilled job classifications. This political plum for unionized construction virtually eliminated

Law is an
expression of
the will of the
strongest for
the time being.

Brooks Adams
Historian

any opportunity for competitive bidding by open shop contractors on federal projects.

The Kingfish Wins a State Wage-Setting Law

Maryland had no such discriminatory "union-scale" prevailing wage law covering its state government construction work. That fact caused Kingfish Ellis to try to negate open shop competition by forcing Maryland public works into a similar federal-type unionized wage-and-job-classification straitjacket. He lobbied the State General Assembly and Governor William Preston Lane (D-MD) with that goal in mind. They cooperated, the newly formed ABC was unable to mobilize sufficient opposition to the powerful AFL-CIO political machine, and Maryland's "Little Davis-Bacon Act" was passed on the last day of the legislative session in 1950.

This new statute called for a state government agency with broad discretion (following the U.S. Department of Labor model) to create procedures for the administration of its terms. The authority included appointment of a commission that would establish "prevailing" wage rates for all state government construction projects. Kingfish Ellis was among the members appointed to this commission by his friend, Governor Lane, and the meetings soon became hostile.

The building trades labor boss lost no time in applying political pressure to make certain that trade union wage scales, along with strict craft work rules and frozen job classifications "prevailed" on all state public construction work. Some of the more conservative commissioners feared, however, that their government building program would be badly hampered by adopting the costly federal scenario. They were reluctant to agree with the Kingfish, but it soon became futile since he controlled the votes of a majority of the commission members.

Ellis won and the young ABC had another *cause celebre* thrust upon it. ABC's founder and first president, Charlie Mullan, decided to seek the advice of an attorney on how to solve this problem. He chose Wilson K. Barnes, a colorful trial lawyer from Maryland's conservative "right wing" Eastern Shore. Since ABC had failed in the political and legislative arenas, court action challenging the legality of the new statute was the only possibility remaining. ABC's leaders explained to Counselor Barnes that open shoppers were being discriminated against by the new so-called prevailing wage law—which ignored the lowest qualified bidder—and they wanted it declared unconstitutional. Mullan added that since its passage in 1931, the Davis-Bacon Act was a thorn in the side of non-union contractors in Maryland who worked on federal construction projects:

> We struggled with senators and representatives to get them to realize that "prevailing" wages were really not. But we got the cold shoulder. Some open shop contractors went to Washington to see the head of the Davis-Bacon Section of the Department of Labor ("DOL") and try to obtain justice. The director shook his finger-fist at them and said: "We'll tell you what to pay!" I learned later from an insider that the DOL staff had been instructed to determine the always-inflated union rates as "prevailing" and thumb their noses at the real world.[2]

On any given day, 50 percent of the lawyers in American courtrooms are losers.

THOMAS W. KELLY
ATTORNEY

ABC Attacks Maryland's Prevailing Wage Statute

Attorney Wilson Barnes agreed to take the case at an ABC board meeting on August 25, 1950, with the understanding that the chance of victory was slim in liberal Maryland, and even more so because this type of pro-union labor legislation had been upheld in several other states. Undaunted and confident of the able guidance of Barnes, Charlie Mullan forged ahead as the plaintiff in a lawsuit filed in the Circuit Court for Baltimore City—both as a protesting taxpayer and as the chief executive of Mullan Contracting Company. He was joined in the litigation by three other ABC members, their firms, and ABC itself as a "corporate citizen," in an attempt to nullify the new Maryland legislation.

They contended that this Little Davis-Bacon Act was unconstitutional for two reasons: Procedurally, it was enacted in the "wrong" session of the General Assembly, and substantively, its discriminatory pro-union intent and administration would unconstitutionally increase the cost of state construction work at Maryland taxpayers' expense and undermine the sovereign power of the state. On the procedural issue, evidence presented by Attorney Barnes showed that the law was passed at a short "even year" legislative session (thirty days) that only applied to "laws affecting the general welfare of the whole state." The new statute did not comply "because it exempted state road construction in three of Maryland's twenty-three counties," Barnes contended.

To ABC's gratification, the circuit court agreed and enjoined the state from enforcing the new law. The state's attorney general promptly appealed this decision and was rebuffed again. The Maryland court of appeals agreed with the trial court on ABC's technical procedural contention and said that there was no need to go further with a ruling on the substantive constitutional issue.

A legislative fluke thus ended the case favorably for the open shoppers. Chief Judge Marbury delivered the opinion of the state appellate court. He wrote that this prevailing wage law was "unconstitutional" because procedurally "it was not within the power of the legislature to pass at the [short] 1950 session."[3]

This legal decision, on the first birthday of ABC, was a tremendous victory at substantial financial sacrifice. By the ruling, Maryland's highest court allowed the young Association's members to continue to win state construction projects on a fair and competitive basis whenever they were the lowest qualified bidders. And Big Labor—despite its political clout—failed to lobby a legally enforceable "Little Davis-Bacon Act" through the Maryland legislature until eighteen years later.[4]

The embryonic ABC once again proved its worth as defender of the open shop movement. Association members continued to construct state government buildings and Maryland taxpayers saved millions of dollars in the cost of their public edifices.

CHAPTER 6

ABC HIRES JOHN TRIMMER

BY THE SPRING OF **1952**, ABC of Maryland had expanded sufficiently in membership—210 contractors—to afford a full-time professional as its executive vice president. The applicant selected at a board of directors meeting chaired by President Edward Colwill on March 20th of that year, John P. Trimmer, was a fortunate choice for all concerned.

John was a native of York, Pennsylvania. His first job was as editor (and sole reporter) of the *York Gazette and Daily News*. He also studied organizational management at Yale and Michigan State Universities. In due course his obvious talent with the written word secured his employment by the Associated Press to cover the Maryland legislature and Maryland's court of appeals. Subsequently he became the first director of the Maryland State Department of Information.

The scholarly and conservative John Trimmer arrived on the ABC scene at the age of thirty-eight and immediately began to provide the young Association with both the administrative and ideological leadership it needed to succeed. Although he took a reduction in pay from his previous job, he told himself that he "admired the contractors' entrepreneurial spirit and believed that he could build the organization." With one secretary as his total staff, Trimmer began a program of ABC name recognition, organization building, and legal battles to protect the members' right to work from autocratic trade union control by the construction industry.

"They were picking up the wheat while we took the chaff," he observed.

ABC Opens for Business

On the internal operational side, Trimmer vitalized and expanded existing ABC committees related to membership, public relations, ways and means, finance, and entertainment. He also created new committees and workshops on legislation, labor and employee relations, safety, professional ethics, wage and benefits surveys, apprenticeship training, and internal audits.

A "plans room" was established at the ABC office, sponsored by some of Maryland's prominent architects and engineers. They cooperated by making their plans and specifications for hundreds of building projects available, free of charge, to contractors and their subcontractors to review and formulate their bids.

According to ABC's corporate minutes, in 1952 the board of directors approved "large sums of money for monthly operating expenses." The dollars appropriated included: Trimmer's salary—$600; secretary's salary—$250; utilities—$100; office rent—$50; travel—$25; furniture—$30; legal fees—$43; printing—$50; and miscellaneous—$50.[1]

Trimmer also increased communications and networking through a classified membership roster and a monthly magazine he called the *ABC Contractor*. With paid advertising, the latter publication soon yielded much-needed income while covering major events in the construction field and activities of the Association. This magazine, which Trimmer and his wife, Ann, penned together in the beginning, soon became ABC of Maryland's official voice, "dedicated to promoting, protecting, and defending the free enterprise construction industry."[2]

The subscription price was $2 per year.

Trimmer Prepares Contractors for Union Avoidance

Major impetus for ABC's creation and growth came from the united front of its founders against attacks by the building trades to attain monopoly status in the construction industry. Since the managerial restrictions caused by operating on a unionized basis were much greater, and therefore the costs much higher than operating the same firm on a non-union basis, ABC members were asking how to avoid confrontations with organized labor.[3]

John Trimmer saw to it that ample practical advice was available. He created an ABC Fact File written in laymen's terms with helpful hints on "positive" employee relations and "what to do when a union knocks on the door."

Through ABC's retained attorneys, additional counsel on labor problems was donated as a service of the Association's membership dues. This "pro bono" guidance usually stopped short of actual litigation. If an issue was of major consequence to the industry, however, members of ABC's board of directors and other leaders contributed personal financial assistance to the contractor involved in any precedential legal battle.

Government is too important to let politicians run it unwatched.

WILL ROGERS
HUMORIST-ACTOR

Action on the Political Front

Trimmer also emphasized that "Big Labor has its own leftist legislative agenda and ABC must be on the watch constantly for these radical activities at the local, state and federal levels." He pointed out that laws, regulations, and executive orders were being considered that affected the business community adversely and he believed ABC should have a voice in determining what kind of legislation was being passed. Trimmer's contacts with like-minded conservative organizations such as the American Institute of Architects, the Maryland Highway Contractors Association, the Baltimore, Maryland, and United States Chambers of Commerce, and the National Association of Manufacturers also gave ABC access to vital information and mutual action.

Through the *ABC Contractor* magazine, Trimmer suggested ten criteria for judging the merits of every law under consideration that could affect his members:

ABC CONTRACTOR
John Trimmer, "Mr. ABC," senior staff executive of ABC from 1952 to 2002.

(1) Is it necessary? (2) Can we afford it? (3) What will it cost? (4) How will it affect free enterprise and basic liberties? (5) Is it in the best balanced interest of all? (6) Is it a dangerous "foot-in-the-door" proposition? (7) Does it place too much power in the hands of one individual or group? (8) Does it recognize the importance of the individual and

35

The greatest
things ever done
on earth have
been done
little by little.

THOMAS GUTHRIE
WRITER

minorities? (9) Is its appeal based on emotional propaganda and selfish politics or relevant facts? (10) Does it square with moral convictions?[4]

An article that was reprinted in the *ABC Contractor* in November of 1953 summed up the political obstacles faced by free enterprise in our nation. This essay on "Big Labor and the Democratic Party" was authored by the nationally syndicated columnist, Frank R. Kent. It appeared originally in his home-based *Baltimore Sun*. It could have been written today:

LABOR BOSSES

WASHINGTON, D.C.—There are many public people whose position on political issues is sometimes vague and confused. Their views occasionally shift with the political currents.

Concerning one group, however, this is not accurate at all. This group is composed of the so-called "Labor Bosses," who are sometimes cheap and unsavory fellows. No citizen capable of reasoning from the clear political facts should have any difficulty in coming to three firm conclusions about these gentlemen.

One is that they are completely identified with and quite dominant in the Democrat party. This has been true for the years during which they had the run of the White House and the personal support of its incumbents. In that period Democrat candidates as well as Democrat policies were—and still are—cleared through them.

The second conclusion is that they are supported by the biggest, best financed and most effective propaganda machine in the country. In these respects it is superior to both the Democrat and Republican party machines and far superior to those of the National Association of Manufacturers, the United States Chamber of Commerce, or any other private organization.

The power of this labor publicity is such that it has put the Labor Bosses into politics in a big way. They not only push their views on labor legislation, which is their right, but they attempt to dictate on taxes, farm measures, foreign policy and practically everything else.

They have lists of candidates who are called "Friendly to Labor" and lists of those called "Unfriendly to Labor." They go into districts and states to support and oppose. Interviews, speeches and statements flow steadily.

The third conclusion is that what these Labor Bosses really want is to run the country. Here, too, they are within their rights—if they can do it. In the back of their minds there is the idea of an American Labor Party similar to the British Labour Party, which, ultimately, will take over the government . . . This, of course, is a bluff since the obvious strategy for these labor organizations is to achieve their objectives through the Democrat party.

Member Training and Benefits

Labor relations was not the only arena in which John Trimmer and ABC pioneered. It became apparent that the senior executives and managers of some member firms received their early training inside building trades unions. They had little formal education and no management experience. To satisfy this need, Trimmer provided seminars led by professionals who volunteered their time for courses on operating a construction business as well as seminars on how to solve people-problems. He recalled that members trooped to a workshop entitled "Why Contractors Go Broke and How to Avoid It."

Group hospitalization insurance was virtually unknown in the open shop side of the construction industry in the 1950s. It caused union agents to seek to organize non-union firms by pointing to their inferior employee benefits. That vulnerability and the legitimate need to improve worker health protection motivated another major initiative in the young association's expansion. ABC's first "Security Plan" was created in 1956, with the able assistance of Charles Herget, a Baltimore-based insurance consultant and ABC member. It was underwritten by the Connecticut General Life Insurance Company of Hartford and was superior to existing trade union benefit plans because of its breadth of coverage. It provided Association members with an excellent means of recruiting and retaining employees. And its low group premium rates through ABC's ever-broadening group purchasing base induced participating firms to continue their Association membership.

It takes twenty-five years to make an overnight success.

EDDIE CANTOR
COMEDIAN

Social Activities

In keeping with Maryland's claim to be "the land of pleasant living," ABC was soon sponsoring crab feasts, oyster roasts, bull roasts, dinner dances, golf outings, and a bowling league. Trimmer knew that these social functions served many purposes: fun and relaxation for all, business networking, promotion of the open shop cause, membership *esprit de corps*, and income to help the Association's tight operating budget. There also were ABC-sponsored construction fairs featuring exhibits of the latest accessories, materials, and equipment that attracted hundreds of the industry's representatives as well as some of the general public. These trade shows and social outings, wrote Trimmer, "reflected the amazing vigor of the young organization and the enthusiasm and loyalty of its members."[5]

On the critical issue of increasing the size of the Association, the following advertisement appeared in the *ABC Contractor* magazine of November 1953. It helped to attract many members, reaching a total of 478 new ABCers by 1954:

WHY DON'T YOU JOIN ABC?

Here's one building trades organization that draws no lines on race, color or creed. It doesn't ask whether you are union or non-union. If you're in any phase of the building business—doing $50,000,000 a year or just supplying knotholes to carpenters—you can benefit from ABC.

You may ask how we are so sure? Well, many firms in Maryland agree that the ABC is important and beneficial enough to remain as members.

What's in it for you? Will you get more business? Let's say you have a problem that you don't know how to tackle. You don't know the ins-and-outs of government officialdom or you may be at a loss on a technical procedure. Well, if you're an ABCer, you can get the answer from our office or ask any member. You'd be surprised at the help you get, without charge, from other members. And sometimes that can be worth many a dollar in your pocket.

In today's modern swirl of business life, you may wonder what's really on the way in the future. Where are the real opportunities? How can costs be cut? What are your competitors doing? ABC is constantly studying such questions as these. What about taxes and punitive schemes dreamed up by selfish politicians, often goaded by improper interests? Or you have some labor problems. Who's going to help you to solve them? Well, the ABC for one.

As people like you join ABC, it becomes stronger all around. It becomes powerful enough to give the special-privilege boys a hard time. And we always tell a new member: "We need you as much as you need us."

Sign up today! Schedule of Annual Dues: General Contractors $50; Sub-Contractors in the Baltimore Area $25; Counties $15; Suppliers and Associates $10.[6]

> **There is no force so powerful as an idea whose time has come.**
>
> SENATOR EVERETT DIRKSEN (R-IL)

Trimmer Creates ABC's Celebrated Epithet

On the philosophical side, John Trimmer reaffirmed that ABC was organized "to support the open shop" and its chief purpose was "to gain a business climate where union and non-union firms can work together in harmony." Then, as ABC moved into heavily unionized areas, he added: "I found that 'open shop' connoted 'anti-union,' and so I coined the phrase MERIT SHOP." The objective, he explained, as reported in the prominent *Engineering News-Record* magazine, "was to emphasize that these new words denote a fair and economical way of workplace life." He added: "They mean that construction projects are awarded on the competitive basis of meritorious performance rather than an employer's union or non-union status and employees are rewarded on the basis of their individual merit." It's "a way of life worth clinging to and fighting for in an era when special interests threaten to engulf the free enterprise system," he concluded.[7]

Trimmer's original draft of the four principles upon which the ABC merit shop movement was founded still serves as an entrepreneurial beacon today:

First, it is in the public's best interest that all construction contracts be awarded to the lowest responsible bidder through open and fair competition, regardless of union or non-union affiliation. This practice assures the consumer of the best possible job for the dollars paid.

39

Courage is the
first of all
qualities
because it is
the quality
which
guarantees
all others.

WINSTON CHURCHILL
BRITISH PRIME
MINISTER

Second, management has the right to direct the activities of its business according to the policies and goals established by its own leaders, searching for efficiency and productivity every step of the way.

Third, each employee in a merit shop company should have the voluntary choice to belong or refrain from belonging to a labor organization and should be paid and promoted based on his or her skills, initiative and responsibility for individual accomplishment rather than on employment seniority alone.

Fourth, discrimination based on race, color, nationality, sex, religion or creed is contrary to the spirit of the Republic of the United States and harmful to our nation both morally and economically.[8]

ABC's Rapid Growth in the 1950s

With John Trimmer at the helm, the Baltimore-based ABC advanced at a remarkable pace. He and his voluntary team of ABC contractors traversed the neighboring countryside, organizing and providing support for new members and new chapters. The objective was to nurture them, provide assistance and legal advice on labor problems that arose, attend promotional functions, and generally encourage the enthusiasm that characterized the young association.

Many of these initial confabs with potential new members were held in a secretive atmosphere to prevent hostile unionists from observing who was present and jotting down license plates of the attendees for future harassment. Trimmer's car was tailed by every kind of vehicle from motorcycles and pick-up trucks to black limousines with shaded windows. Once he returned to his hotel room late at night after an ABC meeting and discovered that the adjoining guest room had been firebombed. His only comment was: "They obviously weren't even smart enough to get the room number right."

The first national convention of ABC members was held at the Claridge Hotel in Atlantic City in 1958. Charles Harbaugh, president of the U.S. Chamber of Commerce, and Jerome Fenton, general counsel of the National Labor Relations Board, were the featured speakers before enthusiastic attendees from Maryland, Pennsylvania, Delaware, and the District of Columbia.

Coincidentally, on that same day Edward Kelly, a leader of the unionized Associated General Contractors Association of America, was telling agents of the federal Small Business Administration in the nation's capital: "Putting non-union men on a job with union men is a ridiculous experiment like trying to mix oil and water."[9]

Twelve contractors formed the first ABC Chapter outside of Baltimore. It was chartered in 1957 and is still based on the Eastern Shore of Maryland, in Salisbury. Norman Holland, Sr., of Pocahontas Concrete Co., Roland Dashielle of Dashielle Construction Co., Elias Nuttle of Nuttle Lumber Co., Bill Schwartz of Goslee Roofing Co., Charles Brown of Brown Glass Co., and John Briggs of Briggs Construction Co. were among the founders, with the assistance of John Trimmer.

A year later, chapters were chartered in Anne Arundel County/Southern Maryland (now renamed the Chesapeake Chapter), in Western Maryland (renamed in 1964 with Southwestern Pennsylvania and West Virginia as the Cumberland Valley Chapter), and in the District of Columbia area (called the Metropolitan Washington Chapter). The Keystone Chapter was established in 1959 in Lancaster County of south-central Pennsylvania, and ABC's banner moved into the metropolitan Philadelphia area (Delaware Valley and Lehigh Valley) plus New Jersey and Northern Virginia about a year later.

This interstate expansion caused the original charter of ABC to be amended on July 28, 1959. The words "of Maryland" were deleted and the organization's current official name of Associated Builders and Contractors, Inc. was recorded.[10] Due to the spectacular growth, Baltimore contractors needed a separate entity to deal with their own local construction issues and services. So ABC reorganized itself and the original founders of ABC of Maryland became members of a newly created Baltimore Metropolitan Chapter. Ira Rigger, a specialty contractor, was its first president.

By the end of the 1950s, ABC had grown to eight hundred members and the internal support staff was increased. A new and improved national headquarters office located at 2323 Maryland Avenue in Baltimore City was donated by Ed Colwill, a co-founder and third national president.

According to the corporate minutes of ABC's board of directors as signed by its eighth president, Larry Best, the Association's income for the year 1959

To grow and know what one is growing towards—that is the force of all strength and confidence in life.

JAMES BAILLIE
PUNDIT

COURTESY MULLAN FAMILY

The Carrollton Apartments complex at Greenway and University Parkway was completed in 1954 by Mullan Contracting Co. at a cost of $1,500,000. It was the first air-conditioned, elevator-type housekeeping apartment complex with an underground garage ever built in Baltimore.

(in rounded numbers) totaled $74,000. It consisted of membership dues—$38,000; the *ABC Contractor* magazine advertisements—$22,000; social affairs (bull and oyster roasts)—$6,200; equipment distributors—$2,000; consulting service to utility contractors—$2,000; insurance trust fund—$2,300; membership directory—$2,300.

Major expenses that same year included the total combined annual salaries of John Trimmer and his staff of five employees—$37,865; staff health insurance—$580; legal fees—$6,800; printing, stationery, and office expenses—$2,000; publishing the *ABC Contractor* magazine—$11,000; rent, telephone, gas, and electric, and postage—$4,100; travel and entertainment—$2,200; public relations and publicity—$1,000; taxes—$650; and accounting—$650. (Yes, ABC operated "in the black".)

ABC Defeats a Union-Only Construction Bid

An early example of trade union intimidation occurred that same year of 1959 in the metropolitan Washington, D.C., area. ABC's new chapter there was led by a future national ABC president, Tracy Coleman. The encounter involved Suburban Trust Company, a large bank that was planning to build a branch office but neglected to invite any non-union construction firms to bid on the project.

This snub riled Coleman, Trimmer, and other leaders of the ABC chapter. They immediately sent a delegation to call on bank officials. These naïve executives explained that "several trade unions had substantial trust funds deposited in the bank and the bank didn't want to offend them." The ABC visitors pointed out that many of its own association members and other businesses not involved with unions were important Suburban Trust customers too. But the bankers refused to back away from unionized contractors as "the better choice" to be their builder.

Much to the surprise of these Suburban Trust Company executives, ABC promptly asked its own local members and their customers to threaten to withdraw their bank checking accounts in protest. ABCers also encouraged independent business people to do the same. Within two weeks' time, bank accounts subject to withdrawal from Suburban Trust had mounted to $8 million—and the bankers begged ABC to stop its boycott.

In return, Suburban Trust invited three ABC members to compete in the bidding on the bank's branch office construction job. Eventually the project was awarded to the lowest qualified bidder, namely, ABC member H. O. McAllister. His firm completed the job—despite substantial union harassment—and the bank was pleased with the result. A collateral benefit was that Tracy Coleman's fledgling Metropolitan Washington ABC Chapter became respected in local business circles.

The Distinguished Career of "Mr. ABC"

Little did John Trimmer realize when he was hired in 1952 that he was beginning a heroic, lifelong journey which would become instrumental in creating one of the largest and most influential employer associations in the United States. When contractors asked him years later if he was one of ABC's founding fathers, he would answer, with a twinkle in his eye: "No, but I came in with the second load of bricks."

Trimmer never tired of reminiscing about those early years when he helped to unite what he called "an upstart group of free-spirited builders" who gathered together with him in a small storefront office in Baltimore in 1952. And the fledgling association had its growing pains. Legal battles against Big Labor and Big Government depleted the meager treasury to the point that dissolution of the organization seemed imminent on several occasions.

Association dues were raised modestly to pay the increasing expenses and the general membership total plunged. But whenever times seemed the bleakest, a small but loyal cadre of dedicated ABC officers and board members would step forward to solve the problem at hand with generous contributions of their own time and money.

We were overwhelming underdogs.

YOGI BERRA
N.Y. YANKEES
CATCHER-PHILOSOPHER

Opinions cannot survive if one has no chance to fight for them.

Thomas Mann
German essayist and Nobel Prize recipient in 1929

The following words that appeared in the May 1954 issue of the *ABC Contractor* magazine summed up John Trimmer's own thoughts on his treasured Association:

The ABC is not an aggressor. We are not starting fights with labor unions. We are not trying to keep people from voluntarily working for other people. We include both union and open shop firms in our membership but without any compulsory affiliation. We include men and women of every race, color, and creed without discrimination. And we call our Association the "merit shop."

It may be a hard pill for some labor bosses to swallow that there is a group of businessmen who won't go along with a contractual set-up under which one side does the dictating and the other side knuckles under.

The strength of ABC is the strength of free enterprise itself. So long as the Association continues to hold to its policies and practices, it cannot but benefit the entire industry. And ABC will stand up for its rights. Through cooperation and the strength that attends it, we will continue to serve the entire industry. ABC wants labor peace, not chaos and terrorism. We want to spend our time coping with the real problems of building in a modern economy. We want to build a better Maryland and a better nation. That is task enough!

Trimmer served as ABC's executive vice president for over twenty-five years. Thereafter, from 1982 until his death in 2002, he was designated "assistant to the president." This title actually meant that he was the mentor, critic, cheerleader, visionary, and conscience of the merit shop crusade.

John Fielder, ABC's twenty-fourth national president ('82) and the CEO of South Coast Electric Company based in Costa Mesa, California, described how Trimmer helped him to succeed in the construction business:

When I wanted to start an open shop business thirty years ago in Southern California, John Trimmer was the first person I called. I visited him and he helped me set up meetings with other successful open shop contractors so that I could learn how they operated effectively. He also helped prepare me for the trials and tribulations to come, and there would be many challenges ahead. At that time, the "construction atmosphere" in California was not good for open shop companies.

There couldn't have been a more perfect individual to head ABC than John Trimmer. He brought dignity to a rough and tough industry and he represented us well. He was a large part of the reason I stayed in business for 30 years—a hero to many, including me.[11]

The greatest use of a life is to spend it for something that will outlast it.

WILLIAM JAMES
PHILOSOPHER-
PSYCHOLOGIST

Charlie Mullan, ABC's founder and first president added: "ABC needed a man to shape our ideas and lead us forward. John Trimmer stepped into that role and became a major industry leader. No one else could have accomplished what John did for the Association."[12]

Phil Abrams, ABC's national president in 1975, described Trimmer as "a brilliant man who never overwhelmed people with his brilliance but let his actions speak instead. He took a rag-tag group of contractors and turned them into a united free market ideology, a cause that forever changed the face of the construction business in the United States."[13]

During his career, Trimmer received many distinguished service awards. To name just a few of the most recent honors, in August of 1999 the editors of *Engineering News-Record*—the construction industry's prestigious publication—named him one of its "Top Construction Leaders of the Past 125 Years." The reason given: "He developed the merit shop philosophy, made that concept and ABC an important part of the dynamics of construction procurement today, and helped to shape this nation and the world by pioneering uncharted territory."

A year or so later, the "Trimmer Award for Teaching Excellence" was endowed through contributions from the John Trimmer Fellows to ABC's Construction Education Foundation. This Foundation presents an annual award to a college faculty member "who best combines teaching skills with the merit shop philosophy, interacts with the merit shop construction community and possesses knowledge of merit shop construction." The winner is announced at ABC's annual national convention and receives a check for $3,500, along with a handsome plaque.

On June 3, 2000, at ABC's 50th anniversary convention in Baltimore, Trimmer was saluted as one of the Association's "leaders of the twentieth century who significantly influenced and strengthened the merit shop construction industry throughout the United States."

These words of Jim Campbell, ABC's seventh national president, say it all about "Mr. ABC": "There are two basic reasons for the success of our Association as the voice of merit shop construction. The first, our cause is morally just. And the second, John Trimmer is on our side!"

If you can talk with crowds and keep your virtue, or walk with Kings—nor lose the common touch...If you can fill the unforgiving minute with sixty seconds' worth of distance run, yours is the earth and everything that's in it.

FROM RUDYARD KIPLING'S POEM "IF"

CHAPTER 7

THE STOVER STEEL
BOYCOTT DEFEAT

IN THE **1950s**, the Associated General Contractors of America was composed of builders committed to the exclusive employment of union labor. It was suffering from open shop competition in Baltimore and throughout the state of Maryland. Naturally the AGCA leaders urged Kingfish Ellis and his Baltimore Building Trades Council to make another try at "correcting" the serious situation.

Ellis agreed. His strategy was to try and force a prominent ABC general contractor—Henry A. Knott, Inc. (owned and managed by the family of ABC founder Charlie Knott)—and its affiliate Garden Construction Company, to operate on a union shop basis or go out of business. The two firms normally worked the "merit shop way," using either qualified non-union or unionized subcontractors on specific jobs as needed, working together as a team.

Big Labor's "Magna Carta"

Kingfish Ellis knew that back in 1935 a pro-union Congress had passed the landmark National Labor Relations Act, also called the "Wagner Act." He understandably revered it as labor's "Magna Carta." For the first time in labor-management relations in the United States, it broadly protected and strongly encouraged the right of unions to organize workers and bargain collectively over wages and working conditions as their "exclusive" representative.

This Wagner Act also contained a first-time list of employer unfair labor practices that prohibited management from interfering with certain specified "union rights." The Building Trades Legal Department also assured the Kingfish that the Supreme Court had declared "peaceful picketing is the workingman's means of communication" and therefore protected by the Constitution's First Amendment guarantee of freedom of speech.[1]

As previously noted, the Baltimore Building Trades chieftain favored a "top-down" attack on the non-union contractor, Henry A. Knott, Inc., whose employees were working on the same projects in harmony along side unionized craftsmen of other contractors. That meant posting union pickets around all project entrances and enforcing Big Labor's unbreakable rule against any union member ever crossing any union picket line anywhere at any time. The Kingfish's anticipated result would be a work stoppage at the construction job site's and surrender by the non-union employer.

But he misread both the applicable law and his targeted opponent.

A New "Slave Labor Law" Bans Secondary Boycotts

Ironically, the stated purpose of the Wagner Act was to end all strikes and other forms of "industrial warfare," but that goal was never fulfilled. While the number of employees organized by labor unions rose dramatically under the Wagner Act's protection and encouragement, so did the number and intensity of strikes and violence that caused most of these union successes. A national wave of work stoppages occurred which shut down steel mills, auto assembly plants, seaports, communications operations, and other facilities critical to a World War II victory.

By 1946, these confrontations had led to public sentiment that labor organizations were abusing their privileged bargaining status—and the Democratic Party was considered to be their political pawn. The uproar caused a newly constituted Congress led by Republicans to pass the amendatory and soon-to-become equally renowned Labor-Management Relations Act of 1947, commonly referred to as the "Taft-Hartley Act."

Kingfish Ellis detested what little he knew about this revised statute which Big Labor nicknamed the "slave labor law." It was adopted by a bipartisan coalition of Republicans and conservative southern Democrats who were able to override the veto of a furious Harry Truman. The President told news media that he resented the "audacity" of the new law. Why? It leveled the labor relations playing field by adding both a new list of union unfair labor practices and new legal protection for certain rights of employees and their employers.

One of the technically drafted amendments had a critical effect on the "top-down" unionization ploy planned by Kingfish Ellis—and he jumped into a legal quagmire. Ellis understood all about a "primary" economic strike attack against an employer whose workers a union actually represents, but so-called "secondary" union activity that coerces a non-union employer was his goal. Such action, as contemplated by the Kingfish, had suddenly become illegal under Section 8(b)(4)(ii)(B) of the 1947 Taft-Hartley law.

Although the section does not specifically mention the term "secondary boycott," it prohibits union threats or coercion (including picketing) to induce certain types of strikes. The illegal act occurs when the union's objective is to force a "secondary" or "neutral" unionized employer to cease doing business with or perform services for a targeted "primary" non-union employer with whom the union has a so-called "labor dispute."[2]

The '47 Taft-Hartley statute also includes two remedial sanctions against these new "top-down" union boycott violations. Section 10(l) states that if the National Labor Relations Board has "reasonable cause" to believe that a Section 8(b)(4) unfair labor practice [secondary boycott] charge is true and that a complaint should issue against the picketing union involved, the Labor Board must immediately petition a federal district court for a "temporary" injunction against such picketing.

This court order will restrain the allegedly illegal boycott and picketing "pending the final adjudication of the Labor Board with respect to such matter." During that time period, the Board is required to investigate and process the secondary boycott charge on a "priority basis over all other cases" since project completion time is critical at a construction site. And Section 303 of the Taft-Hartley Act allows the "injured" contractor to sue the "guilty" union in a federal district court for damages sustained because of such unlawful picketing activity.[3]

Union Picket Lines and "Scabs"

Human nature seldom changes. It has proven time and time again that permitting hostile union strikers to congregate and picket at the scene of their labor dispute—regardless of whether adjudged to be primary or secondary

If you can think of something which is connected with something without thinking of the something it is connected to, you have a legal mind.

THOMAS REED POWELL, ESQ. PROFESSOR AT HARVARD LAW SCHOOL

activity—is to invite coercion and violence. That's what Judge Henshaw meant when, in reviewing the evidence in a case many years ago, he said:

> A picket line in its very nature tends and is designed by physical intimidation to deter other men from seeking employment in the places vacated by the strikers. It tends and is designed to drive business away from the boycotted place, not by the legitimate methods of persuasion, but by the illegitimate means of physical intimidation and fear. Crowds naturally collect, disturbances of the peace are always imminent and of frequent occurrence.[4]

Another realistic jurist, Judge McPherson, added back in 1905:

> At times the paths and walks are obstructed. At times the pickets are near by, making grimaces, and at times acting as if violence were intended, and at times uttering profanity and vulgarity. There is and can be no such thing as "peaceful picketing," any more than there can be chaste vulgarity, or peaceful mobbing, or lawful lynching.[5]

The ultimate goal of a union's secondary boycott in the construction industry always was—and still is today—to use "neutral" third party leverage to force a targeted non-union contractor either to accept the compulsory unionization of its workforce and sign a labor contract or go bankrupt. Kingfish Ellis knew that when a craft union sets up a picket line at a building project where both non-union and union members are working, it immediately threatens the required coordination between contractors and their employees who have all been working in harmony at that common situs. The refusal of unionized carriers and suppliers to make deliveries or pickups at the picketed facility adds to the tension.

Ellis also knew that a picket line causing a work stoppage of even a few days at such a common situs could be the difference between the targeted non-union contractor making a profit and losing money in the pressurized construction business. And he counted on the fact that the cardinal sin within the labor movement—punishable by monetary fine, expulsion, and/or bodily harm—is for a union member to become a "scab" by crossing the union picket line and thereby undermining "labor solidarity."

A rugged character named Jack London, who wrote great novels like *Call of the Wild* about life on the Alaskan frontier, agreed. This ardent supporter of organized labor described a "scab" in a lengthy speech in 1903 to the Oakland Socialist Party called the "War of the Classes." Here is an excerpt from that ten-page-long diatribe:

> After God created the rattlesnake, the toad and the vampire, He had some awful substance left with which He made a traitorous two-legged animal with a cork-screw soul, a waterlogged brain, and a backbone of jelly and glue. Where others have hearts, the "scab" carries a tumor of rotten principles. When a scab comes down the street, people turn their backs, angels weep in Heaven, and the Devil shuts the gates of Hell to keep him out.... Esau was a traitor to himself; Judas Iscariot was a traitor to his God; Benedict Arnold was a traitor to his country; a SCAB is a traitor to his God, his country, his wife, his family and his class.[6]

Three-quarters of a century later, the Supreme Court ruled that constitutional law gives every labor organization a "free speech" license to use Jack London's definition of a scab. Any such "truthful but intemperate, abusive or insulting language is legally permissible without fear of restraint or penalty," said the nation's highest court, "if the union believes such rhetoric is an effective means to make its point in uninhibited, robust debate."[7]

Paradoxically, the dictionary definition of a "scab" in the union-free world has always been "a crust or protective covering that forms over a sore or wound during the healing process..."[8]

The New Law Backfires on Ellis

During the period in which the Kingfish began to mount his campaign to unionize the employees of Henry A. Knott, Inc. and its affiliated Garden Construction Company in Baltimore City by top-down pressure on their management, the Taft-Hartley Act's Section 8(b)(4) ban on a secondary boycott had not been tested locally. As noted before, these non-union general contractors

If unions hold the whip hand, upon whose back does the lash fall?

MARGARET THATCHER
BRITISH PRIME
MINISTER

51

He who is his own
attorney will have
a fool for a client.

ANONYMOUS

made a frequent practice of using qualified unionized subcontractors from time to time that worked peacefully alongside non-union subs in other crafts at a common job site. The over-confident Kingfish ignored that profitable custom as well as the negative implications of the new statutory secondary boycott amendment. Even management's side of the unionized construction industry appeared oblivious to the Taft-Hartley Act's new provisions.

On March 25, 1953, Kingfish Ellis established picket lines surrounding the Claremont and Jessup projects of the targeted merit shoppers in the early morning as both union and non-union tradesmen reported for work. The Carpenters Union claimed that the job sites were being picketed for the purpose of "organization" of non-union employees. Significantly, however, no notice was given by union signs or otherwise that the picketing related only to Knott and Garden Construction—the two "primary" non-union generals against whom the Building Trades had targeted a "labor dispute." The picket signs simply read: WORKING CONDITIONS ON THIS JOB UNFAIR TO CARPENTERS DISTRICT COUNCIL.

Non-union craftsmen of the Knott and Garden Construction firms and their non-union subcontractors on the two job sites paid no attention to the peacefully conducted picketing at all entrances to the projects and crossed the union lines to report for work. But as the Kingfish anticipated, unionized craftsmen employed by so-called "neutral" or "secondary" subcontractors working at the sites refused to "scab" by crossing the picket lines. Instead, they struck the projects.

Stover Steel Defies the Building Trades

Then something happened that the Kingfish hadn't counted on. A tiny but brave *unionized* subcontractor called Stover Steel Company and owned by John Piezonki had assigned six ironworkers to the Knott and Garden Construction jobs. Defying Big Labor's "unbreakable rule," they crossed the picket lines and continued to team up with the non-union Knott and Garden Construction tradesmen who were still working at the two job sites.

That "scab treason" came about because John Piezonki was meagerly capitalized and his faithful employees knew that he faced the loss of his construction contracts plus monetary penalties if he failed to complete the projects on time. And predictably, Charley Muntain, business representative of Local 16 of the Ironworkers Union, refused to honor Piezonki's plea to make an exception in his dire financial situation by easing the picketing order on Stover Steel employees.

Piezonki was in such desperate economic straits that he finally turned to Charlie Knott for help. The upshot was that Knott and other ABCers agreed to assist Stover Steel. They began by retaining a prominent local labor lawyer named Earle Shawe to challenge the legality of the picketing against this "neutral" unionized subcontractor.

Initial encouraging news for ABC was that the Baltimore Regional Office of the Labor Board investigated the case and decided that there was "reasonable cause" to believe that Stover Steel's unfair labor practice charge of an illegal secondary boycott in violation of the new Section 8(b)(4) of the Taft-Hartley Act was valid. At that point, the Labor Board's Regional Office was required to petition a federal district court for a temporary injunction against the allegedly illegal picketing until the Labor Board held a formal hearing on the dispute.

Luckily for Stover Steel, the Labor Board's request for injunctive relief was heard by District Court Judge William C. Coleman, a legend in his own time. One biographer of the famous jurist described him this way:

> His opinions were never dull. They seemed to ripple along, full of color, and my god, how full of conviction! His unyielding distaste for New Deal legislation and all it stood for [which he consistently ruled "unconstitutional"] earned him the reputation of "an extreme right wing reactionary" among the liberal community.[9]

Judge Coleman's ultra-conservative rulings also proved that he was equally disgusted with all kinds of "socialistic labor union shenanigans" against America's free enterprise system. In this case, his "world-class" temporary injunction required the complete removal of all picketing from the Knott and Garden Construction job sites involved in Stover Steel's unfair labor practice charge. Even more unprecedented, the judge restrained "every AFL-CIO affiliated trade union in America from attempting to picket or otherwise interfere with

You can observe a lot just by watching.

Yogi Berra
N.Y. Yankees
Catcher-Philosopher

any construction subcontractor doing business with any general contractor within the entire State of Maryland."[10]

The trade unions involved went into a state of shock.

Stover Steel's Rocky Road to Final Victory

Eventually, with all picketing eliminated on a temporary basis by Judge Coleman, Stover Steel's unfair labor practice charge came before the Labor Board's trial examiner, George Downing, for a full hearing on its merits. Following a lengthy trial that attracted area-wide publicity, Downing agreed with Judge Coleman that the boycott was illegal:

"He has a reputation for swift justice."

The record shows that the [Baltimore Building Trades] Council had long been engaged in a campaign directed at the non-union general contractors in the Baltimore area (including Knott and Garden) to require them to employ members of its affiliated building trades unions. The Council's tactics included both purely persuasive efforts (e.g., the conferences between Clark Ellis and Knott) and attempts to force the general contractors to capitulate by depriving them of the services, i.e., business, of union subcontractors by causing the removal of the latter's employees from the job.

The object of the latter tactics was not only to force or require such union subcontractors to cease doing business with the general contractors, but in practical effect it prevented them from doing business on the job sites during the course of the dispute, since they were rendered helpless to proceed under their contracts in the absence of labor supplied by the crafts unions...

Though the evidence shows that the Council set upon its new course of ["organizational"] action with full awareness of the pitfalls and problems presented by the secondary boycott provisions of the Taft-Hartley Act...yet its objectives remained as before. What was changed was the quality of the means it employed to attain them.

But the change in methods could not disguise the objects of the action which was sought to be induced. Plainly, those methods still envisioned one objective which was illegal, i.e., to force or require the union subcontractors, *who were in no way involved in the dispute*, to cease performance—indeed to prevent performance—of their contractual obligations to the general contractors. Thus the [union] subcontractors, *helpless and impotent neutrals*, became the chief victims of a dispute which they were powerless to resolve."[11] [emphasis added].

Following appeal of this ruling by an incensed Kingfish Ellis, the Labor Board's top brass cooperated with the building trades unions by reversing the decision of its own trial examiner. And so on June 28, 1954, just a year after the initial picketing took place, the five member Labor Board in Washington, D.C., ruled that the effect of the picketing on the "neutral" union subcontractors was to be regarded as legal. It was "merely incidental to the [legitimate] union organizing campaign conducted against Knott and Garden Construction Companies."[12]

ABC Wins Final Round

With ABC's continued legal, financial, and moral support, Stover Steel appealed the Labor Board's decision to the appropriate federal court. Justice prevailed about eight months later. On February 26, 1955, Chief Judge Parker of the Fourth Circuit Court of Appeals (writing for himself and fellow Judges Soper and Dobie) agreed with the Labor Board's trial examiner (plus Judge Coleman and the Knott family) that an illegal secondary boycott had occurred. In overruling the Labor Board, Judge Parker concluded that it was "no answer" to say that the picketing was merely "an organizational campaign" (and therefore constitutionally protected freedom of speech):

Here the main purpose as well as the effect of the picketing was to drive the employees of the [neutral] union subcontractors from the job. This was clearly engaging in a *secondary boycott* within the prohibition of the statute. The consequences thereof may not be avoided by reason of the fact that the ultimate purpose was to organize the workers of the [non-union] general contractors at the work sites where the picketing was carried on.[13] [emphasis added]

Judge Parker also outlined and confirmed all of the conditions necessary for lawful picketing to occur at a "common construction situs" just as they were established in the Labor Board's previously decided *Moore Dry Dock* case. Then the judge held that at least one of these necessary factors was violated by the Baltimore Building Trades Council since the picket signs were directed at the entire project. They erroneously failed to clearly and truthfully identify and disclose that the labor dispute was only with the targeted "primary" employer, namely general contractor Henry A. Knott, Inc. and its subsidiary, Garden Construction Company.[14]

First, proper identification of the targeted firms, other common situs picketing requirements that the building trades unions must adhere to as established in the Labor Board's landmark *Moore Dry Dock* decision (and as Judge Parker reaffirmed), were and still are, second, picketing can only be carried on when the targeted primary employer with whom the union has a dispute is engaged in its normal business at the situs, and third, the picketing must be limited to places reasonably close to the construction situs where the targeted primary employer and its employees are working.[15]

The Famous "Reserved Gate" Doctrine

Under *Moore Dry Dock*, in order to obtain injunctive relief and monetary damages against an illegal secondary boycott and the resulting strikes, the picketed primary contractor must also establish a separate entrance/exit gate reserved exclusively for its own employees, business visitors, and suppliers. Then a second notice must be posted requiring all other contractors and subcontractors, plus their employees, business visitors, and suppliers, to use another separate "neutral" reserved entrance/exit gate.

At the same time, the picketing union, all other local craft unions, their local building trades council, and all unionized subcontractors working at the job site must be notified of the separate dual-gated means of access at the project's common situs. For further leverage and legal protection, involved ABC contractors are also advised to notify international parent unions of the ongoing picketing by their locals. If the picketing union fails to comply with this "reserved gate" system, it amounts to an unlawful secondary boycott that may be enjoined by the courts, as heretofore mentioned.[16] "The pivotal issue in each case," said a federal appellate court in later litigation won by ABC's seventeenth president, Phillip Abrams ('75), "is the union's intent."[17]

When the federal appellate court handed down its ruling favorable to ABCers in *Stover Steel*, a local news weekly called the *Labor Herald* announced that "one of the blackest pages in the history of the Baltimore Building Trades Council has just been written." And in Washington, D.C., the Building Trades Department of the AFL-CIO protested publicly against the federal court's "outrageous decision."

The Supreme Court Protects Picketing Restrictions

In reaching its Stover Steel ruling, Chief Judge Parker's federal Circuit Court of Appeals in 1955 cited and relied on the Supreme Court's benchmark case in *NLRB v. Denver Building & Construction Trades Council*. There the Supreme Court had held, four years earlier in 1951, that (1) a "neutral" unionized general contractor and a "targeted" non-union subcontractor working on the same project were separate legal entities; (2) that secondary boycott provisions of the Taft-Hartley Act [Section 8 (b)(4)] prohibited a trade union from picketing the entire "common job site," and (3) that "unoffending employers and others should be shielded from pressures in controversies not their own."

The Supreme Court in Denver thus spelled out the legal cornerstone that infuriates Big Labor because it permits ABC's merit shop movement to defeat common situs picketing. As the Court concluded:

> The fact that the contractor and subcontractor were engaged on the same construction project and that the [primary] contractor had some supervision over the [secondary] subcontractor's work did not eliminate the status of each as an independent contractor or make the employees of one the employees of another.[18]

The minute you read something you can't understand, you can almost be sure it was written by a lawyer.

WILL ROGERS
COMEDIAN-
PHILOSOPHER

Shake and shake
the catsup bottle,
none will come,
and then a lot'll.

Richard Armour
Writer-post

It soon became apparent that the fledgling ABC was more than a petty nuisance to the building and construction trade unions. Speaking for the victors in the *Stover Steel* case, ABC's third president, Ed Colwill ('52), was jubilant. But he also noted that this legal fight with the trades unions hadn't been easy: "One of our toughest challenges was financing the litigation. Money was never a problem for Big Labor, with its membership dues treasure-trove and battery of lawyers, but in the early days there was just a handful of us contractors who kept the cash flowing. We dug down deep to give something extra and protect free enterprise."[19]

ABC Executive Director John Trimmer added triumphantly:

> *ABC was responsible for helping to validate the new secondary boycott provisions of federal labor law. It was quite a feather in the cap of the young Association at a critical point in the growth of the merit shop. Our philosophy of the freedom of non-union and union contractors to work together voluntarily in harmony is concomitant with the best interests of all parties concerned and America's capitalistic society.*[20]

CHAPTER 8

SELBY-BATTERSBY & CO. OVERCOMES A "STANDARD AGREEMENT"

THE STOVER STEEL CASE VICTORY BY **ABC** caught the attention of the premier national trade journal covering the building and construction industry. *Engineering News-Record* or "ENR." It began to notice and report on the activities of ABC just five years after it was founded. In 1955 this prestigious and impartial magazine, published by a division of McGraw-Hill Company[1] and frequently quoted herein, made an ominous prediction:

> Baltimore will soon see a joint effort on the part of unionized con-
> tractors and the building trades to improve the competitive position
> of union shop operations in an area where non-union construction
> has been a source of costly labor strife.

ENR's forecast was all too accurate. The article went on to discuss the constitution and by-laws of the Building & Construction Trades Council of Baltimore. They included an unused policy that had long been a powerful
organizational weapon of the construction trades in the Chicago area. These
documents urged that an agreement should be reached between all unionized
contractors, their subcontractors, and the local trades council (consisting of
approximately nineteen craft unions in Baltimore) that "no member of any
affiliated union will be allowed to work on a job where there are non-union

Justice is always in jeopardy.

WALT WHITMAN
WRITER-POET

personnel of any craft at work except by special dispensation of the Council." This so-called "Chicago Plan" or "Standard Agreement" was established in 1926, years before passage of the Wagner Act of 1935 or the amendatory Taft-Hartley Act of 1947 and its secondary boycott prohibition discussed in Chapter 7.

Chicago's Standard Agreement was not being enforced in Baltimore and unionized general contractors began to complain to Kingfish Ellis that many of their union subcontractors were working for non-union generals without the required Trades Council clearance to do so. That "disloyalty" gave ABC's general contractors a competitive advantage by accepting bids from both union and non-union subs. Together, working in harmony, they were performing much of the available construction work on a merit shop basis.

Union Coercion "Chicago Style"

Kingfish Ellis had learned the hard way (in the *Stover Steel* case) that it would be legally difficult to break up this mutually profitable arrangement. Nevertheless, in March of 1955, with the support of Baltimore's unionized Associated General Contractors, he decided once more to take "corrective" action. This time he would implement Chicago's Standard Agreement.

The new ruse simply meant that unionized general contractors in the Baltimore area would agree to do business only with union subcontractors and these union subs, in turn, would work only with union generals. A model Standard Agreement was drawn up by the Kingfish and his Trades Council for signing by all local unionized contractors and their subs. They would operate as the "Joint Conference Board for Associated Construction Employers of Maryland and the Baltimore Building and Construction Trades Unions."

For added support in this third "top-down" attack to force the unionization of ABC members, the Kingfish invited all of the international craft union general presidents to come from their headquarters offices in Washington, D.C., and "pay uh friendly visit ta Bawlmer." He figured that they would help "pasuade" every union subcontractor to sign the Standard Agreement and "clobba all da stinkin' open shop bums."

Frank Bonadio, who was Secretary-Treasurer of the AFL-CIO's National Building & Construction Trades Department at the time, directed the international union "coaxing" process. Pressure was brought to bear on friendly architects and project owners to cooperate, with special attention also given to commercial and industrial construction users whose own personnel were unionized. Managers of manufacturing plants were threatened with slowdowns if they continued to do business with any open shop contractor. The Teamsters Union cooperated by stopping deliveries of supplies and materials to non-union construction projects that were targeted.

In due course Chicago's Standard Agreement became effective throughout the metropolitan Baltimore area. All of the unionized generals in Baltimore complied with its terms. And one by one the unionized subs capitulated and signed up. The only balkers were members of the Tile, Terrazzo, and Marble Subcontractors Association. Eventually even these union subs reluctantly caved in too, except for one lone holdout (as in the *Stover Steel* case).

A small union subcontractor by the name of Selby-Battersby & Co. refused to sign the Standard Agreement under any circumstances. It was no coincidence that one of ABC's founders, Phil Cloyes, was associated with the owners in the management of this plucky little firm.

Selby-Battersby complained that it performed most of its work for non-union general contractors and could not afford to be deprived of those lucrative jobs. Its employees were veteran craftsmen who were accustomed to working amicably side by side with non-union workers and did not want to see their paychecks stopped for any reason. That defiance caused Kingfish Ellis and his Trades Council to give the union journeymen working for Selby-Battersby a Hobson's choice: either surrender their union membership cards or go on strike against their own employer. They reluctantly chose obedience to the Trades Council and a work stoppage occurred on April 21, 1955, that shut down the entire merit shop construction project where they were working.

At first the bantam Selby-Battersby firm attempted to resolve this "labor dispute" through conferences with the Kingfish and national craft union officials. When the mediation effort failed, once again a unionized sub and ABC faced a major decision.

Selby-Battersby Fights Back

At a dramatic conference of the ABC board of directors on April 28, 1955, the vote was unanimous to support Selby-Battersby and jointly pursue a legal

Be sure you're right—then go ahead.

Davy Crockett
Frontiersman

challenge to the Standard Agreement. An unfair labor practice charge was filed on May 3, 1955, with the National Labor Relations Board in Baltimore, again assisted ably by the law office of Earle Shawe. Under the charge, Selby-Battersby and ABC sued three local trade unions, their parent internationals, and the Kingfish's affiliated Baltimore Building Trades Council who allegedly were in "conspiratorial liaison" with the newly created Joint Conference Board for Associated Construction Employers of Maryland.

The ABC charge further claimed that the labor organizations were inducing a general strike of their own craftsmen in order to force targeted non-union firms to sign the "Standard Agreement" in violation of the new Section 8(b)(4) secondary boycott provisions of the Taft-Hartley Act.

ABC's John Trimmer remembered the tense situation this way:

> It is hard to conceive the uproar that this Labor Board charge caused in the construction industry in the Baltimore area. Strong merit shop bonds between generals and subcontractors were strained. The union subs were facing substantial losses in business. Open shop subs who had enjoyed working with union generals were likewise out in the cold."[2]

A month after the unfair labor practice charge was filed, the Labor Board's regional director in Baltimore, John "Doc" Penello, found sufficient merit in it to seek a temporary federal district court injunction on behalf of the charging parties (Selby-Battersby and ABC) pending the Labor Board's formal hearing on the complaint. It soon became obvious to the Building Trades Council and its affiliated unions that they were facing a federal court restraining order—presumably to be embellished by the renewed wrath of their mortal enemy, the aforementioned Judge William Coleman.

The Council agreed hastily to avoid that potential humiliation by stopping all picketing, work stoppages and other pressure tactics until there was a final decision in the case. It also consented to revert to the "status quo" as to normal job site work rules and practices until a Labor Board–appointed trial examiner had time to decide the case at a full trial on its merits and issue an "intermediate report" to the Labor Board in Washington, D.C.

On the forty-fifth day of the hearing on this unfair labor practice charge before Trial Examiner Albert Wheatley, Selby-Battersby and ABC gained a partial victory. The three initially charged local trade unions and their affiliated international unions capitulated and jointly accepted a settlement agreement. As approved by the federal court, it ordered them to "permanently cease and desist" their illegal conduct required by the Standard Agreement or risk contempt-of-court action. But the Kingfish, his Baltimore Building Trades Council (supported by the "parent" AFL-CIO Building Trades Department and the recently formed Joint Conference Board for Associated Construction Employers of Maryland) refused to admit responsibility for any violation of the law.

They contended that they were merely "innocent bystanders . . . "

The hearing of that unsettled portion of the charge before the Labor Board's trial examiner lasted eighty-four more days—making it the longest secondary boycott case on record at the time. Towards the end of the litigation, Kingfish Ellis actually pleaded "the Fifth Amendment" and refused to answer any more questions on the ground that his "responses might incriminate him and his organization."[3]

A Trial Examiner Initiates Victory

On May 11, 1956, the Labor Board's trial examiner, Albert Wheatley, issued his "intermediate report" pertaining to this unfair labor practice charge. He minced no words with respect to the "illegal joint venture" between Kingfish Ellis's local Trades Council and the unionized contractors it represented:

> The record reveals that the Standard Agreement was unlawfully devised by the Joint Conference Board for Associated Construction Employers of Maryland and the Baltimore Building and Construction Trades Unions as a means of forcing contractors operating under open shop conditions to change their ways and utilize the services of members of building crafts unions.[4]

On appeal of this intermediate report by the unions, the biased Labor Board in Washington, D.C., took nine more months to review Wheatley's opinion

An incompetent attorney can delay a trial for several months. A competent attorney can delay one even longer.

EVELLE YOUNGER, ESQ.

and issue its own decision. Just as this same Labor Board had done in the *Stover Steel* case, it again overruled its own trial examiner, agreed with King-fish Ellis, and dismissed all unfair labor practice charges against his Trades Council members and its partner, the unionized Construction Employers of Maryland.[5]

Sixteen months later, following an appeal of the Board's ruling by Selby-Battersby and ABC, the federal Fourth Circuit Court of Appeals finally reviewed the Labor Board's decision and (as the same court had done in *Stover Steel*) reversed it. That meant that the Kingfish, his Baltimore Trades Council, and the Construction Employers of Maryland were ordered to refrain permanently from conducting secondary boycotts and all other illegal activities related to their Standard Agreement.

Fourth Circuit Appellate Judge Clement Haynesworth wrote the court's unanimous opinion (joined by fellow Appellate Circuit Court Judges Morris Soper and the aforementioned Simon Sobeloff) on September 12, 1958. The court concluded that Kingfish Ellis's actions on behalf of the Building Trades Council and the Construction Employers of Maryland encompassed an unlawful joint venture against non-union contractors whom they tried to force into unionization or destroy:

> Belief in the effectiveness of the Standard Agreement as an organizing weapon arose out of the fact that some trades in Baltimore, among them, terrazzo mechanics and apprentices were completely organized. If open shop general contractors could be deprived of their services, it would be difficult or impossible for the generals to bid upon construction projects where those skills were required. It was hoped that such pressures would compel open shop general contractors to capitulate to union demands, forcing their own employees to become members of the union.
>
> If the open shop general contractors could be forced, by this means, to accept the Standard Agreement, non-union subcontractors would be confronted with the alternative of capitulation or liquidation. The purpose of the Standard Agreement required that the pressures behind it be directed against those union subcontractors who

employed workers in the fully organized trades, as the terrazzo mechanics and apprentices. If the purpose was to be accomplished, it was essential that each employer of those trades be brought into compliance or put out of business.

From what is before us, there seems little doubt that the conduct was in violation of the [Taft-Hartley] Act . . . *and the order of the Labor Board will be set aside.*[6] [emphasis added]

On March 30, 1959, the Supreme Court silently exercised its right to refuse the request of the Building Trades Council (called *certiorari*) to review the federal Fourth Circuit Court of Appeals decision. On December 30 of that same year, the Labor Board reluctantly adopted this ruling by the Court of Appeals. That finally ended the litigation.[7]

From the inception of the unfair labor practice charges by Big Labor before the Labor Board in the *Selby-Battersby* case until that victorious moment, almost five years had elapsed. ABC's financial "war chest" was depleted and the Association's membership dues needed to be raised to replenish it. Most contractors contributed to the critical ABC victory, but some balked and a few even resigned from ABC.

John Trimmer wrote for posterity:

> *There is little question that unionized contractors and subcontractors in the Baltimore area lost millions of dollars to merit shoppers by colluding with the Building Trades Council to enforce Chicago's Standard Agreement. The* Selby-Battersby *case was a great victory for ABC—the result of courageous, persistent and sacrificial pursuit of free market principles in the face of powerful, illegal union conduct.*[8]

People who win may have been counted out many times, but they didn't hear the referee.

RON HUBBARD
WRITER

CHAPTER 9

BIG LABOR KILLS
A STATE RIGHT TO WORK BILL

IT IS PARADOXICAL THAT MARYLAND—known as the "Free State" and "Cradle of the Merit Shop"—is not generally recognized to be one of the states that have passed a so-called "right to work law" banning compulsory union membership dues.[1] Section 14(b) of the Taft-Hartley Act provides the key sentence on this important subject:

> Nothing in this Act shall be construed as authorizing the execution or application of agreements *requiring* membership in a labor organization as a condition of employment in any State or Territory in which such execution or application is *prohibited* by State or Territorial law. [emphasis added]

The property which every man has in his own labor. As it is the original foundation of all other property, so it is the most sacred and inviolable.

ADAM SMITH
SCOTTISH ECONOMIST

These forty-four words express the doctrine of the merit shop movement, and Section 14(b) has become an anathema to labor union officials. They claim that it jeopardizes their "union security." That's because legislatures or ballot referendum voters in twenty-two states have defied Big Labor and its powerful political cronies by prohibiting all forms of forced unionism.

In these twenty-two conservative states, individual working men and women may choose *voluntarily* whether or not to join and give *financial support* to a labor organization. Put another way, these state right-to-work laws uphold the historic freedom of Americans—and ABC's merit shop credo—to earn a livelihood without being compelled by a collective bargaining agreement to tender union membership dues as a condition of employment or be discharged.[2] Even

The primary aim of all government regulation of the economic life of the community should be, not to supplant the system of economic enterprise, but to make it work.

CARL BECKER
HISTORIAN

in these twenty-two "voluntary unionism" states, however, many unions deviously negotiate and enforce the standard "compulsory" membership clause in their labor contracts. They perpetuate the ruse by hiding at the end of these contracts a legally protective "CYA" clause like this: "Any provision in our agreement which is ruled illegal by a court of law will not adversely affect the remainder of the agreement and it remains in full force."

For many years ABC has participated in the successful political battle to protect Section 14(b) of the Taft-Hartley Act from repeal by Big Labor and its fellow travelers. They contend that the "right-to-work" nomenclature is semantic nonsense which really means the "right-to-wreck." Truthfully, however, the hated phrase denotes a revered legal doctrine of long standing.

The Constitutional Right to Work

More than a hundred years ago, Supreme Court Justice Joseph Bradley's concurring opinion in *Butchers' Union Slaughter-House Co. v. Crescent City Live-Stock Co.* declared that "the right to follow any of the common occupations in life is an inalienable right; it was formulated as such under the phrase 'pursuit of happiness' in the Declaration of Independence.[3] And in the case of *Truax v. Raich*, decided in 1915, Supreme Court Justice Charles Hughes wrote: "It requires no argument to show that the right to work for a living in the common occupations of the community is of the very essence of the personal freedom and opportunity that it was the purpose of the [Fourteenth] Amendment [of the Constitution] to secure."[4]

In *Smith v. State of Texas*, litigated at about the same time, the Supreme Court held unconstitutional a local statute that discriminatorily prohibited certain qualified persons from becoming railroad conductors. The nation's highest court explained:

> Life, liberty, property and the equal protection of the law, grouped together in the [Fourteenth Amendment of the] Constitution, are so related that the deprivation of any one of those separate and independent rights may lessen or extinguish the value of the other three. Insofar as a man is deprived of the right to labor, his liberty is restricted, his capacity to earn wages and acquire property is lessened,

and he is denied the protection which the law affords those who are permitted to work.... The constitutional guarantee is an assurance that the citizen shall be protected in the right to use his powers of mind and body in any lawful calling.[5]

In 1949, the Supreme Court upheld the constitutionality of state right-to-work laws in *Lincoln Federal Labor Union v. Northwestern Iron & Metal Co.* when it dismissed labor union opposition to them in these words:

> We deem it unnecessary to elaborate the numerous reasons for our rejection of this contention of Appellants [the unions]. Nor need we appraise or analyze with particularity the rather startling ideas suggested to support some of the premises on which Appellants' conclusions rest. There cannot be wrung from a constitutional right of workers to assemble to discuss improvement of their own working standards, a further constitutional right to drive from remunerative employment all other persons who will not or cannot participate in union assemblies.[6]

In 1954 in the case of *Barsky v. Board of Regents*, Justice Douglas confirmed and defined the right to work:

> The right to work, I had assumed, was the most precious liberty that man possesses. Man has indeed as much right to work as he has to live, to be free, to own property... It does many men little good to stay alive and free and propertied if they cannot work. To work means to eat. It also means to live.[7]

Unfortunately for the cause of free enterprise, the Supreme Court also has voiced its approval of compulsory union dues. They are held to be a legitimate means of financial support of the labor union (i.e., as a statutorily created exclusive and privileged collective bargaining agency) from whom all of its members receive "benefits" at work, said the Court in its *Hanson* case.[8] It thereby contradicted all the constitutional law previously cited herein.

No man is good enough to govern another man without that other man's consent.

Abraham Lincoln
16th president

Gompers and Meany Supported Voluntary Unionism

As can be seen, the inalienable right to work traces its origin to a solid foundation in the Declaration of Independence and the Constitution of the United States. Samuel Gompers, architect of the trade union movement in the United States as first president of the American Federation of Labor ("AFL"), repeatedly applied this precept to the relationship between an employee and a labor organization. Writing in 1919 in his trade union publication, the *American Federationist*, Gompers said:

> I want to urge devotion to the fundamentals of human liberty—the principles of voluntarism. No lasting gain has ever come from compulsion. If we seek to force, we but tear apart that which, united, is invincible...
>
> There may be here and there a worker who for certain reasons unexplainable to us does not join a union of labor... It is his legal right and no one can or dare question his exercise of that legal right.[9]

The success of the American Federation of Labor and its member craft unions during forty-three years of Gompers's leadership in the last two decades of the nineteenth century and first quarter of the twentieth century is ample testimony to his labor statesmanship and his defense of the inalienable right to work. It caused George Meany, a patriotic journeyman plumber who rose to become president of the united American Federation of Labor and Congress of Industrial Organizations ("AFL-CIO") from 1952 to 1979, to say of this trailblazer with whom he agreed:

> Gompers founded the American Federation of Labor on the bedrock of voluntarism. Lenin called it a "rope of sand." Gompers retorted that this rope of sand would prove more powerful than chains of steel. He believed with his whole soul in personal freedom, in democratic government, and in the ultimate triumph of voluntary human cooperation over any form of compulsion or dictatorship.[10]

The National Right to Work Committee

For many years there has been a politically *incorrect* non-profit organization dedicated to defending voluntary unionism in the United States. Founded in 1968, this figurative dagger in Big Labor's side is called the "National Right to Work Committee" and is based in Springfield, Virginia. It is led by two able and courageous senior executives, Reed Larson and Mark Mix, and it claims to speak for 2.2 million rank-and-file American workers.[11] The Committee has taken a leading role across the nation in protecting the inherent employment rights of disenchanted and intimidated union members.

In performing this entrepreneurial service, the Committee has been in the forefront of the passage and protection of the 22 state right-to-work laws that have adopted the aforementioned "Gompers Creed" by making compulsory union membership illegal. About 40 percent of America's private sector employees work in these states. And in 1998, the Committee established a "Samuel Gompers Endowment Fund" in honor of the great labor leader's capitalistic ideology. The Fund ensures that a portion of each contributor's estate will be utilized to pursue the ultimate goal of voluntary unionism in all fifty states.

CABLE RISDON PHOTOGRAPHY AND MATTOX COMMERCIAL PHOTOGRAPHY

Reed Larson, chairman (left) and Mark Mix, president, National Right to Work Committee.

There is a statute of Samuel Gompers located at Eleventh Street and Massachusetts Avenue, Northwest, in Washington, D.C. It was sculpted by R. Aitken, and below Gompers's right side is the following inscription:

> So long as we have held fast to voluntary principles and have been actuated and inspired by the spirit of service, we have sustained our forward progress and we have made our labor movement something to be respected and accorded a place in the councils of our Republic. Where we have blundered into trying to force a policy or a decision, even though wise and right, we have impeded, if not interrupted the realization of our own aims.

The chairman of the board of directors of the National Right to Work Committee, Charles Serio, learned about Big Labor's mandatory membership abuses from bitter personal experience. As his story is described in the June 2004 issue

PHOTO BY ANNE SOROCK

Statue of Samuel Gompers, founder of the American Federation of Labor, sculpted by R. Aiken, in Washington, D.C.

of the *National Right to Work Newsletter*, Serio worked in the telecommunications industry in Maryland for more than thirty years. When he accepted a job offer in Baltimore from the old Chesapeake and Potomac Telephone Company in 1966, he voluntarily signed on as a dues-paying member of the Communications Workers of America ("CWA") union. But five years later, he and other employees at C & P Telephone (now part of Verizon) ceased to have a choice.

In the 1971 labor contract negotiations, CWA's leaders convinced C & P management to force nonmembers to pay union dues (euphemistically referred to as "agency fees") or face termination. In exchange, CWA officials agreed to accept a smaller wage increase than the one C & P had originally proposed. That was the beginning of Serio's disillusionment with CWA union officials, he said. His let down deepened a few years later when "the differences between my public policy preferences and those of the union became a source of concern for me."

After fighting unsuccessfully for fifteen years to "reform the CWA union from within," Charles Serio resigned his membership in 1986. He asserted his right as a union nonmember, affirmed in the Supreme Court's *Beck* ruling in favor of several employees represented by the National Right to Work Legal Defense Foundation, to stop the CWA from spending his forced "agency fees" on union politics to which he objected. When CWA officials ignored Serio's legal right to refuse to pay "fees" for such non-bargaining purposes, he asked for and received assistance from Foundation attorneys.

Serio and his lawyer kept on fighting until the day he retired from Verizon in 2004, but they enjoyed only limited success. In the end, his personal dealings with officials of the CWA, whom he once supported, convinced him that "completely banning forced union dues is the only genuine way to protect a worker's right—currently more theoretical than real—not to bankroll objectionable Big Labor's politics."

Creating a Favorable Labor Climate in Oklahoma

In 2000 and 2001, ABC joined with this National Right to Work Committee and local statewide "freedom fighters" in an all-out effort to bring one of these right-to-work laws to Oklahoma. ABC directed an aggressive campaign to educate its member contractors and their employees in that state about the

> **In any assembly, the simplest way to stop the transacting of business and split the ranks is to appeal to a principle.**
>
> JACQUES BARZUN
> PHILOSPHER

The fundamental reason that organized labor and its allies failed to block enactment of the Oklahoma Right to Work law in 2001 is that they couldn't explain why the law should protect one employee's right to support a union but at the same time authorize the firing of another employee who chooses not to support the union.

STAN GREIR AND CHARLES BAIRD, *CCH LABOR LAW JOURNAL*

needed legislation. And ABCers from across the country donated more than $235,000 to the cause of union volunteerism.

These dollars included an in-kind donation from the Association's Free Enterprise Alliance for the production and mailing of right-to-work "ammunition" to every builder in the state. ABC national headquarters also sent five staff members from Washington, D.C., to Oklahoma's ABC Chapter. They teamed up with member firms to help distribute significant right-to-work information to the news media and the general public.

Many schoolroom teachers defied the policy of their so-called "professional education associations" (which are professional labor organizations) and participated actively in the campaign in favor of an Oklahoma right-to-work law. Other retired teachers called radio stations or wrote letters to newspaper editors to express their views and tell "war stories" about the abuses of compulsory unionism. This ground swell debunked Big Labor's claim of speaking for all unionized workers.

On September 25, 2001, Oklahoma became the twenty-second state to adopt a right-to-work law. Its voters approved a public referendum, which passed by 447,072 to 378,465 or 54 percent to 46 percent. This action reversed a similar vote taken thirty-seven years earlier. In political defeat, the AFL-CIO's negative propaganda machine outspent proponents of the new law by an estimated $18 million to $7 million. Big Labor also lost a constitutional challenge to the new law.[12]

ABC National President Henry Kelly ('01) of Austin Industrial, Inc., Houston, Texas, summed up the victory: "This was a great day for free enterprise. We congratulate our Oklahoma Chapter and its members for waging an outstanding effort to ensure that workers have the fundamental right to choose whether to join a union."[13] The Oklahoma Commerce Department reported that new and expanded manufacturing and processing investment exceeded $209 million in the third quarter of 2002, a nearly 40 percent increase over the same time period in 2001.[14]

Public Support of These Laws

There is substantial grassroots support for the enactment of right-to-work laws in Colorado, Indiana, Kentucky, Delaware, Montana, and New Hampshire.

Even registered voters in the Big Labor–dominated northeastern United States support them by nearly a two-to-one margin, but the legislation is blocked from passage by pro-union politicians. Midwestern workers, including those in union strongholds like Michigan and Ohio, favor them by nearly four to one. "The record thus shows that Americans from all walks of life and every part of the country oppose forced unionism whenever given a chance to vote on the issue," concludes Mark Mix, president of the National Right to Work Committee.[15] And a survey commissioned in 2004 by the National Institute for Labor Relations Research and conducted by Del Ali (a leading authority on American elections) confirmed that the endorsement of these statutes cuts across geographical regions as well as occupational lines. The survey found that a 79 percent majority of regular voters support a person's right to hold a job "regardless of whether or not he or she belongs to a union."[16]

Economic Benefits of a Right to Work State

Of equal importance, these laws prove to America's corporate community that a state whose legislature has the political and entrepreneurial courage to defy Big Labor by adopting a voluntary unionism policy is a desirable place to do business on a relatively even economic and political playing field. There are many ideological and economic correlations between right-to-work law states and less governmental bureaucracy, less regulations, less restrictive labor laws, more jobs, more new businesses, lower taxes, and more personal responsibility of the citizenry.

These desirable free market components send a clear message to America's business sector about the political slant and personal character of a state's legislators. A right-to-work statute thus has become the litmus test of a politician's willingness to accept Big Labor's wrath by supporting a law that favors a more profitable business community and its development of more jobs. The presence of a state right-to-work law today is synonymous in corporate circles with the term "favorable labor climate."

Some years ago a survey by a Johns Hopkins University task force on the question of Maryland as "a good place to establish a business venture" gave a discouraging report. It found that "labor issues were dominant in discussions with businessmen who had relocated their companies in Maryland and that

You may have to fight a battle more than once to win.

MARGARET THATCHER
BRITISH PRIME
MINISTER

75

wage rates and union activity figured prominently in the companies' evaluation of alternative state locations." The Hopkins study concluded that in many cases "the lack of a right to work law automatically eliminated a state like Maryland from consideration."[17]

Peter Phillips, a vice president of one of the country's largest relocation firms, the Fantus Company, also described how disadvantaged the compulsory unionism states have become in the competition to attract new businesses. A letter he wrote to the Greater Twin Falls, Idaho, Chamber of Commerce explained:

> Approximately 50 percent of our clients indicate that they do not want to consider locations unless they are in right-to-work states. As a result, these states and the communities in them are eliminated from consideration in the initial phase of the site selection process, no matter how strong their other advantages for a facility might be."[18]

The economic benefits of a state right-to-work law were highlighted again in the May 2000 issue of *Site Selection* magazine, a valued guide for business location decision-makers. The editor of this publication, Jack Lyne, profiled top ten capital investment deals and found that eight of them brought their new operations into a right to work law state. The eight companies and their locations were Amazon in Kansas, BMC Software and Sabre Group in Texas, Dell Computer in Tennessee, Microsoft in North Carolina, Volvo in Virginia, American Honda in Alabama, and Chase Manhattan in Florida.

Gary Nelson, president of Advanced Financial Solutions, told the *Wall Street Journal*: "Without right to work, when a corporation looks to relocate or build a new facility, you [and your state] don't even make the list." And Governor Frank Keating of Oklahoma boasted that "since passage of our state's right-to-work law in 2001, there's been a blizzard of interest in us that didn't exist."[19]

Robert Hunter, director of labor policy at the Mackinac Center in Michigan (and a former member of the National Labor Relations Board, former chief counsel to the Senate Committee on Labor and Human Resources, and a professor at Johns Hopkins Graduate Business School) wrote in the year 2002 a summary of "The Effect of Right to Work Laws on Economic Development."

His article attributed "the better economic performance of right-to-work states to greater labor productivity." The "net effect," Hunter confirmed, "is increasing pressure for firms to seek geographical regions with lower cost structures."[20]

It must be understood, however, that a right to work law is not an automatic panacea for all of management's labor problems, as many businesspersons are led to believe. These laws do not prevent labor organizations from (1) conducting aggressive campaigns to organize employees, or (2) from negotiating labor contracts with inflated wage and employee benefits increases, restrictive work rules, and voluntary union dues "check off" provisions, or (3) from ordering work stoppages to gain their economic objectives.

A planned economy: where everything is included in the plan except economy.

CAREY MCWILLIAMS
EDITOR OF *THE NATION*

ABC's '50s Campaign for a Maryland Right to Work Law

One of the early supporters of the merit shop movement and voluntary unionism in Maryland was Roland Stolzenbach, ABC's sixth president in 1956. He

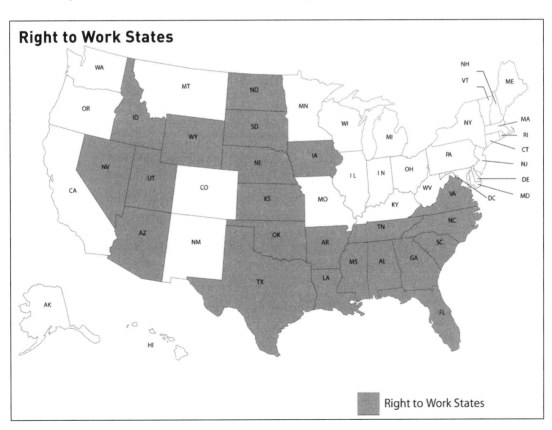

Right to Work States

Right to Work States

was described by John Trimmer as "a fearless fighter who lived and breathed free enterprise, opposed government interference in the workplace, and saw every liberal-labor victory as a portent of national disaster."[21]

Stolzenbach also was active in the Maryland Manufacturers Association, composed of small industrial firms and led by John Fitzpatrick, a Frederick, Maryland, attorney. This group was considering the possibility of passing a right-to-work law in Maryland, and adopted neighbor Virginia's statute as a model.

In 1954, a policy committee composed of Stolzenbach and ABC founder-presidents Charles Knott and Ed Colwill, along with Charles Feihe of the Mullan Contracting Co. and forth president of ABC ('54), recommended to the ABC board of directors that a state right-to-work bill should be drafted and introduced for legislative action. That caused formation of the "Maryland Right to Work Committee," with Colwill as chairman, Fitzpatrick as legal counsel, and Trimmer in charge of coordination and public relations. Campaign headquarters were established in Baltimore, replete with signs, posters, and banners promoting the cause.[22]

An enthusiastic band of ABC members chartered a bus to the Tidewater Inn in Easton on Maryland's conservative Eastern Shore for the Right To Work Committee's first official meeting and, coincidentally, to drum up support for an ABC chapter there. The colorful affair was covered by the news media—most of whose leftist reportorial and editorial views were opposed to these laws—and the political battle began.

More Arguments "Pro and Con" Voluntary Unionism

Union leaders claimed that the whole campaign for this "phony" law was created by Big Business to destroy organized labor by means of a "right-to-wreck" bill. They also called it "blatant union busting" and "insidious right-wing deception." They claimed that if the bill passed, it would produce thousands of "free riders" who unfairly reaped the employee benefits of collective bargaining representation without paying any union "service charge."

Right-to-work proponents responded that forced union membership and union dues actually destroyed employees' individual "constitutional independence and freedom to refrain from association" while replacing it with "captive passengers" (rather than "free riders") in the workplace. "Labor unions," the proponents explained, "like a chamber of commerce or a church and all other private organizations in America, should obtain their members voluntarily by establishing a record of outstanding performance on behalf of their constituents rather than through coercion and compulsion."

Ed Colwill added that "a right-to-work law would bring a new measure of democracy to union members because when union officials realize that their members are looking to them for responsible leadership, they will have to toe the line." And Roland Stolzenbach, in support, cited the opinion of Supreme Court Justice Felix Frankfurter in the case of *American Federation of Labor v. American Sash & Door Company* when he wrote:

> It is not true that the "success of a labor union" necessarily means a "perfect monopoly.". . . Absolute power leads to excesses and to weakness. Neither our character nor our intelligence can long bear the strain of unrestricted power. The union attains success when it reaches the ideal condition, and the ideal condition for a union is to be strong and stable, and yet to have in the trade outside its own ranks an appreciable number of persons who are non-unionists. In any free community the diversity of character, of beliefs, of taste—indeed mere selfishness—will insure such a supply if the enjoyment of this privilege of *individualism* is protected by law. Such a nucleus of unorganized labor will check oppression by the union as the union checks oppression by the employer.[23]

Stolzenbach also pointed out that when union leaders went before Congress in the 1920s and 1930s in their successful lobbying to legalize the compulsory union shop for all of their members, they willingly agreed to "underwrite the burden" of representing the "minority" of employees who did not want any union bargaining agent. But as soon as Congress awarded Big Labor this unique "exclusivity privilege," union leaders reversed themselves and began to press hypocritically for labor contract clauses mandating dues payments by these dissidents (now labeled "free riders") for the union's "negotiating services" to them that they did not seek or want.[24]

The idea of imposing restrictions on a free economy to assure freedom of competition is like breaking a man's leg to make him run faster.

Morris Sayre
President, National Association of Manufacturers

79

One of the most important factors in the eventual outcome of the celebrated right-to-work debate in Maryland in the 1950s was that New Dealism was strongly embedded in the state's political fabric. As John Trimmer put it, "Annapolis [the state capital] and Washington's nearby metropolitan community were full of pro-union liberals. Most of these leftist legislators had little or no practical knowledge of labor relations but counted on the financial and electoral support of the labor union movement for political survival rather than respect for constitutional principles, worker democracy and economic reality."[25]

On the proponents' side, Congressman Fred Hartley (R-NJ) and the National Right to Work Committee in Washington gave substantial assistance. And another effective promotional aid to right to work advocates was ABC's *Contractor* magazine, which had gained an increasing readership. A third important forum was the *Labor Herald*, oldest independent labor newspaper in the nation and published in Baltimore City. This periodical opened its commentary columns to both proponents and opponents of the bill.

An Unexpected Source of Worker Support

To the consternation of union leaders, it soon became evident that there was smoldering interest in the right to work movement among rank-and-file union members throughout Maryland. A few brave employees surfaced from union locals at such giant companies as Bethlehem Steel Corporation and the Martin Aircraft Company to join the fight against their union "bosses." Some of them had the courage to write the *Labor Herald* and express public approval of the proposed labor law.

An especially fearless letter from a local Teamster truck driver declared that the biggest hindrance to union progress was the fact that members "did not have the backbone and gumption to demand their democratic rights and dethrone the labor union dictators." This disillusioned Teamster added in the *Labor Herald*:

> Forced union membership is prevalent in the trucking industry. I am sure that if one were to take the time to canvass the labor field today in regard to the so-called right to work privilege, it would be astounding to find the majority of workers in favor of such legislation. One could rest assured that if such a law was adopted, the big bosses of the

union organizations would need to get off their buttocks and earn the fabulous salaries that they now fleece from their memberships.

To get the true picture of labor's real view on the proposed right to work law, let union members speak for themselves (instead of a few of their arrogant so-called leaders).

Big Business Fades Out

"The fat was surely in the fire," in John Trimmer's words. Members of the Maryland Right to Work Committee traveled throughout the state, talking to groups of citizens at all levels and winning apparent support for their bill. As Big Labor turned up the political pressure, however, many large corporations lost their incentive for the fight. It became apparent that their fear of union reprisals took over. Only a few principled small businessmen plus ABC, its members, and the National Right to Work Committee continued to stand tall and fight publicly for the bill's passage.

Even Baltimore's Chamber of Commerce—the largest representative of the business community in Maryland at the time—ended by lamely adopting a position of what could only be described as "vigorous neutrality." During an internal debate of the issue, the Chamber's legislative committee voted to support the right to work bill but its board of directors refused to follow the recommendation of its own committee. The corporate behemoths that controlled the Chamber's board were either already unionized and didn't want to incur the AFL-CIO's wrath in their own workplaces or their open shops feared union retaliation through organizational campaigns and product boycotts. In short, Big Business sacrificed entrepreneurial freedom and succumbed feebly to Big Labor's threats and intimidation in the legislative fight over mandatory union membership in Maryland.

A Notorious Legislative Hearing

As ABCers lobbying for the right to work bill walked through the legislative halls of Maryland's capitol in Annapolis, they were shadowed by menacing union lobbyists who had an opposite mission. As the time approached for presentation of the bill in the Maryland General Assembly, another dilemma faced proponents: no legislator had the political courage to introduce it. Even

To escape criticism, do nothing, say nothing, be nothing.

ELBERT HUBBARD
WRITER

The enemy who forces you to retreat is himself afraid of you at that very moment.

ANDRÉ MAUROIS
WRITER

the most conservative members from districts that had never felt the tread of a union organizer's foot didn't want any part of the bill's sponsorship. It was rumored generally—but never proven specifically—that union lobbyists scared them by not-too-veiled threats and other forms of intimidation.

In February of 1955, ABC finally found a fearless sponsor for the bill by the name of Senator James Weinroth (R-Cecil County). During his college days in Philadelphia, Weinroth had driven a taxicab and suffered through enough personal "experiences" with Teamsters compulsory unionism to make him dare to publicly oppose its unfairness and hypocrisy.

Next, the right to work bill was handed over to the state's Legislative Reference Bureau for final drafting and printing, as was the practice on all bills. Somehow it was "lost" mysteriously in the internal staff processing for three days. (Rumor had it that a union lobbyist "borrowed" the bill, killing precious time before it could be polished into proper legal form for publication and consideration.)

Eventually the formal bill was referred to the Labor Committees in each house of the Maryland General Assembly. Campaigning efforts increased and a joint hearing of the Senate and House of Delegates Labor Committees was set for March 22, 1955. This unusual political ploy to limit debate broke procedural precedents.

On the day of the hearing, ABCers and other advocates of the bill were confronted with mobs of hostile union men who had been bussed from the Baltimore area and primed for the occasion. They jammed the House Office Building where the hearing on the bill was scheduled to take place. Legislators in charge of the hearings permitted the unionists to usurp all the chairs, line the walls of the room and recline on the floor. A union militant was allowed to photograph ABC's supporters, using a flash camera. The obvious purpose was to intimidate them. Both the building's access halls and the hearing room itself were blocked by these belligerent opponents to such an extent that some of ABC's witnesses could not even find a place to sit.

All of this intimidation caused one key ABC witness, a timid professor of economics at a local college, not to testify. He ducked out of the hearing room because of the riotous union conduct he observed and the fear it implanted in him for both his safety and his future "politically correct" job security. When other right-to-work witnesses were presenting their testimony, sarcastic comments and rude gestures were permitted by the politicians in charge to emanate freely from surly unionists throughout the hearing room.

Legislative "Laissez Faire" Prevails

The proponents' case in favor of the right-to-work bill was ably presented in a dignified manner at the hearing by Attorney John Fitzpatrick. But the politicians he addressed were a prejudiced, discourteous, sarcastic, and bored group of "public servants" who were official members of the Maryland General Assembly's two Labor Committees. Fitzpatrick's witnesses included several railroad employees who had lost their jobs because they refused to join an AFL-CIO union. There was also an aircraft industry employee who was fired for refusing to tender union dues and another aircraft worker who said hundreds of his fellow workers were forced to pay union dues against their will. As they testified, well-coached union heckling and supportive legislators' rudeness continued unabated.

Other right to work law proponents were three small businessmen who were required by contract to employ union labor and several African Americans who charged union officials with racial discrimination. As these witnesses made their way out of the hearing room, they were subjected to verbal insults, profanity, and threats from the bill's AFL-CIO opponents, who were still obstructing both the room and the corridors in access halls of the House Office Building.

The *ABC Contractor* reported on this disgraceful affair, which was ignored by the left-wing news media in attendance:

> The hearing was marked by extreme bias and vicious questioning on the part of Senator DiDomenico, chairman of the Senate Committee, and Delegate Kirkland, chairman of the House Committee. Conducted in a constant uproar, boos, hisses and jeers from the pro-union contingent present, the hearing foreshadowed the kind of report on the status of the bill one might expect from such committees.[26]

Witnesses on behalf of the AFL-CIO who testified against passage of the right to work bill consisted of several statewide salaried union officials, a union lawyer, and two union-supported politicians. Their remarks were received by the joint Senate and House Labor Committees with contrasting courtesy in a suddenly hushed and respectful hearing room.

Criminal Union Conduct Ignored

It was obvious that the proponents' constitutional right to an orderly presentation of their right to work bill had been denied and the safety of their witnesses was jeopardized. More specifically, Big Labor's conduct at the hearing violated the Maryland Code, State Government Article, Title 2, Section 1702(a), which provides, as cited also in the State Legislature's own Rules at page 131:

2-1702. Interference with legislative process.

(a) A person may not willfully disrupt, interfere with, attempt to disrupt, or attempt to interfere with a session, meeting, or proceeding of the General Assembly, the Senate, or the House or any of their committees, by: (1) making, alone or with another person, a noise that tends to be disruptive; (2) using abusive or obscene language; (3) making an obscene gesture; (4) engaging in violent, tumultuous, or threatening behavior; (5) refusing to comply with the lawful order of the police to disperse; or (6) doing any other disruptive or interfering act.

The AFL-CIO's conduct also violated Art. III, Sec. 23, of the Maryland Constitution, cited in the State Legislature's Rules at page 84, which adds criminal penalties:

Punishment. Each House may punish by imprisonment, during the session of the General Assembly, any person, not a member, for disrespectful, or disorderly behavior in its presence, or for obstructing any of its proceedings, or any of its officers in the execution of their duties; provided, such imprisonment shall not, at any one time, exceed ten days.

The elected politicians in authority at the joint legislative session on the right-to-work bill ignored these constitutional due process safeguards that were called to their attention—and the bill was dead on arrival.

Following this infamous hearing, the Senate Labor Committee met alone and greased the way for an unfavorable report on the bill. It was adopted by the full Senate on a voice vote. Republican Senator Weinroth (who introduced the bill) and Senator William James (a respected Democrat from Harford County who eventually became the Senate's president) were the only legislators who supported the bill.

Senator Weinroth sought a roll call to record each vote for public consumption. But Senator Louis "God-bless-you-all-real-good" Goldstein (D-Calvert County), who was acting as temporary chairman, ruled that the voice vote was final, thus averting an embarrassing record of the votes cast for the public's review. Goldstein later was rewarded for his parliamentary skill by what turned out to be a lifelong job as state comptroller of Maryland. In that capacity he sat on the powerful board of estimates (along with the governor and the state treasurer), which (not coincidentally) awarded all state government construction contracts.

In the House of Delegates, the rigged legislative procedure differed only in detail. The right to work bill was reported out of committee and actually reached the floor of the House where a roll call vote was obtained. Among the elected politicians opposing it were all thirty-four Baltimore City delegates plus the entire delegations of Prince George's and Montgomery Counties—home to thousands of federal government bureaucrats. The tally was overwhelmingly against voluntary unionism.

John Trimmer wrote in the *ABC Contractor* that "the Legislature's action was an example of official cowardice that had few parallels in Maryland history." He concluded:

> Defeat of the right to work bill in the Maryland General Assembly spotlighted a shameful situation that every thinking citizen should be aware of: We have a Senate composed of members who lack the courage to vote publicly against a legislative proposal. We have in the

It could probably be shown by facts and figures that there is no native American criminal class except a legislative body.

MARK TWAIN
HUMORIST-WRITER

two "big" counties of Maryland cowardly legislative delegations that showed themselves to be putty in the hands of the labor lobby.

The Baltimore City delegation—Senators and Delegates—slavishly follow the union boss line, work actively in favor of pro-labor legislation, and apparently leave no stone unturned to defeat any bill that would interfere with labor prerogatives.[27]

Big Labor had administered a resounding defeat to ABC and the rest of the right to work law proponents. A few months later, a rumor spread that an AFL-CIO lobbyist had bragged in a labor publication about how "a hundred thousand dollars was distributed in the right places to kill ABC's right to wreck law campaign in Maryland." He also confided that the victory was achieved in part because he relied on what he claimed was an old southern political stratagem:

> Nevah say to uh politician what ya c'n grunt; nevah grunt what ya c'n wink; nevah wink what ya c'n nod; nevah nod what ya c'n shrug; and nevah shrug when it ain't necessary.

Subsequent attempts to revive the right to work law issue in leftward-tilted Maryland have failed, most recently in 1995. We did, however, subsequently use the above-noted statutory procedural rules on proper conduct to silence the disgraceful lobbying tactics of the forced unionism protagonists and their political protégés. Vigorous support for our efforts came from the state's leading free enterprise voice, Maryland Business for Responsive Government, under its able leaders, President R. O. C. Worcester and Chairman Larry Jenkins, also chief executive of Monumental Life Insurance Company at the time.

Two Conflicting Solutions

It is conceded by supporters of voluntary union membership today that the most practical way to outlaw compulsory unionism is by passage of a National Right to Work Act such as was proposed in the House of Representatives as H.R. 391 in 2004. This bill, sponsored by over 120 members of Congress, would protect the unfettered right to hold a job anywhere in the United States and impose a uniform national standard abolishing mandatory unionism and membership dues forever. An identical bill (S. 1765) has been introduced in the Senate.

By way of counter-attack in February of 2003, the AFL-CIO's executive council agreed to join an effort by seven international union presidents (including James Hoffa of the Teamsters) to create an allegedly tax-exempt organization that will be called the National Rights AT Work Committee. "It will launch an education and litigation strategy and serve as a counterpoint to the National Right to Work Committee," according to the Bureau of National Affairs.

This new committee will be governed by "a board of directors composed of union leaders, labor lawyers, labor-friendly academics, religious leaders, and other supporters." It will focus on "promotion of direct action and events that coordinate with the AFL-CIO and its affiliates and allies, such as Jobs with Justice, to raise the noise level on the issue" and defend "union security."[28]

Individual "voluntarism" in a free workplace, on the other hand, is at the foundation of our constitutional heritage and honored by the creator and first president of the American trade union movement, Samuel Gompers. It is the essence of capitalism. Yet today, under federal policy that remains effective in twenty-eight of the United States that do not have right to work laws, more than 7.5 million private sector employees can be forced against their will to tender membership dues for use by a labor union as a condition of their employment—or be discharged.[29]

In politically correct labor parlance, this statutory privilege of exclusive and compulsory unionism is sanitized and labeled "union security."[30] When verbally and factually unspun, this mandatory union membership (1) defies the union voluntarism of AFL Founder Sam Gompers; (2) ignores worker security by invading minority employees' constitutional civil rights; (3) overrides their political independence; (4) causes a discriminatory manpower monopoly; and (5) fosters corruption and violence in the construction industry.

It ain't over 'til its over.

YOGI BERRA
N.Y. YANKEES
CATCHER-PHILOSOPHER

CHAPTER 10

MERRY-GO-ROUND PICKETING BREAKS DOWN

UNION LEADERS—ANXIOUS TO INCREASE their dwindling ranks—cursed the federal Taft-Hartley Act as they watched their picket lines and common situs secondary boycotts meet defeat after defeat. When sabotage of this amendatory labor statute failed under subterfuges like bogus "informational" picketing (as exemplified in ABC's aforementioned *Stover Steel* legal victory) they began to try a maneuver called "merry-go-round" picketing.

An early example of this phony tactic involved Irwin-Kuntz Company, a general contractor from Castanea, Pennsylvania. This firm was one of the founding members of ABC's Central Pennsylvania Chapter in 1964 and a client of mine. In the spring of 1967, Irwin-Kuntz bid successfully on the construction of a science building for Lock Haven State College. This project was controlled by the General State Authority. Irwin-Kuntz, as was its merit shop tradition, assigned some of the specialty craft work including heating, plumbing, electrical, and bricklaying work to *unionized* sub-contractors. When the job began, the local Ironworkers Union established picket lines at all entrances of the job site. That created a work stoppage intended to make Irwin-Kuntz "go union all the way."

This targeted general contractor responded by instituting the secondary boycott "reserved gate" ground rules established by the Labor Board in its *Moore Dry Dock* case and affirmed in *Stover Steel*.[1] More specifically, Irwin Kuntz Company properly acted as follows at the picketed project: (1) established a separate entrance/exit gate reserved for its own personnel and business

Laws too
gentle are
seldom
observed;
too severe,
seldom
executed.

BEN FRANKLIN
FOUNDING FATHER,
STATESMAN, INVENTOR,
AND WRITER

visitors; (2) posted a notice requiring all other employers plus their employees and business visitors to use a separate "neutral" entrance/exit gate; and (3) advised the picketing union, all other local craft unions, their local building trades council, and international affiliates as well as all unionized subcontractors working on the Haven State College project about this strictly enforced dual-gated separate means of ingress and egress at the situs of the science building on the college campus.

Big Labor Ignores Picketing Restrictions

The building trades involved in this labor dispute knew the established legal ground rules. They understood that under *Moore Dry Dock* they only had the right to peacefully picket Irwin-Kuntz (the targeted "primary" employer) at its separately identified and reserved gate. They also knew that under *Moore Dry Dock* they could not coerce any unionized "neutral secondary" employers or their employees and business visitors at the common job site to force Irwin-Kuntz to capitulate to unionization. Nevertheless, the Iron Workers Union ignored this settled labor law on common situs dual entrance gate notices[2] and continued to maintain its picket lines at both of the project's entrances.

Picket signs simply announced that IRWIN-KUNTZ PAYS SUB-STANDARD WAGES. That move caused every craftsman working for the four union subcontractors on the common situs to refuse to "scab" by crossing a brother craft union's picket lines. Because of the highly integrated nature of the project, all work came to a standstill.

The General State Authority's demand that the job resume immediately was ignored by the trade unions involved, and, with my assistance, a secondary boycott unfair labor practice charge was filed on behalf of Irwin-Kuntz at the Pittsburgh, Pennsylvania, Regional Office of the National Labor Relations Board. We requested injunctive relief to remove the illegal picketing immediately. The Labor Board's investigation soon proved that Irwin-Kuntz's charge was valid because the union was "contaminating" the special gate reserved for neutrals in violation of *Moore Dry Dock*. The Ironworkers Union thereupon complied by withdrawing all of its pickets—and the Labor Board dismissed our charge.

A few days later, just as construction work was returning to normal, the scenario repeated itself: a "brother" Carpenters Union began to picket both gates, the entire project came to a standstill, Irwin-Kuntz filed another unfair labor practice charge, and the Labor Board again acted favorably on it. At that point the Carpenters Union dutifully removed its pickets and the Board once again dismissed Irwin-Kuntz's secondary boycott charge. Three more times—ignoring our protests to the Labor Board—a different local craft union took the picketing union's place (Operating Engineers, Plasterers, and Sheet Metal Workers) and continued the illegal harassment until a legitimate unfair labor practice charge was brought against it at the Labor Board—in "merry-go-round" fashion. The science building construction proceeded slowly at best.

Following Irwin-Kuntz Company's request, the General State Authority ("GSA") called the disputants together for a meeting in Harrisburg to resolve the impasse amicably. In response, representatives of the local building trades council demanded that Irwin-Kuntz (which had been attempting to legally fulfill its construction contract with Loch Haven State College on a timely basis) should be banned from the project. And they threatened that no union craftsmen would ever work on the project so long as any entrance at the common situs was picketed. Neither the GSA nor Irwin-Kuntz would capitulate to that attempted union blackmail.

An informal "last chance" meeting followed between Irwin-Kuntz and representatives of the building trades council at which the council made another unequivocal demand for union recognition by Irwin-Kuntz. The council's only concession was that the company would be "permitted" to finish the college project if it signed an agreement "to always work union in the future." Irwin-Kuntz refused to comply with this proposed extortion.

The Labor Board Finally Takes Action

As a result, the merry-go-round picketing continued and work on the GSA project limped along sporadically. Eventually—after several conferences with the Labor Board's chief law officer at the regional office—we convinced the Labor Board to require the immediate cessation of all illegal picketing by any trade union at Loch Haven State College. As Irwin-Kuntz Company had

When you come to a fork in the road, take it.

Yogi Berra
N.Y. Yankees
CATCHER-PHILOSOPHER

Diligence makes good luck.

BEN FRANKLIN
FOUNDING FATER,
STATESMAN, INVENTOR,
AND WRITER

contended all along, the Board finally ruled that there was "overwhelming evidence of a premeditated joint venture and collusion in the illegal secondary boycott activity due to the rotation of picketing by brother craft unions acting in concert as the agents of the same local building trades council."[3]

John Trimmer reported that "through this prolonged confrontation, ABC won the right to work on mixed jobs in the merit shop tradition." He added:

> The entire situation was a gruesome experience for this brave general contractor. Irwin-Kuntz was a firm that never had worked strictly non-union. It consistently employed cooperative and qualified union subcontractors, providing many jobs for union men. The mental, physical and monetary cost of Irwin-Kuntz's defense of managerial prerogatives and employee rights in this case was great. But in the end, despite all of the building trades union bedevilment, this courageous firm successfully completed the State College building—with the cooperation of union subcontractors working in harmony—and regained its position as a leading merit shop contractor in the area.[4]

By victory in the Irwin-Kuntz case, ABC helped to create another favorable legal precedent and passed another major milestone. As time went on, tradesmen working for "neutral" unionized subcontractors at a common situs began to lose interest in playing Big Labor's illegal game of secondary "sympathy" strikes and "merry-go-round" job shut downs. In many situations, after a few days spent honoring a brother union's picket line which deprived them all of their weekly paychecks, the sympathy strikers would defy their union bosses. Ignoring author Jack London's famous sermon against "scabs," they would go back to work of their own accord.

A separate positive result of the Irwin-Kuntz case was the motivation for creation of ABC's "open shop project performance clause." Under its terms, the project agreement of the property owner or the merit shop general contractor controlling the common situs requires any union subcontractor whose employees are picketing, striking, or engaged in a labor dispute of any kind to order them back to work or face the substitution of another subcontractor obtained by the general contractor to do the struck work. "Failure to perform" means that the union sub involved in the labor dispute loses the work, the union craftsmen lose their jobs, and any monetary damages resulting from the unionized sub's strike in breach of its construction contract are paid by it.[5]

That's how ABC broke down the building trades union merry-go-round.

CHAPTER 11

APPRENTICESHIP TRAINING MEETS FEDERAL STANDARDS

S KILLED MANPOWER HAS ALWAYS BEEN a primary need throughout the construction industry at all levels in both its unionized and non-union sectors. During the early years as ABC members began to perform larger and more sophisticated projects, it became evident that they could not depend on the fortuitous hiring of capable workers.

To solve this problem, by the 1960's ABCers began to embark on novel training programs to meet quality standards and gain greater productivity. John Trimmer explained the situation this way:

> The merit shop concept introduced a fresh element to the manpower equation. In order to compete with the archaic trade union apprentice training programs and their mandatory hiring halls, ABC members began to direct their efforts toward providing secure year-round employment for a substantial number of skilled workers. As they did so, rigid traditional hiring methods slowly diminished and became more diversified.
>
> Use of state or private employment services often proved unsatisfactory. Veterans Administration programs under which trainees' wages were supplemented and related instruction courses held in public schools were poorly administered, with accompanying low attendance. ABCers soon found that they had to develop their own multi-skilled workforces even though it meant taking some projects at little or no profit.[1]

An Association-wide workplace study confirmed the obvious: only a small percentage of the required number of apprentices was being trained properly. Contractors' in-house programs lacked proper standards and non-union employers faced a dilemma. They believed then—and still do today—that the traditional trade union methods of training apprentices to become skilled craftsmen perpetuate practices that have become obsolete due to Big Labor's refusal to adopt the industry's advances in techniques, tools, equipment, and materials. Non-union contractors whose multi-skilled craftsmen, trainees, and other helpers did not meet these required union-created training standards found themselves at a competitive disadvantage in bidding on government construction work controlled politically by Big Labor.

The National Apprenticeship Act

The well-intentioned National Apprenticeship Act of 1937 (coupled with the farcical federal Davis-Bacon "Prevailing Wage" Act discussed hereafter in Chapter 16) combined to become bureaucratic "villains" against the open shop. The apprenticeship statute provides that:

> The Secretary of Labor is directed to formulate and promote the furtherance of labor standards necessary to *safeguard* the welfare of apprentices, to extend the application of such standards by encouraging the inclusion thereof in contracts of apprenticeship, to bring together employers and labor for the formulation of programs of apprenticeship, [and] to cooperate with state agencies engaged in the formulation and promotion of standards of apprenticeship... *The Secretary of Labor may publish information relating to existing and proposed labor standards of apprenticeship, and may appoint national advisory committees to serve without compensation.* [emphasis added]

In order for the federal government to "safeguard apprenticeship standards" that were delegated to the Secretary of Labor, the Bureau of Apprenticeship and Training ("BAT") was established within the Department of Labor. The designated purposes of BAT are "to aid labor and industry in developing, expanding and improving apprenticeship programs in certain skilled trades, to provide some degree of uniformity in the skills necessary for a particular industry, and to rekindle a sense of pride of craftsmanship." (BAT's name was changed recently to the Offices of Apprenticeship Training, Employer and Labor Services or "ATELS," but "BAT" will be used throughout this chapter.)

The programs are registered and monitored in accordance with regulations established by BAT under the National Apprenticeship Act or through a BAT-approved state apprenticeship agency or council. Apprentices who graduate receive a certification that they have satisfactorily completed a registered program. Some states (such as Maryland) have passed laws providing for the establishment and operation of state apprenticeship councils.[2] Where this is the case, BAT is supposed to aid the state agency in devising and operating an effective local plan.

Big Labor's Control of Apprenticeship Councils

The bad news for ABC was that the Bureau of Apprenticeship Training within the Department of Labor had been union-dominated since its inception. Prior to the arrival of the Nixon administration in 1969, BAT would not consider approving any apprenticeship program from a non-union organization even if it were modeled upon a union program.[3] And in most state jurisdictions, the advisory joint labor-management councils similarly have been stacked by political appointees, a majority of whom are trade union officials and unionized contractors.

With the building trades in virtual control of these apprenticeship training councils and their eligibility standards, approval of "independent" ABC programs has been delayed or vetoed repeatedly over the years. When eventually certified, ABC programs are subjected to prejudiced official government "compliance reviews" under union influence to determine "conformity" with the restrictive and outmoded union training standards. These unnecessary audits are disguised under BAT's official regulatory goal of "improving apprenticeship programs" and "rekindling a sense of pride in craftsmanship." Organized labor also looks for friendly courts to protect its own BAT-approved manpower training cartels from "unfair" open shop competition.

This administrative and judicial partiality caused an incredulous John Trimmer to write: "Seldom in the annals of shenanigans in government agencies

> **It is difficult to conquer the forest when you're just one of the unnoticed trees.**
>
> GERALD LEE STEESE
> WRITER

In these days it seems hard to realize that there ever was a time that the robbing of our government was a novelty.

Mark Twain
HUMORIST-NOVELIST

has so much power been given to a private organization such as Big Labor for competitive advantage in a market as in the arena of apprenticeship training standards."[4]

Baltimore ABC Chapter Initiates Training Program

By 1955 George Meany was the leader of the united AFL skilled trades unions and the CIO industrial unions (now known as the united "AFL-CIO"). Organized labor had become a powerful economic and political force. Pent-up post-World War II need for all types of construction spurred a strong building boom that would last through the 1950s. Union membership was at an all-time high and local craft unions finally began opening the exclusive familial ranks of their apprenticeship programs to "outsiders" to meet the demand for more manpower.

This initiative, which expanded building trades hiring halls, would prove to be a key to continued trade union strength. Non-union contractors as a group had no standardized method of training for preparing craftworkers for union-styled government project certification or for sophisticated private sector work. This disadvantage limited their ability to take on large and complicated projects.

In 1960, to solve the problem, ABC appointed an apprenticeship committee in Baltimore's newly formed local chapter. It was co-chaired by Gordon Barnes of Nelson Barnes Company and Anthony Gallo of Heer Brothers, with instructions to develop appropriate apprenticeship training methods and benchmarks.

The committee was given authority to instruct, direct, and discipline the trainees while monitoring their progress and workplace welfare. One of the most important results of the committee's report was the indenturing of apprentices to the committee itself rather than to contractor employers. ABCers Cas Sippel, Norman Miller, Frank Barry, Samuel Jackson, Samuel Lipman, and Charles Stinchcomb led the development of the craft courses and certification tests. Another novel aspect of the program was that the committee assumed the responsibility for providing the trainees with stable employment. John Trimmer wrote that "this practice complemented perfectly the merit shop policy of doing everything possible to provide year-around jobs for all personnel."[5]

An Honest Government Servant Surfaces

From almost the first day of this new program, the building trades unions—with the acquiescence of friendly bureaucrats in controlling government agencies—undermined ABC's training efforts at both the local and national levels. Luckily for the Association, one ethical federal agent who supervised the state of Maryland's training activities involving BAT fought tirelessly for the certification of *qualified* open shop apprenticeship programs. He believed that it was immaterial whether the standards were union-controlled or employer-controlled, so long as the criteria "safeguarded the welfare of apprentices" as required by the National Apprenticeship Act.

This courageous government agent—Louis Nemerofsky—finally shamed his pro-union superiors into awarding ABC's Baltimore Chapter a BAT certificate of registration in 1962 for the more flexible open shop trade classifications of plumber, electrician, sheet metal worker, and carpenter. To do otherwise, he contended, "would have been legally and morally discriminatory by impeding the legitimate training of much-needed construction workers." Nemerofsky was "rewarded" for his integrity by demotion and transfer to a lower-paid government job.[6]

ABC's first federally certified apprenticeship training program thus began in Baltimore. Study groups were conducted at the city's premier vocational institution, Mergenthaler Trade School. The project started as a two-year course and soon expanded into a full-scale four-year curriculum combining two thousand hours of on-the-job training and 144 hours of related classroom instruction. In the beginning, Mergenthaler only graduated journeymen craftsmen in the four above-mentioned federally approved trades.

By 1964 the chairman of the Baltimore ABC apprenticeship program was Theodore Clark of Heer Brothers and it had 233 trainees enrolled. An ancillary Skills Development Organization was formed to give the handicapped and other disadvantaged people a basic knowledge of skills used on a construction site and to help solve their workplace problems. Each such special trainee was assigned an experienced craftsman "buddy" for support on a personal one-on-one basis.

My client, Mack Trucks, Inc., donated equipment valued at $25,000 to be used in the overall training plan. It included a six-cylinder diesel engine, a

Character is the only secure foundation of the State.

CALVIN COOLIDGE
30TH PRESIDENT

twelve-speed transmission, two carrier assemblies, and a front wheel drive assembly. Mack Trucks also donated its own Mechanics Service and Maintenance Manual to the Baltimore Chapter for training use.

Charles Chamberlain, the Baltimore ABC Chapter's energetic executive director, and John Trimmer's newly created National ABC office jointly supervised the creation of similar formal apprenticeship programs in the Metropolitan Washington Chapter, spearheaded by Tracy Coleman and James Long; in Western Maryland and the Cumberland Valley Chapter led by Ray Danzar, John Lecron, Jack Barr, and Bob Lukin; and in Pennsylvania, directed by Fred Schnabel and Joseph LaMonaca.

ABC National Coordinates Apprentice Training

The first national ABC apprenticeship seminar was held in 1970 at Friendship (now "Baltimore-Washington International") Airport's companion hotel near Baltimore. Nine Association chapters were represented. Both federal and state government officials in the training field addressed the group. ABC also appointed a national apprenticeship committee composed of Gordon Barnes, Ted Clark, and Frank Williams to prepare national standards in nine crafts,

Charles Chamberlain, executive director, Metro Baltimore Chapter, and thereafter National ABC's director of education from 1960s to 1970s.

with Charlie Chamberlain serving as advisor.

Another national ABC program for the promotion of apprenticeship involved a motion picture film. Through a grant given to Stanford University, a post-graduate student named Mark Steinberg created the color film and called it "Careers In Construction." It was produced in Baltimore.

The film's story line illustrated the pride felt by a young black apprentice in performing construction work. His economic, educational, and personal advancements through his chosen trade were described. In the film's "happy ending," his progress eventually encouraged a friend who was dissatisfied with his own advancement as an office clerk to consider the merit shop construction industry and its unlimited employment opportunities.

When this outstanding film was completed, it was distributed to all ABC chapters and promoted through a public relations agency. Thereafter it was shown at numerous film festivals and on national television networks as well as at many high schools. It also was used in prisons to motivate inmates to help themselves by preparing for a productive career after their release from incarceration.

The film won many awards and brought public acclaim to ABC. Entry into the construction industry was encouraged among hundreds of thousands of high school students and other potential candidates for construction work. In conjunction with the film, ABC also sponsored regional career workshops around the country. Youngsters were given a chance to lay brick, drive nails, cut and glue pipe, and even try their hand at computer-aided design. The goal was to make a connection with youth who were considering career choices and also with their parents.

In every rank, both great and small, it is industry that supports us all.

JOHN GAY
WRITER

DOL Certifies Nine ABC Training Programs

Combined pressures from growth of the merit shop and discrimination by unions against minorities led to good fortune for ABC during the Richard Nixon administration in 1969. Under the president's leadership, BAT's enforcement of the National Apprenticeship Training Act finally began to resemble its original impartial intent. In March of 1970, Nixon issued a statement that criticized the rampant construction inflation and directed the Labor Department to make a study of BAT's certified apprenticeship training programs. The stated objective was improving and expanding them, while controlling labor costs.

ABC's fifteenth National President, Joe LaMonaca ('71-'72), took advantage of Nixon's encouraging action by issuing the following public statement:

> By Department of Labor Statistics, it has been projected that apprenticeship under the Bureau of Apprenticeship Training will fill less than one sixth of the anticipated openings for craftsmen in the construction industry during the next five years. Government certified apprenticeship training as it now exists is prevented from accomplishing its purpose by outmoded standards, quotas and training procedures. In many states a legitimate program without the endorsement of organized labor is next to impossible to obtain.
>
> The Department of Labor is well aware of these facts, yet control of the programs remains in the hands of those whose only interest is

I think we have
more machinery
of government
than is necessary;
too many parasites
living on the labor
of the industrious.

THOMAS JEFFERSON
3RD PRESIDENT

personal greed and power. Apprenticeship training has become a tool of discrimination and intimidation which creates labor shortages without any responsibility for the public interest. It is time that apprenticeship be re-examined and that it begin serving the function for which it was intended. This important instrument for training our workers must be taken away from the control of organized labor and placed into the hands of open-minded government agents who will look after the public interest and offer this training to more and more deserving citizens.[7]

On May 5, 1971, John Trimmer and his hard-working executive assistant, Woodrow Moats (with the support of several civil rights groups and after many weeks of negotiations), convinced Nixon's under secretary of labor, James Hodgson, to override powerful building trades political pressure and move ahead with the national certification of nine ABC apprentice training programs. They included the crafts of bricklayer, carpenter, cement mason, electrician, painter, plasterer, plumber, pipefitter (i.e., refrigeration, heating, and air conditioning), and sheet metal worker.

This DOL action was the first time that the federal government accepted on a national basis any so-called "unilateral" apprenticeship program. That meant the program was under the sole supervision of the contractors involved, without any labor union co-representation or influence. The newly certified and modernized Hodgson apprenticeship standards also provided for the installation of ABC training programs in those states which did not already have a local apprenticeship council and assisted in obtaining approval of ABC apprenticeship programs in those states with existing apprenticeship agencies.

At the formal presentation of the certificate of registration of ABC's national craft standards in Washington, D.C., President Joe LaMonaca asserted:

ABC is delighted that the Bureau of Apprenticeship and Training under the Nixon Administration has recognized that independent trade associations are entitled to register their own apprenticeship courses and operate them in the interest of the employees of their members. BAT has now opened the door to the employment of more minority workers and others in areas in which ABC is now active, as well as in new development areas.

The construction industry holds great potential of meaningful employment with real opportunity to advance. And this approval of the new apprenticeship standards will supply the "ammunition" needed by ABC members to fight the "war" against the artificial shortage of manpower caused by union race and sex discrimination, nepotism and other restrictions upon apprentices entering the union building trades.

Under these new standards, ABC contractors also will be permitted to expand opportunities for more apprentices because of a lowered allowable ratio of one apprentice for every three journeymen. At the same time ABCers are offered an opportunity to invest in the future of their businesses. When the long fight ahead is finally won, the entire industry will reap the benefits. It will be an end to the tremendous inflation in wage rates.

The ascending spiral of greatness in America has risen because industry has produced profit, which in turn has supported educational institutions, which in turn have supported leadership in industry to produce more wealth.

WALLACE F. BENNETT
SENATOR

In response, Hugh Murphy, the supportive new administrator of BAT, told Joe LaMonaca and the assembled ABC contractors:

I congratulate you and the Association which you represent on your efforts to provide a systematic and uniform method for training throughout your industry. Your continued interest and initiative in providing guidance to ABC members through your certified national standards should bring you lasting credit and satisfaction. The staff of the Bureau of Apprenticeship and Training and the cooperating state apprenticeship agencies are available to assist your local chapters in formulating apprenticeship systems in line with your national policy.[8]

A Famous Texas Case

In spite of the Nixon administration's exemplary non-partisan apprenticeship training policy, the ultimate in callous union obstructionism occurred shortly afterwards in Houston, Texas. It was there that an individual craftsman and

ABC Contractor

Presentation by Bureau of Apprenticeship Training, U.S. Department of Labor, of certificate of registration of all ABC apprenticeship standards to ABC's President Joe LaMonaca (far right) and ABC national training director, Woodrow Moats, (far left) on May 5, 1971.

two local trade unions filed a class action lawsuit in a federal court against the U.S. Department of Labor. The two-fold objective of the litigation was to block ABC's Houston Chapter from inaugurating its own registered and certified apprenticeship training program and force it to ignore the new national standards.

The trade union plaintiffs in the case attempted to rely on previous authority given to an earlier secretary of labor under the National Apprenticeship Act to issue circulars outlining the "guidelines" that BAT used in determining if a training program qualified for registration. Some years earlier, during the administration of President Lyndon Johnson, union political pressure caused BAT to issue Circular 66-67, which favored only *one* registered program in any designated area. It required that any competing "independent [non-union] group" desiring to establish an apprenticeship program in an area where one already existed (i.e., a joint union-management program) had to prove its compliance with the exact terms of that union-controlled program before it could start one of its own.

This tilted rule was an attempt to force ABC's state-of-the-art training programs into the obsolete building trades apprenticeship mode. It was an open loophole for union sabotage of ABC's attempts to gain certification of legitimate merit shop training programs under the new Nixon-Hodgson standards.

With urging from John Trimmer and Woody Moats, the Nixon administration soon recognized the incongruity of BAT Circular 66-67 and promulgated an overruling Circular 70-26. It provided that, in order to be certified by BAT, any "independent" apprenticeship training program was required to meet *national* standards rather than local standards and that *the existence of a competing local union program was irrelevant.*

It was this new Circular 70-26 that the local building trades attacked in the Houston, Texas, litigation. They sought an order from a federal court that would prohibit ABC from registering its own sheet metal and electrical apprenticeship programs in Houston. Big Labor contended that a local registered program in those trades which met BAT's national standards already existed and therefore the ABC program was unlawful because it had different standards from those under the registered local union program. In short, the Houston Building Trades Council sought to prohibit the federal registration of any ABC apprenticeship plan that conflicted with their certified local program (under the overruled Circular 66-67) even though ABC complied with the new national guidelines of BAT's revised Circular 70-26.

Texas Justice Prevails over Union Autocracy

ABC intervened to join Nixon's Department of Labor in defense of its action, and in a memorable decision, Texas District Judge Woodrow Seal *dismissed* the plaintiff building trades case in its entirety. In doing so, the judge gave the local AFL-CIO craft unions a severe lecture on both the economic worthiness and the unquestioned legality of ABC's independent, non-union, federally approved Houston apprenticeship training programs:

> The Court is of the opinion that the broad, loose statutory language of the National Apprenticeship Act compels the conclusion that the Act grants an extremely wide discretion to the Secretary to determine what labor standards shall be "necessary to protect the welfare of apprentices." 28 U.S.C. § 50. From the information which has been provided the Court on apprenticeship programs and the construction industry in general it is clear to the Court that the decision on registering an apprenticeship program requires a substantial amount of judgment and expertise, and may turn on many technical facts. These are matters which Congress has left to the discretion of the Department of Labor and matters in which the Court should not interfere and substitute what would amount to a *de novo* decision on its part . . .
>
> The Court is of the [further] opinion that the Plaintiffs [trade unions] have totally failed to make out a case in point of fact that the actions of the Secretary of Labor, including the proposed action of

The law itself is on trial in every case as well as the cause before it.

Supreme Court Justice Harlan F. Stone

This case proves our justice system works—if you have the money and influence to go all the way.

ROBERT ALUM, ESQ.

registering the Defendant Associated Builders and Contractors' program, are in any manner unlawful. The Plaintiffs have introduced a great volume of evidence . . . [b]ut at most this evidence only shows that there are differences of opinion as to the content of standards; *it does not show an abuse of discretion or arbitrary, capricious action by the Department.*

The Plaintiffs [trade unions] have offered no proof that programs which meet national standards will fail to turn out craftsmen skilled in their particular craft. In fact the Court is convinced from the evidence that the change in policy evidenced by [the Nixon-Hodgson] Circular 70-26 may very well have a positive effect on apprentices and apprenticeship programs by bringing to an end the *monopoly situation* which seems from the evidence to exist now for the existing union-sponsored registered program.

An increase in the number of registered programs in a given area will provide more opportunities for people to be apprentices, to learn and practice the skills of the trade which they desire to enter in apprenticeship programs that they can be confident meet certain minimum standards because they have been registered and are continuously monitored by BAT. Further, the evidence indicates that the registration of Defendant Associated Builders and Contractors' programs as well as other programs meeting national standards will result in wider *minority* participation in apprenticeship programs. [emphasis added] [9]

Big Labor Continues To Challenge ABC Training Programs

Although Judge Seal's ruling in this early case was a major victory for ABC, it did not discourage trade union obstruction of the certification of ABC apprenticeship training programs throughout the United States. As recently as the year 1999, in *Associated Builders and Contractors v. Alexis Herman, Secretary of Labor*, the Bureau of Apprenticeship Training ("BAT") and Road Sprinkler Fitters Local Union 669 contended that Grinnell Fire Protection Systems Company could not enroll its strike replacement workers in existing BAT-approved ABC apprentice training programs but rather had to enroll them in the Union's BAT-approved training programs. Speaking for the U.S. Court of Appeals for the District of Columbia Circuit, Chief Judge Harry Edwards *overruled* President Bill Clinton's Secretary of Labor Herman and the Sprinkler Fitters Union—and gave BAT a stern reprimand for its pro-union prejudice.[10]

In this case Chief Judge Edwards began by noting that "throughout this litigation, BAT and counsel for DOL have consistently misrepresented the [regulatory] language." The judge therefore approved a District Court's ruling that "BAT had no statutory or regulatory authority to block Grinnell employees from participating in [ABC's] existing apprenticeship programs." He added that BAT's contention was "blatantly disingenuous" and "consistently misrepresented the language" of its own published regulations. This falsification was not "a simple oversight," continued Chief Judge Edwards, but "BAT's desire to give one side an advantage in an ongoing labor dispute." In short, concluded the judge, BAT's biased action was "at best, incomprehensible"—and he allowed Grinnell to establish its own ABC-certified apprentice training programs.

Undeterred by that humiliating defeat, the building trades unions continue to sabotage legitimate merit shop training programs. One such scheme is to take advantage of the dual control of apprenticeship between some state government agencies and the federal Bureau of Apprenticeship Training. For instance, in the recent case of *Baltimore Metro Chapter of ABC v. Maryland Apprenticeship and Training Council*, the secretary of labor of the state of Maryland was obliged to admit that the decision of its State Training Council to deny ABC's proposed revision to its BAT-certified craft training program and standards should be reversed because its pro-union tilt was "arbitrary and capricious."[11]

In another ABC apprenticeship case culminating during 2001, it took eighteen years for non-union training programs developed by the Construction Industry Training Counsel of the state of Washington—ABC's training partner in the western half of the state—to overcome building trades union opposition. According to Kathleen Garrity, executive director of ABC's Western Washington State Chapter, located in Bellevue, "an audit by the U.S. Department of Labor was required to expose the truth that the administration of Washington State's apprenticeship law was in violation of federal standards." Reminiscent of Judge Seal's Texas ABC case decided in

Some see private enterprise as a predatory target to be shot, others as a cow to be milked, but few are those who see it as a sturdy horse pulling the wagon.

WINSTON CHURCHILL
BRITISH PRIME
MINISTER

Monopoly is business at the end of its journey.

Captain
Henry F. Lloyd
NAVAL AVIATOR

1974, a local Washington state statute had made it impossible for non-union "unilateral" employer-employee training programs to be approved and certified. A parallel development occurred in California's former union-biased training programs.

The battle with the building trades over government-approved ABC apprenticeship programs never ends.[12] One of the latest all-out attacks by the Building and Construction Trades Department ("BCTD") began with a letter from its president, Edward Sullivan, to Elaine Chao, the U.S. secretary of labor, on October 27, 2003. Sullivan charged that as a result of his BCTD's six-month study of Department of Labor statistics ("DOL"), "something is wrong and ABC's flawed and failing apprenticeship training programs clearly warrant further scrutiny." A copy of the trade union's study was sent to members of Congress "to alert them to this situation and seek their support for an investigation by DOL."[13]

In response to the BCTD's "study," Kirk Pickerel, ABC's President and Chief Executive Officer, said that the building trades "have once again issued a politically motivated and misleading attack on ABC's apprenticeship programs. This is due, we believe, to their anger about DOL's efforts to effectively address the bias that many state apprenticeship councils have had favoring union-only apprenticeship training."[14]

Pickerel added that DOL "has the responsibility and authority to regulate the state apprenticeship councils, many of which have given "sweetheart deals" to union programs in the past. He concluded:

> The bottom line is that the president of the BCTD fears competition in the apprenticeship arena and will do anything he can to try to preserve the virtual monopoly the unions have had over apprenticeship programs in states like California.
>
> Building trade unions represented over 87 percent of the construction workforce in 1947 but represent less than 18 percent of those workers now. Even at full capacity, unions could only train a minor fraction of today's construction workforce. With more than four out of five construction workers choosing to work in merit shop construction, it is vital that innovative apprenticeship programs, like

those provided by ABC and its member companies, continue to be given the same opportunity for federal and state approval that union programs have traditionally received.[15]

More than two centuries ago an American patriot by the name of Thomas Paine penned these prudent words which still ring true today: "Those who expect to reap the blessings of freedom must undergo the stress and responsibility of supporting it."

A nation is the more prosperous today the less it has tried to put obstacles in the way of the spirit of free enterprise and private initiative.

LUDWIG VON MISES
PHILOSOPHER-
ECONOMIST

CHAPTER 12

TRADE UNION AUTOCRACY VERSUS MERIT SHOP PRODUCTIVITY

I N THE YEAR **1964, ABC'S** NATIONAL CONVENTION was held at the famous Homestead Hotel and Spa in the Shenandoah Mountains of Virginia on a theme called "The Challenge of Merit Shop Maturity." Total Association membership had climbed to over one thousand firms. Many of them were gaining prestige through the increased size and importance of their projects. Major inroads on industrial, commercial, institutional, and public school construction were being made throughout the Middle Atlantic States.

An announcement at the convention that ABC Founder Charlie Mullan's company had erected a $12 million high-rise apartment and shopping plaza complex in the center of union-building-trades-dominated Baltimore City was electrifying. The fundamental principles that created this achievement were obvious then and still exist today: *open shop contractors recruit, train, compensate, utilize, and manage their workforces much differently than their unionized competitors do.*

For many years there had been a feud simmering between craft unions and industrial unions representing the "blue collar" employees of manufacturing firms within their jointly shared parent American Federation of Labor ("AFL"). The conflict exploded ten years after the death of AFL Founder Samuel Gompers, at a rancorous 1934 convention. Industrial unions were organized on a plant-wide production-and-maintenance jobs basis under the aggressive leadership of John L. Lewis (of United Mine Workers Union fame) and Walter Reuther (soon to become president of the United Auto Workers Union). Eventually these "wall-to-wall" unions broke away from the AFL,

There can be no economy where there is no efficiency.

BENJAMIN DISRAELI
BRITISH PRIME MINISTER

The path to oblivion often goes through a triumphal arch.

DON-AMINADO
WRITER

which Gompers had structured on a rigid craft-by-craft basis, to form the Congress of Industrial Organizations ("CIO").

The schism between these two labor conglomerates continued for twenty years, but today there is a united American labor movement known as the "AFL-CIO." It is a federation of about 75 international (U.S.A. and Canada) labor organizations which claims to represent over thirteen million men and women in the United States and acts—through its local unions—as their exclusive workplace spokesperson.[1]

Within this AFL-CIO hierarchy is a Building & Construction Trades Department ("BCTD") consisting of international craft unions, with a combined total of about two-and-a-half-million members. In 2001, according to the *Bureau of National Affairs,*[2] the BCTD included the following special trades: Asbestos Workers (15,557), Boilermakers (39,452), Bricklayers (62,275), Carpenters (530,000—reported elsewhere), Electrical Workers (676,611), Elevator Constructors (23,093), Iron Workers (90,546), Laborers (310,468), Machinists

ABC CONTRACTOR

High-rise apartment and shopping plaza built by Mullan Contracting Company in Baltimore in 1964.

(not reported), Operating Engineers (280,000), Painters (101,617), Plasterers and Cement Masons (29,500), Plumbers and Pipe Fitters (219,800), Roofers (20,888), and Sheet Metal Workers (93,000). James Hoffa Jr.'s infamous International Brotherhood of Teamsters (1,217,880) is affiliated with them. Few, if any, of the labor organizations listed here have increased in size since that date.

These international craft unions, in turn, coordinate their activities with the umbrella BCTD over them in the nation's capital and with hundreds of affiliated regional building trades councils and thousands of affiliated local craft unions reporting to them from locations throughout the United States. Working together, this labor cartel has raised billions of dollars for political power and caused unionized contractors to abdicate their inherent managerial right to control their own workforces.

Union "Security" and the Union Hiring Hall

The government-supplied glue which binds the organized labor movement together is *compulsory union membership* or, as its nomenclature is sterilized by today's politically correct labor spin: "*union security*."[3] In 1947 Congress passed the Taft-Hartley Act. Sections 8(a)(3) and 8(b)(2) permit a labor union recognized as the "exclusive" fiduciary representative of all employees in an "appropriate bargaining unit" to compel a unionized employer—by an economic strike if necessary—to sign a so-called "union shop agreement."

That means, with the legal—but frequently ignored in practice—exception of a "right-to-work" state,[4] a recognized union can force that employer to sign a collective bargaining agreement containing a so-called "union security" clause. Under this clause, the tender of periodic membership dues to the union becomes *required* as a condition of continued employment of all employees in the bargaining unit, regardless of whether they favor or oppose unionization. The employer is also obligated by this union security clause to deduct the membership dues from the paychecks of "consenting" employees (called "dues check-off") and turn that money over to the union. If an employee fails to tender the periodic dues, the union can force the employer (because of the negotiated "union security" clause) to fire that employee.

The federal government protects union security in the construction industry even further under Section 8(f) of the Taft-Hartley Act. This provision allows management's recognition of a craft union *before* it represents a majority of that employer's workers and even *before* they are hired, provided that a full bargaining relationship is "expected" in the near future. Section 8(f) also permits a unionized contractor to sign a "hiring hall" agreement that it will employ workers referred to it by the union.[5]

The Business Roundtable Opposes Hiring Halls

These hiring halls encouraged the building trades to establish a monopoly over the construction manpower pool. And the surrender of management's inherent right to select its employees based on its own judgment of their qualifications

A man convinced against his will is not convinced.

LAURENCE T. PETER
HUMANIST

In a trade union there is no reward for doing a job faster or better.

JOHN TRIMMER
"MR. ABC"

began to cause many of the nation's leading industrial firms to rebel against the ever-increasing cost of their capital building projects. Expenses were rising at the rate of 1 percent per month—double the national increase in the cost of living.[6]

The result, in 1972, was creation of the influential Construction Users Anti-Inflation Roundtable by two hundred chief executive officers of prominent manufacturing companies. Led by Roger Blough, former chief executive of U.S. Steel Corporation, the stated objective was "to gain a better understanding of the root causes of runaway inflation in construction and help promote research, stability and efficiency in the industry."[7]

A task force formed by the Construction Users Committee of the Roundtable wrote in its first national report that the union "hiring hall" procedure had been so dominated by the building trades unions and so politicized by their administrators that it placed unionized contractors "at a severe disadvantage in performing their role as employers." The study warned that problems relating to union hiring halls were substantial enough to warrant "a very high priority effort to minimize or eliminate them."[8]

The Roundtable report went on to say:

> The day-to-day operation of a hiring hall administered by a union official can be ruthless. Referral lists can be manipulated, contractors enticed to order craftsmen by name or specialty skill in order to avoid the next craftsmen on the list, dissident members or "permit" craftsmen referred constantly to jobs of short duration, and many similar injustices perpetrated.
>
> Control over the referral process also may have a direct impact upon the layoff of employees. For example, instructions from a union official to quit a job are quickly honored if a member hopes to obtain a referral to another job in the future. *In reality, contractors who are dependent on the hiring hall have substantially lost the right to hire or terminate their employees.*[9] [emphasis added]

John Graney, the Roundtable's executive director in charge of construction, explained that the impetus for creation of its taskforce came from the National Conference on Representatives of Local (unionized) Construction User

Groups. They had concluded that "the compulsory hiring hall was the most serious impediment to solving problems relating to manpower supply, discrimination against minority groups, on site management rights, and balanced collective bargaining relationships."[10]

According to the Roundtable's task force report, many of the hiring hall's maladies were a "direct result of the misconception that a union official can properly function as an unbiased employment agency." And trade union control of this referral system "resulted in unions being the repository of virtually all available information concerning the quality and quantity of the construction manpower pool within a labor market but the same information was not accessible to contractors or construction users." The task force report added: "This imbalance in the availability of construction manpower information prevails throughout the organized segment of the construction industry, regardless of the form of the hiring hall." One of the most important features of this Roundtable study in 1972 was its recommendation that "Congress should change the law on hiring halls by outlawing them"[11]—but this politically incorrect action has never happened.[12]

Trade Unions Control Right to Manage

Unbelievable as it may seem to the rest of the business world, building trades unions still treat their special crafts like ancient European guilds. They not only dictate *whom* a contractor is permitted to employ from the union's hiring hall but also *which* workers can advance on a "seniority-only" basis; *which* craft union and *which* journeyman, apprentice, or laborer therein must perform each specific task at every job site; *what* the job ratio of the number of journeymen to apprentices will be on each project; *what* the contractor's wages, employee benefits, work rules, and other conditions of employment will be under area-wide labor contracts; and *when* a work slowdown or stoppage will occur.[13]

Unnecessary labor costs in these collective bargaining agreements also have featured bloated wage and benefits increases, maladministered medical and retirement plans, and inflexible non-productive job duties. Primeval union customs still include: worker advancement only on a seniority (length-of-service) basis, regardless of merit; overuse of skilled journeymen for tasks that

The possession of power inevitably spoils the free use of reason.

IMMANUEL KANT
GERMAN PHILOSOPHER

We all belong t' th' union whenit comes t' wantiing' more money and less work.

HUBBARD

could be performed at less cost by apprentices or laborers; a ban on the employment of lower paid "helpers" to assist journeymen and perform menial work; a guaranteed work week "rain or shine"; show-up pay, overtime pay at double time, subsistence pay, and acceptance of binding arbitration decisions by a liberal "outsider" for all labor dispute resolution. Other wasteful union customs protect prolonged rest breaks and lax disciplinary rules.

A presentation by Sal Palmeter—the manager of construction at GPU Service Corporation in New Jersey—during a meeting of the American Nuclear Society in 1978 estimated that only **31 percent** of every construction dollar billed by unionized firms went into "direct productive work." The rest of the dollar, he reported, was spent in activities such as: late starts and early quits—6.6 percent; personal and "coffee" breaks—3.5 percent; waiting and idle time—29.7 percent; traveling—13.9 percent; transporting—5.4 percent; tools and materials—3.3 percent; and instruction and reading drawings—6.6 percent. (See graphic.) Palmeter added that labor-related costs associated with construction indicated a savings of $100 million or more if non-union contractors who had abandoned the antiquated craft traditions were used in building a 1,000-megawatt nuclear power plant.[14]

Non-Productive Union "Featherbedding"

Many of the costly trade union practices fall within a labor relations term called "featherbedding." Robert's *Dictionary of Industrial Relations* defines it as "making work for union members through the limitation of production, the amount of work to be performed, or other make-work arrangements." Roberts goes on to explain that "some of these practices have come about because workers have been displaced by mechanization and the union has sought some method of retaining the employees even though there may be no work for them to perform or their services may not be required."[15]

An *Engineering News-Record* survey reported in 1972 that "low productivity was causing the construction industry to move in reverse." It listed five general categories of featherbedding practices which are required under trade union labor contracts: (1) prohibiting labor-saving machinery and equipment; (2) requiring unnecessary work or the duplication of already completed work; (3) encouraging excessive non-productive time; (4) restricting employee workloads,

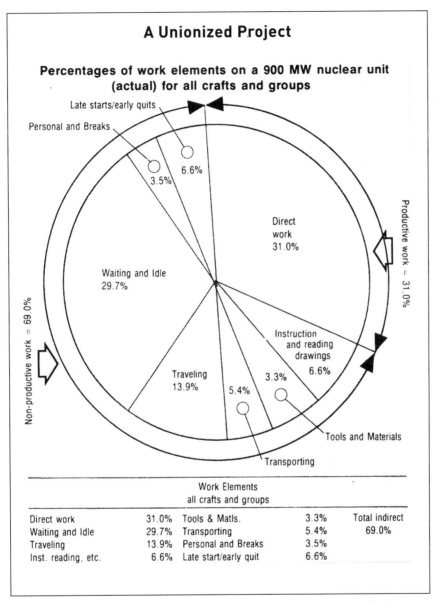

A Unionized Project

Percentages of work elements on a 900 MW nuclear unit (actual) for all crafts and groups

Late starts/early quits

Personal and Breaks

6.6%

3.5%

Direct work 31.0%

Productive work = 31.0%

Waiting and Idle 29.7%

Non-productive work = 69.0%

Instruction and reading drawings 6.6%

Traveling 13.9%

5.4%

3.3%

Tools and Materials

Transporting

Work Elements all crafts and groups					
Direct work	31.0%	Tools & Matls.	3.3%	Total indirect	
Waiting and Idle	29.7%	Transporting	5.4%	69.0%	
Traveling	13.9%	Personal and Breaks	3.5%		
Inst. reading, etc.	6.6%	Late start/early quit	6.6%		

ABC CONTRACTOR

Prepared by Sol Palmeter, manager of construction at GPU Service Corporation, July 1978.

duties, or the number of machines they can operate along strict craft lines; and (5) requiring unneeded workers. The *ENR* survey concluded that low productivity caused by these inefficient trade union practices wasted up to *40 percent* of every construction dollar—and labor costs represent at least *one third* of the price of every construction contract.[16]

On a billion-dollar project in Albany, N.Y., for instance, Teamsters fought with Operating Engineers to determine who should hold the nozzle that controlled the flow of gasoline from a tank truck to the fuel tank on a small engine. In another dispute, the Carpenters and Electricians Unions in Philadelphia battled to determine which union would install a chain-hung lamp on a particular motel project. A carpenter ended up putting the two required hooks in the wall and draping the chain while the electrician placed the plug in the socket.

A strike involving the International Union of Operating Engineers and contractors in Massachusetts idled 20,000 building tradesmen and tied up work on approximately $800 million worth of construction projects. The only issue in dispute between the union and four contractor associations related to "featherbedding." Operating Engineers were paid for "just watching" padlocked air and steam valves as well as for "operating" automatically controlled elevators and for "manning" electric pumps which "they couldn't repair and sometimes couldn't even find."[17]

Literally hundreds of thousands of these trade union featherbedding examples have existed over the years. They contribute to inflationary building costs, higher taxes, and misapplied national income. Professor Emeritus Herbert R. Northrup of the University of Pennsylvania's Wharton School and a nationally recognized authority on construction industry labor relations explained why these costly and unnecessary union devices dupe construction users and the consuming public:

> Essentially, union deployment provides that skilled craftsmen perform nearly all the work involved in an expansive definition of a job, even though much of the work is semiskilled or even unskilled. Thus an electrical crew on a union job is likely to consist of three to five journeymen who not only perform the skilled work but also unload materials, nail up conduit, pull wire through the conduit, etc., although they may be aided in some of these latter functions by apprentices who are studying to be journeymen.

On an open shop job, the same work will be done by a crew consisting of one journeyman, one or two helpers, and one or two laborers. The journeyman may be paid the equivalent of the union wage rate, or even more, but the helpers and laborers are paid much less. Moreover, incidental work considered as "belonging" to other crafts will be done by the open-shop electrical crew, but on a union job will require the services of a journeyman in another classification who may be paid a full day's wage for a few hours actual work.[18]

If at first you don't succeed, try hard work.

WILLIAM FEATHER
WRITER

Dr. Northrup's obvious conclusion was that "open shop contractors have significant advantages in the deployment of personnel on the job."[19] But the most ironical fact of all is that a provision of federal law—Section 8(b)(6) of the Taft-Hartley Act—was intended to restrict featherbedding by making it an unfair labor practice for a union "to cause or attempt to cause an employer to pay or deliver any money or other thing of value, in the nature of an exaction, for services which are not performed or not to be performed." In that sentence, Congress thought it had outlawed these non-productive practices, but biased interpretation by the National Labor Relations Board and the courts has rendered the provision practically ineffective and meaningless.[20]

Misuse of Management Foremen

Unionized contractors' own supervisory personnel—called "foremen" in the trades—are required to be union members, pay union dues, and abide by the union's constitution, by-laws, work rules, and disciplinary policies. These foremen—being unionized—neglect a supervisor's customary managerial duty to increase productivity, to oppose the wasteful allocation of labor, and to direct and discipline craftsmen.

This accepted protocol of forcing front-line company supervisors to be represented by a labor organization defies a basic principle of efficient management. It creates obvious conflicts of interests and loyalties at the workplace between employers and their unionized craftsmen that actually are *forbidden* by Sections 2(3), 2(11) and 14(a) of the Taft-Hartley Act. These provisions *exempt* management from any obligation to recognize its supervisors as union members under any collective bargaining agreement or labor

law. In further support of this protection of traditional management functions, the U.S. Supreme Court has ruled that employers "may condition a
supervisor's employment upon *non*membership in a union or *non*participation in union affairs."[21]

Craft Jurisdiction Conflicts

Strict work jurisdiction boundaries between trade unions create another controversial issue. Zealously guarded craft rules about which union performs
what work—down to the most miniscule task—are marked by slowdowns or
strikes to protest job assignments given to a rival craft. These workplace inter-
ferences occur frequently despite the availability of mediation, arbitration, and
Section 8(b)(4)(D) of the Taft-Hartley Act to settle the problems amicably.
Such jurisdictional rivalries constitute the basis for about one-third of the work
stoppages in the construction industry in any given year. They leave unionized contractors in the middle of a labor dispute not of their making and over
which they have no control.

After studying this jurisdictional problem, the Business Roundtable Construction Industry Cost Effectiveness Project concluded as follows:

> Exclusive jurisdiction—which is based on the notion that every task
> can be performed only by members of a particular union—is a major
> source of inefficiencies in construction. It may well be the greatest
> handicap faced by union contractors as they attempt to avoid further
> losses in their shrinking share of the construction market...
>
> Costly jurisdictional disputes...impose major costs on union con-
> tractors. Mechanisms for their voluntary settlement have only
> increased the problem by developing ever more precise craft assign-
> ments of work that could be performed by any of several crafts. And
> use of the Labor Board is impractical in many disputes because the
> Board takes so long to act, if it chooses to act at all.[22]

In one case, relations between unionized painters and carpenters exploded
as recently as July of 2004. These rival trades contested the right to represent
craftsmen who perform "wall finished work" and the jurisdictional dispute

jeopardized production team work all the way up the hierarchy to the two international unions and their leaders.

According to Painters Union President James Williams, his members were "targeted" by aggressive Carpenters Union organizers to switch their allegiance and craft membership. "It's easier to steal workers someone else has organized than do real [grassroots] organizing," he claimed. Carpenters Union President Douglas McCarron's staff denied the charge.[23]

Union Opposition to Technical Progress

The building and construction industry in America began to undergo substantial changes in the last half of the twentieth century. Modern techniques, materials, and equipment in an age of electronics, computerization, and automation began replacing antiquated construction practices, equipment, and materials. The trade unions reacted negatively to this inevitable progress as they fiercely protect outmoded building codes and new manning practices. Responding negatively to modernization in the same way that they protect featherbedding, trade unions either fight against any efficiency changes in their traditional craft work or demand special compensation before permitting new practices or tools to be introduced that speed up production, improve work quality, and/or reduce the need for skilled manpower.

Big Labor in Big Trouble

The June 4, 1979, issue of *Fortune* magazine featured a remarkably frank article on this subject by Gilbert Burch. It's entitled "A Time of Reckoning For the Building Unions." Pertinent excerpts included the following observations:

> The current predicament of the seventeen building trades unions is both astonishing and portentous. A dozen or so years ago they were enthroned in what seemed like an impregnable monopoly position. They ran the U.S. construction industry, the nation's largest, like a conquering army. Today they are in disorderly retreat, and it is not pulling the nose of reality to describe them as preparing to do battle for their existence. Open shop contractors, who in 1973 accounted for about *30 percent* of the industry's dollar volume, now plausibly claim

A society of sheep must in time beget a government of wolves.

Bertrand de Jouvenel
Historian

121

**Mock the time
with fairest show;
false face must
hide what false
heart doth know.**

Shakespeare
Macbeth, I. vii

to dominate the industry… An open shop trade group, the *Associated Builders and Contractors*, estimates that open shop contractors will not only account for *60 percent* of construction this year but will continue to grow at the expense of the union shop. What happened?

To begin with, what happened was that the building unions became classic examples of the adage that "monopoly has no use save abuse." Their monopoly was based on their ability to control the industry's manpower supply. They decided how many apprentices would be trained to become journeymen—that is, skilled workers—and how long it would take to train them, and they recurrently used that power to keep the supply short of demand. They operated the pools of manpower known as hiring halls, from which they supplied contractors with all their help—including foremen who frequently worried more about staying in the good graces of their brothers than about doing an efficient job for their employer. Thus management was shorn of prerogatives and forced to abdicate crucial responsibility. The arrangement was accepted by contractors who were willing to pay dearly to be relieved of the responsibility for hiring and training so long as they could pass the bill along to their customers.

By the middle 1960's, all U.S. unions were beginning to vie with one another in exacting highly inflationary wage increases. As might have been expected, the construction unions were in the van of the movement. Some local contracts called for increases totaling 100 percent over three years. Worse, the unions flooded the industry with make-work rules and jurisdictional distinctions even more preposterous, perhaps, than the restrictions that have all but ruined the railroads. According to findings of a yearlong study published by the *Engineering News-Record*, in 1972 these practices padded the national construction bill by $12 billion to $16 billion.

At about the same time as the *Fortune* article was written, Richard Wiggins, a partner in an architectural-engineering firm in Grand Rapids, Michigan, and a member of the National Council of Architectural Registration, praised the construction work of ABCers:

A way to minimize construction costs is to involve merit shop contractors. We have had some of our greatest success in our projects by working with them. I am convinced that merit shop firms, generals and subs, are one of the best building costs alternatives we have today. These craftsmen are basically much more responsive to the tasks and more responsive to getting the job done on time.[24]

The world is full of cactus but we don't have to sit on it.

WILL FOLEY
PUNDIT

Unfortunately for the AFL-CIO, little, if any, correction of these building trades productivity problems occurred. As long ago as 1975, Dean Sooter, general vice president of the United Brotherhood of Carpenters, warned: "We frankly tell our members that union construction is going down the tubes and only they can reverse this ominous trend."[25] And a few years later the Texas Building Trades Council sent a no-punches-pulled letter to its thousands of rank-and-file members. The admonition about a serious decline of union shop construction was clear:

The world's full of thorns and thistles. It's all in how you grasp them.

ARNOLD GLASOW
PHILOSOPHER

> It is becoming apparent that we union tradesmen may be our own worst enemy. The reports and statistics of high absenteeism, low productivity, and lack of initiative and pride in ourselves and in our union is apparent. Is it expecting too much that we as union craftsmen do less than abide by our obligation to give a respectable day's work for a respectable day's pay? Protect your job and your future![26]

An Answer to the Building Trades Dilemma

A two-fold peaceful, practical, and legal solution to organized labor's grave craft union predicament is available but ignored. First, union membership, as envisioned by the AFL's founding father and first president, Sam Gompers, should be *voluntary*.[27] Such an "open" labor organization selected by and dedicated to the workers necessarily is more democratic and more responsive to the needs and beliefs of its members than an autocracy operated for the power and security of its professional leaders. Supreme Court Justice Felix Frankfurter emphasized this fact in the aforementioned *American Sash & Door Company* case.[28] Secondly, the building trades should return all basic management functions to unionized contractors, including: supervisory responsibilities of

The open shop meets the psychological needs of workers by recognizing and rewarding above average employees through pay increases and more responsibility.

JOHN HEIZELMAN
CONSULTANT

their foremen, the right to deploy flexible work rules that abolish outmoded craft union practices, and respect for a fair and reasonable wage and employee benefits structure that is needed to remain competitive in the marketplace.

Instead, the construction unions still seem to regard their antiquated trades and inflationary employee benefits as sacrosanct. Their unwavering answer, since the founding of ABC in 1950, has been an attempt to make the policies and practices of the merit shop construction movement irrelevant through partisan politics, coercion and terrorism, leading to monopolistic unionized mastery of the entire industry. That goal justifies whatever means is necessary to attain it—and thereby wipe out the merit shop crusade.

Open Shop Wage and Benefits Cost Advantages

An obvious threat to the building trades over the years has been the lower wage and employee "fringe benefits" costs of ABC competitors. But specific comparisons are difficult. In a compulsory union shop, all employees in each of three standardized job classifications (journeyman, apprentice, and laborer) receive the identical wage negotiated in the labor contract, regardless of individual comparative qualifications and work performances.

Non-union firms have no rigid job descriptions and no uniform industry-wide or even local job classifications, wage scales, or employee benefits, so they are more difficult to survey. Every contractor determines these factors on the basis of the type of construction work performed, the profitability and productivity of its own workforce, and the individual merit of each employee. There is respect for length of service ("seniority") but unlike trade union policy, only when the ability of employees under consideration is relatively equal.

In recent years this labor cost margin has decreased as skilled mechanics in many open shop construction firms are being employed at higher wage levels with incentive pay due to a rising cost of living, severe labor shortages, and a building surge. Some non-union contractors even pay their best mechanics at a rate above the union scale but still maintain a labor cost advantage over unionized competitors through more diversified and utilitarian management of personnel overall. Most importantly, annual take-home pay consistently runs equal or higher in the non-union sector. That's because each contractor provides year round employment for its basic workforce even in slow business periods as opposed to the unionized side of the industry, with its uncertainty of placement referrals due to dictatorial hiring hall practices and seasonal workload variances.

Employee fringe benefits, like wage rates among ABC contractors, vary by local standards, by craft, by size and success of the company, and are equally difficult to catalogue. There also is an upward trend to provide "perks" that are on a par with other industries. All but the smallest firms offer paid holidays and vacations, health and life insurance protection, and some type of profit sharing or retirement plan. Insurance premium cost sharing between employers and their employees continues to grow. ABC's own state-of-the-art group insurance program takes nationwide advantage of competitive independent carriers to offer the large population of its members lower group premium rates under efficient internal administration. This is another open shop labor cost advantage.

As an inducement to recruitment and an incentive for efficiency and against workforce turnover, many open shop firms include a six-day workweek with premium overtime pay, night and holiday shift premiums, special per diem pay, and a variety of bonuses based on productivity, attendance, safety record, profitability, job completion, or special wage rates for certain projects. Larger ABC members frequently pay the cost for employee education tuition, annual physical examinations, free health club memberships, day nurseries for employees' children, and other worker-and-family benefit programs. Additional benefits for employees that improve morale include low rates on insurance premiums and checking accounts, interest-free equipment purchases, plus payroll deductions for children's future education and for health insurance add-ons such as eye or drugs coverage.

Superior Open Shop Manpower Management

Today the competitive edge that the open shop offers to construction users over a closed union shop results less from the traditional wage and employee fringe benefits margin than from the vast difference in *human resources utilization*. Non-union firms have none of the previously described restrictive union controls over supervisory and executive prerogatives, no featherbedded labor union agreements or practices, no rigid hiring hall or other manpower

Even if you're on the right track, you'll get run over if you just sit there.

WILL ROGERS
COMEDIAN-
PHILOSOPHER

For employee success, energy, morale, and integrity are equally as important as ability.

Harry F. Banks
Humanist

restrictions, and no labor slowdowns or strikes. Instead, people-oriented ABC contractors practice firm but fair employee relations in a harmonious modern-day environment that places emphasis on "good will" factors such as:

- Mutual respect and two-way communications from top management to rank-and-file employees.
- Priority emphasis on safety and health.
- Front-line supervisors (foremen) practicing positive employee relations and job site management without any union control.
- A humane company culture and trustworthiness that boosts employee morale by solving people-problems quickly and fairly.
- Training of employees at a pace based on individual merit and ability to master multi-skilled tasks that cross traditional union craft lines.
- Flexible deployment of work crew mixes, including liberal journeyman-apprentice ratios, and the extensive use of helpers and laborers for semi-skilled and unskilled tasks.
- Opportunity for career development and growth.
- Job security provided by steady work in a year-around "home" at one construction firm.
- Concern for the personal and family life of all employees.

Business Roundtable Praise for the Merit Shop

In 1982, members of retired U.S. Steel CEO Roger Blough's Business Roundtable urged the business community of constructions users to hear the ABC "merit shop story" and to use non-union contractors as part of a "Construction Industry Cost Effectiveness Project." This authoritative Roundtable report proclaimed that its statistics showed the general business sector favored an "open shop" approach in the construction industry and regarded union power as too great. It undoubtedly had an impact on the decreasing union density in construction.[29]

The Business Roundtable report also emphasized ABC's outstanding apprentice training programs and praised the cost-efficient use of "helpers" as opposed to the nonproductive exclusion of this semi-skilled job classification by unionized contractors:

Open shop contractors have a significant economic advantage because of their ability to fully utilize *helpers* for unskilled and semiskilled work in all crafts, and to add manpower to labor pools . . . Using a high percentage of subjourneymen, properly screened, may bring labor cost savings on a particular job *as great as 20 percent*. The long-range benefit may be equally important because it offers the construction industry a new tool for meeting future manpower needs. Open-shop contractors have demonstrated an ability to train large numbers of workmen, *including minorities and beginners*, in a relatively short time by a variety of successful methods.[30] [emphasis added]

Education makes people easy to lead but difficult to drive; easy to govern but impossible to enslave.

HENRY BROUGHAM
SCOTTISH POLITICIAN
AND REFORMER

Use of "Temps"

Severe shortages of skilled craft workers in today's marketplace are fueling the growth of another burgeoning trend in open shop construction: the use of independent private labor agencies that supply non-union contractors with a temporary array of supplemental skilled workers. Richard Pomeroy, president of Construction Workforce, Inc., an Oregon-based "temp" agency or "labor supplier," reported that he has "a database of 57,000 skilled non-union craftsmen and can supply everything it takes to run a construction project in twenty-seven states." He claimed that he is using technology at its fullest "to give his clients the most versatile personnel available."[31]

Outsourced labor is taking hold.[32] And according to *Engineering News-Record*, "a labor battle is brewing today" over this practice:

> The Building and Construction Trades Department of the AFL-CIO estimates that there are more than 450 of these temp agencies across the U.S., providing about 250,000 workers daily in almost every construction craft. Temp agency sources say the numbers are even greater.
>
> Unions fear these agencies are enticing workers and employers with a smorgasbord of services designed to make daily labor hassle-free. "It's becoming more and more of a problem," says Thomas Fischbach, business representative for Sheet Metal Workers' Union Local 22 in Cranford, N.J. Fifteen [international] building trades unions have launched a multicraft organizing campaign aimed at workers and

The closest a person ever comes to perfection is when he fills out a job application form.

STANLEY RANDALL
PUNDIT

employers. But some insiders say unions should expand the services they offer employers as a way of countering the temp firms.[33]

Engineering News-Record's prediction of a "labor battle" over temporary employees has come true. During the late 1990s, the Clinton administration's National Labor Relations Board and its General Counsel began to make it easier for unions to organize these "temps."

Recruitment, Education, and Training Programs

One of the main causes of labor shortages in the construction industry is the fact that the heroic public image of skilled workers braving the elements to "build America" has fallen on hard times. It's a growing fact that the "baby-boomer" population is retiring in the next few years and we are losing a large part of the construction work force."[34] It's also true that cultural, social, and technological changes have altered the way that young people entering the workforce choose a career. They are reluctant to abandon the well-paid cocoon of a computerized high-tech world for an outdoor job they consider too physical, dirty, dangerous, seasonal, low-paying, and unsuitable to a stable family life.

ABC recruiters visit and team up with schools, community colleges, and universities to change the industry's poor image and explain its challenging lifework advantages. Construction users also are becoming involved. The impact of a tightening labor supply and declining skills can produce low quality work that comes to rest on the doorsteps of customers who foot the bills.

These factors also have led to a growing emphasis by merit shop contractors on offering their employees technological advances and job versatility within a planned career path. The work environment features upward mobility within a state-of-the-art education and training program. ABC has become a leader in attaining these goals.

As early as the 1960s, the Association helped to found both the American Council for Construction Education ("ACCE") and the Associated Schools of Construction ("ASC"). ACCE is an accreditation body that, with ABC's assistance and advice, establishes construction curricula and sets industry standards. Its programs cater to youth who are entering college and seek a future in the construction industry. ASC is a professional-fraternal organization of professors and other instructors who teach the accredited programs. Some eighty schools of higher education (such as the University of Florida, Auburn, Clemson, Texas A&M, and Georgia Institute of Technology) are members of both organizations, as is ABC.

The student curricula of ACCE and ASC include safety, communications, people-problem solving, time management, job planning, scheduling, bidding, production, and cost control, as well as computer use. Role-playing is used to add a touch of realism to lessons in employee relations. Graduates from an ACCE-accredited institution receive a bachelor's, master's, or doctorate degree in Construction Technology or Construction Management. Condensed courses are offered to construction employees on leave from their firms.

ABC's Unmatched "Wheels of Learning" Program

Of even more importance in today's technical revolution is one of the crown jewels of ABC: *a world class construction trades teaching method originally called "Wheels of Learning."* The name was coined in 1978 by Scott Robertson, ABC's able director of public relations at the time, and the program was developed over several years at a cost of millions of dollars. It is defined as "a competency-based, task-oriented training program covering twenty-one crafts that provides a modular format allowing contractors to design their training procedures to suit their needs and their workers' interests." (The program has recently been renamed *"NCCER Contren,"* and is under new ownership, as discussed later.)

This massive project—called "a truly pioneering effort" by John Trimmer—was initiated in the late 1970s by three future ABC presidents: Ted Kennedy of BE&K ('80), Robert Turner of Paisan Construction Company ('79), and Franz June of Gulf States, Inc. ('81). These foresighted contractors were ably assisted by fellow ABCers Leo Anhalt of SSI, Inc., and John Smith of Lake Mechanical Company. Their task was to oversee the drafting and standardization of model apprenticeship training programs by a team of professional tradesmen and university curriculum writers covering all of the crafts on a national basis.

According to Roger Liska, ABC's national director of education and safety in 1980, this Wheels of Learning program was made available to all types of personnel in the industry at a negligible cost:

Life is an escalator: You can move forward or backward; you cannot remain still.

PAT RUSSELL-MCCLOUD
MOTIVATIONAL SPEAKER

**Take the tools
in hand and
carve your
best life.**

DOUGLAS LORTON
CONSULTANT

It is the most flexible training program available because it can be used in a formal classroom setting or in an individual private setting, and that is what makes our program so unique. It can also be used by an individual to gain skills in a number of trades. And experienced workers are given the opportunity to utilize modules to update their knowledge of seldom-used skills or learn income-producing skills in a completely new field. There are no other training programs available which provide this flexibility.[35]

Major funding for this gigantic project began with a $50 levy on every ABC member firm in order to raise a million dollars. Subsequent financing of the program came from educational and construction foundations, private users, and other ABC supporters.[36] In 1982, ABC gave a presentation on the Wheels of Learning program to U.S. Secretary of Labor Ray Donovan and received high praise.[37]

A modular-oriented format allows contractors to hand-tailor the Wheels training program to their own specific projects and special employee requirements. Apprentices learn how to read plans, use tools, and become skilled mechanics in the shop or field. Safety is an integral part of each curriculum. Because of the unique instruction concept, students can be cross-trained in many skills within a single craft as well as in other crafts, thus greatly enhancing their value to merit shop employers.

Through this combination of classroom and on-the-job tutelage, Wheels of Learning students move on as soon as they have mastered a skill. Individual merit of each student is the key factor and there is no union-style frozen time period for progressing on a seniority basis only. Courses covered today are available in textbook or module format and include: core/basic construction fundamentals, boilermaking, carpentry, concrete finishing, drywall, construction craft labor, electronic systems, glazing, heavy equipment operations, heating–ventilation–air conditioning, industrial maintenance, instrumentation, insulation, ironwork, masonry, metal building assembly, millwright, mobile crane operations, painting, pipefitting, plumbing, roofing, sheet metal, sprinkler fitting, and welding.

President Ronald Reagan was so impressed by the Wheels of Learning plan during a meeting with his Task force on Private Sector Initiatives that he told the group: "I have just left a meeting of the Associated Builders and Contractors and you might be interested to know that this is an association of 17,000 independent contractors who have a program in which they are training and educating people who want to learn how to become craftsmen." Reagan added that such programs encouraged him because they show: "We're witnessing a rebirth of concern and involvement that historians may describe as a reawakening of the American spirit. For the first time in decades, people are starting to realize they have an important role to play and that they can make a difference."[38]

Today the apprenticeship training curricula of Wheels of Learning are completely standardized, portable throughout the United States and abroad, accessible to the general public, competency-based, self-paced on merit, task-driven, and career-directed. They also meet official craft certification standards of the U.S. Department of Labor's Bureau of Apprenticeship Training for work on government construction projects.

Thousands of young apprentices and trainees have completed these courses. Many of them start as early as high school or vocational school and continue on into engineering colleges through "School-to-Career" programs sponsored by local ABC chapters and their numbers. More than 1,500 master trainers and 15,000 certified instructors are teaching in accredited training centers across the nation.[39]

A Companion Construction Jewel: NCCER

A second ABC masterstroke, the *National Center for Construction Education & Research* ("NCCER"), was created in 1991—with the aid of eleven major contractors—as an educational affiliate. The goals, according to ABC member Fluor Daniel Construction Company's President Dan Buck, are threefold:

> To educate the construction user community on the value of investing in training; to develop and publish state-of-the-art construction and maintenance curricula that set national standards in every craft; and to attract qualified young people into construction's ranks.[40]

All who have meditated on the governing of mankind have been convinced that the fate of sovereignty depends on the education of youth.

ARISTOTLE, GREEK PHILOSOPHER

My education began with a set of blocks which had on them the Roman numerals and the letters of the alphabet. It is not yet finished.

CALVIN COOLIDGE
30TH PRESIDENT

Fortified by $11 million in initial funding, the first major action by NCCER was its adoption of administration of the ABC Wheels of Learning's nationally certified training program for use throughout the construction industry. Because of the magnitude of this reorganization and the need for broad-based participation, ABC invited other construction industry associations to join with it under the National Center umbrella, and the program's name has been changed to "NCCER CONTRENS."

Ensuring its independence from any single industry group, NCCER became a separate entity in 1994 and established a working relationship with the Rinker School of Construction at the University of Florida on its Gainesville campus. Today, twenty-eight industry associations are partners in NCCER CONTRENS, with ABC acting as its general partner. BE&K's Ted Kennedy (ABC year '80 President) served as chairman of the organization's board of trustees in 2003 and Austin Industrial's Henry Kelly (ABC year '01 President) was the 2004 chairman. From offices in Gainesville, the National Center publishes and maintains standardized training in more than twenty-five crafts. It also houses a National Registry documenting proof of the successful completion of training by would-be construction workers.

Former ABC and NCCER Leader Turns Educator

Daniel J. Bennet was NCCER's President from its inception in 1996 until he resigned in 2003. He had previously been the highly proficient executive vice president of ABC from 1983 to 1997 and was a driving force behind the standardization of open shop craft training for the Wheels of Learning program. Under Bennet's leadership, annual sales of the NCCER curricula reached $7 million. The NCCER's National Registry processed 1.5 million training transcripts and NCCER certified more than 21,000 individuals as craft instructors. During Bennet's watch, it also was honored with many citations, including the industry's prestigious NOVA award by the Construction Innovation Forum "for excellence in innovation that improves the quality, efficiency and cost-effectiveness of construction."

In 1992, Dan Bennet was named by *Engineering News-Record* as a leader who has made a "mark" on the industry. In 1995 he received the highest citation of the Construction Industry Institute: its Carroll H. Dunn "Award of

Excellence" for his "singular and notable responsibility for significant advancement in improving the cost effectiveness of the industry." In the year 2000, he was chosen as one of nine "ABC Leaders of the twentieth century who significantly influenced and strengthened the merit shop construction industry located throughout the United States."

The list of NCCER-CONTRENS partnering industry associations, along with ABC, has included The Business Roundtable, the Associated General Contractors of America, National Association of Minority Contractors, National Association of Women in Construction, Merit Contractors Association of Canada, Construction Industry Institute, National Utility Contractors Association, U.S. Army Corps of Engineers, Vocational Industrial Clubs of America, Women Construction Owners and Executives, U.S.A., and the National Vocational Technical Honor Society.

As reported by *Engineering News-Record*, NCCER also coordinates the National Construction Image Steering Committee. It was established in 2001 to devise proposals for improving the industry's ethnic and gender diversity, minority language barriers, safety training, wages and benefits, employee and public relations, and youth outreach.[41]

Financing NCCER Operations

The funding of NCCER-CONTRENS has occurred in three ways. The *first* stage is $20 million in contributions that the National Center is currently in the process of raising. The *second* method is the sale of information and materials used in craft management and safety training. The Wheels of Learning curricula "sell themselves" and bring in millions of dollars. The *third* aspect of funding occurs through voluntary cents-per-hour-of-work contributions that come from individual contractors and construction users. It is a trusteed program that donates money for craft training based on estimated hours worked as part of bid specifications. This is the most critical part of the financial equation, and potential for revenue is almost unlimited. The

If you want to earn more—learn more. If you want to get more out of the world, you must put more into the world.

WILLIAM J. BOETCKER
HUMANIST

ABC CONTRACTOR

Daniel Bennet, executive vice president, ABC (1983–1996); NCCER president (1997–2003); and winner of ABC's award as one of its nine "leaders of the twentieth century."

fund supplants the negotiated labor contract requirement placed on many unionized contractors to provide similar funds for craft training through paycheck deduction from union workers' earnings.

Under a National Training Service Agreement (endorsed by The Business Roundtable) contractors are provided a fiduciary depository of this training fund administered by NCCER to ensure customers that the financial contribution is being used on training. Due to the current shortage of skilled manpower, this practice is becoming popular on major open shop projects.[42] Prestigious firms such as Kellogg Brown & Root, Fluor Daniel, BE&K, Inc., Clark Construction Group, Adena Corporation, TD Industries, Hess Mechanical, Zachry Construction, Wilmar Electric, Suitt Construction, Austin Industrial, the Nova Group, Inc., Grinnell Fire Protection Systems, Harkins Builders, Jack Jennings & Son, Miller & Long, Vos Electric, and many other ABC-member generals and subs have volunteered to contribute fifteen cents per every employee hour worked as part of all successful project bids.

Kent Underwood, former chairman of the Construction Committee of The Business Roundtable and currently an executive at Solutia, Inc., urges that "owners should do business only with contractors who are actually investing in professional training and maintaining the skills of their workers."[43] And Dan Buck of giant Fluor-Daniel Construction Company summed up the Wheels of Learning–NCCER program this way:

> It is absolutely world class and has been given rave reviews by everybody that has used it. I would say that almost every major contractor in the United States is using the Wheels of Learning. Some of us are using it overseas and have converted it into foreign languages. This standardized, portable, self-paced curriculum is the absolute first building block for our success. Our challenge in the future is that we keep it updated and relevant as we go forward.[44]

ABC School-to-Work Training

One of the most important activities of NCCER-CONTRENS affiliates like ABC's Cumberland Valley Chapter, under the competent leadership of its president, Joan Warner, is a partnership with area school districts. Each year her chapter participates in a "Careers In Construction Teleconference" broadcast live to thousands of schools across the United States on the great opportunities available to young people in the construction industry. The viewing audience is estimated to be several million students and construction workers. And a School-to-Work Program allows high school students to begin construction craft training in their locality as part of their education. This program is sponsored by local construction companies, and students are placed in jobs during the summer months before their senior year. Their education continues during their senior year, and after graduation they are placed in construction jobs. They then continue the remaining required courses in evening adult training programs until graduation as skilled mechanics.

This photo from the *ABC Contractor* of November 8, 1995, was sent across the country to promote careers in construction. These students attended NCCER's school-to-work program at Western Technical High School in Baltimore County, Maryland.

Engineering News-Record recently devoted an entire issue of its weekly magazine to "Looking at Construction Education." It pointed out that learning could be "fun" if:

> . . . curricula are timely, pertinent, and meaningful. They also must produce graduates who have skills that employers need and are willing to pay for and which will produce better projects to meet the needs of our society. But that is only half the battle—and may be the easier part. The most important struggle is over how to engage students, hold their interest and make the subjects come alive. Without that component, all is lost, including the many students who may wander away to other fields and industries.[45]

To increase contractors' interest in supporting these training programs, ABC National's School-to-Career Committee ("S-T-C") assembled a list of national partnerships that local ABC chapters and their members work with

A writer asked me, "What makes a good manager?" And I answered: "Good players."

YOGI BERRA
N.Y. YANKEES
CATCHER-PHILOSOPHER

Leadership is action, not position.

DON MCGANNON
MANAGEMENT
CONSULTANT

to attract more young people into the industry. They include SkillsUSA-Vocational Industrial Clubs of America (which educates 250,000 students enrolled in trade and technical programs), Junior Achievement, ABC's College Student Chapters, and ABC's latest partnership with Learning for Life–Explorers, a skilled trades program subsidiary of the Boy–Girl Scouts of America. A successful S-T-C program recruits future workers, enhances the image of the industry, trains the next generation of industry leaders, and promotes the merit shop philosophy to local school board members and government officials.

ABC's National Craft Olympics

In 1985, all of Florida's ABC chapters banded together and held a statewide Craft Olympics to salute the Association's "best of the best" craft trainees. It was so popular that in 1987 the first national competition was held at ABC's annual convention in Orlando. Only four trades (sheet metal, plumbing, carpentry, and electrical) were showcased that year, but today it is one of the main attractions at ABC's annual national convention, offering a dozen or more trades. Individuals enrolled in apprenticeship or craft training programs that represent ABC chapters or member companies compete in a series of craft-related exercises that test newly developed skills and award prizes.

The National Craft Olympics (recently renamed National Craft Champions) thus promotes job training for all ABC member firms, focusing on skilled craftsmanship and creating a positive image for the construction industry. The ability and knowledge of individual entrants representing ABC chapters or member firms is judged by using NCCER's Wheels of Learning curricula. And this popular annual event gives ABC an added bonus: Winners say that the competition "was an enjoyable experience, enhanced their careers, and helped them to grow as people." From starting as helpers to becoming journeymen and moving on to management positions, or, in some cases, owning their own businesses, the National Craft Olympics keeps on producing many of tomorrow's leaders.[46]

Craft Training Portability and Tracking

Another major factor in the success of the Wheels of Learning–NCCER-CONTRENS program is its aforementioned portability. Through a national registry "bank," each student craft worker's training history can be verified and tracked. Over 900,000 transcripts have been issued, allowing a novel continuity of training when these student-apprentices move from one contractor to another as the job market fluctuates, without interrupting their training schedules. NCCER-CONTRENS, under its associated partners, represents more than 100,000 construction and construction-related businesses and maintains this national registry with transcripts and certificates to verify that all of its graduates are trained to industry standards with portable skills.

One pound of learning requires ten pounds of common sense to apply it.

Persian Proverb

Training for Corporate Executives

Also under the auspices of NCCER-CONTRENS are a series of management training programs and workshops in subjects such as leadership, human resources, cost scheduling and scope control, pre-project planning, design, environmental issues, construction site safety, technology and decision analysis, material oversight, productivity and quality standards, modularization, team building, and industry image promotion. These courses have graduated more than 3,000 project managers, superintendents, and other corporate executives. NCCER and ABC produce a series of programs for them on the latest information about workplace safety, including interpretations of ever-changing federal and state laws and regulations on the subject.

Many of these educational courses take place on the campus of the University of Florida, Clemson University, and other participating educational institutions. Through them, construction professionals are given the opportunity to gain additional management training and skills that can increase their on-the-job performance and advancement opportunities within their own firms. A master's degree in Construction Science and Management is offered through Clemson University in partnership with NCCER.

ABC's "Task" Training Programs

As described before, ABC believes that training programs in the construction industry should be "competency-based, flexible, and career-oriented." That is why ABC members also engage in a substantial amount of so-called "task," "multi-skilled," or "building block" training. The learners (whether apprentices, helpers, or laborers) acquire all-around knowledge by combining classroom study with on-the-job instruction. Trainees can progress as far as they desire at a pace based on their own ability and motivation to master chosen jobs. Job featherbedding is eliminated and the training can be customized or upgraded for a particular contractor to satisfy a special need or particular work crew mix.[47]

The Business Roundtable has praised this versatile and cost-effective training approach:

> An important difference between labor-management apprenticeship programs and training done by open-shop contractors and their associations is the greater use of 'task' training by non-union employers. Training of workers merely to accomplish specialized tasks has, in many instances, proven to be more efficient and economical for specific projects than the training offered by [traditional craft union] apprenticeship programs. Trainees can reach necessary levels of skills much faster when they concentrate on specialized tasks.[48]

Recruiting Military Veterans

One of the most desirable sources of manpower to be explored recently is the employment of veterans as they separate from heroic duty in the armed services. Kirk Pickeral, ABC's president and CEO, reported that he has been in touch with many construction firms which are proud to employ them and that "ABC itself is planning our own national initiative." The National Center for Construction Education and Research, with aforementioned strong ties to the merit shop movement, also offers extensive training programs and recruiting relationships with America's military forces. "These young men and women are well-skilled, have time-honored core values, are responsible, and maintain an excellent work ethic," confirms a private job placement service known as The Destiny Group.

The building trades unions, to their credit, are also spending significant time and effort in recruiting war veterans.[49]

Why "The Merit Shop Builds Best"

To sum up ABC's operating philosophy, the merit shop is based on a blend of entrepreneurial independence, management vision, and operational teamwork in an open and competitive marketplace. In 1985, to mark the thirty-fifth anniversary of ABC's birth, the Association's national magazine, *ABC Construction*, sponsored a roundtable discussion on this subject with some of its founders. ABC patriarch and first president, Charlie Mullan ('50), offered these words:

> Never in all my expectations did I dream of the Associated Builders and Contractors being as large as it is today. It was flexibility and efficiency in the use of the work force—breaking outside the rigidity of union craft jurisdictions—that made the difference. But I'm just amazed and proud with how it has grown. The goals that have been set and reached are tremendous. But the biggest contribution of ABC, I think, is to be able to keep general contractors and subcontractors independent and operating together as open shop team players rather than being told by trade unions who will work for them and how they have to work.

ABC's co-founder and second president, Charles Knott ('51), also reminisced about this harmony:

> An important characteristic of ABC membership in those early days was that we encouraged subcontractors to join the Association. We generals knew that for us to be strong, these subcontractors had to be strong. So if they were working on one of our jobs, we would be sure that they were paid on time and help them with their financing. We scratched each other's backs and this drew the subs to ABC in droves. We thought the Association would grow, but we never thought it would expand to what it is today.

Ed Colwill, another founder and the third president of ABC ('52-'53), explained his merit shop ideology this way:

> The perception that ABC was "non-union" was definitely not true. This was proved by the fact that we all worked with union subcontractors. We asked for only three things in hiring a subcontractor. One

All truth passes through three stages. First, it is ridiculed. Second, it is violently opposed. Third, it is accepted as being self-evident.

ARTHUR SCHOPENHAUER
GERMAN PHILOSOPHER

was a price upon which we both agreed. Second, that the work be done properly and on time. Third, that it would pass plans and specifications from the architect. Whether the sub was union or open shop, black or white, made no difference to us. If a worker elected to be union of his own volition, okay. But he should not be forced to go union. That's it in a nutshell.

I'm more proud of what we've done for free enterprise than any other goal we set. There's one word in the English dictionary that really makes a person forge ahead and that's "accomplishment." When I look at ABC today and I know that I had a part in launching it, I feel that's the greatest accomplishment of my life. Competition is the most powerful tool to secure a fairer and more prosperous society.

The Henry Lewis Story

The traditional work ethic of ABC's founders has been instilled in the Association's modern-day leaders. Success stories of "coming up the hard way" and dedication to "merit shop free enterprise" abound. A typical example is Baltimorean Henry Lewis who says he was "lucky to be at the right place at the right time."

After graduating from high school, Lewis was hired by ABC founder Ed Colwill in 1947 as a laborer. He soon progressed to apprentice mechanic status. At the same time, he received an architecture certificate from the Maryland Institute by attending classes three nights a week for four years. Colwill paid Lewis' tuition fees and then promoted him to the front office where he began to learn estimating.

In 1951, Lewis left Ed Colwill (with his blessing) for a career advancement as an estimator in the Charles Tovell Company and then for W. H. Ward Company. He soon became Ward's representative at ABC functions and also faced job site picketing and violence by local building trades unions.

In 1966, Lewis established his own firm—Henry H. Lewis Contractors, Inc.—and immediately became an active member of ABC's Metropolitan Baltimore Chapter. Today he still remains one of the leaders of his chapter and an ardent advocate for the merit shop as a spokesman, a financial supporter, and a highly successful builder. In 2001, he was given the chapter's first "Lifetime Achievement Award" which stated:

> Henry Lewis exemplifies all that is good about the merit shop: As a builder, he enjoys an unparalleled reputation for quality and value; as an employer, he inspires loyalty and exemplary performance among his employees; and as an ABC member, he has emerged as an ardent and articulate defender of the merit shop. Fiercely independent, Henry's tireless support of the merit shop and his quiet leadership has sustained the Association during the good times and the bad.

When soliciting new ABC members, Lewis asks prospects to consider this question: "Where would our industry be without ABC?" Then he gives his answer, which always begins like this: "The nominal amount of membership dues you pay to ABC for its outstanding services and benefits will come back to your business many times over. You will also have the satisfaction of protecting the cause of free enterprise from increasing control by Big Government and Big Labor."

Some of the landmark buildings recently constructed or restored by the Henry Lewis firm are located at Johns Hopkins University, Western Maryland College, Loyola College, Gilman School, Sheppard Pratt Hospital, and Monticello, the historic home of Thomas Jefferson.

A Unique Glass Banner

Another crowning achievement of the Lewis company was a recent contract to build the unique $3.7 million addition to the Star-Spangled Banner Flag House Museum at 844 East Pratt Street in downtown Baltimore City. This historic national landmark features the home of Mary Pickersgill and a 30-by-42-foot glass wall (1,260 square feet) nearby that displays a likeness of the great banner with fifteen broad stripes and fifteen bright stars. It is an exact replica of the huge American flag sewed by

Hats off! Along the street there comes a blare of bugles, a ruffle of drums, a flash of color beneath the sky; Hats off! The flag is passing by!

HENRY BENNETT
POET

PHOTO BY ALAN JARAMILLO

Henry H. Lewis, president of Henry Lewis Contractors, LLC. In 2001, he received the first "Lifetime Achievement Award" given by his Metro Baltimore Chapter of ABC.

Mary Pickersgill that waved over Fort McHenry during the Battle of Baltimore in 1814. It was intentionally made big enough for the enemy to see. Francis Scott Key—who was held as a prisoner of war on a naval vessel in the Baltimore harbor, caught a glimpse of the mammoth banner and was inspired to write the poem that became our national anthem. (See color photo of this glass banner at end of Chapter 52.)

The *Baltimore Sun* of October 29, 2001, described the unusual construction project as follows:

> Instead of making a building that would be an enclosure for a flag, it was decided that the flag should be the building. This flag-wall will be a structural glazing system in which glass is put in place without mullions. Instead of being clear, the glass will be colored with a ceramic "frit" material designed to depict the flag with thin, red, white and blue stripes. The stripes will be spaced far enough apart that people will be able to see in and out of the glass wall, but close enough that the flag image will be discernible from a distance.

In a subsequent article written on the forth of July, 2002, The *New York Times* added: "Michael Vergason, the Flag House Banner project's landscape architect, will include a fountain with a three-and-a-half-foot-high bronze spool of thread and water jets that look like sewing needles." As this one-of-a-kind project neared completion in May of 2003, the *Baltimore Sun* featured a story on it headlined: **GLORY IN GLASS.** Here is a passage from that article:

> America has had dozens of different flags over the years, but it's never had anything like the one taking shape as a huge window near Baltimore's Inner Harbor. Henry Lewis Contractors of Owings Mills is the general contractor. The window is actually the south wall of the building and the special glass was made by a German company. Each of the 28 colored panels weighs 400 pounds. They arrived in Baltimore via ocean vessel and barge.
>
> Everyone involved in this patriot project seems to believe that it is a once-in-a-lifetime experience to see; the only monument of its kind

in the world. It's being counted on to spark greater interest in the American flag and its remarkable history.[50]

Jennings Describes the Merit Shop

Another prominent second-generation ABCer has restated the half-century-old merit shop philosophy in modern terms. At a meeting in 1997 of the Southern Nevada Chapter, John Jennings, ABC's thirty-ninth national president and vice president of Jack Jennings & Sons of Orlando, Florida, delivered an important merit shop message in Las Vegas. It occurred at the time of a craft union organizational effort in the area that was promoted by national AFL-CIO leaders. Here is a quotation from the Jennings speech to local ABCers:

> We believe that every individual and company has the right to succeed based on skill, dedication and determination. We believe in a level playing field. We believe that every American has a right to decide, without any coercion, to join a union or refrain from joining one. And we believe that management has the right to operate its own business without outsider sabotage and violence. We also believe that any responsible contractor who can do a quality job in a timely fashion and submits the lowest bid should be awarded the project: *that's the merit shop creed.*

An unusual headline and two paragraphs from the January 2003, issue of ABC's award-winning new *Construction Executive* magazine corroborate this creed, in miniscule:

TEAMSTERS BUILD UNION HALL
WITH MERIT SHOP LABOR

AFL-CIO officials in Houston, Texas, expressed disappointment over Houston Teamster Local 988's decision to build its new 16,246-square-foot union hall using open shop labor, including members of ABC. The Teamster local told its leaders that "union contractors cost too much."

> **Employees are human beings first, citizens of our nation second, and factors in production third... The great working force of any business is a collection of people with individual rights and individual problems worthy of consideration by management.**
>
> *THE POWER OF PEOPLE* BY CHARLES P. MCCORMICK, CEO, MCCORMICK & CO.

In an interview with the *Houston Chronicle*, Dale Wortham, president of the Harris County AFL-CIO, said: "I just can't believe the cost issue outweighed the right thing to do." Last year, Local 988 withdrew from the local AFL-CIO under mounting pressure to use only union labor despite costs.[51]

Superior manpower policies and practices show that ABC's free market construction forces have been at work for more than fifty years with devastating results to the autocratic and archaic trade union movement throughout the United States.[52]

As the proud slogan goes, "Merit Shop Builds Best!"

CHAPTER 13

FROM UNION BOSS TO ABC CONTRACTOR

THERE IS NOTHING UNUSUAL about unionized contractors "going open shop" or union members "putting their membership card in their shoes" and working for open shop contractors. But a novel news story was created about thirty-five years ago when a frustrated union business agent named Joseph DiCarlo opened his own non-union subcontractor's firm—and then joined ABC.

This remarkable event was reported by *Engineering News-Record*[1] and revisited in the *ABC Contractor* magazine. It seems that from 1971 to 1975, DiCarlo was the business manager of Bricklayers' Local Union No. 1 in Baltimore City. Unlike the other labor leaders, he was quick to realize that militant resistance wouldn't stop open shop growth in Maryland. In order to survive and prosper, he believed that trade unions should cooperate with contractors whose craftsmen the non-union sector of the industry represented and reach friendly accommodations with them on a project-by-project basis.

DiCarlo allowed brick subcontractors whose tradesmen his union represented to ignore restrictive work rules and union-only contracting clauses in their labor agreements so that they could bid competitively to open shop general contractors. He also urged more productivity from his members. "We realized that if we were going to survive, our contractors had to be able to compete," DiCarlo said. "Instead of wasting time trying to fight the open shop, I concentrated on improving the productivity and craftsmanship of our own members."

Sometimes life-changing values come to us in moments of contact with high-potential personalities.

WALTER MACPEEK
SCOUTS LEADER

DiCarlo Relaxes Union Work Rules

One of the first steps DiCarlo took was to reduce the traditional apprentice-to-journeyman ratio from five-to-one to three-to-one. This move created more jobs for higher paid workers and at the same time reduced the employers' "featherbedded" labor expenses. Then he created a pre-apprenticeship and helper-type program that taught basic skills so that his newest recruits could be useful as soon as they were sent to a job site. "I told all our members that they have a dual obligation to our union and to their contractors." And DiCarlo noted: "That meant that when a worker is sent to a job he's got to produce, to hustle."

In an effort to back up this promise of productivity, DiCarlo included in all of his labor contracts an unheard-of clause permitting contractors to unilaterally discharge—in their own discretion—any workers who were not performing their jobs satisfactorily. This unusual entrepreneurial attitude helped DiCarlo to bid competitively on all area projects, including those led by non-union general contractors. Even more importantly, as he emphasized: "The merit shop ABC was good to us and our contractors so my policy was that we wouldn't picket. If we had a problem, we'd sit down with management and settle it amicably."

Merit Shop Harmony

DiCarlo drew further conservative media attention when he asked both union and non-union contractors to recommend to out-of-town general contractors that they use his union for masonry work in the Baltimore region. One of the many firms that endorsed his Local Union No. 1 was William Wilke, a non-union Baltimore general contractor who was a member of ABC. In a letter to a prospective out-of-town contractor, Wilke wrote:

> The fact that we operate an open shop endeavor does not deter us from commenting on our use of journeymen and apprentices represented by the local Bricklayers' Union. Without hesitation, we recommend them to you because they are completely trustworthy and sensitive to the contractor's problems.

This daring and unorthodox strategy paid off for DiCarlo. Membership in his union increased from 480 in 1971 to 1,209 in 1974. But obviously not everyone was pleased with this maverick approach. His refusal to follow union contractual work rules or to honor picket lines set up by other craft unions enraged the Baltimore Building and Construction Trades Council—and DiCarlo removed his union from affiliation with that body.

This "heresy" led in turn to a federal lawsuit by the Baltimore Building Trades Council seeking a permanent injunction restraining the defendant, Bricklayers Local 1, from withdrawing from the Trades Council. Raymond Bergan, attorney for Local 1, denied an accusation that the decision by DiCarlo to work with non-union firms was "traitorous" to the Trades Council. Instead, Bergan claimed that the lawsuit was merely the union's "exercise of its legal right to self-determination" and nothing came of the litigation.[2] But Local No. 1's "disloyal" action against the Council did lead to threats of violence that prompted DiCarlo and his assistant business agent to obtain pistol permits and arm themselves.

Looking back on the trying times, DiCarlo admitted it was at that point that his family began to pressure him to quit the construction business. And he was also disgusted with the way his members expected him to automatically defend them from discipline when they were wrong. "Sometimes," he complained, "I'd be asked to go to bat for a member and fight to get him eight hours pay when he wasn't worth eight cents pay. That used to gnaw at me."

From Compulsory Unionism to Free Market Competition

A major schism between DiCarlo and his Bricklayers' Local No. 1 finally came to pass in 1975 as the Baltimore Building Trades Council's executive committee was developing strategy for upcoming bargaining sessions involving his union. DiCarlo was concerned about protecting his members' competitive position against the open shop and urged a wage freeze. When his own union's bargaining committee rejected that idea, he knew it was time to go. Without waiting for the next internal election of union officials, DiCarlo resigned his business agent's post in the fall of 1975 and left the trade union movement that he'd belonged to for twenty-five years. After his departure, Local No. 1's membership decreased substantially.

> **It is a blessed thing that in every age a few people have courage enough to stand by their own convictions.**
>
> ROBERT INGERSOLL
> ORATOR

We must build a new world, a far better world—one in which the eternal dignity of man is respected.

HARRY S. TRUMAN
33RD PRESIDENT

The following February, Joe DiCarlo and his wife created Master Masonry Corporation in Hamilton, Maryland, and began bidding on construction work in the Baltimore area. At first he used union scale wage rates, but losing bids for several jobs convinced him to "go open shop." Many longtime buddies of DiCarlo from his former Bricklayers' Local 1 joined Master Masonry. Some of them even offered to work for DiCarlo without pay temporarily to get the new company off the ground. Although the Baltimore Building Trades Council and its Local No. 1 tried to coerce and fine these craftsmen for their "disloyalty" to it, most of them decided to stay with DiCarlo and allowed their union membership to expire.

During its first fiscal year—1976—Master Masonry completed more than $300,000 worth of work for private and public owners, including a classroom job at the U.S. Naval Academy. Twelve months later, DiCarlo's non-union firm signed up more than $800,000 worth of work. All of it was performed for open shop general contractors. Typical projects were school jobs, shopping centers, and warehouses. In 1978, Master Masonry became a member of the Baltimore Chapter of ABC and soon employed fifty-five journeymen, apprentices, and helpers on a regular basis.

To the chagrin of the AFL-CIO, its Baltimore Building Trades Council and especially its Bricklayers Local No. 1, Master Masonry Corporation operated profitably until Joe DiCarlo retired.

He was a merit shop hero many years ahead of the times.

CHAPTER 14

WOMEN AND MINORITIES IN CONSTRUCTION

ABC HAS BELIEVED FROM ITS INCEPTION that the construction industry's historical "all-male-all-white" image must be overcome. The Association's goal is to reflect fairly and profitably America's diversifying society and, at the same time, to help satisfy the demand for skilled personnel at all levels.[1] As noted before, one of the principles upon which the merit shop was founded is that "discrimination based on sex, race, color, nationality, creed, or compulsory unionism is contrary to the spirit of American democracy and harmful to our nation morally and economically."

Engineering News-Record and other noteworthy publications have confirmed that "the construction industry must attract more women and minorities if it expects to meet its labor needs."[2] Nearly half of all privately held U.S. businesses today are women-owned[3] and during the first decade of the twenty-first century, women will make up approximately half of the nation's workforce. But not more than 10 percent of them are employed in building and construction. It has been described as "among the last great bastions of maleness."[4]

Civil Rights Pioneers

Back in 1973, a far-sighted television show on this subject caught the attention of David Mears, an officer of ABC's Florida Gold Coast Chapter and owner of a plumbing business. There had been a shortage of labor in his area and he was intrigued by a promotional film about women working on an assembly line in a northern state. Mears made a "radical" decision and the Fort Lauderdale *Sun Sentinel* reported the rest of the story:

> The first time Adam had a chance, he laid the blame on women.
>
> NANCY ASTOR
> BRITISH POLITICIAN

If particular care
and attention are
not paid to the
ladies, we will
not hold our-
selves bound to
any laws in which
we have no voice
or representation.

ABIGAIL ADAMS
FIRST LADY

The back shop of David Mears's Atlantic Plumbing is hot, dirty, and crowded. It's like most back rooms where physical labor and pipe welding go on. However, the women don't seem to mind. One employee, Shirley Corbin, has only been working for Mears as an apprentice plumber for two months. But she's on her way up. She has already been promoted to the pre-fab shop and received an increase in salary. Shirley, at thirty-five, isn't working for a lark. She has children to support...

Contractor Mears says: "I figured if women can work on an assembly line, why not put them to work in the plumbing field? So I put an ad in the paper. I guess you could say I discriminated for, instead of against, women. I wanted to try my idea out. Now I have 17 of them. They adapt readily and do a fantastic job. Within a year I'd like to make about half of my work force women." (Mears employs 265 people so he isn't speaking of small numbers.)[5]

A year later, in another part of the country, there was an unusual scene in front of the office of Local Union No. 469 of the United Association of Plumbers. Nine shapely female pickets were marching around this building located in Phoenix, Arizona. They were performing "a strike in reverse." The temperature was 110 degrees and—to the delight of male passersby—they were wearing abbreviated attire.

According to Twila Thompson, owner of Mother Thompson's Plumbing Company and the instigator of this unusual protest, Local 469 had been trying to unionize her employees for some time. When Ms. Thompson refused to capitulate to the union's demand for representation, it accused her of paying "substandard wages." She denied the charge and produced proof from her financial records that supported her statement.

Local 469 countered by establishing picket lines at all of Ms. Thompson's construction jobsites in an attempt to shut them down. This union strategy backfired when the Arizona news media featured a close-up photo of the sexy picket line at Local 469's office and an article with this headline: **WOMEN GIVE UNION A DOSE OF OWN MEDICINE.**

Ms. Thompson, a licensed master plumber, was quoted to the effect that she would remove her female pickets from the union's business office as soon as the union removed its male pickets from her construction projects. They did (sheepishly) and she did (triumphantly).

Another situation that occurred in 1978 involved Karen McDermott, a typical first-year carpenter's apprentice except for one thing. She's female.

McDermott was employed by Accent Builders, a merit shop contractor in Gaithersburg, Maryland, and she told ABC about her first year of the job: "I've always liked working with my hands and I hated being in an office, sitting all day long." When a friend who was also looking for a construction job told her about the ABC apprenticeship program through its Metropolitan Washington chapter, she "jumped at the chance."

McDermott didn't go into construction blindly. Her husband was a carpentry foreman until injuries in a motorcycle accident forced him on the sidelines for two years. McDermott decided she didn't want to take just any job; she wanted one with a future in it for her. "I'm not making much money now," she said, "but the farther up the line I go, the better it'll be. People just don't seem to be paying women much these days in most lines of work but in construction you can go about as far as you want."

According to McDermott, she didn't receive much harassment from the men with whom she worked. "Some of them were worse than others. But the guys I team up with now are great. I haven't had any trouble at all." And McDermott's superintendent added: "It doesn't matter to me whether I've got men or women working for me. As long as they do the job, I don't care. Karen is an excellent worker and that's all that counts."[6]

Barbara Franke, another "pioneer," gave an interview on "Women In Construction" for ABC's *Contractor* magazine in October of 1973. This twenty-six-year-old owner of B. J. Franke Landscaping Co. and a member of ABC's Anne Arundel–Southern Maryland Chapter reported: "I had a belly full of clerical desk jobs with little challenge and no money." And so one day, out of curiosity, she applied for a position as a laborer for a local landscaping company and got the job. She soon discovered that she could gain more personal satisfaction in landscaping than in any type of "pink collar" work she had previously trained for or performed.

Shortly after Barbara was hired, the financial bottom fell out of the firm and she was out of work. "It seemed at the time to be the same old story—find

She who hesitates is last.

MAE WEST
HOLLYWOOD
FILM LEGEND

the thing you want to do the most and something happens to mess it up," she admitted. "Having tried different jobs working for other people long enough," at the age of twenty-three she decided to open her own landscaping business.

"One thing led to another and soon I found myself with a shovel in my hands," Ms. Franke says. "My first job took two days to complete and netted a profit of $300 which I immediately spent as a down payment on an old car. Then I put on my best clothes, drove around in my car, sold a few more jobs, and started enjoying work again."

Eventually Barbara Franke was asked how she felt about women in construction, and she began with a predictable answer: "I think it's like any other field that requires a lot of perseverance and a desire for independence. These days women are reevaluating their roles in life." She also conceded that "women face lots of problems" in trying to break into male-dominated construction ranks: "It's unusual to see a woman competing in an industry predominantly controlled by men and some of them even resent the thought of women in the construction field. One of their biggest concerns is that a woman is physically incapable of dealing with certain situations." But Ms. Franke hastened to rebut that "unfair" conclusion: "I've lugged fifty-pound rolls of sod many times."

When it comes to dispensing advice to other women thinking of entering the construction field, Barbara Franke's contributions were frank and to the point:

> First, get used to four-letter words and keep sexist heckling mild. If you're planning to run a crew of men, be really prepared to lead them. Second, example by performance is the key to success. And third, thank the Lord, because with *Her*, all things are possible—even lady hardhats![7]

Women in Construction Are Increasing

Those four stories about female workplace "pattern-breakers" taken at random from *ABC Contractor* magazine heralded an important trend. The hand that traditionally rocked the cradle was beginning to put bread on the table from open shop construction work. Females working in the industry increased *20 percent* between 1995 and 2000, reaching a total of *913,000*, according to the National Association of Women in Construction.

Although nearly half of these females are employed in sales, administrative, and technical support positions, the other half work in the field as helpers, apprentices, skilled mechanics, supervisors, safety directors, project managers, or line executives. And a growing number of new start-up construction companies are owned by women, as reported by U.S. Department of Labor statistics.[8] They generate income not only for themselves and their families but for thousands of other employees.

A rough-and-tough work environment, male skepticism and jealousy, discrimination, sexual harassment, unequal pay for equal work, and lack of a corporate family leave policy are some of the causes of female detours along the way. But as courageous and ambitious women proved their capability to perform male-dominated work, they gradually gained respect and workplace equality. Today enlightened management welcomes them as valuable members of the merit shop construction team. Women also serve diligently as officers and board of directors members of ABC as well as on the professional staffs of ABC National and its local chapters.

The way I see it, if you want the rainbow, you gotta put up with the rain.

DOLLY PARTON
COUNTRY SINGER

A National ABC President

Jean Hails is an ABC pioneer who broke the industry's chauvinistic mold at the highest executive level. She became the Association's first female national president in 1986. Her Hails Construction Company in Atlanta, Georgia, has been licensed in ten southeastern states, specializing in office buildings, shopping centers, and light industrial facilities. Its prestigious clients have included McDonnell-Douglas, Martin Marietta, Georgia Power, the Kroger Company, Volkswagen of America, and General Electric Company.

"There's no hiding the biological facts, not that I would ever want to," says this mother of six children. "I *am* a woman but I'm also a contractor, a businessperson, and an achiever. I may

ABC CONTRACTOR

Jean Hails, first female national ABC president, in 1986, and CEO of Hails Construction Company in Atlanta, Georgia, with President Ronald Reagan at the White House.

Once made equal
to man, woman
becomes his
superior.

Socrates

have had to work a little harder to prove myself but that comes with the territory."

Jean Hails received her start in the mortgage industry, which provided her with a solid understanding of the financial aspects of building and construction. That experience helped when she and her husband formed a partnership to found Hails Construction Company in 1970. And she adds with enthusiasm: "The more we became involved in ABC and followed the merit shop principles, the more our business grew and prospered. Our investment in ABC was repaid many times over."

As a charter member of ABC's Georgia Chapter, Mrs. Hails has been active in the Association's affairs. She served on various committees and held a number of leadership roles on both a chapter and national basis for over fifteen years. She logged 40,000 travel miles during the year of her presidency, spreading ABC's merit shop message from coast to coast: "The construction field has allowed me to prove my abilities and by my involvement with ABC I hope I have put something back into the industry that has given me so much," she says.

In addition to valuable service to ABC, Jean Hails has been active politically both within Georgia and nationally. She campaigned throughout the United States on behalf of the Reagan-Bush ticket in the 1984 election. She was a member of the Presidential Advisory Committee on Women Business Owners and the Republican National Committee's Small Business Advisory Council.[9]

On March 7, 1987, as ABC's immediate past national president, Jean Hails addressed the Association's annual convention in Orlando, Florida, and told her fellow ABCers:

The past year was truly for me one of the most exciting and rewarding of my life. As a girl

"*We can still be friends, Roger. I just don't want you to be one of my vice-presidents anymore.*"

growing up in a small country town in Tennessee, never once did I think that I might someday sit at a conference table next to President Ronald Reagan. Yet I have, and it was an opportunity afforded to me not only because of who I was but also because of whom I represented.

As a general contractor who happened to be a woman in a male dominated industry, never once did I think that I would someday have the opportunity, in a nationwide forum, to help other businessmen and women understand and better cope with the problems we all face today in the workplace. But I have been given that opportunity as national president of ABC, the cornerstone of the American construction industry.[10]

Female Chapter Presidents of ABC

Another outstanding example of women in construction is Clarice Cornett, ABC's Hawaii Chapter President in the year 2000. She joined forces with Honolulu Habitat and her state's department of public safety in creating a program to train women in pre-apprenticeship. This venture accepts females from all walks of life. Under the supervision of Ms. Cornett's own construction firm, Wahine Builders, it combines classroom theory of the trade with on-the-job task training. The course on house building involves all of the applicable skills such as excavation, concrete, framing, plumbing and electrical, drywall, finish work, painting, and landscaping. Hawaii Chapter members donate materials, time, and money to the effort, and ABC National President Thomas Musser ('00) has provided electrical materials. Even the wife of Hawaii's Governor Benjamin Cayetano joined a work crew.

"I believe this is just the sort of program that we need to diversify our industry and increase the number of apprentices coming into the trades," Hawaii's Chapter President Cornett observed. "My company has contributed our staff, tools, vehicles, components, and effort because we believe that the private sector is where programs like this must come from. Every ABC member who can do so should become involved."[11]

Similar female officerships exist throughout all of ABC's chapters. The chapter in Baltimore, as an example, has had three outstanding female presidents:

Audrey Bolyard ('86) of Automatic Sprinkler Co., Marilyn Rainey ('93) of Crown Electric, and Mary E. Easto ('99) of Henry H. Lewis Contractors.

More Female Success Stories

Businesswoman Judy Kumler recently told the *ABC Contractor* about her rewarding experience in the construction industry:

> In the early 1990s, I became the comptroller of a small construction company in Ohio. I had never heard of ABC until my bosses told me that because of my never unvoiced opinions, one of my responsibilities would be to represent my employer at ABC functions. I didn't know what to expect at my first general membership meeting. I truly was surprised when everyone stood respectfully for an invocation and then joined in the Pledge of Allegiance. I was also amazed when I discovered that this organization to which I had been assigned was dedicated to furthering the cause of free enterprise and educating its members in the art of political action by writing, faxing and e-mailing legislators prior to critical votes.
>
> I was like the proverbial kid in a candy store. I communicated with legislators and my messages always made reference to the fact that I was an ABC member. As an individual, I had little or no clout but as an ABC member, I felt that I was "a force to be reckoned with." My letters did not go unanswered. I joined the Ohio Valley ABC Chapter's Membership Committee and later chaired it. Then I joined the Programs Committee and later chaired that. I attended virtually every general membership meeting, contributed to and attended the annual political action committee auctions and drove to Indiana to participate in long-range planning at regional conferences of the Association.
>
> I was extremely sad when I attended my last ABC meeting before moving to Nevada. It simply never occurred to me that I would ever again have an affiliation with ABC. Three months ago, ABC of Southern Nevada hired me as the chapter's membership director. Once again, I am like a kid in a candy store![12]

Being a woman is a terribly difficult trade, since it consists principally of dealing with men.

JOSEPH CONRAD
WRITER

At the age of thirty, another "pattern-breaker," Katherine Penn of Takoma Park, Maryland, set foot on her first building project as an employee of ABC-member firm Donohoe Construction Company. Although she had been involved in the industry in several capacities for more than ten years, she says she finally found where she wanted to be. "Donohoe is big, but not so big that you get lost," she explains. "I have enough responsibility to challenge me and just the right amount of direction if I need it." As an assistant project manager, she negotiates business contracts, determines the scope of work, oversees change orders, and supervises jobsites.

Ms. Penn was asked by Donohoe Construction to join the Metro Washington Chapter's craft training committee and eagerly accepted the assignment because she "recognized the importance of bringing quality people into the industry." She also admits that over the years she has "experienced some challenges" because she is a woman, "but they've been nothing more than little bumps in my career path. In the construction field, people respect hard work."

At ABC's national convention in Maui, Hawaii, in 1998, Katherine Penn's Metro Washington Chapter received the top award for its outstanding human diversity program. Chapter Executive Director Debra Schoonmaker and Chapter President Kathy Teitel of member firm Hess Mechanical Corporation made a special effort to promote the capabilities of women like Katherine Penn to prime open shop contractors. "We see it as business development opportunities," said Ms. Teitel. "We target the bigger general contractors like Donohoe who have more employment opportunities and we meet with them to promote the advantages of diversification."[13]

Rich Conlon is an owner's representative who appreciates the valuable contributions of women in the building industry. Conlon is vice president of construction for the Baltimore/Delaware region of one of America's largest house builders, Pulte Homes. He has high praise for ABC Chesapeake Chapter's Pamela Volm, a partner and co-owner of Annapolis Carpentry Contractors of Glen Burnie, Maryland. "She's a role model for the industry," says Conlon. "I'd rather work with one Pam Volm than ten average guys," he adds frankly.

Traveling between 150 and 200 miles each day in her truck, Ms. Volm makes it a point to visit each of her jobsites. "I'm physically active in the field," she explains, "because I need to see what's going on." She notes that

When a man points his finger at someone else, he should remember that three of his fingers are pointing at himself.

ANONYMOUS

Life is easier than you think. All that is necessary is to accept the impossible, do without the indispensable, and bear the intolerable.

KATHLEEN NORRIS
NOVELIST

I'm furious about the Woman's Liberationists. They keep getting up on soapboxes and proclaiming that women are brighter than men. That's true, but it should be kept very quiet or it ruins the whole racket.

ANITA LOOS
ACTRESS

communication, safety, partnering, and employee benefits are her key focus areas, emphasizing that her workers come first: "You've got to have good human relations—and ABC has provided us with great support and advice in solving our people problems."

Pam Volm received her Chesapeake Chapter's STEP Safety Award in the year 2000 for outstanding commitment to keeping her employees free from harm's way. She gives much of the credit to her female safety director, Bobbie Hann, whom she hired to oversee all jobsites. And Ms. Volm's chapter "partners" with the minority business enterprise office of Anne Arundel County, Maryland, on seminars covering effective methods of developing a diversified business climate for small contractors.[14]

Two Corporate Mentor Programs

In Birmingham, Alabama, twenty-five high school girls spent a day with engineers from BE&K, Inc., a leading ABC member firm. In 2001 this giant contractor expanded a program that featured engineering careers for women. It includes visits to project teams and computer-aided design demonstrations. This "Girl Power" event ends with a tour of a Honda auto manufacturing plant in Lincoln, Alabama, where BE&K was the designer of the 1.2-million-square-foot factory that can produce 500 Odyssey vans per day.[15]

ABC member TD Industries of Dallas, Texas, is another example of a diversity success story. Over 15 percent of its skilled workforce is made up of women and the number is growing. Jessie McCain, the vice president of TD's human resources department for over seventeen years, says: "The culture of our company is to provide equal opportunity and give everyone a chance to achieve his or her full potential. We have some female stars here."

TD Industries has received the Crystal Vision Award from the National Association of Women in Construction for this philosophy of nondiscrimination, and one of its budding luminaries is twenty-one-year-old Rebecca Gonzalez. This spunky five-foot-two-inch youngster began her construction career at age sixteen when she read a brochure on joining the construction trades. She leaped at the opportunity and enrolled in a vocational school during her senior year of high school.

Ms. Gonzalez said she knew nothing about what to expect, but that didn't stop her. Once at the new institution, it didn't take her long to realize that "this construction deal is neat." And the teacher made her the class leader of the carpentry school. "The boys there would joke with me but I could handle it," she confides.

After a short stint with an electrical contractor, Ms. Gonzalez received a part-time job at TD Industries. "They really were excited about having me in their craft training program," she says. "Management was letting people know I was here so they received me well. People kept telling me to be tough so that I could do it."

Within three years Ms. Gonzalez proved that a TD woman could do field work equal to or better than a TD man. And she was the first female to mentor other women in TD's plumber apprentice training program. Today she is a group leader on a project installing polypropylene piping systems. "I've never met any resistance from the men, but if I did, I would just give them a piece of my mind," she jokes.

Ms. Gonzalez sums up her success as a journeyman plumber by recommending that employers tell the real truth to women about construction when they are being recruited: "It's hard going. The temperature can be 110 degrees or ten below zero. You've got to really want to accept some rugged conditions. If you do, the payoff is great—I just love seeing the finished product."[16]

There are hundreds more success stories like these that can be told about female employees in ABC construction firms.

National ABC Liaisons

In support of women's equal right to work, ABC National is a member of and works closely with many government and private sector agencies, including the National Association of Women in Construction. NAWIC is an organization whose members are motivated by a desire for self-improvement and ambition to learn their profession. It places women in all kinds of construction jobs and at all levels of responsibility. An ever-increasing number of them also serve as staff personnel for ABC National and its local chapters across the country.

In protecting women, courts and juries should be careful to protect men, too, for men are not only useful to general society but to women especially.

Humphrey v. Copeland 54 Ga. 543, per Blackley, J.

After all these years, I see that I was mistaken about Eve in the beginning. It's better to live outside the Garden with her then inside without her.

Mark Twain
Humorist-Writer

The objectives of NAWIC and ABC are simple and direct: to unite all women who are actively employed in construction and promote their education and service in the industry. "You don't have to be a big husky man these days," says NAWIC executive director Dede Hughes. "Brawn has less and less to do with it. It's brainpower that counts now since many of the jobs are automated."[17]

A Special Tribute to Female War Veterans

In the state of Virginia on the outskirts of Washington, D.C., situated on four acres of land at the ceremonial entrance to Arlington National Cemetery, is a unique monument. It honors the two million women who served in America's armed forces during all of its eras, beginning with the Revolutionary War. The cemetery's sixty-five-year-old, 25,000-square-foot granite gateway and building had deteriorated and was in dire need of repair, but that disgrace began to be corrected in 1997. A 37,000-square-foot Women in Military Service Memorial ("WIMSM") to be located beside the giant structure was proposed to remedy the problem.

ABC member firm Clark Construction Company of Bethesda, Maryland, won the right to build this prestigious memorial in 1998 and assembled a *female* team to oversee the challenging assignment. USAF Brigadier General Wilma Vaught (also WIMSM's President) emphasized that she wanted women to build the memorial, and Clark Construction named its Stacy Chuang as project manager. Ms. Chuang worked with project partner Lehrer McGovern Bovis, Inc., from New York, which assigned Margaret Van Voast as onsite representative, Michelle Stuckey as assistant on-site manager and Joan Gerner, a Bovis vice president, as project head. Beth Leahy, a historic preservationist, also helped to guide this important undertaking.

The dedication and opening date was set before the project began, and it promised to feature many national dignitaries. Clark Construction, led by Stacy Chuang, had to meet that date and did—one week before the ceremony. After completion of the project, ABC's *Award of Excellence* was given to Clark Construction "for restoring and rebuilding a monumental tribute to all women who have served their country in time of war."[18]

Through the professional skill of female personnel, Clark Construction led the design and construction of this memorial—the entryway to some of

America's most revered ground. From an ignominy, the site became a cherished monument honoring courageous and patriotic American women and a permanent national treasure in its own right.

A Steadily Growing Field in 2004[19]

As has been noted, although the construction industry is not an easy business for women to break into, successful recruits are increasing in numbers. Jackie Horowitz, a project manager for Pavarini McGovern, a construction management firm headquartered in New York, was always good with statistics. When she came to the United States from Puerto Rico, searching for work, she was encouraged to give construction a try. Now she oversees three major projects in New York City and finds it rewarding to "take something from a conceptual aspect to a three-dimensional building."

Horowitz is also an instructor for New York University's Real Estate Institute Construction Management program, has worked on the $300 million U.S. Federal Courthouse in New York, the renovation and expansion of Continental Airlines Global Gateway, and many large residential buildings. "More men are retiring, and there is a real opportunity for women," she says. "But it's up to us. We have to promote ourselves and bring more women into the industry. It's a constant challenge about how you're doing. Women have to prove themselves every day."

Some women have a head start on others. They grew up around construction and engineering, so that they observed a family business at a young age. Kristina Swallow, a land development manager at Poggemeyer Design Group, Las Vegas, followed in her father's engineering footsteps and says the industry was not difficult for her to get into:

> It's more about developing the communications pipeline and encouraging young women to take the classes in college and joining the workforce. It's more about making the construction field a friendly place and women choosing to stay.

The Ultimate Challenge

In 2004, Susan Tianen, a chief safety officer for the U.S. Army Corps of Engineers ("USACE"), took on the role, single-handedly, of sanitation engineer

If I was asked to what the prosperity and growing strength of the Americans ought mainly to be attributed, I should reply: "To the superiority of their women."

ALEXIS DE TOCQUEVILLE
DEMOCRACY IN AMERICA

for the City of Baghdad in Iraq. The USACE was ordered to monitor the City's utility contracts for water, electricity, oil, and buildings operations.

While serving in this job and working with Iraqi engineers, Tianen also was responsible for trash and refuse removal. It included clearing away war wreckage such as tanks, artillery, buses, and cars off the streets. It also included clearing out human waste and animal slaughter. In sum, it involved the removal of all outward signs of war from major city arteries, the creation of a building demolition program, and the development of a system that would allow Iraqi engineers to evaluate buildings for removal or repair.

As a woman in construction and engineering in charge of a $423,000-per-week budget in addition to $11 million for hire laborers, Tianen faced challenges in Iraq the likes of which she never saw in the United States. "Iraqis are a proud people and starving to learn a trade," she says, and the City of Baghdad has hired nine Iraqi engineers and trained them to do their own work:

> I had to explain to them that as a part of the government of a city, they must work together as a team. Iraq is taking baby steps to allow women to work, but the degree of tolerance is improving. Iraqi men are observing female American soldiers and engineers who are respected for their work.

The liberal mainstream news media spins its pessimistic reporting of the global war on terrorism by constantly headlining American casualties (which are heartbreaking but miniscule when compared to previous wars)[20] and ignoring heroic victories by American troops and support personnel. At the same time, courageous service women like the USACE's Susan Tianen quietly and efficiently perform their jobs. That means putting their lives on the line every day to help Iraq build a safe and independent democracy out of Saddam Hussein's horrendous gestapo.

Minority Workplace Development and Expansion

On the equally critical issue of human relations discrimination within the United States, the U.S. Bureau of Labor Statistics predicts that blacks in the total workforce will grow at more than twice the pace of whites. An even greater expansion in the future workforce will come from Hispanics and Asian-Americans. It is estimated that by the year *2009*, the nation's employees will be composed of *20 percent* Hispanics, *14 percent* African-Americans and *6 percent* Asians.[21]

ABC always has taken an active role in the employment and advancement of minorities in the construction industry. An early example of recruiting African-Americans[22] occurred during the regime of Fred Schnabel, ABC's thirteenth national president in 1967–1968. Here are some quotations from an editorial he wrote to all members that appeared in the April 1968 edition of the *Contractor* magazine:

Summer is just around the corner—despite the little kicks that Old Man Winter is still putting out—and when it does come, the tough problem of jobs for Negro youths will assume ever greater proportions. ABC members have always found the Negro worker to be a valuable member of the team. Some use them as laborers, others as cement finishers, some as carpenters, electrician and plumbers helpers. Our apprenticeship courses have opened the door further to Negroes with vistas of journeyman opportunity that the union closed shop has denied them for years.

Yes, it's hard to believe, but it's not new. Remember how we told you we had proof that AFL-CIO trade unions boasted in print to their members that they had kept ABC from getting certified apprenticeship courses? Well, the same tactics are being used against our effort to hire the disadvantaged. But we're not going to give in just because of these obstructionist tactics. The truth is they just make us more earnest.

ABC is currently striving to join with various organizations that are providing job opportunities for Ghetto residents. Preliminary meetings have been held with public and private interests towards this end. We are serious about this—it's not window dressing—and we are constantly appalled by the union political pressures that try to bar us from doing a good turn for the minority. This summer we need to make an even greater effort to open the doors to untrained Negroes who really want a job and are willing to work if given a chance.

Few things help an individual more than to place responsibility upon him and to let him know that you trust him.

Booker T. Washington
Educator and Civil Rights Leader

In June of 1968, Fred Schnabel gave a practical example of this ABC non-discrimination policy in action to the Reverend Leon Sullivan, an African-American founder of the Opportunities Industrialization Center ("OIC") based in Philadelphia. Under Sullivan's leadership, OIC operated sixty-five centers across the country to train the underprivileged for jobs.

Schnabel began by showing the minority leader ABC's award-winning apprenticeship film—"Careers in Construction"—which featured the training of a black youth. Sullivan reviewed the movie enthusiastically and emphasized its impact from an integration point of view. "This film," he said, "will instill positive attitudes in young African-Americans toward entering the construction business."

The Reverend Sullivan also toured several ABC jobsites and was impressed with what he saw. Coming upon black workers engaged in drywall construction and masonry work, he questioned them intensively and remarked about the zeal they showed for both their jobs and their employers. At some of the sites Sullivan visited, skilled African-American workmen outnumbered the white workers. Summing up ABC's goal, Fred Schnabel told the prominent clergyman:

> We want to join forces with you. If you help us to recruit the youths, we'll hire them and give them on-the-job training under expert foremen and supervisors. They'll earn more, progress further and live better.[23]

Two months after Sullivan's workplace tour, ABC selected Mark Battle as the keynote speaker at its eleventh annual convention held in Freeport, Grand Bahama Island. This African-American administrator of the Bureau of Work Programs of the Federal Manpower Administration saluted ABC's minority employment program. He also lamented that "the apprenticeship guilds of the trades unions are exclusive white clubs where it is easier to qualify for entrance into college."[24]

In September of 1968, ABC presented its "Man of the Year" award to the Reverend Leon Sullivan at the OIC's first annual banquet held in the Convention Center in Philadelphia for his "outstanding assistance to minorities in the workplace." That same year Baltimore's Mayor Tommy D'Alessandro commended ABC's Metropolitan Baltimore Chapter and its executive director, Charlie Chamberlain, on their minority initiatives in these words:

> I want to take this opportunity to thank you for the outstanding service you have rendered to the City through your past and present participation on committees and groups concerned with expanding employment opportunities for minority group members. Without your support and cooperation we in government would have had little success in providing more jobs for the less advantaged members of our community.[25]

ABC Contractor

Reverend Leon H. Sullivan accepts ABC's 1968 "Man of the Year" award.

A few years later, Paul King of the National Association of Minority Contractors described ABC Presidents Joe LaMonaca ('71-'72), Mike Callas ('73-'74) and Phil Abrams ('75) as "new friends working very closely with NAMC representatives in developing a dynamic joint training program."[26]

The Merit Shop Foundation—a non-profit tax-exempt institution—made its debut in 1971. It was charged with "the promotion, development and defense of America's free enterprise system by improving technology, productivity and labor peace." It also was created "to let the public, owners and architects know the advantages of merit shop construction."[27]

The Foundation's initial project sought to develop practical solutions for the problem of "employment imbalances." It was believed that many high school dropouts, children of disrupted families, and less-educated communities have potential leadership qualities that the Foundation, through its educational mechanisms, hoped to bring to the surface.

In addition, the program strove to research optimum manpower utilization. It developed new methods to determine the positive and negative factors of private sector and governmental programs and public understanding of the construction industry. According to ABC President Tracy Coleman ('63-'64), who spearheaded creation of the Foundation:

One source of the difficulties in developing much-needed journeyman mechanics is a lack of understanding among young people as to the advantages of working in the construction industry and how to obtain jobs therein. We have also encountered the belief among minority groups that because of their discriminatory treatment by the trade unions, the rest of the construction industry also offers meager hope for their advancement. We believe that it is necessary to dispel this idea through action, not only to appeal to minorities to enter the industry, but to be responsible for educating them in various trades.[28]

ABC's Newest Minority Integration Programs

Since those early days, many African-Americans and other minorities have become craftsmen, supervisors, managers, and owners in ABC member firms. As reported in its official national magazine, the *ABC Contractor*, the Association is on the cutting edge of this rebirth. Besides internal civil rights initiatives, ABC's Diversity Task Force published a manual on minority integration-building through networking, training, and joint organizational initiatives. This Task Force works through the Association's local chapters and their programs to link with other supportive organizations such as the National Association of Minority Contractors, the National Black Chamber of Commerce, public school systems, universities, and community organizations to bring more minorities into the building and construction workplace. There is also assistance to minority contractors in solving their historic problem of obtaining financial backing. And ABC teams up with a bonding service foundation that places many of them in the mainstream of the construction industry by qualifying them for surety bonds on projects of significant size.

Because of a six-year involvement with ABC's integration program, Sam Carradine, the black executive director of the National Association of Minority Contractors, affirmed that ABC is ready for the "changing make-up" of the labor market. "I'm very pleased with the training that local chapters of ABC are providing to minorities and I'm using ABC as a role model for craft programs with other groups," he concludes.[29]

The Florida First Coast Chapter of ABC, which frequently partners with local minority associations on seminars and other outreach programs, has made recruitment of these groups "a priority," according to Chapter Executive Director Gerald Dykhausen. One of the chapter's former presidents knows about this initiative firsthand. He is Carlton Jones, an African-American contractor who remains an active chapter member and is the president and owner of ABC-member firm Renaissance Design-Build Constructors of Jacksonville. Jones joined the Florida ABC chapter because, as he says:

> I felt it was a sincere effort by the leadership to be very pro-inclusive, trying to recruit qualified minority enterprises. ABC also encourages subcontractors to become involved with the Association and that provides a good networking opportunity which is vital to the growth of minority businesses.[30]

For many years ABC's Kentuckian Chapter has publicized and practiced its slogan: "Get more minorities and women in construction." Chapter President Phil Anderson works with a local county office of economic development and a minority resource center to promote the use of these groups, and some one hundred emerging and current minority contractors have benefited from the chapter's help. "We've tried to cover all the bases, such as how to set up an office, finances, legal issues, marketing, estimating, bidding strategies, and more," claims Anderson. "Following the training sessions, our program graduates are matched with an experienced mentor contractor to foster liaisons and locate work."[31]

Ronney Spencer was an outstanding professor in construction management for many years on the faculty of the University of Maryland Eastern Shore ("UMES"), which has a predominantly black student body. He also served as executive director of ABC's Eastern Shore Chapter from 1982 to 1990, doubling the chapter's membership during his tenure. With the help of Mike Callas, the dedicated general contractor from Maryland's Cumberland Valley Chapter who subsequently became ABC's sixteenth national president ('73-'74),[32] they created a substantial endowment fund for UMES students to become trained in construction management. In 1991, UMES became—and has remained—the only historically African-American institution that is fully accredited in this field, according to its current executive director, Carol Mills.

I have a dream that my four children will one day live in a nation where they will not be judged by the color of their skin but by the content of their character.

REVEREND MARTIN LUTHER KING, JR.
CIVIL RIGHTS LEADER

Work and family are at the center of our lives, the foundation of our dignity as a free people.

RONALD REAGAN
40TH PRESIDENT

This Nation will not go back to the days of simply shuffling children along from grade to grade without them learning the basics. I refuse to give up on any child, and the No Child Left Behind Act is opening the door of opportunity to all of America's children...

PRESIDENT GEORGE W. BUSH IN HIS 2004 STATE OF THE UNION ADDRESS

Secure an education at any cost.

BOOKER T. WASHINGTON EDUCATOR AND CIVIL RIGHTS LEADER

In Loretto, Minnesota, ABC-member firm Shinkopee Builders makes minority recruitment a key practice. Native Americans are a substantial portion of the population there and 30 percent of the firm's workforce are Indians. This makeup is no coincidence. The company's owner, Gae Veit, is a female Crow-Creek Sioux. As an ABC Accredited Quality Contractor, she has won state and national awards for her work with minorities, including National Female Entrepreneur of the Year in 1991 and the Governor's Certificate of Commendation in 1992.

Don Mar, a member of ABC's Chapter Integration Committee in the state of Washington, has been another leader in the minority mentoring effort. Mar is a partner in the Marpac general contracting firm in Seattle. Of Chinese descent, he has been in the industry since 1981, and in 1993 began a construction firm with his brother. Mar says the focus of the Washington Chapter's diversity committee "is to truly reach out to minorities and women to try to get them involved. He adds proudly that "we have many things to offer here—networking and classes—and we are making a concerted effort to diversify and integrate." Mar has faced severe racial discrimination throughout his career but he says, "ABC encourages us to integrate."

There are 32 million Hispanics living in the United States today. This heterogeneous population represents many nationalities and ethnicities, including Mexicans, Cubans, Puerto Ricans, and Spaniards as well as people from the Dominican Republic and other Central and South American countries. Some of them want to work in construction. To assist their integration into the industry, ABC National and its Virginia Chapter have developed a series of seventy taped English/Spanish "Toolbox Talks" for contractor members throughout the nation. Other ABC chapters taking a lead in integrating these workers include Georgia, South Alabama, Greater Houston, South Texas, Arkansas, and Northern Illinois.[33]

ABC's Diversity Task Force

As ABC enters the twenty-first century, it is seeking to further diversify its membership by increasing the number of minorities and women operating under the merit shop umbrella. The Association's Diversity Task Force is chaired by Diane Quimby of BE&K. It is charged with promoting and ensuring access to business and career opportunities in construction-related industries through craft and management education, training, mentoring, and other programs to maximize each individual's potential success. Chairperson Quimby is a role model whose own career from the front line trades to employee trainer to managerial ranks has been exceptional.[34]

ABC also recognizes that different personal backgrounds and learning styles require different training models. Non-traditional workers are hard to attract and retain in construction. Many underprivileged youngsters are intimidated by attending formal courses in a school environment. They lack confidence, academic records, and/or language skills.

An article in the March 2003 issue of ABC's newest monthly magazine, the *Construction Executive,* by Pam Hunter describes the Baltimore Metro Chapter's answer: "a training program for economically disadvantaged individuals from Baltimore City." Here are some passages from the story:

> The Chapter's JumpStart program provides individuals who have little or no experience in the electrical industry with an intense five-day, four-hour "boot camp" that combines hands-on training with classroom learning. Following the training, participants, who go through an intensive interviewing process to qualify, possess the ability to work as a semi-skilled helper for an electrical contractor. A grant provided by a local, private workforce development agency in Baltimore, STRIVE, pays for the first year of apprenticeship training for successful participants who complete the program and stay with their employer.
>
> Struever Bros. Eccles & Rouse of Baltimore believes strongly in using local labor and in recruiting workers from economically disadvantaged neighborhoods. Kate McShane, the company's community outreach coordinator, says it uses its clout in the Baltimore area to encourage subcontractors to hire local labor, including participants in the JumpStart program: "We have all these people who are desperate to find work in the neighborhoods where there is not a lot of opportunity," McShane notes. "The question is, how do we begin to get them out of this morass of dead-end jobs?" She works closely with a community hiring coordinator who is out in the field . . .

My dream goes on to say another thing that ultimately distinguishes our nation and our form of government from any totalitarian system in the world. It says that each of us has certain basic rights that are neither derived from nor conferred by the state. They are God-given, gifts from His hands... It started way back in 1776 and God grant that America will be true to her dream.

REVEREND MARTIN LUTHER KING, JR.
CIVIL RIGHTS LEADER

McShane says most of the candidates who go through JumpStart are highly motivated. "We have about a 50 percent success rate, which is good when you consider the disadvantaged population we are working with." She adds, "All of the individuals who wanted to be placed were placed."

Leadership by Example

In the March 2003 edition of ABC's *Construction Executive* magazine, there was another excellent article entitled "Leading by Example." It starred a remarkable African-American ABCer, and here is a summary of it:

Raised by a single mother in the 1950s and turbulent 1960s, Randy Bosley proved to be an anomaly in the poor black neighborhood of Seattle where he grew up. He was a hard worker, determined to rise out of poverty: "I remember thinking even then, as a young man, that all these construction projects were going on around us and no one in my community was working on them. I didn't see one black person. They were all unemployed," he says. "I didn't want that."

Bosley's early years were a blueprint for his life to come. Throughout his teens, he usually held two or three jobs: coordinating paper routes, working as a waiter, and performing maintenance at the naval base. He saved his money and by the age of seventeen, moved into an apartment and owned two vehicles. "Life was brand new but I already had a jump on it," he confides. By the time he left junior college, he and his younger brother had opened a restaurant. It was just a little barbecue pit on Main Street. "My brother was the professional cook and I was the professional food tester," Bosley says.

It wasn't until Bosley truly involved himself in the world of construction that he began to see the inequities around him. Once he encountered what he calls "the old boys network," he began to understand some of the huge roadblocks that minorities faced. He says it was difficult being accepted as a quality contractor by a business force made up largely of white, male contractors with years of experience. It didn't stop him, but it was "a new reality."

Having his first taste of true business ownership—albeit small—Bosley was ready to accept a proposal from a successful black developer, John Parrish, to

---

If we expect to succeed, we must look to ourselves and not to government...What truly defines the civil rights movement today isn't whether you can get a seat at the lunch counter. It's whether you can own that lunch counter in order to create legacy wealth for your children.

Maryland Lt. Gov.
Michael Steele

Either I will find a way or I will make one.

Sir Philip Sidney
Statesman

170

CONSTRUCTION EXECUTIVE

Randy Bosley, general contractor, real estate developer, community leader, and "teammate" to emerging contractors. He has also been an active member of Washington State's Western ABC Chapter.

enter the real estate business. Parrish taught him how to buy buildings and properties and renovate them to lease or rent. Bosley credits much of his success to Parrish and other entrepreneurs that he met during those early years: "I was fortunate to have all kinds of people—black, white, Jewish, Asian—in my life. They mentored me and coached me, keeping me motivated."

In 1993, more than ten years after first entering the building market, Bosley moved into his third construction business. It was the first firm he actually owned, called Sovereign Enterprises—a small carpentry and finish-out contractor. It won many projects in the heart of Seattle, including libraries, colleges, and theaters. Today Sovereign Enterprises, a twelve-person business, counts among its prestigious projects a subcontractor's agreement at the Seattle Opera House.

A Community Leader

As a business owner and community activist, it didn't take Bosley long to discover the benefits of networking relationships with organizations such as ABC and the Urban League. "I realized I needed to get more involved in my community. I had seen things, witnessed problems, and had a background and knowledge that could help other minorities succeed."

Bosley joined the state of Washington's Western Chapter of ABC in 1998. It had been reaching out to the minority community and, according to Chapter President Kathleen Garrity, "he was just the person it needed." He, in turn, noted ABC's commitment right away: "It's a front-runner in the area of minority recruitment. I had looked at other organizations but ABC stood out."

Success isn't measured by the position you reach in life; it's measured by the obstacles you overcome.

BOOKER T. WASHINGTON
EDUCATOR AND CIVIL RIGHTS LEADER

Americanism is a question of principle, of idealism, of character: it is not a matter of birthplace or creed or line of descent.

THEODORE ROOSEVELT
26TH PRESIDENT

Soon Bosley was appointed to serve on ABC's local chapter board of directors and worked with ABC in selecting struggling area contractors to participate in a free course in the ABC Construction School of Management ("CSM"). The training covered all aspects of starting and running a successful business, and its first class graduated in May 2002.

Today CSM has given way to a new organization, called the Contracting Development and Competitiveness Center ("CDCC"), which Bosley helped to launch. It is housed at Seattle's Urban League headquarters and partly funded by the city. Minorities gain an even greater level of support by working directly with city and state politicians, insurance companies, and bonding agents to address issues facing such emerging contractors.

In 2003, Bosley began to divide his time between Sovereign Enterprises and the CDCC. He even hints that he may reduce Sovereign's business volume in order to focus almost exclusively on the CDCC: "I see it this way—I've had so much success along the way, I'm ready to do something for my community and environment to make a difference."

ABC Diversity Manual

It is apparent that ABCers believe the future of the construction industry depends more and more on the skills of a diverse but integrated work force, including women and racial and ethnic minorities. Adopting the policy of ABC National's Diversity Committee, the Association has codified this belief in a *Diversity Manual*. It "assists chapter leaders and members in their efforts to expand on diversity-building to deliver the high quality of construction services expected by customers and also increase the well-being of the overall industry."

The manual is divided into three "modules" for ease of use. Module I deals with diversity-building through ABC networking. Module II covers the subject through joint organizational initiatives with counterpart construction-related organizations. And module III addresses the issues associated with building diversity through training.

ABC chapters follow and expand the manual's policies and practices through their own minority business enterprises committees. They reach out to construction users and owners, government agencies, safety consultants, and general contractors. Local chapters also engage in community service activities, joining with vocational and religious institutions and public school-to-work programs that adopt the Wheels of Learning curricula to encourage low income/minority youngsters to try construction work.

Making Diversity An Advantage

In the February 2005 issue of *Construction Executive* magazine, Lauren Pinch's excellent article on "Diversity Advantage" reports as follows:

> Robert Capps, director of field recruiting and retention at American Infrastructure, a heavy civil infrastructure contractor in Worcester, Pa., has witnessed the changing workforce dynamic. He says companies realize that the workforce of the future will retain fewer white males than it did during the past decades.
>
> "The associations and businesses that make adjustments by incorporating more minority and women contractors are going to be the ones that are able to attract the key people that they need to grow their business. If you don't do this right, then another company will," Capps adds.
>
> The bottom line: diversity creates a strategic business advantage. Both the construction company and its employees benefit when women and minorities are trained and promoted within the industry.
>
> Jeff Donohoe, director of business development for Donohoe Construction Company, Washington, D.C., agrees. "If you don't have any cultural background, you'll be out of place. In an ever-evolving workplace, you have to evolve with it or you'll be left behind," he predicts.
>
> "More and more companies are beginning to understand that the construction world has changed," Owen Tonkins, executive director of the National Association of Minority Contractors (NAMC), Washington, D.C., says. "The workforce should reflect the diverse communities contractors are working in, especially in urban centers. It just makes good business sense."

Sex and Race Discrimination by Big Labor

In contrast to ABC's long-established merit shop policy and practice of equal employment opportunity for all qualified workers regardless of sex, race, color,

You cannot strengthen the weak by weakening the strong. You cannot help the wage earner by pulling down the wage payer. You cannot further the brotherhood of man by encouraging class hatred. You cannot help the poor by destroying the rich. You cannot build character by taking away man's initiative and incentive. And you cannot help men permanently by doing for them what they should do for themselves.

MARYLAND'S LIEU-
TENANT GOVERNOR
MICHAEL STEELE

or creed or voluntary union affiliation, the building trades unions have been perennial civil rights offenders. For many years, both contractual and unspoken practices have restricted the number of women who can even become eligible for membership in their male chauvinist organizations. Because of exclusive union hiring halls and self-monitored limitations on the number of "qualified" apprentices allowed to complete traditional "good old boy" craft training programs, women have faced an uphill battle merely to be accepted, much less graduate as skilled mechanics.

One case actually required legal battles in three separate federal courts of appeal before a women's class action lawsuit finally obtained a judicial order to increase access for females into a local Carpenters Union apprenticeship training program in Northern California. After twenty-one years of costly and ludicrous defenses pleaded by Big Labor, a federal appellate court finally ruled that the union-controlled "two tier" apprenticeship committee had "a hunting license" to do "everything in its power to avoid leveling the playing field so that women can compete for admission to the apprenticeship program as equals with men. Under these circumstances, a monitor [court appointed] is necessary."[35]

Similar illegal and immoral action by the building trades has created artificial labor shortages by limiting the number of non-Caucasian males who can enter the union building trades as apprentices and progress to qualified craft persons. One such example involved Jack Robinson, the African-American owner and chief operating officer of Robinson Construction Company as well as a member of ABC's Yankee Chapter in Massachusetts. He was supportive of equal opportunities for minorities and ran an integrated operation employing about 50 percent black craftspersons and 50 percent white.

Robinson bid and was awarded a school rehabilitation contract in Belmont in an open competition over seven white contractors. He also conquered typical minority financial hurdles in obtaining a million dollars in bonding for the school job. When Robinson's firm began work on the project, it immediately faced picketing by the local building and construction trades council to force it to hire union workers.

Robinson was understandably angry—and rejected what he called "the unparalleled arrogance of these white racist unionists." He explained that the

ABC CONTRACTOR

Former Chairman of the Joint Chiefs of Staff Colin Powell (later U.S. Secretary of State) addresses ABC's 50th anniversary celebration in Baltimore in 2000.

labor leaders involved "had the unmitigated gall to come to me, a black non-union contractor, ask me to become a unionized contractor, and then force me to hire only white union journeymen from their racist training programs and hiring halls. They have systematically excluded all blacks from the building trades unions here for the last hundred years." Robinson refused to capitulate and completed the project successfully.[36]

When Paul King, another African-American, was chairman of the National Association of Minority Contractors Labor Committee and owner of a painting firm in the 1970s, he summed up the racial discrimination that had he observed this way:

> The building trade unions, who have traditionally controlled entry into and training for the skilled crafts, show a long and ugly history of discrimination against minority groups. Hence there are simply fewer minority craftsmen available to mature into qualified contractors. Similarly, these same trade unions contribute to the lack of skilled labor accessible for the minority contractor to build his work force.[37]

According to the University of Wisconsin's industrial relations professor, Herbert Hill (who was the NAACP's national labor director for twenty-eight

The conscience of the Conservative is pricked by anyone who would debase the dignity of the individual human being.

BARRY GOLDWATER
U.S. SENATOR (R-AZ)

> **Our nation's historical commitment to freedom has always angered and frustrated those who have wanted to impose their ideology on the rest of the world. From age to age, these enemies may wear different masks, but they all have the same face—the cold face of totalitarianism.**
>
> CONGRESSMAN J. C. WATTS, JR. (R-OK) IN HIS FOREWORD TO "AMERICA STRONG"

years), the nation's construction trade unions have "viciously" resisted compliance with the Civil Rights Act of 1964. In his book, *Black Labor and the American Legal System*, he charges that trade unions were using restrictive membership practices in the late 1970s to exclude large numbers of blacks and other minorities from employment.[38]

Time has done little to change this illegal and immoral ideology. In 1999, a federal appellate court ruled that both a local building trades union and its international parent union were responsible for a "despicable and egregious history" of excluding African-Americans from local union membership in violation of Title VII of the Civil Rights Act as well as in defiance of a project labor agreement. For a decade, this Laborers' Local 496 had followed the nepotistic practice of admitting relatives of white members to its ranks while ignoring qualified African-American applicants for union membership.

Such a policy is "explicit evidence of disparate treatment," ruled the federal court, and added: "We are baffled and amazed as to how [the international union] can contend that it did not instigate, support, ratify or encourage a policy it created in its own international constitution." Eventually the black plaintiffs in the lawsuit were awarded $1.8 million in damages from the two unions involved under a settlement agreement.[39]

Harry Alford, President of the National Black Chamber of Commerce, added his testimony before Congress that "we're in the year 1999 and Jim Crow is alive and well in the building trades."[40] And Edward Sullivan, national president of the AFL-CIO Building & Construction Trades, admitted publicly in 2000 that "too many local unions still retain barriers to membership [that] include high initiation fees, complicated job referral policies and entrance examinations that keep people out."[41]

This persistent trade union hostility to minorities and women was summed up by Dr. Herbert Northrup, Professor Emeritus of the University of Pennsylvania's Wharton School of Business, in an address to the U.S. Chamber of Commerce. He told the leaders of business and industry that "there have been more public demonstrations, more civil rights lawsuits, more federal equal opportunity cases, and more state human relations commission cases in the construction industry than probably any other, with the building trades unions the principal offenders and targets."[42]

Colin Powell Praises ABC

In stark contrast, Colin Powell addressed ABC's fiftieth anniversary celebration in Baltimore on June 1, 2000. As keynote speaker, he complimented ABC's diversified training programs and compared them to a recent phase of his own distinguished career. The retired general explained that he was helping to instill integrity and values in young people from all walks of life through "America's Promise," a non-profit organization which he created and led as its president. This former chairman of the nation's Joint Chiefs of Staff—and subsequently President George W. Bush's secretary of state—concluded his remarks this way:

"The choice is simple. We either build kids or we build more jails. If America really wants a future, we must develop all of our youth—and I believe that ABC will continue to be an important part of this initiative."[43]

CHAPTER 15

DEDICATED COMMUNITY SERVICE

"**N**EVER TOO BUSY TO GIVE BACK**"** is a traditional commitment among ABC members. While they are vigilant in the crusade to protect free enterprise and the merit shop from mandatory unionism, they also make time to practice good citizenship by helping to improve life in their communities.

Generous donations of professional expertise, skilled labor, materials, equipment, and financial assistance are provided by ABCers to an endless variety of worthy causes. And the Association gives special recognition to contractors who demonstrate an outstanding level of civic and charitable services. ABC's professional chief of staff (recently renamed President and Chief Executive Officer[1]), Kirk Pickerel, reconfirms the Association's belief that:

> Construction can be a key component in the transformation of communities as well as a catalyst in changing the quality of people's lives. Our role in this dynamic process is one of the highlights of working in the construction business.[2]

The mission statement of Corpus Christi–based Repcon Construction, Inc. in Texas proclaims: "The Company and its individual employees have an obligation to provide active support of worthwhile community and industry-related activities." Since the firm's inception, this "ABC Accredited Quality Contractor" has donated its services and $50,000 annually to non-profit charities and other humane groups. Repcon's president, Bob Parker, helped to

Without civic morality, communities perish; without personal morality their survival has no value.

BERTRAND RUSSELL
ENGLISH
PHILOSOPHER

No act of kindness, no matter how small, is ever wasted.

AESOP'S FABLES

establish ABC's Texas Coastal Bend Chapter which—through Repcon and other member companies—donates time and dollars to organizations such as The United Way, Jerry Lewis Muscular Dystrophy Association Telethon, the Boy Scouts of America, the Kidney Foundation, and the Nuecess County Youth Rodeo.

R&H Construction of Portland, Oregon, decided to focus on disadvantaged children, according to its president, John Bradley. His approach to charity allows clients to decide which organization to support and then R&H makes a contribution to it in the client's name. Among the beneficiaries are the Boys and Girls Club of Portland, the Junior Diabetes Foundation, and the YMCA.

Periodic issues of the publication *ABC Today* have listed many more instances of merit shop altruism at work through local ABC chapters. In Pennsylvania, 150 member contractors recently raised thousands of dollars for the Make-A-Wish Foundation. In Mississippi, two hundred contractors built and furnished houses for needy families sponsored by Habitat for Humanity. Over one hundred contractors in Florida delivered free bicycles to poor children. In Washington, D.C., thirty-five contractors contributed labor and equipment to revitalize public parks. An ABCer in Vernon, Connecticut—New England Mechanical Services—donates $50,000 each year to community causes such as the Kid Safe project, a land preservation trust, and the World Affairs Council, which promotes non-slanted understanding of international issues.

Some sixty contractors in Wisconsin gave cash, materials, and labor to design and construct a million-dollar ranch facility for troubled teenagers. In Sierra, Nevada, an ABC chapter joined forces with the City of Reno's Fire Department to purchase a mobile trailer and preach fire safety education from schoolyard to schoolyard, talking to twenty thousand children every year. Toys for Tots, Handlebars for the Holidays, Rawhide Boys Ranch, and Christmas in April are other events sponsored by Nevada ABCers.

Recently the Georgia Chapter of ABC rejuvenated the landscape at a local nursing home. More than a dozen volunteers spent a Saturday at the Roswell Nursing Home, spreading mulch, planting seeds, and laying brick to enhance the beauty and accessibility of the nursing home's courtyard.

Georgia ABC members donated more than $10,000 in labor and materials to the project. Shrubs now decorate the courtyard, flowers bloom in new flowerbeds, and a stone walkway makes its way to a new brick barbecue pit. The Georgia Chapter also expanded the nursing home's concrete patio and added an awning. "This has been a great project for everyone," says Sam Stiteler, chair of the ABC of Georgia's Community Service Involvement Committee.

And the Chapter's commitment to its community does not end with its work at the Roswell Nursing Home. Each year, the committee joins forces with the Chapter's Program Committee to organize and host the "Holiday Dinner and Chinese Auction." In the past two years, the event has raised $10,000 to fund community service initiatives. In addition, the Committee has organized a number of community service activities with various outside organizations, including the Atlanta Community ToolBank that provides no-cost repairs to elderly and disabled low-income homeowners in downtown Atlanta.

Examples of these merit shop humanitarian acts throughout the nation are endless.*

Constructing High-Profile Projects

Merit shop contractors also combine technology, design, and craftsmanship to build projects that make news headlines and are seen by millions of people all over the world. When 20th Century Fox executed a nearly impossible feat for its movie *Titanic* by sinking a turn-of-the-century luxury liner replica weighing more than 1,000 tons, ABC was there. Industrial Mechanical of Downey, California, built, installed, and secured the support framing system for this four-story-high, 410-ft-long ship look-alike. Movie effects specialists still applaud the realistic spectacle that was created on the movie screen.

When George H.W. Bush was honored by the construction of presidential library buildings on the campus of Texas A&M University that documented his life, ABC was there. Manhattan Construction of Dallas built the dignified structures that encompass more than 300,000 square feet and are arranged in a "village scheme" to allow touring visitors easy access.

---

*The author is indebted to ABC's national montly magazine for its excellent reporting used here and frequently throughout this book. (Kirk Pickerel, Publisher; Lisa Nardone, Editor; and Amy Ingram, Assoc. Ed.)

America is a land of wonders in which everything is in constant motion... No natural boundary seems to be set and in man's eyes what is not yet done is only what he has not yet attempted to do.

ALEXIS DE
TOCQUEVILLE
FRENCH PHILOSOPHER

Blake Construction, Inc., of Washington, D.C., was chosen to build the U.S. Holocaust Memorial Museum depicting atrocities committed by the Nazis during World War II. For an authentic expression of the time period and the horrors experienced, Blake Construction installed brick, concrete, and steel to symbolize German industrial construction before World War II. The firm received awards from four construction organizations, including the American Institute of Architects. Today this museum in the nation's capital is one of America's most frequented memorials. And ABC was there.

A national community service initiative called "ABCares" has been established to promote the many and diverse public-spirited activities undertaken by ABC chapters nationwide. The promotional pamphlet proclaims:

> ABC would like to highlight your company's community relations projects on the ABCares web page. We want to share your achievements with a much broader audience. ABC chapters and members are actively involved in a wide range of community service activities each year, including projects such as: Habitat for Humanity, Rebuilding Together, Handlebars for the Holidays, and Make a Wish. (Visit ABCares from the ABC National home page, or go directly to *www.abc.org/abcares*.)

ABC Partners with FEMA

Floods, hurricanes, fires, earthquakes, and blizzards damage almost every community in the country. When an area falls victim to such a natural catastrophe, merit shop contractors step up to the challenge of restoring hard-hit locations. They pride themselves on a long record of assistance in disaster remediation.

This basic reconstruction work usually is supervised by the U.S. Army Corps of Engineers. It achieves primary objectives of the Federal Emergency Management Agency ("FEMA") to provide temporary housing for uprooted residents and to rebuild damaged infrastructure such as streets, bridges, and highways. ABC chapters and their contractors in areas stricken by these tragedies work side by side with local, state, and federal authorities under harrowing conditions to bring local facilities back to normal.

ABC also has agreed to partner with FEMA on its "Project Impact" program to help communities across America withstand the damage of natural disasters. In a joint announcement at the National Press Club in Washington, D.C., in 1997, FEMA Director James Lee Witt told the news media:

> I am especially pleased that ABC—one of the nation's largest contractor associations and whose member firms employ over a million workers—is becoming a FEMA partner. ABC brings the science, experience and knowledge to build disaster-resistant communities and fill one of the biggest pieces in the disaster prevention puzzle.[3]

Project Impact also builds awareness of disaster prevention by educating the public on how to plan for avoidance, mitigation, and risk reduction. This initiative includes coordination with transportation and infrastructure experts, local police and firefighters, elected government officials, and civic and religious organizations.

"Project Impact is far from a band-aid or a hand-out solution," said ABC's year 1999 National President David Bush: "It's a leg-up solution that encourages communities to become disaster resistant throughout the world by building better and building wiser." That same year FEMA Director Witt led a White House conference at which Dave Bush's Adena Corporation of Mansfield, Ohio, was recognized for its efforts as a "good neighbor" in Latin America by assisting in the construction of a medical clinic after Hurricane George struck the Dominican Republic.[4]

The Oklahoma City Bombing Disaster

Worthy of special mention is the gallant role ABCers played over a period of many months after bombs set off by convicted vigilante Timothy McVeigh destroyed the Alfred P. Murrah Federal Building in Oklahoma City on April 19, 1995. He murdered 167 people and injured many more. The punishment he received was a jury-and-court-ordered death sentence. It was carried out much less painfully than the one he dealt to his victims.

In that Oklahoma City tragedy, from split-second stabilization of the crippled structure for the rescue of victims pinned beneath the rubble to providing

What do we mean by patriotism in the context of our times? A patriotism that puts country ahead of self... But remember it's often easier to speak up for principles than to live up to them.

GOVERNOR ADLAI STEVENSON (D-IL)

I feel that the greatest reward for doing is the opportunity to do more.

Jonas Salk
Physician-Research
Scientist

needed supplies and equipment to contributing services and financial help to the memorial reconstruction and a relief fund, ABC members did what they do best. They responded with their expertise, their generosity, and their courage.

Space (and memory) do not allow acknowledgement of every ABCer who helped in the Oklahoma City disaster, but some of them came from ABC member firm Flintco, Inc. Tom Maxwell, president of this general contractor that has its corporate headquarters in Tulsa, said:

> I'm very proud of Jay Harris, our senior project manager and our entire office in Oklahoma City. Jay didn't wait to call us. He gathered a group of our brave people and went straight to the federal building after the explosion to offer the company's help.

Working under the direction of the Oklahoma City Fire Department, Tom Maxwell's Flintco personnel placed equipment close to the scene—with company logos intentionally removed. The bombed building's structural stability was of immediate concern to the safety of surviving victims and rescue workers because the blast crippled three major support columns. Flintco employees worked continuously throughout the first night and into the next day, helping to place horizontal braces on these columns to protect what was left of the building. After the most pressing safety concerns were addressed, Flintco workers built temporary on-site offices for the Fire Department and the Federal Emergency Management Agency.

As this nightmare unfolded, other selfless acts of ABCers came into play. Flintco contacted several of its ABC sub-contractors, including Midwest Wrecking, Murphy & Hibbs, and Quickway Excavating, to provide more manpower and special equipment for the recovery project. It soon became a twenty-four-hour-a-day operation and lasted nearly three weeks.

The Eastern and Western Oklahoma Chapters of ABC sought much-needed supplies and materials from their members. In a matter of hours, chapter staff personnel transported necessities from Tulsa to Oklahoma City. They included hard hats, gloves, blankets, shovels, rain suits, safety goggles, and construction-related materials. "We had offers of help from chapters and members throughout the country," noted Jeri Kolke, executive director of the Western Oklahoma

Chapter. Carl Williams, executive director of the Eastern Oklahoma Chapter, agreed: "The outpouring of help was tremendous."[5]

And ABC was there.

Global Terrorism Invades the USA

Six years later, when the world stopped in shock and disbelief on that fateful day of "9-11-01," ABCers mobilized again to assist at the air-crash murder sites of thousands of innocent people in the Pentagon in Washington, D.C., and the World Trade Center in New York City. Without hesitation or reservation, they volunteered in efforts to rescue injured people and start the devastating recovery process. A number of ABC-member firms actually were working at or near these two "Ground Zeroes" when all hell broke loose.

AMEC of Bethesda, Maryland, had almost finalized its three-and-a-half-year multi-billion-dollar renovation on the Pentagon Wedge 1 Project in Washington and was supporting the government staff's move back into a renovated area when the stolen terrorist-controlled commercial jet hit the Pentagon. AMEC's Assistant Superintendent Dan Fraunhelter was thrown off his feet by the impact of the plane exploding against the building only thirty yards away. As flames and choking smoke poured out, he and his construction teammates provided immediate assistance to emergency teams in the gruesome search and recovery operations.

AMEC's personnel rarely left the Pentagon site in the first few days after the tragedy. Eventually they moved to a "more comfortable schedule" of six days a week, on two rotating ten-hour shifts, with some crews holding over on Sundays. By September 15, the Pentagon Renovation Office ("PENREN") had awarded a major contract to AMEC to rebuild the damaged core and shell of the Pentagon's Wedge 1 and 2 areas. Secretary of Defense Donald Rumsfeld—who called the recovery effort the "Phoenix Project"—was often seen onsite. His reference was to the mythological Phoenix bird rising from the fires of Hades. In every way, the Project would prove to be a symbol of endurance and excellence born out of horrific times. The Phoenix Project mantra reads: *From the ashes of the worst act of terrorism on American soil, a safer and stronger Pentagon will rise.*

AMEC was not the only ABC-member firm that rushed to assist at the Pentagon on that dastardly September 11th. Equally oblivious to the danger as

In the long history of the world, only a few generations have been granted the role of defending freedom in its hour of maximum danger... The energy, the faith, the devotion which we bring to this endeavor will light our country and all who serve it— and the glow from that fire can truly light the world.

35TH PRESIDENT JOHN F. KENNEDY'S INAUGURAL ADDRESS IN 1961

185

Emergency repair and restoration of the Pentagon.

they voluntarily contributed their services to the rescue effort were employees of Hensel Phelps Construction Co. (Chantilly, Va.); HITT Construction Co. (Fairfax, Va.); Springfield Rental Crane (Springfield, Va.); M.C. Dean Electrical, Inc. (Chantilly, Va.); Prospect Waterproofing Co. (Sterling, Va.); and Bovis Lend Lease (Bethesda, Md.). Fortunately all of these workers remained safe and accounted for.[6]

One of AMEC's first calls for special assistance at the Phoenix Project was to Facchina Construction of LaPlata, Maryland. Ken Wyman, the firm's project manager, said: "We were asked to provide manpower and support to FEMA [the Federal Emergency Management Agency], the FBI and the Department of Defense. We had 50 people on the site right away."

Next, the Facchina firm received a request to perform continuous civil and structural construction work during the rescue, crime scene demolition, and reconstruction phases of the emergency project. Under the company's guidance, demolition was accomplished in four weeks instead of the eight months that a project of this scope was estimated to take.

Two days after the September 11th attack, ABC-member Forrester Construction of Rockville, Maryland, joined the Phoenix Project team. This company was contracted by the Department of Defense to supply a temporary roofing structure for areas destroyed by explosions and fires. Forrester's work was completed one month ahead of schedule.

Other ABC members who contributed to the Pentagon's Phoenix Project included: ACM Services, AMEC and AMEC Earth & Environmental, C. J. Coakley Co., Chesapeake Firestopping, Commercial Hardware, David Allen Co., ECB, Ltd., Irvine Access Floors, J. D. Long Masonry, Jefferson Millwork & Design, John J. Kirlin, Inc., Masonry Arts, Material Distributors, Overhead Door Co., Sun Control Systems, and Superior Iron Works, Inc.[7]

As recovery and rebuilding efforts continued, appreciative Pentagon employees held up signs of encouragement to the exhausted construction workers. At one key location the message simply read: **LETS ROLL!** This motivational message honored Todd Beamer, who heroically led the passenger counter-attack which forced another terrorist plane to crash on "9-11" in rural Pennsylvania near the town of Shanksville, killing the flight crew and the hundreds of commercial jet's passengers. That aircraft was on a murderous mission to destroy the United States White House or the Halls of Congress . . .

The Pentagon originally estimated that it would take $740 million to execute and complete the Phoenix Project. Because of the skill, talent, forethought, and dedication of the ABCers who were managing the project, work was completed for $550 million. These contractors also found a way to condense what would have normally been a three-year project into one year.

A federal PENREN office spokesperson said: "We kept serving up bigger and bigger challenges and the contractors kept coming back with better and better solutions. The construction community has responded to this emergency in a manner unparalleled in our experience." And the Phoenix Project received a congressional commendation. The award paid tribute to "the 2,000 workers who performed at the site as well as the innovative construction practices and high quality workmanship."[8]

"Ground Zero" in New York City

At the World Trade Center's almost simultaneous terrorist attack in the Wall Street area of New York City, two pirated commercial jetliners crashed into the World Trade Center's twin towers on September 11, 2001, murdering the crews, the passengers, and over a thousand office workers and police and

No man is worth his salt who is not ready at all times to risk his body, to risk his well-being, to risk his life in a great cause.

THEODORE ROOSEVELT
26TH PRESIDENT

Life is an escalator: You can move forward or backward; you cannot remain still.

PAT RUSSELL-MCCLOUD
MOTIVATIONAL SPEAKER

firemen on valiant rescue missions there. Within an hour, Nu-Way Crane owner Mike Sackaris of Wantagh, New York, received a crisis call from the New York City Fire Department. Without hesitating, ABCer Sackaris volunteered to help immediately.

A few minutes later, George Kunkel, a safety director with the New York City Fire Department (and a former Nu-Way Crane employee) told Sackaris from a mobile phone in an impromptu fire station set up a few blocks from Ground Zero: "Do what you've got to do, but get in here fast. We not only need cranes, we also need cables, shackles, and rigging gear." At the moment, Nu-Way Crane had only one crane and ancillary equipment in Manhattan. The other Nu-Way cranes were on projects on Long Island.

Sackaris immediately replied: "No problem. I'll have the cranes ready for you." There was not any mention of reimbursement. Then he went out and bought $8,000 worth of supplementary supplies needed to cope with the catastrophic situation. The Suffolk County police cooperated by closing off thirty miles of the Long Island Expressway and personally escorted Sackaris, his crew of seven men, and their outfitted cranes to Ground Zero within three hours.

Mike Sackaris said that when he and his crew reached the site they simply stared, stunned by what they saw: "It was unbelievable. There was total chaos, like a war zone." They climbed into their cranes (the first ones to reach Ground Zero) and worked around the clock for three days, slowly and carefully lifting and moving dozens of mangled bodies, tons of debris, and thousands of cars that had been parked in the garage. "We were hoping to save at least one person," Sackaris recalled sadly. But all he saw was "body bag after body bag."

ABC equipment supplier-member Caterpillar of Peoria, Illinois, also provided people power and equipment to support the rescue and restoration efforts. Within hours on that fateful "9-11," Caterpillar's New York dealer, H.O. Penn Machinery, had forty technicians on site and sixty-five more on standby. A crew from Penn worked alongside the New York City police the first night to set up fifty light towers and twelve generator sets. These technicians stayed on the job day and night until it was completed. Caterpillar also donated five truckloads of work tools, one thousand hard hats, and two thousand pairs of gloves for relief workers.

Another member, ABC National Associate/Supplier firm Williams Scots-man, of White Marsh, Maryland—a nationwide lessor of mobile offices—vol-untarily sent eighty-five portable units to New York. They were used by teams that needed to work in close proximity to Ground Zero, such as rescue and repair organizations, emergency management agencies, and criminal investi-gation units.

ABCer Bill Watterson, of Watterson Construction in Alaska, donated $6,900 to "9-11" disaster relief. Even though he was a thousand miles away, Watterson matched dollar-for-dollar contributions made from his employees in the months following the attacks.

Later on, ABC's senior staff executive, Kirk Pickerel, joined fifty of the nation's top association executives in New York City to share a message with the world that "despite the events of September 11th, America is stronger and more united than ever." During that meeting, Pickerel hand-delivered a letter to Mayor Rudy Giuliani. It offered ABC's continued support of the recovery and reconstruction effort at Ground Zero. "We will not let terrorists bring America's business to a standstill," Pickerel promised the mayor.

Most of ABC's eighty-four local chapters representing approximately twenty-four thousand members also took some part in the relief effort involv-ing these New York and Washington, D.C., tragedies. They offered services, supplies, and equipment. They coordinated blood drives and held fundrais-ers. They also encouraged member participation in ABC's Foundation "9-11" family relief fund which soon donated $145,000 to the charities listed for needy victims' families.

"It's been very satisfying," said ABC's 43rd National Chairman, Henry Kelly ('01), and chief executive officer of Austin Industrial, Inc., a general con-tractor based in Houston, Texas. "But it's what we expect from those who uphold the free enterprise philosophy and true American spirit."

Morghan Transue (age seventeen), winner of the 2003 *Idea of America* essay contest, wrote these stirring words:

> In a nation established by peoples of differing languages, ethnicities,
> and religions, Americans find unity in the democratic principles of
> the founding fathers; principles that united the thirteen colonies after

One of the strongest impulses in man is patriotism. It is the instinct that has ever inspired men to make great and heroic sacri-fices—to give up interests, posses-sions, dear ones, and even life itself. Patriotism lifts men above the level of expe-diency, safety, and profits.

SAMUEL GOMPERS
AFL PRESIDENT

189

Liberalism...tries to think its way past danger, decadence and despair to reach some other shore, however vaguely imagined that shore might be on a global humanistic horizon.... **Most Americans of faith simply don't believe it's out there.**

PHILLIP MCMATH, ESQ., *WALL STREET JOURNAL* EDITORIAL

the American Revolution and continue to unite America during such crises as the attacks of September 11, 2001.

Three weeks after these fanatical Islamist assaults, President Bush addressed the General Assembly of the United Nations and declared: "My hope is that all nations will heed our call and eliminate the terrorist parasites who threaten their countries and our own. Some governments will be timid in the face of terror. But make no mistake about it: if they do not act, America will!" And the President added, soon after:

> We will persevere through this national tragedy and personal loss. In time, we will find healing and recovery. In the face of all this evil, we remain strong and united, "one Nation under God..." America will never seek a permission slip [from the United Nations or any other international body] to defend the security of our people.

A year later, ABC's 44th National Chairman, Ken Adams ('02),[9] and the CEO of Pace Electric of Wilmington, Delaware, issued a special letter of thanks to "All Construction Heroes." These are excerpts:

> On the anniversary of September 11, 2001, the construction industry's support of the victims of the terrorist attacks continues—in more ways than one. From the very beginning, the construction community was there to assist with search and rescue, to donate much needed services, supplies, and equipment, to contribute to relief funds. Today, that same construction community is still there, in the form of renovation and memorial construction assistance.
>
> Our industry was hit hard that awful September 11th day. More than 150 construction workers died on the job: Three construction association and business offices, including the Port Authority offices, were destroyed at the World Trade Center.
>
> More than 5,000 construction workers helped recover the World Trade Center and Pentagon sites. These brave people were continually exposed to heat, dust, poisonous fumes and physical exhaustion.

Crisis centers, some run by ABC members, were set up at both sites to counsel construction workers suffering stress-related illnesses. The only order that was disobeyed involved instruction to "go home and get some rest." Many of the workers lived on the site, sleeping in their vans, cars, or hotels in the area.

ABC chapters should be recognized for their generous donations of supplies and money over the past year. They also continue to offer support to members through various post-September 11th educational programs on safety vigilance and new building techniques in an age of global terrorism.

The unprecedented acts of murder by fanatical Muslim terrorists and the reactive acts of bravery by victims, survivors, and rescuers on and after "9-11" must never be forgotten. Among the heroes were many ABC volunteers who risked their lives while donating their services to this unparalleled world crisis.

For over fifty years ABC contractors have recognized the economic benefits of investment in communities where they do business. Constructing quality edifices, strengthening client relations, peer networking, improving contacts with government officials, and generating goodwill with the public all make good business sense. A bottom-line motivator for merit shoppers, however, has always been the enthusiastic donation of assistance to others who deserve a helping hand and show dedication to their beloved United States of America in times of need.

COVER STORY

"Freedom itself was attacked this morning. Freedom will be defended."
— PRESIDENT GEORGE W. BUSH, *Sept. 11, 2001*

REPRINTED WITH PERMISSION OF AP WIDE WORLD PHOTOS

CHAPTER 16

THE "PREVAILING WAGE LAW" FARCE

FROM THE TIME **ABC** WAS FOUNDED in 1950 to today, a federal "prevailing wage law" known as the Davis-Bacon Act and its state and local counterparts have been the Association's nemesis in the field of public construction work. Simply stated, these labor laws destroy free market competition. They adopt rigid union-scale wages work ruler, and fringe benefits almost automatically, thus discriminating against non-union workers and minorities while artificially increasing government building costs underwritten by American taxpayers.

An "evil sought to be remedied" by this Davis-Bacon Act, according to Congress when the law was enacted in 1931 in the midst of the Great Depression, was that "lower [non-union] wages led to labor strife" and "the workmanship of cheap [non-union] labor was very inferior."[1]

The bureaucrats claimed that this statute was passed as "a protective economic response to certain unscrupulous contractors." These "villainous builders" were accused of hauling around the countryside many non-union, migrant, *black* southern workers who were allegedly "exploited at substandard wages" in a time of widespread unemployment. This practice was said to "undercut" local northern firms that employed higher-paid *white* union workers on federal public works projects.[2] AFL President William Green agreed: "Colored labor is being brought in to demoralize wages."[3]

The practical effect of arbitrary "super" minimum wages imposed discriminatorily by the biased administration of this Davis-Bacon legislation allowed northern contractors to bid successfully. They could employ white unionized craftsmen against lower-paid but qualified non-union African-Americans or non-union whites—without suffering legal or financial consequences.[4] And the deplorable truth is that Davis-Bacon remains essentially unchanged since its enactment over seventy years ago. It still causes non-competitive, inflationary union-scale raises in labor costs and in tax costs used to finance public projects such as highways, bridges, government office buildings, low-income housing, hospitals, and prisons. And it still discriminates against minorities and non-union contractors.[5]

This arcane prevailing wage law—which ABC's John Trimmer called "the biggest boondoggle in the history of the construction industry"—applies to all agreements with prime contractors and subcontractors for the construction of federal public works projects over $2,000. It requires that such contracts

> . . . shall contain a provision stating the *minimum* wages to be paid various classes of *laborers and mechanics* shall be based upon the wages that will be determined by the Secretary of Labor to be *prevailing* for the corresponding classes of laborers and mechanics employed on *projects of a character similar* to the contract work in the city, town, village, or other civil subdivision of the state in which the work is to be performed. [emphasis added]

reprinted with permission from Cartoon Features Syndicate

"I'd like to pay you what you're worth Jackson. But the minimum wage law has teeth in it."

The scam is that over the years the Secretary's Department of Labor ("DOL") seldom uses the true "prevailing" free market scale paid to the majority of construction workers in an applicable locality by properly taking into account both non-union and union labor rates.[6] Instead, DOL traditionally favors the higher wage scales negotiated by unions and unionized contractors, using an unspoken presumption. DOL—unless challenged—assumes that the uniform collectively bargained building trade union rates for three specific trade union job classes (certified craft journeymen mechanics, their apprentices, and laborers) are the *exclusive* work categories allowed by the Act and provide

**Politics is an
excellent career,
unless you
get caught.**

Robert Half
Entrepreneur

the prevailing wage rates to be adopted by all successful bidders on federal government projects.

In other words, contrary to sound business and accounting practices followed in the private sector, Congress rejected the award of government construction projects to the lowest qualified bidders, on a level playing field, regardless of their union or non-union status. This political rip-off continues even though unionized workers and their wage scales in the United States today only factually "prevail" on less than *18 percent* of the nation's similar private sector free-market-oriented construction projects.[7]

An amendment of this Davis-Bacon statute in 1964 added a further inflationary burden on America's taxpayers. Congress obliged Big Labor by redefining "wages" to include a combination of both wages and union-negotiated "fringe" benefits. The cost of entitlements such as pensions, medical and hospital care, apprentice training set-asides, paid holidays, and vacations are added together to make up DOL's union-scaled "prevailing wage" determinations.

Without debate, Congress endorsed this amendment *viva voce* into law. President Lyndon B. Johnson (D-TX), creator of the nation's "Great Society," proudly announced at the signing ceremony: "Today is a glad moment for the eminent leader of the Building Trades Department, C. J. Haggerty. We've come a long way since the original Davis-Bacon Act became law, and the record through the years confirms the wisdom and value of that Act . . ."[8]

A Certified Weekly Payroll Report

The companion Copeland Anti-Kickback Act passed by Congress in 1934 requires contractors performing Davis-Bacon projects to assume the additional business burden of submitting to the government a weekly certified payroll report covering the exact wages and fringe benefits paid to each employee working on the project. If a non-union contractor fails to (1) pay DOL's prevailing wage and benefits rates, or (2) misclassifies a union-scale mechanic's work as the work of a lower paid non-union apprentice or laborer, (3) or takes improper credit for non-union fringe benefits contributions, or (4) otherwise fails to comply with the payroll reporting requirements, that contractor is penalized. He will pay upwardly adjusted back wages and benefits that the government claims are "due" his employees. In a "flagrant" case, the contractor can be debarred from

The Congress is constitutionally empowered to launch programs the scope, impact, consequences, and workability of which are largely unknown, at least to the Congress, at the time of enactment. Then the federal bureaucracy is legally permitted to execute the congressional mandate with a high degree of befuddlement as long as it acts no more befuddled than the Congress must reasonably have anticipated.

U.S. District Court Judge Robert Kelleher Central District, California, in *American Petroleum Institute v. Knecht*

federal government work. There are also criminal penalties against contractors for "willful" violations of the two laws.

All of these strictures encourage frivolous trade union charges and litigation claiming that ABCers working on Davis-Bacon projects have acted illegally. But no punitive or actual damages are recoverable by the accused non-union contractors for the lost work time and cost due to their successful legal defense against these unfounded claims by Big Labor and DOL.

Prejudiced "Prevailing Wage" Determinations

The statutory procedure, when a government construction project nears the bidding stage, requires the contracting federal agency involved to secure a prevailing wage determination from DOL (or its state law counterpart). These determinations are published in the *Federal Register* and, unless amended or challenged, apply to "all projects of a similar character in the designated area."

The Davis-Bacon Act itself provides no administrative guidance as to a statistical computation to determine such a "prevailing wage." Instead, it delegates to the secretary of labor and DOL—as one court said, "in the broadest terms imaginable"—the regulatory mandate to make all rate determinations.[9] DOL's findings are conclusive unless appealed, and thousands of horrendous examples of administrative "errors" favoring the building trades abound.

In one case the secretary of labor's administrator actually ruled that the construction of a huge aluminum processing plant qualified as an exemplary "project of a character similar" to remodeling a small office building and several tiny animal shelters in the locality. In other absurd situations, high union scale "city" wages have been designated as "prevailing" for rural and far-out suburban areas or for areas in adjoining states where union strength was minimal and open shop rates were prevalent.

Sometimes the "area" used is expanded or contracted arbitrarily to fit a union wage scale. It is not unusual for DOL bureaucrats to designate a local negotiated union scale as prevailing without any database whatsoever, or import the union scale from a non-contiguous metropolitan area into an open shop locality, or base the prevailing rate on one large but long-outdated unionized project in an area currently dominated by open shop labor.[10]

The secretary of labor's operative policy for fifty years in determining any local prevailing wage rate was a three-step process endorsed enthusiastically by the building trades. *First*, if any single-to-the-penny (union contract scale) wage was "determined" by DOL to be paid to a *majority* of the workers in a class, that union wage became "prevailing." *Second*, if there was no such single (union contract scale) wage paid to a majority of the workers, any to-the-penny (union contract scale) wage paid to just *30 percent* of them became the "prevailing" wage. *Third*, if no single wage was paid to a 30 percent "plurality," then a *weighted average* combining all union and non-union wages blended together was supposed to be used.[11] (This last procedure, of course, required more computation work on the part of the bureaucrats.)

> **Nearly everything the government touches turns to solid waste. After the government turns something to solid waste, it regulates it and turns it into natural gas.**
>
> Gaffin's Paradox

The Emasculated Reagan Rule

In 1983, due in large part to respect for voluntary unionism and the merit shop by President Ronald Reagan's administration plus a supporting federal court victory participated in by ABC, the second-step union-minority 30 percent rule was eliminated. Under the current *"majority rule"* policy, if DOL determines that more than *50 percent* of the workers in a given class (mechanics, apprentices, or laborers) in a locality are paid at the same to-the-penny union contract wage and benefits rate, that rate will be considered "prevailing." But if no such single 50 percent rate exists, then DOL is supposed to use "old" step three and calculate the prevailing rate based on a *weighted average* formula that includes a blend of all workers' wages and benefits—union and non-union—in each job classification.[12]

Unfortunately for American taxpayers and open shop contractors, this weighted average step usually is ignored or avoided. DOL relies almost entirely on the factual submissions of contractors, both union and non-union, to obtain information regarding the rates prevailing in the more than 3,000 counties in the United States and in the three union-designated statutory categories of construction workers for each county. All the unionized contractors and their trade unions have to do to comply is send DOL the applicable local labor contracts.

Partisan government agents justify their preferential use of these inflated union-scale rates as "prevailing" because of what they openly admit is "a lesser administrative burden." They simply accept the "easily accessible" local union

Bureaucracy defends the status quo long past the time when the quo has lost its status.

LAURENCE J. PETER
WRITER-PUNDIT

collective bargaining agreements that always contain identical wage and fringe benefits rates for all workers employed in the three rigid craft union job classifications as the "presumptive majority rates."

The scam evolves because non-union employees' pay and fringe benefits vary widely from employer to employer, based on each contractor's judgment of each employee's comparable merit and versatility of performance in one or more trades or multi-skilled job classifications. DOL thus negligently (if not fraudulently) rejects its legal obligation to obtain *bona fide* prevailing rates because of what it calls the "time-consuming chore" of collecting individual wage surveys from all open shop construction workers in the applicable locale. This unpopular chore (required under DOL's own regulations) seldom is performed because it means categorizing, tabulating, and fitting the variable job classifications and differing wage rates of many hundreds or thousands of multiskilled open shop craftsmen into the three rigid statutory union-style job modes. The same bureaucratic chore applies to computing the diverse and variable open shop fringe benefits.

This farce is further complicated by the fact that ABC is limited in the time and cost necessary to assist or challenge DOL by obtaining comprehensive wage and benefits data from its contractor members. Many of them are unconvinced as to the value of participation. They visualize government bias in the bid procedure, a tremendous amount of time and expenses in accurately computing the "weighted average" in a given locale, followed by a substantial chance of bid rejection.

An Early Example of Government Negligence

In 1964 I was retained as labor counsel to the Metropolitan Baltimore Chapter of ABC. One of my assignments was to challenge the dubious prevailing wage determinations for public construction projects of Baltimore City. Under the municipality's "Little Davis-Bacon Act," a Personnel Policy and Wage Advisory Committee followed political tradition by presumptively adopting the building trades union wage scales. The committee gave this justification for its decision:

We have determined that wage scales established by the U. S. Bureau of Labor Statistics were adopted after extensive research, investigation and survey of both union and non-union wage rates in this locality and a proper weighing of the data collected.

In view of the fact that the said Bureau employs an army of statisticians, a great number of whom have advanced degrees with access to some of the most sophisticated computer machinery in the world, and continuously collects, collates and analyzes all of the available data, this Personnel Committee is of the opinion that no consultant would have access to any better information.[13]

I decided to verify the accuracy of this glowing report and the actual facts about the City's prevailing wage determinations. My worst suspicions were confirmed. The so-called "extensive research, investigation and survey" of union and non-union wages consisted of a few telephone calls between City officials, the U.S. Department of Labor office in Baltimore, local unionized contractors, and the Baltimore Building and Construction Trades Council. No effort whatsoever was made to check the volume of non-union contractors' open shop wage structures or, alternatively, to compute a "weighted average" of union and non-union rates in the locale as required if no union scale majority rates "prevailed."

Next, I made a trip to Washington, D.C. The alleged "army of statisticians with advanced degrees" in the U.S. Labor Department main office who made the original wage determination consisted of one wage analyst and his assistant. Their investigatory jurisdiction covered not only Baltimore, Maryland, but fifteen states. Neither of them had "an advanced degree" or used a "sophisticated computer." Not even an adding machine was in view.

The City's Board of Estimates Reacts

With this evidence in hand, I requested and gained a hearing on the wage determination issue before the Baltimore City Board of Estimates, which awarded all of the City's construction contracts. I charged that the new union-scale wage schedules for municipal construction work "were erroneous and based on conjecture rather than fact." I added that "the City's Personnel Policy and Wage Advisory Committee report was geared intentionally for Big Labor, which was trying to obtain inflated rates at the expense of free enterprise and the City's taxpayers."

> **If experience teaches us anything at all, it teaches us this: that a truthful politician is quite as unthinkable as an honest burglar.**
>
> H. L. MENCKEN
> SYNDICATED
> COLUMNIST-CRITIC

It was fortunate for ABC that Joseph Allen, Baltimore's city solicitor and chairman of the aforementioned Personnel Committee, happened to preside over my meeting with the Board of Estimates. This respected attorney seemed shocked when he heard my charges. He apparently had been duped by pro-union municipal flunkies whom he relied on to gather the data for his Personnel Committee's report. Allen hastily advised the Board of Estimates and me that his Committee would "restudy" its recommendations. "Mr. Cook's arguments will be reviewed point by point, and if we can't answer them, I will confess error," he concluded.[14]

True to his word, City Solicitor Allen soon issued a report admitting that his Personnel Committee could *not* truthfully rebut my charges. He therefore ordered the prevailing wage scale of Baltimore City construction projects to be reduced to portray the lower weighted average wage rates established by an independent accounting firm.

A Cumberland Valley ABC Prevailing Wage Victory

Four years later, in 1968, I was retained as labor counsel to ABC's Cumberland Valley Chapter, covering Western Maryland, Southwestern Pennsylvania, and the Panhandle of West Virginia. My first assignment was to challenge prevailing wage rates established on a federally financed Davis-Bacon Act nursing home project in Waynesboro, Pennsylvania. In its typical lazy and prejudiced fashion, the U.S. Department of Labor ("DOL") had automatically adopted the local building trades union labor contract scale and ignored the multitude of open shop construction projects in the locality.

DOL refused my request to reconsider its decision. Then the U.S. General Accounting Office ("GAO") advised me that it would take eighteen months to review DOL's action unless GAO received a request for such an investigation from a member of Congress. With the assistance of the ABC Chapter's executive director, John Lloyd, we persuaded Senator Scott (R-PA) and Congressman Mathias (R-MD) to pursue our charge. Within a week, DOL sent a single "statistician" to Waynesboro and—to our amazement—he recommended that an even higher "prevailing" wage scale should be established.

Only one course of action was still available to ABC. With the help of William Barton, a vice president and general counsel of the U.S. Chamber of

Commerce, we petitioned DOL's Wage Appeal Board in Washington, D.C., for a hearing. There we resubmitted Executive Director John Lloyd's well-documented survey of lower open shop job classification rates for similar projects in the applicable locality.

Justice finally triumphed as the Wage Appeal Board reversed DOL and accepted our overwhelming evidence of open shop wage scale prevalence. Here is a comparison of the original and second (final) revised prevailing wage determinations established by DOL for the Waynesboro nursing home project in 1968 at ABC's request:

Practical politics consists in ignoring facts.

HENRY ADAMS
HISTORIAN

Craft	DOL's First Determination	Revised Final DOL Determination
Carpenters	$4.52	$2.35
Electricians	$4.40	$2.25
Laborers	$3.10	$1.40
Painters	$3.42	$2.00
Roofers	$3.55	$2.00
Plumbers	$4.62	$2.75
Sheet Metal Workers	$4.75	$2.65
Truck Drivers	$2.32	$1.40
Backhoe Operators	$5.77	$2.00

The happy ending of this left wing scam was that Michael Callas of Callas Contractors (who would become ABC's sixteenth national president in '73-'74) was awarded the nursing home job—and the taxpayers saved $1,944,000.[15]

Defusing a Building Trades Union Myth

These two early Maryland examples are typical of many Davis-Bacon Act area prevailing wage determinations and their state law equivalents to this day. Embedded government servants still try to parrot the uniform union wage rates, classifications, and fringe benefits found in collective bargaining agreements without any regard for their accuracy or blended union and non-union scale "weighted averages." The typical government findings under this antiquated law bear no resemblance to economic, statistical, or statutory reality and negate the greater work force flexibility, economy, speed, and savings to taxpayers that merit shop contractors provide.

Prejudiced politicians and organized labor leaders circulate the myth that union scale wages and fringe benefits are needed in public construction projects "to ensure labor peace and quality workmanship." Nothing could be further from the truth. The actual facts are that labor disputes—in violation of contractual "no strike" pledges—are resulting regularly in costly work slowdowns and work stoppages on many public construction projects controlled by the Davis-Bacon Act and its state counterparts.

Open shop construction workers, on the other hand, don't engage in work stoppages. And their wages and employee benefits are responsive to competitive market-place standards plus individual merit and qualifications. Simply stated, most open shop construction employees have excellent skills, high productivity, work harmoniously in teams, and make a good living for themselves and their families. That all results in "labor peace and quality workmanship" at its best.

As further rebuttal to the union charge of "poor quality work" by the open shop, graduates from ABC's state-of-the-art training programs regularly win awards for superior performance and outstanding safety records. Ultimate proof of the high quality of non-union workers' productivity is the established statistic that over *80 percent* of all *private sector* industrial, commercial, and institutional construction work performed throughout the nation (and not controlled by any artificial prevailing wage law) is awarded competitively to the lowest qualified and responsible bidder, namely, a *non-union* contractor.[16]

The "live-better-work-union" claim which perpetuates the leftist political justification for Davis-Bacon's inflated union-scale prevailing wages-and-benefits paid on government construction projects "to ensure labor peace and quality workmanship" is simply false propaganda circulated by Big Labor and its controlled politicians.

Mandatory Adoption of Restrictive Union Work Rules

A lesser known but equally discriminatory and costly burden on non-union contractors and the taxpaying public which foots government construction costs is another partisan DOL requirement under the nonsensical Davis-

Bacon Act. Whenever union labor rates are determined to prevail in a locality, the archaic and featherbedded building trades labor contract *work rules and practices also must be followed*. In some cases DOL adopts these union workplace rules even though a weighted average open shop wage and benefits rate is found to prevail. The absurd result is that non-union builders who are awarded a government construction job must eliminate the normal and flexible multi-skilled work assignments of their versatile employees to comply with the inhibiting and rigid union-style conditions of work that restrict productivity and increase labor costs.[17]

There is nothing in the Davis-Bacon Act itself or its regulations that requires DOL's practice of paying high-skilled journeymen mechanics to do semi-skilled or menial work which could be performed with no adverse impact on "output" or "quality workmanship" or "labor peace" by lower-skilled workers such as apprentices, helpers or laborers at much lower cost. Philip Abrams, ABC's seventeenth president ('75), addressed this bureaucratic nightmare in testimony at a U.S. Senate hearing in 1979. He told the legislators:

> The problem with restrictive work practices is difficult to quantify, but in general, if union wages have been determined and published, any such work practices that are part of union collective bargaining agreements are then made a requirement in the name of "area practice" and are the responsibility of the contractor.
>
> The requirement, basically, is that skilled people do unskilled work and that arbitrary rules like "the tools of the trade" determine the hourly wages that a working person receives. For instance, in one particular project, the fact that laborers were using hammers caused DOL and HUD [Department of Housing and Urban Development] to conclude that the workers should be paid as carpenters, even though they were in fact doing laborers' work...
>
> The sum and substance is that you lower productivity on construction sites by enforcing featherbedded union work practices, by not allowing "helper" job categories, and by refusing, for example, to let unskilled people nail up insulation or carry pieces of steel or pull wire or unload plumbing fixtures.

The difference between a politician and a statesman is: a politician thinks of the next election and a statesman thinks of the next generation.

JAMES FREEMAN CLARKE
MINISTER, AUTHOR, AND REFORMER

The worst and most pernicious part of these DOL requirements is that they are *unwritten*. There is no place where you can find these area practices anyplace in any government manual for anybody to reference. You're simply expected to comply with these [union] area practices which are enforced by the contracting officer and DOL arbitrarily and without any previous notice to the contractor.[18]

Union "Audit Scams" on Wage Law Compliance

A typical organized labor ruse to harass ABC members who bid on federal prevailing wage construction projects is seen in the following letter (with disguised identities) from a building trades council's alleged tax-exempt "foundation" to an ABC general contractor:

> This is to advise you that the Affiliated Construction Trades Foundation is interested in insuring fair competition among contractors involved in prevailing wage work. As a non-profit organization acting on the public's behalf, we function within our legal right to review public works projects. We understand that you have bid on this project and we wanted to let you know that it is among those projects which our staff will monitor.
>
> Our intention is to investigate possible infractions, independent of state and federal agencies, and forward any violations to the appropriate agency. Our monitoring activities will include, but will not be limited to, site visits, reviewing certified payroll records for proper classification of employees, verification of apprenticeship ratios, and proper payment of overtime. We have informed the owner of our intentions and our contact with you.
>
> We believe that the majority of contractors who work on prevailing wage projects make every attempt to abide by the laws. However, we know that there are some companies who will stop at nothing to make more money. If you have information regarding questionable practices and would like us to investigate, or have any questions, please feel free to call.

Targeted ABCers are advised that this type of self-serving letter must be reviewed by labor counsel who should either draft a short "denial" answer to be sent to the union "foundation" or ignore the letter completely.

Another bogus union communication is a variation on the previous letter and should receive the same type of response. In this ploy, a local organizer of the Sheet Metal Workers International union advised the chairman of a West Virginia County's Board of Education (with disguised identities) that a non-union contractor employed on a school construction project within the county was not classifying or paying its employees properly under the state's prevailing wage law:

Dear Mr. Chairman:

It is our understanding that Smith Construction Company has been awarded a contract to perform heating, ventilation and air condition work on your South Western School project. I am writing to supply you with important information that you may not be aware of.

I have enclosed copies of sections of the West Virginia Prevailing Wage Law and a Regulation that I believe will prove the serious claims I am making in this letter. This information will show that your School Board and it's agents have a responsibility to verify that workers performing the work on this project are properly classified and paid the legally established prevailing hourly wage as well as receive the prevailing amount of fringe benefits. Please realize that if Smith Construction Company does not offer a qualified wage and fringe benefit package that equals the amount that "prevails" in your locality, its employees are entitled to additional wages and benefits equaling the amount that does "prevail."

According to law, moreover, if a worker on a West Virginia "public improvement" project is classified as an *apprentice* sheet metal worker, that worker must be enrolled in a bonafide apprenticeship program that is recognized by the Bureau of Apprenticeship and Training. Through contact with that Bureau, I have learned that Smith Construction Company does not have such a registered

You are never so easily fooled as when trying to fool someone else.

Francois de la Rochefoucauld
statesman

205

The American people are demanding that we change the way the federal government operates. It doesn't work well, it costs too much money and it performs very poorly.

VICE PRESIDENT
AL GORE

apprenticeship program in place for its sheet metal workers at this time. This means that all Smith Construction employees who perform the work of a sheet metal worker will be entitled to the higher prevailing wage and benefits rate for a journeyman sheet metal worker. It is illegal for a worker that performs the work of a sheet metal worker to be classified and paid as a laborer or any other lower paid classification.

If you would like to learn more about the prevailing wages and fringe benefits of apprentices on West Virginia Prevailing Rate Projects, you may contact the Bureau of Apprenticeship and Training at 304-123-4567. Also please feel free to contact my Local Union if you have any questions about the information we have provided or if we may be of assistance to you or the Board of Education.

Very truly yours,
John Smith
SMWU Local 13

How Labor and Government Fleece Taxpayers

About one-fifth of the total non-residential construction market in the United States resides in public works and government contracting. It amounts to billions of dollars. In 1980 Nobel Prize–winning economist Milton Friedman summed up the Davis-Bacon Act's multi-billion-dollar swindle of taxpayers as a "source of union power":

How do unions raise the wages of their members? What is the basic source of their power? The answer is: the ability to keep down the number of jobs available, or equivalently, to keep down the number of persons available for a class of jobs. Unions have been able to keep down the number of jobs by enforcing a high wage rate, generally with assistance from government. They have been able to keep down the number of persons available, primarily through licensure, again with government aid . . .

To return to the wage rate, how can a union enforce a high wage rate? An easy way is to get the government to help. That is the reason union headquarters are clustered around Capitol Hill in Washington, why they devote so much money and attention to politics.

A major form of government assistance to construction unions is the Davis-Bacon Act. The reach of the act has been extended by the incorporation of its prevailing wage requirement in numerous other laws for federally assisted projects, and by similar laws in thirty-five states covering state construction expenditures. The effect of these acts is that the government enforces union wage rates for much of construction activity.[19]

In 1985 the state of Michigan provided a unique opportunity to study the economic impact of its own state prevailing wage law—a "Little Davis-Bacon Act"—like the one in Maryland. This Michigan law was passed in 1969 but suspended in 1994 for a period of thirty months following a federal district court ruling in a case brought by ABC. The court held that the prevailing wage law was nullified and preempted by the Employee Retirement Income Security Act.[20]

In 1997 a federal appellate court reversed this lower court and reinstated the prevailing wage law.[21] Then a study released by the Mackinac Center for Public Policy (an independent organization based in Midland, Michigan) reported that during the thirty-month invalidation period when the prevailing wage law was not in effect, more than eleven thousand new construction jobs were created and at least $275 million was saved annually in the cost of state construction work. That savings amounted to 10 percent of the state's total annual outlay for construction.[22]

A similar report by the Kentucky Legislative Research Commission found that "currently [December, 2001] neither prevailing wages set by the Kentucky Labor Cabinet or the U.S. Department of Labor yield prevailing wages that are representative of local wages." The rates used, continued the Kentucky report, "are biased upward."[23]

A prominent business consultant and Adjunct Professor of Management at the University of Baltimore, Dr. Armand J. Thieblot, Jr., summed up the prevailing wage law racket recently: "While changing technology is forcing the whole construction industry toward a more fluid, more variable structure of

The world's greatest lie: "I'm from the government and I'm here to help you."

ANONYMOUS

new specialties and multiple levels of skill and reward, prevailing wage laws are helping to preserve an anachronistic earlier phase of the industry's evolution at which the union side has solidified." Dr. Thieblot went on to explain the discriminatory nature of Big Labor's prevailing wage law bonanza:

> The existence of prevailing wage legislation and the unions' apparent ability to make government an active participant on their behalf in the administration of them has long sustained construction unions by simultaneously increasing the costs of non-union contractors, diminishing the competitive advantage their flexibility in job deployment offers, increasing non-union contractor risks of enforcement and penalty actions, and rigging the contractor-selection process in favor of government preferment for the union way on public works. The construction unions' continuing ability to influence the administration of and set the agenda for prevailing wage laws, particularly the seldom-examined details of the rate setting process, is perhaps the most important factor for their continuing viability.[24]

A Discouraging Appeal Process for ABCers

DOL has provided a small ray of hope to disillusioned open shop builders who have the fortitude to bid on government projects. The agency tolerates a ponderous mechanism to challenge whether bureaucrats can be held responsible for their dishonest wage and benefits determinations. This "grievance procedure" is basically a fact-finding process that eventually ends before a Wage Appeals Board. Its decisions are final and binding.

Aggrieved non-union contractors who are under construction project bid-time constraints but want to challenge a phony DOL decision must produce their own rebuttal evidence before this Board. That means conducting a detailed private survey of local wages and employee benefits. The ritual consumes a tremendous amount of investigatory time, resources, and money.

Successful contractor challenges against DOL are rare, and a victory does not assure that the protestor who paid for the litigation will actually win the bid for the government contract involved. Many construction firms have neither the time, the expertise, nor the funds to undertake such an appeal. Even those contractors who try to challenge an outrageous DOL wage ruling frequently find that the government's review of their appeal isn't returned to their offices until after the project has been scheduled to begin. Most of the successful protests against DOL rulings have been achieved through expert assistance by ABC on behalf of its wronged members.

Federal Construction Exclusion of Semi-Skilled "Helpers"

Another archaic Davis-Bacon Act practice allows DOL to maintain a policy that only the three restrictive classes of workers noted before as provided in building trades union collective bargaining agreements (journeyman mechanics, their apprentices, and laborers) are applicable to prevailing wage determinations and only they can perform work on government projects.

Semi-skilled "helpers," whose role is to assist journeymen mechanics or other personnel, have been a subject of controversy in the construction industry for many years. They are used regularly by non-union builders for dozens of routine tasks in private sector construction work. On one particular day, for example, giant ABC member Kellogg Brown & Root employed 33,425 construction workers. In addition to journeymen mechanics and their apprentices, ten thousand of these KB&R employees were *helpers* who would not legally be allowed to perform Davis-Bacon work. Only 2,830 were laborers.[25]

Building trades leaders long before the reign of Baltimore's "Kingfish" Ellis in the 1950s consistently opposed the employment of helpers so that they didn't learn a trade and qualify to compete with union apprentices and journeymen mechanics for available work. Dr. Herbert Northrup, Professor Emeritus of Management at the Wharton School of the University of Pennsylvania, summarized the non-productive trade union rationale this way:

> "Helpers," as the name implies, assist craftsmen in their work by doing a variety of tasks including the "grunt work" of lifting heavy loads, service work, fetching materials, and picking up coffee, or even performing part of the craftsmen's work. The nature of the job requires the helper to toil close to the craft job and to the journeyman performing it. Consequently, the helper who is alert and ambitious learns how to perform much of the skilled work. In the terms

One of the most striking differences between a cat and a lie is that a cat only has nine lives.

MARK TWAIN
WRITER-HUMORIST

Government is the only known vessel that leaks from the top.

JAMES RESTON
COLUMNIST

of the trade, the helper "picks up" the skill. Therein lies the root of the controversy...

The helper who picks up the trade threatens the skilled craftsman. He not only provides competition for jobs in a business in which job-scarcity consciousness is a way of life, but if the former helper is accredited and admitted to the craft union, he is a potential replacement for the journeyman.

More commonly today, helpers are employees of open-shop contractors vying for the available work with union-trained skilled craftsmen. By accepting less remuneration than union journeymen, helpers restrain union wage acceleration. The determination of construction unions to eliminate such competition and potentially decisive strike-breaking has been at the heart of negative union policy toward helpers for almost a century.[26]

DOL Endorses a Ban on "Helpers"

DOL policy for many years—under conservative lobbying influence—grudgingly permitted the use of helpers on rare occasions. It only accepted proof that (1) "the scope of the helper's duties—meaning the physical tasks performed—was defined; (2) it could be differentiated from that of journeyman duties; (3) and it "prevailed" in the area."[27] To meet this heavy burden of proof, helpers could not use any "tools of the trade" and DOL did not consider the term "helper" to be synonymous with its approved "apprentice classification." In the realities of the construction industry, this rigid and impractical test was DOL legalese for an implicit declaration that use of the dreaded open shop helper job classification usually was forbidden on Davis-Bacon Act work.

This biased barrier meant that much semiskilled government construction work was wasted on the unneeded talents of skilled mechanics at their high-paid journeyman wage. And it limited employment access to needed entry-level jobs and upward training opportunities. The discriminatory and costly result was that non-union contractors working on federal projects faced a Hobson's choice of either not using their helpers at all or overpaying them at taxpayers' expense. The latter choice also creates bad employee relations. It causes jealousy among the same contractor's helpers who were not used on the government project and continued to perform private sector work at their lower regular rate of pay.

In response to vigorous advocacy by ABC, DOL finally revised the helper regulation in 1982 on the recommendation of the Ronald Reagan administration. With the approval of Secretary of Labor Raymond Donovan, this amended policy recognized that helpers are widely employed in private sector construction and it redefined a helper as a "semi-skilled worker who works under the direction of and assists a journeyman." The new Reagan "helper" regulation also permitted overlap of certain duties between the "assisting" helper and the "supervising" mechanic and allowed helpers "to use the tools of the trade."[28]

A Temporary "Helper" Victory for ABC

The AFL-CIO's Building Trades Department challenged this regulation's broadened helper class policy in the federal courts—and lost. The case was filed against Secretary of Labor Ray Donovan and his DOL. ABC supported DOL's new regulation with an *amicus curiae* (friend of the court) brief filed in the *Donovan* case by my law firm, and Senior Circuit Judge McGowan wrote the appellate court's unanimous affirmative opinion. He began by pointing out the Secretary's estimate that "the expanded use of helpers would save the government $363 million in construction costs."[29]

As further justification, Judge McGowan continued, "he [the Secretary] stated that the new rules will increase job opportunities for less skilled workers, including young people, women and minorities; encourage training; increase productivity; and enable more contractors to compete for government work." The judge also cited with approval an affidavit by the aforementioned Professor Herbert R. Northrup of Pennsylvania University that was filed in the case to the effect that "more efficient deployment of labor [such as by allowing extensive use of helpers] is one reason why open shop construction today [1983] controls 65 percent of all construction . . ."[30]

National ABC President Ed Frohling ('83), a Tucson, Arizona, mining contractor, reported the impact of this victory in the *Donovan* case to ABC members:

Labor disgraces no man; unfortunately, you occasionally find men who disgrace labor.

Ulysses Grant
18th president

When the U.S. Court of Appeals for the District of Columbia ruled last week in favor of most of the [Donovan] Labor Department's proposed regulations for administering the Davis-Bacon Act, they did more than just overturn an erroneous lower court ruling—they struck a blow for free enterprise. The mere fact that ABC has been able to push the Davis-Bacon issue to this level is a great step forward.

We have won the public's support for our position, and now have strong judicial backing as well. That's certainly a far cry from where we started out over 30 years ago! For ABC, naturally, this is an important milestone. But this is as much an individual victory as it is an Association achievement. All ABC members can take pride in their own contribution to the Davis-Bacon effort. We made a difference![31]

Infuriated by Judge McGowan's reasoning in the *Donovan* case, Big Labor lobbied a Democrat-controlled Congress in 1991 to sneak a rider into a supplemental appropriations bill which prohibited DOL from spending funds to implement the Reagan-Donovan helper regulation.[32] This tactic eventually backfired when it was reviewed by the same federal appellate court that decided the *Donovan* case. With the support of another *amicus curiae* brief for ABC by my law firm, not only was a broadened helper regulation approved again, but the unanimous decision of the court included these remarks by Circuit Court Judge Sentelli:

> Before discussing the substance of the regulations, we first note that the unions object to the authority of the Secretary [of Labor] to implement the helper regulations...The unions argue that the rider is permanent legislation [but] a provision contained in an appropriations bill operates only in the applicable fiscal year unless its language clearly indicates that it is intended to be permanent...In short, nothing in the rider affects the ability of the Secretary to promulgate the present regulation.[33]

Clinton Eliminates Government Use of "Helpers"

With the arrival in Washington of the pro-union Clinton administration in 1993, this expanded Reagan-Donovan helper regulation became "suspended indefinitely pending further review" under presidential executive edict.[34] In 1996, ABC, represented by my law firm, filed a lawsuit attempting to make DOL implement its own court-approved Reagan-Donovan helper regulation. The agency's secretary of labor—Alexis Herman—refused to do so "because of the policy's negative impact on formal [union] apprenticeship programs." Her inaction was upheld by a liberal federal district court because, among other reasons, "it was not arbitrary, capricious, or an abuse of discretion."[35]

ABC thereupon urged legislation in Congress (supported by the *Donovan* case victory) that would provide for the creation of helpers as an entry level fourth class of workers which would involve a separate DOL prevailing wage determination. Reporting to journeymen mechanics, helpers would assist at the job site by carrying and furnishing materials, tools, equipment, and supplies as well as cleaning and preparing work areas. They could also use the tools of the trade under a mechanic's supervision.

The Clinton administration blocked this proposal[36] and, in December of 2000, it resurrected an anti-taxpayer policy that reverts to the pre-Reagan-Donovan era definition of "helper" previously described. Under it, DOL protects a political payback to Big Labor by essentially eliminating helpers as a legitimate job classification to perform public sector Davis-Bacon work. In response, ABC's 42nd National President, Tom Musser ('00), told the news media:

> By refusing to designate wage rates for helpers who assist skilled journeymen, this new regulation forces employers to pay artificially inflated journeyman wages for entry level jobs, thereby pricing out and excluding much needed entrants into the industry.
>
> It is inexcusable that the [Clinton] Labor Department has promulgated a rule which codifies an obsolete, unworkable definition of helpers and fails to recognize prevailing practices throughout the industry. It is also troubling that this regulation, which will impede American workers who are seeking careers in the construction field, was enacted so that it goes into effect only a day before a new Bush [George W.] administration is to be sworn in at the White House.[37]

Political shenanigans and demagoguery are nothing new. What is new is the staggering hypocrisy and boldness of some elected officials today. They and their spinmeisters turn the truth into an appalling game of "parse the sentence."

BILL O'REILLY
THE O'REILLY FACTOR

Helpers Used in Private Sector Construction

In private sector open shop construction more than a half-million helpers are used regularly throughout the country today to reduce labor costs. As previously explained, they are job-rated between apprentices and laborers and perform both semi-skilled and unskilled tasks. At the same time, they provide a source of much-needed entrants into the industry and the opportunity to receive hands-on training as a stepping-stone to eventual journeyman status.

ABC recently told a House Oversight and Investigations Subcommittee that helpers are a vital stepping-stone to a career in the construction industry and should be recognized on public projects just as they are on private projects. Ronald Kinning, president of ABC member firm RK Mechanical of Colorado Springs, Colorado, testified that "despite what the current U.S. Department of Labor tries to claim, helpers exist and are widespread in the construction industry." Then he outlined results from a Bureau of Labor Statistics pilot study in Jacksonville, Florida, which found that helpers comprise more than 10 percent of the private sector construction labor force.

Kinning gave several examples of successful employees at his company who began their careers as helpers, including a vice president. And he, too, started out as a helper: "If I did not have that opportunity as a young man to learn and grow in the construction business, I may not have been able to establish and maintain my $70 million company today," he concluded.[38]

The National Labor Relations Board has long accepted the fact that helpers are an integral part of an employer's workforce in the private sector and qualify for representation by a craft union. In its landmark *U.S. Potash Company and International Association of Machinists* case, the Labor Board held as follows, with regard to diesel mechanic helpers:

We believe that the record in this case impels a different result with respect to the *journeyman helpers*. It now appears that the journeyman helpers are normally assigned to work with specific journeymen of a particular

REPRINTED WITH PERMISSION; *WASHINGTON TIMES* GRAPHICS (VALEO I.P.)

craft, and devote their time, with insubstantial exceptions, to assisting them. Moreover, the employer's policy is to promote journeyman helpers to journeyman status whenever possible, and such promotions have occurred in numerous instances.

It is thus clear that the *journeyman helpers* are the type of employees whom we would customarily include with craftsmen in directing a self-determination [union representation] election, and we shall therefore afford these employees the opportunity, at this time, to indicate their desires with respect to joining the crafts to which they are regularly assigned . . .[39] [emphasis added]

Clinton Tries to Expand Union Scale Coverage

As recently as the year 2000—to further reward political supporters in organized labor—President Bill Clinton and his administration attempted *unsuccessfully* to broaden, complicate, and increase the cost to taxpayers of federal (union-scaled) prevailing wage coverage under the Davis-Bacon Act by *expanding* the "site of the work" in the "designated area." This radical ploy would have included wages and benefits paid for third party material and supply services located at tool yards that were "dedicated to the covered project" or "adjacent or virtually adjacent to the project." It would also have included "secondary sites other than the project's final resting place at which a significant portion of the public construction is performed."[40]

The national news media remained voiceless on the subject.

Racial Discrimination by Big Labor under Davis-Bacon

It is also paradoxical that alleged racial bias that was the original impetus for passage of the Davis-Bacon Act "still echoes seventy years later." Nationally, African-American workers account for more than 10 percent of the total workforce, but in the construction industry these blacks represent "only 6.4 percent of all workers" and have been "contractually shut out of unions."[41]

According to the Center for the Study of American Business, there is "considerable evidence that the Davis-Bacon Act and state prevailing wage laws [with their ban on helpers] serve to reduce employment opportunities for minorities, particularly African-Americans."[42] Another review of "Minority

Employment in the Construction Trades," by Farell Bloch, estimates that "across 162 large U.S. metropolitan areas...repeal of the Davis-Bacon Act would increase construction employment for 27,000 minorities and 10,000 laborers."[43] This discrimination is sustained by union hiring halls, restrictive union journeyman-apprentice ratios, and union contractual bans on the use of helpers.

Harry Alford, president of the National Black Chamber of Commerce, testified on this sensitive subject before a subcommittee of the House Committee on Education on July 21, 1999. He predicted that allowing helpers to participate at federally funded workplaces would improve participation of low-income minority workers "by promoting an environment that more closely resembles the make-up of America and also helps small minority-owned businesses to compete for federal contracts." And Alford concluded: "The Davis-Bacon Act has racist roots...and contributes to the under-representation of blacks. The bitterness and disgust of capable black workers and black business owners is starting to boil."[44]

Similar charges of racial discrimination under Davis-Bacon have been made by the Institute of Justice as well as the National Association of Minority Contractors, located in Washington, D.C. A 1995 treatise recommending repeal of the Davis-Bacon Act by Professors Richard Vedder of Washington University at St. Louis and Lowell Gallaway of Ohio University called the Davis-Bacon Act "arguably one of the most insidiously racist forms of federal legislation ever passed in the United States."[45] And writing in the *Journal of Labor Research* in 2003 on "Race and Prevailing Wage Laws In Construction," Dr. A. J. Thieblot concluded statistically that "between 1970 and 1990, blacks fared better in construction employment in states where prevailing wage laws were weaker, and best where there were none."

Auditors and Congress Lambaste DOL Today

To sum up this fossilized Davis-Bacon Act travesty, one-sided determinations which rubber-stamp inflationary union-scale wages and fringe benefits as well as their restrictive work rules and job classifications frequently originate from survey information that is outdated or non-existent. At other times the determinations are the result of the solicitation, transcription, and interpretation of data that is provided in sloppy, inaccurate, or fictitious form by government drones and their favored union contributors.

Both innocent and intentional "mistakes" thus frequently occur. These bureaucratic machinations cause most open shop contractors to become discouraged and refuse to bid on projects covered by the Davis-Bacon Act. This decision, in turn, deprives the taxpaying public of savings achieved through free market competition. It would result in lower government construction costs because of projects awarded to the lowest qualified bidders, regardless of union or non-union affiliation.

In 1979 the Comptroller General of the United States testified frankly about this rarely publicized and politically incorrect scandal before a Senate oversight hearing on Davis-Bacon:

> After nearly 50 years of administering the Act, the Department of Labor has not developed a system to plan, control or manage the data collection, compilation, and wage determination issuance functions under the Davis-Bacon Act. In fact, the policies, practices and procedures developed by DOL for establishing wage rates under the Act have only rarely implemented the legislative intent.[46]

In 1996 the U.S. General Accounting Office ("GAO") reemphasized the seldom publicized fact that DOL's process for determining wages under Davis-Bacon "includes weaknesses that could permit the use of fraudulent or inaccurate data for setting prevailing rates." Such "central weaknesses in the system can lead to increased government construction costs not required by law," declared GAO, stating the obvious.[47] Its study found errors in 70 percent of the wage determination forms submitted to DOL, thus inflating the prevailing wage estimates by an average of seventy-six cents an hour.[48] A similar report by the U.S. Office of the Inspector General, conducted at the request of ABC, concurred.[49]

The Congressional Budget Office ("CBO") options report for 2001 estimated that the federal government could save $9.5 billion from 2002 to 2011 if Congress repealed the Davis-Bacon Act. In addition, reported CBO, "it would increase the opportunities for employment that federal projects would offer to

Energy and efficiency are equal to desire and purpose.

SHERYL ADAMS
WRITER

less skilled workers." Even by raising the Act's threshold coverage from the current $2,000 to $1 million, concluded CBO, "the federal government could save $1.3 billion in federal outlays over the 2002 to 2011 period.[50] Comparative cost savings would be made by repeal of "Little Davis-Bacon Acts" at the state level.[51]

Adopting a report unveiled on October 2, 2003, by House Budget Committee Chairman Jim Nussle (R-IA), a majority of the members of the House Education and Workforce Committee recommended the repeal or curtailment of the Davis-Bacon Act as one way to eliminate waste, fraud, and abuse in the federal government. "The application of Davis-Bacon has been demonstrated to inflate construction costs on average from five to 15 percent, and in some instances up to almost 40 percent," the Workforce Committee said. "Moreover, the determination of 'prevailing wages' by the Department of Labor has been documented to be rife with abuse."[52]

In spite of these irrefutable charges against the operation of the Davis-Bacon Act, this seventy-five-year-old federal travesty is still given the silent treatment by the elite news media and all branches of government.

One Brave and Honest Government Official

No discussion of the nation's statutory prevailing wage law subterfuge should end without honorable mention of Brenda Reneau, a former ABC chapter executive director who became Oklahoma's secretary of labor. She was lauded for her courage because she exposed flagrant Davis-Bacon Act fraud. In the process, she also saved her state's taxpayers millions of dollars while undergoing threats of bodily harm and loss of her life. A *Wall Street Journal* editorial in 1996 reported her courageous story, but it was ignored by the left wing mainstream media:

> Economists have shown that Davis-Bacon freezes out many lower-skilled workers, primarily black or Hispanic, from jobs on these projects. What hasn't been known until now is that many Davis-Bacon "prevailing wages" appear to have been calculated using fictitious projects, ghost workers and companies set up to pay artificially high wages. Taxpayers may be paying top dollar for construction projects but getting fewer schools, prisons and bridges built than they should.

Brenda Reneau, Oklahoma's secretary of labor, found that many of the wage survey forms submitted to the U.S. Department of Labor to calculate federal wage rates in her state were simply wrong. Records showed that an underground storage tank was built using 20 plumbers and pipefitters making $21.05 an hour. No such project was ever built. In another case several asphalt machine operators were reported to have constructed a parking lot at an IRS building and been paid $15 an hour. In reality, no asphalt operators were used to build the concrete lot and the actual Davis-Bacon wage should have been $8 an hour.

Speaker Newt Gingrich (R-GA) discusses revelations of fraud in the administration of the Davis-Bacon Act in Oklahoma. At right is Oklahoma Labor Commissioner Brenda Reneau, who received ABC's Distinguished Public Service Award for her leadership in bringing Davis-Bacon fraud into the public eye.

Ms. Reneau says she was thwarted for months in her efforts to learn whether union officials or contractors submitted the bogus forms. She notes that federal labor officials "completely stonewalled" her by claiming much of the information fell into the same category as "trade secrets." "They have publicly denied the fraud and resisted our investigation," she maintains. Back home, she has been threatened with physical harm for her troubles. "I've been told my life is worth about $1,000, and that my legs could be broken for $500," she says. . . .

Ms. Reneau has established that two of the inflated wage reports were filled out by union officials. They, in turn, claim that any mistakes were either innocent or the fault of government officials. . . . Ms. Reneau would like to end Davis-Bacon. She calls it a "welfare program" that is being used to "lie to federal officials and steal from taxpayers." But the White House has been an arch-defender of Davis-Bacon, with President Clinton himself promising to veto any repeal effort. The Clinton Administration talks about the need to create jobs. At the same time, it is preserving a fraud-riddled program that blocks employment opportunities for unskilled inner-city residents.

Our cause is noble: it is the cause of mankind's freedom. The danger is allowing it to be undermined by ourselves.

GEORGE WASHINGTON
1ST PRESIDENT

This Administration's rhetoric is at war with the reality it is helping to create.[53]

This valiant "whistle blowing" action of Oklahoma's state secretary of labor, Brenda Reneau, caused Congressman J. C. Watts (R-OK) to salute her as "an outstanding government official who believes in the merit shop and has the backbone to take a stand against government waste, not just give it lip service."[54]

To this day ABC fights for repeal of the Davis-Bacon Act farce and its state law counter parts. The Association regularly defends its members against phony union allegations of violations of these labor statutes and leads the attacks by ABC members and chapters on government's discriminatory and/or fraudulent enforcement of the legal relics. But so far, only ten states have repealed or eliminated their "Little Davis-Bacon Acts" (after Arizona became the first to do so in 1979), while fourteen states have passed new or stronger pro-union prevailing wage statutes.[55] Congress still keeps the "parent" act alive and well as a political payback to Big Labor.

It would seem that times haven't changed much since Mark Twain defined public servants as "persons chosen by the citizenry to distribute the graft."[56]

CHAPTER 17

SAFETY FIRST!

BUILDING AND CONSTRUCTION has always been a dangerous field of endeavor. For the careless worker, there are potential hazards everywhere. Even the careful worker must be vigilant. About 6 percent of the nation's workforce is employed in this industry yet it accounts for a disproportionate 20 percent of all occupational fatalities and 12 percent of the disabling injuries. More than three-fourths of these accidents are the result of human error rather than failure of a physical system.[1]

Employees must scale heights, perform on busy highways, around heavy moving equipment, in tunnels or deep earth cuts, and in other confined spaces. They work in water, heat, and frigidness, near toxic substances, high noise levels, extreme electrical voltages, and powerful explosives. There can be an errant step on a girder set hundreds of feet above ground level...or an automatic saw buzzing a few inches from hands and torso...or a forklift swerving around a blind corner and dropping a load of metal slats...The list of precarious situations is endless.

From the day of its founding in 1950, the watchword of ABC has been "safety first, last and always." In order to receive a charter, each new chapter must have in place an active safety committee. A staff safety director is hired as soon as the local budget permits.

It comes as no surprise that the hostile building trades have attempted to characterize open shop contractors as grossly negligent in safety matters. These unions often keep records of alleged safety "missteps" by ABCers and then file trumped-up complaints or encourage unnecessary inspections by government

There are safe and unsafe ways of doing nearly everything. The knowledge or the knack of doing things safely is gained by experience, properly directed.

RALPH BUDD
RAILROAD EXECUTIVE

regulatory agencies at construction sites where ABCers are working. It doesn't cost a union anything to file a frivolous or exaggerated charge, but the ABC contractors involved must defend and defeat each case. Legal fees mount and valuable work time is wasted.

The only authentic nationwide study of construction fatalities available seems to be the one conducted by Charles Culver (Ph.D., P.E.), a former director of the Office of Construction and Engineering of the federal Occupational Safety and Health Administration ("OSHA"). It was reported in OSHA's Integrated Management Information System Data Base of 1985–93. Culver's study of 5,564 deaths found that fatality rates for unionized contractors' employees based on the number of deaths per 100,000 workers ranged from 20 percent to 35 percent higher than those for open shop contractors over each of the nine years studied.[2]

A National Safety Conference

Adopting the theme "Your Future Stake in Safety," ABC's sixth annual convention in 1963 was held at Atlantic City's Claridge Hotel and used to launch a national safety program. It featured employee education, training, and accountability. As an incentive to gain broad worker compliance, safety hard hats bearing the ABC emblem and other relevant prizes were given to employees to honor their long record of no lost-time accidents. Convention attendees also applauded these words of John West, a vice president of U.S. Fidelity and Guaranty Company in Baltimore:

> Every person prefers to work where the company has regard for him or her as a human being. The best means at the disposal of management to indicate this is to provide a safe place in which to work. This agenda also assures greater cost effectiveness on the job site through increased productivity and reduced insurance costs.
>
> The cooperative machinery of accident prevention—safety committees, managing stress on the jobsite, complying with safety laws, the coming together of supervisors and employees in safety meetings, the constant insistence on the fact that accidents can be eliminated only through cooperation between management and personnel on the

60 stories high. 10-inch girders.
18 mph winds...

The fire at the manufacturing plant was due to friction caused by a large inventory rubbing up against an insurance policy.

ANONYMOUS

job sites—all these help to bring about, in the minds of executives and workmen alike, a realization that they have common self-preservation interests to a high degree.[3]

A Union Tradesman's Accident Report

On the lighter side of a serious subject, it was reported at this same Atlantic City convention that one of the merit shop's most popular safety directors had adopted an amusing technique to gain the attention of enrollees in his basic training course on injury prevention. His pitch included the following fictitious "accident report" by a union tradesman who hoped to receive a substantial compensation award from a government agency:*

Dear Commissioner Safeway:

I am writing in respectful response to your request for additional information. In Block Number 3 of the Accident Report form, I wrote "Poor Planning" as the cause of my injuries. You said in your letter that I should explain more fully. I hope the following facts will help.

I am a union journeyman by trade and proud to be a member of Local 13 of the Benevolent Bricklayers Brotherhood. On the day of the accident, my apprentices were AWOL and so I was working alone on the roof of a new six-story building. When I completed my job, I noticed that I had about 400 pounds of brick left over. Rather than carry the bricks down to the first floor by hand, I decided to lower them in a nearby steel drum by using a rope and pulley (block and tackle) which was attached to the roof of the building.

After securing the pulley rope at ground level, I returned to the rooftop, swung the drum out, and loaded the bricks into it. Then I went back to the ground and untied the rope, holding it tightly to provide a slow descent of the 400 pounds of brick. (You will note in

---

*This fable did not originate with the author.

We're only here for a spell, so get all the good laughs you can.

WILL ROGERS
COMEDIAN-PUNDIT

A typical Laurel and Hardy construction project.

Block Number 10 of the Accident Report form that I weigh 145 pounds.)

Due to my surprise at being jerked off the ground so suddenly, I forgot to let go of the pulley rope. Needless to say, I proceeded at a rather accelerated rate up the side of the building.

In the vicinity of the third floor, I met the steel drum filled with bricks as it was proceeding downward at an equally high speed. This explains the 28 stitches for the gash in my skull, the skin graft of a new left ear and my broken collarbone, as listed in Block Number 3 of the Accident Report. Slowed only temporarily as I bounced around the drum, I continued my rapid ascent up the side of the building.

You cannot escape the responsibility of tomorrow by evading it today.

ABRAHAM LINCOLN
16TH PRESIDENT

At approximately the same time, however, the drum of bricks hit the ground—and the drum's bottom fell out. Without the load of bricks, the broken drum now only weighed about 50 pounds. (I refer you again to my own weight in Block Number 10 of the Report.) As you might imagine, I immediately began a swift drop down the side of the building.

In the vicinity of the fourth floor, I met the drum again, this time on its way back up the block and tackle. That accounts for my bruised groin, four broken teeth, two fractured ankles, severe lacerations of my legs and lower body, and the ruptured spleen. (See Block Number 4.) Fortunately this second encounter with the drum slowed my descent enough to avoid any fatal injury. As I fell onto the pile of bricks, on the ground, three vertebrae were cracked. (See Block Number 5.)

I'm sorry to report, however, that at this point I had some really bad luck. As I lay there on the pile of bricks, in considerable pain and unable to stand up—while watching the empty drum swaying six stories above me—I lost control and let go of the pulley rope. Since the steel drum weighed more than the rope, the drum immediately gravitated back down on me and broke both my kneecaps plus five ribs. (See Block Number 6.)

I hope I have furnished the information you needed as to how the accident happened. Therefore, I respectfully request that the first Worker's Compensation Award check for my 99 percent permanent partial disability be forwarded to me promptly...

Yours in Brotherhood,
Joe Union

Some Practical Safety Guidelines

Returning to a serious vein, the following safety rules were distributed to the Atlantic City conventioneers and published in ABC's *Contractor* magazine in 1963:

• Establish a new-hire safety orientation program.

- Train supervisors to recognize safety hazards, make regular field safety inspections for corrections, and never take dangerous short cuts.

- Provide an ongoing program to teach employees about safe working conditions and the safe use and proper maintenance of tools and equipment.

- Insist that employees follow established safety regulations as to all work procedures, including hard hats, safety shoes, glasses and special clothing. Add penalties for violations and rewards for accomplishments.

- Review all workers compensation cases and lost-time accidents. Talk to the employees involved and their supervisors. Discover whether the cause was failure of equipment, negligence on the part of some employee, or an unavoidable accident.

- Remember that the entire workplace team has a human relations responsibility as well as a legal obligation and a profit motive to operate safely at all times.

It is a truth but too well known that rashness attends youth as prudence does old age.

CICERO
LAWYER, POLITICIAN,
PHILOSOPHER

ABC also encouraged the conventioneers at Atlantic City to use a series of safety talks prepared for their employees that featured videotapes, "how to" manuals, and other instructional materials. Topics discussed included accident investigations, demolition, "horseplay" at the jobsite, and working on scaffolds.

Since drug and alcohol impairment are a great threat to workplace safety, ABC unveiled an onsite "rapid response" testing procedure for new job applicants plus a program for random and post-accident testing of current employees. That service has expanded today into a comprehensive and cost-effective substance abuse testing program on a national basis.

Nixon's Safety Statute

In 1970, a major new law in the safety field—the Occupational Safety and Health Act ("OSHA")—was passed on President Richard Nixon's watch. Its stated objective is "to ensure so far as possible every working man and woman in the nation safe and healthy working conditions." And "a general duty to furnish a place of employment free from hazards" was placed on all employers.

**Incongruous:
where laws
are made.**

BENNETT CERF
HUMORIST-WRITER

While ABC endorsed the Act's overall goal, it opposed the reams of onerous and unnecessary rules, regulations, postings, record keeping, and reporting requirements that accompanied it. ABC also objected to the government's hostile enforcement attitude that included unannounced jobsite inspections, unreasonable non-compliance citations, exorbitant fines, and unnecessary threats of felony prosecution.

Under OSHA's terms, the secretary of labor and his inspectors became analogous to all-powerful policemen who were given the authority to act as legislator, prosecutor, judge, and jury. They promulgated workplace safety and environmental standards and enforced them through injunctive, monetary, and criminal sanctions. The employer under investigation frequently was faced with a presumption of guilt and risked a series of protracted intra-agency appeals to defend itself.

ABC National reacted by holding a workshop for all chapter safety directors and safety committee chairpersons. It briefed them on highlights of the legislation, outlined effective employee training programs, and concluded with a question-and-answer session. A prominent safety consultant and trainer led the seminar. He stressed the need for ABC National to develop a uniform safety agenda for all of its members "because OSHA is legislation with crocodilian teeth."

Next, ABC's National Safety Committee established a legal counseling system through its network of Chapter attorneys to assist members in explaining and complying with the complexities of the new statute in its embryonic and constantly changing stage. Even a former chairman of the Occupational Safety and Review Commission who resigned in disgust, Robert Moran, asked: "Why can't OSHA administrators say what the Act means—if they know?" He charged that "the standards are vague, sloppy, meaningless and useless. They make employers the scapegoats for work accidents and make employees guinea pigs."[4]

ABC's executive vice president, John Trimmer, described the critical impact of this poorly drafted but far-reaching national safety law on member contractors:

> When the OSHA regulations became effective, many in the construction industry were stunned and confused. In the rough and tumble

of daily work, most of these new regulations were outlandishly impractical or confusing and, at times, trivial too. The bureaucrats who drafted them seemed to make an effort to complicate normal work on the jobsite.

Nonproductive construction costs to comply with the new standards reached 30 percent or more on new safety devices, new environmental controls and the administrative burden of compliance.

ABC members also were wary of federal agents in view of their close relationship with trade union officials. It was feared that the new regulations would provide another excuse to meddle with contractors' right to operate on a merit shop basis. These fears were eventually confirmed. An Associated Press study of 778,000 OSHA inspections conducted from 1989 to 1995 showed that one-third of the inspections prompted by complaints turned up no violations at all. In fact, more than half of all complaints filed failed to find any serious violation.[5]

It's not too long; it just seems like it is.

YOGI BERRA
N.Y. YANKEES
CATCHER-PHILOSOPHER

A Management Representative Sounds the Alarm

One of the summaries of the absurdities promulgated by Congress in its passage of OSHA (and an exposure of unnecessary government restrictions on free enterprise) was written by Arch Booth, executive vice president of the Chamber of Commerce of the United States in 1972. He called his critique "OSHA Hunts Flies with an Elephant Gun."

Here are a few excerpts:

> A law should not be so complex that it cannot be understood by those who must live under it. But many of OSHA's regulations are a mystery to any small business, which cannot afford to keep a staff of highly trained experts, as do the big corporations. For example, there are 11 pages of regulations relating to ladders, their construction and use. How many different ladders should the average small business use? How long would it take the firm to see if it's in compliance with just this one regulation?

Arch Booth concluded with a ray of hope:

The business of government is to keep government out of business.

Will Rogers
Humorist-Actor

Congress, which passed this law in haste, under intense pressure from labor unions and other special interest groups, is now taking a second look, under equally intense pressure from outraged small businesses. The Occupational Safety and Health Administration might find that is a wise course to follow with respect to its own practices, too. It clearly needs to become more educational and less punitive. After all, nobody wants accidents, but there are legitimate grounds for disagreement on the best ways to prevent them.[6]

To establish a practical guide through this maze of safety audits, edicts and reporting requirements and to counteract the government's pro-union interpretive "spin," ABC published a first-of-its-kind "Guide to Construction Safety." The indexed manual soon became a best seller throughout the industry—and publicly embarrassed the federal government into a fairer administration of its new safety law. "Safety-grams" were sent to all ABC members whenever newly released OSHA information was of sufficient importance to warrant immediate concern, and chapter safety directors worked directly with member contractors in their compliance programs.

Reacting to this flood of criticism from the construction industry, in 1976 the U.S. Department of Labor provided ABC with the first OSHA instructors' course in the nation. In addition to classroom training, ABC chapters were able to sponsor mock safety inspections, relying upon this OSHA compliance guide to determine potential violations. Feigned citations were issued in an effort to provide members with an insight into what they might anticipate during an actual inspection by a government agent.

The "Fortune 200" Business Roundtable, discussed previously, instituted an annual National Safety Excellence Award in 1988. Prizes are presented during the ABC national convention. Since that first award, 75 percent of the winners of this prestigious citation have been ABC members. Some of them are BE&K, Inc. of Birmingham, Alabama; Kellogg, Brown & Root of Texas; Bancroft Construction Company of Wilmington, Delaware; Industrial Services of Mobile, Alabama; and Gulf States, Inc. from Freeport, Texas.[7] All in all, ABC contributed a giant step out of the chaos in the construction workplace caused by OSHA and its discriminatory enforcement.

A Modern ABC-OSHA Agency Partnership

Today—in stark contrast to those early years of prosecutorial presumption and bureaucratic bungling—ABC members have learned to live with "enlightened" OSHA agents under the George W. Bush administration. They are construing the law in a more reasonable manner, and the Association has become a member of the agency's Employer Advisory Committee. To advance the mutual goal of providing a safe and healthful work environment in the construction industry, OSHA and ABC also have developed an unusual relationship that provides ABC member firms with a step-by-step program to attain excellence in safety and avoid biased government inspections followed by prejudiced punitive actions.

The primary incentive in this partnership is a first-of-its-kind agreement that awards a privileged "STEP Platinum" status to ABC contractors who meet certain safety standards. Once OSHA verifies through an audit that a contractor has met these fair-but-strict safety goals, its work sites are removed from OSHA's targeted inspection list for the next twelve months.

OSHA also will agree that unprogrammed target inspections are conducted only in response to legitimate reports of imminent danger, fatalities, catastrophic accidents, or signed complaints. No penalties are issued for non-serious violations that are promptly abated, and citations are reduced by the maximum amount for the employer's "good faith."

This public-private sector partnership agreement between OSHA and ABC also requires that local ABC chapter safety committees visit construction sites and verify data submitted by contractors seeking to qualify as STEP Platinum members. It is the responsibility of ABC's national safety director to sponsor random site verification visits and submit annual reports to OSHA's construction directorate. In turn, OSHA will inspect less than 10 percent of the applicable construction sites to verify STEP Platinum program compliance.

Under what OSHA calls "a model plan for future employer collaborations," ABC chapters have become key players in administering the provisions of this novel initiative. Four of the earliest qualifiers were the Ohio Valley Chapter (Dennis Nutley, president, and Kathleen Somers, executive director); the Oklahoma Chapter (James Beeman, president, and Carl Williams, executive director); the Hawaii Chapter (Clarice Cornett, president, and Carl Williams,

The only real security that a person can try to have in this world is a reserve of knowledge, experience, and ability.

HENRY FORD
INDUSTRIALIST

231

Behavior is a
mirror in which
everyone shows
his image.

JOHANN WOFGANG VON
GOETHE
PHILOSOPHER

executive director); and the Wisconsin Chapter (Robert Stephenson, president, and Stephen Stone, executive director).

In liaison with its affiliated National Center for Construction Education and Research ("NCCER," discussed in chapter 12), a state-of-the-art modular program provides industry-based training for the safety directors of ABC members and all other personnel throughout their firms. This program is recognized by OSHA as equivalent to or better than its own agenda.

The national OSHA Agency-ABC partnership has received recognition in construction trade magazines and newspapers, including *Engineering News-Record* and the *Wall Street Journal*. And every year ABC recognizes its member companies whose safety accomplishments are exemplary. As further recent evidence of a more fair and balanced administration of U.S. Department of Labor policies, the *Bureau of National Affairs* reported as follows in June 2002:

> Labor Secretary Elaine L. Chao (R-KY), appointed by President George W. Bush, plans to unveil a strategy to "bring transparency" to what she describes as a "regulatory jungle." In a speech that Chao delivered before the National Federation of Independent Business on June 14, the Labor Secretary pledged to the business group that there "is a new culture of responsibility being built at the Department of Labor—a responsibility for us to help you understand our exhaustive list of regulations." The new initiative, according to Chao, involves a "process of painstakingly and deliberately" making information in the extensive regulations promulgated by DOL more understandable to employers.
>
> Secretary Chao, in her remarks, also plans to announce creation of a new and permanent senior agency within DOL: a director in charge of compliance assistance. With respect to specific enforcement agencies, Chao also intends to create an agency within the Occupational Safety and Health Administration that will be "dedicated to small business and function absolutely separately from inspection officers."[8]

Affordable Health Care

Safety and health care are twin requisites in the workplace. ABC's Region 5 Vice Chairman Bill Fairchild (president of R.W. Murray Co., Manassas, Va.)

met with President George W. Bush and a panel of four other small business owners recently to discuss the health care needs of small business owners and their employees. Fairchild shared his firm's experience in the health care arena and expressed the need for Congress to pass association health plan ("AHP") legislation:

> We had a great plan through ABC, and if we can get it passed again, it will allow my business and the other 23,000 members of our Association to pool together and get better coverage at a better price. That will put us on a level playing field with big businesses, labor unions, and other entities that are able to get coverage nationwide.[9]

President Bush agreed: "Another way to make sure that small businesses can survive and provide care for their employees is through association health

CONSTRUCTION EXECUTIVE PHOTO, APRIL 2004

President George W. Bush and Bill Fairchild, far right, ABC's Region 5 vice chairman and president of R.W. Murray Co., meet with ABCers to discuss safety and health issues.

Things are not as bad as they seem. They are worse.

BILL PRESS
COMMENTATOR
(MSNBC)

plans. These would provide small businesses the same opportunity that big businesses [and other organizations] get."[10]

Workplace Dangers Increase

Unpredictable workplace violence by hostile employees, ex-employees, and their family members is a growing concern to management in the workplace. Mirroring today's amoral society, each year hundreds of employees are victims of crimes, beatings, stabbings, shootings, rapes, homicides, and other physical assaults at their jobsites.

Consider this incident: A former employee at a manufacturing plant returned to the worksite, shot and killed four employees, wounded several others—and then shot himself. The motive: he had been discharged after thirty-nine years of service.

From an economic perspective, workplace violence poses more than a safety issue. It creates recruitment and retention problems, lowers employee morale, increases absenteeism, disrupts productivity, and fosters litigation. It also contributes to psychological traumas and other mental health problems of employees, both bona fide and feigned. While no amount of precaution, planning, and training can totally eliminate these physical and emotional tragedies, a security audit is the obvious first step in preventive action since the cost of construction has increased by millions of dollars annually. An excellent article on "Workplace Violence Versus Employee Rights" by attorney Jerry Goldstein of Bethesda, Maryland, appeared in the January 2002 issue of the *Maryland Bar Journal*. He began the treatise this way:

> According to the Bureau of Labor Statistics, homicide is the second leading cause of fatal occupational injury in the United States. Nearly 1,000 employees are murdered and 1.5 million are assaulted in the workplace each year. In 1998 there were also 386,000 aggravated assaults, 51,000 rapes, and 84,000 robberies in the workplace. These figures mandate that employers take all reasonable precautions to protect their employees from harm and themselves from liability. However, an employer's precautionary efforts can clash with employee privacy and statutory rights.

Violence in the workplace can arise in four different contexts. The *first type* involves criminal intent where the perpetrator has no legitimate relationship with the employer or the employees and is usually committing a crime in connection with the violence. The vast majority of workplace homicides, some 85 percent, fall into this category, and the employees most at risk are those who exchange cash with customers as part of their job, work at night, or work alone.[11]

If you have a job without any aggravations, you don't have a job.

MALCOLM FORBES
PUBLISHER

Goldstein then listed *type two* violence as involving "a customer or client who has a legitimate relationship with an employee but becomes violent while being assisted by the employee." *Type three* is "worker-on-worker, where an employee or former employee attacks or threatens another employee in the workplace." *Type four* occurs "where the perpetrator has a personal relationship with an employee but usually does not have a relationship with the employer." This fourth situation, concludes Goldstein, "typically arises out of a domestic dispute involving a current or former spouse or close friend and the majority of the victims are female."[12]

In 2002, the National Institute of Occupational Safety and Health ("NIOSH"), a part of the Centers for Disease Control, issued a "current intelligence bulletin" on violence in the workplace. It stated that major factors which increase workers' risk for assault in the workplace include: contact with the public, exchange of money, having a mobile workplace, working with unstable or volatile persons who are in heath care or criminal justice settings, working alone or in small groups, working late at night or during early morning hours, in high-crime areas, guarding valuable property or possessions, and in community based settings.

Management's Duty to Provide a Safe Workplace

For many years, violent acts involving employees in the workplace were considered outside the scope of employment and employers were not held responsible for "resulting repercussions." In today's liberal age of personal entitlement, however, the legal ground rules have changed. Under the expanding common law of "employment rights" that punishes "negligence" in hiring, retention, and discipline "plus occupational safety and health statutes and

No doubt Jack
the Ripper
excused himself
on the grounds
that it was
human nature.

A. A. MILNE
WRITER

workers' compensation laws," employers now are required to provide "a reasonably safe work environment for their personnel."[14]

In *Gant v. Security USA, Inc.*, for example, a divided federal Court of Appeals recently held that a female Maryland security guard who was kidnapped from work—and then raped and tortured—could take an employer's "intentional infliction of emotional distress" claim to trial. A majority of the judges held she could allege that her employer, despite a protective order, placed her in danger when she was assigned to an isolated location where she feared for her life.[15] Today OSHA asserts that "an effective safety and health program for preventive workplace violence must include components for (1) management commitment and employee involvement; (2) work-site analysis; (3) hazard prevention and control; and (4) training."

To a lesser degree, outsiders such as business visitors, family, friends, and the general public also may be entitled to protection. Politically correct Big Brother Government is turning from punishing the perpetrators of these crimes to forgiving them as politically favored plaintiffs' tort lawyers and leftist judges are creating new defenses. Criminals are avoiding responsibility for their premeditated actions because they have become "the victims of society" and rely on an "abuse excuse" allegedly related to their heredity or environment. *The truth is that socialistic employment law is paralyzing the American workplace.*[16]

International Terrorism Intensifies Safety Needs

As all the world knows, international terrorists hijacked three American commercial airplanes and kamikaze-style bombed the twin 110-story skyscrapers known as the World Trade Center in New York City and the Pentagon in Washington, D.C., on September 11, 2001. The heroic passenger-created crash of a fourth terrorist-stolen airliner at Shanksville in southwestern Pennsylvania (about ninety miles short of its intended White House or Congress target) occurred the same morning. These devilish deeds, committed by fanatics of Arab, Middle Eastern, and South Asian origins and Muslim religious backgrounds, collectively murdered *3,025* civilians from *80* different nations and the American workplace showed its vulnerability to an immeasurable new danger: *international terrorism.*[17]

Our nation and the entire planet were the direct or indirect victims of a traumatic event. It required assessment of the human, physical, emotional, and economic toll exacted by these combination suicide-murder missions and potential new atrocities that the future holds. Amidst the carnage and rubble, one thing became certain: the safety level of our nation and its infrastructure has changed forever.[18]

On September 20, 2001, President George W. Bush addressed a joint session of Congress about this vital subject. Here are a few words from that speech which was televised and radioed to over 100 million Americans. It is considered to be one of the great presidential orations of modern times:

> All of this horror was brought upon us in a single day—and night fell on a different world, a world where freedom itself is under attack. Our grief has turned to anger and anger to resolution. Justice will be done...
>
> As long as the United States of America is determined and strong, this will not be an age of terror; this will be an age of liberty, here and across the world. We will not tire, we will not falter, and we will not fail...In all that lies before us, may God grant us wisdom and may He watch over the United States of America.

Three weeks later, President Bush addressed the General Assembly of the United Nations and warned its members about a worldwide "Axis of Evil." Here are excerpts from another historic speech:

> Every nation has a stake in this cause. As we meet, the terrorists are planning more murder—perhaps in my country or perhaps in yours...This threat cannot be ignored. This threat cannot be appeased. The very civilization we share is threatened. For every regime that sponsors terror, there is a price to be paid. And it will be paid. The allies of terror are equally guilty of murder and equally accountable to justice. The time for sympathy has passed; the time for action has arrived. Freedom and fear are at war!

We dare not tempt our enemies with weakness

JOHN F. KENNEDY
35TH PRESIDENT

On the six-month anniversary of September 11, 2001, President Bush warned the world of the greatest of all perils—*terrorist access to and use of biological, chemical, and nuclear weapons of mass destruction*: "These facts cannot be denied and must be confronted. There is no chance to learn from mistakes [and] inaction is not an option. People who have no regard for life must never control the ultimate instrument of death."

The Construction Industry Reacts

In March of 2002, *Engineering News-Record* reported positive news that the lethal attacks of "9-11"

> . . . brought America together in ways that the terrorists could not have imagined in their fog of religious and political zeal. The construction industry responded immediately and heroically to assist in the recovery of the dead and injured and later in the removal of about 1.5 million tons of debris. They worked in exceptionally dangerous conditions, yet there were so many volunteers that they had to be turned away in droves.[19]

The workplace obviously no longer has any luxury of complacency. All Americans are on the front lines in an endless war against international terrorism. ABC National, its local chapters, and member firms responded heroically to the "9-11" crisis with emergency persoanl assistance at "ground zero" in New York City and Washington, D.C., with a victims' relief fund, and with research on new materials, equipment, practices, and techniques for the protection of America's construction projects. (See Chapter 15.)

It is obvious that owners and managers of potential future targets for the religious and political Muslim fiends who despise America and all it stands for must employ skilled contractors. They will restore, rebuild, and modernize public and private facilities to lessen the vulnerability of the nation's people, facilities, and infrastructure from these evildoers.[20] And, as James Loy, head of the Transportation Security Administration added, in an order issued by the White House which made the AFL-CIO building trades furious: *"Mandatory collective bargaining [between labor unions and government] is not compatible with the flexibility required to wage war against terrorism."*[21]

A National Safety Conference

The consensus of a multi-disciplinary panel of public and private-sector construction professionals meeting in New York City shortly after September 11, 2001, was: "We will be more prepared when and if there is a next time." This conference, organized by *Engineering News-Record* and the *McGraw-Hill Construction Information Group*, reviewed the horrendous events of 9-11 and resulted in an action plan for dealing with the new terrorist threat to America's buildings and infrastructure. The symposium included senior officials from construction, design, and architectural firms, government procurement and construction offices, construction employer associations, and industry analysts. Participants addressed the immediate impact of the murderous attacks on the future of the construction industry and offered ideas on how the design and building of facilities might change.

Robert Prieto, a civil engineer and chairman of Parsons Brinckerhoff, based in New York City, ended this national conference as follows:

> A major challenge facing the design community will be to develop performance levels for myriad edifices from infrastructure to public, commercial and residential buildings. Remember the three Rs of threat design: "Design to *resist* the threat. Design to *respond* to the threat. Design to *recover* from the threat."[23]

ABC will continue to play a major role in educating and training the construction community and the public about new techniques, tools, materials, manpower, instrumentation, and accommodations to protect America's workplace. In the deadly serious business of building and maintaining facilities and infrastructure, there is no greater guardian of security, morale, productivity, and profitability than a premier safety program firmly and fairly enforced for the benefit of all concerned.

The Patriot Act takes account of the new realities and dangers posed by modern terrorists. It will help law enforcement to identify, to dismantle, to disrupt, and to punish terrorists before they strike.

PRESIDENT GEORGE W. BUSH AT PATRIOT ACT SIGNING CEREMONY ON OCTOBER 26, 2001

CHAPTER 18

FROM BOYCOTTS TO BALLOTS

TWO FACTORS MOTIVATED some of the building trades unions to try a change in their organizational tactics against ABCers in the 1960s. First, the young Association's *Stover Steel* legal victory in 1955 solidified the Supreme Court's *Denver Building Trades* case which forbad secondary boycott picketing at a common construction site.[1] Second, these union boycotts even began to alienate "neutral" union members by forcing them out of work and out of pay on a so-called "sympathy strike" caused by a labor dispute not of their own making and not involving their own union or their own employer.

In desperate straits due to ABC's rapid growth, the trade unions turned to a *legitimate* employee representation procedure that they had traditionally ignored. It simply consisted of an exercise of their legal and democratic right to unionize workers by majority vote of the eligible employees. This method— called "bottom up" organizing—has been used regularly by industrial unions ever since the passage of the original Wagner Act of 1935 and its successor Taft-Hartley Act in 1947, with some success.

Under the labor law's government-sponsored procedure, a union can set in motion the National Labor Relations Board's secret ballot election mechanism by filing a "representation election" petition. The document must be accompanied by union membership authorization "pledge cards" signed individually by at least 30 percent of the employees in what the union contends is an "appropriate bargaining unit" within the targeted construction firm.

Union organizers obtain this required 30 percent "showing of interest" to initiate an election procedure in many ways. Their tactics run the gamut from "coaxing" workers to sign a card during fraternal beer parties held at the union hiring hall to one-on-one "sales pitches" featuring promises of future wage and benefits increases to be "forced" on the employer at the bargaining table, and— if all else fails—threats of dire consequences for a worker's failure to "sign up." Veteran union organizers know how to cope with the "fuzzy" legal distinction in this card-signing procedure between permissible "persuasion" and illegal "coercion" of the targeted employees. It thus becomes difficult for management to challenge and prove improper union campaign conduct to the Labor Board.

Once the petitioning union has proffered this 30 percent "showing of interest," in order to win an election, it must comply with Section 9(a) of the Taft-Hartley Act. This section provides that a union "selected [through a secret ballot election] for the purposes of collective bargaining by the *majority* of the employees in a *unit appropriate* for such purposes [as determined by the Labor Board] shall be the *exclusive* representatives of all the employees in such unit."

No other private organization has ever received such a unique and monopolistic privilege.

Determination of the Appropriate Unit

The size and composition of the "appropriate" bargaining unit for the election often becomes a subject of dispute between the petitioning union and the non-union employer-defendant in the representation case. This decision is critical since it determines whether the petitioning union may be entitled to proceed with any election in the targeted contractor's workforce. The union may enjoy majority support within some "incompatible group" of the workers (such as crossing craft lines) but may not be able to establish sufficient proof (30 percent) of representation in a different but legally "appropriate" unit. When the targeted employer and the union involved in the legal proceeding disagree on this issue of voting eligibility, the Labor Board makes the final decision after an administrative hearing with the parties. The Board's primary concern is to group together all non-supervisory employees who have "a substantial mutual interest in wages, hours, and other conditions of employment."

Trade union organizers thus faced the difficult problem of how to blend the open shop's flexible, multi-skilled, multi-craft journeymen, helpers, laborers, and pre-apprentice trainees into an "appropriate" bargaining unit which the organizers contended should be composed of the traditional, predetermined building trades apprentice-to-journeyman single craft groups and their separate trade unions.

As one construction trades union manual phrased the dilemma:

> Unfortunately, unorganized workers do not fall into the neat categories of [single craft] journeymen and apprentices recognized by our collective bargaining agreements and whom most unions are equipped to process as new members under their normal craft systems . . . Some local unions have attempted to deal with this problem by taking into membership only those craftsmen who passed journeyman examinations and proved minimum qualifications, while expecting or requiring contractors to get rid of and replace all others by using the [union hiring hall] referral procedure.

Then this union manual frankly posed two questions:

> How, then, does the union approach the organization of [legally appropriate] bargaining units which include subjourneymen categories? Must the union fail in recruiting majority support because the organizer cannot guarantee [to the non-union workers] a classification in jobs covered by the labor agreement or because certain workers must be told that they cannot be accepted into membership?[2]

The manual concluded that "this problem is one of the toughest to solve and is the single most damaging obstacle to both top-down and bottom-up construction union organizing."

At times, in desperation, a craft union has sought (illegally) to influence the result in a representation election campaign by trying to ignore the dilemma. Eligible voters are given a union membership card that allows them to work as skilled craftsmen without pretending to go through the requisite formal training and work experience required in the particular craft. "This gift," at least two federal courts have ruled, "smacked of an illegal purchase of votes."[3]

Salesmanship starts when the customer says "no."

GEORGE R. BOULÉ, JR.
PHILOSOPHER

Election Campaign Claims and Counter-Claims

In the course of these Labor Board–monitored representation election campaigns, the building trades union professional organizers would boast to targeted ABC employees about guaranteeing them "fair treatment" plus the higher wages and greater fringe benefits provided in their union's area-wide collective bargaining agreements. They even encouraged powerful left-wing politicians to support their cause. Here's a copy of an actual letter written by a Democratic African-American Congressman:

> Dear Employees,
>
> On September 26, it is my understanding that you will have an opportunity to take an important step toward making a big change in your life through a secret ballot election. Your vote for Union No. 88 would be one of the most positive moves you could make.
>
> Collective bargaining with your employer through your union is the best method I know of to get better wages, benefits, conditions and security, and to give you a better quality of life. Your right to this self-betterment is protected by federal laws. I sincerely hope you will not let fear deny you this great opportunity.
>
> I wish you the best in this wise endeavor.
>
> Sincerely,
>
> Parren J. Mitchell
>
> Member of Congress

ABC contractors countered by exercising their constitutional right to free speech by cautioning their employees to be careful about "what they signed" and by reminding them what they already enjoyed: equivalent or better income from steady, year-round employment and good fringe benefits in a stable, harmonious, long-term relationship. It was also pointed out that they worked the year 'round for one employer in a multi-skilled job with an opportunity to be promoted on individual ability, regardless of length of service.

ABC employers further explained, by way of comparison, that the trade unions usually provided intermittent work handed out by their business agents on a preferential project-by-project basis to senior favorites from union-controlled hiring halls. The Labor Board has ruled that "mere negligence" does not constitute an abuse of "union power." Therefore a trade union does not violate its statutory duty of "fair representation" when its negligent conduct in the operation of an exclusive hiring hall results in a union member's loss of an employment opportunity and when, after becoming aware of the dire consequences of its negligent action, the union failed to remedy the loss.[4] This disadvantage, said the ABCers, was combined with compulsory union membership dues and fines, loss of individuality, internal union politics, and strict union rules. There could also be under-the-table union "work permits" and "special assessments" paid in cash to union officials to hold jobs plus the risk of union-led strikes causing more loss of earnings.

To increase morale and productivity, most ABCers had instituted incentive bonuses and profit-sharing plans long before any union organizational drive occurred. They also bolstered their employees' *esprit de corps* through informal "rap sessions" with senior management on job-related problems as well as through purely social outings. No labor union contract contained these benefits, they noted.

Candid words from Mark Erlich, a member of Carpenters Local Union No. 40 in Chicago, exposed in detail many facts that are still true about building trades difficulties in organizing non-union construction workers:

> For all the physical hardships, it is the psychological insecurity of uncertain employment that drives many [union members] out of the trades. The boom-and-bust nature of the business means that no one can ever count on long-term security. Regional variations in job prospects are staggering, and the booms in any one area never last long. Even in the best of times, the oasis of overtime in the summer often is not enough to compensate for the wasteland of the winter months. Building trades workers average eight or nine months a year of employment, reducing the impact of their comparatively high hourly wages . . .
>
> An AFL-CIO official once remarked to a reporter that so little organizing took place in construction that "if you ask the 17 craft unions how to do it, you will get 17 different answers." In the prosperous

We are salesmen every day of our lives. We are selling our ideas, our plans, our enthusiasms to those with whom we come in contact.

CHARLES M. SCHWAB
PRESIDENT OF
BETHLEHEM STEEL CO.

A sample management "flyer" sent to employees' homes for the legally permissible purpose of attempting to persuade them not to sign union representation election authorization cards.

1950s, union leaders ignored trades workers outside their ranks, preferring to assure relatively stable employment through limits on membership size. Whatever organizing did occur was of the "top-down" variety—that is, "convincing" employers to sign a union contract.

The official attachment to top-down organizing and the reluctance to embrace "bottom-up" organizing cannot be simply attributed to post–World War II complacency. Organizing in construction *is* very difficult. Unlike potential bargaining units permanently ensconced in factory or office settings, a typical building employer's workforce is small and transient. Tradespeople shift from site to site, company to company, and city to city. Even on the largest sites, a full-blown organizing campaign with card-signings and Labor Board elections would almost invariably take longer than the life of the project.

There is another reason that building trades officials, particularly on the local level, resist grassroots ["bottom-up"] organizing. Given the economic insecurity of construction, rank-and-file union members hesitate to welcome unlimited numbers of new members. In an industry with no provisions for seniority, older union members frequently conclude that restricting membership is the only road to job protection.

Then Erhlich honestly listed more union organizational problems:

As understandable as the restrictive memberships point of view may be, it has proved disastrously counterproductive in the current era of the open shop. Many qualified non-union trades workers know the building trades unions only as institutions that have barred them. Thus, even the local unions that muster the courage to mount genuine "bottom-up" organizing campaigns must overcome hostility from the people they hope to organize. "*You don't want me, you just want the work*" is a standard comment hurled at building trades organizers. Given their limited bottom-up organizing experience and lukewarm membership backing, few organizers are able to overcome both non-union worker skepticism and union member fears while waging a difficult campaign against an anti-union employer...

A salesman minus enthusiasm is just a clerk.

HARRY BANKS
CONSULTANT

There is no
wisdom like
frankness.

BENJAMIN DISRAELI
BRITISH PRIME
MINISTER

What is clear is that decades of closed doors and restrictive union regulations have not prevented a devastating weakening of construction unions. They have, on the other hand, bred hostility among non-union trades workers, minorities, and other groups who have been the victims of exclusionary union policies.

Construction unions need to loosen restrictions and crack open their doors. This applies to the internal life of the union as well as outside. Since business agents are often in a position of referring workers to jobs, their political power is augmented by the economic control they hold over members' lives. As a result, internal democracy has not always flourished in post-war building trades unionism. This has had the effect of reducing participation in union activities and creating a large body of members who pay dues as a *pro forma* matter.[5]

The employees of ABC contractors who were undergoing Labor Board–supervised bottom-up organizational campaigns and union representation elections in the 1960s and 1970s listened intently to both sides of the "debate"—and consistently voted "**no union**." Like a prognosticator of future events, Judge Haynesworth wrote in ABC's *Selby-Battersby* secondary boycott case victory that "soliciting voluntary affiliation by employees of unorganized employers is not the traditional organizing means in the construction industry."[6]

That judicial divination proved to be the labor-management relations understatement of the twentieth century.

CHAPTER 19

A NEW LAW FIRM ENTERS THE FRAY

IT WAS AT ABOUT THIS TIME, coincidentally, that I resigned from my full-time job as in-house labor counsel to W. R. Grace & Co. I had been traversing North and South America for several years while tangling with both industrial and craft unions on behalf of that international corporation's chemical plants and sugar cane plantations. On June 15, 1961, to be exact, I reentered private law practice in Baltimore City by way of partnership with an astute and respected local labor lawyer, H. Raymond Cluster.

We flipped a coin to decide the name of the firm and I won the toss. Many of Cook & Cluster's early clients were leaders of the newly created Metropolitan Baltimore Chapter of ABC. Among these ABCers were its first and second presidents—Ira Rigger ('63-'64), a specialty contractor, and Ralph Ensor ('65), the CEO of John K. Ruff, Inc., a general contractor. We defeated building trades unions seeking to represent their employees through "bottom-up" secret ballot elections conducted by the Labor Board.

After one victory celebration, my clients presented me with a copy of an alleged olde english scroll dated 1750 and containing these words of wisdom:

> The compleat barrister should have a quick mind but unlimited patience, know how to dissemble without being a liar, inspire trust without trusting others, be modest but assertive, charm others without succumbing to their charm, and possess plenty of money and a beautiful wife while remaining indifferent to all temptation of riches and women.

"In my youth," **said his father,** **"I took to the law** **and argued each** **case with my wife.** **The muscular** **strength which it** **gave to my jaw** **has lasted the** **rest of my life."**

LEWIS CARROLL
AUTHOR

Today the most useful person in the world is the man or woman who knows how to get along with other people. Human relations is the most important science in the broad curriculum of living.

STANLEY C. ALLYN
PRESIDENT, NATIONAL
CASH REGISTER CO.

One of my responsibilities in those days was to conduct "pro bono" seminars for ABC members on how to avoid unionization while following the required legal ground rules during building trades organizational campaigns. These workshops emphasized that there is no compulsion in human behavior that automatically leads people irresistibly and inevitably into labor unions of their own free will. Worker dissatisfaction that can lead to unionization usually is the result of ineffective management, I explained. It is not so much the wages and other employee benefits but rather the more subtle matter of handling people-problems that causes most worker unrest and discontent.

I reminded my audience that the average supervisor spends over three-fourths of the working day dealing with—*people*. The largest single cost in most firms is—*people*. The most valuable asset any organization has is its—*people*. And all operational plans are carried out—or fail to be carried out—by *people*. Then I cautioned management about the message of a sign on the desk of a veteran maintenance foreman servicing the Baltimore & Ohio Railroad. It read:

If you want productivity and the financial reward that goes with it, you must treat your workers as your most important asset.

THOMAS PETERS AND
ROBERT WATERMAN'S
*IN SEARCH OF
EXCELLENCE*

> They don't let me run the train,
> the whistle I can't blow.
> I'm not allowed to work the switch
> or make the engine go.
> I'm not allowed to let off steam
> or even ring the bell.
> But let the damn thing jump the track
> and see who catches hell!

After that, I cited a survey of 5,000 front line hard-hat construction workers who rated their six causes of job satisfaction in the following order of importance this way: (1) workplace safety and security; (2) a feeling of belonging; (3) good working conditions; (4) competitive wages and employee benefits; (5) promotion opportunities; and (6) fair discipline.

Next I outlined some of the traits of a successful manager, such as being people-oriented, innovative, open-minded, communicative, a good listener, a goal-setter, compassionate, and dedicated to free enterprise. Other topics discussed in my ABC workshops included the following:

- How professional union organizers operate and how to legally discourage the signing of union authorization cards
- The Labor Board's role in conducting a union representation election in an appropriate bargaining unit
- The many negative facts of worklife as a trade union member
- What both employees and their supervisors would lose if the union wins
- How to communicate and motivate employees
- How to conduct a legal counter-campaign to defeat the union
- How to practice permanent union avoidance

Human action can be modified to some extent, but human nature cannot be changed.

ABRAHAM LINCOLN
16TH PRESIDENT

Most importantly, I closed my workshops by asking the ABCers to follow my own version of the biblical "golden rule" as applied to the workplace: *All employees must be treated as honorable individuals; justly rewarded; offered a friendly, safe, and healthy workplace; given equal employment opportunity; properly trained and fairly assigned; sincerely motivated; encouraged to advance; openly heard; fully informed; and evenly disciplined.*

Legal Rules for the "Campaign"

The technical formula required of management at the time of a union's organizational drive was simple. On the negative side, under the election policies of the Labor Board, management must never **spy** on union meetings, never **promise** employees increased wages or new benefits to avoid unionization, never **interrogate** employees about their own union activities, and never **threaten** or engage in **retaliation** against employees because of their pro-union activities. (Just remember the letters in the expressive word **SPITR**.)

On the positive side for victory, ABCers needed to do two things: First, actively exercise their constitutional right of free speech by telling employees true facts about the many previously described disadvantages of work in the building trades unions as compared to the steady employment and fair treatment by open shop firms.[1] Second, apply my "golden rule" to daily operation of their firm and solve the causes of worker job satisfaction within the permissible bounds of the Labor Board's "SPITR" rules.

Another key part of my long-range employee relations program was a recommendation that ABC contractors provide all of their personnel with an

Happiness has many roots, but none more important than security.

EDWARD
STETTINIUS JR.
SECRETARY OF STATE

employee handbook based on my state-of-the-art model. It contains straightforward non-legalese designed to fit any size employer from a "mom and pop shop" to an international corporate giant. Without such a handbook, inadequate employee-management communications can result in workers having no comprehension of company policies, rules, and employee benefits; not knowing how to communicate with management to air problems; and not understanding what is expected of them.

One of an employer's best defenses in a union organizational campaign, moreover, is the ability to counter the alleged "worker security" of a labor contract as advertised by the union involved. An employee handbook completely rebuts this claim because it sets forth in friendly and readable language all of the contractor's fair employee benefits, reasonable work rules, and an informal employee complaint procedure, plus real job tenure and security.

The absence of such a handbook can lead to inconsistent application of daily workplace decisions by supervisors, including discriminatory discipline. These errors eventually may provoke a union organizational campaign or costly civil rights litigation instigated by disgruntled workers, union organizers or hostile government agencies. Jury verdicts against employers who violate the myriad of federal, state, and local employment laws and regulations in force can result in actual and punitive damages in the millions of dollars.

Our ABC clients listened, took our advice, and none of them ever succumbed to unionization. The voluntary and uncoerced no-dues-paid-for-outsider-representation preference of employees proved their confidence in their ABC-member employers and in a union-free workplace.

The labor relations practice of our little Cook & Cluster law firm exploded. We began to represent open shop contractors throughout Maryland and along the East Coast, primarily in Pennsylvania, Delaware, New Jersey, New York, Virginia, West Virginia, and the Carolinas. They all wanted to learn how they could legally make labor unions unnecessary and unwanted. I was "on call" twenty-four hours a day, seven days a week, fifty-two weeks a year in the practice of compulsory union shop avoidance.

A Building Trades Boss Attacks ABC "Union Busting"

Within a few years, a senior official of the Building & Construction Trades Department of the AFL-CIO in Washington, D.C., by the name of Robert Georgine became so disturbed about his organization's unbroken string of defeats by the employees of ABCers at the Labor Board's secret ballot boxes that he took his complaint to a sympathetic labor subcommittee of the U.S. House of Representatives in Washington, D.C. It was (not coincidentally) investigating so-called "Pressures in the Workplace."

Georgine testified that both ABC and I, as one of its attorneys, were engaging in "illegal tactics" by teaching member contractors "how to stay non-union." He lamented to Congress that such "union-busting" had become a rapidly expanding industry—and it should be made illegal:

> Today, I would like to turn my attention to the role of employers' trade associations. These associations are literally becoming "think-tanks" for their employer-members in which lawyers, psychologists and consultants create and formulate methods which can later be utilized by employers to "bust" unions. . . . And nowhere is "union-busting" by trade associations more apparent than in the construction industry. I recently received a circular which advertises one of the mass-marketed anti-union seminars called "Managing in a Union-Free Environment". . .
>
> The seminar instructor is Samuel Cook. He is billed in the seminar pamphlet as an attorney and consultant for the U.S. Chamber of Commerce, the American Hospital Association, the National Association of Manufacturers, the Maryland Association of Counties, and none other than ABC. . .
>
> The ABC claims not to be anti-union but if this kind of seminar activity is not anti-union, I really do not know what is. The ABC, like other trade associations, disseminates these types of anti-union tactics through manuals, how-to booklets and teaching seminars. It encourages its staff and lawyers like Sam Cook to publish articles providing practical and legal advice to employer-members on how to

Luck is the residue of preparation, action, and discipline.

Anonymous

AND NOW COMES THE COMPANY'S "OUTSIDE LABOR CONSULTANT!" or . . .

"THE MADISON AVENUE HUCKSTER!"

WHY?? - - READ ON . . .

This cartoon was distributed by a union agent during an organizational campaign involving one of the author's construction clients.

operate non-union. I would submit to you that this type of advice demonstrates a profound disregard for our laws, for our collective bargaining processes, and for workers.[2]

A not-too-flattering cartoon likeness of me and my alleged tactics was circulated, entitled "The Company's Outside Labor Consultant—or the Madison Avenue Huckster." AFL-CIO President George Meany added that "today's labor relations consultants carry briefcases instead of brass knuckles and leave no visible marks on their victims. But their job is the same—to frustrate human hopes and nullify human rights."[3]

I immediately contacted the office of Frank Thompson, Jr., (D-NJ) the congressional subcommittee chairman who was holding the hearing on "pressures in the workplace," and offered to appear personally and testify in rebuttal to Robert Georgine's charges. I also wrote a letter to Thompson's congressional subcommittee, stating that neither my ABC clients nor I had ever been found "guilty" by the National Labor Relations Board of any unfair labor practices because of our activities in these union representation election campaigns. And my letter reminded Congressman Thompson and Georgine that Section 8(c) of the Taft-Hartley Act confirms the First Amendment of the Constitution in protecting freedom of speech by both labor and management during these election campaigns.[4]

Next, my letter to Thompson cited dozens of examples of Georgine's own AFL-CIO–affiliated building trades unions which, *when acting as employers*, had illegally "busted" other labor organizations that were trying to organize these trades unions' own internal staff personnel. All of these hypocritical "union-employers" were pronounced guilty of flagrant unfair labor practices by the National Labor Relations Board and/or federal courts of appeal.[5]

Union President Meany as "Union Buster"

Finally, as the *piece de resistance,* I told Thompson's Subcommittee what happened when AFL-CIO President George Meany's trained staff of 215 union organizers located throughout the United States decided that they were not being treated fairly by their own *employer,* namely Big Labor. In frustration, they formed the Field Representatives Union to bargain with AFL-CIO's management over wages and other working conditions.

The professional organizers naturally assumed that their request would be honored by a sympathetic Head of the House of Labor without the need for any secret ballot election. Instead, making noises like the irate capitalist that he really was, George Meany "laid off" several ringleaders of the Field Representatives Union and refused to recognize and bargain collectively with the rest of them. Then Meany actually told the National Labor Relations Board (in defiance of his staff employees' perfectly legitimate "bottom up" representation election petition) that "it would be contrary to the best interests of the labor movement for the AFL-CIO to recognize a union of its own organizers." He explained lamely that there would be "a danger of promoting power blocks of organizers within the international unions..."[6]

Even George Meany's loyal friends at the Labor Board couldn't swallow that duplicity and they ordered Big Labor's Boss to submit his AFL-CIO—as an employer—to its staff employees' representation election. This vote resulted in an overwhelming secret ballot victory by the Field Representatives Union, but Meany still balked at recognizing the legal unionization of his own internal personnel. Eventually another Labor Board order was required to force Meany and his fellow AFL-CIO executives to sit down on management's side of the bargaining table—and stay there until they negotiated a labor contract covering the wages and working conditions of their own union employees.

As the New York Yankee's colorful manager, Casey Stengel, used to say to a skeptical national press corp: "Ya can look it up."

Congressional Silence Reigns

As I anticipated, after receiving my rebuttal to Georgine's union-busting charges, Congressman Thompson never responded to my request to testify before his subcommittee on "Pressures In The Workplace." But I made certain

> **If your employer is getting advice from labor relations consultant Sam Cook, you have a better chance to join a union in Poland.**
>
> THOMAS BRADLEY, JR.
> PRESIDENT, AFL-CIO
> OF MARYLAND AND
> D.C.

that ABC submitted a formal statement to it for the record. We explained the merit shop philosophy of voluntary unionism and construction site harmony among union and non-union contractors. We also denied Robert Georgine's charges of illegal anti-union activities on ABC's part as an employers' trade association. And we cited ample evidence of illegal secondary boycotts and other coercive and violent labor activities to show that the trades union movement itself—rather than ABC—was a primary source of the hearing's issue of harmful "pressures in the workplace."

The upshot of all this union "anti-ABC" activity and political hypocrisy was that no employees of ABC members "went union" and no pro-union legislation resulted from the ignoble House of Representatives hearing. Eventually leftist Congressman Frank Thompson was jailed for two years on evidence of bribery while in office.[7]

And, so far as I know, neither AFL-CIO President George Meany nor the Building Trades Department's Robert Georgine ever attacked me publicly again.

CHAPTER 20

MAN-BITES-DOG STORY

IN THOSE DAYS I WAS WORKING sixty to seventy hours a week. Some of my clients continued to be involved in defeating union representation election cases that were supervised by regional offices of the National Labor Relations Board located throughout the middle-Atlantic states. It therefore was with some amusement and considerable satisfaction that I read from time to time about the internal miseries of senior Labor Board officials when they were caught acting illegally as an employer.

The Board's national field staff, including in-house lawyers stationed regionally throughout the United States, were members of a federal government workers labor union. And it seems that negotiations between the Board's management team and this field staff employees' union over the terms of a new labor contract had reached a deadlock at their in-house bargaining table in Washington, D.C.

The staff negotiators team finally became so upset with the Labor Board management's delaying tactics during these bargaining proceedings that they set up local picket lines in Washington and at the Board's regional offices across the country. This picketing caught the attention of the local news media and one headline in the *Baltimore Sun* blared out: **LABOR BOARD PERSONNEL PROTEST PACE OF NEGOTIATIONS**. There also was a photograph of angry local Labor Board staff employees waving picket signs that read: **THEY SAY CUT BACK—WE SAY FIGHT BACK!** Here are some excerpts from the *Sun's* article:

> **Life may not always be the party we hoped for, but while we're here we might as well dance once in a while.**
>
> ANONYMOUS

No matter what we are going through or how much time we have, Lord, let us never forget how to laugh.

WES KING
COMPOSER

Federal employees who work for the agency charged with protecting union rights were out picketing for their own union this week. Lawyers and clerical workers for the National Labor Relations Board set up informational pickets outside their regional offices at 109 Market Place [in Baltimore City] on Tuesday, Wednesday and yesterday. The pickets were up in the morning, during lunch, and in the evening.

These workers, who are members of the Labor Board Union, were protesting the slow progress of negotiations on [nationwide] agreements. In Baltimore, there are about 45 members. There were similar pickets at other Labor Board offices in Washington and around the country, union officials said.

The dispute involves two labor contracts, one that covers 1,000 professional employees and another one that covers 500 clerical workers. Both contracts had an expiration date of February 4, but they have been extended by mutual agreement between the Union and the Labor Board's management.

Nathan Albright, a Labor Board field attorney and vice president of the Baltimore local union, said the contract dispute involves efforts by the management of the agency to circumvent seniority rules, slash upward mobility programs, eliminate flexible work schedules and restrict the activities of union officials. Albright said the pickets are intended to publicize the dispute. "It certainly shows the irony in our situation," he added.

The Labor Board Staff Union also distributed a letter to all Labor Board personnel in Washington, D.C., and throughout the country. I received an anonymous copy of this letter:

LABOR BOARD IGNORES RIGHTS OF OWN EMPLOYEES

The National Labor Relations Board—the agency which is supposed to protect the rights of employees, employers, and union—is now acting in complete disregard for the rights of its own employees. The Labor Board Union, which represents all field employees, has been negotiating [for months] with Board management in an effort to reach agreement on a new contract.

The Labor Board has adamantly opposed any improved working conditions for its employees and has instead continuously sought to take away benefits contained in our current agreement. Illustrative of the Board's bargaining stance is its ongoing refusal to agree to such commonly accepted labor principles as seniority, just cause for discipline or discharge, and increased job opportunities for its own minority and female employees.

The employees of the Board will no longer tolerate the agency engaging in unfair tactics which the Board itself was established to discourage. The Board has already been found to have committed numerous unfair labor practices in violation of its employees' rights "by failing to bargain in good faith." The Federal Labor Relations Authority, another government agency, is presently prosecuting the Board in several such cases and we are prepared to take similar legal action.

Please join us in demanding that the National Labor Relations Board treat its employees in the same lawful manner that it requires of other employers by contacting the Board's Regional Director in this city and the Board's General Counsel in Washington, D.C.

Eight months after unfair labor practice charges were filed in this dispute with the Labor Board's own management for "bad faith bargaining under federal public sector labor law," its senior officials finally capitulated by signing a miserly new collective bargaining agreement with their unhappy staff.

Oh, well, nobody's perfect except thee and me.

> **There is no trick to being a humorist when you have the whole government working for you.**
>
> WILL ROGERS
> HUMORIST-WRITER

CHAPTER 21

DEFLATING PHONY UNION "WHISTLEBLOWERS"

THE DISCLOSURE OF ILLEGAL EMPLOYER PRACTICES to the public or to a prosecutorial government agency is known as "whistleblowing." A number of federal and state statutes presumably protect persons engaged in this bona fide activity from retaliation. Even without such a specific law, some courts have held that whistleblowers are shielded by the Constitution's First Amendment and public policy considerations.

Capitalizing on distortion of this honorable protective cover, a timeworn tactic of the building trades unions has been to contact some solicitous government regulatory agency and make a frivolous "whistleblower" claim that an ABC member is violating a law that the agency administers. These "anonymous" tips from union business agents or a disgruntled worker fronting for the union can result in political or media embarrassment and a costly remedial process for ABCers.

The targeted contractor receives bad publicity and gets dragged through expensive litigation of fictitious or exaggerated claims related to alleged workplace violations. Safety and health issues, civil rights, prevailing wages on government construction projects, proper pay for straight time and overtime work, as well as environmental, zoning, and building permits are some of the favorite union whistleblower targets.

The investigatory strategy frequently adopted by government auditors in these situations, after receiving a union's "confidential tip," is to make an unannounced visit and to invade the home office of the startled contractor.

> **Never answer an anonymous letter.**
>
> YOGI BERRA
> N.Y. YANKEES
> CATCHER-PHILOSOPHER

The biggest liar in the world is "They Say."

DOUGLAS MALLOCH
WRITER

An on-the-spot review of company records and practices involving proof of compliance with the regulation in question is demanded.

We warned ABCers not to capitulate to this unethical (if not illegal) ambushing tactic and provided them with protective and practical guidelines to follow in the event such a future "inspection" was about to occur. Our initial advice was that the contractor should hold the government bureaucrat at bay and contact his labor counsel before allowing any such investigation to proceed.

While most of these whistleblower claims turn out to be false, occasionally some legitimate technical violation by a contractor is uncovered. Then the local building trades union which initiated the charge threatens litigation or contacts employees of the non-union contractor involved, and brags about how the union can get the workers "some back pay" and at the same time correct "a dangerous safety hazard" in their workplace.

The union whistleblowing pitch to targeted employees is always the same: "If we can get these workplace benefits for you without even representing you officially, think how much more we can do for you if you join our organization." The union may also try to embarrass the allegedly guilty employer by negative publicity in the news media and in the eyes of its employees, its customers, and the government agency involved.

ABC contractors who are subjected to union whistleblowing tactics should refuse to discuss the matter with anyone and make no concession without first consulting their labor counsel. They should also exercise self-control, courtesy, and firmness when confronting hostile investigatory bureaucrats—while keeping their powder dry at all times.

CHAPTER 22

A RISKY CONSTITUTIONAL CONVENTION

I N 1967, ONE OF MY ASSIGNMENTS as labor counsel to the Maryland ABC and the Maryland Chamber of Commerce was to take on Big Government and Big Labor again. Maryland's Democratic Governor Millard Tawes and the Maryland General Assembly (also controlled by the Democrats) had called a Constitutional Convention.

Its 141 delegates elected by the citizenry from all walks of life prepared an analysis of the state's existing constitution, which was originally adopted in 1867. Four left-wing delegates who earned their livelihood as professional members of the internal staff of labor unions immediately proposed the inclusion of a "Bill of Rights" for organized labor in the revised document.

This potential union amendment began by acknowledging "the right of government employees to organize and bargain collectively through an exclusive union representative." Then it inserted a "Little Davis-Bacon Act" prevailing wage determination policy for *private sector* construction in the Constitution. It also recited "the right of the state to establish a system of workers' compensation unemployment compensation and health insurance protection against inadequacy of income." It ended with "the right of all employees in a free enterprise system to strike in order to share fairly and equitably in the profits and increased productivity of their employers and of society generally." (The inherent common law right of employers to manage their businesses profitably was ignored.)

Many liberals accept their opinions, ideas, and evaluations as others accept revealed truths. The facts are preserved to conform to their doctrines, so why discuss the facts?

WILLIAM F. BUCKLEY, JR.
WRITER AND PUBLISHER

A Labor-Versus-Management Constitutional "Draw"

In opposition to the union delegates' bill, I appeared at a hearing before the Constitutional Convention Commission in Annapolis, the state capital, on behalf of my two clients. My opening statement included the following observations about Big Labor's "Bill of Rights" constitutional amendment:

> The ploy of inserting these perennial statutory failures regarding exclusive and compulsory union recognition plus union scale wages and benefits for public building projects into the Convention *potpourri* will be recognized by those of you who have served in our State Legislature. AFL-CIO-sponsored mandatory collective bargaining bills and prevailing 'union-scale' wage bills have been defeated on many occasions over the past years. No sound economics in or out of government to our knowledge has ever advocated that such inflated labor cost increases should "prevail" in the private or public sector of our state.

I added that:

> As to the union bill's health insurance provisions, detailed workers' compensation amendments and unemployment compensation laws are already on the statute books of Maryland and are constantly being amended and revised, with the "assistance" of the AFL-CIO. Health insurance and a statewide "union war on poverty" are just as obviously subjects for the Legislature's consideration rather than for this Constitutional Convention. Lastly, the mandatory procedure for "exclusive" labor union representation in both the public and private sector and the equitable distribution of a private corporation's profits among its employees and stockholders certainly do not properly belong in the constitution of any free state such as Maryland.

In further rebuttal to the AFL-CIO bill of rights proposal, I offered my own counter-constitutional amendment. It asserted "the inalienable right of every person to hold a job without being forced to join and pay dues to any type of private organization such as a labor union, a religious group, a chamber of commerce or a political club." Here are some edited excerpts from the National Municipal League's coverage of that debate:

A strong movement developed in the Convention to give constitutional recognition to the right of all workers—in the public and private sectors—to organize and bargain collectively. A provision to this effect was adopted in the Committee on Personal Rights, but that adoption generated a bitter and extensive counteraction. Both on the floor and off, debate became acrimonious, arguments emotional, and lobbying rampant. All efforts to achieve a workable compromise failed...

Debate on October 19 in the Senate Chamber attracted hundreds of spectators, most of whom were connected in some way with labor organizations. Those who testified were Charles A. Della, president of the Maryland-D.C. AFL-CIO [and also a delegate to the Convention], Albert J. Mattes of the United Automobile Workers, and Samuel Cook, Esq., representing the Maryland Chamber of Commerce and the Associated Builders and Contractors of Maryland.

Della proposed a labor "Bill of Rights" which would not only protect the right of all workers to organize and bargain collectively, but would guarantee their right to strike. Cook in turn proposed a counter-amendment to protect the "right to work," that is, a constitutional guarantee that no one could be forced into joining a union and tender union dues in order to hold a job.

The issue between labor and management thus was clearly joined in a long and heated discussion. Agitated by the tone of the session, Pro-Tem Committee Chairman Kiefer insisted at one point: "I'm not about to have a debate between labor and management. I know this is a touchy issue, but we are here to get light, not heat, in this area." A bitter debate ensued anyway.

The Maryland Chamber of Commerce board of directors held an extraordinary New Year's Day meeting and, prior to the Convention session the following day, the Chamber mobilized its resources. Charles Della's controversial labor Bill of Rights was finally dropped

Socialism works best in the beehive and the anthill.

Jean-Francois Revel
French politician

A Republic is the worst form of government except all others.

WINSTON CHURCHILL
BRITISH PRIME
MINISTER

by the convention delegates when it failed to muster a majority on passage at second reading. The vote was **69** to **69** ...

Delegate Beatrice Miller, who had been at the center of the fight since its beginning, charged that the Convention had failed in its duty "because of the most ignominious reason of all—the business community's selfish and shortsighted threat to scuttle the Constitution, and we responded to this pressure."[1]

A similar fate awaited the final redraft of the entire Constitution as revised and adopted by the Convention. Personal endorsements in favor of passage of the complicated document read like a "who's who" of Maryland legal, business, civic, and political leadership. Even among opponents, few predicted its defeat, but Maryland's citizens rejected it by a substantial margin on May 14, 1968.

The actual vote against the new Constitution was **367,101** to **283,033**, with **46 percent** of the electorate participating. And, for the record, although this unpassed final version of the redrafted Constitution did not contain my "right to work" proposal, it had helped to block (by a tie-vote margin of the convention delegates) any constitutional mention of Big Labor's socialistic "Bill of Rights."

There is an old maxim that sometimes we learn more from our failures than from our successes. ABC discovered that a genuine political counterattack can serve as a good defense against the schemes of radical special interest groups such as Big Labor.

CHAPTER 23

DUAL SHOPS—AN ESCAPE PLAN

THE MANY ECONOMIC DISADVANTAGES of operating a *unionized* construction firm created another type of legal challenge and a new variety of construction clients for me in the 1960s. I began to receive calls from frustrated builders who asked my advice on how to solve their labor relations crises. They saw only two possible choices: First, operate in a major urban market where union economic strength and undue influence on law enforcement still kept open shop rivals from serious competition, or second, try to break completely from the building trades and operate in a less-unionized suburban area on an open shop basis.

I suggested to these unionized contractors that an alternative solution was available: the creation of what became known as a *dual shop* or *double-breasted operation.* This legal concept refers to a contractor's ownership of two distinct companies performing in the same field of work. The original "parent" firm is party to a typical area-wide labor contract negotiated on its behalf by a local unionized contractors' association. The second firm is established and operates on a non-union basis, with its own separate and distinct wage scale, employee benefits, and work rules. By owning such a "dual shop," the contractor may open a broader market and the overall business can become more profitable—while joining ABC's merit shop movement.

The proprietor of such a dual shop, I advised the harassed contractors, must follow stringent guidelines imposed by the National Labor Relations Board. And if—as happens sometimes—a building trades union challenged the legality of such a "double-breasted" establishment, the Labor Board and the courts look beyond the corporate veil to decide certain legal questions: Is ownership of the second firm—which operates on a non-union basis as it performs the same type of construction work in the same locality as the parent unionized firm—considered a *bona fide* separate business venture? Or will the Labor Board call the non-union firm a "sham" and "alter ego" created illegally to evade a collective bargaining agreement with a building trades union?

An affirmative answer to the second question would make the parent unionized contractor vulnerable to substantial financial risks. If a trade union's unfair labor practice charge proves that the new non-union business is not legally constituted, the Labor Board can hold the parent contractor subject to contractual and monetary penalties, retroactively to date of creation of the second firm. The supplemental remuneration to employees of the new non-union firm would include all "underpaid" wages and "delinquent" reimbursements to various labor union funds covering a pension, a health and welfare plan, and other fringe benefits mandated under the parent unionized company's collective bargaining agreement.

The second firm could also face a Labor Board order merging its non-union employees into the parent company's labor contract, including all of its more costly wages, benefits, and restrictive operational provisions as well as its compulsory union membership, without any secret ballot election to test the free choice of the firm's workers.[1]

Ground Rules on Operating Dual Shops

The ultimate legal resolution of these sensitive and costly issues usually turns on the degree of *separation* versus the degree of *integration* of operation of the two firms as evidenced by a "total circumstances" test of each case. In reaching its decision, the Labor Board relies on four basic factors that have been confirmed by the U.S. Supreme Court. These controlling criteria are "interrelation of operations, common management, centralized control of labor relations, and common ownership or financial control" of the two firms.[2]

Years of challenging litigation by organized labor have led the Labor Board and the courts to place varying degrees of emphasis on these four factors. Seemingly insignificant activities such as common use by both firms of the same clerical personnel, buildings, vehicles, telephones, mail facilities, or tools may lead the Labor Board to require the newly established open shop company to "go union" and apply the parent's collective bargaining agreement.

Of even more concern, the Labor Board ruled as early as 1956 that evidence of "operational integration" and "joint control of labor relations" in the two companies tip the scales *against* permissive dual operations. Proof as to this illegal exercise of "common management" is found in the daily operation of the business. If supervisors or executives of one company perform similar managerial or labor relations functions for the second enterprise, or employees are transferred back and forth between the two firms, "illegal common management and excessive interrelation of operations" will be found to exist.

The Labor Board's position on the fourth factor, "common ownership," is good news for ABC dual shoppers. Unless there are other indications of "joint oversight," the same corporation, person, or group *can* maintain a 100 percent financial ownership of two enterprises engaging in the same type of business in the same locality without illegally subjecting the second corporation to the terms of a collective bargaining agreement entered into by the parent firm. As a general rule, it thus can be said that "common ownership" is much less risky, legally, than the other three factors.[3]

In the much-litigated *Peter Kiewit Sons* series of cases in the 1970s, the Labor Board offered factual guidance on whether a dual non-union firm could be legally created and operated by a unionized construction firm or, instead, the employees of both establishments should be included in one collective bargaining unit within the parent firm:

> … Where, as here, we are concerned with more than one operation of a single employer, the following factors are particularly relevant: the bargaining history; the functional integration of operations; the differences in the types of work and the skills of employees; the extent of centralization of management and supervision, particularly in regard to labor relations, hiring, discipline, and control of day-to-day operations; and the extent of interchange and contact between the groups of employees.[4]

Lawsuit: a machine which you go into as a pig and come out as a sausage.

AMBROSE BIERCE
WRITER

Only painters and lawyers can change white to black.

JAPANESE PROVERB

Some Practical Issues

While the discussion here only deals with broad legal guidelines for successful dual shop operations, it should be noted that the pro-union Labor Board during the Clinton presidential years vigorously opposed dual shops and at least temporarily made the legal ground rules more difficult for a contractor's compliance.[5]

Harsh political and economic realities also require contractors who want to "go dual shop" to weigh additional practical questions: When a powerful building trades union hears about a new double-breasted corporate setup that affects the work of its own members, how will it react? Will the contractor's attempt at union "avoidance" bring down the economic, political, and/or corporeal wrath of the building trades on both operations? Will the union representing the parent firm's employees file a costly unfair labor practice charge at the Labor Board? Will the contractor's corporate duality cause work stoppages or other forms of union intimidation and violence?

A trade union's response to questions like these and its reaction in any particular situation depends upon the character, personalities, and power of the union representatives involved, their relationship with the dual shop contractor, the number of union tradesmen out of work in the area, the strength of the merit-shop movement in the locale, and the degree of impartial law enforcement needed to maintain labor peace where the two companies operate.

Careful Planning Produces Dual Shop Winners

Some owners of dual shops have endured and survived threats, property damage, boycotts, picketing, litigation, and other types of union coercion and sabotage. The temptation of contractors is strong to ignore the legal ground rules and to take shortcuts to reduce costs by excessive blending and interconnecting of operations of the two firms. As a practical matter, fortunately, most unionized firms who have gone double-breasted find that the building trades do not become bothersome so long as they continue to get their "fair share" of local construction work. Prominent examples of ABC members who have operated dual shops successfully are three of America's largest general contractors: Fluor-Daniel, Bechtel-Becon, and Clark Construction Company (formerly Hyman and Omni).

A double-breasted operation is not a sure bet for every firm. It is also true, however, that sophisticated contractors who have made a successful switch to operate simultaneously in both the union and non-union sectors of the construction field believe that the increased versatility was worth the legal and financial risk. But these same contractors warn against making a spur-of-the-moment decision and forming a dual shop too hastily.

Without proper planning and effective legal implementation, double-breasting can be doomed to expensive failure. But set up and administered properly, a dual shop operation sometimes becomes the key to a contractor's survival—while adopting the principles of the merit shop crusade.[6]

Woe into you also, ye lawyers! for ye lade men with burdens grievous to be borne, and ye yourselves touch not the burden with one of your fingers.

LUKE 11:46

CHAPTER 24

NEW CHALLENGES IN THE 1960s

THE DECADE OF THE **1960s** began with ABC facing the end of Dwight D. Eisenhower's two-term presidency and the victory of John F. Kennedy. Riding a wave of Big Labor's support, the "New Frontier" Democratic Party also gained substantial majorities in both houses of Congress.

This restyled political climate even affected an inaugural celebration cake for JFK that was designed to be ten feet high and six feet across, with a sugar-walled White House on top. The gastronomical masterpiece was intended as a gift from an admiring open shop Massachusetts baker but the presidential banquet committee refused the generous offer. It seems that unionized cooks employed by Camelot's caterer threatened to go on strike rather than serve any cake without a "union-made" label.

That feisty episode in 1961 actually set the tone for the incoming Kennedy administration's pro-labor legislative agenda. A union-endorsed bill was introduced immediately in Congress to repeal the protective "separate-gate" secondary picketing and boycott ground rules of the Taft-Hartley Act. As previously discussed, these rules were formulated by the National Labor Relations Board in its 1950 *Moore Dry Dock* case, solidified by the Supreme Court in the landmark *Denver Buildings Trades* decision in 1951, and followed in ABC's *Stover Steel* victory of 1955.[1]

In *Denver*, the Supreme Court declared that a "neutral" unionized general contractor and a "targeted" non-union subcontractor working on the same project were separate legal entities and that secondary boycott provisions of the Taft-Hartley Act prohibited a trade union from picketing the entire "common job site."[2]

In an attempt to reverse the opinion of the nation's highest court, a union-sponsored bill to "overrule" the *Denver* decision against common situs boycotts and picketing was supported by President John F. Kennedy and his secretary of labor, Arthur Goldberg. This former general counsel to the United Steelworkers Union testified before the House Labor Committee to urge an amendment to Taft-Hartley that would permit a craft union which has a dispute with a single contractor to picket and shut down an entire construction project where many "neutral" union and non-union contractors and their employees are also working. Goldberg's remarks described ABC as the villain because its non-union contractors destroyed "union wage standards":

> Graphic evidence was presented before this committee in the 86th Congress of the impact of the *Denver Building Trades* rule on the ability of the construction employees to protect their hard-won standards. In nearby Baltimore, a small group of non-union contractors formed the Associated Builders and Contractors shortly before the *Denver* decision.
>
> Membership rose to over 1,000 firms in ten years, but the number of union general contractors dropped from 58 in 1951 to five in 1959. Non-union wage rates, ranging from 25 percent to 70 percent below union scale in 1951, still persist in that city today. I submit that the *Denver* rule against "common situs boycotts" invites such efforts to undermine union standards not only in Baltimore but also in every community in the country.[3]

Goldberg's pro-union statistics (other than the growth of ABC) were grossly exaggerated but his political loyalty to JFK eventually gained him a seat on the Supreme Court of the United States. From ABC's point of view, being "featured" by the secretary of labor at a congressional committee hearing at least showed grudging respect for the budding merit shop movement.

Campbell, Best, and Knott Lead Boycott Opposition

Three National ABC presidents—Jim Campbell ('57), Larry Best ('58-'59), and John Knott ('60)—united the lobbying forces to prevent passage by Congress of this "common situs boycotts" bill in 1961. Within the state of Maryland, they brought together such organizations as the Baltimore Chamber of Commerce, the Maryland Motor Truck Association, the Home Builders Association, the Maryland Highway Contractors Association, and, remarkably, ABC's old unionized foe, the Baltimore Chapter of the Associated General Contractors. Together, they conveyed ABC's opposition of the common situs bill to Maryland's representatives in Congress.

At the national level, John Trimmer reported that "ABC publications bristled with bulletins on the controversy and members in all chapters were urged to express their views to Congress." ABC National also teamed up with the U.S. Chamber of Commerce and the National Association of Manufacturers to lobby against the bill. Testifying before a Special Subcommittee of the House Committee on Education and Labor, ABC's Jim Campbell cautioned the legislators:

> There is a record number of 1300 boycott cases in dispute at this time, but that is not the whole story. Those of us in the construction industry are well aware that there are thousands more *threatened* common situs secondary boycotts that achieve the purposes that these illegal secondary boycotts had hoped might be achieved when we were forced to go to court. It is the threat of the secondary boycott that in many cases does the jobs the union wants to do. This is particularly true of suppliers. Unions can, by threatening a secondary boycott, control suppliers on a construction site to just those they prefer, which will always be union suppliers exclusively.[4]

Luckily for ABC, the contest over this proposed building trades legislation became embarrassing to the Kennedy administration. Industrial unions similarly affiliated with the umbrella AFL-CIO were opposed to the picketing bill's passage because they thought it would threaten their own job security. They reasoned that if the bill passed, a craft union could force work that was normally performed in their unionized factories to be done at a construction job site. One enraged industrial union president testified that the building trades were "seeking preferential treatment from Congress."

States' Rights, the cornerstone of the Republic and our chief bulwark against encroachment by Big Government on individual freedom, is fast disappearing under the piling sands of absolutism.

Senator Barry Goldwater (R-AZ)

James Campbell, ABC President (1959)

Our task now is not to fix the blame for the past but to fix the course for the future.

JOHN F. KENNEDY
35TH PRESIDENT

The White House finally saved face in this embarrassing political stalemate through the efforts of Congressman Adam Clayton Powell, an influential African-American Democrat. As chairman of the House Labor Committee dealing with this common situs picketing legislation, Powell said he would not report out of his committee a bill on which there was no agreement between the AFL-CIO's affiliated building trades and industrial unions. And John Trimmer explained the Congressman's unspoken second motivator: "There was little question at the time that the recurrent criticism of racial discrimination in the apprentice training programs of the building trades unions played a role in Powell's refusal to support their common situs picketing bill."[5]

JFK Encourages Federal Unionism

When President Kennedy failed to gain congressional approval of this legislation, he placated the AFL-CIO hierarchy by issuing a novel executive order that encouraged U.S. government agencies to recognize labor unions and bargain with them over the working conditions of their public employees.[6] Organized labor capitalized further on this favorable political climate to secure work for its members by gaining exclusive jurisdiction over defense-related construction projects arising from the Cold War and the Space Race. "We didn't call them project labor agreements then, but that's what they were," said Building Trades Department President Robert Georgine. Using these "PLAs" on major jobs like the Hanford Nuclear Facility and the Cape Canaveral Space Center, the building trades ensured that all federal construction work in Kennedy's administration was performed on a union-only basis.

Marsh and Coleman: Contrasting Leaders

ABC's first national presidents to face this renewed Big Labor–Big Government–Democratic Party partnership were Charles Marsh ('61-'62) and Tracy Coleman ('63-'64). The personalities of the two leaders differed in many ways. Marsh was a blunt, rugged individualist from the Maryland Chesapeake Bay watermen's school of hard knocks and fierce independence. He never would use a scalpel (so to speak) if a sledgehammer were available to settle a free enterprise issue. In contrast, Coleman, a graduate engineer, four-year class president, and captain of the football team at the University of Maryland, was more diplomatic, suave, and articulate. But their dedication to the merit shop philosophy was identical.

On one occasion I represented Charlie Marsh's elevator construction company at a union representation election hearing held in the offices of the National Labor Relations Board in Baltimore. Many of Marsh's employees had signed legitimate union "authorization cards" (because he was a rough and tough boss) but he blamed the federal government "for allowing such a damn rip-off to occur."

During the course of this administrative hearing to determine which of this company's elevator mechanics were eligible to vote, Marsh lost his temper because of what he called "bullshit pro-union questions" that the Labor Board's hearing officer was asking him. At one point he jumped out of the witness box and, like a wounded bull, actually charged the government official. I caught Charlie's upraised right fist just as he was about to take a swing at the startled bureaucrat. Then I ushered my frustrated client back to the trial table—and rested both Marsh and our case.

As we retreated, I'll never forget Charlie yelling at me: "Damn it, Cook, isn't this a free country?" I had to admit to him, gently but firmly, "No, sir, it isn't *totally* free."

After we left the Labor Board hearing, I managed to get Charlie's temper under control. From then on, I supervised a legally pro-company campaign lasting two months—while keeping Charlie muzzled and leashed, figuratively speaking. This strategy resulted in a substantial majority of Marsh's employees voting in a secret ballot election to *reject* the Elevator Constructors Union.

Looking back at the rumpus, I dread to consider what might have happened to my career as a labor lawyer if we had lost that union representation election case involving a fiery ABC president's own employees. But Charlie's unbounded spirit and forceful leadership served ABC well, as his record of accomplishment and the accurate prediction in his final President's Report to the members attested:

> Because of our phenomenal growth, we must completely revise the structure of ABC. It has been a great experience to see the

One thorn of experience is worth a whole bramblebush of warning.

JAMES RUSSELL LOWELL
POET AND ESSAYIST

Charles Marsh, ABC President (1961-62)

vitality of the new chapters. Contractors all over the nation are catching the original free enterprise enthusiasm and there is no stopping them. As management and workers in construction see what can be accomplished by teaming up together voluntarily, many more contractors will rally to our standards and free enterprise will be protected.[7]

Marsh's successor and ABC's eleventh national president, Tracy Coleman, was the first builder from outside the metropolitan Baltimore area to be chosen for this honor. As chief executive officer of the Silver Spring–based general contracting firm of Coleman & Woods, he led the chartering of ABC's Metropolitan Washington, D.C., Chapter in 1958. Tracy was a motivational leader of people and, during the term of his presidency in 1963, he articulated his frank views on labor-management relations in these memorable—and still timely—words:

> During ABC's emergence as a nationwide organization, we face new challenges in addition to those that originally caused us to band together. First and of course foremost, is the immediate necessity for planning and implementing a real national organization with a philosophy to match.
>
> In planning for the future, however, we must never forget the past. The formation of labor unions was hastened if not directly caused by the greed of the 19th century industrial barons and the inhuman treatment they accorded large numbers of the workclass. It is easy for us to overlook the historical fact that the trade union movement brought about a veritable revolution of the laboring class, raised the living standards of millions, and provided vast new markets to nurture our lusty young economy. For these and other contributions we are, and should be, grateful to the forces of organized labor.
>
> Now, however, the pendulum has swung too far in the other direction. Our people, who once were dominated by tyrannical Big Business, now are in danger of succumbing to a dictator-

Tracy Coleman, ABC President (1963-64)

ship of the czars of Big Labor. The greed of these men for political power, for control of our government, for more money with less responsibility, and for the debilitating principle of socialism, may eventually destroy our country's ability to compete in a belligerently aggressive world economy.

It seems to me that if our free enterprise system is to survive, we must return as a nation to the entrepreneurial principle that a worker's pay should be based on individual ability to produce. We must avoid any exploitation of labor and give each employee an honest assurance that his wages are directly related to his productivity, that these wages are truly a fair and meritorious share of the income of our system, and that each worker is provided with the opportunity to share a job security program.

If we backers of the merit shop philosophy make certain that our own house is in proper order and will bear the searching scrutiny of critical eyes, we will be assured of the best in labor productivity and morale.[8]

Character is destiny.

HERACLITIS
GREEK PHILOSOPHER

A Task Force Reviews ABC's Growing Pains

Corroborating Coleman's concerns, John Trimmer wrote in his treatise, *ABC: Profile of a Philosophy*, that "toward the end of 1964 some ABC leaders were having misgivings about the escalating pace of the Association's progress." They "believed," he continued, "that there was a lack of definition of goals and the relationship between the national organization and its chapters was affected by other problems that are characteristic of expanding federated associations."

To examine these issues and consider ABC's future, a task force was established. President Tracy Coleman led the group, along with John Trimmer and ABC National Presidents Charles Fiehe ('54), Fred Schnabel ('66-'67), James Long ('65–'66), and John Lochary ('69–'70), plus Ira Rigger (Baltimore Chapter president, '60). During a three-day meeting in Boiling Springs, Pennsylvania, the task force sought ways and means to clarify national objectives, improve the organizational structure, and solidify the Association's financial situation.

Competition is
the cutting edge
of business,
always shaving
and conserving
the costs.

HENRY FORD
INDUSTRIALIST

Their report showed that ABC, despite its youthfulness, was beginning to assume the responsibility of coordinating open shop construction industry activities throughout the country. The Association had contacts not only in the Middle Atlantic states but also with contractors in Florida, Massachusetts, and Texas. And meetings with various builders' groups in Pittsburgh, Pennsylvania, and Grand Rapids, Michigan, indicated that ABC had broad appeal in those areas.

The Association also was playing an important role in federal legislation affecting construction, and working closely with right-to-work law movement leaders in several states. Internal programs of ABC included an expanded stepped-up annual national convention, Davis-Bacon prevailing wage surveys, and merit shop construction business promotion. For its members, ABC also acted as an information clearinghouse, administered the national health insurance plan, and offered advice on labor relations, industrial training, and safety.

New Association Directions in Five-Year Plan

Major new projects also resulted from the task force report. One conclusion was that ABC could never advance nationally without more active membership participation. Business promotion also was increased, ABC's relationship with other open shop organizations was broadened, and a special fund was created to promote new chapters. It was further decided to designate 1965 as "Year of the Leader" and train members to become the activists that the organization needed.

Under ABC President Tracy Coleman's direction, another major result of the task force was the evolution of a "five-year plan." In the preface it was noted that both ABC membership and the budget had more than doubled during the previous five years. National and chapter office staffs had grown substantially, too, but much time had been spent "putting out fires" in labor relations and legislation. More long-range programs were needed to protect the merit shop philosophy and give steady impetus for member participation and growth.

Geographical areas designated by Tracy Coleman for expansion were Pennsylvania, New England, the Midwest, and the Midsouth, with the expectation of moving into the Southwest by 1970. Membership services also were increased in the fields of legal aid, management education for company executives, and training programs for multi-craft employees.

James Long Carries the ABC Torch

Ably following Tracy Coleman as national president in 1965 and 1966 was Jimmy Long, founder of the first open shop concrete manufacturing firm in metropolitan Washington D.C. In order to control the rapid expansion and protect the business standards of ABC, the following Code of Ethics was drafted by Long and his national board of directors:

The essence of belief is the establishment of a habit.

CHARLES S. PEIRCE
PHILOSOPHER

As a member of the Associated Builders and Contractors, Inc., I will strive to observe the following principles in the conduct of my business:

- Maintain a high standard of performance consistent with the customer's best interests and my obligations to them.
- Cooperate to the fullest extent with the architect and other agents of the owner toward fulfillment of a common goal.
- Quote only realistic prices and completion dates and perform accordingly.
- Solicit quotations only from qualified firms with whom I am willing to do business.
- Make all payments promptly within the terms of the construction contract.
- Observe and foster the highest standards of safety and other working conditions for my employees.
- Establish meritorious wage and benefits programs for my employees commensurate with their ability and work ethic.
- Actively participate in the training of skilled tradesmen for the future welfare of the merit shop industry.
- Promote voluntarism rather than compulsion as to union membership on all construction work sites while working in harmony on a merit shop basis.

In the May, 1966, issue of the *ABC Contractor*, President Jimmy Long reported on the Association's growth as a national organization. There were fourteen chartered chapters with full-time executive directors and other staff personnel. Membership had grown to *1500* firms, which employed over

80,000 workers in virtually every construction trade. As part of the continuing expansion drive, a group called the Beam Club was formed to pay tribute to members who secured a substantial number of new ABCers. These "Beamers" were awarded a handsome blue or maroon blazer with a distinctive ABC emblem on the lapel pocket.

Along with expanding the national headquarters staff to provide adequate help for local chapters, Jimmy Long set up a new category called "membership at large" for firms outside any area in which a chapter had not yet established formal jurisdiction. The national board of directors added an "ABC affiliate" status for compatible independent employer associations. The dual purpose was to join forces as rapidly as possible with like-minded organizations that favored the merit shop principle in order to increase ABC's regional and national effectiveness.

During President Long's congenial but forceful tenure, ABC's first formal business brochure was published under the title *You Be The Judge*. It was a forty-eight-page pamphlet containing photographs of award-winning building projects by ABCers that highlighted the diversity and capabilities of merit shop contractors. This publication was mailed to architects, potential construction users, and insurance and bonding companies.

In addition, ABC's first national legislative conference to become acquainted with congressional representatives was held in Washington, D.C.; a modernized construction safety program was developed for adoption by all chapters; and an expanded classified membership directory was distributed. New seminars and programs were initiated for members on subjects such as labor relations, apprenticeship training and personnel supervision, employee benefits, business management, job site safety, lobbying, and legislation.

On the lighter side, an issue of ABC's *Contractor* magazine carried a headline announcing that "The Builders Meet the Bunnies." The article featured a photograph of three enthusiastic ABC members surrounding a Hugh Hefner protégé. She was wearing her official Playboy Club uniform: a black bow tie, a starched white collar, and a skimpy

The Contractor
ABC '65-'66 President James Long gives the 1500th ABC member an award.

costume featuring generous décolletage, long black silk stockings, and a cottontail derriere. In dignified contrast to the perky pin-up, an accompanying article described a widely publicized new Playboy building project this way:

> To ABC member Finglass Construction Company of Baltimore went the honor of building the Baltimore Playboy Club, latest in the cross-country chain of such clubs and the only one on the East Coast between New York and Miami. The Baltimore facility, which opened its doors in July, is composed of six floors in what was known as the H. E. Crook Mechanical Building on Light Street, with three of the floors used as working areas for the club.
>
> The Finglass Company, one of the early members of ABC, spent six months in extensive remodeling and renovating of the premises, using many other ABC members as subcontractors. Décor of the swank new club is set by the latest idea in wall treatment: solid 16-inch sections of Gold Crest walnut from Georgia-Pacific's hardwood operations in Savannah, Georgia.

ABC's Annual Convention Urges Political Action

One of the high spots of the year 1966 was ABC National's annual convention at Grossinger's in the Catskill Mountains of New York state. President Jimmy Long emphasized the need for increased member participation in the political process. Long warned that under the radical left wing political climate of the times, the merit shop needed to become more deeply involved if it was to survive. A course in "practical politics" prepared by the U.S. Chamber of Commerce was used effectively. Chapters responded with an intensive counter-attack by members who were concerned about the socialistic direction in which government programs were heading.

Under this new agenda, ABC National for the first time established an independent political fund-raising committee called the Political Education Program or "PEP." It began to raise modest sums that were channeled to candidates for government office who supported free enterprise goals and objectives. ABC members were well aware that the dollars they were able to gather were not going to influence many votes when compared to the huge monetary

Too much of a good thing can be wonderful.

MAE WEST
HOLLYWOOD FILM
LEGEND

The political machine triumphs because it is a united minority acting against a divided majority.

WILL DURANT
HISTORIAN

clout of Big Labor, but the contributions at least provided politicians with an introduction to the merit shop's entrepreneurial point of view.

Echoing and assisting Jimmy Long's push for action on the political front, his predecessor ABC President, Tracy Coleman, added insightful advice. It still rings true today and should be preserved permanently, lest we forget:

> The great weakness of our political system seems to be the ability of vociferous minorities to organize pressure groups that impress on the vote-hungry office seekers that theirs is truly the voice of the people and must be obeyed. This, plus the smallness of character found in far too many aspirants to public office, results in government by and for minorities which we have come to know as the "welfare state," the "socialist state," "pork barrel government," and so on and on *ad nauseam.*
>
> The issues as defined by Democrats and Republicans are so mixed and entwined that the parties are no longer distinguishable one from the other. A far clearer and more important division exists between the philosophy, on the one hand, of the leftist exponents of big government and socialism, and, on the other, of conservative thinkers who support free enterprise and the theory of Abraham Lincoln that government should do nothing for the people which they can do better for themselves.
>
> Here in this political arena and in these two conflicting theories of government, there exists a real challenge for ABC members and all who think as we do. Will American free enterprise as we know it flourish and mature, producing evermore goods for the use of those who produce them, or will it wither, die and be replaced by the big brother paternalism of the socialist state? Only we, the American people, have the ability to influence the decision positively. Upon our willingness to pledge our intellects, time and our money to this battle will rest the success of our free enterprise system and hence the American way of life.[9]

At the same 1966 convention, ABC named Senator Everett M. Dirksen (R-IL) as its first "Leader of the Year." In making the award, President Jimmy Long praised the Senator's "extended debate" (i.e., filibuster) in the Senate that killed an AFL-CIO attempt to repeal the right-to-work proviso of the Taft-Hartley Act.[10] Then Long lauded Dirksen's major role in the victorious fight to keep Big Labor's common situs picketing bill from being enacted into law and read the inscription on the ABC's plaque given to the senator. It honored Dirksen for his "courageous fight in defense of our constitutional liberties" and his "devotion to the principles of the signers of the Declaration of Independence." A sample of the famed Dirksen oratory made an impression on an enthusiastic ABC audience as he responded graciously:

> Frankly, I'm overwhelmed by this award coming from so fine an organization and to be called Leader of the Year is indeed a high and very impressive tribute. I can only hope for one thing and that is that perhaps I might even in a modest degree be deserving of the esteem and confidence which certainly is implied in the award.
>
> To me it will bring a great inspiration to be constant to the basic calls of our country, to its priceless traditions of freedom, and to what the scriptures call the ancient landmarks which our Founding Fathers set. They must be reasserted. They must be kept![11]

Schnabel and Higgins: Two More Great Leaders

Another highlight of the 1966 annual convention was the election of Fred Schnabel, a tough, hard-driving, open shop general contractor from Lansdale, Pennsylvania. He was the first non-Marylander to become ABC's national president. In addition to many years of outstanding service to his local chapter and to ABC National, he valiantly withstood the wrath of the building trades unions against his expanding open shop firm in later years.

In one situation—at about the time that Schnabel Associates ranked No. 263 on the *Engineering News-Record* list of the 400 largest general contractors in the country—the Philadelphia Building Trades picketed five of the firm's projects simultaneously. They were located in Boothwyn, Radnor, and Haverford, all suburbs of Philadelphia. Schnabel began videotaping this picketing activity and he maintained a journal of the day-to-day events that transpired at all of the work sites. After viewing many hours of these photos, a reporter for *Engineering News-Record* wrote:

The worst crime against working people is a company which fails to make a profit.

SAMUEL GOMPERS
AFL PRESIDENT

Many of life's noblest enterprises might never have been undertaken if all the difficulties could have been foreseen.

THEODORE L. CUYLER
WRITER

The tapes show pickets beating company employees, spiking and slashing tires, throwing rocks and even a stolen chain saw through the windows of cars and trucks entering the jobsite. In the films, union business agents involved in the picketing appear to be directing part of the activity, and local law enforcement officials are seen standing idly by as pickets violate court injunctions against mass picketing and violence.[12]

Fred Schnabel eventually won that bloody battle, and served aggressively as ABC's 13th president in 1967 and 1968. He began by envisaging and receiving board of directors approval of a new internal administrative set-up featuring six regional directors and by expansion of the national staff's services to members. His acceptance speech announced a bold agenda for ABC's future as a national force:

> Like the man said: "you ain't seen nothin' yet!" We of ABC are about to embark upon a gigantic building program. Our past administrations, under extremely capable leadership, have constructed strong foundations with solid piers and footings and have established the means of financing our merit shop programs for the present and future. Now we are ready to erect our structure with chapters in every state in the union.[13]

ABC CONTRACTOR

Fred Schnabel, ABC's 13th President (1967-1968)

It was ABC's further good fortune to hire Eugene Higgins two years later. A keen, conservative, and hardworking graduate of Bowling Green State University, he became a key factor in the Association's growth. Gene's administrative ability, integrity, and dedication to the merit shop cause soon earned him a promotion as assistant executive vice president, reporting directly to John Trimmer.

While holding that position from 1968 to 1980, Higgins assumed overall supervision of both the internal and service operations of National ABC. His areas of responsibility included accounting, financial matters, legal-labor relations, public relations, education, public affairs, insurance and pension benefits,

286

legislation, safety, and business development. In this key job, he also relieved Trimmer and ABC presidents on interstate missions as ABC's national spokesperson.

During the twelve-year service span of Gene Higgins, ABC grew from 2500 members to over 16,000 members. His departure in 1980 to become executive vice president of and later president of Joseph J. Hock, Inc. (an active ABC member constructino hauling and land development firm) left a difficult-to-fill void. John Trimmer praised him as "an outstanding association executive who was a privilege and pleasure to work with." Everyone who teamed up with Gene Higgins at the National ABC office and in the local chapters agreed.

Eugene Higgins, ABC national assistant executive vice president (1968–1980) and president of a member of ABC, Joseph J. Hock, Inc., (1981–1999).

Charlie Feihe Is Honored

In 1967, ABC honored another one of its most competent, loyal, hardworking, and longtime members by presenting its first *Distinguished Service Award* to Charles Feihe for contributions "above and beyond the call of duty toward the success of ABC." Charlie was vice president and treasurer of the Mullan Contracting Company in Baltimore, one of the founding firms of ABC. He also served as the first secretary on ABC's national board of directors in 1950 and as ABC's fourth national president in 1954. In addition to Feihe's outstanding work as an officer and member of the national board over a long period of time, he was active in the promotion of ABC's minority training initiatives and also established the Association's first accountancy committee.

The *Contractor* magazine couldn't resist these additional comments on the popular Charley Feihe:

> This good-natured and enthusiastic ABCer has frequently been a great master of ceremonies at our get-togethers of various sorts on both the national and chapter levels. In the early days of ABC, he also could be seen as an active participant at Samplers' Night. Newer ABC members might be interested to know that this was in reality "KP duty" to peel potatoes, prepare vegetables and pat the crab cakes for these seafood feasts. (As an incentive, tasting the finished products was allowed.)

A Model Employee Security Program

One of the major reasons for ABC's continued growth in the late 1960s was its excellent employee benefits program, called the ABC Security Plan. It featured group medical, disability, and life insurance and soon added a retirement program. The plan completed a banner year in 1967, with over a 100 percent increase in the number of participative member firms. It provided a choice of three levels of insurance benefits for ABC members, their employees, and families. The broadest coverage included life insurance, accident and sickness weekly income, daily hospital bed-board-services-and-supplies, surgical fees, doctor's attendance in the hospital, and maternity, obstetrical, accident, and medical catastrophe benefits. It also covered full-time students until age twenty-three and qualifying retirees as eligible dependents.

To complete this outstanding security plan, there was a benefit tailored to fit a special need of the construction industry called "portability." An employee working and covered by one ABC member firm who moved to a different area of the country could go to work for another member firm in the new locality and continue insurance coverage with no lapse in coverage protection.

According to officials of the underwriter, Connecticut General Life Insurance Company, ABC's security plan was their most successful program. In 1967 it protected 617 member firms covering 7,500 employees, with the annual premium reaching the $3,000,000 mark. Trustees who served as caretakers of this

ABC Contractor
Charles Feihe, ABC's 4th President

ABC insurance benefit fund included Maryland ABC members Casper Sippel, Harold Hogg, John Sands, James Green, Oscar Schneider, and Baltimore-based insurance agent Charles Herget. ABC's able insurance director, Woodrow Moats, supervised day-to-day promotion and administration of the plan, and it became one of the Association's most important member solicitation and retention components. President Fred Schnabel had this to say about the state-of-the-art Security Plan:

Since its inception, many changes and improvements have been made so that the coverage provided would be sufficient to keep pace with rising hospital and medical costs. We are now charging less for the Plan than we were in 1964 and giving more coverage. Many of our members have found that the savings they realize from participating in the Plan over their own private plans is enough to pay their annual ABC membership dues.

The Security Plan also has been helpful to those members working on jobs which come under the Davis-Bacon Act or state prevailing wage laws. The money paid by ABC contractors for their employees under the Plan qualifies for "health and welfare fringe benefits" in determining prevailing rates. Moreover, the insurance trustees act as a watch dog committee to see that the Plan is operated in the best interests of our Association. They also function as a decision-making body on any proposed changes or additions to the insurance program, acting in consultation with the ABC Executive Committee.[14]

New Retirement Benefits

Another major benefit for ABC employers and their employees was created in 1967 when Fred Schnabel signed the master trust agreement covering a retirement program as a companion part of the ABC Security Plan. The expanded retirement plan was underwritten by Massachusetts Mutual Life Insurance Company and administered by ABC's national office. ABC's Investment Trust was controlled by W.L. Gardner and Associates and the Equitable Trust Company of Baltimore. A companion pension program was established for internal ABC staff personnel.

Under the Security Plan's terms, "member employers were able to provide their employees with profit-sharing or almost any other kind of lawful hand-tailored security blanket desired. The program emphasized individual selectivity and flexibility in design, in tax benefits, and in portability of its protection among employees who move from one ABC firm to another."

This dual health insurance and retirement benefits package was the first of its kind in the open shop movement and second to none in the construction industry.

By the late 1960s, Fred Schnabel, John Trimmer, and other ABC leaders were flying all over the United States to trumpet the merit shop story and spearhead this period of steady growth for their popular Association. Trimmer also brought prestige to ABC as a member of the Labor Relations Committee

Goodwill is the one and only asset that competition cannot undersell or destroy.

MARSHALL FIELD
BUSINESS LEADER

289

In the arena of human life, the honors and rewards fall to those who show their leadership qualities in action.

ARISTOTLE
GREEK PHILOSOPHER

of the U.S. Chamber of Commerce and several national employer executives' organizations.

Another Schnabel-Trimmer initiative was the direction of ABC's lobbying efforts in a labor-dominated Congress. Some of the major goals achieved were as follows: *first*, another defeat of the AFL-CIO's perennial common situs picketing bill which attempted to legalize secondary boycotts at construction projects; *second*, defeat of the passage of a barrage of anti-merit-shop construction law bills; and *third,* federal certification of several ABC chapter apprenticeship training programs. A substantial portion of each local chapter's membership dues helped to finance these national accomplishments.

John Lochary Takes the ABC Helm

In 1969 John Lochary—the quiet, hardworking chief executive officer of Property Construction Company located in Baltimore County, Maryland, and a longtime leader in ABC's Baltimore Chapter—became ABC's 14th national president for a two-year term. His first monthly "President's Letter" to all members contained these grave words of warning about the building trades unions:

> In many parts of the United States, a "shadow" government has taken over control of the construction industry. We refer to the building trades union leaders, with their unbridled power to compel membership and levy 'taxes' in the form of exorbitant wage increases. Victor Riesel, the syndicated columnist, who was blinded with acid thrown by labor goons, wrote in his column: "The building and construction trades unions are restructuring society at their own pace and pay."
>
> What can be done to break this shadow government with its nefarious effects upon the economy as a whole? Systems people are sitting back and watching. Big companies are considering how they can get their own work done less expensively. Open shop contractors are benefiting in the competitive market and as union wage rates escalate, they can be expected to benefit even more.[15]

John Lochary took advantage of these national economic circumstances as he continued to focus ABC activity on membership and chapter growth plus improved services to its merit shoppers. He also moved ABC's legislative office from the Dickinson Building at Friendship International Airport near Baltimore to the Cafritz Building at 1621 I Street, N.W., in Washington, D.C., on November 1, 1969, for convenience in servicing the Association's increased national political activities.

ABC CONTRACTOR

John P. Lochary, ABC's 14th president (1969-1970).

The results of this aggressive leadership caused *Engineering News-Record* to select Lochary as the first ABC president to be featured on the prestigious magazine's cover. And *ENR* ran a companion article that heralded ABC's success, with Lochary at the helm, "in reinvigorating the construction industry by introducing real competition into its monopolistic practices which had brought on inflation." The article accused the trade unions of escalating labor costs and observed, significantly: "AFL-CIO construction workers and union contractors don't scare easily but they're scared now by the growth of the open shop movement."[16]

Five of ABC's national presidents in the 1960s, Charlie Marsh, Tracy Coleman, Jimmy Long, Fred Schnabel, and John Lochary—with outstanding administrative help from ABC's two senior staff executives, John Trimmer and Gene Higgins—diagnosed and cured the Association's teenage growing pains. Under their joint leadership, ABC became a major entrepreneurial force in the construction field.

This success also brought with it increasing respect by America's business community. At the same time, it intensified the hostility of Big Labor, its supportive left-wing politicians, the liberal national news media, and ivory tower academia.

CHAPTER 25

ABC GOES NATIONAL

THE YEAR **1968** was filled with catastrophic human events. A disastrous undeclared Vietnam War was still dragging along. A 10 percent surtax on American taxpayers' income was passed to support it. The nation was recovering from shock at the assassination of President John F. Kennedy.

Although President Lyndon Baines Johnson was still in the White House, he had bowed out of the re-election presidential race in the face of certain defeat. Soon after, Robert Kennedy, JFK's brother and a presidential hopeful, as well as the Reverend Martin Luther King, Jr., were assassinated. In the wake of Dr. King's murder, riots broke out in 125 cities. About 150 people were killed, 2,600 were injured, arson was rampant, and over 21,000 arrests were made.

National morale hit the bottom.

On the labor relations front, a rash of violent strikes spread across the country. Federal mediators attempted to settle over one hundred work stoppages involving 77,000 construction workers. These labor disputes involved Davis-Bacon "union-prevailing-wage-scale" projects as well as private sector free market "lowest-qualified-bidder" sites. A reported 142,000 construction man-hours were lost on NASA's space program alone.

The building trades unions, flexing political and economic muscle, were in the vanguard of these strikes—and the cost of their labor contract settlements was considered outrageous. George Romney, a Republican presidential candidate, told the public that construction wage agreements were "two to three times the increase in gross national product" and that "reward based on contribution had been replaced by reward based on raw power." An economic upheaval was

To suffer and to endure is the lot of humanity.

Pope Leo XIII

The cost of living has gone up another two dollars a quart.

W. C. FIELDS
COMEDIAN, IMBIBER, AND MOVIE STAR

beginning, coupled with tremendous financial outlays for the Vietnam War and for President Johnson's ineffective "war on poverty." John Trimmer explained the grave national situation and its ironic beneficial effect on ABC:

> During this incubatory stage of cost-price escalation, our successes were a forerunner of things to come. As raging inflation was later to prove to everyone, ABC was among the first groups speaking out on America's need to turn back from its governmental juggernaut of centralized economic controls toward the basically free enterprise economy that had nurtured its greatness. The year 1968 brought both challenges and victories for ABC on the national scene.[1]

Labor strikes continued and financial outcry on the industrial front grew more strident. The resulting inflated wage and benefits settlements set off alarms in executive suites throughout America over spiraling building and construction expenses. By July of 1968, the National Association of Manufacturers was declaring a "cost crisis" and claiming that trade union wage settlements were "a substantial contributing factor."[2]

One prominent firm, Dow Chemical Company, announced that it was shutting down more than $90 million in new building projects "because of unsettled labor conditions." Dow President H. D. Dean emphasized that "this situation is of such broad national consequence that additional action is required." And so his firm promulgated its own internal wage stabilization goals and procedures which it decided were necessary "to turn back the tide of inflationary construction spending."[3]

The Roundtable Fights Big Labor and Inflation

Many other leaders of major industrial firms denounced the wage demands of the trade unions as extortionate, and a sense of catastrophe prevailed. In 1969, led by U.S. Steel Corporation's retired board chairman, Roger Blough, two hundred of the nation's chief executive officers formed the previously mentioned Construction Users Anti-Inflation Roundtable, later known as the Business Roundtable.[4] Its members, in addition to U.S. Steel, included General Electric, Exxon, DuPont, and many other corporate luminaries with sizable construction budgets. Their goal was to reduce skyrocketing costs for building new plants because of—as described that year by *Fortune* magazine—"the collective bargaining strength of the most powerful oligopoly in the American economy."

The solution, according to U.S. Steel's Roger Blough, was to ally the Roundtable with ABC, offer bid opportunities to open shop contractors, and support their congressional lobbying against "unfair" labor legislation. He emphasized the "enthusiasm" with which the open shop movement had been accepted throughout the nation "as an alternative to solve the economic crisis."[5]

The unionized side of the construction industry, on the other hand, said Blough, is "one of the most uneconomic and inflationary types of workmanship that we have anywhere in the country and much of the increase in building costs can be laid to this serious imbalance in labor relations." A widely distributed publication of the Roundtable criticized unionized contractors who capitulated to exorbitant and inhibiting labor contracts for their inability to prevent unions from "usurping the employer role normally reserved to management in other industries."[6]

During this national financial debacle, surprisingly favorable attention also became focused on ABC by some of the national news media, including *Time* and *Newsweek* plus the more impartial *Fortune*, *Reader's Digest*, and *Engineering News-Record* magazines. The primary reason for this favorable publicity was obvious: Open shop projects of high quality were being completed on schedule while building trades strikes idled unionized construction projects, wasted man-hours, and were resolved by excessive labor cost settlements. As *Fortune* explained, ABC was providing "an antidote to the economic distortions brought about by trade union monopoly and its medieval work rules."[7]

The situation became so serious that even President Johnson's pro-union Council of Economic Advisors criticized the building trades:

> The rise in construction prices has exceeded the advance in most other industrial sectors by a substantial margin. This is principally due to the fact that wages of construction workers have been rising more rapidly than those of industrial workers while improvement in [unionized] construction practices and techniques has lagged seriously...

A nickel ain't worth a dime anymore.

Yogi Berra
N.Y. Yankees
Catcher-Philosopher

People forget how fast you did a job—but they remember how well you did it.

HOWARD W. NEWTON
CONSULTANT

At the same time, changes in construction techniques which would improve productivity and afford at least a partial offset to rapidly rising wages have been slow in coming. This has been especially true in many urban areas where standards are rigidly controlled under local building codes. They have retarded the advances made possible by developing technology and have preserved high-cost techniques. The construction trade unions have resisted changes in these codes [and] have been especially opposed to changes in the allocation of work among different categories of craftsmen and to the use of prefabricated parts.[8]

Meanwhile, at a meeting of the AFL-CIO Building Trades Department in New York City, Paul Wechter, president of the National Contractors Association (whose members operated on a 100 percent unionized basis) was telling the unionists in attendance that "three undeniable facts" were giving his NCA members grave concern: "Open shop competition for industrial plant construction projects is increasing; there are more non-union workers in construction than ever before; and in-plant factory workers are doing more construction work." Therefore Wechter cautioned:

> In the face of these truths, we can only conclude that unions perhaps have reached a turning point in their function as a service organization for the construction industry. And we are forced to admit that if the present trends continue, trade unions as we know them today will not exist in the not too distant future.[9]

The Twenty-Year Accomplishments Of ABC

The dire analyses of the trade union movement by the President's Council of Economic Advisors and Paul Wechter of NCA were accurate. Meanwhile, on the merit shop side of the construction industry, by the end of 1969 ABC had grown phenomenally. The Association chartered *twenty-one* chapters. Five of them were located in Maryland (Eastern Shore, Baltimore Metro, Anne Arundel–Southern Md., Cumberland Valley, and Metro Washington, D.C.). Four were in Pennsylvania (Central, Delaware Valley, Keystone, and Lehigh Valley).

Two were in Florida (Gold Coast and Gulf Coast), two in Michigan (Central and Western Michigan), and two in Louisiana (New Orleans and Monroe). There also were single chapters in Northern Virginia, New Jersey, Massachusetts, Central Ohio, Texas, and Arizona, plus pre-charter recognition and individual contractor members-at-large in *fourteen* other states and Puerto Rico.

The first of many statewide ABC affiliates were established in Maryland and Pennsylvania to coordinate legislative and marketing activities on a broader basis. Meanwhile a thousand future journeymen were pursuing ABC apprentice training programs, with *18 percent* of them from minority ranks. And the total contractor-membership count exceeded *3,000*, with a workforce estimated at *350,000* employees.[10]

To briefly recapitulate, ABC's successes in its formative first twenty years included: (1) flexible use of multi-skilled mechanics, apprentices, trainees, and helpers on private sector construction projects; (2) the recruitment, training and employment of women and minorities in construction work; (3) a national award-winning safety program; (4) a precedent-setting construction industry health, medical, and retirement security plan; (5) increased political action in the defense of free enterprise against monopolistic unionism; (6) relocation of national ABC offices to Washington, D.C., for closer contact with government officials and their agencies; and (7) voluntary civic and community services donated throughout the nation whenever a legitimate need arose that could be helped by the expertise and resources of ABCers.

Many other ABC achievements previously discussed were the direct result of labor law victories, such as: (1) defeat of "top-down" construction situs secondary picketing and boycotts; (2) defeat of a compulsory union-only "Chicago-style" standard agreement; (3) defeat of union common situs "merry-go-round" picketing; (4) government certification of ABC's national and local apprenticeship training programs; (5) defeat of Maryland's union-slanted "Little Davis-Bacon" prevailing wage law; (6) defeat of vindictive union "whistleblowers"; (7) defeat of a socialistic labor union "Bill of Rights" in a proposed new Maryland constitution; (8) creation of successful "dual" union and non-union construction operations; and (9) defeat of "bottom up" union organization drives initiated through employee secret ballot representation elections conducted by the National Labor Relations Board.

Progress in industry depends very largely on the enterprise of deep-thinking people who are ahead of the times in their ideas.

Sir William Ellis
English clergyman
and author

These major accomplishments in the 1950s and 1960s launched and solid-ified the Associated Builders and Contractors throughout America. Within 20 years after being created, it had truly "gone national." Its premier position as the merit shop voice in the nation's workplace was undisputed.

News of ABC's growth and victories over compulsory building trades labor spread throughout the land. Contractors in many states wanted to know more about this singular organization. But it also was true that these AFL-CIO craft unions were still performing half of America's industrial, commercial, and insti-tutional construction work.

And they wanted desperately to regain control of the other half by whatever means was required.

"Let's organize."

298

PART TWO

MOBOCRACY ON THE PICKET LINES

"There is no reason for people to resort to the kind of mob action or physical injury to persons and property that have caused one whole segment of the construction industry to put security against violence as its foremost problem."

ENGINEERING NEWS-RECORD
(MCGRAW-HILL PUBLICATIONS)

CHAPTER 26

UNION TERRORISM ERUPTS IN THE WORKPLACE

COMPARATIVELY PEACEFUL LABOR SCHEMES to either unionize or destroy open shop contractors were backfiring in the 1950s and ABC membership was continuing to grow by leaps and bounds. As a desperate response, in the 1960s and 1970s the building trades unions reverted to their traditional strong-arm tactics. They called it "going back to basics."[1]

Labor terrorism—"the use of force or threats to demoralize, intimidate, and subjugate"[2] non-union contractors—has been a fact of life in the construction industry for many years. Its effects have resulted in severe personal injury, murder, property destruction, lost work opportunities, reduced production, and dissipated corporate profits. It has even jeopardized the nation's safety, health, and welfare. Unfortunately, the perpetrators frequently are given governmental immunity from punishment for their misdeeds.[3]

The physical and temporary nature of the work, the vulnerability of jointly used work sites, union jurisdictional disputes, and the insecurity of the hiring hall employment relationship controlled by the building trades unions all provide a natural setting for hostility to erupt. Union threats, coercion, and physical force are used for many reasons: as an organizing device, as a collective bargaining tactic, as a mechanism to ensure solidarity among recalcitrant union members or crafts, as a public attention-getter, and—most of all—as leverage to force capitulation by every opponent of compulsory unionism.

In an authoritative text on this little-publicized subject, Professors Armand Thieblot, Thomas Haggard, and Herbert Northrup of the University

"Scab labor—get the hell out!"

"Tools of the trade."

"If we don't defend ourselves, who will?"

Families are being threatened.

"No more freeloaders!"

A collection of photos of building trades unions "going back to basics" against ABC member contractors in the late 1960s and early 1970s.

of Pennsylvania's Wharton School, described some of the purposes of union violence:

> . . . *First*, it is intended to frighten contractors and employees from working open-shop; *second*, violence serves to frighten construction users from awarding contracts to open-shop builders; and *third,* its purpose is to increase the costs of open-shop builders if they win contracts by requiring rework for damaged jobs done; purchase of new equipment for that destroyed or damaged; extra costs for safety provisions, guards, legal assistance; and other expenses such as recompense to employees for damages to their property or person.[4]

ABC's leading members were chosen as the primary targets of this terror. There was intimidation of the construction company owners, managers, supervisors, rank-and-file employees and their families, clients, business associates, and suppliers, coupled with mass picketing, personal assaults, sabotage, extortion, and property destruction wherever ABC firms were thriving and expanding.

To make matters worse for these ABC standard bearers, when they sought protection from government agencies that were responsible for public safety, the bureaucrats displayed a *laissez faire* attitude about organized labor's illegal activities. John Trimmer recalled the merit shop's dilemma in trying to protect the security and property of ABC members as he wrote:

> Law enforcement was slow and sporadic. It has been said that "a public official sees many votes on the blue-collar picket line but few in the corporate front office." I remember the frustrating times we had trying to convince district attorneys, police chiefs, sheriffs and other political office holders to do their duty and enforce the law against union violence, arson, personal assault and other illegal pressures.
>
> It was not uncommon for them to claim that "labor problems were none of their business." Occasionally, the wind would shift the other way and I was offered a cushy position if I would leave ABC, but I wasn't buying. I do admit that time and again I was scared, but perhaps just too naive to cave in.[5]

Many of the same people who have no difficulty in finding extenuating circumstances to account for the violence of the hardhats find it impossible to accept any explanations for violence of the general public.

NORMAN COUSINS
CONSULTANT

In response to this increasing trade union savagery, John Lochary, ABC's fifteenth national president, sent a letter to all ABC members that included these memorable words:

> The turmoil which many of us have been predicting for a number of years has become a reality all along the country's eastern seaboard. The Constitution's protection of the right of the people to assemble peaceably and speak freely is not a license for revolution. "Freedom of speech" does not mean freedom to shoot. "Peaceful assembly" is not defined as the hurling of firebombs or bricks by unruly mobs. The condoning of this violence by law enforcement officials leads to glorifying anarchy and can only result in the destruction of democracy. We cannot let that happen![6]

Not only had ABCers become the mortal enemies of the building trades unions but they were also regarded, in John Trimmer's words, as "misfits from the wrong side of the tracks" by unionized contractors, their architects, engineers, financial institutions, and bonding companies. Some construction suppliers and users, many career government officials, most elected politicians, and a majority of government labor agencies, the courts, and the mainstream news media agreed.

Trimmer described the irony of the situation:

> There were union firms in ABC from the beginning and we used many union subcontractors on our jobs, but it is hard to describe what the slur "non-union" meant in political circles. "Leprosy" would have been far more acceptable. The New Deal under Roosevelt, which continued under Truman and was renewed under Lyndon Johnson's Great Society and John Kennedy's New Frontier kowtowed to organized labor. Union bosses walked in and out of the White House at will. They dictated presidential and vice presidential candidates. They held veto power over nominations for offices such as the Secretary of Labor, members of the National Labor Relations Board, the United States Supreme Court, and a host of lesser positions.

How can you guarantee yourself a future in public service? Be willing to sell out for campaign money.

BILL O'REILLY
THE O'REILLY FACTOR

Pro-union legislators nationally and in the states did Big Labor's bidding. Had it not been for southern conservative elements of the Democrat party who held important committee chairmanships in Congress, I have no doubt that our national government would have drifted even further to the political left.[7]

Defying all the odds, this brave troop of ABC merit shoppers persisted. They gained my constant admiration and my all-out legal assistance night and day, weekends and holidays, whenever and wherever I could help. We fought against terrorism at the jobsites, prejudice in the executive and legislative halls of government, and partisanship in the courtrooms. Sometimes bloody but never bowed, not one ABCer that I know of was forced to abandon the principles of free enterprise and surrender to legalized terror and compulsory unionism.

The result—as John Trimmer put it modestly—was that "in spite of the stacked deck against us, the ever-growing band of construction gypsies began to become respectable throughout America."[8]

CHAPTER 27

THE BUILDING TRADES DECLARE INTERSTATE WAR

I T CAME AS NO SHOCK TO **ABC** that building trades union chieftains labeled Baltimore City "the blackest spot in the nation." To emphasize this accusation, on Saturday, April 25, 1964, about four thousand construction workers attended an emotional rally at Baltimore's Fifth Regiment Armory on the corner of Howard and Preston Streets. The objective was to publicize a massive "top-down" effort to force the unionization of all local open shop contractors, especially members of ABC.

This event was sponsored by the Baltimore Building & Construction Trades Council and was preceded by a colorful parade. It featured hundreds of automobiles decked with union banners and slogans plus forty-five pieces of heavy construction equipment driven for a mile or so from the formation arena at Memorial Stadium on 33rd Street to parking lots near the rally site at the Fifth Regiment Armory.

According to the *Baltimore Sun* newspaper, AFL-CIO officials at the big powwow were furious because their member craft unions represented an ever-decreasing minority of Baltimore's seventy thousand construction workers. They vowed "to make Baltimore the union city it used to be." And fiery James O'Neill, president of the Philadelphia Building & Construction Trades Council, intensified the angry mood of the audience. He was followed at the podium by Cosimo Abato, the able and dedicated labor attorney for the Baltimore Building Trades Council.

Abato warned the unruly throng that "unless something is done in the next five years, your standard of living will evaporate and your union as you know

> **Wars almost never end the way starters had in mind.**
>
> MALCOLM FORBES
> PUBLISHER

it today will not exist." And he urged all union members to be "salesmen of the accomplishments of the labor movement and help to reverse the atmosphere of anti-unionism."[1]

Other Baltimore Trades Council speakers at the 1964 rally named ABC as "the chief devil of the labor movement" and outlined a program to "stop ABC and put unionism on the offensive." The *Sun* reported that this plan consisted of three major objectives:

> First, leaders of the construction trades unions would "pin-point" certain key general contractors and present them with an "either or" proposal. In other words, either these contractors and their subcontractors would hire union members 100 percent of the time or no union member would work on their jobs.
>
> *Second*, the Trades Council would establish a geographical area in the heart of the city where all contractors doing business would be compelled to sign this "standard agreement" and hire only union workers.
>
> *Third*, the Trades Council would solicit more open shop builders to join the Associated General Contractors, a rival employers' association whose members hired only union workers—the union's answer to ABC.[2]

The mood of the assemblage at the armory coupled with a mandatory expansion of funds created by a special assessment deducted from the paychecks of all union members reinvigorated the Building Trades Council to defy law and order in reaching its goals. Every strong-arm tactic imaginable began to be used to coerce ABC members into a choice of unionization or bankruptcy. The peaceful, democratic, and legal secret ballot election procedures of the National Labor Relations Board to convince non-union construction workers to unionize were forgotten by the building trades as merit shoppers and their employees were bullied and savaged. Shakedowns, physical beatings, and even homicides occurred. Open shop job sites throughout Baltimore City and its surrounding counties were picketed, raided, pillaged, burned, and dynamited.

A senior executive of the Mullan Construction Company who also was ABC's fourth national president, Charles Feihe ('54), recalled the treacherous times:

> We could only bid on jobs where we were reasonably sure of some police protection. When you left your office—unless you were a careless contractor—you kept looking over your shoulder in all directions until you got into your car and locked the doors. Those were dangerous days.

And Donald Fritz, another Baltimore ABC member, added: I served on active duty during two wars but was never hurt physically. Then I came home and went into the family construction business only to become shot at and beaten up by union goons. It didn't make any sense.[3]

All-Out War Declared at Union Convention

The first public announcement of a nationwide attack on ABC by the Building and Construction Trades Department of the AFL-CIO came at its 54th annual convention in December of 1967. It was attended by international, regional, and local trade union officials from all over the United States. It took place in the plush quarters of the Americana Hotel in Bal Harbour, Florida, and was financed by the dues of non-attending rank-and-file union members.

After calling the convention to order as its chairman, National Building Trades Department President C. J. Haggerty recognized the first speaker, Guido Iozzi, Jr., a rugged iron worker who became the feared boss of the Baltimore Building Trades Council. His assignment was to give the hundreds of trade union leaders gathered there a first-hand review of the growing ABC movement and rally them for "an all-out battle against this major menace to the security of every unionized building tradesmen."[4]

Iozzi began by charging—in typical union dialect of the times—"that tha merit shoppas hava multa-million dolla budget an evry damn dolla goes ta finance dere fight against da labor muvment." He bemoaned the fact that "I'm doin' my part in Balamer but becuz uv tha laziness uv da udder trade unions, ABC is makin' big gains. And he warned that "unless dis damn union-bustin' bunch is stopped, it'll be coitins for all ovus."[5]

We denounce and oppose violence. If any individual in a union commits a crime, we expect officers of the law to enforce the law... I am fully convinced that there is nothing so hurtful to the interests of organized working men as the use of physical force in their efforts to secure justice—attacks upon life or property.

Samuel Gompers
president, AFL,
on June 7, 1903

Opinions founded on prejudice are usually sustained with the greatest violence.

FRANCIS JEFFREY
SCOTTISH JUDGE

Reprinted here are excerpts from Delegate Iozzi's formal remarks that memorable December day as recorded (in purified English translation) within the recorded minutes of the Building Trades Department convention proceedings:

Chairman Haggerty, I speak in order to alert the Building Trades Unions throughout the country to prepare now to defend themselves against destruction by a vicious organization of non-union contractors, which is the Associated Builders and Contractors, otherwise known as the "ABC." This union-busting outfit is determined to destroy the organized building trades movement—and it makes no bones about telling the world of its evil intentions.

Until recently, each time ABC has been mentioned, the building trades have considered it a problem affecting only the unions in Baltimore. Today, however, it must be recognized that ABC is no longer just a problem for Baltimore. It has spread throughout the Atlantic Seaboard and into the Midwest, and unless it is stopped it will become a nation-wide organization bent upon destroying all building trade unions everywhere...

In every state that the ABC enters it points to Baltimore and tells the contractors and owners about how it defeated the trade unions in the nation's sixth-largest industrial city and third largest seaport. ABC describes how it grew from a couple of contractors who installed store fronts to a giant organization whose member contractors can now erect $12 million dollar buildings....

ABC is a major menace to the security of all union building tradesmen—not just the Baltimore building tradesmen, and it is even more. It is a menace to the public generally because it wants to have the legal right to erect buildings with unskilled, untrained men without any regulations regarding quality of construction or standards of safety. Such structures would jeopardize the lives of all the people who entered them.

The Building Trades Department knows full well how dangerous the ABC is, because the Department tried several times to fight it in

Baltimore, but ABC won the fight. It had grown into such a powerful union-busting organization that the unions entered the battle too late, with too little with which to fight back.

Delegate Iozzi then urged an immediate call to action:

> If we continue the same laxity today that we demonstrated in the '50s, ABC will grow just as powerful throughout the country as it now is in Baltimore. Unless we want to witness the destruction of all the standards of skill and wages and working conditions that unions have gained through the years, ABC has got to be stopped—and stopped now.
>
> Therefore, Mr. Chairman, I would like to see this Convention take action to expose ABC for the evil force that it is; I would like for this Convention to take action to prepare for an all-out battle to counter the union-busting war the ABC is now waging against us. If we wait until the next convention, it may be too late.
>
> In conclusion, I urge this Convention to heed my warning. We have both the power and the know-how to turn back this vicious attack; let's use them to get the job done.[6]

Speaking in support of Guido Iozzi's call to arms against the "evil union-busting ABC" was Peter Brennan, a former master painter, then president of the New York Building Trades Council, later appointed U.S. secretary of labor by President Richard Nixon. Martin Graham of the Ohio trade unions also echoed the call for "war on ABC." These leaders were followed on the Bal Harbour podium by concurring union chieftains from Washington, D.C., Pennsylvania, Delaware, New York, New Jersey, Ohio, Michigan, Florida, and Tennessee—all locations where ABC members were making major inroads.

After these tirades about ABC's "vicious attack on union security" had been completed, officials of the seventeen assembled international craft unions and their state union delegates unanimously adopted and publicly distributed the following ominous resolution designed to motivate the defeat of ABC's merit shop movement:

Like a mounting devil in the heart, so rules unreined ambition.

NATHANIEL WILLIS
AUTHOR

It's difficult to argue you are for working men and women when your policies prevent them from working by destroying the businesses that would employ them.

JACK KEMP
CONGRESSMAN (R-NY)
AND VICE-PRESIDENTIAL
CANDIDATE

Whereas in recent years a serious menace to the working conditions and the very existence of our building trades unions has made its presence felt in no unmistakable terms; and

Whereas the sole stated purpose of this organization is to undermine and undercut working conditions and wages of union craftsmen employed in the building and construction industry, and to eventually destroy the Building and Construction Trades Department and its affiliated International Unions; and

Whereas this organization has made great progress and growth since it was established a few years ago in the Baltimore area and now has charters in over ten states; and

Whereas this challenge to our livelihood must be met head-on;

Now therefore be it resolved that there be appointed a Special Committee comprised of officers of the state and local councils directly affected by ABC, with the objective of formulating an effective organizing campaign to combat the ABC and to report to the Executive Council of the Building and Construction Trades Department.[7]

ABC Rebuts the Building Trades "Declaration of War"

The Board of Directors of ABC immediately released a counter-statement to the news media denouncing the Building Trades resolution as "false, hostile and conspiratorial." This press release also reaffirmed ABC's belief in the merit shop principle "where union and non-union construction firms work side-by-side in harmony."

Here is more text from ABC's historic public declaration:

> The Associated Builders and Contractors condemns the action of the Building Trades Department as an obvious effort to destroy the livelihood of employers and employees in "merit shop" construction. The vitriolic attack against ABC on the floor of its recent convention was completely unjustified. The shibboleths repeated against ABC are indications of intellectual bankruptcy and the resolution adopted is a tissue of misrepresentations hardly paralleled in union history.

It is high time that the American government and people be informed as to just what Building Trades Department unions are doing to the construction industry. We, as an Association, are far from alone in observing the disastrous course upon which the building trades unions are embarked. There is no question that under the guise of "work preservation" contract clauses, they have obstructed the introduction of time-saving prefabricated equipment and materials on construction sites. The practice has resulted in further acceleration of the already greatly inflated construction costs.

This obstructionism follows right along with the exorbitant wage demands that have been universally condemned. In fact, even the largest general contractors association in the nation [the unionized Associated General Contractors] has expressed alarm at the thrust of wage settlements during the current year.

In the troublesome area of discrimination, the U.S. Labor Department has exposed the fact that the building trades unions have been far behind the times in admitting minority groups to their membership rolls.

The Building Trades Department representatives also have been active in apprenticeship councils to prevent training of apprentices in the merit shop construction industry. By these tactics they have prevented opportunities for minority and majority youths alike to undertake gainful employment.

Furthermore, the Trades' Department's resolution completely distorts the policies and practices of the ABC and its thousands of member firms. The Association's policies have been public information for years.

ABC's press release concluded with its voluntary "live-and-let-live" policy between labor and management:

> We stand for the "merit shop" in construction, a method of operation in which union and non-union firms work side by side in harmony, and we are opposed to any form of compulsory unionism.

Success is simply a matter of luck. Just ask any failure.

EARL WILSON
COLUMNIST

History is a race between education and catastrophe.

H. G. WELLS
ENGLISH AUTHOR
AND HISTORIAN

We are well aware that employees have the legal right to organize and bargain collectively for their benefit. At the same time, we believe that management should be aware of its own entrepreneurial rights under the law. Moreover, we have promoted the installation of fringe benefit programs including health and welfare, pension plans, profit sharing and others, some of which do not even exist in the unionized segment of the industry.

We recognize the importance of the union movement in the nation. But we believe along with the vast majority of Americans that no private group should arrogate to itself a power so autocratic that individuals who may disagree are deprived of their right to earn a living.

We believe, furthermore, that the individual rights granted under the U.S. Constitution are sacred rights, that among these is that of the individual to work at his livelihood without interference from or compulsion to join any private organization, no matter how well intentioned.

We are sure that, contrary to the expectations of the Building Trades Department, the Associated Builders and Contractors will continue to prosper because the "merit shop" means sound construction at a fair price and true opportunity for the disadvantaged. It is this type of construction that we believe the American people want and deserve."[8]

The battle lines were drawn for a labor war between ABC and the AFL-CIO's building and construction trades hierarchy. It would rage from their Washington headquarters to dozens of international craft unions and their hundreds of regional councils to their thousands of local craft union members throughout the nation. Big Labor's conspiracy to unionize or destroy the merit shop crusade was intended to engulf the entire United States—and continues to this day.

CHAPTER 28

THE FALL AND RISE OF A LABOR CZAR

DURING THE OUTBREAK OF VIOLENCE against ABC members in Baltimore, a militant thirty-five-year-old ironworker named Guido Iozzi, Jr. succeeded Clark "Kingfish" Ellis as president of the Baltimore Building Trades Council. Iozzi had gained national attention in the labor movement by his attack on "the ABC menace" at the aforementioned national building trades convention in Florida in 1967 and also by his friendship with Jimmy Hoffa ("Sr.") of Teamsters Union notoriety. This Baltimore Trades Council was now an organization of twenty-six local craft unions, with a total membership of fifteen thousand journeymen and apprentices.

Iozzi grew up in East Baltimore's "blue collar" Highlandtown and attended a vocational school near there. He and his brothers were a pugilistic team who took on all comers and controlled a neighborhood gang. Iozzi enlisted in the U.S. Air Force in 1948 and was honorably discharged as a sergeant in 1952 after serving in Korea. Upon returning home to Baltimore, he became a skilled iron worker—one of the most dangerous construction crafts—and moved rapidly through internal union ranks to become the business agent of Ironworkers Local 16. He held the job from 1961 to 1963.

In 1964, Iozzi was elected the undisputed leader of the Baltimore Building Trades Council, representing all of the local craft unions. The aggressive tactics of this rising union star struck fear in the hearts of foes and friends alike. He organized contractors previously regarded as "untouchable" and rammed through a mandatory union membership dues increase that bolstered the Trades Council's net assets from $18,000 to $115,000 in four years. The fee also contained an extra "penny-per-hour-worked" for union political action in the Democratic Party.

On one occasion, as the story goes, a leader of Iozzi's Iron Workers Local 16 named Angelo "Crowbar" Caroletti was observed enforcing the dues increase in an unusual but effective way. The method used was dangling a delinquent fellow union member by his heels from the tenth floor of a building still under construction. The reluctant "brother" changed his mind and promised to pay in cash immediately upon his return to an upright position.

Iozzi Indicted for Murder

Iozzi was built like a middleweight prize fighter, wore tailored clothes with fancy jewelry, chain-smoked Viceroy cigarettes, lived a tumultuous life, and was rumored to have underworld ties. He landed in major legal trouble in the fall of 1965 when he was indicted by a Baltimore City grand jury.

The charge against Iozzi was conspiring to murder the forty-three-year-old Kenneth Hatfield, a respected local Bricklayers' Union business agent and member of the Baltimore Building Trades Council. He was shot once in the chest and twice in the back by an unknown man whom the victim's wife heard ask, "Are you Ken Hatfield?" Then she heard three shots that went through the Hatfield home's front screen door and ended her husband's life.[1]

This shocking "gangland-style killing" made news media headlines. It was motivated by events that occurred in mid-summer when Baltimore building tradesmen established a picket line around a construction project at the facilities of my client, The Johns Hopkins Hospital. The union goal was to prevent non-union carpenters from continuing to work there.[2]

It seems that this particular Hopkins project was "pin-pointed" as a 100 percent union job under the Baltimore Building Trades Council's "standard agreement." Union leaders claimed that the scheme had been rendered legal—in spite of ABC's *Stover Steel* and *Selby-Battersby* secondary boycott case victories—due to a subsequent (Landrum-Griffin) amendment of the Taft-Hartley Act. But Ken Hatfield's bricklayers only honored the pinpointed hospital picket line for one day and then he ordered them to "scab" by crossing the picket line and returning to work. Hatfield said that his union was not bound to respect this type of "ideological dispute" aimed at reducing open shop competition when it jeopardized patient care and safety in the hospital.

The *Baltimore News-American* newspaper reported what happened next:

> In order to force Hatfield and his bricklayers out on strike again, a 27-year old steelworker "with contacts" was hired to get somebody to scare Hatfield by wounding him. The contract went to an ex-convict for a sum thought to be about $500. Five times the trigger-man went to Hatfield's home with a pistol that had been supplied him. Each time he lost his nerve at the last moment. He bowed out when he was picked up for violation of probation and sent back to jail, and the contract went to another unnamed person.
>
> Two days later the new "hit man" earned his money, but overstepped his obligation in a fit of nervousness by shooting Hatfield three times through the front screen door of his home. As the bricklayer official breathed his last, the killer fled across Radecke Park and dropped the 22-calibre murder weapon as he ran. [His own bullet-riddled body was found later in a country road ditch.][3]

Guido Iozzi pleaded "not guilty" to the murder charge and requested a speedy trial because the indictment was "injurious to his reputation in union labor circles." His able and aggressive young lawyer, Peter Angelos, eventually became the chairman of a large regional law firm that he created by the prosecution of claims of industrial asbestos victims and other tort class action plaintiffs. (Angelos also became majority owner of the Baltimore Orioles baseball team, a civic leader devoted to Baltimore, and a national power in the Democrat Party.)

The Contest Is Removed to Eastern Shore

On the eve of Iozzi's trial, Angelos suddenly asked for a change of venue from the Baltimore courts "because of adverse publicity preventing a fair hearing." In view of the possibility of a death penalty if Iozzi was convicted, Judge Dulany Foster granted the location change and the trial began on December 15, 1965, in the town of Princess Anne on Maryland's Eastern Shore. The

The world turns and the world changes, but one thing does not change, however you disguise it: the perpetual struggle between Good and Evil.

T.S. ELIOT
IN "THE ROCK"

Mine honor is my life; both grown in one; take honor from me and my life is done.

WILLIAM SHAKESPEARE
POET-PLAYRIGHT

opening statement of the prosecutor of the case, Deputy State's Attorney George Helinski, told the court that his star witness—an unemployed oiler named John Keller who had not been charged with any criminal offense—would testify that Iozzi gave him $800 and told him that Hatfield "had to be roughed up." [4]

Prosecutor Helinski also claimed that Iozzi went to Keller's house a few days after the murder and told him to "forget everything you know about this." When called to the witness stand, Keller stunned Helinski by refusing to testify on grounds of self-incrimination. As reported by the news media: "Keller pulled the clam act and took the fifth after he previously had promised the State that he would waive his constitutional rights and answer all questions."

Faced with Keller's refusal to cooperate in exchange for immunity from prosecution, Helinski told the court he had no evidence to offer and rested his case. Judge McMaster Duer and Judge Daniel Prettyman of Maryland's First Judicial Circuit Court immediately granted a defense motion by Peter Angelos for acquittal of Iozzi on all charges stemming from the murder.

The trial ended on the same day that it began.

Keller, the reluctant witness, subsequently was indicted, tried, convicted, and sentenced to ten years in the Maryland Penitentiary for perjury as an accessory before the fact and a conspirator in the Hatfield murder. During December of 1967, however, the Maryland Court of Appeals reversed the conviction because Keller's statements induced by a promise of immunity could not be used later to convict him of a crime. [5]

Based on this turn of events, Iozzi's mentor—"Kingfish" Ellis—attempted to promote a $25-per-plate "testimonial" dinner for his meteoric protégé by the local building trades unions, with the net proceeds allegedly going to "charity." The dinner was cancelled after heated debate in which some union members charged that "the banquet was just an excuse to pay Iozzi's legal fees in the Hatfield murder case." [6]

The Feds Put Iozzi behind Bars

Four years later, in 1969, Guido Iozzi was indicted again, following a nine-month-long federal grand jury investigation of union racketeering. This time it led to his conviction following prosecution by an astute and courageous young U.S. attorney, Stephen Sachs. The charge was extorting thousands of dollars from contractors in cash payoffs "under the table in exchange for labor peace," in violation of the Hobbs Anti-Racketeering Act. Sachs based his case against Iozzi on the sworn testimony of a parade of twenty-nine witnesses who described "a drumbeat of pressure by the trade union leader."[7]

Terror tactics used, Sachs said, included work slow-downs, illegal picketing, threats of physical violence, use of harassing "safety inspection squads," clipping of power lines, breakage of automotive equipment, and the display of a hangman's noose on a construction job site. Iozzi even shook down Dominic Piracci, a builder who was the father-in-law of Baltimore Mayor Tommy D'Alessandro.

A reporter covering the trial described the thirty-five-year-old Sachs as "wearing a baggy, tweedy suit, with a shock of thick dark hair and a casual stance that made the young prosecutor look like Dustin Hoffman playing Perry Mason." And the newsman added: "His court demeanor and questions to witnesses became increasingly tough."[8]

According to Sachs (who subsequently served two terms as Maryland's attorney general) this president of the Baltimore Building Trades Council was an "outlaw driven by the need for cash and by a passion for personal power to ride roughshod through the construction industry in Baltimore." He "misused the conventional tools of organized labor," claimed Sachs, "by converting them for his arsenal of extortion while selling out his own union members by allowing non-union contractors to work on unionized jobs."

Iozzi pleaded "not guilty" to the federal charge while publicly professing "shock and surprise" at the indictment. On a motion of his new defense counsel, Raymond Bergen from the Washington law office of Edward Bennett Williams, the trial was removed by Judge Alexander Harvey in December of 1968 to a federal district court located in the city of Alexandria, Virginia.

Walter Skopp: Hunter or Hunted?

Attorney Bergen had contended that "an unusual event made the selection of an impartial jury in Maryland impossible." That event, he said, was the wide

> **Physical bravery is an animal instinct; moral bravery is a much higher and truer courage.**
>
> WENDELL PHILLIPS
> ORATOR AND
> SOCIAL REFORMER

publicity given to the sudden death of a key witness for the prosecution, namely the business agent of Electrical Workers Local 24, one Walter Skopp. It was front-page news that Skopp had been shot to death by a shotgun blast at point blank range. It came, presumably, from the weapon of one or the other of two federal marshals who were assigned to protect Skopp's safety prior to the trial. The dramatic demise occurred while all three men were huddled together in a duck blind on the western shore of the Chesapeake Bay near Reno, Virginia. Skopp, an avid hunter, was in the middle in more ways than one.

After a brief government investigation that reported "an apparently accidental death," the two marshals resumed their regular duties. A federal official in Washington observed: "They have to guard a lot of funny people at times. Just two weeks before this accident, they had gone deer hunting with Skopp."[9]

The *Baltimore Sun* of December 16, 1968, carried these headlines: **SKOPP DEATH PROBE UNABLE TO FIX BLAME** and **SKOPP DEATH MYSTERY YET**. The article went on to report the Virginia medical examiner's opinion that "the shotgun blast almost squarely in the back of Skopp's head apparently ruled out the possibility of suicide or death from an accidentally self-inflicted wound."

U.S. Attorney Sachs acknowledged that Skopp's untimely demise eliminated his critical testimony that he was the payoff "bag man" for Iozzi in many of his shakedowns of non-union contractors in exchange for labor peace. But Sachs told Judge Harvey that he was prepared to go forward with the trial because the government's case against Iozzi was still supported by substantial evidence of "a pattern of illegal conduct that defied any legitimate labor objective." It included, Sachs explained, testimony by William Kirchoff, business agent of Operating Engineers Local 27, who had personal knowledge of Skopp's extortion activities. Several contractors and construction users involved in the ripoffs were prepared to corroborate Kirchoff's statements.

A Holiday Affair

After Iozzi was indicted for this crime and free on bail before the trial began, he held a Christmas party for "four hundred close friends," including labor union members and supportive politicians. One incident in this colorful event was described by the *Baltimore Sun*:

Shortly after this evening party began, the Hilton North meeting room was beginning to fill. A small orchestra played soft dance music, while several groups of persons entered the hotel. They were met at the door by two men sitting at a table with a list of those invited.

These two ticket-takers checked names against the list while Mr. Iozzi stood in the doorway of the meeting room, shaking hands and conversing. The uninvited people who stood near the doorway to look inside the room were escorted down the corridor by another man who said: "There are some travel posters down here I think you'll enjoy looking at."[10]

> **I could not tread these perilous paths if I did not keep a saving sense of humor.**
>
> LORD NELSON
> BRITISH ADMIRAL

A few days later, the Baltimore Building Trades Council approved a 50 percent pay raise for Iozzi. At first it was explained as "a routine incremental increase" called for in Iozzi's ten-year contract with the Trades Council that had been "in the works" before the grand jury indictment was presented. Later on, a union source admitted that in the previous year, his raise in pay was $3,000.[11]

Iozzi was not called by his attorney to testify as his trial on union racketeering proceeded, but three members of the executive board of his Building Trades Council contradicted some of the testimony given by witnesses for the prosecution. They claimed that any "harassment and pressure" by Iozzi was merely "a legitimate collective bargaining tactic aimed at persuading non-union contractors to sign the Building Trades Council's standard union shop agreement."[12]

"A Danger to the Community"

The trial lasted two weeks but the jury of seven men and five women took only three hours to bring in a guilty verdict. In the course of sentencing Iozzi on March 25, 1969, to serve fifteen years in prison and pending his appeal of the conviction, Judge Alexander Harvey cancelled Iozzi's $30,000 bail and sent him to jail. The judge called him "a danger to the community who sold unionism down the river." Iozzi's attorney took the trade union leader's appeal for a release on bail all the way to the U.S. Supreme Court, where it was denied by Chief Justice Earl Warren.[13]

The *Baltimore Sun* editorialized on February 15, 1969, about Iozzi's conviction as a "labor racketeer":

Murder, though it hath no tongue, will speak with most miraculous organ.

WILLIAM SHAKESPEARE
HAMLET II. II.

Guido Iozzi, Jr., chosen by his fellow construction workers to be their leader throughout Baltimore, is found instead to have undertaken the low-road career of labor racketeer. A United States District Court trial ends in his conviction on half a dozen charges the background of which is extortion, shakedown, physical injury and property destruction (as threat and sometimes as occurrence) and other shameful abuses of the whole labor-management process ...

Doubtless the verdict will be appealed, and doubtless labor racketeering did not begin with the regime of the incumbent president of the Baltimore Building Trades Council nor will it necessarily all cease as and when he is deposited inside the walls of a federal penitentiary. Nevertheless, the instances brought to light in recent testimony in an Alexandria (VA) courtroom, thanks to the courage of Iozzi's victims, have fitted together to form a pattern of cynicism, greed, terror and contempt for the law and the unions themselves—a pattern which the Baltimore public has regarded with shock and disgust. And Iozzi, no outsider but a life-long Baltimorean, has brought discredit upon his city; he has hurt and diminished the working man's cause.

For bringing these scandals out into the open, for producing testimony that would stand up in court and lead to a hard clear finding of guilt, the United States attorney for this district, Stephen Sachs, and his assistants and staff deserve earnest thanks. The removal of so festering an evil offers a real improvement to life in this community.

On May 7, 1969, the incarcerated Iozzi was honored by "union members and some business executives" at a rally in the Fifth Regiment Armory. Here are excerpts from the *Baltimore Sun's* report of that event:

A commemorative plaque honoring Iozzi's leadership of the 15,000 members in 26 building trades unions was presented to his son and wife who said simply: "On behalf of Guido, we accept this." After an ovation for Iozzi's family, Edward J. Courtney, the business agent for Local 438, Steam and General Pipe Fitters Union, assumed the Trades Council leadership ... and called for "brotherhood" among the local unions.

Three weeks later, while Iozzi's appeal of his conviction was in the hands of the Fourth Circuit Court of Appeals in Richmond, Virginia, union members were asked to contribute ten dollars each to the "Guido Iozzi Defense Fund." In the months that followed, a dozen contractors and several local trade union officials were convicted and fined or imprisoned for their participation in what the court found to be illegal payoffs masterminded by Iozzi.[14]

Publicity surrounding this lawsuit caused State's Attorney Charles Moylan, Jr. to comment on his concern about the "lack of safeguards" against contractors who routinely incorporated pay-off money to labor leaders into their bids for construction projects. Reporter Thomas Edsall of the *Baltimore Sun* interviewed Moylan and summarized his views this way:

> The first problem is that the responsible agency, the Police Department, is "totally unequipped to handle the job." The department lacks auditors and financial investigators of the kind necessary to do the digging into accounting books. The second problem, Mr. Moylan said, is that it is questionable whether there is any law against incorporating expected pay-off demands into bids. Federal law under the Hobbs Act covers demanding, making and receiving pay-offs, Mr. Moylan said, but simply planning on an expected demand is not covered.[15]

An editorial in the *Baltimore Sun* which appeared on the same day, simply entitled "Iozzi," added the following observations:

> Why don't contractors report extortion demands to the authorities? One reason in some cases may be that the contract carries a performance clause, with money penalties for default. Performance may fail if labor troubles develop. Can the contractor be sure the authorities will work fast enough to catch the extortioner and abort his plans? Will the police control illegal picketing at his construction site and protect him and his family against the open terrorism that sometimes features these cases—threats of property damage and even bodily injury?
>
> The questions raised are obvious and so are the answers. Contractors must agree collectively and singly to prompt and faithful collaboration

Angry men are blind and foolish, for reason at such time takes flight.

PIETRO ARETINO
ITALIAN WRITER

We often place too high a premium on "flexibility" as a value itself. In America's relativistic climate, the person who hedges or splits the difference regardless of the circumstances receives acclaim as a "moderate." But the person who adopts a strong unyielding position gets labeled "extreme" or "radical."

KATHERINE HARRIS
CONGRESSWOMAN
(R-FL) AND AUTHOR,
CENTER OF THE STORM

with the law as one of the risks of their trade. But law enforcement officers must minimize such risks by prompt and rigorous action on complaints and energetic protection of complainants. (Obviously taken for granted is equally energetic action against contractors who don't complain but do collaborate with extortioners.) The public's stake is clear enough: to smash corruption and squeeze its very high costs out of the price of building.

Iozzi Loses the Appeal of His Conviction

A famous trial lawyer named Melvin Belli defended Iozzi in the appeal to reverse his conviction of extortion on constitutional and evidentiary grounds. But Judge John Butzner of the federal Fourth Circuit Court of Appeals (joined by Judges Simon Sobeloff and Albert Bryan) denied the request on January 12, 1970. In this major victory for free enterprise and the merit shop, Judge Butzner explained that as president of the Baltimore Building Trades Council, Iozzi had

... used his position to foster the impression that he had sufficient power to slow down or stop construction projects unless his demands were met. With respect to Count 1, the evidence is clear that Iozzi demanded and received $10,000 in cash from the president of Morrow Brothers Construction Co. With regard to Count 3, he demanded, but did not receive, $20,000 from Ames-Ennis, Inc., another [ABC] general contractor. . . .

Work stoppages and picketing on the contractors' other jobs, Iozzi asserts, had nothing to do with his demands for money, but, on the contrary, were designed to persuade the contractors to sign a Building Trades Agreement. He, however, never explained this nice distinction to his victims. They quite justifiably believed that their difficulties with labor, his demands for cash, and his insistence that they sign a labor agreement were inextricably mixed. The evidence discloses that Iozzi forcefully drove home the point that the alternative to the contractors' financial and economic loss was payment of the tribute he levied. His conduct transgressed the bounds of legitimate labor tactics and violated the Hobbs Act. . . .

Count 5 involved the payment of $3,000 so construction on an office building in Towson, Maryland, could proceed. Walter Skopp, business manager of a local union of electrical workers, conducted the negotiations and made the demands for payment. He represented that he was acting for Iozzi, and that unless payment was received, the Mafia, with whom he said Iozzi was linked, would sabotage the job. . . . Significantly, it was Iozzi, not Skopp, who pocketed the money and sent back a message through the intermediary that he, Iozzi, was not going to be bought for chicken feed like $3,000. Iozzi's receipt of the fruits of Skopp's extortion gives credence to the government's assertion that Skopp was Iozzi's agent. As Judge Learned Hand said of a similar situation, "There may be honor among thieves, but there is no maudlin munificence."[16]

Iozzi was paroled from prison in 1974 for "good behavior" after serving five years of his fifteen-year sentence at the Allenwood Prison in Lewisburg, Pennsylvania. He was barred for five more years from holding elective office in a labor organization because of his conviction under the Hobbs Act and, for a short time, became the superintendent of a non-union Baltimore-based concrete distributor.

Iozzi's Triumphant Return from Allenwood

My own meetings with Guido Iozzi over the years in the representation of clients had always been "above the table" but tense. He was one of the most intimidating union leaders I ever confronted. To my amazement, however, one fall day in 1983 Iozzi telephoned to ask me for a draft of a personnel policies manual for use by the non-union concrete firm that had employed him. Fortunately for all concerned, it seemed that he had "reformed." After considerable soul-searching, I gave him a copy of my model employee handbook and other effective employee relations material.

I never heard from him again.

A short fling in the open shop environment apparently didn't change Guido Iozzi's deep-rooted loyalty to the trade union movement and the power it gave him. He soon left the managerial job, and in 1991 he became manager of his

Adversity makes a man wise, not rich.

JOHN RAY
WRITER

alma mater, Ironworkers Local 16. He was interviewed that year by columnist Dan Rodricks of the *Baltimore Evening Sun*, and the unusual event proceeded something like this:

"Here we go again," Guido Iozzi said. "Whenever youse come around, I know you're gonna be diggin' up tha past. They put that poison pen in you peoples' hands." I [Rodricks] hadn't said a word but "hello"...

"When we gonna say it's over? Why don't you deal in today's news, not somethin' that happened 20-somethin' years ago? Why don't cha write that he was a veteran of the Korean War, he served his country, and he gave a lot of money to the Israel people? Why don't cha write that and leave what I paid society back for outta this?" Iozzi continued.

Good question. Easy to answer.

When Iozzi was paroled from federal prison, he was restricted from holding union office [president, vice president, treasurer, etc.] for five years. By the spring of 1979, he was running for business manager of Local 16. He lost that election. But, 12 years later, in a development that might be quintessentially American—a nation of second and third chances—he's set to assume the post he long coveted.

Iozzi gets a salary and a car. He sits on the boards of the local union's multimillion-dollar pension and annuity funds; he's even a trustee of the local's apprenticeship program. He's a national convention delegate as well...

Why did Guido Iozzi persist in seeking office in his old trade union local?

He says "tha past is tha past. I paid tha price, I gotta family, I gotta live. They needed good leadership. And I'm tha best."

By Bo Rader in 1990/Photo reprinted with permission of *Baltimore Sun*

Still militant! Baltimore Building Trades Boss Giudo Iozzi's former Ironworkers Local No. 16 picketing L. R. Wilson & Sons, Inc., an ABC contractor, at a hospital construction site.

CHAPTER 29

BALTIMORE LABOR DUELS OF THE 1970s

EDWARD **C**OURTNEY, **THE BUSINESS MANAGER** of Steamfitters Local Union No. 53, was Guido Iozzi's handpicked choice to succeed him as president of the Baltimore Building Trades Council when the long arm of the law sent him to jail. The same pattern of union intimidation, mass picketing, bodily assaults, and property desecration continued in the metropolitan Baltimore area under his successor. It was endorsed again at the AFL-CIO's Building Trades Department annual convention in 1971.

Inflammatory remarks at that time, as in the 1967 convention, were focused on "busting" the open shop rival—and this time the chief "hatchet man" was Courtney. He submitted to the powerful union assemblage a Resolution 22 labeled "Defeating ABC Attack on Building Trades Unions." It described the Association as a "viciously anti-labor group of open shop contractors dedicated to the destruction of building trades unions as effective bargaining agencies."[1]

Resolution 22 referred to Guido Iozzi's similarly militant resolution that was adopted at the 1967 building trades convention. It also reemphasized ABC's tremendous expansion. Then the resolution called on the Building Trades Department and all of its affiliated international and local unions "to initiate immediate and effective programs to combat the ABC and thus defend the building trades unions from ABC's union-busting attacks while reclaiming the historic jurisdictions which have been lost to the ABC by local unions in many areas."[2]

Finally, Ed Courtney's 1971 Resolution 22 proposed that this nationwide scheme against ABC should be implemented by the following carefully phrased "organizational" activities:

> **A man's worst difficulties begin when he is able to do as he likes.**
>
> THOMAS HUXLEY
> BRITISH SCIENTIST

(1) Revise geographical jurisdictions so that boundaries of local unions conform with those of the local building trades councils with which they are affiliated; (2) Make it mandatory that all local unions be affiliated with local building trades councils in their area; (3) Require all local building trades councils to establish per capita tax systems sufficient to maintain financial strength; (4) Require all local councils and local unions to negotiate "standard project agreements" in conformity with Section 8(e) of the Taft-Hartley [National Labor Relations] Act; (5) Insist that local unions coordinate their activities through their respective local councils; and (6) Establish a permanent committee to coordinate organizational activities, with membership to include officers of local building trades councils where the ABC or any other anti-union trade association is active.[3]

Courtney's Resolution 22 was adopted unanimously and referred to the central office of the National Building Trades Department in Washington, D.C. There its Committee on Organizations promptly recommended that "the affiliated International Unions fully support the need of affiliation with the Local Building Trades Councils by their respective Local Trades Unions; that such affiliation should be on a full membership basis in the Local Council's jurisdiction; and that these affiliates should cooperate upon an organizational basis to strengthen their membership in every Trades Council jurisdiction and otherwise support and cooperate with their Local Trades Council."[4]

Union Terrorism at Morgan State College

Two of my clients, John K. Ruff, Inc. (the largest non-union general contractor in the Baltimore area) and Lawrence Construction Company (another major merit shop firm), soon became primary targets of Ed Courtney's Building Trades Resolution 22. The Ruff firm was led by its resolute chief executive officer, Ralph Ensor, who (by no coincidence) also had been the first president of ABC's newly formed Baltimore Metropolitan Chapter.

The series of unprovoked attacks against Ensor's company began on January 26, 1972, at the campus of Morgan State College, where a $3.4 million library building was being constructed. More than 150 members of Ed Courtney's Steamfitters and Pipefitters Local Union 438 arrived at that job site and began destroying construction equipment. Trailers were toppled and burned, sand was poured into fuel tanks of heavy equipment, and a storage shed was set afire. The blaze was not extinguished until it reached a construction trailer where it destroyed blueprints and other valuable accessories.

On the morning after the Morgan project was closed down, members of Steamfitters Local 438 formed a massive picket line featuring signs claiming that "union wage standards are being sacrificed." When Albert Marani, vice president of the non-union Lawrence Construction Company, arrived to inspect the site, he was attacked and beaten severely. A few minutes after Marani was rescued by reluctant Baltimore City Police patrolmen, ten molotov cocktails blew up a Lawrence Construction trailer.

Ralph Ensor of the Ruff firm immediately sent a telegram to Maryland Governor Marvin Mandel, a Democrat, requesting the stationing of National Guardsmen on the Morgan State College site. This request was denied by Mandel. A representative of the Baltimore City Police Department's Public Information Division explained that they couldn't help either "because the college campus was on state property."[5]

During a press interview, the business agent for Steamfitters Local 438 suggested that the damage was caused by the elements: "It was very windy that morning and maybe it blew over the trailers and some crossed wires started the fire." As this union official was giving the news media his weather report, another union representative added that the picketing was "purely informational" and was only intended to "inform the public" that a non-union subcontractor on the project (ABC member Ingleside Plumbing and Heating, Inc.) was "failing to pay union scale wages."[6]

Keswick Nursing Home Targeted

When mass picketing and violence began again at Morgan State College on January 27 (the next day), I filed the necessary legal papers for a court injunction to restore law and order. That move caused the building trades unions to abandon their illegal activities at Morgan State College and turn their hostility on another John K. Ruff, Inc., project in Baltimore City: the Keswick Nursing Home. Some 350 enraged unionists from the same Steamfitters Local

The measure of a man is what he does with power.

Pittacus
Statesman

Baltimore ABC chapter firms hit by trade union terrorism in 1972-1973

438 converged upon a recent addition to that health care facility for the aged and the incurable. Two construction trailers were torched and a large crane was firebombed.

The helpless patients panicked.

I immediately requested a Baltimore City Court to extend my previous petition for injunctive relief at Morgan State College to this Keswick Nursing Home project and any other Baltimore City construction location attacked by the Baltimore Building Trades. A week later Judge Meyer Cardin granted my petition. He forbad all trade union representatives from "threatening, blocking, or assaulting" ABC employees attempting to enter or leave any construction job site within Baltimore City. The judge also limited the number of pickets on any such project site to four persons at each entrance.

Towson University Attacked

After a relatively peaceful weekend, the Ruff firm's work at Towson State Teachers College (now called Towson University) on its newly constructed $6 million fine arts building in Baltimore County was disrupted at six o'clock in the morning by more riotous picketing, arson, and other property destruction. About 375 union tradesmen blocked ingress and egress at the Towson State job site, forming what the news media called "a solid wall of human flesh"[7] to prevent the fires from being extinguished. A construction trailer and a crane were overturned and burned. Baltimore County firemen summoned to extinguish the blazes were physically blocked from entering the construction site by the enraged pickets. A fire hose forced through the hostile picket line to put out the fires was cut in half with an axe. Rocks and other debris were thrown in all directions.

Some of the unionists involved at the Towson State project carried signs disclosing that they represented Ironworkers Local 16 (Guido Iozzi's and Ed Courtney's trade union). Picket signs also proclaimed that the Ruff firm paid wages that were "below union scale" and "endangered union standards." My legal petition to a Baltimore County Court for an extension of the Baltimore City Court's restraining order was denied when a county judge relied on his distorted interpretation of Maryland's antiquated "Little Norris-LaGuardia" Anti-Injunction Act. The continuing brawl eventually required fifty county

> **A mob will be no less a mob if it is well fed, well clothed, well housed, and well disciplined.**
>
> RUSSELL KIRK
> *THE CONSERVATIVE MIND*, 7TH EDIT.

All seems
infected that th'
infected spy, as
all looks yellow to
the jaundic'd eye.

ALEXANDER POPE
ENGLISH POET

police plus twenty-five riot-trained state troopers with K-9 guard dogs to restore law and order.

Four days later, about one hundred pickets ignored the previously issued Baltimore City court injunction and massed at the municipal site of a new Fire Department Pumping Station near the landmark downtown Bromo Seltzer Tower. My ABC client, William F. Wilke, Inc., was the general contractor on this project. Three non-union craftsmen were assaulted while attempting to cross the picket line and two policemen were beaten severely for trying to protect them. It was the fifth attack in nine days at a Baltimore City non-union construction project in January and February of 1972. A state police helicopter monitored the devastation and front-page headlines of the *Baltimore Sun* blared out: **FOUR HELD AFTER VIOLENCE ERUPTS AT CITY BUILDING SITE**.

I persuaded a representative of the City sheriff's department to show my citywide court injunction to the union leaders involved and they claimed they "had no knowledge of it." Upon being advised by the sheriff's emissary that the injunction was "valid," they reluctantly left the project site but no arrests were made. On my recommendation, ABC called a press conference, led by the Ruff Company's Ralph Ensor. He charged that there was "a reign of terror by the local building trades unions because the police and the courts were failing to furnish adequate protection."[8]

ABC Goes on the "PR" Offensive

The next evening Ralph Ensor and other ABC contractors spent from 9 p.m. to midnight describing the union violence on radio station WCBM's talk show hosted by Alan Christian. His four call-in phone lines to WCBM were never silent during that three-hour program. Over the airwaves, ABC President Ensor set to rest the building trades' false charge that his company was paying sub-standard wages (i.e., below union scale). All of the picketed projects were federally funded and required payment of the prevailing (union) wage scale under a Davis-Bacon Act determination.[9]

During this time of crisis, State Senator John Bishop (R-4th Dist.), Delegate Robert Latshaw (R-4th Dist.), and Delegate Robert Strobel (R-3rd Dist.) announced the introduction of bills in the Maryland General Assembly requiring full union restitution for all damages stemming from their violent and otherwise illegal activities.[10]

The resulting publicity caused Maryland's Governor Marvin Mandel to announce at a hastily called press conference that he had "received assurance from Ed Courtney of the Building Trades Council that the union leader would make every effort to see to it that further violence was avoided." As reported in the *Baltimore Sun*, Mandel concluded that "there is no need for any new action or legislation to deal with this labor situation." And Maryland's Attorney General Francis Burch (D-Balto. City) was quoted to the effect that "his hands were tied since the Legislature has not seen fit to give him any grand jury investigative power over union strong-arm tactics."[11]

Big Labor's political influence on most of Maryland's elected officials was then—and still is—awesome.

Green Contracting Company Assaulted

Another client of mine, Green Contracting Company, was the victim of arson at about the same time. James Green (the company's brave CEO and a subsequent Baltimore ABC Chapter president) discovered early one morning that his business headquarters on Old York Road plus a job site trailer and thirty pieces of construction equipment located nearby had been severely damaged by fire bombs. The explosions "coincidentally" occurred at 1:30 a.m. on the eve of an ABC legislative get-together on Capitol Hill in Washington, D.C., led by Jim Green. But the arson didn't keep him from testifying before Congress a day later against a perennial AFL-CIO-sponsored "common situs" picketing bill to legalize secondary boycotts at construction projects and overrule ABC's previously discussed *Stover Steel* case legal victory.

A reward of $10,000 for information leading to the arrest and conviction of the persons responsible for the $30,000 bomb damage to Green Contracting Company was underwritten by members of the Baltimore ABC Chapter. Meanwhile Green praised the ABC staff and members, many of whom called him to offer "money, tools, and other help." He said: "When you have trouble, it's a great comfort to know people with whom you're associated are so ready and willing to come to your aid."[12]

Of all the tasks of government, the most basic is to protect its citizens against violence.

John Foster, Dulles
Secretary of State

Courage in danger is half the battle.

Plautus
Roman philosopher

ABC Contractor

"Greetings from the arson team!" This is the office that greeted ABC contractor James Green the day before he testified in Congress against illegal trade union activities.

ABC's local executive director, Charles Chamberlain, who was working closely with Baltimore police and fire departments on the Green case, noted that larceny and arson damages involving ABC members over the previous year amounted to over $300,000. On my recommendation, Green and Chamberlain re-issued a joint statement reminding all ABC contractors that they should:

(1) Establish liaison with local police in every job location area to assure more than a casual spot-check by patrolmen assigned to the area; (2) Employ watchmen to report suspicious acts in or around each site and record license numbers of vehicles lingering in the area; (3) Make maximum use of high pole lighting, especially in the rear areas of their places of business or work sites; and (4) Impress upon employees the need for reporting all remarks, including threats of union abuse; and (5) all incidents of coercion, property damage, or violence should be reported to Charlie Chamberlain at ABC's local Baltimore

headquarters to compile evidence of a continuing building trades conspiracy and potential cause for legal action.

A Mysterious Visitor

A number of ABC contractors reported to me that before any "trouble" began at their construction projects, they were visited by a burly individual of Hawaiian extraction. He would introduce himself as Alfred Kaleo, a business representative of the Baltimore Building Trades Council,[13] and ask whether they would sign a collective bargaining agreement with the Trades Council. When they refused, Kaleo silently left the premises—and shortly thereafter union foul play "coincidentally" began.

We attempted to obtain a photograph of Kaleo to pass on to ABCers so that they could be on the lookout for a visit from him. We even scrutinized news media photos of mass picketing in order to identify Kaleo, but he never showed his face.

By coincidence, one of my law partners, Lawrence Wescott, happened to be teaching a course in labor relations at Essex Community College when this labor turmoil was taking place. At Larry's opening lecture, as was his custom, he began by asking the students to stand up, identify themselves, and indicate where they worked. Much to Larry's amazement, one of them arose and identified himself as "Alfred Kaleo of the Baltimore Building Trades Council."

After each student had introduced him or herself, Larry gave a brief biographical summary of his own experience in the labor field and—staring directly at Kaleo—announced the name of our law firm. When Kaloo heard the words "Venable, Baetjer and Howard," he skulked out of the classroom and, so far as we could determine, never appeared at Essex Community College or at any ABC job site again.

More Building Trades Terror Targets

Some of the other Baltimore merit shop contractors and subcontractors who were subjected to union insurrection in the 1970s were L.R. Wilson & Sons, Pikesville Electric Company, Leimbach Construction Corporation, Dance Construction Co., Joseph Trionfo and Sons, and High Steel Structures. Five

Violence is the last weapon of the incompetent.

ISAAC ASIMOV
AUTHOR-CRITIC

non-union ironworkers received major injuries from being attacked with pick handles and iron pipes at a $7 million Pennington Avenue bridge project. Trailers were burned at a pyrolysis plant on Russell Street.

One construction worker employed by High Steel Structures was overcome by a mob of union goons in South Baltimore. He suffered a broken jaw and a detached retina in one eye. His firm had been working on the Curtis Bay Bridge project for only one day when the violence occurred. According to newspaper reports, at least five more of High Steel's employees were attacked by the gang who wielded pick handles, iron pipes, and two-by-four boards as the crew reported to work. These workers suffered broken bones and had to be hospitalized. High Steel was the only merit shop firm on the project and its employees were told by the thugs: "We're here to take over the job."[14]

Ingleside Plumbing and Heating, Inc., and its president, Charles Ruth (who became president of ABC's Metropolitan Baltimore Chapter in 1983–1984), were singled out by "unknown sources" for terroristic activities. And Ruth received several death threats from a local trade union boss. His firm's office plus an Anne Arundel County Junior College job site in Severna Park also were seriously damaged in fires set by professional arsonists.

One day about two hundred members of Ed Courtney's Steamfitters Union Local 438 picketed a Baltimore job site of ABC member Lawrence Construction Company. Just before seven o'clock on that morning, the company's vice president saw a trailer toppled over by the mob and attempted to cross the picket line and protect it. He didn't make his goal. The moment he reached the bullies, he was attacked, pummeled to the ground, and remained there in severe pain until rescued by a local policeman. Despite this physical confrontation between the patrolman and unionists who perpetrated the assault, it was decided by law enforcement officials that "the action did not warrant an arrest." The explanation was that "the officer-witness involved had been on the force for only one week and was vague about what actually happened."[15]

The *Maryland Coast Press* of Ocean City reported that a labor dispute there between Glen Construction Co. (an ABC member) and Ironworkers Local 46 "nearly erupted into major violence." The company was unloading steel by non-union workers when the job was blocked by union members who went "head to head" at the 88th Street construction site of the Sea Terrace Motel.

Instead of continuing the fight, Glen management allowed union members to unload the truck "because guns were flourished." Two weeks later, Ocean City police discovered a mysterious fire in the cab of a crane at the site. The trailer office had also been broken into and Police Chief Lee Duggan said his department was investigating the case: "Without a doubt it was definitely set on fire, but we have not been able to learn the identity of the arsonist."

No legal action ever was taken.

James Grant of the *Baltimore Sun* also reported that on Maryland's Eastern Shore "violence against non-union builders resulted in beatings to at least a dozen men and local police quietly advised two contractors to carry guns." The builder hardest hit was MLM Company. One of its mechanics got assaulted by pickets as he prepared to drive away from a jobsite and gave the following statement:

> I started to get into my car and I was knocked to the ground. I got up and started running to the dual highway but only got part way when I was thrown down from behind and hit a few times. While I was on the ground some men started stomping and kicking me.
>
> After a while the thugs let me up. I felt blood running down the back of my head where I had been struck. I needed five stitches to close up the gash in my head and a cast on my right leg due to a break where I had been kicked.[16]

No one was arrested in this fracas either. It was just one of many such ignored "incidents" during four days of mass picketing.

Crossgates, Inc. and Cumberland Are Invaded

These violent trade union raids also spread as far west as the city of Cumberland, Maryland. In 1972, an ABC client of mine, Crossgates, Inc., began building a high-rise complex for the elderly in the center of this union-controlled municipality, and the project came under severe siege by the local building trades council. I immediately issued a public statement for the benefit of the community. It was published in the *Cumberland News* and produced positive results for ABC and my client:

Neutrality, as a lasting principle, is evidence of weakness.

Louis Kossuth
CONSULTANT
AND WRITER

Crossgates—a merit shop employer—gave unionized subcontractors every opportunity to bid on this job and made awards to the lowest qualified bidders. At least two of the subcontractors who were awarded jobs actually employ union labor. Crossgates also met informally with representatives of the building and construction trades unions and told them that jobs would be available for qualified, local construction workers in the various crafts, as needed, regardless of their membership or non-membership in any labor union. Union members could apply at the job site for these positions as they became available. The answer given to Crossgates by spokesmen for the building trades unions and its trades council was "either you do this job all union or it will not be done at all."

Under the circumstances, Crossgates would like Cumberland area citizens to know that as this building progresses—and we will never be intimidated by union bullyism—we will be employing more and more local construction workers, local truck drivers and local suppliers. The citizens of Cumberland should also know that upon completion of this $4.3 million structure, the taxes paid into the Cumberland government on what was formerly a vacant lot and the personnel hired to care for the elderly will be of substantial benefit to the community.

Because of the hostile and dangerous situation created by these labor organizations, Crossgates has instructed us to file unfair labor practice charges with the National Labor Relations Board against both the local building trades unions and their international parent unions in Washington, D.C. We will also take whatever other federal and local legal action is necessary to insure the orderly and safe continuation of this major building project for the elderly. The mass picketing, vandalism, blocking of streets, threats to persons crossing picket lines, hurling bricks and stones, air rifle shots and other terroristic tactics will not be tolerated.

We are sending a copy of this release to Cumberland Mayor George Wyckoff, Police Chief G. P. Giles and Economic Development Director Richard Mappin in order to guarantee their cooperation in keeping this project and the persons on it working safely, without fear for their lives and property.

It is a shame that organized labor, when it loses out in fair and competitive bidding, attempts to take the law into its own hands and uses fear to try and force unionism on workers who oppose it. The reputation of Cumberland as a desirable place for new businesses to locate and the welfare of the entire community (including the elderly) is at stake.

Cumberland residents and the local government reacted favorably to this statement for Crossgates; the building trades backed off; and justice triumphed. Completion of the first merit shop building within the city was assured without any further strong-arm "incidents."

The only noticeable reaction of the building trades regarding this defeat in Cumberland was to move their terrorism to other ABC locales. In a follow-up editorial a few months later entitled "Trouble on the Job," the *Baltimore Sun* (a conservative news medium in those days) suggested that organized labor was engaged in a dangerous "conspiracy" against the merit shop movement:

> Intimidation, sabotage and arson are criminal acts that have no place in labor-management disputes. Yet an unusual and unhealthy number of such acts have been recorded by public officials on and off construction sites around the state. Individual beatings and destruction of property following threats are tactics directed at non-union contracting firms, the record shows. Builders estimate losses in man-hours and property damage at more than $500,000 this year alone; some workers who defied threats have been seriously injured. And of 16 men convicted on charges connected with these and other crimes, not one has served a day in jail, according to a survey by reporter James Grant of the *Sun*.
>
> Given the established pattern, Marylanders should be appalled. Why haven't the prosecuting arms of federal, state and local governments been more effective in stopping such blatant abuses? . . .
>
> As state Attorney General Francis Burch points out, nothing under existing Maryland law permits a statewide investigation. Still, one is clearly needed if hard hats and their employers are to live in peace and

Our first duty is to war against dishonesty. Corruption in every form is the arch enemy of the Republic.

THEODORE ROOSEVELT
26TH PRESIDENT

341

Man behaves as if he is the missing link between the ape of yesterday and the human of tomorrow.

MARTIN GROTJOHN
PSYCHOLOGIST

solve their differences at the bargaining table, not the battlefield. The Governor and his legal aides must make every effort in this instance to safeguard potential victims and prosecute the criminals, by whatever means available.

For the most part, federal investigators have been turning over their findings to local state's attorneys. Isolated indictments and convictions, however, don't seem to offer any remedial effect. And the larger question of whether or not a conspiracy exists deserves immediate attention.[17]

Neither that public rebuke by the *Baltimore Sun*, nor ABC's local court injunctions against trade union violence and public relations campaign in the news media, nor the incarceration of Baltimore Building Trades Council President Guido Iozzi, nor threatened legislative action by three valiant Maryland delegates discouraged the ever-burgeoning AFL-CIO Building Trades war against ABC.

The fortuitous question raised in that Baltimore Sun *editorial about whether Big Labor was engaging in a "conspiracy" of terrorism against the merit shop movement turned out to be exceedingly timely and would soon be answered.*

CHAPTER 30

UNION BRUTALITY IN THE CITY OF BROTHERLY LOVE

PHILADELPHIA, LIKE **B**ALTIMORE and many other older cities along the East Coast, had been a "union town" for many years. The local building trades unions held a virtual monopoly on metropolitan construction work. It was not a coincidence that they were ardent supporters of successive leftist mayors and enjoyed a close relationship with city hall. Labor union officials received lucrative appointments to local government agencies dealing with housing, zoning and building codes, craft apprenticeship programs, and prevailing wages.

Philadelphia was also a municipality where construction union threats, physical abuse, and sabotage against open shop employers were beginning to flourish. A major labor-management confrontation arose during 1963 in a geographical area covered by the newly established Delaware Valley Chapter of ABC. Its jurisdiction encompassed the entire metropolitan Philadelphia area.

As John Trimmer told the story, "the Philadelphia Building & Construction Trades Council was thundering against ABC's invasion of their territory." He noted that "a cartoon created by the Trades Council pictured us as an octopus from the south, spreading tentacles out of Baltimore and into Philadelphia." In "defiance," concluded Trimmer, "the Trades Council promoted and enforced a mass meeting of 10,000 of its members in historic Convention Hall for the purpose of arousing opposition to ABC and the merit shop movement."[1]

This rowdy powwow was addressed by such dignitaries as the pro-labor mayor of Philadelphia and Jimmy Hoffa, Sr., president of the rackets-infiltrated

False conclusions which have been planned are infinitely worse than blind impulse.

HORACE MANN
EDUCATOR

343

Where law ends,
tyranny begins.

WILLIAM PITT
THE ELDER
BRITISH STATESMAN

International Teamsters Union. In an hour-long diatribe, Hoffa guaranteed to "fight shoulder-to-shoulder for union scale wages." Then the mayor promised the unruly mob that "as long as I am in office no ABC contractor will ever do a lick of work for our city."[2]

Fisher Construction Company Is Assaulted

Not long after that hostile labor rally was held in the shadow of the Liberty Bell in Independence Square, the Fisher Construction Company—a non-union general contractor that ordinarily performed residential work—began building a $630,000 motor lodge in Lester, Pennsylvania, near Philadelphia's international airport. The Fishers (father and son) tempted the fates by engaging non-union subcontractors for the project, with the sole exception of a union subcontractor who was needed to perform pilings work.

Affronted officials of the Philadelphia Building Trades Council and its affiliated Steamfitters, Operating Engineers, and Teamsters Unions demanded that the Fishers take three actions: (1) sign a labor contract covering their employees; (2) revoke their construction contracts with all non-union subs; and (3) give all work on the airport motor lodge project to unionized contractors and subcontractors whose craftsmen were affiliated with the Trades Council.

The Fishers were warned that "we're gonna maka youse go union or ruin ya," but they refused to capitulate. On August 15, 1963, the Trades Council established a small group of so-called "informational" pickets who claimed they were peacefully exercising their constitutional right to free speech at the motor lodge site. Their signs protested: **THIS BUILDER IS DESTROYING INDUSTRY STANDARDS BY NOT OBSERVING PHILADELPHIA AREA WAGES AND CONDITIONS.**

On the tenth of September, the number of pickets at the motor lodge construction site zoomed to over four hundred. They massed arm-in-arm, encircling the entire project and making access impossible. Then they ignored a local court "cease and desist" order against this violence that limited the number and manner of picketing. Instead, they continued to destroy new construction already in place, assault Fisher's employees, wreck expensive construction equipment, and forcibly prevent jobsite deliveries. The garage of a subcontractor was dynamited while homes of the Fishers and the owner of the motor lodge were paint-bombed. Neutral firms and their employees who persisted in doing business with the Fishers were threatened with reprisals.

In order to continue work on the motor lodge to meet a completion deadline, the frustrated Fishers decided that they would obtain concrete and cinder block from non-union sources by sending their own pick-up trucks to several open shop block-manufacturing plants. But roving union tradesmen followed the trucks and set up picket lines at public entrances into the non-union block plant facilities. This caused the fearful plant management to refuse to load Fisher Company trucks.

Soon after that, a homemade bomb shattered twelve units of the Lester motor lodge project. It tore out the roof, walls, and floor of a thirty-foot section in the middle of the building. The Lester township police chief said his six-man force could not cope with the situation and Pennsylvania's Governor William Scranton refused to give any assistance.

"Intolerable" was the word used by the *Philadelphia Daily News* in an editorial that described the Fishers' fracas and urged Scranton (unsuccessfully) to provide necessary police protection against the "coercion and vandalism." The newspaper concluded that "individual acts of violence are bad enough, but when explosives hurl debris in all directions, the public safety is endangered. We hope those responsible for the latest outrage will be caught and punished promptly."[3]

The Fishers offered and publicized a $1,000 reward "for confidential information leading to the arrest and conviction of the persons responsible for the bombing," but there was no response. At this point, the distraught contractor was on the verge of capitulating to the union demands but fortunately decided to make a last minute appeal to ABC for advice and assistance. Delaware Valley Chapter members, led by President Jim McGee and Executive Director Ralph Miller, immediately rallied to the Fishers' cause.

These resolute ABCers, along with John Trimmer and other staff from the national office, helped the father and son to solve many jobsite problems so that normal work could resume. They also bolstered the Fishers' resolve to mount a legal counter-attack. Trimmer remembered the tense situation as "the essence of ABC contractors joining together to protect their right to freely operate their businesses."[4]

> **I got problems wid da woid "violence." Whatsit mean?**
>
> ACTUAL ALIBI OF A UNION REPRESENTATIVE

The Fishers Win a Legal Battle

With ABC's assistance, a secondary boycott unfair labor practice charge was filed and approved by the Philadelphia office of the Labor Board against the offending unions. About fourteen months after the labor siege began, the picketing and other illegal activity was enjoined temporarily by a federal district court, followed by a hearing on the merits of the Fishers' charge before the Labor Board.

On December 11, 1964, the Board finally ruled that the Building Trades Council's "informational" picket signs protesting the company's failure to pay so-called area wage rates and observe industry standards actually were just a

ABC CONTRACTOR

Some of the vehicles wrecked by rioters.

"sham." The real purpose of this union "venture," the Board held, was an illegal secondary boycott to force the Fisher Construction Company to stop doing business with its chosen neutral subcontractors and recognize a labor organization as the exclusive representative of its employees.[5] Eventually a federal appellate court reaffirmed the Labor Board's decision requiring the Trades Council and its member craft unions to cease and desist the picketing and all other illegal activities.[6]

John Trimmer summed up the impact of this early victory over compulsory unionism in Philadelphia: "There was no question that if the Fishers had not come to ABC for help, their firm would have succumbed to labor coercion and violence. The final result also protected and extended geographically the merit shop concept of entrepreneurial freedom to build harmoniously on either a union or non-union basis without interference by either with the other."

CHAPTER 31

THE ORDEAL OF ALTEMOSE CONSTRUCTION COMPANY

ONE OF THE MOST BRUTAL UNION ASSAULTS on a business firm in the history of American labor annals occurred in the same "City of Brotherly Love" eight years after the Fishers' motor lodge confrontation. It involved the prolonged torture of another non-union employer known as Altemose Construction Company.

This enterprise was founded by Leon Altemose at the age of twenty-two. He had graduated from Eisenhower High School in Norristown, Pennsylvania, studied engineering at Penn State University for three years, and then decided (for financial reasons) to leave college and become a general contractor. Under his soft-spoken leadership, the Altemose firm grew in ten years from a small homebuilder to a multi-million-dollar construction giant. It moved into big-time commercial and public building projects along the Philadelphia Main Line suburbs, with several subsidiaries and three hundred employees.

Leon Altemose was a dedicated merit shop practitioner who farmed out the bulk of his work to whichever qualified subcontractors—either union or non-union—bid the lowest prices. His firm's gross sales rose from $250,000 in 1963 to $35 million in 1972.

The reign of union terror against Altemose, a member of ABC's Delaware Valley Chapter, began in August of 1971. A labor dispute arose with the Building & Construction Trades Council of Philadelphia over the company's refusal to sign a "subcontractors' agreement." It would have obligated Altemose to subcontract only to firms using union labor, no matter how high their

Liberty is one of
the most precious
gifts God has
bestowed upon
Man. No treasures
the earth contains
or the sea con-
ceals can be
compared to it.
For liberty one
can rightfully
risk one's life.

MIGUEL CERVANTES
SPANISH POET-
PLAYWRIGHT

charges. Underlying this action were the hundreds of labor agreements between the local Trades Council and its business allies in the General Building Contractors Association ("GBCA") of Philadelphia. These contracts required GBCA-member contractors to hire union employees exclusively, to employ them under the terms of the Trade Council's collective bargaining agreements, and never to do business with subcontractors whose names did not appear on the Trades Council's "fair contractor" list.

It was irrelevant to the Trades Council that Leon Altemose utilized union subcontractors whenever their craft skills were needed and paid his own employees wages and benefits equal to or better than the local trade union scales. In true merit shop fashion, however, Altemose was unwilling to deny bidding rights to qualified non-union firms. As an alternative solution, he told the Trades Council that he would consent to an election conducted by the National Labor Relations Board and abide by the secret ballot choice of a majority of his employees on the question of union representation. The answer of Tom Magramm, business manager of the Trades Council, to Altemose's democratic counterproposal was: "Sign our union-shop deal or we'll shut down all youses mutha-fuckin' goddamn job sites."

The Labor War Begins in Prospect Park

Leon Altemose refused to surrender to this blackmail. On January 24, 1972, (reportedly "just to soften Altemose up") several hundred trade union pickets congregated and blocked roadways at an elementary school in Prospect Park, Pennsylvania, where the firm was constructing a new wing for the main building. Five Altemose trucks were burned and threats on his life and the lives of his employees began.

One employee told the news media: "I've been warned on three occasions by members of the Trades Council. One of them claimed he would come back to my home and cut me and my family into little pieces and put us in plastic bags to get rid of us." Another craftsman volunteered: "My wife got a phone call at home telling her that if I didn't quit working for Altemose acid would be thrown in her face and my baby's face." An employee of a non-union Altemose subcontractor was attacked by six building trades pickets when he attempted to cross their line surrounding the Prospect Park

School project. This victim suffered multiple fractures, lacerations, and a brain concussion.[1]

A secondary boycott charge was filed immediately at the Philadelphia regional office of the National Labor Relations Board against the Trades Council by a prominent local labor lawyer, John Pelino, on behalf of Altemose. This charge was accompanied by the customary request that the Labor Board seek immediate injunctive relief in a federal court to stop the illegal activity. It motivated the Trades Council to enter into a settlement agreement that limited peaceful picketing to the Prospect Park school jobsite's primary gate and by no more than a dozen persons at a time.

Ten days after this legal document was signed—on February 3, 1972—an Altemose office trailer at this same school project was set afire by an incendiary device. And an additional $3,000 in property sabotage was inflicted on construction work in progress. Then on March 5, five trucks belonging to Altemose were drenched with gasoline and burned, resulting in $35,000 worth of damages. On April 10, a truck driver working for a subcontractor arrived at the school construction site and was stopped at the entrance by "strange men." When the driver identified himself and the non-union firm he worked for, he was yanked out of his truck and beaten sadistically. As he was regaining consciousness, a policeman arrived at the site, looked around—and filed an official report that the trucker had injured himself "in a fall from his vehicle."

Valley Forge Plaza Project Is Challenged

Finally the school addition at Prospect Park was completed, but the labor war against Leon Altemose had just begun. It reached a state of total anarchy during the summer of 1972 after his company was awarded a contract to build an $18 million Sheraton Hotel and office building complex plus retail stores and a movie theatre. It would become known as "Valley Forge Plaza." This project was situated on a twenty-four-acre site in a western suburb of Philadelphia called King of Prussia, adjacent to the famed revolutionary war battlefield.

The fact that a prominent non-union contractor would "dare" to build such a visible high-dollar volume project in "their" Philadelphia suburbs domain sent tremors through the Philadelphia Trades Council's high command. Tom

> **Truth is the cry of all but the game of few.**
>
> GEORGE BERKELEY
> ENGLISH PHILOSOPHER

One man with courage makes a majority.

GENERAL ANDREW JACKSON
7TH PRESIDENT

Magramm told a union rally at the Spectrum that "as long as I'm da business manager ah dis Council in no way—an' I mean, in no way—will Philly or da close counties become anotha Balimore." And he announced plans to amass a "war chest" of $200,000 (through a special monetary assessment on each union member) "ta wipe out dat rotten bastard."

News of the Altemose construction contract at Valley Forge even jolted the Building & Construction Trades Department's national headquarters in Washington, D.C. This "contemptible scab action," Big Labor reasoned, would encourage open shop firms to gain jobs in other locales that the AFL-CIO had staked out as "exclusive union country."

The Building Trades Demand a Union Shop

An enraged delegation from the local Trades Council paid Leon Altemose a visit at once, demanding that Valley Forge Plaza and all future projects be built "100 percent union." In a last-ditch effort to avoid more labor trouble, Altemose offered to build the Plaza and its Sheraton Hotel using trade union subcontractors on three-fourths of the project work. He refused to unionize the job further than that because, as he explained, "I will not fire my own employees working there who tell me they don't ever want to be members of any union."[2]

The Trades Council officials ignored this more-than-reasonable compromise and responded publicly again that Altemose was "destroying area wage standards." He denied the accusation, explaining that his employees were guaranteed year-round employment and that their take-home pay was better than the trade union wage scale. His company's liberal employee benefits, Altemose also noted, included paid holidays and vacations, accident and sickness expense protection, fully funded family hospitalization, and major medical insurance coverage. In addition, as an incentive bonus, the company matched 10 percent of its employees' earnings out of the first corporate profits earned each year.

"Many of my workers," Altemose reminded the Trades Council leaders, "are former union members. They know, as I've frequently told them, that if they think they can make more money in a trade union all they have to do is ask for a secret ballot election at the Labor Board to decide the issue."[3]

At a press interview later reported by Commentator Mike Wallace on the television show *60 Minutes*, Altemose described portions of that critical meeting with Building Trades Council leaders in more graphic terms:

> They showed up in two big black cars with about eighteen men, half of whom refused to identify themselves. The other half gave their names reluctantly. They told me that the Valley Forge Plaza Project would never be built; that I would never live to see it built.
>
> The head of the Trades Council, Tom LeGrand, was present. He said that I would have problems of every type imaginable. In the interest of avoiding that type of situation, I made a proposal that the Plaza job be built 70 percent using union men and 30 percent non-union. Then LeGrand told me: "I don't reprasent 70 percent uv noth'n. I reprasent 100 percent uv dis Trades Council, period."[4]

After the Council rejected Altemose's counteroffer to settle the labor dispute and fearing that bigger trouble was on the way, he strung a mile of chainlink fence topped with barbed wire around the company's entire project at Valley Forge Plaza. It was a wise decision. He had heard a rumor that a "demonstration" was scheduled to take place against his firm and ordered all of his employees and subcontractors to stay away from the Plaza job site.

Altemose also requested protection from Upper Merion Township—which had jurisdiction over the Plaza project—because of the potentially dangerous situation. The Township's police chief declined to help, explaining that "any show of force would only be provocative."[5]

The chief would soon regret those words.

In matters of principle, stand like a rock.

THOMAS JEFFERSON
FOUNDING FATHER AND
3RD PRESIDENT

CHAPTER 32

A BATTLE AT VALLEY FORGE

IT WAS OBVIOUS THAT THE Philadelphia Building Trades Council never became interested in pursuing any of the fair compromises offered by Leon Altemose to end the labor impasse between them. Union leaders knew they couldn't win a majority vote if they petitioned the Labor Board to conduct a secret ballot election on the question of the militant Trades Council's representation of the company's well-treated employees. And no Trades Council official would "allow" 25 percent of the construction work to be performed "open shop." In their minds, Altemose was "a rotten union-bustin' scab." They vowed "he would neva live to see da Sheraton built" and promised "an all-out war ta make da goddamn pimp go broke." Nothing less than 100 percent compulsory unionism would satisfy Big Labor, regardless of the preference of his employees for individual independence as to their job benefits and workplace issues.[1]

At dawn on the morning of June 5, 1972, the Trades Council launched what the Supreme Court of Pennsylvania would later describe as "a virtual military assault." It was "marked by a degree of violence and destruction reflecting little improvement in the state of labor relations during the three quarters of a century since the Pullman and Homestead strikes."[2] Spearheaded by the Trades Council's corrupt Roofers Local Union No. 30, a hostile but well-disciplined mob of a thousand construction workers poured out of a caravan of private cars and seven buses chartered by Local 30. They had precise orders on how to destroy the Valley Forge Plaza project of Altemose Construction Company.

Choices are the hinges of destiny.

EDWIN MARKHAM
PHILOSOPHER

353

Cry "havoc" and let sip the dogs of war.

SCRIPTURER 736:16

According to testimony by eyewitnesses, the onslaught was coordinated by a bunch of roughnecks dressed in flashy business suits who arrived at the scene in Cadillac Fleetwoods. Many of their young "troops" were wearing printed cardboard signs identifying them with the Trades Council and repeating their claim that Altemose wages were "destroying industry standards." Then they tore down five thousand feet of chainlink fence surrounding the project, marched over the top of it and followed colored smoke signals to designated targets within the site. Union mobsters were equipped with wrecking bars, Molotov cocktails, and hand grenades as they laid waste to everything in sight.

The annihilation was beyond belief.

Forty-Five Minutes of Hell

Al Haas, a reporter for the *Philadelphia Evening Bulletin* who covered the siege, wrote the next day:

> I felt like a war correspondent. The scene at that construction site was right out of Vietnam . . . For openers, union tradesmen threw rocks at the first group of Upper Merion policemen who appeared, tore down eight-foot high cyclone fences around the tract, and set fire to a futuristic housing module which previously had been on display for civic and promotional purposes at the Franklin Institute. Then they began

We are a kind of chameleon, taking our hue—the hue of our moral character—from those who are about us.

JOHN LOCKE
ENGLISH PHILOSOPHER

The widely distributed photo of the Philadelphia Building Trades Union attack on the Sheraton Hotel construction site of ABC contractor Leon Altemose at Valley Forge, Pennsylvania, on June 5, 1972.

It is not our freedom that is in jeopardy in the first instance; it is our public order. If that breaks down, freedom will be lost and so will the prospect for greater justice.

ERIC SEVAREID
NEWS COMMENTATOR

destroying everything in sight. It was planned pandemonium and scared the hell out of me.[3]

In the initial wave of this insurrection, a guard hut, trucks, and construction trailers were firebombed to the ground. Bulldozers, graders, and other large earth moving equipment were set afire or battered. Lime was poured into their fuel tanks. Two security guards were pelted with rocks and their vehicles were ruined. Smoke from the burning facilities and equipment could be seen for miles around.

During the first forty-five minutes on that fateful morning, more than $300,000 worth of property destruction occurred. Many of the union marauders cheered as they watched or committed the pillage. Unable to restrain them, local police directed municipal fire trucks to turn away from the chaotic site because the safety of the firemen was endangered.[4] An editorial in the *Philadelphia Inquirer* called the demonstration "arson, violence, malicious mischief and vandalism—a gross, indefensible assault on public order and the process of law by a rapacious mob."[5]

The enraged union horde continued to rampage over the Valley Forge project until midday, when state troopers in riot gear finally arrived on the scene. Then, suddenly, at a signal from the labor bosses in business attire, the battle was over. Sandwiches and soft drinks appeared out of nowhere and the intimidators wandered quietly around the edges of the smoldering shambles as though nothing had happened. Meanwhile peaceful picketing by other trade union members continued outside the job site on public property, still protesting that Altemose "destroyed industry standards."

The company's veteran labor attorney, John Pelino, figured that more sabotage and brutality would be coming soon. In defense, he filed a complaint that same day—June 5th—in the Montgomery County Court of Common Pleas at nearby Norristown to restrain any further unlawful action by the Trades Council. Following an immediate *ex parte* hearing on Counselor Pelino's complaint (ignored by attorneys for the Trades Council), Trial Judge Vincent Cirillo granted the company's requested injunction at 5 p.m., on a temporary basis. He ruled that the assault was part of a "broader proclivity on the part of the Trades Council and its members to achieve their goals by violence and intimidation." Based on this "vicious pattern," Judge Cirillo ignored legal precedent by drafting an unusually broad order. It forbad all picketing and all congregating within a mile of the Valley Forge Plaza site or any other Altemose project or the firm's headquarters office at Center Square.[6]

The judge also concluded that the Trades Council's actions violated the secondary boycott provisions of the federal Taft-Hartley Act but that neither that statute nor Pennsylvania's Anti-Injunction Act preempted his court's "equitable jurisdiction" to forbid the illegal conduct:

> ... The defendants' picketing had become so enmeshed with violence, harassment, intimidation and property destruction that an atmosphere of fear and terror survives even in the absence of picketing ... Peaceful picketing was so inextricably interwoven with acts of violence as to render impossible the maintenance of domestic peace and order in the community.[7]

Big Labor Defies a Court Order

As Altemose Attorney Pelino had predicted, the lawlessness of the Building Trades Council was far from over. But this time the combined state and local police were better prepared to cope with it. On June 6—just one day after Judge Cirillo issued his preliminary restraining order—two hundred union picketers congregated around the Altemose Construction Company's main office at Center Square. They threatened to burn it down and shouted obscenities at Leon Altemose and his seventy staff employees located there. Some of the mobsters were arrested for violating the previous day's court injunction and fined $100 for civil contempt. According to nationally syndicated labor columnist Victor Riesel, "about 40 percent of those arrested had previous convictions for criminal offenses of assault and battery, arson and worse."[8]

Members of the Trades Council also put pressure on personnel employed by firms servicing the Valley Forge Plaza construction project to make them stop working for Altemose. A union business agent contacted one of the non-union subcontractors on the site, Richard Czeiner, to warn him that the unions would "prefer" that he not work there. Czeiner refused to quit—and several of his vehicles were ruined by firebombs.

The art of life is to know how to enjoy a little and to endure much.

WILLIAM HAZLITT
ENGLISH ESSAYIST

Despite increased security measures, construction on the project continued to be plagued by sabotage. And Leon Altemose and his employees continued to receive anonymous telephone threats against their lives and the safety of their families.

On June 13—a week after the initial union attack—John Trimmer and several members of ABC's Central Pennsylvania Chapter (who had been communicating daily) met with Altemose and his attorney at the downtown Philadelphia Sheraton Hotel to discuss more effective ways and means to counteract the dangerous situation.

That same day, a group of "unknown persons" checked into the same Sheraton under aliases. They smashed all the furniture in four rooms, ripped carpets, slashed mattresses, and clogged the toilets with concrete. Then they fled, after spray-painting the hotel walls with a threatening message: **THIS PAINT IS FOR ALTEMOSE—NEXT TIME FIRE**.

A "Spontaneous" Labor Holiday

When the original temporary restraining order of June 5 against the Building Trades Council was allowed to continue "indefinitely" by Trial Court Judge Cirillo, infuriated officials of the council and their attorney, Bernard Katz, held a press conference. They announced that a "spontaneous mass demonstration" would soon take place. To make certain that all of their members showed up for the event, the union chiefs decreed June 22 as a "labor holiday." And they warned that a fine of one day's pay would be levied on any union member who did not leave his job and report for the "grass roots protest."

Union strategy called for a march on the Montgomery County Courthouse in Norristown to vilify Judge Cirillo and his court order that outlawed all building trades union picketing and congregating within a mile of any Altemose construction site. Right on cue, an army of *twenty-five thousand* Hurricane Agnes–soaked union hardhats who had been collected from across several states descended on the courthouse. They well knew that they were in defiance of the judge's injunction because the building was located less than a mile away from an Altemose construction project. The mob shouted epithets like:

"We want da Judge," "Carrillo's a rotten scab," and "dey'll neva' build dat stinkin' hotel."

To guard against another rebellion such as occurred at Valley Forge on June 5, Pennsylvania's Governor Milton Shapp declared a "state of emergency." The union mob was confronted by a corps of *two thousand* state troopers in riot gear, combined with a reinforced local police force, to maintain law and order around the county courthouse. A "strike expenses" bill paid by taxpayers for providing emergency police deployment in connection with this labor war included motel rooms for troopers ($24,713), their meals ($26,150), transportation ($8,970), and overtime pay ($85,800)—for a total of $145,633.

Union officials leading the angry marchers announced that their tradesmen soon would begin to boycott all Sheraton Hotels across the state and nation in protest of the chain's use of Altemose and other open shop construction firms. Threats also were made to withdraw union funds from banks that financed any Altemose project. These ploys failed because local banks and the hotel chain pledged their continued support to him.

Union Goons Beat Up Altemose

On August 17, Leon Altemose was attacked while going through a line of trade union pickets outside the First Pennsylvania Bank, a major financier of his Valley Forge project. About two dozen of the ruffians mobbed the contractor on Chestnut Street in downtown Philadelphia, shouting threats like: "Ya goddamn union-bustin' scab, we'll teach ya not ta show youses face in Philly" and "get da hell back ta Norristown, ya no-good sonovabitch," and worse.

As fists flew, Altemose slumped to the ground. "They kicked him in the face and body-punched him so hard that he had to be taken to the nearest hospital for treatment," said one eyewitness. Three union hoodlums identified by both Altemose and the police at the scene as the culprits were arrested and charged with assault. But a union-friendly judge freed the bullies for "lack of evidence."[9]

When interviewed later by the news media about this judicial farce, Building Trades Council President Tom LeGrand responded, with a smirk, "I dunna who bloodied up dat fella Altemose—maybe one of our wives done it."[10] On

Fight on, fight on my heroes all, I am a little hurt, but I'm not slain. I will lay me down to bleed a while, then I'll rise and fight by your side again.

"The Ballad of Johnny Armstrong"

the same day, the First Pennsylvania Bank's management was advised that union members were withdrawing their deposits and that all of its branches would continue to be picketed.

About three months later, on November 29, the Pennsylvania Supreme Court released its opinion arising out of an appeal by the Building Trades Council to rescind Trial Judge Cirillo's broad ban of June 5th against mass picketing and congregating at Altemose construction project sites. The appellate court began with good news by upholding Judge Cirillo's injunction against this illegal activity. On the evidence presented of a pattern of violence, the lower court "was fully warranted in its action," the State Supreme Court ruled. "We hold," the Court declared further, "that even defendants' peaceful picketing, indistinguishable and inseparable as it was from acts of violence, is not the type of activity which is protected by the First Amendment. Along with and because of the violence which accompanied it, picketing itself was a proper subject for this preliminary injunctive relief."[11]

The sad news in the ruling for Altemose Construction Company began with the State Supreme Court's reduction of Judge Cirillo's one-mile circular no-picketing zone around each of the company's construction projects to two hundred yards. The appellate court also incredibly declared that the 125 picketers who were arrested for violation of the injunction on the morning of June 6 at the Altemose office building fracas and fined $100 each for contempt of court made the payments "under duress" and therefore "were not afforded their constitutional due process rights." Based on "technical violations of multiple arrest procedures" by the police—as contended by the Trades Council—the state's highest court ordered all of the monetary fines to be returned to the toughs.[12]

As a result of the constant trade union atrocity at Valley Forge Plaza and elsewhere, many subcontractors withdrew from Altemose's Sheraton Hotel construction project. Even ready-mix concrete firms geographically situated close enough to serve the company's jobsite refused to do so. Anonymous phone calls threatened the lives of corporate executives if they dared do business with Altemose, and their homes were spray-painted.

When one more distant concrete firm did begin to help, the tires of fifty-eight of its trucks were slashed while they were in the firm's own parking lot.[13]

Appearance of the First Union "Salts"

By this time Leon Altemose had difficulty in obtaining qualified journeymen who were willing to risk their safety by working for him. In desperation, without checking personal references, he hired two unknown workers off the street. They claimed to be plumbers and their names were John Zaleski and Norman Young. Soon after coming on the job they complained to fellow employees about "the company's lousy wages and working conditions." Then they bragged that pay and benefits at union jobs were much better and pointed out what they viewed to be many other advantages of unionization.

At the same time, Zaleski and Young demonstrated a lack of competence in their alleged craft. They knew little about installing plumbing equipment, were not familiar with tools of the trade, and produced sloppy work behind schedule. After tolerating many months of their pro-union agitation during working hours and continued unsatisfactory job performances, Leon Altemose discharged the two union sympathizers on February 28, 1973. The reason he gave was "lack of productivity resulting from either their incompetence or their intentional efforts to slow down and sabotage the job in furtherance of the Building Trades Council's attempts to prevent completion of the Valley Forge Plaza project."

The two plumbers responded by filing an unfair labor practice charge at the National Labor Relations Board, with, of course, the assistance of the Trades Council's attorney. On the first day of the hearing before the Board's trial examiner (now called an administrative law judge), more than one hundred union rowdies gathered outside the entrance to the federal building where the hearing was being held to jeer and intimidate witnesses called to testify on behalf of Altemose. But despite his request to the police for protection from these rabble-rousers, neither the Labor Board nor the trial examiner permitted any security assistance to occur.

When the same "company" witnesses arrived at the hearing the next day, the gang of brawlers screamed obscenities, rushed them, prevented them from entering the building and forced them to run away for their safety. A police squad car finally rescued them. From that time on, all Altemose personnel attended the Labor Board hearings through an underground entrance into the government building under the protection of armed U.S. marshals.

> **For a plot hatched in hell, don't expect angels for witnesses.**
>
> ROBERT PERRY, ESQ.

During the course of this unbelievable trial, the two discharged plumbers contended that they were not terminated for poor performance (which they claimed was a "conjured pretext" by the company) but rather were fired for engaging in "legally protected union organizational activities." Norman Young testified that after he told Leon Altemose's brother that he (Young) was a former union president, he and Zaleski were advised that they were being terminated "due to their union activity."

The company countered with a supervisor's uncontradicted testimony as to the unsatisfactory work performance by Zaleski and Young. There also appeared to be numerous inconsistencies in their own testimony, but the Labor Board's trial examiner mysteriously "reconciled" the conflicting statements of the fired workers. He also "discredited" management's unchallenged testimony on its "proper cause" for the terminations. Then he ordered both unionists reinstated to their jobs—plus back pay for time lost from work during the board's hearing. The truth was that the threatening circumstances surrounding the hearing made a fair trial before the left-wing Labor Board agent impossible.

In this biased case—which helped to plant the seeds of organized labor's present-day tactic called "salting"[14]—on April 18, 1974, a three-member panel of the Labor Board in Washington, D.C., denied Altemose Construction Company's appeal to review the dubious return-to-work ruling of its trial examiner and summarily affirmed his decision.[15]

A welcome victory for Altemose came a year later when a federal appellate court castigated the Labor Board and *reversed* its decision in the case. The court reasoned that "conducting a hearing in a mob atmosphere demeaned the legal process" and "may have had an intimidating influence on the testimony of witnesses." The court added that the Labor Board's ruling "raised serious questions about the propriety and impartiality of the [evidentiary] investigation" as did its refusal to believe "the Altemose defense that the unfair labor practice charge was fraudulent."[16]

By January of 1975, the Trades Council and its Teamsters Union affiliate had begun to picket Altemose's main office again and also resumed picketing—on a comparatively peaceful basis—at the Valley Forge Plaza project. Union members displayed signs at entrance gates bearing the following legend:

NOTICE

ALTEMOSE CONTRACTOR

refuses to enter into

a sub-contractor's

agreement with the

Philadelphia, Pennsylvania

Building & Construction

Trades Council, AFL-CIO

THIS IS A

TEAMSTERS

PICKET LINE

PLEASE HONOR IT AND

SLOW DOWN—

LOW WAGE

AREA AHEAD!

> **A helpless sparrow can drift with the wind, it takes an eagle to fly against the storm.**
>
> ANONYMOUS

The Building Trades Gain a Court Triumph

While rejuvenated picket lines did not bring construction activities to a complete halt, the Teamsters slowed down deliveries and otherwise disrupted work in progress. Leon Altemose's attorney finally convinced the Labor Board to obtain a temporary restraining order against this alleged "recognition picketing" because it continued for more than thirty days without filing a petition for a union representation election conducted by the Labor Board, in violation of Section 8(b)(7)(C) of the Taft-Hartley Act.[17]

Unfortunately for Altemose, the Labor Board's Philadelphia Regional Director settled the dispute by permitting the picketing to resume on the tongue-in-cheek "pledge" of the Building Trades Council and the Teamsters that there no longer was any "recognitional or organizational objective as forbidden by Section 8(b)(7)(C)." Altemose was not even allowed to intervene in the case to challenge the impropriety of the Labor Board's prejudiced settlement.

Encouraged by this legal victory, the Philadelphia Trades Council ignored the Labor Board's settlement agreement and renewed its coercion and intimidation. Non-union subs again were "urged" to cease doing business with Altemose. Frightened suppliers capitulated and advised Altemose they would no longer

The CONTRACTOR
THE VOICE OF MERIT SHOP CONSTRUCTION

MARCH 1974

"They'll never build that hotel"...
THE SHERATON VALLEY FORGE HOTEL COMPLEX COMPLETED BY ALTEMOSE CONSTRUCTION CO. page 20

The Sheraton Hotel that Leon Altemose "would never build," in the threatening words of the Philadelphia building trades unions.

furnish material for his projects. Construction users were "warned" not to put Altemose on their bid lists. Investors in his projects were "requested" to withdraw their monetary support. Union members and the general public were "encouraged" to withdraw deposits from First Pennsylvania Bank, the major financier of the Valley Forge Plaza project. Hotel guests were "coaxed" to cancel reservations at the newly constructed Sheraton Hotel in the Valley Forge Plaza complex.[18]

Under these turbulent conditions, Altemose Construction Company had difficulty in obtaining performance bonds for new jobs. Bids on some building projects were rejected even though the company was the lowest qualified bidder. Union coercion also was directed toward lending institutions that might furnish funding for such future projects.

In spite of this tremendous union pressure, Leon Altemose eventually completed all of his construction work at the Valley Forge Plaza and it became a popular shopping center. His state-of-the-art Sheraton Hotel was dedicated and unveiled to the public in September of 1973. But Altemose and his business associates continued to be terrorized by the Trades Council's illegal activities for many more years, led by its notorious Roofers Local 30 which had spearheaded the initial lethal attack in 1972.

Pro-Union Politicians and Judges

There is no doubt that the far-left agenda of Philadelphia politicians during the time of the building trades battle over the Valley Forge Plaza construction work contributed to the gross neglect by the City and its surrounding counties of responsibility for the safety and general welfare of their residents. The pro-union stance of the mayor was well known. As previously noted, building trades leaders were represented on many key municipal agencies dealing with building issues.

More proof of the degree to which the mayor encouraged union turbulence to solve a "problem" occurred at a Democrat Party celebration in 1974 in the City of Brotherly Love. "Hizzoner" had not been invited to sit on the dais at the shindig because of a dispute with a hostile city party chairman. This obvious slight caused the following scene to evolve:

> While over 4,000 Democrats were gathering at the Civic Center to dine and hear speeches, a flying squad of Roofers [union members] burst into the hall. They overturned tables, beat up a 60 year old [opposition party member] and ignored a number of deputy sheriffs who were serving as ushers while the police looked the other way.
>
> A few minutes after the Roofers had set the tone, the mayor pulled up in his city limousine. The business agent of Roofers Local 30, the president of the Building and Construction Trades Council, and the business agent of Teamsters Local 107 were riding with him.
>
> Led by a fife and drum corps, the mayor and 500 union toughs stormed into the Civic Center, completely upstaging the Democrat politicians and scaring the hell out of everyone there. They encircled the diners and dignitaries, chanting obscenities and knocking people down along the way. The union chiefs formed a phalanx around the mayor, who boasted that it was the greatest night in his life.[19]

Even the governor of Pennsylvania, while acting as the host of his peers at an annual governor's conference, ordered the national event to be moved away from the Valley Forge Plaza so that the Altemose-built project would not receive patronage.

I never cease being dumfounded by the unbelievable things people say they believe.

LEO ROSTEN
WRITER-PUNDIT

To make matters worse for the merit shop cause, a Pennsylvania appellate court reversed the conviction of eleven members of Roofers Local 30 whom a jury had found guilty of charges ranging from rioting and malicious destruction of property to conspiracy and assault during the Valley Forge battle of June 5, 1972, against Altemose. The court held as a matter of law that without proof of actual participation or encouragement, photographic evidence of mere presence of workers at the scene of a riot is not adequate proof of the offense.[20]

As previously described, on that occasion trade union rioters trampled down thousands of feet of cyclone fencing and the prosecution introduced in evidence a photograph of one of these union defendants running alongside the fence while it was being destroyed. The prosecution's theory was that the defendant "had been alternatively jumping onto and from the fence and the cameraman just happened to take the picture while the man was running beside [rather than onto] the fence." This same evidence, coupled with the defendant's membership in the militant Roofers Union, had been held sufficient to support the jury's verdict of "guilty" in the lower court.

The appellate court disagreed. It concluded instead that the photography was "mere guesswork" and "one could also conjecture that the defendant was running along the fence urging his comrades to dismount it and stop breaking the law."[21] (Compare the photo of the riot in this chapter.)

The same leftist Pennsylvania appellate court also said it was "concerned" that the trial judge did not "appreciate fully the nature and character of inherently prejudicial newspaper articles and television broadcasts" allowed in evidence. They published some of the defendant unionists' criminal records and "cast a general impression that they were members of a dangerous criminal organization." Therefore the appellate court held in vaguely spun legalese:

> Considering that this all happened while the jury was not sequestered and not properly instructed or questioned, especially during the days when the trial was suspended, we find that the trial court's denial of the motion for sequestration of the jury, without predicating that decision on adequate cautionary instructions and without proper inquiry into all the matters that came to its attention concerning the publicity of this case, was an abuse of its discretion.... *The sentences are reversed, the*

defendants are discharged and the case is remanded for a new trial.[22]
[emphasis added]

Leon and Carol Altemose: National Heroes

Ironically, on the famous (and usually liberal) television show *60 Minutes*, commentator Mike Wallace told a nationwide audience the truth about who Leon Altemose was, what happened to him, and why:

> Lately the building trades unions have fallen on hard times. Their employment rate hereabouts is less than 30 percent, and as big jobs begin to wind down in the city, the jobs in the suburbs that they never used to bother about began to look more attractive....
>
> Leon Altemose is a quiet-spoken, independent, and very successful building contractor in suburban Philadelphia and Leon Altemose says he is afraid. Afraid for his life. Afraid for his family too. He's so fearful of what his enemies may have in store for him that he starts his car each morning by remote control in case a bomb may have been wired to the ignition.
>
> Who is Leon Altemose afraid of? Men he calls thugs. Men, he alleges, are in the pay of the construction unions. He has fought those unions for an open shop and that fight has cost him over $2 million and big trouble besides.
>
> Altemose is only one of a growing number of open shop builders and his battle only one of a growing rash of violent confrontations in the construction industry around the country. The fact is that last year almost half the total dollar volume of construction—and construction is this country's biggest industry—almost half was open shop.[23]

Beginning in 1971, Altemose had laid his business career and his personal safety on the line in the City of Brotherly Love. Threats, intimidation, and violence against the thirty-three-year-old contractor, his loyal employees, and his loving kin continued to be commonplace. This constant pressure and persecution took its toll. There were millions of dollars owed in the replacement

He serves most who serves his country best.

HOMER
LEGENDARY GREEK
POET OF THE EIGHTH
CENTURY B.C.

of sabotaged construction property, materials, and equipment as well as legal expenses. His firm lost customers who were fearful of labor terrorism, the company became reduced in size, and its future as a major general contractor seemed questionable for a while—*but he never gave up.*

Family and friends wondered why Leon Altemose elected to undergo this horrendous ordeal rather than capitulate to the compulsory unionization of his tradesmen. This was the answer he gave to one and all:

> It's a matter of principle. Three informers have told me I'm supposed to be dead, but I won't change the way I live. My strongest support comes from my family and my employees. And ABC is the only organization that stood up for me from the day it all began. The American people simply cannot knuckle down to corruption and terrorism any longer. Someone has to make a stand for American free enterprise and the merit shop. To the extent that I can, I pledge that I will.[24]

In February of 1973, Leon Altemose was featured on the cover of *Engineering News-Record* as its "Construction Man of the Year" for his bravery and perseverance in the face of the Philadelphia Building Trades Unions onslaught of hit-and-run terror tactics. An accompanying lead article's headline read: **LEON ALTEMOSE—STAKING HIS LIFE ON THE RIGHT TO WORK OPEN SHOP**.

This freedom fighter also received an award at *Engineering News-Record's* annual banquet that year in New York City. It was followed by a standing ovation from a thousand fellow contractors. The plaque cited Altemose as "a fearless champion of the right-to-work merit shop and an inspiration to the growing number of contractors across the United States who have determined to face up to the same kind of lawless opposition." ENR added that he was "a champion for a cause that has become more important for him than personal safety, labor peace or life itself."

Then, in what *ENR* termed "an appropriate violation of tradition," the magazine gave a similar plaque to Leon's wife, Carol, for her "gallant role" in the ordeal. This "Construction's Woman of the Year" award—the first in

ENR's history—was inscribed: "With Grace Under Pressure, A Full Partner In A Courageous Cause." [25]

History has recorded that Leon and Carol Altemose kept their pledge of workplace voluntarism and harmony as opposed to building trades compulsion and terrorism. In doing so they protected and defended their construction business, their employees and families, their way of life, and the integrity of the merit shop crusade.

Cover of February 15, 1973, issue of *Engineering News-Record* naming Leon Altemose (shown here with his armed bodyguard) as "Construction's Man of the Year."

CHAPTER 33

RODGERS SAVES
THE GRAND OLE OPRY

IN STARK CONTRAST TO THE PROLONGED TORTURE of Leon Altemose, his company, his family, and his business associates by organized labor is the short but savage saga about the construction of Opryland USA. It was completed on a merit shop basis within a twenty-four-day deadline—while facing the tension of an opening day commitment and the fury of the Nashville Building & Construction Trades Council.

The Associated Press News Service carried a release across the nation that announced this major labor crisis. It read like this:

> NASHVILLE, TENNESSEE, April 28, 1972: Construction on a multi-million dollar family entertainment park, one of the largest in the country, was halted recently just a few weeks prior to completion as a result of continued labor strife. A national publicity campaign had been started months in advance and, as a result, a capacity crowd is expected for opening day ceremonies on May 19 at Opryland USA.
>
> NBC-TV also is about to begin production of a one-hour Danny Thomas television special to be aired nationally, using the entertainment park as its central theme. In order to meet these commitments, owners of the park have turned to a general contractor who they believe can complete the project on schedule without labor disputes, restrictive work practices or excessive construction costs.[1]

In music, one must think with the heart and feel with the brain.

GEORGE SZELL
COMPOSER

The unanimous choice to cope with this emergency was Joe M. Rodgers, an articulate, vigorous, and patriotic southerner who was born to be a leader. After graduating from the University of Alabama with a civil engineering degree in 1956, Rodgers served a three-year stint in the U.S. Coast and Geodetic Service. Next, with his last $250 in his pocket, he landed a job for a Birmingham, Alabama, contractor. He remembers it as "a great experience" because he "had to learn to operate every piece of equipment and prove to the boss that my college degree didn't hurt me."

Within a few years Joe Rodgers left A. E. Burgess Company in Birmingham and went to Nashville, Tennessee, where he worked in production and sales for his brother Ed's unionized Dixie Concrete Pipe Company. It was to be only temporary, since Joe wanted to go into business for himself.

In 1966 five local Nashville businessmen each contributed $250, Rodgers invested his last $250, and a $1,000 corporation named Joe M. Rodgers & Associates was founded. Two years later Rodgers met Dr. Thomas Frist, Sr., and that event turned out to be a crucial moment in the success of the new construction company. It seems that Dr. Frist had a dream of building a huge chain of hospitals at lower cost and in less time while improving the delivery of quality health care. So he and some friends put up the seed money to begin construction. Then Frist—who was impressed with the young man's "strength and humility"—gave Rodgers an opportunity to build the first five hospitals of the chain without any contract. Each was a $650,000 project and, on mutual trust, he received his pay "out of the cash flow."[2]

The Rodgers Firm Expands

That's how the giant Hospital Corporation of America ("HCA") was created and that's why Joe M. Rodgers & Associates (which eventually built 90 percent of HCA's projects across the nation) experienced an increase in completed construction work from $2 million to $27 million in just one year. His firm was growing so fast, says Rodgers, that "we worked from daylight to dark just to keep up with it." He always believed that it was his professional responsibility to create "a quality team effort on a fast track incorporating the individualism and creativity of the owner, contractor, architect, engineer, subcontractors, and suppliers." Using that policy, by 1970 he had completed fifty-eight state-of-the-art hospitals for HCA.

In August of that year, after many months of planning, the construction was about to begin at Opryland USA near downtown Nashville. It was the first phase of a 369-acre family entertainment park. This $19 million section was being developed by the NLT Corporation (hereinafter "NLT").

As the result of a labor strike at the same time on a separate and unrelated NLT headquarters construction project which was also located in Nashville, trade union leaders proposed a settlement package deal with NLT. There would be no more work stoppages in completing the NLT headquarters project if the contemplated Opryland USA project also would be awarded exclusively—with "guaranteed" labor peace—to unionized contractors.

NLT agreed and its headquarters building was completed, but the Opryland project was continually plagued by labor problems. Job featherbedding, craft jurisdictional disputes, and work slowdowns occurred in spite of the "harmony" pledge. With the trade unions honoring each others' picket lines, progress on the job was severely delayed and construction costs mounted unnecessarily.

Nashville in those days was 90 percent "union built." On April 23, 1972, less than a month before the announced grand opening date of Opryland, the local building trades unions shut the project down again and gave NLT another ultimatum: "We won't come back to work until you guarantee that we will represent all permanent Opryland employees after the park opens."[3]

NLT said "no" and informed the union contractors that their services were terminated as of April 28. Michael Downs, the General Manager of Opryland, told the news media: "We have been treated most unfairly and are sadly disappointed by the union leaders who ignored their promise of labor peace and simply didn't live up to their responsibilities."

Joe Rodgers Accepts a Challenge

At this point, knowing that the entertainment park had to be completed by May 19th for filming a Danny Thomas TV special, Opryland officials contacted Joe M. Rodgers, a founder and first president of ABC's Tennessee Chapter. They believed "with confidence that this outstanding merit shopper would

Peace is an armistice in a war that is continuously going on.

THUCYDIDES
GREEK HISTORIAN

Courage is the universal virtue of all those who choose to do the right thing over the expedient thing. It is the common currency of all those who do what they are supposed to do in a time of conflict, crisis and confusion.

Florence
Nightingale
English nurse

get the park opened on schedule and get it done right." In a subsequent conversation with the news media, Rodgers described what happened next:

As soon as I was contacted, I looked the Opryland project over and the place was in the biggest mess imaginable. It looked impossible to finish the job in the time allotted.

There were about 750 union workers on the project when they struck and shut it down. We couldn't jeopardize our other jobs by taking our workers off of them, so we would have to hire all new employees. I knew, however, that we would not need anywhere near 700. But I'll never forget that frustrated feeling, riding back from Opryland's office to our office. I had been preaching the merit shop concept constantly and now I was faced with this challenge.

I felt there was no way I could win, really. I told Opryland officials that I would come back the next morning and give them my decision. But neither was there any way I could turn down the project. No way at all—if I believed in what I had been preaching.

Twenty-four hours later I accepted the job, with two understandings: first, that I be in full control of construction, and second, that I receive a bonus of $25,000 for every day that we completed Opryland before the May 19th deadline. I added that I would donate half of any such bonus to the Boy Scouts and half to the Girl Scouts. My wife and I had been active in the Scouts movement and so had several NLT executives. I also felt it would help to gain public sentiment on our side because we would have a big problem with union opposition.

Springing into action on April 30, Joe Rodgers refused to jeopardize his other construction projects and decided that he needed at least four hundred new workers as soon as possible, putting crews together from scratch. His firm contacted other ABC members plus high schools and colleges for volunteers. The presses of the *Nashville Banner* newspaper were stopped in order to insert a large "help wanted" advertisement. It announced that the Opryland project would be going twenty-four hours a day, seven days a week, and that all personnel would be on twelve- or fourteen-hour shifts, with time-and-a-half pay for all work beyond forty hours.

Prompt responses were received from ABC members throughout the Southeast. They offered manpower, equipment, and materials. Construction workers and students came from as far away as other states to participate. Three of the union subcontractors who originally worked on the project agreed to cooperate on a merit shop basis and were retained. Ten ABC member subcontractors were added to help meet the challenge. Opryland USA soon became a *cause celebre* as a result of the national publicity, the employment opportunities, and the challenging possibility of a substantial donation to the great Scouts organizations.

Work began on the project twenty-four hours after Joe Rodgers was contacted by Opryland. About 430 people were hired within four days and one concrete pour lasted fifty-four straight hours. On Monday, May 1, however, more than three hundred militant trade union pickets arrived at the job site. That number swelled throughout the day to one thousand. Merit shop workers were threatened, pelted with rocks and assaulted, equipment was damaged, car tires were cut, and delivery trucks were run off the road. Rodgers maintained private security guards at his home and office for eighteen days.

Both local police and the Tennessee Highway Patrol were contacted to ensure the safety of personnel crossing the hostile picket lines when entering and leaving the Opryland site. But "little cooperation was given by local law enforcement authorities," according to Terry Brooks, the accomplished labor attorney for Joe M. Rodgers & Associates. "The police," Brooks said, "argued that they could not become involved in a labor dispute and refused to cooperate even when we explained that criminal laws as well as labor laws were being violated."

In a speedy letter to Tennessee Governor Winfield Dunn, Rodgers wrote that he was not asking police to become involved in the labor dispute nor was he asking them to break their policy of "total neutrality." But he also emphasized that the display of a picket sign did not grant a person immunity from prosecution for having committed a criminal act. His letter to the Governor concluded: "I ask for nothing that is not due any Tennessean when faced with personal violence and property damage." Shortly thereafter a local court issued a temporary

> **Courage is resistance to fear, not absence of fear.**
>
> MARK TWAIN
> HUMORIST-WRITER

What counts
is not the size of
the man in the
fight but the
size of the fight
in the man.

DWIGHT D.
EISENHOWER
34TH PRESIDENT

restraining order against the building trades, which helped to disperse the mass picketing. Only four pickets were allowed to remain at each entrance gate. According to Attorney Brooks:

> Upon hearing the plans for mass picketing, we immediately sent telegrams to the presidents and business agents of the various construction trades unions and their international affiliates, telling them that separate gates had been established and that mass picketing would be in violation of federal labor law. The Labor Board Resident Officer in Nashville arrived at the Opryland site, where he investigated the situation and accepted four unfair labor practice charges.
>
> They included illegal mass picketing by the Carpenters Union and the Nashville Building Trades Council. They also included charges of an illegal secondary boycott against these two labor organizations since they carried picket signs against Joe M. Rodgers & Associates but prevented the employees and suppliers of other contractors from entering the common job site. The Labor Board's Regional Director in Memphis determined that reasonable grounds for the charges did exist and was prepared to take action when a Nashville court ordered the unions to behave peacefully.

Work continued on the Opryland site from then on with only occasional minor labor problems. All shifts were increased from twelve hours to fourteen hours. During the week, volunteers arrived after completing their normal 7 a.m. to 3 p.m. workday elsewhere to assist at Opryland until 10 p.m. or later. On Saturday and Sunday mornings, workers from other merit shop projects arrived at the Opryland site to do what they could to help meet the tight construction schedule.

Throughout this crisis, thousands of hamburgers and chicken dinners were delivered to the project by local caterers and restaurants. On Saturdays, more than 250 Girl Scouts working in their own homes would make special meals for the construction workers. Then a truckload of these scouts would arrive at the site, cross the picket lines, and serve the hungry and exhausted crews.

ABC Contractor

Part of the completed Grand Ole Opry construction site, showing also the victorious J. M. Rodgers construction team members.

Rodgers and His Team Meet the Deadline

By that time there were 520 people working on the site. Some 280 were employees of Joe M. Rodgers & Associates and the remaining 240 were both union and non-union employees of the subcontractors. The bottom line was that because of marvelous teamwork, expertise, and planning, this $19 million project was completed on May 17—*two days ahead of schedule*. On May

19, a check for $25,000 was presented to the Boy Scouts and a check for $25,000 was presented to the Girl Scouts by NLT and Rodgers.

Discussing the completed project, Opryland's Michael Downs proudly proclaimed: "Joe M. Rodgers & Associates did what other contractors could not do; that is, they performed high quality work and completed the project on time under very trying and difficult circumstances. The project managers, subcontractors and their employees all worked hand-in-glove with our people, in an area where they were thoroughly unfamiliar, to complete the emergency job." Daniel Brooks, Chairman of the board of NLT, added: "We are seriously considering this fine merit shop firm for additional construction work"—and that promise soon came to fruition. For his outstanding achievement, Rodgers also was awarded the Associated General Contractors–Motorola "Build America" Award. And *Engineering News-Record* displayed his photograph on its cover of August 21, 1975, along with a feature article about him entitled "A Merit Shop Contractor with the Midas Touch."

Opryland USA opened to the public with great fanfare, complete with amusement rides, animal sanctuaries, specialty foods and, above all, country music. NBC's Danny Thomas TV special was filmed during the last week of construction and, like the project itself, was completed on schedule.

An Outstanding ABC President, Civic Leader, and Businessman

In 1976, Joe Rodgers became ABC's eighteenth national president. Meanwhile his construction firm was becoming one of the largest general contractors in the United States and also operating overseas in the Middle East. During his ABC presidential year he visited every chapter, flying 250,000 miles in his Learjet. He achieved his goals of expanding the Association's membership roots to all fifty states and ten thousand members.

Rodgers had this to say about ABC and his own professional success:

> The merit shop is as American as anything I know. Paying people based on their qualifications rather than their title or union membership; training people so they can grow in their occupation and their compensation; providing people profit-sharing plans and other incentives so that they

Cover of August 21, 1975, issue of *Engineering News-Record*, featuring Joe M. Rodgers, ABC's national president in 1976, and founder-owner-chief executive officer of J. M. Rodgers & Associates in Nashville, Tennessee. [Reprinted from *ENR* with permission, copyright the McGraw-Hill Companies, August 21, 1975, all rights reserved]

To sit in silence
when we should
speak out makes
cowards out
of men.

ELLA WHEELER WILCOX
AUTHOR-POET

are motivated to produce to their fullest; and stressing the importance of the individual so those people become loyal to their company rather than to some labor union broker are all important to the future of the construction industry. Owners also must truly feel they are getting the best for their money and the principles of the merit shop give them that. My businesses will always respect and live up to these standards.

We know that the merit shop's struggle for freedom under American law and ethics is being challenged by those who favor compulsion and terrorism but we are sure that the Spirit of '76 is not smoldering. It remains a light in all that merely needs rekindling in some. It represents the culmination of the struggle toward liberty whose price is eternal vigilance.

Rodgers also coined the phrase **GET INTO POLITICS OR GET OUT OF BUSINESS** and led ABC's expanded public involvement at the local, state, and national levels. His commitment included a "Contract for Political Action" in which each ABC member agreed to write, call, and meet with elected officials, support pro-free-enterprise candidates and voter registration through donations of time and financial resources, and attend ABC legislative action conferences. He would tell one and all: "Politics is not a spectator sport. Together we have the power—*so use it or lose it*!"

Practicing what he preached, Rodgers selected presidential candidate Ronald Reagan as the keynote speaker at ABC's annual convention in Houston, Texas, in 1976, and Senate Majority Leader Robert Dole (R-KS) was the keynote speaker when Rodgers went out of office at the year's end. Both of these distinguished political leaders had become friends of his in 1975 when he served as chairman of "Citizens for Reagan" in Tennessee. He gave similar support to Senator Howard Baker (R-TN).

It was because of Ronald Reagan that Rodgers became national finance chairman of the Republican Party in 1979 and served until 1981. He also served on President Reagan's Foreign Intelligence Advisory Board and on the U.S. Trade Representatives, Foreign Investment Advisory Board. President Reagan appointed Rodgers as the U.S. ambassador to France in 1985 and he served until the end of Reagan's administration in January of 1989.

In 1979, Joe Rodgers' firm ranked as *Engineering News-Record's* ninetieth largest general contractor and was among the nation's top twenty firms that specialized in health care construction. He sold the company in 1980 and today it is known as Centrex-Rodgers. He continues to serve on nationally prominent corporate boards of directors and civic organizations and receive many professional and civic awards.

To name a few of these honors, Rodgers is a member of the state of Alabama Engineering Hall of Fame and a recipient of "The Citadel Sword for Distinguished Service." In 1988 Francois Mitterand, the President of France, personally made Rodgers one of eight living Americans to become a Grand Officer of the Legion of Honor; in 1990 he received the Herbert Hoover Medal awarded by nine national engineering societies; and at ABC's annual convention on June 3, 2000, in Baltimore, he was named one of ABC's "Leaders of the 20th Century."

When Joe Rodgers reminisces, he never forgets a certain construction endeavor that helped to bring him fame and fortune, while also gaining a major victory for his customer and for ABC:

> *Nashville was 90 percent union at the time we took over the Opryland USA project in 1972. It had been shut down by the unions in a blackmailing effort to organize the permanent employees of the Opryland Theme Park. ABC members along with several cooperative unionized contractors did the near impossible. It was a great showing of spirit and dedication. Strength and loyalty in numbers is very important when you are facing union coercion and violence.*
>
> *The Grand Ole Opry project gave members of ABC throughout the United States the courage and determination to build their companies based on free enterprise principles. Within a few years after that victory, Nashville became 90 percent merit shop and it remains so today.[4]*

Author's P.S: See end of Chapter 52 for color photo of the beautiful Coutry Music Hall of Fame and Museum built by the J. M. Rodgers Group in Nashville recently.

CHAPTER 34

BROWN & ROOT—A PARAGON OF FREE ENTERPRISE

SINCE ITS FOUNDING IN **1950**, ABC has attracted thousands of outstanding construction and engineering firms to its membership rolls. Many valiant leaders of these companies are mentioned within these pages. As a global luminary among a galaxy of stars, the firm of Brown & Root has played a special role in the success of ABC since almost the beginning.

This phenomenal story began in Texas in 1919 when fourteen mules helped to put Herman Brown in the road-building business. The contractor for whom he had been working went broke and gave him the mules, four Fresno scrapers, a pair of plows, and six wagons in lieu of nine months back pay for services rendered. Then the young road-gang foreman grew a handlebar mustache to make himself look older than his twenty-one years and talked the Freestone County Commissioners into giving him his first construction contract.

From the start, Herman Brown planned "to make it big." To him that meant "all out guts and gristle—the willingness to tackle the impossible and the ingenuity to make it happen." Luckily for him, it was a good time to become a road builder. Henry Ford had cranked up his assembly line and Model T's were on the turnpikes to everywhere. Within two years, the Federal Road Act was passed and a year after that the Texas Highway Commission was appointed. With construction prospects bright, Herman Brown married Margaret Root. Two years later, her brother, Dan Root, became an investor/partner—and one of the world's future headliners in engineering and construction was created.

In 1922 George Brown joined his brother Herman and Dan Root in the company business. While Herman was known for being the blunt working-

A man began by believing something; not by debating and arguing over many things.

THOMAS CARLYLE
SCOTTISH HISTORIAN

Success in any
enterprise
requires the
right product,
methods and
people—and
each must com-
plement the
others.

JOSEPH BURGER
HUMANIST

man's man, George was the smooth talker destined to walk and talk with presidents and royalty. Later in the decade, the two Brown brothers acquired Dan Root's interest in the firm and formally incorporated as Brown & Root, Inc. (B&R).

In 1929, while the nation reeled under the Great Depression, the small company managed to stay afloat. During World War II, it branched off into other services while doing its best to support the war effort. With an appetite for big projects, B&R made a tremendous leap when it built the Corpus Christi Naval Air Station and then constructed and launched 360 U.S. warships.

After the war, the firm continued its winning ways by setting building records, creating new technologies, and regularly "doing the impossible." In 1946 B&R built its first petrochemical plant and its first paper mill. In 1947 it constructed and launched for Kerr-McGee its first offshore platform out of sight of land in the Gulf of Mexico, offshore Louisiana.

The 1950's were marked by another series of firsts for B&R—most notably construction of the first $100 million polyethylene plant plus Louisiana's Lake Pontchartrain Causeway (the longest bridge of its kind) and the world's first

ABC CONTRACTOR

Herman (left) and George Brown, founders of Brown & Root, Inc. Texas, 1919.

supertanker terminal. B&R also assumed responsibility for architect-engineering of the Manned Spacecraft Center in Houston.

That decade also established the fundamental merit shop labor relations policy that still guides B&R today. A Texas building trades union council provoked an early philosophical and economic showdown with Herman Brown when it promulgated the following resolution on May 10, 1950:

> This Trades Council and all of its affiliated local unions will insist that all men working on any job coming under the jurisdiction of this Council be declared 100 percent union. Each respective local union will support this policy and insist that all of their members have working Building Trades cards"[1]

Texas Labor Federation Attacks B&R

At the time that this decree was announced, B&R was performing construction work on a non-union basis at five projects: a compressor station on the Little Inch gas pipeline, a power plant for the city of Austin, the Port Authority highway, Rice Stadium, and the Bull Shoals dam. It was not a coincidence that a news column called "Man Behind The Scenes," sponsored by the Texas State Federation of Labor, soon appeared with the following not-so-veiled threat:

> Herman Brown, the stud buck of the Brown & Root Construction Co., has finally run into a situation he is hard put to get out of. He moved a scab crew to start a compressor station on the Little Inch gas pipeline which he also partly owns. Some of the boys in Beaumont didn't have anything else to do so they put up a picket line around the job. Later that day, as the imported workers were being taken back into Beaumont by bus, the bus had an accident. It collided with a car, and somehow the bus got showered with beer bottles in the process. There were indications that some of the Brown scabs got struck by the shower of bottles . . .
>
> Of course, Brown hasn't asked us for advice. He has two or three law firms hired all the time to give him that, for a fee. But we'd give

Bravery is being the only one who knows you are afraid.

Franklin Jones
PUNDIT-HUMORIST

We can't always control our circumstances, but we can always control our reactions.

NAOMI JUDD
COUNTRY SINGER
AND HUMANIST

him a bit of advice, for free: If he really wants that compressor plant built, he'd better find himself a union sub-contractor to build it.[2]

Mass picketing and sporadic incidents of coercion, property damage, and violence occurred at most of the above-named job sites. A special assessment of forty cents per union member per month was levied by the Houston Trades Council "for the duration of the program" against B&R. But Herman Brown repeatedly refused to capitulate and sign a collective bargaining agreement proffered jointly by the local trades council and the entire state and international hierarchy of the AFL building trades unions. It would have required B&R "to go 100 percent union on all of its projects throughout the United States," Brown said.

At this point, B&R's attorneys went into a local Texas court for injunctive relief and damages based on "an AFL conspiracy to destroy the company." Union activities cited by the lawyers as cause for legal relief included placing the company's name on an "unfair" list; attempting to force the company to deny employment to non-union craftsmen; boycotting persons and firms doing business with the company; and refusing to perform work on any construction project where the company's personnel were employed.

The district court trial judge granted B&R's temporary restraining order against all of these alleged illegal labor practices. He added that his local court had jurisdiction of the case because monetary damages were requested (which required jury determination) and therefore there was no preemption of the matter by the National Labor Relations Board under the federal Taft-Hartley Act.

The Texas State Federation of Labor appealed this adverse decision—and was rebuffed again. The Court of Civil Appeals of Texas upheld the trial judge's injunctive order, sent the case back to him to determine recoverable damages by B&R, and confirmed the following findings of fact and law:

> The dispute or so-called "fight" of appellants [labor unions] with appellee [B&R] is widespread and has continued for some years past... [But] there is little, if any, evidence that B&R does not maintain excellent working conditions... [and]... there is no evidence that

B&R is engaged in a campaign to flout the labor laws or to destroy labor organizations.[3]

Most importantly, the appellate court in effect ruled in 1952 that the activities of the AFL building trades consortium *amounted to an unlawful conspiracy in restraint of trade.* Here is some of its reasoning:

> We have already shown that the dispute of the trades unions with B&R at Beaumont, Houston and Austin was in opposition to its open shop policy and was for an unlawful purpose. As to these local unions, the evidence shows that they were united in their respective local fights against B&R and that the picket lines on B&R's jobs in those localities were supplied and supported by the concerted action of those respective groups.
>
> The affiliates of these local unions—the Trades Councils of those respective areas, the State Federation of Labor, the Internationals, and the AF of L—were carrying on a fight against B&R to force it to enter into [illegal] closed shop contracts and agreements. In the furtherance of this common purpose and design, the various affiliates furnished encouragement and aid to the locals, and the acts done by the one in an effort to accomplish a common purpose became the acts of all.[4]

While this was a highly significant victory for B&R, the building trades unions never gave up their brutal tactics. In the 1960s, for example, after B&R was purchased by the Halliburton Company and had become the largest engineer-constructor firm in the United States, hundreds of union marauders mobbed and mass-picketed its job sites. They harassed and brawled with the open shop workers, damaged property and equipment, and blocked jobsite ingress and egress in attempts to bring the projects to a standstill.

On these occasions B&R was forced to persuade reluctant governors or attorneys-general to bring about law and order because timid or corrupt local sheriffs "had gone fishing." At times construction would be under siege for several weeks until B&R could convince National Labor Relations Board

Risk more than others think is safe. Care more than others think is wise. Expect more than others think is possible.

West Point cadet maxim

agents or local judges to enforce established legal procedures to protect B&R projects. During some of these encounters, B&R's loyal employees continued to work, eat, and sleep inside the jobsite twenty-four hours a day under the watchful eye of private security guards and military-style protective devices.

B&R Assists New Texas ABC Chapter

I'm May of 1969, National ABC representatives rolled into Houston, Texas, for their first membership foray into the southwest—a rally aimed at establishing a chapter in the troubled labor area. This critical event had been in the planning stage for several months under the guidance of Marvin Woodfin, senior vice president of B&R. Several ABC staffers and George Heit, administrative assistant to Woodfin, played an important role in motivating the turnout of 175 businesspersons. They consisted of a wide array of generals, subs, and suppliers from Houston and other parts of Texas.

A dinner meeting at the Americana Hotel was a huge success. It was chaired by B&R's Woodfin. Also participating in the program were ABC President John Lochary ('69–'70), past presidents Jimmy Long ('65–'66) and Fred Schnabel ('67–'68), Vice President Ralph McClelland ('68), and Executive

ABC Contractor
Marvin Woodfin, senior vice president of Brown & Root and first president of ABC's Texas chapter in 1970.

Vice President John Trimmer. Another prominent ABC staff official, Woodrow Moats, was in attendance to provide expert guidance on the introduction of the ABC Security Plan and Pension Program.

By the time this general meeting occurred, a local ABC budget committee had finished its work and set up a membership dues schedule. Incorporation was in process and office space had been established. Three months later, ABC President Lochary administered ABC's oath of office to the first president—Marvin Woodfin—and the board of directors of the new Texas Chapter. John Trimmer proudly summed up the good news:

Spearheaded by the fearless leadership role of Marvin Woodfin of Brown & Root, ABC put down a large merit shop foot in the southwest. It gave our Association a new anchor, with the potential to move to the far west and at the same time consolidate with southeastern states which either had or needed chapters.[5]

Trimmer's prediction soon came true. Woodfin saw to it that B&R helped to keep the Merit Shop Foundation solvent. He also assisted in expanding apprentice training on a national basis; began meetings with chapters-in-formation in Arizona, Nevada, Oklahoma, California and almost everywhere else west of the Mississippi River—while also giving ABC an entrée to the great technical schools of the southwest.

Woodfin was succeeded by Emil Zerr as B&R's senior representative with ABC. Zerr rose from a young construction engineering graduate of the University of Texas in 1957 to become chief operating officer of the giant firm in 1992. He served on both the ABC's local Texas chapter and its national board of directors from 1971 through 1980, and his advice and support were invaluable to the overall growth of the merit shop. Zerr said that B&R, because of its size, "preferred to keep a low public profile, behind the scenes, but always acted as a strong supporter of the merit shop and particularly ABC's smaller members who needed a leg up."

B&R Features Positive Employee Relations

According to Foster Parker, president and chief executive officer of B&R in the 1970s and a graduate of the business school of the University of Texas, four factors underlie the growth of his Houston-based company into one of the world's largest general contractors:

> Open shop, diversification, single responsibility and promotion from within made Brown & Root unique. Herman and George Brown believed that the number one key to success in business was the direct relationship between management and employees. They thought it important to communicate with employees and to learn if they have any complaints. . . .
>
> And one of the many advantages in open shop operation is that an employee can do more than one job. With what construction costs today, the emphasis is on speed up of production. We're seeing a

The strength of a cause or creed lies in the true sense of loyalty it can arouse in the hearts of its people.

LOUIS GERSTEIN
WRITER

greater and greater penetration of the open shop. Companies that in the past used only a union shop are moving to the open shop.

In concluding this interview with Anne Lundren of the *Houston Post*, Parker also described B&R's outstanding apprentice training program:

> This year, 1975, B&R will have 6,000 persons in its craft training program and expects to have some 10,000 next year. Minority groups account for 20 to 25 percent of the employees in the program—about the same percentage as in the Houston area. They are the greatest source of labor left in our area.
>
> We conduct our own training school and give concentrated courses. We believe that an employee can be trained to be a skilled journeyman in much less time than unions think is necessary. Retention of trained employees runs about 90 percent.[6]

During more recent years, the company's general manager of construction and maintenance, Don Griswold, has served with distinction on both ABC's national board of directors and the Greater Houston Chapter's industrial committee. B&R was a primary factor in the creation and financing of ABC's state-of-the-art "Wheels of Learning" craft training curriculum. And in 1994, B&R was one of eleven companies involved in founding ABC's companion National Center for Construction Education and Research ("NCCER").[7]

Today B&R continues to donate professional expertise and millions of dollars to NCCER's success. Frank Yancey, the company's senior vice president of construction, made the following comment in this regard:

> All of us in my firm feel that the single most important issue in the global construction industry today is to develop a well-trained workforce. This is an issue in which we desire to be a global leader, not a follower. We applaud the National Center for the great strides it has made in advancing the construction industry and fully support its goals and ideals.[8]

A historic merger of engineering and construction titans occurred in 1998 as Brown & Root joined forces with a complementary firm founded by Morris Woodruff Kellogg. This merger produced Kellogg Brown & Root (KB&R), recognized today as one of the largest, most versatile, and most resourceful technology-driven engineering and construction firms in the world.

KB&R, like B&R before it, is a paragon of free enterprise. Under the Halliburton Company banner, it operates as a merit shop employer and major member of ABC. It has consolidated revenues of over $17 billion and a workforce of approximately 100,000, located in more than 120 countries.

Back in 1919, the "guts, gristle, and ingenuity" of Herman Root tackled the impossible and made it happen. [9]

CHAPTER 35

BRAVERY ALONG THE BAYOU

MY FOND MEMORIES OF **NEW ORLEANS** date back to the 1950s. In those days, among other assignments, I was the chief negotiator for W.R. Grace & Co. at the bargaining table versus the militant International Chemical Workers Union and equally combative regional Building and Construction Trades Councils.

Production and maintenance employees of Grace's chemical manufacturing plants located in Baton Rouge and Lake Charles, Louisiana, were represented by these labor organizations. In order to reach the union-dominated cities, the first leg of my journey was a non-stop flight (on non-union Delta Airlines) from my home base in Baltimore to New Orleans. Whenever possible, I made a point of staying overnight in that wondrous city of Mardi Gras fame to fortify myself for the stress and strain of imminent labor confrontations.

With the advantage of a generous business expense account (for the first time in my life), my joyous ritual in the Nawlins Big Easy usually began with a Sazerac cocktail and some crawfish bisque at the Hotel Roosevelt bar or a Hurricane Punch and sing-alongs with the boisterous crowd surrounding twin pianos at Pat O'Brien's Place. Then I would commence more serious gastronomy at Antoine's Restaurant in the French Quarter. Seafood gumbo and a glass of Chateau Lafite were followed by a combo-plate of Oysters Rockefeller and Bienville, succeeded in turn by a main course of Pompano En Papillote and Trout Meuniere Amandine with stuffed Mirliton. All of this was accompanied by a Famous Ramos Gin Fizz (or two). Dessert consisted of Bananas Foster and a Creole pecan praline with Café Brûlot on the side. As a grand finale, I walked

No man can be a victor on an empty stomach.

WILLIAM COWPER
ENGLISH POET

along Bourbon Street and bolstered my morale on a nightcap snifter of Le Cognac de Napoleon, blended with the famous jazz music and Cajun stories of trumpeter Al Hirt, clarinetist Pete Fountain and their Dixieland Six.

The practice of labor relations can be fun at times...

Louisiana Becomes Industrialized

The movement of giant petrochemical and refining firms into the Pelican State at that time was the result of a booming post–World War II economy, antiquated plants, and higher labor costs in the North and East, cheap natural gas from new offshore production, and deep channels to the open Gulf of Mexico, plus an eager workforce. Louisiana's two-hundred-year-old agrarian economy was giving way to massive industrialization. Historic plantations handed over their thousands of lush Mississippi River acres to companies such as W.R. Grace & Co., Exxon, Dow Chemical, Georgia Pacific, DuPont, Union-Carbide, Monsanto, and many more corporate giants.

When building their new plants, these Fortune 500 companies used the largest unionized construction firms belonging to the National Construction Association, which had a nationwide collective bargaining agreement with the National Building and Construction Trades Council headquartered in Washington, D.C. As a result, thousands of local Louisiana workers were automatically blanketed into the compulsory labor union movement. After the plants were put online, the newly hired maintenance employees similarly were herded into local building trades unions and the new production workers were allocated to OCAW.

In 1956, two significant events occurred. Democratic populist Earl Long became governor of Louisiana while the fiery Victor Bussie was elected president of the state's division of the newly merged AFL-CIO. Long and Bussie were ideological brothers under the skin. While Long's leftist shenanigans lasted only four years, Bussie built a juggernaut that virtually dominated business, industry, and politics for the next quarter-century—and he saw to it that a compliant pro-union majority controlled the state legislature. By the time another ultra-liberal from North Louisiana named John McKeithen was elected governor in 1960, Louisiana was the most heavily unionized state in the South.

The Building Trades Flex Political Muscles

Even so, the entrepreneurial rush to the sunbelt continued, and by 1967 more than 130,000 Louisianans belonged to labor unions. The Catholic Archdiocese of New Orleans required union-only labor on its building projects. And the trades unions, grown rich and powerful through control of the politicians and the police forces, demanded and got exorbitant wages, skyrocketing employee benefits, and featherbedded work rules.

Labor costs were ignored as industries scrambled to get their facilities into production first. But still unsatisfied, the trade unions began bickering and fighting among themselves. Inter-union craft jurisdictional fights and violent walkouts became the norm. Contractors and construction users were at the mercy of an oppressive and, oftentimes, criminal union leadership. Cost overruns of 30 percent to 40 percent were common. In Lake Charles and Baton Rouge, hundreds of workdays were lost, and more than $250 million in construction was idled because of irresponsible and illegal activities of the building trades. Some manufacturing plant owners even threatened to shut their new construction gates permanently.

Not content with this dominance, Big Labor set out to organize the local oilfields and offshore industry. They chose Lafayette and Southwest Louisiana to begin—and immediately met with resistance. The "oil patch" people were accustomed to running their own businesses. They didn't know or care about "union standard agreements" or "national labor councils." Hiring halls, mandatory membership, antiquated work rules, excessive crew size, autocratic union stewards, and the like would not work there. This union collectivism concept also was rejected by most of the conscientious workers themselves.

The building trades responded with threats, intimidation and finally, beatings and dynamitings. Two people were killed. There were twenty-three serious explosions in twenty-one months. The oilfield companies fought back with a new organization of their own called the Oilfield Contractors Association. And official Acadiana offered rewards for conviction of the terrorists. Notice was served that Cajun country would not tolerate such violence. Within two years most of the offenders were in jail or awaiting trial. Local trade unions had their first taste of failure—and it marked the turning point in labor-management relations in Louisiana.

Now I know what a statesman is: he's a dead politician. We need more statesmen.

BOB EDWARDS
JOURNALIST

The next piece of bad news for the building trades unions (although they had no way of knowing it at the time) was the appearance of a new adversary described by one of his peers as "a man so fearless he would charge the fires of hell with a bucket of water." The gentleman's name was Archie Lyles and he had been the regional director of government affairs for Brown & Root for thirty-four years. Throughout Lyles's remarkable career, he was a leader in the following organizations, in addition to ABC: a founder of the Louisiana Political Action Committee, where he served as past president and member;

PHOTO COURTESY OF MARY LYLES ADAIR

Archie Lyles, a founding member of ABC's Louisiana-New Orleans-Bayou Chapter in 1970, and regional director of government affairs at Brown & Root.

the South Political Action Committee, where he served as chairman; the Louisiana Policy and Advisory Council, where he served as an executive committee member; a founder of the Construction Industry Legislative Council, where he served as president; the Louisiana Right to Work Committee, where he served as founder and board member; and a founder of the Louisiana Oil Field Contractors Association, where he served as chairman of the board in 1988–1989.

"Why and How ABC Came to New Orleans"

The rest of this story is the amazing account of an ABC chapter's creation and establishment in New Orleans. It is told here in Archie Lyles' own words as recorded by Lisa Nardone, editor of the *ABC Contractor,* in its September 2000 issue, and later repeated to me:

During October of 1969, I (Archie Lyles) was in Houston, Texas, on business. My boss at Brown & Root asked me if I had a clean shirt. He wanted me to stay there overnight to meet a group of open shop contractors from Baltimore who had started something called the "merit shop." We got together in a downtown hotel with ABC Executive Vice President John Trimmer, President John Lochary, and former President Jimmy Long. They impressed me and I realized immediately that many of ABC's policies and strategies were the same as those used by Brown & Root to remain "open shop" over the years.

I returned to my New Orleans base and the next week invited six oilfield contractors—Buster Hughes, Monroe Wolfe, Nolty Theriot, Ken Wallace, Jim Bean, and Ben Baldwin—from Belle Chase to our conference room to discuss the exciting facts I had heard in Houston. That powwow turned out to be the first ABC meeting in the state of Louisiana. Two weeks later we rounded up a few more Westbank contractors, including Ray McDermot, to meet with Trimmer and Lochary. ABC's Louisiana Chapter (known today as the New Orleans/Bayou Chapter) was born the next year—1970.

We immediately set out to devise a formula for an open shop climate that would ultimately include all of Louisiana. We had won in the oilfields of South Louisiana by pulling together, but we were not strong enough to take on the Baton Rouge and Southwest Louisiana Building Trades Councils at their industrial bases. We reasoned that we must first bring the New Orleans commercial builders into the fold to establish a broader organization. Once we had solidified on the Westbank and South Louisiana, with about fifty to sixty firms, we went into New Orleans and Metairie. We talked to contractors Joe Scheyd, Emille Littinger, the Favrets, "Ace" Legardeur, Jack Donahue, and others. Our growth was slow but steady. We had financial problems from the beginning, so Monroe Wolfe gave his office space to us rent-free.

We in the oilfields—Brown & Root, McDermot, Avondale, and a few others—had always worked open shop. We had no union agreements and we were large companies. It took guts for smaller guys like Scheyd, Littinger, Donahue, Legarde, and the Favrets to "bite the bullet" by risking all that they had owned on the line against Big Labor's terrorism. And they believed there was no turning back once the commitment was made.

Our members didn't just run out and sell long-suffering contractors into the "blessed sanctuary" of ABC. What we told them sounded good—all this new freedom to manage their own companies. But union contractors decided they had much to think about before changing completely the way they had always done business. They knew any final victory was far down the road, but

The human spirit is stronger than anything that can happen to it.

C. C. Scott
HISTORIAN

the alternative of the status quo—*compulsory unionism*—had become unacceptable. Any past satisfaction a builder could gain from watching his handiwork come out of the ground to become a functional living thing had too long been soured by a sullen and non-productive workforce. They were loyal to their bosses who, at every turn, demanded more and more and gave less and less. And so once these contractors made the ABC commitment, it was total.

They never looked back.

We went on the attack to restrict picket lines by using ABC's "reserved gate" secondary boycott legal strategy on member projects. It worked and we became bolder. We notified law enforcement agencies and unions by telegram and registered letter of our plans in advance of our actions. We recorded all suspicious actions on film and our project managers kept accurate logs. They were schooled on what to watch for. When picket lines were set up at the wrong gate, they were legally challenged. We operated as though we knew exactly what we were doing—and the Lord must have been with us!

New ABC member "Ace" Legardeur was given the task of bringing in competent open shop ready-mix concrete suppliers who would cross a union's so-called "informational" picket lines. Edson Davis became our first East Bank supplier and Vernon Dowdy's West Bank firm had always been non-union. Now we could meet that basic materials demand on an area-wide basis. All of us worked at our businesses twelve hours or more every day and then spent three or four more hours every night talking to ABC prospects. These were some of the most fulfilling years of my life in the construction business.

Archie Lyles Leads New ABC Chapter

I became president of the Louisiana Chapter of ABC in 1971 and we continued to expand. A dozen general contractors served notice that they would not renew their contracts with the building trades when they expired. Not-so-veiled union threats and sabotage occurred on some of their jobs, but we stood together. We, like they, were now well organized. Large contractors like McDermott, Avondale, Prestressed Concrete, and Crain Brothers became ABC members.

Within two years' time, we had overcome our initial growing pains. During Joe Scheyd's presidency of our new ABC Chapter, we hired Terry Gee to be our executive director. He brought with him true professionalism and organizing skills. His outstanding leadership turned the Louisiana Chapter into a model for the entire national association. At the legislative level, with help from a new Louisiana Political Action Council, we were able to thwart labor union initiatives at the state capitol in Baton Rouge. We couldn't beat them but they couldn't beat us either, and so an impasse resulted. In 1974, the business community formed an umbrella organization called the Louisiana Association of Business and Industry.

We had united at last.

On January 15, 1976, Big Labor made another critical mistake. An outrageous and senseless act of raw criminal violence occurred on that day in Lake Charles. During a dawn attack with heavy construction equipment, rifles, and shotguns, trade union members stormed a Jupiter Chemical Company work site and Joe Hopper was killed. His offense was being in a non-union construction trailer while applying for a job.

ABC Wins in the State Legislature

A huge cry went up from every corner of the state. People were fed up with union coercion, compulsion, and terrorism. Somebody had to do something—and this time we in ABC were ready. Two months after the bloody incident occurred and during the regular session of the Louisiana Legislature, we lobbied for a state right-to-work law forbidding compulsory unionism[1] and the amendment of six anti-violence statutes to make them include illegal labor union activities.

Our ABC chapter played a key role in the victory that followed. On "Open Shop Day" just before the final House vote on the right-to-work legislation, 1500 non-union workers from our chapter member firms invaded the state capitol at Baton Rouge. We came by the busload and packed the legislative halls in an orderly fashion. The cadre of sullen trade union supporters on hand were shocked as we filled both hearing room galleries. Then we looked lawmakers in the eyes and told them: "We have rights, too."

The Louisiana Legislature was impressed and got the message.

I never was more proud of ABC in my life than on that day. Our state right to work bill and an anti-union-violence bill both passed with plenty of votes

Wherever law ends tyranny begins.

JOHN LOCKE
17TH CENTURY ENGLISH
PHILOSOPHER

399

Bravery, the Cajuns say, is endurance for just one minute more than your opponent.

ANONYMOUS

to spare, and our young contractors association became a respected member of the state's business community.

Brown & Root's Archie Lyles, the trailblazer of merit shop bravery along the bayou, concluded his remarkable story this way: "That's why and how ABC began in Louisiana. It took dedication to free enterprise, coalition building, political action, and legislative involvement. It still amazes some people that everything turned out just like we said it would!"

CHAPTER 36

THE MERIT SHOP
BRIDGES AMERICA

THE DECADE OF THE 1970S COMMENCED with newly elected President Richard Nixon facing—like his four immediate predecessors in office—the political power of Big Labor.

An early sign of the formidable influence of the AFL-CIO's construction trades unions was present (albeit inconspicuously) along the inaugural parade route that Nixon traveled through the capital city of Washington, D.C. The same invisible sign was present in the ceremonial stands where he took the oath of office, at the White House stand where he reviewed the parade units, and in the grandstands seating the parade's spectators.

This silent harbinger of labor-management crises to follow in the 1970s was described in the *Washington Report on Labor*, a monthly publication of the Chamber of Commerce of the United States:

> A non-union construction firm was the original low bidder for the job of erecting the temporary reviewing stands for the Nixon inauguration. Enter the Washington Building Trades Council, spokesman for the AFL-CIO construction unions in the District of Columbia. Complaining that the reviewing stands contract always went to a union firm, the Trades Council successfully demanded that the contract be increased

Government is the only known vessel that leaks from the top.

JAMES RESTON
JOURNALIST

$50,000 above the original bid and stipulated that it contain exclusive union hiring hall provisions.

Furthermore, the successful low bidder—a small open shop builder—was compelled to agree to use only union labor on all jobs the firm undertakes for a full year. The unions, disputing the meaning of the overtime clause in the non-union firm's contract, demanded extra money to pay double time instead of time-and-a-half for work on weekends and holidays. Pressures of the inflexible January 20 inaugural deadline forced the Nixon Inaugural Parade Committee to acquiesce to the Building Trades Council ultimatum.[1]

The concluding sentence of the U.S. Chamber's report of the event was: "This incident may seem insignificant as compared to those dramatic foreign and domestic issues facing the new Nixon Administration and Congress, but the problem it represents is massive."

The accuracy of that prediction was evidenced by rampant inflation facing the Nixon Administration after it had been nourished by the "Great Society" economic policies of the previous Lyndon Johnson administration. Two prestigious employer organizations—the National Association of Manufacturers and The Business Roundtable—placed much of the blame for this financial crisis on the "irrational bargaining systems and outmoded apprenticeship programs" espoused by the building trades unions.[2]

Wage increases of up to 50 percent spread over three-year-long collective bargaining contracts were negotiated. During the first six months of 1970 alone, union construction wages rose 87.5 cents an hour. These inflated deals frequently were the result of strike pressure. They also restricted the number of apprentices in training and forbade the introduction by management of improved equipment, materials, and production methods at a time when construction represented 14 percent of the nation's gross national product.

George Romney, the chairman of American Motors who became governor of Michigan and later secretary of Housing and Urban Development (R-MI), held a meeting with AFL-CIO leaders and begged them to do something to reduce the excessive wage and fringe benefits settlements, but they booed him out of the union hall. They also ignored a warning by Secretary of Labor (and later secretary of state) George Shultz (R-CA), that they were engaged in "a formula for suicide" as well as his pleas that they permit contractors to initiate more flexible work rules and train more African-Americans for skilled construction jobs.

ABC Benefits from Trade Union Excesses

One significant result of this union arrogance and the inflation it created was a surge in the growth of ABC. It had the approval and endorsement of *Fortune* magazine, which set the stage for what lay ahead in its feature article entitled "The Building Trades versus the People." Bemoaning the fact that craft unions had created an artificial labor shortage and used that shortage to push construction wages up more rapidly than any manufacturing or other industrial wage, *Fortune* predicted that "in many instances wages are slated to double in the next three years."

A "side effect of construction wage spiraling," *Fortune* continued, "is that it induces a wage rise in other industries and, since these increases are not supporting a comparable increase in productivity, an automatic inflationary situation is created." But, *Fortune* noted, "resistance to the unions is beginning to show up among both contractors and big construction consumers." The magazine added, significantly, that ABC was a growing "antidote" to trade union malpractices and concluded:

> Public opinion, as manifest in the press, is growing against the building trades. A showdown with the construction unions is long overdue. But it will not be an easy task to cut down their grass-roots political and economic power. The building trades' counter-strategy at this point is to make it appear that they are bowing to public and judicial opinion while, at the same time, they are working behind the scenes to preserve their control over the labor force.[3]

In February 1971, *Time* magazine similarly attacked "the 17 AFL-CIO construction trades unions which consist of three million members in ten thousand local councils and trades that have forced construction costs to climb at a rate of almost double that of all other U.S. industries." This "soaring inflation,"

Inflation is a form of hidden taxation which is almost impossible to measure.

JOHN BECKLEY
1ST LIBRARIAN
OF CONGRESS

The exploitation of money has never been charged, so far as I know, with assuring the triumph of open and competitive markets.

ALBERT CAMUS
PUNDIT

continued *Time*, "has caused many firms to defer plans for new buildings and factories or shift their production to foreign countries, thus depriving the United States of revenue and American citizens of jobs. And the larger engineering and construction firms that employ 100 percent union labor have reported that in the last two years they lost $7.5 billion in contracts to open-shop, non-union operators." Immediate action needed to be taken, according to *Time*, "since it was predicted that there would be a 14 percent wage hike in the construction industry during the coming year." The *Time* article, like *Fortune*, concluded with praise for ABC's merit shop "as a key to untangling the dilemma."[4]

Presidential Deferment of the Davis-Bacon Statute

Public indignation against Big Labor reached a boiling point on March 3, 1971, when President Nixon suspended the union-slanted Davis-Bacon Act

"We also think there should be an escalator clause to meet any cost-of-living increase that may result from the granting of our wage demands."

to help curb unbridled inflation. Section 6 of that "prevailing wage law" authorizes the president to take such an action "in the event of a national emergency."[5] Nixon's proclamation stated bluntly that "construction industry collective bargaining settlements are excessive and showing no signs of decelerating." He also concluded that "increased unemployment and more frequent and longer work stoppages have accompanied the excessive and accelerating union wage demands and settlements," threatening the basic economic stability of the nation's economy.[6]

Several industrial unions within the parent AFL-CIO supported the president's executive order but the building trades were enraged at it. They called his suspension of their favorite labor law "an obvious attempt to destroy union wages and conditions on government work." AFL-CIO President George Meany loyally supported his building trades department by describing the president's action as "personal and punitive against the welfare of American workers."[7]

Within four weeks' time, Nixon capitulated to this attack by Big Labor and reinstated the arcane Davis-Bacon Act, with one caveat: "Organized labor" would participate with "management" and "government" in a tripartite Construction Industry Stabilization Committee ("CISC"). No place was established on this committee for merit shop representation, but seventeen craft boards were included that covered every segment of the unionized side of the industry. Despite constant internal bickering, these boards managed to slow down the pace of negotiated wage rates and fringe benefits somewhat, but the "uniform national work rules" of the craft boards designed to reduce union "featherbedding" and increase productivity usually were ignored.

A National Wage-Price Freeze

Six months later, President Nixon was still under political pressure to do more about curing the country's inflation, and he imposed a "temporary" wage and price freeze on August 15, 1971. While this move also was vehemently opposed by the AFL-CIO's George Meany and the Democrat party as "contempt for the well-being of the average American employee," the President's Cost of Living Council and Pay-Price Commission had some beneficial impact on the nation's economy.[8]

> **After order and liberty, economy is one of the highest essentials of a free government.**
>
> CALVIN COOLIDGE
> 30TH PRESIDENT

The wage control machinery set up under the aforementioned CISC also continued to function, but received scathing criticism from an *Engineering News-Record* editorial. It pointed out that "union members of the CISC approved first-year increases as high as 15 percent while an aggregate increase in wages and salaries under any merit or non-union salary administration plan—where no labor agreement existed—was subjected to the 5.5 percent standard." And in response to CISC's explanation that labor union settlements required "different treatment," the *ENR* editor scoffed: "As a cynical statement of the rules of power politics, that proposition has a certain gruesome appeal. As the basis for a system of controls, it is horrifying."[9]

A year or so before these trying times began, ABC National officials had scanned the economic horizon and warned all Association members of the possibility of wage-price controls. Members also were advised to establish a "paper trail" documenting their firm's pay and fringe benefit policies and practices to avoid a wage freeze that would render them unable to continue to pursue their normal practice of periodic merit pay increases and productivity bonuses for deserving workers.

Meanwhile, as events unfolded, ABC kept its members informed through its *Contractor* magazine about regulations and administrative rulings affecting the construction industry. ABC also handled appeals before the CISC and frequently succeeded in bringing a touch of equity into that agency's biased decisions. Government efforts to regulate wages and prices dragged on as late as 1974 before they were removed, while ABC continued to monitor all of these federal actions.

Joseph LaMonaca, ABC's 15th president

LaMonaca Takes Over as ABC's President

Joseph LaMonaca, a quiet-mannered, thoughtful, and dedicated general contractor based in Lancaster, Pennsylvania, who had been an admiral's aide-de-camp in World War II, became ABC's fifteenth national president in 1971. He served the Association with distinction for two years and his acceptance speech at the annual convention in San Juan, Puerto Rico, was well received. Excerpts from it bear repeating. LaMonaca began by quoting the opening lines written by Charles Dickens in his famous novel, *A Tale of*

Two Cities. These words, LaMonaca said, were "timely and analogous" to the irony of the merit shop's mushrooming popularity during a national period of calamitous construction inflation caused by the building trades unions:

> It was the best of times, it was the worst of times, it was the age of Wisdom, it was the age of Foolishness, it was the epoch of Belief, it was the epoch of Incredulity, it was the season of Light, it was the season of Darkness, it was the spring of Hope, it was the winter of Despair...

The forceful message that followed in LaMonaca's address in 1971 is still applicable today. It mirrors our fractured society in the twenty-first century. First, he likened the free enterprise system to a "three legged stool." Those legs, he said, are "government, labor and management and the seat of the stool is the public interest." Support given to this seat is "determined by the influence exerted by each of the three legs, and the seat," he charged, "is badly tilted." In other words, LaMonaca explained, "the influence of government and organized labor is expanding while private sector management grows weaker and weaker." And he elaborated:

> During the past 40 years we have allowed our concept of freedom to change drastically. By freedom, we used to mean that one could pursue his own economic and social bent without interference, so long as he lived within the basic rules of society. It was this concept of freedom that made us the melting pot of the world and our people prospered.
>
> This is no longer the case. Today's concept is a freedom from want, from fear, and from insecurity. We of the "merit shop" cannot accept this concept because it destroys that sense of accountability and responsibility. For too long, we have been asking our government to assume this responsibility for us as an "entitlement." But our Founding Fathers intended that the government should do only those things that we could not do ourselves.
>
> Government now sees only one side of an issue, depending upon the superior political power of various pressure groups. From their

The real problem with which modern government has to deal is how to protect the citizen against the encroachment upon his rights and liberties by his own government; how to save him from the repressive schemes born of the egotism of public office.

WILLIAM BORAH
U.S. SENATOR

leverage, government has become involved in nearly every facet of our free enterprise system. It has created such a morass of legislation that it now finds itself unable to cope with the real problems at hand.

Today we find ourselves in the position where a handful of willful and powerful union bosses can literally bring this nation to its knees. It is time government began to realize that organized labor is only one fourth of our working force and a small minority of our total population. It is time that we examine our labor laws and return to each individual those basic inalienable rights of our Constitution: the right to decide voluntarily and of one's own free will to belong or not belong to a private organization; and the right to work and pursue one's own niche within our free enterprise system without government interference.[10]

ABC Moves Westward

On November 29, 1971, ABC was featured in the *Chicago Tribune* newspaper with this headline: **OPEN SHOP DRIVE EXPANDS IN MIDWEST**. As the *Tribune* reported: "You don't hear too much about open shops in Chicago because the city is a stronghold of unions. But about 3,500 contractors across the country have joined ABC and the membership drive shows no sign of slackening." The article quoted John Trimmer to the effect that "management throughout the United States is fed up with the escalating wages, jurisdictional disputes, make-work rules and other abuses of the building trades unions."

The *Tribune* noted that the open shop's entrepreneurial freedom allows contractors to determine the size of a workforce they need and retain the critical managerial prerogative of making job assignments. Again quoting John Trimmer, the story emphasized that the open shop movement gives management much more flexibility and productivity than a union shop, which—continued the *Tribune*—was one of the reasons why open shop contractors were performing an estimated 40 percent to 50 percent of all commercial and industrial work throughout the nation. The *Tribune* also reported that the unionized National Constructors Association had lost jobs valued at $7.5 billion dollars to open shop contractors in the previous two years.

ABC Increases Its Publications and Member Services

In the public relations arena during Joe LaMonaca's regime as president, ABC's national periodicals reached new heights. The *Contractor* magazine, which had served as the "voice" of the merit shop construction industry for eighteen years, now was becoming the most widely read publication in its field in the nation. Distributed monthly, it provided its readers (as its successor publications do today) with reports on important subjects such as modern building techniques, labor and construction legislation, precedent-setting court decisions, effective employee relations, safety and health, successful internal management practices, the growth of the merit shop, and the accomplishments of ABC member firms throughout the nation and the world.

Because of newsworthy features such as these, circulation of the *ABC Contractor* was constantly increasing. Key employees in every subscribing firm read it regularly. The magazine also enjoyed popularity among construction workers at all levels through ABC's gift subscription program for its members. Because of this circulation popularity, an increasing number of articles appeared regularly which were of particular interest to mechanics, foremen, and field supervisors. Moreover, many members of Congress received the *ABC Contractor* regularly. Their subscriptions were presented to them as donations by their concerned contractor constituents. The magazine also was sent to colleges and universities that offered an introduction to the construction industry and/or engineering curricula.

Another valuable publication prepared and published by ABC was the *Annual Membership Directory*. In expanded format, it listed every member firm in the Association (contractors, suppliers, and supportive services) according to local chapter and construction classification as well as alphabetically. The *Directory* was read regularly by major construction users throughout the country to locate contractors and invite their bids on projects. In addition, general contractors began to refer to the *Directory* to locate subcontractors in a specific locale who specialized in a particular trade they needed to use. Supplemented by paid advertising, this publication became an essential tool for every merit shop contractor and an important source of ABC revenue for operating expenses.

> Words are the most powerful drug of mankind.
>
> RUDYARD KIPLING
> AUTHOR-POET

Good teaching
is one-fourth
preparation
and three-fourths
theatre.

GAIL GODWIN
AUTHOR

New internal ABC activities in the early 1970s included the first national public relations program and the first national apprenticeship seminar. To assist members in gaining government certification of ABC craft training programs, the Association's national headquarters published its first craft-training manual. It detailed the steps required to establish an effective and approvable local plan. In further support of training new journeyman mechanics, ABC's national board of directors passed an "apprenticeship statement of responsibility." It pledged all ABC member firms to the promotion of careers in construction by providing the best quality training available to all apprentices.

Several Canadian trade associations expressed interest in these ABC programs and an ABC movie on the merit shop philosophy was circulated to business groups and service clubs throughout Canada as well as the United States.

By this time ABC also had developed an outstanding health and medical insurance package for its members. They could look to the Association as a one-stop center with protection that was hand-tailored for their individual needs. The program considered location, demographics, industry specialty, and business objectives. It was priced competitively and reduced the amount of tedious paperwork by individual contractors through its coordinated administration at the national level. It offered flexibility and choice of coverage by using nationally and regionally based carriers and focusing on top-rated insurers with a reputation for prompt payment of claims. Further security came in the form of a report by trustees of the fund that assets had reached a million dollars.

Robert Hepner Joins ABC National Staff

Another encouraging sign of ABC's growth was the creation of a national office comptroller in 1971. It was ABC's good fortune to hire for this important position a gentleman who turned out to be one of the Association's most capable and popular staff leaders—Robert Hepner. He came to ABC with an excellent background for the job. After receiving his bachelor of science degree in accounting from the Baltimore

ABC CONTRACTOR

Robert Hepner, national ABC controller (1972–1997) and ABC executive vice president (1998–2000).

College of Commerce, he worked for Atlantic Coast Freight Lines, Inc., as an assistant secretary-treasurer and for the Baltimore Transit Company as assistant to the comptroller.

In this new ABC position, the native Baltimorean became responsible for the financial affairs of the national association. Hepner said his reason for seeking the comptroller's position was his confidence that "ABC's growth potential was unlike any other business association in the country." He noted that "there seems to be a definite feeling of pride held by all those connected with the merit shop and I am looking forward to doing my part to help ABC span the nation."[11]

Bob Hepner accomplished that goal. Over the years at various times he assumed responsibility for almost every phase of ABC's national business, including finances, insurance operations, membership recruitment and membership services, business development, public relations, education, training, and safety programs.

In 1998, Hepner was appointed to ABC's highest staff position—executive vice president. In that job he directed a professional team of seventy persons and was in charge of overall planning and management of the Association. In announcing this promotion, David Bush, ABC's forty-first national president ('99), proclaimed Hepner as "an experienced and upbeat coalition builder and association leader and the perfect choice to lead the ABC team into the new millennium."[12]

ABC Goes to Washington

In February of 1972—about a year after Bob Hepner was hired—ABC's first major national legislative conference was held. The goal was to awaken Congress about the needs of the merit shop sector of the construction industry. Members and staff officials from every ABC chapter met in Washington, D.C., to carry the message personally to their senators and representatives on Capitol Hill.

Congressman Philip Crane (R-IL) opened the two-day meeting with a discussion of the best methods of approaching legislators and handling the responses they might give. Speaking candidly, Crane noted that personal visits, monetary donations, and election-time support "would pull more weight on the Hill than the most eloquent letters."[13]

> **Whenever you commend someone, add your reasons for it.**
>
> RICHARD STEELE
> WRITER

> A politician is
> a person with
> whose politics
> you don't agree;
> if you agree
> with him, he is
> a statesman.
>
> DAVID LLOYD GEORGE
> BRITISH STATESMAN

Next, conference attendees met with the congressmen and senators from their home states. These ABCers were armed with policy statements on such issues as the ever-increasing job site violence, pro-union administration of the Davis-Bacon Act, the ineffectiveness of the Construction Industry Stabilization Committee, and discriminatory apprenticeship training program regulations. A large number of ABCers also explained the merit shop story to legislators from areas of the country where there was a lack of familiarity with the movement.

In one of the highlights of this legislative conference, two of ABC's top officials—Joe LaMonaca and John Trimmer—met with Donald Rumsfeld, director of the Cost of Living Council (who became President George W. Bush's secretary of defense thirty years later) to discuss ABC's concern about the council's administrative decisions. Further meetings were scheduled with Rumsfeld and produced substantial cooperation from his COLC.

After completing these strategic lobbying sessions on Capitol Hill, ABC members attended a dinner meeting during which they were addressed by Senator Edward Gurney (R-FL) and Congressman William Archer (R-TX). Both Gurney and Archer informed the attendees that the enactment of much-needed labor reform legislation during that session of Congress was highly unlikely. "The AFL-CIO's Committee on Political Education (COPE) is more powerful than both the Republican and Democrat parties combined," they said, "and it is effective because it makes a strong effort on a national basis. Organized labor's money goes where there's a chance of winning." The senators' final advice was: "Members of ABC must get more involved in politics if merit shop goals are to be realized. The labor unions figured out this strategy to support their causes back in the 1930's. Continual follow-through is the key to the success of your legislative program."[14]

Trimmer's Crusading Travels

Because of Big Labor's inflationary labor contract settlements and its ever-increasing trail of terrorism and property destruction designed to counteract ABC's expanding share of the building and construction market, a deluge of calls began to come to ABC offices. Both dissatisfied unionized contractors and harassed non-union contractors across the nation wanted to join the merit shop crusade.

This tidal wave of interest caused John Trimmer to criss-cross America in jet-style "seven-league boots," preaching the ABC gospel. Not only contractors, architects, and materials suppliers but also a large number of construction users soon became exposed for the first time to the Association's profitable yet non-inflationary philosophy of quality building and construction, regardless of non-union or union affiliation.

This is a diary of a typical month of Trimmer's agenda. It covers January of the year 1972:

In every triumph there's a lot of "tri."

James Tyger
WRITER

Jan. 3	White Plains, N.Y.: Along with Yankee Chapter President Phil Swett, met with representative in charge of construction for one of largest industrial corporations in U.S. Discussed ABC and current problems of large construction users.
Jan. 4	Attended ABC's Metropolitan Washington Chapter meeting and installed chapter officers.
Jan. 5	Held national staff meeting to review current programs and report recent events.
Jan. 6	Washington, D.C.: Met with representative of one of the largest U.S. corporations' public relations executive to assist in presenting merit shop facts for report to be made in the near future.
Jan. 7	Nashville, Tenn.: Attended chapter-in-formation board of directors meeting to develop organizational and operational plans.
Jan. 8	Kansas City, Mo.: Spoke to "User's Conference" concerning Kansas City prevailing wage rate situation and future impact of ABC. Also met with a nationwide firm in construction industry to discuss ABC and the company's potential role in promoting the merit shop.
Jan. 9	Attended Baltimore Metropolitan Chapter's dinner-dance with Anne (Trimmer).
Jan. 10	Met in National ABC Office with assistant in charge of construction for one of top U.S. corporations. Discussed

ABC, the merit shop operation and its role in the corporation's future construction planning.

Jan. 11 Atlanta, Ga.: Met with group of contractors interested in forming ABC's Atlanta Chapter.

Jan. 13 Oakland, Calif.: Participated in two-day seminar of Western Industrial Contractors Association. Was luncheon speaker presenting the ABC merit shop philosophy and was panel moderator on current construction industry problems. During stay in Oakland, met representative of major corporation and was taken to its California office where met with chief executives to present ABC story.

Jan. 14 Whittier, Calif.: Met and spoke to group of general contractors who operate in Whittier area. Told ABC story and benefits of merit shop.

Jan. 16 Monterey, Calif.: Spoke to Western Coast Engineers Association on subject of ABC and its activities, including detailed comparison of merit shop operations as compared to compulsory union shops.

Jan. 17 Scottsdale, Ariz.: Met with "Committee of 100" of Chamber of Commerce of U.S. This is a committee made up of specially chosen executives from one hundred U.S. trade associations. Also met with president of ABC's Arizona chapter-in-formation.

Jan. 19 Long Island, N.Y.: Spoke to Long Island Building Exchange on ABC's merit shop philosophy.

Jan. 20 Syracuse, N.Y.: Met with contractors to develop a promotional meeting pursuant to establishing a Syracuse chapter-in-formation.

Jan. 22 Houston, Texas: Met with Chapter President Travis Reaves, Vice President O.D. Pugh and Executive Director George Heit.

Jan. 25 Nashville, Tenn.: Met in organizational meeting with ABC's Nashville chapter-in-formation.

Jan. 27   Atlanta, Ga.: Met with new board of directors of the developing Atlanta ABC chapter.

Jan. 28-30 Airlie, Va.: Attended ABC National Leadership Conference.

One of the favorite stories circulating around National ABC office water coolers in those days was known as "Trimmer's Travels." It seems that, after a particularly hectic trip to the West Coast, this mild-mannered and erudite gentleman slipped gently into a soft chair in his Washington office to gulp down a cup of high test coffee—and made the following observation to several associates: "Son-of-a-gun, my fatigued derriere resembles the contour of a TWA coach class seat." An hour later, as John Trimmer grabbed his hat, his public relations brochures and his travel bag to head for another jet flight out of the Baltimore-Washington International Airport, he muttered to his secretary: "If my dear wife Anne calls, please tell her I waved goodbye as I passed over our house."

ABC Blankets America

On January 20, 1973, Phil Husted, the president of a highway construction business in upstate New York known as Hogeboom & Campfield, received congratulations from John Trimmer and Joseph Ciorilla, executive director of ABC's Empire State Chapter, as the firm became *ABC's 5,000th member*. The merit shop was bridging the nation, with thirty-two chapters located in sixteen states and the District of Columbia. They included Florida, Georgia, Kentucky, Louisiana, Maryland, Massachusetts, Michigan, New Jersey, New York, Ohio, Oklahoma, Pennsylvania, Tennessee, Texas, Virginia, and Wisconsin. There also was group activity in California, Colorado, and Nebraska, plus lots of individual members-at-large who operated in localities that once were considered impregnable union strongholds.

One of many typical "thank you" letters written to ABC President Joe LaMonaca came from Ralph Huber, president of Glen Construction Company and an active member of the Metropolitan Washington Chapter. Huber summed up his appreciation of the Association's success this way:

If you want to succeed, you should strike out on new paths rather than travel the worn paths of accepted success.

JOHN D. ROCKEFELLER
FINANCIER

415

Valor grows by daring; fear by holding back.

PUBLILIUS SYRUS
ROMAN HISTORIAN

Ten years ago we started a construction business by borrowing $20,000. Today we signed a $7,227,000 contract which was competitively bid. Without ABC, this could never have been done. We are indebted forever to the contractors who had the foresight and courage to create and develop the merit shop.[15]

On November 2, 1972, *Engineering News-Record* published a historic four-page feature article entitled **OPEN SHOP, A GROWING FORCE AND CATALYST FOR CHANGE**. It began this way:

> Organized labor and union contractors have created their own monster and it refuses to go away. In fact, it's growing. Their monster is the open shop and it's changing the industry.
>
> For the past several years, work has been increasingly slipping away from union contractors and fueling the growth of open shop construction... The impact should not be minimized. "I am convinced that the public attention that has been given to the fact that there are substantial open shop construction projects successfully underway has had a far more depressing effect on the highly inflationary wage demands of organized labor than CISC [Construction Industry Stabilization Committee] or any other governmental wage policy," says Nello L. Teer, Jr., a Durham, N.C., contractor who next year takes over the reins as Associated General Contractors president.

Then *Engineering News-Record* described the meteoric rise of ABC and its impact:

> No one really knows how much work nationwide is performed open shop. A good indication is the growth of the Associated Builders & Contractors, Inc., the only national organization of open shop contractors. Its "merit shop" membership, as it prefers to call the open shop, has doubled since 1969 to a total of 4,600, and it expects a 35 percent increase in 1973. ABC estimates that non-union builders

account for about two-thirds of the country's contractors and did $45 billion of last year's $109-billion volume of work.

But this isn't the only evidence of open shop growth. For example: Twenty-one of 28 major union general contractors responding to an *Engineering News-Record* survey reported that they would operate open shop if they could. Of that 21, ten said they are considering going "double-breasted" or operating both union and non-union shops. [see Chapter 23] . . . In the industrial field, members of the National Constructors Association, which all operate union, last year lost more than one-third of their work to open shop contractors, an industry group says.

A spokesman for the Associated General Contractors, whose 9,100 members did $81.5 billion worth of work in 1971, says ABC's $45 billion open shop volume figure is not inflated. AGC estimated in 1969 that 35 percent of its membership operated open shop. It declines to speculate on what that figure is now, but says it is higher.

Next, the *Engineering News-Record* article reported Big Labor's concern over ABC's growth:

> In hard-core union areas, work often is slow since owners are frightened away to outlying areas by inflated costs. Robert Georgine, Secretary-Treasurer of the AFL-CIO Building and Construction Trades Department, says of non-union growth: "It's here, it's a problem, and we don't really know how to cope with it . . ."
>
> Georgine also says that unions want to make their contractors as competitive as possible. "We can't abolish craft lines, but we are entering into project agreements whenever asked," Georgine explains. But he adds: "There's a limit to what you can do. . . . The attraction of operating open shop is the promise of no jurisdictional work stoppages and the ability to use cheaper, unskilled men to back up the highly paid mechanics the contractors keep as the nucleus of their work force."
>
> AFL-CIO Building and Construction Trades Department President Frank Bonadio called for cooperation: "The relationship

Misfortunes always come in by the door that has been left open for them.

CZECH PROVERB

between the union contractor and the union should not be the same as that between a bull and toreador." Sheet Metal Workers General President Edward Carlough and United Association General President Martin Ward have warned their members to increase productivity. But their message is often hard to sell at the local level where, as Ward explains, "Each leader is a political animal, and if he fails to meet or exceed the achievements of other leaders, he cannot survive."

This *Engineering News-Record* story appeared only twenty-two years after ABC was founded in a construction industry that had been dominated (90 percent) by the building trades unions. But the undeniable evidence of the Association's sensational growth was tempered by the magazine article's ominous conclusion:

"Violence is the gut reaction of trade unions to counter the open shop."

CHAPTER 37

AN EXPANDING ZONE
OF UNION TERRORISM

BRUTAL LABOR-MANAGEMENT BATTLES that involved the construction industry in the cities of Baltimore, Philadelphia, Memphis, and locales along the Gulf Coast in the states of Texas and Louisiana were not isolated or random events. As *Engineering News-Record* reported in 1972, the maturing merit shop movement in the late 1960s and early 1970s found itself in "an ever-exploding war" with the building trades over compulsory unionism.

Armand J. Thieblot, Jr., Thomas R. Haggard, and Herbert R. Northrup of the University of Pennsylvania's Wharton School of Business confirmed in their authoritative text, *Union Violence*, that a resurgence of strong-arm tactics in the construction trades was sparked by "the rise of the open shop in the mid-1960s." The "geographic extent of violence is wide," the authors warned, "and it involves most of the traditional building crafts.[1]

A national official of the AFL-CIO's Building & Construction Trades Department, Robert Georgine, reaffirmed that a nationwide attack was authorized at the annual convention of the Building Trades Department and its seventeen International Building Trades Unions in 1967 and again in 1971[2]—and he reminded all union tradesmen:

> Pride in workmanship is almost nil. Productivity is our biggest problem. The construction unions are getting a smaller and smaller piece of the pie each year. This may mean that we must develop a more militant viewpoint. *We have to go back to basics.*[3] [emphasis added]

America symbolizes free enterprise, diversity, and democracy. It is these three factors which cause the worst fears of the fanatics who use violence and terror to destroy them.

BENAZIR BHUTTO
PAKISTAN
PRIME MINISTER

419

I tell ye Hogan's
right when he
says "Justice is
blind: Blind she
is, an' deef an'
dumb an' has a
wooden leg!"

FINLEY PETER DUNNE
(MR. DOOLEY)

Henry Landau, president of the Sheet Metal Workers International Association, added in a letter to his trade union members that vilified ABC and was entitled: "The Honeymoon Is Over":

> We don't plan to give up easy. We are going to fight with everything we have available. *We may get a little bloody,* but if we're all sincere, we will be successful. In the months and years to come, you will all notice and become part of *many necessary changes to preserve our livelihood.* [emphasis added]

Those conspiratorial messages of coercion motivated the trade unions to create a nationwide communications system which allowed them to track new open shop projects coming "on line" and single out the applicable contractors and owners for "special attention." Wherever ABC chapters became active, physical confrontations occurred with relentless rapidity. The nation's eastern, southern, and midwestern states were the locale of most of the battlegrounds.[4]

Uncontrolled mass picketing of open shop projects became commonplace. Local tabloid accounts exposed hundreds of examples of threats, intimidation, extortion, assaults with intent to injure, stonings, stabbings and beatings, extermination of property, arson, sabotage, and dynamiting. There was verbal, physical, and psychological abuse of every kind—all carried out in the legally and politically correct cause of "organizing the unorganized." And law enforcement officials and politicians continued to avoid or evade prosecution of the terrorists.

One of many despicable trade union ploys consisted of telephoning the wives of merit shop workers and threatening their husbands' lives if they continued to report to work. Another scheme was the pillaging and fire bombing of non-union construction sites early in the morning before the regular workday began. This hit-and-run vigilante tactic was especially troublesome because the union ruffians knew which sensitive elements of a construction project to blitz and create the most costly delays.

The "bloody back to basics" outbursts across half the nation that are described in this chapter (and many more like them) have been collected from the news media, ABC publications, Thieblot, Haggard, and Northrup's book,

Union Violence,[5] Northrup's books on "open shop construction,"[6] John Trimmer's *ABC Profile*, featured articles by Charles Stevenson—an editor of *Reader's Digest*, and my own personal investigation.

Stevenson wrote in his four-part "Special Report on Building Trades Terrorism" that shocked the nation:

> In a desperate effort to retain control of the country's largest industry, a number of building trades unions have embarked on a campaign with a clear and violent message: any builder unwise enough to use non-union labor will be knocked out of business.[7]

Union Attacks on "Sunshine State" Contractors

Florida—a "right to work" state[8]—was one of the first regions along the East Coast that the building trades unions targeted for nation-wide construction terrorism against ABCers. When Peter Matthews, president of Matthews Company and first president of ABC's Florida Gold Coast Chapter (now known as the Florida East Coast Chapter), tried to use his own non-union crew to erect a hangar at *Florida's Fort Lauderdale International Airport*, a gang of thirty to forty bullies pulled the crane operator from his machine, injuring him severely. Then Matthews was beaten up when he went to the operator's aid. John Lloyd, ABC's local chapter executive director who was "caught" photographing the fight, also was hurt and had to be hospitalized.

"Despite clear proof," Peter Matthews reported, "I could get no action out of local law enforcement authorities, even after offering them witnesses, photographs of assailants, and a list of their auto licenses. The police shrugged it off as just another labor dispute in which they did not want to become involved." And Douglas Macmillan, chief of the U.S. Department of Justice Strike Force against organized crime in Florida, complained: "Our problem is that labor-related violence alone, however heinous, is not now a federal offense." Only by hiring guards and equipping them with combat dogs was Pete Matthews able to complete the job.[9]

Across the state, in *Marco Island on the West Coast,* seventy-five to one hundred union hoodlums ganged up on eight non-union men who were digging trenches at a condominium construction site. They beat up all the workers

Trade Union Attacks on ABC Contactors in Florida

ABC Contractor

ABC Contractor

and injured one man critically. The goons broke three of his ribs, poured steel shavings into his eyes, and made threats to cut off his hands and put them in his back pockets.

Twenty-six of these hard-core attackers were arrested but only twelve were brought to trial and none were convicted. A law-enforcement officer said "it was just another incident in a continuous stream of violence at Marco Island." The trade unions "claim the island as their own," he added. "In the past two years, there have been fifteen to twenty instances of non-union construction equipment being damaged or destroyed."[10]

In *West Palm Beach*, about a year later, auto dealer Richard Spreen decided to build a new facility on Okeechobee Boulevard adjacent to his foreign auto dealership facilities. Union construction bids exceeded his budget, so he awarded the contract to non-union contractors led by J. W. Petitt Company, a member of ABC's Gulf Coast Chapter. In retaliation, the local building trades council picketed the project for two weeks. When that effort failed to stop any work, the craft unions announced that "a mass demonstration" would take place.

Although advance information of this huge rally was given to local government officials, the sheriff and his deputies failed to take proper security measures and a union-led riot took place at the new building site. Over 2,500 building tradesmen participated in the attack. It was described by the local press as a "miniwar," an "infantry charge," and "nineteenth century labor anarchy."[11]

The unionized workers charged in a wave, ignoring the handful of private guards posted around the property. They flattened a barbed wire chain link fence, ripped up its steel posts to use as battering rams against concrete walls, flailed new cars with sledgehammers, and hurled Molotov cocktails. Fires were set to combustible fluids poured beside the building and the uncompleted steel deck roof was ripped apart. Bands of tradesmen set fire to construction trailers and trucks. Luckily, Spreen had told his employees and contractors not to report for work that day because of the scheduled union "demonstration."

News media reporters on the location were assaulted, their cameras ripped from their hands and smashed. A freelance photographer who was posted atop the building before the riot began succeeded in getting a complete roll of film featuring the attacking ruffians. When he was discovered by the mob, he was assaulted and his camera was broken. Destruction of all photographic evidence was part of the master plan of attack.

The Spreen Auto Company Battle Arouses Citizens, Police, Politicians, and Courts

The effects of this Spreen Auto riot were not limited to the construction job site. Steel trusses were placed across the adjoining public road, preventing thousands of people from using their normal routes to jobs. Congested traffic also made it impossible for police reinforcements to reach the battle scene in time to protect the Spreen Auto property from almost total destruction. The perpetrators blasted sixty new passenger cars, including Audis, Porsches, Volkswagens, a news media cruiser, plus two police vehicles—and left the entire construction project in smoking shambles.

The *Miami Herald* reported that over $1 million worth of construction equipment at Spreen's foreign auto operation was bullet-ridden, shoved into canals, or burned "to give the scabs the word on who should be hired." The union horde was too large and unruly for the local police to control. They were attacked and injured by rioters who used a barrage of pieces of cement block, rocks, and broken bottles. It took an additional force of three hundred sheriff's deputies, West Palm Beach police, and Florida state troopers more than three hours to restore peace and order. They eventually used tear gas to quell the rioters.[12]

The Spreen Auto situation became so tense that Florida's Governor Claude Kirk called out the National Guard on a standby basis. And Senator Edward Gurney (R-FL) condemned the labor insurrection in a speech on the floor of the U.S. Senate on April 15, 1970. It included these excerpts:

It is obvious that we cannot permit repetition of this series of incidents in Palm Beach County. Law enforcement officials must be given the means to prevent such attacks and punish criminal conduct of this sort.

We must once more assert the rights that ordinary citizens have under our body of laws to pursue their trade and go about their business freely without illegal interference from any source. We must put an end to special privileges of the building trades unions that have given these arrogant union leaders the erroneous impression that they are beyond the reach of law and that their rights are superior to those of other citizens.

We must show that unlawful violation of the rights of citizens will be resisted and, where criminal, will be punished. There is no question that these union leaders must learn and understand that the privileges that they now enjoy will be restricted or curtailed if they pursue this line of lawless conduct.

Finally, we must see that construction is returned to its rightful place as an area for honorable employment for all persons capable of performing the job, whether they are union or non-union. We must guarantee that management and employees—whether union or non-union—enjoy the rights they are entitled to as citizens, especially the right to go about their business without fear of violence or intimidation.

A grand jury investigated the union-created Spreen Auto holocaust but witnesses clammed up and nothing came of it at the time. Local businesspeople in possession of important evidence expressed fear of personal injury to themselves or their families, reprisals against them in their businesses, discrimination against them in recruitment of new employees, and other workplace terrorism if they became identified with any information against the trade unions or their rioting members.

Soon ABC contractors and some of their non-union employees journeyed to the state capitol to plead for punishment of the guilty brawlers. Led by National ABC Officials John Lochary and John Trimmer plus Richard Coleman of the ABC Gold Coast Chapter staff, they also urged the passage of laws to make such union violence a criminal offense. There was an uproar in the press but intimidated state legislators—in the face of a powerful AFL-CIO lobby which included three hundred unionists packing the local hearing room and harassing hostile witnesses—refused to act.

Two years later, grand jury indictments of some of the union perpetrators were issued, and a criminal court in *West Palm Beach* found eleven individuals guilty of various charges stemming out of the Spreen Auto uprising. These crimes ranged from "felonious attacks and inciting a riot" to the misdemeanor of "unlawful assembly." There was a huge backlog of penalty investigations under review by the State Probation and Parole Commission at the time, but eventually jail sentences varying from six months to five years were ordered.[13]

A Trade Union Payoff in Tampa

Over in Hillsborough County, the local building trades unions involved in work at the *new $70 million Tampa airport* reportedly were "paid off" to the tune of $129,000, following a jobsite fight resulting in injuries to four non-union men and a general work stoppage at the terminal. The Airport Authority by a vote of three to two decided to pay this "shake-down" sum for a construction change order that required the contractor involved to perform the work with union labor instead of his own open shop personnel. The action was taken in spite of Florida's right to work law.[14] Airport management lamely explained that "the cost to the taxpayers would be greater if the work stoppage was allowed to continue."

Officials of the Airport Authority and the Mayor of Tampa pleaded with the construction union bosses to grant them some assurance that there would be no repetition of the "problem" in the future. The president of the local building trades council responded that he would order his tradesmen back to work, but he could give no assurance that there would not be "trouble" in the future. In fact, he explained, "these workers deserve some consideration too [referring to the union men who had walked off their own jobsites to create the chaos] because there were non-union scabs engaged on the project."[15]

Naples Is Next on the Union Hit Parade

In May of 1972 at *Naples*, Deal Construction Service, a non-union firm, was burying some underground cable for the Lee County Co-op. Because of "coercion" by the Operating Engineers Union, a sheriff's deputy and an undercover officer were placed at the project. Tradesmen later identified as Operating Engineers continued to swarm over the site. Two of them began beating the operator of a backhoe.

That bullying caused the deputy sheriff to fire a warning shot in the air. He was immediately attacked and beaten. And then a detective was hit on the

> **An infallible method of conciliating a tiger is to allow oneself to be devoured.**
>
> KONRAD ADENAUER
> GERMAN CHANCELLOR

427

head with a wrench, thrown to the ground, and kicked. Three days later, a number of men identified as members of the Operating Engineers Union were arrested in connection with this savagery and charged with offenses ranging from inciting and encouraging a riot and aggravated assault against a police officer to destruction of property. There were no convictions but Deal Construction Service refused to capitulate. Subsequent to the attack, the president of Operating Engineers Local Union 675 phoned Deal and told its president that he better "get right" with the union if he hoped to do any more work.

Deal refused to be "blackmailed."

Another Florida Union Shake-Down

A twice-convicted felon named Richard Nell controlled Local 675 of the International Union of Operating Engineers in nearby *Broward County*. The wages of its 2000 members in the 1970s averaged $15,000 a year. But Nell received an annual salary and allowances of more than $50,000 plus a Cadillac and a European vacation for himself and his wife. He also obtained union real estate valued at more than $20,000 for the sum of two dollars.

Any tradesman who failed to obey the orders of this Broward County union boss found life "difficult." Sworn testimony attested to cruel assaults, threatening phone calls, shotgun blasts fired into one worker's home, physical attacks on employees of non-union companies and damage, and destruction of expensive equipment.

On Lincoln's birthday, several hundred of Richard Nell's handpicked hooligans squared off against non-union employees of L. E. Meyers & Co., an open shop construction firm, at a project site just south of *Fort Lauderdale*. A guard was holding the union intruders at bay with a gun when four local patrolmen arrived and ordered the guard to put his weapon away. Thereupon the police officers were beaten, rocks were showered on workmen, equipment was set afire, and autos were overturned.

Not one arrest was made at the L. E. Meyers project, despite the fact that the wounded policemen were able to identify some of their assailants. When the wife of one of Nell's bullies agreed to tell a grand jury what she knew about the violence and sabotage, she received a savage pummeling that "changed her mind." Although a state attorney's investigation resulted in indictments against five union tradesmen, no convictions were obtained. The L. E. Meyers firm suffered $50,000 worth of property damages.

As the mob left the Meyers construction project, further union battle orders sent them to *Fort Myers*. There, at the site of a $1.4 million public housing apartment project, they staged a repeat performance. Editor Charles Stevenson of the *Reader's Digest* described this bold assault in detail:

> They wrecked the construction office, firebombed a crane and lashed the construction superintendent with a chain so that he ended up a hospital case. Amid threats of further violence, Nell brought in pickets. The purpose was to force the local open shop prime contractor, Cassius Peacock, to fire his own steadily employed workers and hire union men instead.
>
> The labor boss warned everyone to stay away from the Peacock job so no one, union or non-union, dared touch it. But Paul Prendergast, a union-shop engineering contractor headquartered in Fort Lauderdale who had been driving the pilings for these apartments, was determined to complete his subcontract. So he asked his own field superintendent, 44-year-old Earl Lassitter, to operate the machinery and finish the work. Result: when Lassitter showed up at his next work site—on the Fort Lauderdale beach—one of Nell's goons gave him such a going-over with leather gloves that he suffered a permanent hearing loss and since then has had to wear a hearing aid.[16]

On October 15, 1972, the *Miami Herald* summed up the conspiracy of labor terrorism against the merit shop this way:

> Labor unions are emerging as a violent force in South Florida as they turn increasingly to mob actions, sabotage, fire bombings and other outlaw measures to make their points... Hardhat tradesmen, stereotyped as tough but honest working men, are engaging in a form of *guerrilla warfare* to stop projects manned by non-union labor.
>
> Most of the labor violence revolves around internal union power struggles and the growing use of non-union labor by the area's

It is bad enough to persevere in barbarism; it is worse to relapse into it; but worst of all to seek it out.

Aurel Kolnai
Philosopher

429

booming construction industry...Bitter battles for union control turn into Godfatheresque intimidation, corruption and murder, and both local and federal law enforcement officers express alarm at the swirling undercurrents of crime in the labor world here.

Arnold Lusky, president of the Industrial Agricultural Union in Miami, said: *"It's a shame the unions in many ways act like the Arab World."* [emphasis added]

Labor Battles in Michigan

Open shop contractors in the state of Michigan also felt the nationally coordinated "back to basics" wrath of the building trades unions. Almost every region was hit. On October 6, 1965, a headline in the *Detroit Free Press* blared out: **UNIONS DECLARE WAR ON NON-UNION BUILDERS**. The article quoted an officer of the local trades council to the effect that "every legal means" would be used to bring all open shop contractors in the *Lansing area* into the AFL-CIO fold.

Five weeks later, the Lansing Building Trades Council publicly declared a three-day "labor holiday" to begin "a major drive to wipe out non-union commercial construction." A general strike followed at all union job sites. Some 2,500 union tradesmen left their work to picket and swarm over non-union building projects throughout the capital city in a three-day "demonstration." This reign of terror began as trailers were overturned and torched, rocks and two-by-fours were thrown through double-paned insulated windows, power lines were pulled down, fistfights occurred, and open shop employees and property owners were mauled. Women and children were hastily removed from the area on advice of the police.

Joseph Davis, the executive director of an ABC affiliate called the Western Michigan Contractors Association, was wounded during this "labor holiday." And a shotgun blast was fired as one job superintendent hid within his job site trailer. Then a missile-like object thrown from outside shattered his trailer's window and the whole office tipped over. Union officials later told the news media that "high winds" uprooted the trailer and "large acorns" broke the window.[17]

National Guardsmen and State Police were considering counter-action in Lansing when the riot finally came to an end, with the help of ABC chapter attorneys who worked day and night on the crisis. It took the lawyers five days to gain a temporary injunction against the insurrection and two more weeks before Judge Sam Street Hughes of Ingham County reluctantly reached a favorable decision. He finally limited the number of pickets at all construction sites to five, and forbade all blocking of entrances to the projects. His court order "permanently" enjoined the Lansing Building Trades Council and its members from "violence, coercion, intimidation or acts of physical strength that would prevent persons from entering upon the free enterprise building projects."

Frank Hand, a staff writer of Michigan's *State Journal* gave the following summary of this Michigan labor crime-fest that had stunned the public: "Three days of tension brought construction in the area to a standstill, resulted in injuries to persons, major damage to property under construction, terror to the hearts of some, and a violence-blotted smear to the image of Lansing."

Although there had been sufficient notice to city officials of the impending union seige, Reporter Hand wrote that "the police appeared to be caught flatfooted and did nothing but stand around." And he added, "by the time reinforcements arrived, the mass picket lines had dissolved and the union workers were back on their respective jobs." Judge Hughes' injunction, concluded newsman Frank Hand, "was like locking the stable door after the horse had been stolen. The damage was done, the injuries sustained, and psychological scars inflicted on innocent men, women and children."[18]

In December of 1972, about 150 unionists massed around the $1 million Pointe North professional building under construction in Lansing. They knocked down walls and destroyed machinery, leaving an estimated $50,000 in damages in their wake. No arrests were made. The *State Journal* reported this attack on January 3, 1973:

> The spree started at 8:30 a.m. when 40 to 50 ruffians descended on the site and began hammering and kicking holes in the gypsum board and wreaking other havoc.
>
> The contractor, James D. Parish Co., Inc., normally had 20 tradesmen on the site, about half of whom are *unionized*. Only six were

All cruelty springs from weakness.

SENECA
ROMAN STATESMAN-PHILOSOPHER

431

Trade Union Attacks on Michigan ABC Contractors

ABC Contractor

ABC Contractor

ABC Contractor

ABC Contractor

ABC Contractor

ABC Contractor

working that morning, some of them *union members*. The gang tipped over two portable offices, damaged a forklift truck and inflicted other damage.

The most serious damage was done to a 1,000-pound propane gas tank on which the valves were opened and the shutoff controls damaged. A spokesman for the Lansing Fire Department said the leaking gas could have caused a serious blowout. "One spark or one cigarette and we would have had an explosion," he said.

Two trucks from the Lansing Fire Department shut off the leaking gas and sealed off the site temporarily. There had been no labor problems between the men working on the site. Patrick E. Kelley, vice president of the Building Trades Council and a member of a group that visited the site Wednesday, said there was no connection. "We were just looking at several sites," Kelley said, "and that was one of four or five we visited."

Not long after this onslaught, about four hundred more roughnecks—many of whom had been drinking heavily—blocked traffic and threatened violence at the main intersection of the little town of *Kalkaska*. It was located on Michigan's southern peninsula, some two hundred miles north of Detroit. The unionists outnumbered the local police force and a county prosecutor tried to persuade them to leave. In response, they overturned his automobile. Property damage reached into the hundreds of thousands of dollars before the rioters departed. And the Teamsters helped to continue the siege of terror there for several months. During this battle, the state of Michigan had to station as many as 350 troopers—20 percent of its total military force—in this small town to protect the public. The cost to taxpayers was $30,000 every day.[19]

Shell Oil and Delta Engineering Are Targeted

While still unchecked at Kalkaska, some of the hoodlums moved three miles down the road to the construction site of a $20 million Shell Oil Company natural-gas processing plant project by non-union Delta Engineering Company of

Houston, Texas. The angry mob set fires, wrecked construction equipment, smashed vehicles, and demolished buildings. Car tires of local people who were not even employed at the projects were slashed and nearby stores were vandalized. Although outnumbered, state troopers attempted to seize three of the rioters. But after they injured two of the troopers, the three offenders were actually released. Despite two court orders to stop this Michigan mayhem, law enforcers permitted it to drag on, even though Governor Milliken described the assaults as "more guerilla warfare."[20]

The superintendent on this Shell Oil project testified that some union men "doctored" his auto so that it stalled on a country road. Then, he said, two carloads of them swarmed around him, cut his car tires, and warned that if he went back to work: "It'll be youse next time." The brawlers also asked him: "Who's gonna take care uv da family afta youses gone?"[21]

Eventually District Judge Noel Fox and Governor Milliken prodded Delta Engineering and Shell Oil to appear in the judge's chambers to "negotiate" with the local trades council. This was a peculiar order since neither company was a party to any litigation or collective bargaining agreement involving any labor union. The result was a "voluntary" settlement in which the trades council called off its picketing and violence while the two companies remained open shop. But the contractors' "compromise" in the deal was an agreement to "donate" $250,000 to the Kalkaska Township "so that it could employ more local [union] workers."[22]

Judge Fox's rationale for mediating the labor assault instead of issuing an injunction (that was indisputably warranted) against it was that "such an order would not be enforced and that he always preferred mediation." This biased approach by the federal judiciary seemed highly questionable to the *Grand Rapids Press* of July 26, 1973. It editorialized that viewpoint:

> Somehow we cannot help but have misgivings about a settlement which, in effect, has been arrived at because members of the Building Trades Council—in order to achieve their ends—were willing to commit acts of violence and vandalism...That such repugnant methods should be rewarded in any way is troubling indeed.[23]

The most costly of all follies is to believe passionately in the palpably not true.

H. L. MENCKEN
SYNDICATED COLUMNIST
AND PUNDIT

Grand Rapids, Lapeer, Rochester, and Madison Heights Are Attacked

At midnight on February 17, 1968, huge fires "of mysterious origin" began raging through the offices of two open shop construction firms at *Grand Rapids* in southwest Michigan. Vital business records and architectural plans were destroyed and the damage was estimated at $80,000. One of the torched establishments was Herrema Plumbing and Heating, owned by Ted Herrema, also the president of the Contractors and Suppliers Association of Western Michigan (an ABC affiliate). The other abused firm was Pioneer Construction Company. Kenneth Harmsen, its vice president, was a delegate to the National Executive Committee of ABC.[24] No one was apprehended.

At about the same time, the Dan Voss Construction Company of Grand Rapids negotiated a contract to construct a food distribution facility at a site near Detroit. Gary Voss, the firm's president (and subsequently ABC's 36th national president in 1996) was aware of the building trades unions' dominance there, and met informally with its local representatives to propose a "merit shop" compromise.

Voss promised the union leaders that he would see to it that 50 percent to 70 percent of his project "goes union." The answer he received was a blunt "Hell no: its 100 percent union or else..." That ended the powwow and a nervous Voss prepared for "the worst":

> We put up an 8-foot security fence around the entire project. There were large lights every 200 feet surrounding the job site's 30 acres and a two-way radio communication system—one for inside the project for security guards and one for my people. We also had a direct radio to the state police force.

The next day Dan Voss employees showed up for work early, but they were soon subjected to violence by a mob. Rocks were thrown, windows busted, trailers defaced, locks damaged, tires slashed, and threatening comments made. Voss' workers couldn't try to leave the site until 9:30 p.m. that night because the goons had locked them in. Eventually seventy Michigan state police escorted the non-union employees to a nearby hotel. The troopers stood guard there to protect their safety all night long.

That was not the end of the rampage. The next day, hostility swelled to major proportions. Union tradesmen showed up with bats, sticks, and other "weapons." By mid-morning an estimated one thousand ruffians had gathered at the site. They came from all over Michigan and the midwest. Meanwhile, local law enforcement agencies were also gathering their troops. A force of one hundred local and state police officers was assembled and others were on standby. One "highlight" of the bedlam was a climbing expedition by two enraged ironworkers. They ripped the American flag from a steel girder and replaced it with a picket sign. That action brought forth cheers from the mob and the bedlam soon brought construction to a halt.

It was too dangerous for workers to cross the picket lines—even with police protection—so the Dan Voss Company pursued another course of action. With ABC's assistance, the firm went to the Livingston County Circuit Court to ask a judge for a temporary restraining order. Eventually Judge Stanley Latrell issued the order against Iron Workers Local 25 and eight hundred unnamed protestors acting in concert with Local 25. The order limited demonstrators to five pickets at each of the two gates of the construction site. It also banned them from trespassing, harassing people entering or leaving the site, and from damaging property.

That legal action worked. No more pickets formed and job site peace returned. Voss and his crew stood up to a union battle and won. Voss said: "it's my business, my employees, and my client." Together they set a standard for courage and completed the project to the satisfaction of their customer. Later on, Dan Voss told the local press:

> I look at it this way; it's a free country. I didn't know there was a boundary in this state that we live in and do business in that says "Voss Construction, you can't go beyond this line." That bothers me because we're a quality contractor and I ought to have that right as an American to go to any place in this country and to make a living at what we're good at. Nobody should have the right to tell me that I can't go beyond

We will never have real safety and security for the wage earners unless we provide safety and security for the wage payers.

WILLIAM J. H.
BOETCHER
ECONOMIST

437

Two ABC Michigan firms fall victims to arson in Grand Rapids area.

ABC CONTRACTOR

At both Herrema Plumbing & Heating and Pioneer Construction Co., senior officials were officers in ABC, locally and nationally.

In war, there
is no substitute
for victory.

GENERAL DOUGLAS
MACARTHUR DURING
WORLD WAR II

a certain point. That's what the building trades tried to do, and that's wrong. We are willing to stand on our merit shop principle. Somebody has to pave the way; and if it's us, so be it.

Four years later, construction union bullies in *Lapeer* dynamited several shopping-center sites, storage areas, and an asphalt plant in an eight-day statewide rampage. More than $250,000 worth of destruction was done to a W. T. Grant & Co. shopping plaza being built by Tri-Cities Construction Company, a member of ABC's Western Michigan Chapter. On October 25 of that same year, 1972, some 200 trade union members formed a ring around the project, set fires, and tipped over a mobile office trailer. They also tore down a 20-foot cement-block wall at a second W. T. Grant site in *Grand Blanc* that was being built by Tri-Cities. Before reinforcements arrived to aid badly outnumbered police, the vandals were speeding back to Lapeer, where they attacked and damaged the almost-completed W. T. Grant shopping center for the second time.

Officials of Tri-Cities Construction placed most of the blame for this brutality on Ironworkers Union Local 25, which had been tormenting open shop workers on the projects for some time. In defense, the business agent for the Ironworkers observed: "I guess da men jus got outta hand." He also admitted that there were three hundred union members involved in the incidents, all of whom were unemployed.

While the mob eventually was dispersed by police at both W. T. Grant shopping center sites, there were no prosecutions.

In *Rochester, Michigan,* meanwhile, about four hundred building-tradesmen stormed the construction site of the Walter P. Reuther Junior High School. They spent two hours ripping out electric wiring and setting fires. And there were racial overtones because 30 black mechanics employed by Auburn Electric Company on the project had been refused membership in the local Electrical Workers Union. "Individual liberty is at stake in this dispute and that is not something to be taken lightly," said the Auburn firm's president, Ed Connop. Property damage: $60,000. Arrests: none.

Soon after that uprising, ABC's Metropolitan Detroit Chapter planned an installation of new officers and a dinner dance in *Madison Heights.* The usual advance notice of the event was dispatched to local ABC members but it fell unintentionally into the hands of Michigan building trades leaders. They quickly planned an attack, after sending "instructions" to their members. The result was that more than two hundred union brawlers mass-marched outside a social club where the dinner took place. They blocked parking lot entrances, approached ABC members menacingly and shouted obscenities at them as they neared the facility.

Police eventually showed up and seventy-three union members were arrested for "loitering." Then several union officials assailed the police "for overreacting to a peaceful demonstration." It was "immaterial," they said, that many of the tradesmen had shown up for the protest brandishing crowbars, pipes, and assorted hostile paraphernalia. The unionists insisted that they were "merely asserting their right under the free speech amendment" of the Constitution to voice their opposition to ABC—and the seventy-three culprits were promptly released from police custody.

One of the union picketers—who also happened to be a local county commissioner—had helped to incite the violent activity by announcing publicly prior to the contractors' dinner meeting: "I support the trade unions here. We worked 50 years to get a secure living and then these ABC scabs come along and hire non-union workers for far below prevailing wage rates. We're not going to let it happen here."

Of the 250 ABCers who had made reservations for the dinner dance, only seventy were present by mid-evening. But those who came said they were not sorry to have braved the union storm. "After we got by the threats and traffic jam at the entrance," commented one courageous lady party-goer, "we had a fine time."

John Doherty, ABC's neighboring Western Michigan Chapter Executive Director for over thirty years, reminisced that "the only time my members used to believe they might be on comparatively equal footing with the building trades unions that were harassing them was when we hired armed security personnel with guard dogs." And Doherty described an incident of union harassment of one of his members, a small welding firm, after it won the first open shop project for a *Dow Chemical Corporation* plant:

> Mobs of pickets appeared immediately. Then these union goons would hop in their cars, follow the construction workers on their way

Don't jump on
a man unless
he's down.

FINLEY PETER DUNNE
(MR. DOOLEY)

home at night and try to run them off the road. It was a very scary time. Eventually the contractor had to hire buses and a state police escort to complete the project under safe conditions."[25]

Reviewing all of this conspiratorial trade union oppression, an article headlined "Hardhat Vandals Reflect Union Battle" in the *Detroit News* began by reporting a dangerous sortie in *Rochester* during January of 1973:

> When several hundred AFL-CIO building tradesmen stormed onto a school construction site in Rochester two days ago and caused damage estimated at $30,000, it was another manifestation of the turmoil in Michigan's construction industry today. The "hardhats" were protesting the presence on the job of so-called non-union workers employed by Auburn Electric Company of Auburn Heights, a Pontiac suburb. They ripped out electrical circuits and tipped over two construction trailers.
>
> It would appear that the confrontation was a relatively minor and isolated incident, but underlying it are basic issues that refuse to go away. First, *there are racial overtones*. Auburn Electric is not non-union. Its president, Edward Connop, has a contract with United Construction Trades Local 124, a union formed here in 1968 by black construction workers who said they were refused membership in the predominantly white building trades. Connop says his 30 employees are paid according to wage rates equal to or better than members of Local 58, International Brotherhood of Electrical Workers...And, as Connop points out, the local has been certified by the federal government as a legitimate bargaining agent.

Then the *Detroit News* article "went nationwide" as to the scope of the union conspiracy:

> So what the dispute really boils down to is the fact, in the view of the building tradesmen, that there has been a resurgence of anti-AFL-CIO sentiment among building contractors, *both at national and local levels*. The Greater Detroit Building Trades Council says the

stimulus comes from the Associated Builders and Contractors, which started in Baltimore in 1950, and has mushroomed across the United States.

Today, the ABC has more than 5,000 contractor members in 26 chapters throughout the nation. Connop, a steely-eyed, angular 6-foot-4 amateur flier, is the head of the Metropolitan Detroit Chapter. Started in 1971 locally, ABC now boasts at least 100 members in the metropolitan area, *a good portion of them minority contractors.*

The union tradesmen charge that ABC is "an organization intent on destroying the AFL-CIO Building Trades and the entire labor movement." Their displeasure was evidenced last October when several hundred of their hardhats swooped down on contractors affiliated with the ABC in Grand Blanc, Fenton and Lapeer, and destroyed thousands of dollars worth of property. It was climaxed two days ago when, ironically, their target was the Walter P. Reuther Junior High School near Rochester.

Meanwhile, the feud shows no sign of abating and Connop isn't about to give up. He's going to ask the Oakland County prosecutor to investigate the Rochester incident. "I've been harassed nearly all my life," he says in clipped tones. *"Individual liberty is at stake in this dispute and that is not something to be taken lightly."*[26] [emphasis added]

Ohio, Rhode Island, Louisiana, and Tennessee Contractors Are Blitzed

Continuing this country-wide collusion against ABC, in the state of *Ohio* at *Columbus* during October of 1972 about 1500 union spoilers using walkie-talkies tied up millions of dollars worth of open shop building jobs as they sabotaged five big construction projects simultaneously. In hit-and-run vigilante style, they threatened workers, mass picketed, battered in walls, cut electric wiring, smashed windows, yanked out plumbing fixtures, set fires, and overturned trailers. But Columbus public officials declined to condemn this planned havoc.[27]

The local *Citizen-Journal* newspaper added that the City's public-safety director was at a loss to explain why police allowed the building trades mob to attack the construction sites. There were only six arrests and no major convictions.

In another *Ohio* fracas, Apex Contracting Company, Inc., also an open shop contractor, began a job in March of 1973 under contract with the State to install guardrails along some highways near *Ashtabula.* Not long after the project was under way, a series of meetings were held with representatives of the Ohio Building Trades Council and their local Operating Engineers and Laborers Unions. These two organizations expressed to state representatives their "dislike" of Apex's use of non-union and out-of-state laborers on the project. By April 26, however, it was clear that Apex would not agree to the Trades Council's demand that compulsory union shop labor contracts be signed with its affiliated unions.

On the morning of April 30, a group of twenty derelicts went to the gas station where Apex had set up a job site trailer and parked some of its trucks. When Apex employees boarded these vehicles and attempted to drive out of the station to begin work, the trailer and trucks were surrounded by the bums. Two Apex employees were struck on the head. That episode caused Apex to send its employees home for their own safety.

On the following day, a similar mob of bullies massed in front of the Apex trucks so that they could not be moved. Antifreeze was leaking out of the radiator of one truck where it had been punctured with a screwdriver. As an Apex employee tried to drive his truck out of the gas station, one of the union thugs smashed the window of the door on the driver's side with a shovel, cutting him with flying glass. As a second Apex truck attempted to leave the gas station, a shovel was thrown through the driver's side window.

At that point the owner of the station told the Apex superintendent that he would have to move his equipment away from the station. The station owner also advised the Apex official that it would be necessary to tow the trucks because most of the brake lines had been cut and sugar had been put in gas tanks.

A few months later, the non-union Hooper Construction Company of *Yellow Springs, Ohio*, was awarded a sizeable building contract by Antioch College. The local Carpenters Union immediately picketed the project site and two trucks packed with goons arrived on the scene. They carried heavy tools in a menacing manner and made threatening remarks to the non-union workers present. Then representatives of the picketing local Carpenters Union and the Dayton Building Trades Council demanded that the work be done by union tradesmen under a union shop contract. When Hooper Construction refused, the car of a non-union worker was set on fire, a concrete block truck was turned back from entering the job site after threats to the driver, and a newspaper reporter who attempted to take photos of the "visiting tradesmen" was roughed up.

The national conspiracy against ABC by trade union councils was evidenced further in *Rhode Island* on February 18, 1973. More than five thousand members of the state's building trades unions crammed into a meeting hall at *Rhodes-on-the-Pawtuxet* in *Cranston* to protest the expansion of the open shop "devil" in their state and throughout the northeast. First the massive crowd sang a rousing rendition of "God Bless America." Then the hostile horde gave a standing ovation to fiery speeches made by their union business agents that outlined "a full scale war on tha stinkin' open shop contractors." So great was the union response to attendance at this rally against ABC's "cancerous growth" that nearby parking lots were packed and normally placid Sunday side streets were lined with the tradesmen's automobiles. Some of the unionists hiked a mile from their cars to reach the meeting site.[28]

Arthur Coia, who at that time was a regional vice president of the International Laborers Union (and currently is a notorious senior official in the parent AFL-CIO and close political ally of Senator Hillary Clinton, D-NY),[29] addressed the huge Rhode Island powwow. He warned the assemblage that open shop contractors were continuing to grow in strength and numbers and frankly admitted:

> Today, our productivity is not as it should be. We wanted a first coffee break and we got it. We should have it. But we wanted a second one. Then some of us forgot to go back to the places where we were working after the breaks.[30]

As this rally to "destroy ABC" continued, the business agent for Local 28 of the Plumbers Union proposed that each member in attendance should contribute

Justice delayed is justice denied.

WILLIAM GLADSTONE
BRITISH
PRIME MINISTER

$5 towards the creation of a statewide building trades council "war chest." The estimated $80,000 raised would be utilized "to take fast action" against open shop contractors and hire a full-time "coordinator" for the battle.[31]

The national confederacy of labor terrorism continued southward. A contract to construct a fuel oil facility in *Port Allen, Louisiana*, had been awarded to Payne & Keller, Inc., a member of ABC's Texas Chapter. Work on the job proceeded on schedule for several months, at which time a few Baton Rouge Building Trades Council pickets appeared at each entrance gate on the common situs. Three days after the first pickets appeared, their number had grown to 150 rampaging tradesmen, making entrance to the job physically impossible. After discussing this situation with the West Baton Rouge sheriff, representatives of ABC were able to obtain a temporary restraining order from a district court judge. His injunction limited the number of pickets to six and stated that they were not to obstruct the passage of persons entering or leaving the site. But the Building Trades Council refused to lower the number of pickets on this Port Allen project despite the court injunction and once again Payne & Keller's employees were physically denied entrance to their jobs.

On the following day, one hundred employees of Payne & Keller formed a caravan and attempted to gain access to the project site. Altercations occurred and severe physical injuries were inflicted on them. Several vehicles belonging to the company's employees were damaged. In the hope of avoiding further confrontation, Payne & Keller flew its employees into the project by helicopters. Because of continued terrorism by the pickets, however, the employees were forced to leave after having worked only a few hours.

The local sheriff finally admitted that there was an insufficient number of deputies to control the growing mass of militant pickets at Port Allen, and he contacted the governor of Louisiana, John McKeithen. State troopers and national guardsmen were assigned to the job site the following morning. That action caused most of the rioters to disperse and Payne & Keller employees were allowed to enter the project again—escorted by sheriff's deputies.

Eventually the governor of Louisiana had to send five hundred national guardsmen to the job site to restore law and order.

Leading the interstate conspiratorial trade union attack in *Tennessee*, several construction job sites were mass picketed. And in 1973 "unknown persons" blew apart a $1.6 million Ramada Inn. It was nearing completion by ABC leader Joe M. Rodgers & Associates and caused $500,000 in damages. As described by Rodgers, ABC's national president in 1976:

> We had experienced union harassment from the beginning so we wire-fenced the project and brought in guard dogs each day after work. They were removed in the early morning. For some reason the dogs did not show up one evening and the Inn was bombed. We were only a couple of months from completion and the bombing almost destroyed the entire facility. No one was ever caught and neither the guard dogs nor their owner could be found.[32]

Senator William Brock (R-TN) asked the U.S. Justice Department "to take immediate action against these Memphis union ruffians." He claimed that they had been responsible for bombing the Ramada Inn, dynamiting a contractor's home, burning down an elementary school, and committing other local acts of violence. He further requested that the Justice Department investigate information that professional arsonists from out-of-state were being hired by the local building trades to conduct a continuing campaign of terror in the Memphis district. "If this action is not taken, we will see a spread of bloodshed by organized crime in other areas," warned the senator. But nothing happened.

Meanwhile, on April 3, 1973, the *Tennessean* reported that work was suspended on TVA's $25 million Normandy Dam project on *Tennessee's Duck River* following a fight between Teamsters Union members and non-union employees of a subcontractor. "We don't have any definite plans for resuming operations," Roy Edwards, TVA's project manager said. He declined to discuss details of the altercation between employees of Ready-Mix Company of Knoxville, which supplied concrete for the dam under a $1.5 million contract, and members of Nashville Teamsters Local 327 employed by TVA.

Frank Pittenger, president of Ready-Mix, told the *Tennessean* that his firm planned to file Labor Board unfair labor practice charges in connection with the battle. Three of its employees—a driver, a safety engineer, and the job

If we are to keep our democracy, there must be one more commandment: Thou shall not ration justice.

JUDGE LEARNED HAND
U.S. COURT OF
APPEALS

superintendent—were severely beaten. "The issue in dispute here is our right to hire the workers we choose rather than have the Nashville union local's hiring hall send us their members," he said. "We also want the right to choose our own foreman who helps to manage our business."

Arson as a Trade Union Tactic

Last but far from least in this nationwide plot of trade union monopoly, a frightening pattern of arson was emerging in western states such as *Colorado, Arizona, Kansas*, and *California*. Union ruffians would ask an open shop contractor to sign an agreement binding the company to employ only union members; the contractor would refuse; the thugs would give him "a middle finger salute" and leave. When the project was taking shape a few months later, it would "mysteriously" be set on fire. Afterward, a union "representative" would appear at the job site and pointedly ask the contractor if he believed that it was "time ta sign up wid da union?"

The blowing up of trucks, polluting internal combustion engines, and setting fire to vehicles were not activities accomplished on the spur of the moment. Sophisticated explosives, contaminants, and other special devices were created and cleverly applied during the night by professional arsonists. These criminals either escaped arrest or were given mild punishment by reluctant law enforcers.[33]

In addition to buildings under construction, the lumber yards supplying them, construction offices, trailers, and even homes of the targeted open shop contractors were torched at one time or another as a "lesson" in the added costs of non-union work. "Hire our members or else . . ." was Big Labor's message to ABCers. The "or else" meant fire.

At 5:33 a.m. on April 12, 1968, a muffled blast in *Denver* ushered in what Charles Stevenson of the *Reader's Digest* called "the most arrogant and costly onslaught of organized arson in American history." Within minutes, oil-primed flames reduced a nearly completed apartment building to smoldering coals.[34] Thieblot and Haggard, in their book on *Union Violence*, amplified the tragic story:

> During the period about 40 such fires were reported which involved open shop builders or contractors [in *Denver, Colorado*] who were

involved in disputes with construction trade unions. The fires usually occurred when they could do the maximum damage—after a building was closed in, but before internal walls and ceilings were in place, for example—and the total amount of destruction during the period was estimated to be over $10 million.

Investigation of these fires was stymied for a considerable amount of time while attorneys for the Northern Colorado Building and Construction Trades Union Council vainly sought to suppress evidence obtained through wiretapping. The Trades Council appealed all the way to the U.S. Supreme Court, but the wiretap procedures were found to have been legal under Colorado law, and the evidence was eventually admitted . . . During the trials, there was considerable evidence that this "arson organizing" conspiracy extended beyond the Denver area, with *Arizona, Kansas*, and *California* mentioned as other sites where it may have occurred. There have been, however, no related indictments or convictions in those other areas.[35]

Michigan also had its share of "coincidental" explosions at non-union job sites. At least four of the "hits" involved arson: the torching of a church under construction in *Grand Blanc* on June 18, 1972; the arson and dynamiting of construction equipment at *Bruce Crossing* valued at over $400,000; the roasting of an apartment project in *Port Huron* on January 8, 1973; and about $80,000 worth of fire damage to the offices of two ABC contractors in *Grand Rapids* the same year. In the *Port Huron* situation, there had been previous general coercion by building trades business agents and mass picketing of the project because it was being built on a non-union basis. As the apartments went up in flames one early morning in January, an estimated 175 ruffians wearing hard hats and the clothes of construction workers milled around across the street and cheered.[36]

Small fires were followed by huge fires. On one day, two blazes that totaled $1.1 million occurred. Arson damages for 1972 totaled $2.1 million in Colorado alone, for 1973, more than $2.7 million. The U.S. Department of Labor knew about this arson but did nothing. The Federal Bureau of Investigation and the U.S. Department of Justice knew too, but gave up on the cases.[37]

> **The only way back to a semblance of normal life is to fight terrorism and win. Pacifism is appeasement, appeasement is defeat, and defeat is the death of the American dream.**
>
> DAVID LOWERY
> COLUMNIST

ABC's "Man of the Year"

In the previously cited series of articles published in 1973 and labeled "The Tyranny of Terrorism in the Building Trades," Charles Stevenson, roving editor of the *Reader's Digest*, described this coordinated nationwide insurrection as "a mockery of law and order, a death knell to the cause of free people." And he summarized his yearlong investigation of the conspiratorial activities as follows:

> In a desperate effort to retain control of the country's largest industry, a number of building trades unions have embarked on a campaign of terror with a clear and violent message: Any builder unwise enough to use non-union labor will be knocked out of business... Cracking heads, smashing equipment, fire-bombing open shop building sites— many construction unions are trying to destroy competition through open violence, while legislators and police do little to stop it. The chilling fact is that case histories of similar terrorism are being recorded in city after city across our land...[38]

Deservedly, Stevenson was honored as ABC's "Man of the Year" in 1973 for his "tenacious investigation and courageous reporting." He summarized his exposition of coordinated trade union savagery with these memorable words:

> After three articles on the current wage of labor-union violence appeared in the *Reader's Digest*, readers by the hundreds wrote in. A few were critical... But the overwhelming majority confirmed the facts as reported, or called attention to similar cases.
>
> Delivered by mail, telephone or in person, these accounts come from contractors forced out of business, from rank-and-file union members victimized themselves by strong-arm dictatorship. In broad outline and in detail, they corroborate the story of union bosses who, having priced construction labor out of the market, now find themselves facing open-shop competition—and seek to crush it by guerrilla warfare...
>
> In a Labor Day message, the Construction Trades Department labeled the *Reader's Digest* documented facts of terrorism as "baseless,"

"absurd" and "a huge distortion of fact..." For six years, violence has accompanied the Building Trades Unions' official campaign to stop open-shop contractors. Yet rarely have the leaders of organized labor condemned the violence—or even acknowledged it...

Here is the shocking conclusion of Charles Stevenson's famous *Reader's Digest* report:

> *This violence has reached epidemic proportions because of the failure of our laws, both unenforced and inadequate, that allow terrorists and racketeers to hide out in unions, engaging in supposedly "legitimate" labor disputes.*[39]

CHAPTER 38

REBUILDING NOAH'S ARK

THERE IS NO DOUBT THAT LUCK plays an important role in the lives of many mortals, including contractors and their lawyers. With regard to my representation of ABC in the early days, it just happened that I was in the right place at the right time to join the fight for voluntary unionism. But I also discovered that the harder I worked for the merit shop cause, the luckier I got.

Another discovery I made along the way was that on occasions of extreme stress and danger caused by Big Labor and acquiesced in by Big Government, ABC members never lost their courage and seldom forgot their sense of humor. When the going was toughest and there seemed to be no light at the end of the legal tunnel, I would tell them forcefully, with a clenched fist: *"Don't worry—if justice triumphs, we'll appeal immediately!"*

While they were still mumbling over that *non sequitur*, I would try to lighten the day by giving these bruised-but-unbowed contractors a "revised" biblical story to read. It was about the world's first maritime builder. And it related some of the trials and tribulations he would have faced if he had been living in the United States today when he was awarded that famous contract to construct a special barge.*

Here is an updated version of the tale I told merit shoppers for solace in their hours of tension:

Once upon a time God spoke to Noah and said: "In one year, I am going to make it rain and cover the entire earth with water until all of the human

---

* This sad tale did not originate with the author, although I have added a few embellishments.

To be ignorant
of the lives of the
most celebrated
men of antiquity
is to continue a
state of childhood
all our days.

PLUTARCH
WRITER

beings on it are destroyed because of their wickedness. But I want you to save your family, who are the only righteous people alive, plus two of every kind of living beast. Therefore I am commanding you to build an ark."

In a flash of lightning, God delivered the specifications for the ark. It would be 450 feet long, 75 feet wide and 45 feet high. *(Gen. 6:14-16.)* Total space aboard the ark would be 100,000 square feet—more room than in 20 standard-sized basketball courts.

Fearful and trembling, Noah took the blueprints and nodded his assent respectfully, on bended knees. "And remember," said God, "You must complete this ark and bring every animal aboard within twelve months."

Exactly one year later, a fierce storm cloud covered the earth and the seas began to swell. At that moment God looked down and saw Noah sulking in his trailer home on a mountaintop, weeping profusely. "Noah," He roared, "Where is the ark?"

"Oh God, please forgive me!" cried Noah. "I did my best but there are so many problems. First, the National Labor Relations Board made me sign an agreement to hire only labor union tradesmen and use restrictive work rules for constructing the ark. Then I needed a building permit and Your plans didn't comply with the maritime building code of the American Bureau of Shipping. So I retained an engineering firm to redraft the specifications. At that stage the Occupational Safety Agency ordered a hearing over whether or not the ark needed a fire sprinkler system and flotation devices plus larger bathrooms for the animals and some more lifeboats.

"At about the same time the U.S. Coast Guard demanded the right to inspect each phase of the construction of the ark. It also ordered me to make a written report to prove that I was complying with every federal, state, and local statute, law, regulation, and any other condition governing the construction, maintenance, and operation of a deepwater vessel.

"Next," Noah sighed, "my neighbors charged that I was violating a zoning ordinance by building the ark in my front yard, so I had to obtain a variance from the County Planning Commission. When I applied for this re-zoning clearance, my property taxes increased so much that my wife had to take a job to help pay the added assessment so she couldn't help me with the ark's construction. And then I couldn't get enough lumber to build the ark because there was a government ban on cutting trees in order to protect the spotted owls. I finally convinced the Bureau of Forestry that I needed the wood for an international emergency. But the Fish & Wildlife Commission wouldn't let me catch any owls for the ark because they are an endangered species under the Rare Animals Protection Act.

"On top of that," Noah moaned, "the Carpenters Union went on strike for a shorter work day, higher pay, more family leave and a better medical plan. They formed a picket line around our trailer, punched me in the nose, kicked my children, and threatened to break my wife's legs. But I still refused to capitulate to the union's exorbitant demands until the National Labor Relations Board ordered me to 'bargain in good faith' and resolve the 'impasse.' So I had to negotiate a quick settlement that meant exceeding Your budget and hiring 16 more skilled carpenters than I need plus two apprentices to 'assist' each of the new carpenters that I don't need. And the Department of Labor ordered me to increase their pay scale and fringe benefits even more to comply with some federal 'prevailing wage law.' That added expense forced me to obtain a Federal Housing Authority mortgage loan on the ark-to-be at 20 percent interest so that I could finance the carpenters' labor dispute settlement.

"And there's more," Noah whined. "When I started rounding up all the animals, I was sued by the American Zoological Society. It claimed that the ark space is too cramped and the animal food rations aren't sufficient. Just as I got that lawsuit settled, the Environmental Protection Agency notified me that I could not complete the ark without filing an environmental impact statement on Your proposed flood. Confidentially and off the record, Your Holiness, one U.S. Senator didn't take kindly to what he called "my extreme right wing idea" that the federal government has no jurisdiction over the conduct of the Creator of the Universe. Moreover, the Army Corps of Engineers demanded a map of Your proposed flood plan. So I sent them a world globe."

"And there's still more," sobbed Noah. "The Society for the Prevention of Cruelty to Animals contends that I have rejected too many handicapped beasts in violation of the American Critters with Disabilities Act. And the Carpenters Union claims that I have violated the Fair Labor Standards Act by employing minors (my own children) on 12-hour shifts without any pay and also violated the Labor-Management Relations Act by not requiring my

Often it seems such a pity that Noah and his party didn't miss the boat.

Mark Twain
HUMORIST-WRITER

In the first place, God made idiots. That was for practice. Then he made politicians.

MARK TWAIN
HUMORIST–WRITER

kids to join the Seafarers Union. Meanwhile, the Internal Revenue Service has seized all of my earthly assets on the theory that I'm building the ark in preparation to flee the world to avoid paying taxes. And I just got a court summons from the Department of Commerce that says that I failed to register the ark as a recreational watercraft.

"Also please listen to this, Almighty God," muttered Noah, on bended knees. "The president of the United States (on his last day in office) promulgated an executive order to make certain that there is a luxurious suite in the bow of the ark for him and four beautiful Hollywood girlfriends plus the Radio City Music Hall Rockettes—and another suite for his wife, at the stern of the ark. On top of that, the American Civil Liberties Union talked a federal court into issuing an injunction against further construction of the ark. The charge was 'multiple violations of the U.S. Constitution and its Animal Bill of Rights.' And the court ruled that since God is flooding the earth, rather than the President or Congress, it is a religious event and therefore politically incorrect under the Constitution's required separation of church and state.

"With the greatest respect and humility, Your Grace, under all the circumstances (including paying the exorbitant legal fees of a dozen trial lawyers), I really don't think I can finish the Ark for another five or six years!" Noah wailed . . .

Suddenly the sky began to clear, the sun started to shine, and the seas became calm. Then a beautiful rainbow arched across the sky. Noah looked up hopefully and asked: "Oh Omnipotent One, does this mean you are not going to destroy the earth?"

"Yes," answered God emphatically. "I don't have to. The federal government already has . . ."

CHAPTER 39

BIG LABOR'S SPECIAL PRIVILEGES

THE YEAR 1970 HOLDS A SPECIAL PLACE in my memory for two reasons. That was the time when I was selected as ABC's first national general counsel. It also was the year that my diminutive Baltimore labor law firm of Cook & Cluster accepted an invitation to merge into one of the country's largest legal establishments: the Maryland–Washington, D.C.–Virginia–based regional firm of Venable, Baetjer and Howard.

I made a wise choice. With excellent legal support and research resources at my beck and call, it wasn't long before I became deluged by merit shoppers seeking preservation for themselves, their livelihoods, and their possessions from workplace terrorism by the building trades. The perennial question that all of these ABC contractors asked me (with expletives deleted) was: *"Whatever happened to America's constitutional protection of life, liberty, and property through due process of law?"*

There was no easy answer—and the search for some practical solution became a frustrating experience. In trying to solve my clients' predicament, I kept looking for a creative way to pierce the veil of special privileges and legal immunities that were conferred on labor organizations by all branches of government whenever non-union contractors were targeted for compulsory unionism or oblivion.

Far from encouraging were the writings of a leading economist of the time, Donald Richberg. He believed that "the greatest concentration of political and economic power is now found in the underregulated, under-criticized,

The laws of a nation form the most instructive part of its history.

Edward Biggon
English historian

Venable, Baetjer and Howard's labor and employment law department twenty-one years later—in1991. The author, kneeling, second from left, plus twenty-one attorneys. Six more lawyers (including today's ABC national general counsel, Maury Baskin) were absent from the photo. The author created this department in 1970 with two lawyers, and thereafter developed, expanded, and chaired it until 1992.

under-investigated, tax-exempt, specially privileged labor organizations and their belligerent, aggressive, and far-too-often lawless and corrupt leaders."[1] Professor F. A. Hayek, a Nobel Prize winner in economic science, summed up my dilemma this way: "Today unions are uniquely privileged institutions to which the general rules of law do not apply. They have become the only important instance in which governments singly fail in their prime function—the prevention of coercion and violence."[2]

Thus challenged, I began to prepare for my counterattack by seeking historical perspective to evaluate ABC's chances of legal success against trade union terrorism.[3] A summary of my research—unavoidably exposing the reader to some legalese that I hope I have succeeded in translating into respectable English—is contained in this Chapter.

An Anti-Union Labor Climate in the Early Years

During the nineteenth century, the essential element of employment law was the common law prerogative of management to control all aspects of the work life of its employees.[4] For over a hundred years employers in the United States retained this freedom to operate their enterprises on their own terms, including the right to discharge employees "at will, be they many or few, for good cause, for no cause, or even for a cause morally wrong, without being guilty of legal wrong."[5] In 1908, the Supreme Court of the United States summarized this common law doctrine as follows:

> The right of a person to sell his labor upon such terms as he deems proper is, in its essence, the same as the right of the purchaser of labor to prescribe the conditions upon which he will accept such labor from the person offering to sell it. So the right of the employee to quit the service of the employer, for whatever reason, is the same as the right of the employer, for whatever reason, to dispense with the services of such employee...[A]ny legislation that disturbs that equality is an arbitrary interference with the liberty of contract which no government can legally justify in a free land.[6]

The grievances of rank-and-file workers in those days were numerous and legitimate, but arrogant management ignored most of their complaints. Employers also won court orders against so-called "criminal conspiracies" which actually subjected their employees to jail time whenever they joined together and attempted to bargain collectively over their wages and working conditions.

This gross inequality of bargaining power in the workplace between the autocratic captains of industry and the robotized men and women on the mass production assembly lines making steel, rubber, autos and other major products continued in the days of the industrial revolution. As recently as the

1920s, the "my-way-or-the-highway" common law of "master and servant" condoned working conditions that were both unfair and dangerous to limb and life.

Attempts by the exploited workers to rebel and form independent labor unions for mutual aid and protection were counteracted by aggressive company-hired "goon squads" of strike-breakers. Management "black listed" the militant workers and enforced individual "yellow dog" employment contracts that legally *forbad* an employee to join or maintain membership in any labor organization.

The aroused union-led workers countered with slowdowns, strikes, and sabotage of company property. Employees who took part in mass demonstrations while seeking bargaining recognition of their union were treated by law enforcement authorities and company security guards like any other type of uncontrollable mob engaged in acts of criminal (later modified to civil) disobedience. These confrontations often became small wars, with fisticuffs, weapons, and bloodshed on both sides.

In 1895, a court injunction enforced by 3,500 federal troops ended a nationwide strike by the newly formed American Railway Union against the Chicago Pullman Palace Car Company for reducing its workers' wages by 25 percent. The union's militant president, Eugene Debs, proclaimed confidently from his prison cell:

> Ten thousand times has the labor movement stumbled and bruised itself. We have been enjoined by the courts, assaulted by thugs, charged by the militia, traduced by the press, frowned upon in public opinion and deceived by politicians. But notwithstanding all this, labor is today the most vital and potential power this planet has ever known, and its historic mission is as certain of ultimate realization as is the setting of the sun.[7]

Negative public reaction to this 20th century workplace upheaval was inevitable, and a new social order began to emerge. Little by little, the feeble labor movement gained legal, political, and economic influence. Workplace reforms began in laws pertaining to collective bargaining, child labor, female labor, rudimentary health and safety, minimum and prevailing wages, maximum hours of work, and workers' injury compensation. Another sign of changing times was the preamble to the Clayton Anti-Trust Act of 1914. It declared that "the labor of a human being is not a commodity or article of commerce."

The Unique New Monopoly Status of Unions

With the encouragement of Franklin D. Roosevelt's Democratic administration, in 1935 a liberal senator named Robert Wagner (D-NY) took major remedial action. Joining with organized labor, he persuaded Congress that it should pass what eventually turned out to be the landmark National Labor Relations Act. It became known colloquially as the "Wagner Act." In it, Senator Wagner sold Congress on the belief that "caught in the labyrinth of modern industrialism and dwarfed by the size of corporate enterprise, the individual employee can attain freedom and dignity only by cooperation with others of his group." The senator concluded that his proposed legislation was "an affirmative vehicle for economic and social progress."[8]

This new Wagner Act—which organized labor called its "Magna Carta"—*outlawed* management's right to require workers to sign so-called "yellow dog contracts" agreeing *never* to join a union. The statute also ironically gave organized labor the antithetical right to *force* all workers into "closed union shops," regardless of their personal choice to remain union-free. The latter political gift meant that any union elected by a single vote or more majority of rank-and-file employees in a Labor Board-supervised election was awarded a "fiduciary privilege" never given before or since to any other private sector organization: as previously noted, a union can become certified to serve as the "exclusive" bargaining agent over wages and working conditions for all employees within "an appropriate bargaining unit determined by the federal government." Included inside the unit can be as much as a 49 percent minority of the workers who voted against such union representation.

The Wagner Act also enunciated for the first time a list of *employer* "unfair labor practices" if it failed to recognize and bargain "in good faith" with a duly certified union. In reviewing and upholding the constitutionality of these

Fight labor's demands to the last ditch and there will come a time when it seizes the whole of power, makes itself sovereign, and takes what it used to ask.

WALTER LIPPMANN
COLUMNIST

461

I think we have
more machinery
of government
than is necessary;
too many para-
sites living on
the labor of the
industrious.

THOMAS JEFFERSON
3RD PRESIDENT

unprecedented privileges, the U.S. Supreme Court conceded that every employee within a union's "exclusive" bargaining unit was forced to give up his or her own workplace independence. Congress, wrote the Court, extinguished the individual's power to order his own relations with his employer, created a power of "exclusivity" vested in the chosen union representative, and "stripped minority employees" of traditional forms of redress.[9]

In other words, Congress weighed the constitutional issues and bowed to Big Labor's political pressure. Congress rationalized that "compulsory unionism's economic benefit to the majority of its members [such as strike leverage at the bargaining table] evened the playing field with management." Brushed aside by these legislators was the deprivation of every minority employee's civil right to free speech, to freedom of association (by refraining from unionization) and to freedom of contract (by entering into his or her own personal work agreement with his employer based on individual merit). These individual rights supposedly are protected by the First and Fourteenth Amendments to the U.S. Constitution.[10]

In this historic Wagner Act of 1935, Congress also emasculated the common law managerial right of employers to operate their businesses as they saw fit in their own discretion. Although rarely mentioned in lofty legal or academic circles, a special three-judge decision in *National Maritime Union v. Paul Herzog* that was affirmed by the Supreme Court left no doubt of this huge entrepreneurial handicap:

> ....[Congress] added to the fundamental right of employees to organize and to bargain with their employers, certain important privileges and benefits that had not existed theretofore. Not only was the right to organize unions and to bargain through them affirmed but also the *privilege* of becoming the *exclusive* bargaining agent of all employees in a bargaining unit was extended to a labor organization favored by a majority of such employees. Moreover, employers were required to bargain collectively with the representative chosen by a majority vote. *This, to be sure, was an abridgment of the minority's fundamental rights, as well as those of employers.*[11] [emphasis added]

Dr. Charles Baird, director of the Smith Center for Private Enterprise at California State University, lamented the "legislative tyranny" by Congress in giving any private association—such as a labor organization—this awesome power over America's workforce: "The sale of a private citizen's labor is not a governmental matter. It is a private matter."[12] Even George Meany, president of the AFL-CIO at the time, admitted: "No longer can we take the position that we are the underdog."[13]

After twelve years of violent labor-management confrontations and work stoppages on an *uneven* battleground created by the Wagner Act, public outrage in 1947 forced Congress to enact the amendatory Labor-Management Relations Act (also referred to as the Taft-Hartley Act.)[14] While this supplementary statute rightfully continued to protect the Wagner Act's right of workers to organize and bargain collectively, Congress gave *employees* the legal right to *refrain* from joining a labor organization. Of equal importance, the new act subjected *unions* to certain unfair labor practices, including a ban against their secondary boycotts at the job sites of merit shop contractors.[15] It also permitted individual states to pass "right to work" laws that *outlaw* compulsory unionism and require membership to be *voluntary*.[16]

This equally renowned Taft-Hartley Act was passed by a majority of the 80th Congress on June 23, 1947, in spite of powerful opposition from the labor movement. A conservative coalition of Republicans and Southern Democrats also overrode the veto of an enraged Democrat President Harry Truman who labeled the amended law "an insult to America's workers."[17]

In a memorable speech before the U.S. Senate, the statute's coauthor, Robert A. Taft (R-OH), rebutted Truman's hypocritical reaction, traced the violent union-management relations history, and summarized the equitable basis for his major revision of the nation's labor relations policy:

> The truth is that originally, before the passage of any of the laws dealing with labor, the employer had all the advantage. He had the employees at his mercy, and he could practically in most cases dictate the terms that he wished to impose. Congress passed the Clayton Act, the Norris-LaGuardia Act, and the Wagner Act. The latter act was interpreted by a completely prejudiced [National Labor

Political ability is the skill to foretell what is going to happen tomorrow, next week, next month and next year. And to have the ability afterward to explain why it didn't happen.

WINSTON CHURCHILL
BRITISH
PRIME MINISTER

Relations] Board in such a way that it went far beyond the original intention of Congress, until we reached a point where the balance had shifted over to the other side, where the labor leaders had every advantage...

All we have tried to do is to swing that balance back, not too far, to a point where the parties can deal equally with each other and where they have approximately equal power. There will be no free collective bargaining until both sides are equally responsible.[18]

AUTHOR'S PERSONAL COLLECTION

Robert A. Taft of Ohio, a brave, brilliant, and conservative leader of the U.S. Senate from 1939 to 1953, known as "Mr. Republican." He authored the famous Taft-Hartley Act of 1947 and was chosen by his peers as "one of the five most outstanding members in the Senate's history."

Taft was revered by his conservative followers and respected by many of his political enemies. Even the mighty labor leader, John L. Lewis, called Taft "a great statesman and a great American." When the U.S. Senate chose the five outstanding men in its 168-year history, it ranked Taft with Webster, Clay, Calhoun, and Robert La Follette.[19]

Robert Taft's legacy—*the monumental Taft-Hartley Act of 1947*—has been a key factor in stabilizing America's workplace for half a century. It does that, when impartially enforced, by maintaining a delicate balance between the conflicting legal rights and responsibilities of individual workers, employers, labor organizations, and the public at large. As stated in the Act's preamble, its equalizing purposes are:

First, to prescribe the legitimate rights of both employees and employers in their relations affecting commerce;

Second, to provide orderly and peaceful procedures for preventing the interference by either with the legitimate rights of the other;

Third, to protect the rights of individual employees in their relations with labor organizations;

Fourth, to define and proscribe practices on the part of labor and management which are inimical to the general welfare; and

Fifth, to protect the rights of the public in connection with labor disputes affecting commerce.

This preamble to Taft-Hartley also explains why it added a parallel list of illegal union activities which were omitted from the original Wagner Act of 1935:

> ... Experience has further demonstrated that certain practices by some labor organizations, their officers, and members have the intent or the necessary effect of burdening or obstructing commerce by preventing the free flow of goods in such commerce through strikes and other forms of industrial unrest or through concerted activities which impair the interest of the public in the free flow of such commerce. The elimination of such practices is a necessary condition to the assurance of the rights herein guaranteed.

Regrettably, for the cause of capitalism, the government agency entrusted by Congress to enforce this revised statute—the National Labor Relations Board—frequently acts as though Senator Robert Taft's equalizing amendments never existed. In 1964, in the *Fibreboard Paper Products* case, Supreme Court Justice Potter Stewart's concurring opinion described the necessity to restate this national labor policy that labor unions and unionized contractors frequently had been allowed to sidestep or ignore:

> It is possible . . . that Congress may eventually decide to give organized labor or government a far heavier hand in controlling what until now

The true interest of Americans is mutual interest. The doctrines that put group against group, class against class, race against race, and worker against employer are all false doctrines.

WILLIAM McMILLAN
CONSULTANT

465

have been considered the prerogatives of private business management. That path would mark a sharp departure from the traditional principles of a free enterprise economy. Whether we should follow it is, within constitutional limitations, for Congress to choose. But it is a path that Congress certainly did not choose when it enacted the Taft-Hartley Act.

Restrictions on Employers' Relief Against Violent Union Conduct

Returning now to the political climate of Congress in the 1930s, its pro-labor slant also was evidenced by passage of the Norris-LaGuardia Act and its progeny of state "Little Norris-LaGuardia Acts." These laws rendered illegal the aforementioned "yellow dog" employment contracts that forbad employers to force their employees to refrain from joining any labor union. The new statutes also severely limited use of the court injunction by management and the general public as an effective defense against union violence and explained the "justification" for their enactment: "Individual unorganized workers are helpless to exercise actual liberty of contract, protect their freedom of labor, and thereby to obtain acceptable terms and conditions of employment." The Supreme Court characterized this legislation as "the culmination of a bitter political, social and economic controversy extending over half a century."[21]

The quandary for free enterprise was that these antiquated, union-biased anti-injunction statutes continued to remain in force in spite of the fact that organized labor became a political power to be reckoned with rather than the "weak sister" of the 1930s. A labor strike that is still permitted to continue uninterrupted under the Norris-La Guardia Act frequently is more than what leftist judges and politicians call "exercising liberty of contract" by "peaceful withholding of labor" whenever the union regards the employer's offer of compensation (or some other benefit) to be "inadequate." In reality, a work stoppage usually is an aggressive and hostile union attempt to prevent customers and suppliers from doing business with the struck firm until the union gains its objectives. A strike causes loss of jobs by employees and causes their employer thousands or millions of dollars in lost sales and profits. Mass picketing during a strike can turn into a riot, jeopardizing the disputants and the public's well being.

In spite of these facts, the antiquated Norris-LaGuardia Act and its state counterparts still contain time-consuming and safety-challenging procedural conditions to this day. This ridiculous ritual must be satisfied by employers and other victims of union intimidation *before* a court's restraining order against any *illegal* strike will be issued. And liberal courts at all levels have been emphatic that the "exceptions" which have been left open to help award injunctive relief to injured employers "should be viewed restrainedly as a narrow field of permissive jurisdiction."[22]

A typical example of this union-slanted ideology is seen in Maryland's "Little Norris-LaGuardia Act" of 1935. The primary concern of any employer victimized by massive picket line coercion or other labor savagery is that the illegal activity should be brought to an immediate end for the safety and welfare of all persons, entities, and properties affected. But the statute does not permit any court of equity to honor an employer's court petition to issue a restraining order against such terrorism in a labor dispute until *after* that injured employer has complied with the following *procedural* requirements:

1. Give prior notice of the employer's petition to the union involved and post a security bond.
2. Attend a formal court hearing with the "alleged" union violator on the employer's complaint.
3. Receive the court's issuance of findings of fact.
4. Allow an automatic forty-eight-hour waiting period "as a condition precedent to equitable relief."

Until these criteria are satisfied—in the court's judgment—union coercion and violence continue uncontrolled, "no matter how loudly the other facts seem to cry out for such relief."[23]

On the *evidentiary* issues, moreover, *before* any injunctive order against a strike will be issued, the employer under siege must produce "credible evidence" that:

People who love sausage and respect the law should never watch either being made.

OTTO VON BISMARCK
GERMAN POLITICIAN

1. The union's unlawful conduct will continue unless restrained.

2. The union enjoined has committed, authorized or ratified the unlawful conduct.

3. There is no other adequate legal remedy.

4. Substantial and irreparable injury will follow the union's misconduct.

5. The local police charged with the duty to protect the injured employer, its employees and property have been unable or unwilling to do so.

6. The employer (even though non-union!) "has made every effort to settle the dispute with the labor organization involved by negotiation or with the aid of any available arbitration or mediation mechanisms."

The height of statutory absurdity is reached by the fifth factor listed above. As can be seen, it requires the victimized employer to obtain an embarrassing admission from police at the scene that they can't perform their own jobs. And the equally ridiculous sixth factor requires the victimized employer to negotiate a compromise settlement with the striking union "mugger" in order to avoid future "muggings."[24]

In a violent labor dispute where an employer's ability to stay in business and operate in a safe manner as well as the general public's right to receive goods and services are jeopardized hour-by-hour and day-by-day, this severe legal burden on management to obtain temporary protection of limb and prosperity is patently unfair. It's the converse of the unfair criminal strike injunctions and "yellow dog" contracts obtained by management in the early twentieth century against peaceful union organizational activities.

Union Exemption from Antitrust Laws

In another important area of the law involving "monopolies," for a century or more there has been a legal proscription in the United States against "combinations in restraint of trade." But it took less than one generation for labor organizations to evolve from illegal criminal conspiracies into legitimate private organizations uniquely privileged to be the "exclusive" representative of workers in their relationship with their employer. As a direct result, unions have become national power brokers exercising monopolistic control of the supply of labor to unionized employees exclusively in many basic industries—including building and construction—*in restraint of trade*.

Eventually these facts forced a union-friendly Congress to "reconcile" two conflicting national policies: antitrust law which "condemns restraints of trade directed toward raising prices and reducing output," and labor law, which "encourages collective action on the part of workers to pursue and protect their employment interests."[25]

A liberal Supreme Court cooperated with Big Labor.

In *United States* v. *Hutcheson*, boycotts by labor unions to keep non-union goods out of the marketplace were held immune from criminal liability for wage-price fixing under the Sherman Antitrust Act of 1890 and the Clayton Anti-Trust Act of 1914 "so long as the union acts alone in its own self-interest and does not combine with non-labor [i.e., business] groups.[26]

Writing for the nation's highest court in *Hutcheson*, in 1941, Justice Felix Frankfurter established the parameters of this union exemption from anti-trust law as he endorsed the court's pro-union philosophy. Frankfurter's widely quoted ruling proclaimed that, under the Sherman Act, a labor organization that does not conspire with non-labor groups has the legal right to use any type of *unlawful* action, including violence, to drive an employer out of business. He explained—in Marxist-style rhetoric—that the end justifies any means: "The licit and the illicit are not to be distinguished by any judgment regarding the wisdom or unwisdom, the rightness or wrongness, the selfishness or unselfishness of the end of which the particular union activities are the means."[27]

In a dissenting opinion in the companion *Hunt v. Crumboch* anti-trust case where the Supreme Court permitted an employer's business to be destroyed by a labor organization, Frankfurter's shocked brother Supreme Court Justice, Robert Jackson, observed:

> Those statutes which restricted the application of the Sherman Act against unions were intended only to shield the *legitimate* objectives of such organizations, not to give them a sword to use with unlimited immunity. With this decision, the labor movement has come full circle . . .

The human race's prospects of survival were considerably better when we were defenseless against tigers than they are today when we have become defenseless against ourselves.

ARNOLD TOYNBEE
HISTORIAN

469

This Court now sustains the claim of a union to the right to deny participation in the economic world to an employer simply because the union dislikes him. This Court permits to employees the same arbitrary dominance over the economic sphere which they control that labor so long, so bitterly and so rightfully asserted should belong to no man.[28]

Union Protection from "Extortion" Statutes

The next major involvement of the federal government in the problem of protection against union terrorism rose in the context of "extortion" statutes. The cases construing these laws have provided a legislative-versus-judicial disunity that leaves federal jurisprudence on this critical subject in a state of confusion even today.

In the Hobbs Act of 1951, Congress tried to broaden the law's coverage by defining "extortion" as "the obtaining of property from another, with his consent induced by wrongful use of actual or threatened force, violence, or fear." There was no exemption in the statute for collective bargaining "pressure" by organized labor, but the Supreme Court's reluctance to punish union brutality surfaced again. This time it was featured in 1973 in the case of *United States v. Enmons.* In that five to four decision, the Court gave unions immunity from punishment for extortion and violence under the Hobbs Act "when used to gain workplace concessions."[29]

Evidence in the *Enmons* case showed that several Teamsters Union officials were indicted for firing high-powered rifles at public utility company transformers and blowing up a transformer substation—all for the purpose of extorting higher wages and other benefits for striking employees. The Supreme Court gutted the Hobbs Act by ruling that it didn't apply to the brutality and sabotage because it occurred in a "labor dispute."

Curiously, one of the Supreme Court's most liberal judicial activists, Justice William Douglas, led the dissent in this *Enmons* case. Douglas wrote that "the regime of violence, whatever its precise objective, is a common device of extortion and is condemned by the Hobbs Act." He added that in ignoring criminal evidence against the Teamsters thugs, "the Court achieves by interpretation what those who were opposed to the Hobbs Act were unable to get Congress to do because the acts [of violence] literally fit the definition of extortion in the Hobbs Act."[30]

This Hobbs statute and its immunity to labor union terrorism remains unchanged today.

That means that under the *Enmons* decision, labor organizations enjoy a special privilege—unique among all private legal entities in the United States—to use coercion and destruction of life and property in achieving their "bona fide" economic goals. Union officials may assault workers and even murder them yet escape federal prosecution under the Hobbs Act so long as their criminal activity is undertaken for what the Supreme Court in *Enmons* calls "a legitimate labor objective."

An aroused U.S. Attorney General Edwin Meese (R-CA) recently observed: "This exemption is otherwise foreign to American law. In no other legal context has it been said that the end justifies the means as it applies to a particular class of criminals or organizations."[31]

The legislature is the proper forum for this debate, and we do not sit as a superlegislature to award by judicial decree what was not achievable by political consensus.

U.S. 11TH CIRCUIT COURT OF APPEALS, JANUARY 27, 2004

The RICO Act—Relevant but Untested

In 1970 Congress provided a new legal weapon to deal with drug lords and other mobsters through enactment of the Racketeer Influenced and Corrupt Organizations Act (RICO). It followed the failure of prior laws and the need for a new approach to patterns of criminal wrongdoing. This statute spells out both criminal and civil sanctions against "persons" at the managerial level of "enterprises" who engage in "a pattern of continuous or related racketeering activity" that injures a business or property. Illegal activities—called "predicate offenses"—include traditional physical crimes as well as more sophisticated and covert white-collar offenses. And a jury (under a lower burden of proof in a civil case) can award *treble* the monetary damages sustained by the victim, plus court costs and reasonable legal fees.

RICO is not a labor relations statute *per se*. While its original purpose was to combat organized crime's widespread infiltration into legitimate organizations, its scope is much broader. That means that a defendant "person" may be a company or a labor union or any one of its respective members, employees, or officers.

In a democracy, only those laws which have the approval of strong groups have a chance of being enforced.

ABRAHAM MYERSON
RUSSIAN-AMERICAN
PSYCHIATRIST

The RICO statute thus appears on its face to be available for combating some types of labor coercion and violence that are protected by the Supreme Court's *Enmons* decision under the Hobbs Act and under the anti-injunction and anti-trust statutes. Unluckily for ABC, there was a judicial reluctance towards honoring lawsuits against any member of the politically powerful House of Labor as an alleged "criminal enterprise full of racketeers." The untested legal breadth of RICO's statutory "persons" and language "enterprise" coverage and evidentiary proof made it an unused weapon of the Justice Department in either civil or criminal cases arising out of labor disputes during the 1970s. And the use of RICO by private labor-management litigants in civil cases did not occur until the late 1980s.[32]

This narrow 1970s view interpreted RICO for over a decade as applying only to organized crime organizations. The American Bar Association's *Developing Labor Law* authors, Hardin and Higgins, explained the subsequent change:

> It was not until 1985, after plaintiffs had begun to use civil RICO more aggressively, that the Supreme Court took the opportunity in *Sedima v. Imrex Company*[33] to end the lower courts' narrow interpretation of the RICO statute. The Court stated emphatically that RICO "makes it unlawful for *any person*—not just *mobsters*—to use money derived from a pattern of racketeering activity to invest in an enterprise, to acquire control of an enterprise through a pattern of racketeering activity, or to conduct an enterprise through a pattern of racketeering activity." Despite *Sedima's* broad reading of RICO and the aggressive use of it since that time, many advocates of the narrow view have continued to criticize the application of RICO to *legitimate* labor organizations.[34] [emphasis added]

Today—in contrast—the American Bar Association's Labor and Employment Law Section calls RICO "the thermonuclear litigation device used in contexts such as pension and welfare plan abuses, union organizational campaigns, wage and commission contracts, union 'corporate campaigns' and other labor disputes."[35]

Union Immunity from Principal-Agent Responsibility

No matter what statute or common law principle is used to attempt to convict labor organizations and their officials of wrongdoing, they cling to their union's nebulous *unincorporated status*. This ploy makes them more difficult to sue for their misdeeds. In the words of Roscoe Pound, the oft-quoted and revered dean of Harvard Law School for twenty years: "By persistent and successful resistance to incorporation, which would make them responsible legal entities, the unions have been able to escape tort liability[36] and liability of funds for breach of contract for abuse of collective power."[37]

As an example, under the federal Norris-LaGuardia (Anti-Injunction) Act and its state counterparts discussed before, a union cannot be held responsible for the illegal acts of its agents unless there is "clear evidence of the union's actual participation in, authorization of, or ratification of the agent's acts." Big Labor knows that it is difficult to prove to any judicial body's satisfaction that a parent labor union—acting formally in its administrative capacity—is careless or stupid enough to get caught giving express prior authorization or subsequent ratification "to acts of coercion or violence by its affiliated unions or their members." With no such direct evidence available, the strong legal presumption by the liberal judiciary is that the alleged illegal activity "was not within the scope of the union or its agent's employment. It's hard to prove that a wink, a nod, a whisper, or an upright middle finger caused broken bones."[38]

In the case of unfair labor practices under the previously mentioned Taft-Hartley Act, however, Congress did adopt—from years of precedential common law—a broader and more easily proven "agency responsibility" test. Section 2(13) provides that:

> In determining whether any person is acting as an "agent" of another person so as to make such other person responsible for his acts, the question of whether the specific acts performed were actually authorized or subsequently ratified shall *not* be controlling." [emphasis added]

The legislative intent of this section was to make certain that both employers and unions are subject to the broad and inclusive common law doctrine

The right to one's day in court is meaningless if the judge who hears the case lacks the talent, experience and temperament that will enable him to protect imperiled rights and to render a fair decision.

WILLIAM H. REHNQUIST
CHIEF JUSTICE,
SUPREME COURT

Genius may have its limitations but stupidity is not thus handicapped.

ELBERT HUBBARD
WRITER

of agency rather than the restrictive and limited agency liability standard of the Norris-LaGuardia Act.[39] In actual practice, this important legal distinction frequently is ignored when applied to union conduct. The U.S. Supreme Court held in the *Cabot Fuel Company* case that an international union was *not* liable for "wildcat" strikes engaged in by its affiliated local unions. The reason given: it could not be proven that the international union actually authorized or subsequently ratified the illegal work stoppages. The High Court also refused to hold the international union to the broad common law principal-agent duty proscribed in Section 2(13) of the Taft-Hartley Act "to use all reasonable means available to it to prevent strikes [by its local unions] or bring about their termination."[40] But—with unabashed hypocrisy—an employer was held liable by the Labor Board for illegal actions of its supervisors because of their "apparent" authority under the same Section 2(13), even when those actions were not only unauthorized and never ratified by the company but also expressly against the written instructions to its agents.[41]

The Landrum-Griffin Act's Double Standard

The corrupt *internal* affairs of labor unions in violation of their role as "statutory fiduciaries representing their members' interests exclusively" were further regulated by passage of the Labor-Management Reporting and Disclosure Act of 1959, also referred to as the "Landrum-Griffin Act." This statute was preceded by extensive hearings in 1956 through 1958 of the "Select Committee on Improper Activities in the Labor-Management Field," chaired by Senator John L. McClellan (D-AR). A monumental record of wrongdoing by many unions, including the building trades, was compiled by this committee. Malpractices uncovered included breaches of trust, corruption, disregard of the rights of individual employees, and other failures to observe fiduciary standards of responsibility and ethical conduct.

This law contains a detailed "Bill of Rights" for union members and specific election procedures designed to guarantee internal "union democracy." It also provides for the appointment of union trusteeships to monitor and correct intra-union corruption and financial wrongdoing, requires fulfillment of every union's fiduciary responsibilities to its members, and bars convicted felons from serving as union officers.

Insofar as the *external* activities of unions are concerned, however, Congress, the courts, and the executive branch of government have continued to allow a legal double standard to exist. While corporations are prosecuted both criminally and civilly for the business malpractices of their officers and agents, comparable actions of labor union officials in the workplace are ignored, condoned, and protected. The Landrum-Griffin Act is silent on improper *external* union conduct affecting employers and the general public.

Professor Sylvester Petro of New York University's Law School described this chicanery in the preface of his treatise on *Power Unlimited—The Corruption of Union Leadership*:

> The McClellan Committee Record demonstrates that governments at all levels in this country have failed to apply the law of the land faithfully and vigorously to [external] abusive union conduct which would not be permitted to other persons or organizations. It further demonstrates that unions have taken great advantage of this special privilege to defy the laws, precepts, and principles of the good society.
>
> Workers have been beaten and robbed. Businessmen have been the victims of extortion. Consumers have been exploited. Political figures and governmental officers and agencies have been corrupted. Few significant areas of society have been left uncontaminated. Out of unlimited power, unlimited corruption is breeding.[42]

Criminal Law Reprieves on Union Violence

In spite of all of these federal exemptions from prosecution and unique privileges bestowed on Big Labor by Congress and the judiciary, it would seem that the general criminal laws of the states should be adequate to deal with most of the people-problems resulting from union-related violence and terrorism. Local laws all over America punish murder, manslaughter, assault, battery, intimidation, arson, trespass, damage to property, looting, and unlawful use of firearms by the general public, *with no exceptions*. While these statutes may be worded differently, ultimately they are all subject to the same human frailty: political reality in the form of pro-union favoritism and discrimination.[43]

Law is a reflection and a source of prejudice. It both enforces and suggests forms of bias.

DIANE SCHUDLER, ESQ.
LAWYER-EDUCATOR

The sad news for ABC was that the U.S. Supreme Court's *Enmons* case protection of union coercion and violence from federal relief under the Hobbs Act (as previously discussed in this chapter) has either been held to preempt local law or it is adopted by local law enforcement authorities in similar circumstances. A sign of the times was recorded in an article published by Frank Stewart and Robert Townsend in a 1966 issue of the University of Pennsylvania's law review:

> An assault is an assault and a battery is a battery. In every jurisdiction in the United States these common-law torts are actionable, civilly and criminally. One is not privileged to strike the landlord, the policeman, or the professor, except in self defense. If one disagrees with an opponent he should seek legal redress—*except in labor disputes*. The mystique of labor law is that violence is an aberration so strange and perplexing that ordinary standards of assault and battery simply will not do. The theory seems to be that, since violence is a traditional part of labor disputes, tradition sanctions its use....As a result, strike violence has achieved a protection afforded no other violent conduct.[44]

The renowned Nobel Laureate economist, Milton Friedman, and his equally distinguished wife, Rose, concur:

> ...[T]he use of violence implicitly involves government support. A generally favorable public attitude toward labor unions has led the authorities to tolerate behavior in the course of labor disputes that they would never tolerate under other circumstances. If someone's car gets overturned in the course of a labor dispute, or if plant, store, or home windows get smashed, or if people even get beaten up and seriously injured, the perpetrators are less likely to pay a fine, let alone go to jail, than if the same incident occurred under other circumstances.[45]

It is a grim fact that many government agencies and judges regard trade union intimidation and physical abuse as a "normal outgrowth" of labor-management confrontations. They look the other way or delay as long as possible in processing the legitimate counter-actions of ABC contractors to defend themselves and their property. One Virginia court justified the absence of union responsibility for the cruel acts of its members this way: "The assaults were not committed to satisfy any personal motives of the assailants but were caused by some emotion which naturally grew out of and was incidental to the performance of strike activities."[46]

Harassed ABCers soon discovered that they had to meet a heavy legal burden in obtaining criminal prosecution for each individual instance of union violence, sabotage, or other coercive activities. Under the requisite strict criminal court standard of "proof beyond a reasonable doubt" (rather than the easier-to-prove civil rule of "preponderance of the evidence") a trial on the merits of a case was slow in coming and uncertain as to conviction. Juries were unsympathetic too. In their minds—encouraged by union attorneys, left-wing politicians, and the mainstream national news media—it was "the poor, abused, and downtrodden workers versus a big, bad, wealthy corporation."

Victims and eyewitnesses suddenly lost their courage to testify against union assailants. Physical evidence somehow "disappeared." Local union officials who swore under oath that they never committed, authorized, acquiesced in, ratified, or had any knowledge of illegal activities were considered truthful even when the credible evidence against their testimony was overwhelming.

Fearful rank-and-file union members often were the only eyewitnesses and their memories suddenly "failed" under the covert pressure of union officials and the glare of hostile judges. Phone threats were made anonymously. Vandalism and arson were carried out by professional thugs in the dark of night. Positive identification of the wrongdoers was especially difficult in cases where the imposition of criminal sanctions was most warranted, such as intentional mob violence and widespread destruction of property.

In his definitive treatise on *Union Corruption*, Carl Horowitz explained:

> A culture of intimidation pervades much of America's unions. And that culture explains why so much corruption is hard to detect and fight. Corruption, by definition, involves illegal activity for personal gain. And in a large organization such as a labor union, no

It's strange dat guys should take up crime when 'dere is so many legal ways ta be crooked.

AL CAPONE
MAFIA GODFATHER

participant, acting alone or in concert with others, will admit to misdeeds. Instead, when under suspicion, they will issue a defiant, "Prove it!"

In the absence of vigilant prosecution and witness protection, the lone dissenting worker is not likely to risk his job, let alone his physical safety, to play the hero. Fear and silence thus enlarge the pie for corruption.[47]

Distressing News for ABC Contractors

It was obvious that the organized labor movement had acquired—from a class-conscious society and its leftist law enforcers—many politically correct privileges and legal immunities which have never been granted to any other private sector entity. *Fortune* magazine's John Davenport described the crisis bluntly: "This inability of the law to cope with and contain the excesses of union power must be counted as one of the great failures of Anglo-Saxon jurisprudence."

Writing in the *Nebraska Law Review*, Professor Thomas Haggard agreed:

Despite the plethora of state and federal laws which potentially touch on the matter, the problem of labor union violence seems to persist... The uneasy feeling remains that the law does not address the problem of labor union violence with the vigor that it should.

This attitude can be seen in all three branches of government. Prosecution under the criminal statutes, especially at the state and local level, is reportedly lax in certain jurisdictions, perhaps because of the political sensitivity of the issue. Moreover, where vigorous attempts have been made to enforce these statutes against labor union violence, the administrative agencies and courts have often either construed the statutes so narrowly as to make them virtually worthless or have judicially excluded labor violence from their coverage altogether. In addition, legislatures, especially Congress, have seemed either unable or unwilling to write statutes prohibiting labor violence with that degree of specificity that is apparently necessary in order to insure judicial and administrative enforcement.

Dean Roscoe Pound of Harvard Law School appraised this vast leftward swing of the labor-management relations pendulum in these words:

> The substantially general privileges and immunities of labor unions and their members and officials to commit wrongs to person and property, to interfere with the use of highways, to break contracts, to deprive individuals of the means of earning a livelihood, and to control the activities of individual workers and their local organizations by national organizations centrally and arbitrarily administered beyond the reach of laws [are] things which no one else can do with impunity.[48]

To sum up, under the laws of the United States as enforced by the courts and government agencies, labor organizations were in the 1970s—and still are—entitled to:

1. Severe delays and other dangerous limitations on court injunctions against them to stop their mass picketing and other violent misconduct.
2. Compulsory and exclusive representation status that denies dissenting minority employees the freedom of choice to refrain from union membership and dues.[49]
3. Protection from their own terrorism and sabotage exercised in disregard of extortion statutes;
4. Exemption from monopoly-busting antitrust laws when acting independently from employers.
5. Immunity from common law principal-agent responsibility for their injurious conspiratorial actions.
6. Reprieve from criminal violence and wrongful tort transgressions applicable to everyone else.

I had been retained to protect ABC members, their families, their employees, their companies, and their customers on a nationwide basis from the physical brutality and property destruction by the AFL-CIO's building and construction

There are risks and costs to action. But they are far less than the long-range risks of comfortable inaction.

JOHN F. KENNEDY
35TH PRESIDENT

trades unions. But my research into the history of labor-management relations failed to disclose any practical, prompt, and inexpensive legal strategy to reach my goal.

For some unexplainable reason, my thoughts turned towards a highly unlikely source to give my clients the aid and protection from labor union terrorism that they deserved.

CHAPTER 40

AN INFAMOUS
GOVERNMENT AGENCY

NOWHERE WERE THE SPECIAL legal and political privileges of Big Labor more apparent than at the controversial government agency which prosecutes union and management unfair labor practices throughout the United States. As previously noted, it is called the National Labor Relations Board (and sometimes the "NLRB," the "Labor Board," or the "Board"). At an early age I became an inside observer of the full impact of this Board's power and how it maladministered the federal Labor-Management Relations Act—the so-called "Taft-Hartley Act of 1947"[1]—which, as noted previously, is intended to resolve conflicts in the nation's private sector workplace on a bipartisan basis.

The story began after I spent several drab years as a young $2,000-per-annum associate in the prestigious Baltimore law firm of Piper, Watkins, Avirett & Egerton. When it merged with the equally prominent firm of Marbury, Miller and Evans, managing partner William Marbury told me that I "could come to work for them but I would never be admitted to his partnership," which featured *magna cum laude* Harvard Law Review editors.

This unflattering news didn't surprise me—a graduate *magna cum difficultate* of the University of Maryland law school. The feelings were mutual. I had quietly decided many months earlier to leave the boring (to me) general practice of business law and enter a brand new specialized field called "labor-management relations." Attempting to solve people problems in the workplace seemed more challenging (and rewarding) than sitting among the library

If you walk up to the bell, ring it.

MEL BROOKS
COMEDIAN-PRODUCER

stacks while researching legal memoranda or drafting corporate by-laws or foreclosing Moss-Rouse Company mortgages on poor widows' homes or persuading traffic court judges not to suspend the driving licenses of the spoiled and reckless kids of the firm's blueblood clients.

I presumed that the best way to gain experience in my newly chosen field was to become employed by the National Labor Relations Board for several years. In my naiveté, I didn't realize that voluntary civic service as a young officer of the conservative, entrepreneurial Baltimore Junior Chamber of Commerce actually made me suspect as an "undesirable" candidate for employment by this union-biased agency. Many months of bureaucratic stalling were followed by outright rejection from Chief Law Officer David Sachs to fill an open low-level legal position (for which I was qualified) at the Fifth Region Labor Board office in my hometown of Baltimore.

I finally was hired and reported for work on the headquarters legal staff of the Labor Board's General Counsel in Washington, D.C. But it took behind-the-scenes "assistance" from Maryland's Republican Senator John Marshall Butler to convince the Board to hire me. Luckily, the conservative Senator was a member of the Senate Labor Committee, which approved the Labor Board's annual budget . . .

The date of my employment was 1951, one year after ABC was founded.

As a tenderfoot slotted at the lowest rung of the Labor Board's legal ladder (GS-9), I had no clue that this federal government service in my chosen field of law practice would become a traumatic experience which affected the rest of my life—both professionally and personally. Within a few months, however, it became obvious that my assumption of professional integrity on the part of this critical executive branch bureau was wishful thinking. I discovered, bit-by-bit, to my amazement, that my new employer, since its inception, had been engaged in unethical, immoral, and even subversive activity against the American free enterprise system.

Dancing with the Devil

The top-ranking personages of that first Labor Board were appointed in 1935 by President Franklin D. Roosevelt, with the advice of his close friend, a Marxist-style union leader named Sidney Hillman. According to documented sources, the persons selected featured a cell of ideological Communists and fellow travelers. Labor Board Member Edwin Smith and the Labor Board's first personnel director, Nathan Witt, were among the clandestine radicals.[2]

Most of the potential seditionists and their followers were placed in positions of influence at the Board's Washington, D.C., headquarters. They held secret meetings on a regular basis to decide policy issues in spinning their one-sided interpretation of the nation's critical labor-management relations law. Their decisions usually favored John L. Lewis's militant Congress of Industrial Organizations (CIO)—which was infiltrating and unionizing national defense industries on a "wall-to-wall" basis—over Sam Gompers' conservative, old-line American Federation of Labor (AFL) craft unions. These government policy makers also favored all labor organizations over all employers and all non-union employees whenever possible.[3]

In the 1946 case of *NLRB v. McGough Bakeries Corporation*, as one example, the federal Fifth Circuit Court of Appeals remanded an unfair labor practice case against an employer to the Labor Board for reversal with the instruction that management's "sworn testimony cannot be over-ridden by suspicion or by slight circumstances that may be given another color." The court pointed out that the Labor Board's trial examiner "with complete consistency... found every witness for the union reliable and truthful and every opposing witness [including the company's president and supervisors] untruthful and unreliable. Witnesses called by the Board were reliable when they testified favorably to the union, but otherwise not reliable."[4]

This unscrupulous left-wing government agency was careful to perpetuate its anti-capitalism philosophy. Although Edwin Smith, Nathan Witt, and many of their Marxist disciples had departed the Labor Board before I arrived on the Washington, D.C., scene in 1951, a distorted administration of the Taft-Hartley Act continued during my sojourn there. Federal courts, when called upon to enforce the Labor Board's injunctive orders against employers' "unfair activities" during that era, chastised the agency for its pro-union partiality and frequently reversed its decisions.

These judges gave the Board stern lectures on its injustices to management and the general public as they disputed its findings of fact and overruled its legal

---

Some people seem to think that there is a great difference between socialism and communism. But Karl Marx used the two words as synonyms. The best definition of a communist I have heard is that he is a socialist in a hurry.

CHARLES E. WILSON
CEO OF GENERAL MOTORS CORP.

Marxism is the equal sharing of miseries.

WINSTON CHURCHILL
BRITISH
PRIME MINISTER

conclusions. Board rulings were described as based erroneously upon "inference piled on inference"[5] or "arbitrary and capricious" actions[6] "inconsistent with the principles of equity."[7] Some Board decisions were held to be founded on "suspicion and conjecture and a kind of cloak and dagger process of reasoning."[8] Other Board orders were "just as immoral and inequitable in labor as in any other human relations."[9] Even the U.S. Supreme Court at times found it necessary to rebuke the Board with observations such as "substantive rights and duties in the field of labor-management relations do not depend on verbal ritual reminiscent of medieval real property law."[10]

An Honorable Government Lawyer Comes to My Rescue

Working as an unsophisticated legal trainee at this evil agency in the 1950's caused me to wonder if I had made a tragic mistake in the selection of labor relations as a career path for my future law practice. Luckily, however, a veteran government attorney by the name of Tom Sweeney quietly adopted me into what he liked to call his "little pro-America cell" at the Labor Board. While it was my observation that Sweeney's professional integrity and conservatism retarded his advancement in the agency, his long service and vested government tenure rendered him immune from any major discipline by his ultra-liberal "superiors." Sweeney also had the respect and support of Maryland's Republican Senator Butler and his capable administrative assistant, Edwin Hood, as added job protection from any Democratic political shenanigans.

Tom Sweeney and I soon became good friends. He taught me the fundamental principles of the Taft-Hartley Act as its primary author, Senator Robert Taft (R-OH), intended it to be enforced—evenly and impartially. In reviewing unfair labor practice charges assigned to me for possible prosecution by the office of General Counsel George Bott, a liberal Democrat, I learned to base my recommendations on the preponderance of the actual evidence and the express statutory language as interpreted by more trustworthy appellate courts. Cases assigned to me were carefully "screened" in advance. Apparently it had become known that I would refuse to embrace the Labor Board's unwritten presumption of the legality of almost every union action, no matter what actually happened, at the expense of the legitimate legal rights of rank-and-file workers and their employers.

Occasionally a "hot" union issue would slipp through to me due to some clerical mistake. In fact national labor peace and productivity could have been jeopardized by one outrageous case I reviewed that involved compulsory unionism in the steel industry. (My recommendation was overruled, of course.) In my view, there were "good" and "bad" employers and "good" and "bad" unions, depending on the evidence and the applicable law in each case. I simply respected and lived by my oath of integrity as an officer of the courts and a member of the Maryland Bar. This professional impartiality soon made me unpopular with my biased Board supervisors, but it never crossed my mind to act otherwise.

A Case Involving the Communist Party

One vivid memory in my political baptism as a government lawyer employed by the sinister Labor Board relates to a precedent-setting case in which I did not participate. It involved the Board's devious strategy in its manner of *defending* the constitutionality of Section 9(h) of the Taft-Hartley Act when it was challenged by the National Maritime Union in 1947. This statutory provision required all labor union officers to sign an affidavit denying their membership in or support of the Communist Party or any other organization "that believes in or teaches the overthrow of the United States Government by force or by any illegal or unconstitutional methods."

Failure to comply with this Section 9(h) prevented the union officials involved (and their labor organizations) from utilizing the Labor Board to conduct employee representation elections or process unfair labor practice charges on their behalf against employers.[11]

Officers of the ultra left-wing National Maritime Union ("NMU") refused to sign such an affidavit and the Labor Board was legally obligated to exclude the union from use of the above-noted Board procedures. The NMU thereupon filed a special action before a three-judge federal district court to enjoin the Labor Board from enforcing Section 9(h) of the Act against it, claiming that this non-communist affidavit section of the statute was "unconstitutional." The union contended that the Communist Party is "merely a political party like Democrats or Republicans," and therefore its members were entitled to protection under the First Amendment's freedom of speech and assembly.

In a very real sense, today's contest between freedom and despotism is a contest between the American assembly line and the Communist Party line.

PAUL G. HOFFMAN
INDUSTRIALIST

In rebuttal, the government attorney who was selected by the Labor Board to represent it in *defending* the constitutionality of Section 9(h), made the following argument to the federal court:

> ...Congress did not find—I might as well make it perfectly clear now—it did not find and it did not purport to find, and it is our position that it did not need to and could not properly have found, that the Communist Party advocates the doctrine of violent overthrow of the Government by force or other unconstitutional means. That is just no part of this case.[12]

This distorted contention caused Associate Justice Prettyman to observe publicly as follows:

> Upon the evidence of which the court takes judicial notice and which the Government presses upon us, *this is a curious diversity of conclusion.* In the Congress and in the public press, there are many declarations that the Communist Party is a subservient tool of a foreign power and, as such, bent upon the destruction of our Government by force or illegal methods. Curiously, part of the evidence cited and quoted by the court in this case as supporting the conclusion that the Communist Party foments industrial strife, is actually that that party seeks to overthrow the Government. *But we are told by the Government [Labor Board] that Congress did not reach the latter conclusion and "could not properly have [so] found."* [emphasis added][13]

The court had no difficulty in upholding the constitutionality of Section 9(h) of the Taft-Hartley Act and rebuffing the Labor Board attorney's misrepresentation of Communist Party objectives. Associate Justice Wilbur K. Miller's majority opinion in this *National Maritime Union* case emphasized that "events on the national and world stages since the Taft-Hartley Act became law on June 27, 1947, have not removed the basis which the Congress then had for deciding that Communistic influence in labor relations was *a clear and present danger to the national welfare and security.* Those events have, on the contrary, *emphasized* the ground for alarm which Congress felt."[14]

It further defied credulity when the government attorney who presumably concocted this twisted argument in the *National Maritime Union* case was promoted to the position of the Labor Board's senior advocate in the presentation of all of its cases argued before the U.S. Supreme Court. And I will never forget that at the year's end, the same attorney received a government citation as "outstanding lawyer at the National Labor Relations Board."

The Making of a Conservative

It is significant to contrast the Labor Board's leftist spin on Communism in those days as "merely another political party" with the modern-day opinion of Russia's own highest court on the same subject. It reviewed and upheld the constitutionality of President Boris Yeltsin's ban on the Communist Party in 1992. In doing so, the Russian court called an expert witness and thereafter endorsed his opinion: Richard Pipes, an eminent Harvard University historian and the Director of Soviet Affairs on President Ronald Reagan's National Security Council, proclaimed:

> From the time it seized power, the Communist Party was an entirely new type of organization. It stood outside the government and yet completely dominated it. It controlled everything, including the country's economic assets, without itself being subject to controls. It was a self-perpetuating totalitarian order of self-elected rulers that provided the model first for Mussolini and Hitler and then for post–World War II dictators around the world.[15]

Sadder but wiser, I left the Labor Board in 1953 following two years of bizarre and disillusioning government service. Soon after, fortunately, I began what turned out to be a rewarding experience in my new field as, first, a chemical plant industrial relations supervisor and, subsequently, as corporate labor counsel of the private sector industrial giant, W. R. Grace & Co. I always respected managerial, union, and workers' rights, operating under the legal ground rules of the statute that I had helped to administer. It was (and still is)

Laws not defended cease to be laws, and rights not defended may wither away.

THOMAS MORIARTY
WRITER

487

The first thing we do, Let's kill all the lawyers.

WILLIAM SHAKESPEARE
HENRY VI, ACT IV,
SCENE II

fair and balanced labor legislation drafted through the legal brilliance, ethical principles, human relations skills, and courageous leadership of Senator Robert Taft. But the unprofessional, falsified, and seditious conduct that I witnessed within a sensitive executive agency of the federal government made an indelible impression on me for the rest of my life.

That experience—and my subsequent exposure to the competitive world of private sector free enterprise under the inspirational leadership of President and Chief Executive Officer Peter Grace,[17] his brilliant Davison Chemical Division President, William E. McGuirk, and the fiery World War I fighter pilot turned industrial relations vice president, H. Barton DeVinney— changed me forever.

From a carefree, naive, apolitical youth I became a conservative and patriotic Republican man, championing traditional American values.[16]

The Pro-Union Board Remains

The same partisan maladministration of the Taft-Hartley Act by the Labor Board that I observed first-hand in the 1950s continued to exist during the 1960s and 1970s—a time when ABC was coming of age as the premier advocate of merit shop construction and I became the Association's General Counsel. Even the impartial national news commentator, David Brinkley, couldn't resist a public observation about the sinister agency. This famous television anchorman told his vast audience that while the Labor Board is supposed to be "an unbiased, adjudicating body somewhat like a court, it usually behaves like a department of the AFL-CIO and is about as neutral as its president, George Meany."[18]

There was no attempt by the Board to respect and adhere to the aforementioned Taft-Hartley Act's declaration of policy stated in Section 1(b) to "avoid industrial strife which interferes with the normal flow of commerce" by requiring that "employers, employees, and labor organizations each recognize under law one another's legitimate rights in their relations with each other." And this policy declaration concludes with the rule usually twisted out of shape or ignored by the Board that the parties must "above all recognize that neither [unions, employees, or employers] have a right in its relations with any other to engage in acts or practices which jeopardize the public health, safety or interest." Of equal importance, Section 7 of the Act guarantees the alternative rights of employees either to engage in collective bargaining or—also overlooked by left-wing Board bureaucrats—to *refrain* from unionization.

Coercive Union Misconduct Is Condoned

Defying this Taft-Hartley Act preamble that establishes a mandate for a level field among all parties and persons involved in enforcement of the nation's premier labor law, the Labor Board continued to spin the policy that union threats of violence to force or protect union representation which were unaccompanied by severe physical acts did not warrant any discipline of the culprits involved. Employers who imposed sanctions on such "mere gestures" were held guilty of an unfair labor practice.

In one case, a non-union employee was attempting to report for work when another non-union employee who was engaging in a strike and walking a picket line shook his fist and called his "brother" worker "a rotten scab." The

Litigation is the basic legal right which guarantees every organization its decade in court.

DAVID PORTER
WRITER

PHOTO FROM THE AUTHOR'S COLLECTION

The Curtis Bay (Baltimore) Works of Davison Chemical Co., a division of W. R. Grace Co. The author worked there in the early 1950s as assistant to the director of industrial relations, Captain Bob Holden, in "shepard-ing" a production and maintenance workforce of 1500 members of the International Chemical Workers Union, AFL-CIO.

striker also warned his co-worker that "he would get the goddamn shit knocked out of him" if he was caught ignoring and crossing the union's picket line again. The Board ordered this abusive striker to be reinstated after his employer discharged him for "inexcusable misconduct."[19] In a related case, the Board ordered an employer to rescind another striker's 20-day suspension from work for jumping on the hood of a non-striker's slowly moving car. The striker had remained on the hood for a mile or so, while repeatedly beating on the car's windshield until ordered off by a police officer.[20]

In still another dangerous situation, several striking employees followed their company supervisor driving home from work at night for fourteen miles. The frightened supervisor, fearful that his wife and children would be drawn into the labor fracas, drove past his own house. He was trapped eventually on a dead-end country road where an escape passage was blocked by the strikers. The Board ruled that the strikers' misconduct did not merit a two-week suspension imposed by their employer. It reasoned that "since the supervisor's fear was eventually put to rest and the intimidation did not in fact ripen into actual physical harm, the threat of violence was not coercive and therefore did not warrant any discipline."[21] Other typical examples of violent union misconduct that should have been punished as "unfair labor practices" but frequently were condoned by the Labor Board because they were considered to be just "the spontaneous outgrowth of confrontation" included mass picketing, blocking of ingress and egress to a job site, and property damage.

At the same time, the Board continued to impose significant limitations on the right of an employer to discipline an employee for engaging in picket line coercion or brutality. In one such case, a striking worker who pulled a knife

"I don't suppose you have one saying something like 'sorry about that NLRB decision'?"

FROM *THE WALL STREET JOURNAL*, REPRINTED WITH PERMISSION, CARTOON FEATURES SYNDICATE

on a non-striker in a picket line ruckus was held to be "engaged in protected activity of self defense."[22]

What's Wrong with Hurling a Brick or Two?

This lack of concern by the Labor Board for union terrorism sabotaged the Taft-Hartley Act's expressed policy that protects the fundamental alternative right of employees to remain "union-free." The Board's twisted reasoning also undermined the Act's protection of the right of employers to enjoy a peaceful workplace and the general public's right to protection from bodily harm. "Unfortunately," explained the Labor Board, once again ignoring the clear statutory policy and intent, "some disorder is not unusual in an extensive strike." And, added the Board, "there must be an allowance for picket line horseplay devoid of sinister purpose" as well as "some leeway for impulsive behavior."[23] "Surely," the Board noted, "minor scuffles and disorderly arguments...and other impulsive behavior on the picket line is to be expected," especially when directed against non-striking employees and strikebreakers.[24]

Even the Supreme Court has agreed that "a trivial rough incident" or "a moment of animal exuberance" is to be expected and protected "when emotions run high in a labor-management dispute involving otherwise peaceful picketing."[25] In short, with the liberal benediction of the Labor Board and the judiciary, union terrorism frequently has been down-played or excused as "a trivial instance of rowdyism"[26] or "natural human zealotry."[27] No such lax and one-sided legal standard has ever been applied in any law related to civil or criminal intimidation or physical injury caused by an employer, the police, or any other segment of the American public.[28]

It is a normal reaction of human nature that, regardless of whether any threatening or actual violent conduct towards an individual is downgraded judicially to "minor" or "insignificant," the victim on the receiving end may well be fearful for his or her safety in the workplace and absorb permanent emotional scars. Such coercive union activity was never intended to be tolerated by Robert Taft's Congress when it provided equally balanced union-employee-management rights and responsibilities through passage of the Taft-Hartley Act in 1947.

Modern liberalism's most powerful position, arguably, is its dominance in the law.

FORMER FEDERAL JUDGE ROBERT BORK IN *THE TEMPTING OF AMERICA*

When you get to the end of your rope, tie a knot in it and hold on.

WILL ROGERS
HUMORIST-ACTOR

The Labor Board's Double Standard on Remedial Penalties

Even when some remedial action was forthcoming from the Labor Board, unequal treatment existed between the penalties meted out to different guilty parties in the dispute. The Board never hesitated to order back-pay awards to unionized employees who were discriminated against by coercive acts of *employers* or their agents during the course of a labor dispute.[29] In *Phelps Dodge Corporation v. NLRB*, for instance, the Supreme Court noted that "making the workers whole for losses suffered on account of an unfair labor practice [by their employer] is part of the vindication of the public policy which the Labor Board enforces."[30] But the most severe penalties that *unions* usually received for their equally coercive and violent illegal activities against employers and non-union employees were innocuous tap-on-the-wrist "cease-and-desist" orders applicable in the future that had to be enforced by expensive and lengthy litigation in the federal courts. Unions might also be required to post notices in their union hall "to behave themselves in the future"—while not admitting any past wrongdoing. "Our powers, which are entirely remedial, are inadequate to cope with [union] violence," weakly claimed the Board.[31]

In the case of *Roofers Union Local 30 and Associated Builders and Contractors*, the Labor Board made this double standard perfectly clear:

> The Board has long held that *employees* legally damaged by the tortious [i.e., wrongful] conduct of unions might be better served by pursuing those private remedies traditionally used for the recovery of such [make whole] damages. We are persuaded that the same policy considerations obtain where *employers* are legally damaged by the tortious conduct of unions. In both instances, private remedies traditionally used for recovery of such damages would bring employees and employers before tribunals which have *more experience* and are *better equipped* than this Board to measure the impact of tortious conduct, including *violence*, and to make the victims whole.[32] [emphasis added]

Violent Secondary Boycotts Are Forgiven

The Board's lax treatment of threats and terrorism when related to illegal secondary boycotts by unions caught the attention of one intellectually honest government attorney, Kenneth McGuiness. This able lawyer, who served briefly as General Counsel to the National Labor Relations Board under an interim appointment by President Dwight Eisenhower, wrote:

> The public, and particularly those individuals who have not become callused to the oddities of the labor-management arena, must find it difficult to understand the apathy with which governmental authorities view violent conduct in labor disputes . . . In the writer's own experience, the Labor Board refused to act where massed pickets completely blocked ingress and egress at a plant for more than a month [and] there had been continual violence. Violence, mass picketing, physical blocking of ingress and egress, and threats have no place in the legal concept of picketing as a means of publicizing a labor dispute . . .
>
> In one case after another, the Labor Board has narrowed the impact of the Act's proscriptions on secondary activity. More often than not, the conflict between the neutral employer's right to be free from industrial strife and the union's right to exert economic pressure has been unbalanced heavily in favor of the union. Despite the intent of the original secondary boycott provisions and the well documented goal of the [Taft-Hartley Act] amendments, Congress has been singularly unsuccessful in convincing the Labor Board that it wants secondary boycott activity stopped.[33]

"Boys Will Be Boys"

This reluctance of the Labor Board to impose meaningful sanctions upon union threats and brutality naturally served to encourage its recurrence. It perpetuated the axiom that "some violence" is a sacrosanct American tradition in labor-management confrontations and therefore legally acceptable. James Bovard pointed out in the *Wall Street Journal* that the Labor Board would charge union officials with an unfair labor practice "only if the conduct was so violent as to render an employee unfit for future service." In other words, Bovard concluded, "short of killing or crippling a non-union worker during a labor dispute, the Labor Board's attitude seemed to be 'hands-off.'"[34]

Unions are so beyond the reach of the law that they can, and often do, resort to violence that coerces employers into giving them what they want . . . Even more disturbing is the fact that the U.S. government lets these terrorist acts go unpunished.

LINDA VALEZ
SYNDICATED COLUMNIST
AND WRITER
IN *BETRAYAL*

493

In their authoritative text on *Union Violence*, Armand Thieblot and Thomas Haggard confirmed that substantial coercion and violence by unionized workers was "tolerated" under the Taft-Hartley Act as interpreted by the Labor Board: "Its attitude seems to be that 'boys will be boys'; that a certain amount of 'animal exuberance' is to be expected in the emotionally supercharged atmosphere of a labor dispute; that while this is to be regretted, the law should not over-react and run the risk of 'chilling' the exercise of the employees' right to organize and strike..."[35]

Despite a continuing pattern of labor coercion and brutality against ABCers, the National Labor Relations Board was reluctant to prosecute illegal union activities. Even when it did, I claimed that its remedy was like "using a peashooter to rout a rampaging elephant." My search for an effective national counter-attack to puncture the shroud of special privileges and immunities that protected the terroristic activities of the building trades unions seemed hopeless at this infamous government agency.

On the other hand, the Bible says that once upon a time an Israelite shepherd boy named David, armed only with a slingshot, faced impossible odds in a fight to the death against a ten-foot-tall Philistine called Goliath. This armor-clad giant was prepared to wield a sword against David. But you know who won...

ABC needed a similar miracle to happen somewhere, somehow—and soon!

PART THREE

ABC COUNTER-ATTACKS

"How many more people must be shot at, beaten, or maimed before public outrage
demands that the union terrorists be brought to justice?"

Charles Stevenson
Roving Editor, *Reader's Digest*, June 1973

CHAPTER 41

CALLAS CHALLENGES THE CONSTRUCTION TRADES

THE PRESIDENT OF **ABC** IN **1973** AND **1974**—Mike Callas—made Association membership expansion and respect for a terror-free, harmonious, and competitive construction workplace in America his primary objectives. Attainment of these two goals would mean the difference between success and failure of the merit shop crusade.

Callas was well aware of the hurdles that lay ahead of him and maintained an itinerary that equaled the globetrotting of ABC's executive vice president, John Trimmer. They both traveled non-stop throughout America from border to border and coast to coast. Callas also focused his agenda on leftist labor legislation coming out of the nation's capital in Washington, D.C. This dynamic leader's ringing salvo to all was *"ABC is on the march!"*

Like most merit shop luminaries, Mike Callas was a self-made man. He was born in Hagerstown in 1921. It was just two years after his parents moved to that bustling Western Maryland borough in the beautiful Cumberland Valley. Their first home after emigrating from Greece had been in New York's Lower East Side. Young Mike worked in the family candy shop and a confectionery store in Hagerstown's public square from the time he was ten years old until he graduated from the local high school. His double workday never ended before midnight.

In 1939 Callas won an academic scholarship to Johns Hopkins University in Baltimore where he received a degree in civil engineering while working as a laborer on roads and bridges during the summer months. Then he served four years in the U.S. Army Corps of Engineers in World War II and returned to Johns Hopkins to earn a master's degree in structural engineering (at the top of his class) in 1947, with the aid of the GI bill. His first full-time job in the construction field with the esteemed Whiting-Turner Contracting Company in Baltimore lasted three years, followed by nine years of work for smaller general contractors in his native Hagerstown.

In 1958, Callas and his wife of fifteen years, Betty, sold their mortgaged house and their DeSoto car to buy a used station wagon, an old pick-up truck, a typewriter, and a hand calculator in order to go into business as Callas Contractors, Inc. Betty acted as manager–receptionist–secretary and, coupled with Mike's experience as a contractor, the little firm grew steadily.

ABC CONTRACTOR

Michael Callas, a life-long director of his local Cumberland Valley ABC chapter (its president in 1968) as well as national ABC's president in 1973–1974 and thereafter a member of its board of directors until his death in 2004.

All of its supervisors and journeymen carried Carpenters Union membership cards.

Callas Goes "Merit Shop"

One evening in 1961, the Carpenters' Local Union—which was controlled by its International Brotherhood representatives in Washington, D.C.—voted to demand a forty-eight-cents-per-hour wage increase for all union carpenters working in Hagerstown and the rest of the Cumberland Valley area. The underlying objective was to help a huge unionized contractor who was engaged in a large local building project in the area to entice additional union carpenters from surrounding large city areas (Baltimore, Washington, Pittsburgh, and Philadelphia) to help complete the local job.

Callas received the union's forty-eight-cents-per-hour demand while his firm was in the middle of a series of fixed-price construction contracts. They included lower labor rates for all of his employees and he faced the same crisis that Charlie Mullan, Charlie Knott, and Ed Colwill had faced in Baltimore eleven years earlier: *Should he give in to compulsory unionism or fight against it?*

Here, described in Callas's words, is the episode that caused him "to go merit shop" in the year 1961:

At that time my company had about $2.5 million worth of work, including a church addition in Clear Spring, Maryland, a project at nearby Mercersberg Academy in Pennsylvania, and a couple of smaller jobs in the Hagerstown area—but I could see that we were going to have a major labor problem. I spent a sleepless night. The next morning I covered all of my job sites (pay day) and told everyone that we could not add the 48 cents per man-hour demanded by the Carpenters Union to the labor cost of our projects because our clients would not tolerate an addition to their fixed-price construction contracts with our company.

I asked my employees to take this information home over the weekend and discuss the serious situation with their families. I cautioned them that if they decided to stay with Callas Contractors while receiving our lower contractual labor rate in defiance of the union's edict, there could be job site "troubles." And surely they would be blackballed from getting a job anywhere in the United States that carried the banner of the Carpenters' Union.

Needless to say, that weekend I paced the floor night and day. Early on Monday morning, I rushed out on the job sites to see just how many of my employees had reported to work. The town of Clear Spring rests in a valley in the hill country of Western Maryland. As I looked down from the road above it, I saw a remarkable sight. All of my carpenters were working at the church project. Then I drove further north about 20 miles to Mercersberg, Pennsylvania. As I peered through the morning haze, there was my yellow pickup truck at the project. I covered the other job sites and our carpenters were working, including my supervisors who also were card-carrying unionists.

They all had made their decision to stay with Callas Contractors.

> **Wherever man goes to dwell, his character goes with him.**
>
> CHINESE PROVERB

> The quality of a man's life is in direct proportion to his commitment to excellence, regardless of his chosen field of endeavor.
>
> VINCE LOMBARDI
> GREEN BAY PACKERS
> COACH

If I recall correctly, we had 44 carpenters who were carrying the Carpenters' local union membership card. Of the 44, 40 of them left the union, remained with our company, and never left us. Because of that display of loyalty, the Carpenters Union gave up and seldom bothered us again.

Civic Leader

In Western Maryland's Washington County where Callas lived until his death at age eighty-three on May 31, 2004, if any worthy civic organization had a problem, the solution was "go see Mike." His community and charitable activities over the years raised thousands of dollars for worthy causes. He also served on the local governing bodies of many institutions, including the Boy Scouts, the County Board of Education, local and state Chambers of Commerce, the YMCA, Convention Visitors Bureau, United Way, Greater Hagerstown Committee, and his alma mater in Baltimore—Johns Hopkins University.

Among the hundreds of civic and charitable contributions made in his own field of work, Callas financed and helped to build Bethel Gardens, a low-income multi-unit housing development for The Homeowners Foundation of Washington County. Under the auspices of the Cumberland Valley Chapter of ABC, he spearheaded a drive for money, materials, and manpower to construct and donate a Boy Scouts Service Center for its Mason-Dixon Council. He also sponsored and helped to build the unique "Children's Village"— a miniature town center devoted to safety education for youngsters under the tutelage of the Hagerstown Fire and Police Departments.

Outstanding Contractor

Callas Contractors has completed major construction projects for clients such as Mack Trucks, Washington County Hospital, the County Court House, Hood College, Rustoleum, Comfort Suites, and Phoenix Color, Inc. On January 4, 5, and 6, 2000, a state-of-the-art Clarion Hotel and Conference Center newly built by Callas Contractors in nearby Shepherdstown, West Virginia, accommodated the president of the United States, Bill Clinton, his secretary of state, and their huge entourage. The occasion was a conference to discuss elusive peace in the Middle East with Syrian Foreign Minister Farouk al Sharaa and Israel's Prime Minister, Ehud Barak.

Merit Shop Icon

Mike Callas had a permanent commitment to ABC. He was the president of his local Cumberland Valley Chapter back in 1968—four years after it was chartered. He remained a lifelong member of that chapter's board of directors and was the longest tenured member of ABC's national board of directors. When traveling throughout the country as he spread the merit shop message, Callas enjoyed telling his audiences this little story at the conclusion of his formal presentation:

> Always remember that neither "profit" nor "security" are dirty words—but they must be earned without forfeiting freedom. America's greatest resource is not material things like wood and coal and fertile farmlands but the magic of independent people working together in a free enterprise society. We are the envy of the whole world.
>
> I know a small businessman from the old country who keeps his accounts payable in a cigar box, his accounts receivable hooked on a nail on the wall, and his day's receipts in a drawer of the cash register. "I don't see how you can run your business this way, Pop," said his son. "How do you know what your profits are?"
>
> "Son," replied the patriotic old immigrant, "When I got off the boat in New York City many years ago, I owned only the pants I was wearing. Today your sister is an art teacher, your brother is a doctor and you just passed your CPA exam. We've got a car, a nice home and a good business. Everything is paid for. So, you add them all up—*subtract the pants*—and there's your profit!"

Surpassing his own goal, during the two-year Callas presidency ABC membership almost doubled; there was a 30 percent expansion in new chapters; and an 80 percent increase of chapters-in-formation. The greatest ABC concentration was solidified along the eastern seaboard and the Gulf States. Most of the new growth came in the South and Midwest, with a new membership base also forming in the Far West.

Meanwhile the open shop's share of the nation's construction dollars had increased from 15 percent in 1950—the year of ABC's founding—to nearly 50 percent by the end of the Callas presidency in 1974. Non-union contractors were even doing major commercial renovation and alteration work in the heart of New York City, one of the most hostile union strongholds in the country. These statistics, coupled with ABC's record-breaking 90 percent membership retention rate and the signing of its first Canadian contractor member-at-large in London, Ontario, were some of the Association's outstanding achievements that were reported in the June 27, 1974, issue of *Engineering News-Record*. It featured a cover photograph of Mike Callas and an article about him entitled "Open Shop Leader Girds ABC To Soothe Growth Pains." The story began this way:

> In 1952, when the ABC national office was first staffed, the Association totaled fewer than 200 companies. That number rose to 1,000 by 1962. For the past several years its membership grew by about 25 percent annually to 5,000 in 1972. But the fastest growth occurred between 1973 and 1974, when ABC boosted its ranks by 40 percent.
>
> To keep up with this growth, ABC, under Mike Callas' leadership, launched a program to sharpen the business and construction skills of its members and their employees, and to provide its contractors with an available pool of manpower. ABC's $1.5 million annual budget has helped fund management seminars across the country to coach contractors in practically all aspects of construction management, including new building techniques. Under another part of its program, ABC has made it easier for its contractors to get financial help from lenders to take on larger projects.
>
> One of ABC's chief concerns is manpower training. Callas says that the building trades unions, despite economic pressures, have not accelerated their apprenticeship programs to meet labor demands. As a result, he says, "union workmen and their employers are standing aside while we do the work."

The thrust of ABC's apprenticeship program is to train a worker to perform several crafts. "The unionized sector of the industry emphasizes craft specialists," observes Callas, "but today construction users can't afford that specialization." He stresses that while skilled work should be done by skilled personnel, "the day has passed when a truck load of pipe must be unloaded by high paid journeymen." That's one reason why ABC members are currently training 5,000 apprentices under federally approved curricula.

We are healthy only to the extent that our lives are humane.

KURT VONNEGUT, JR.
HUMANIST

That same year Callas was named "Contractor of the Year" by *Industrial Contractor* magazine for "guiding the nation's open shop movement to its greatest growth and stature."[1] He received many other honors for his professional, civic and charitable activities over succeeding years. It all culminated on June 2, 2000—ABC's fiftieth anniversary—when he was named one of the Association's nine "Leaders of the 20th Century who significantly influenced and strengthened the merit shop construction industry throughout the United States."

Callas and ABC Confront a National Wage Freeze

On the national economic front in the days of the Callas presidency, ABC witnessed the escalating cost of doing business and the uncertainty of bureaucratic wage controls. Actions by the federal government to freeze wages and other economic benefits led the trade unions into intense bargaining on non-economic issues such as inhibiting work rules, exclusive craft jurisdiction, and other restrictive non-wage issues. Without management's ability to "sweeten" wage and fringe extras packages to sell an agreement, the unions took rigid positions related to these workplace relations. By the time the wage freeze was two weeks old, 365 trade union strikes were in progress despite an unemployment rate of 30 percent and the highest compensation of any industry.

During this crisis, President Nixon surprised his Republican constituents by appointing Peter Brennan as secretary of labor. Brennan had served as president of both the New York City and the New York State Building and Construction Trades Council. He also had been vice president of their parent New York State AFL-CIO. Reacting to this appointment, Mike Callas wrote:

Leadership is the ability to get people to do what they don't want to do and like it.

ANONYMOUS

As President of ABC, I can express nothing but amazement. Mr. Brennan signals a reversal of the policies of the Nixon Administration which have previously won widespread support from the American people. We cannot see how it is possible for Mr. Brennan to separate himself from the ideology of the building trades unions in their drive for monopoly of the industry and destruction of the open shop.[2]

Callas added that "the antiquated craft practices and outrageous wages of the trade unions coupled with their usurpation of management's traditional right to operate its business independently and their sabotage and violence against free market competition are sucking the life blood out of a once proud country."

Mr. Callas Goes to Washington

In December of 1973, Mike Callas was appointed as ABC's representative on the Office of Wage Stabilization's "Non-union Construction Advisory Committee." Other members of this committee included representatives of the Associated General Contractors of America, National Constructors Association, National Association of Minority Contractors, National Association of Home Builders, and National Association of Plumbing-Heating-Cooling Contractors. Through this committee assignment, Callas assured ABC members that, as he put it, "your Association will be represented in the federal office responsible for the government's wage policy."[3]

Callas told this Advisory Committee that the government's economic controls "did not stop rising prices, wage inequities, black markets, a growing list of material shortages and double digit inflation." He also complained that "non-union employers are restricted in their attempts to obtain equal consideration under the governmental guidelines which favor unionized labor." He concluded his remarks by urging "a return to the merit shop competition of the American free enterprise system."[4]

On numerous occasions Callas represented ABC before congressional committees and at White House economic summit conferences. These meetings brought together leaders of American government, business, organized labor, and civic groups to discuss the state of the economy and the construction industry. Mike's persistence influenced the fight to end President Nixon's wage-price controls and on April 30, 1974, Congress allowed them to expire.

Callas also gained new respect for ABC from the national business community and the conservative sector of the news media by his aggressive (albeit losing) battles with a pro-union Congress to abolish the archaic Davis-Bacon (prevailing wage) Act; to modify the overly restrictive Occupational Safety and Health Act; to reform nonsensical pension, health insurance, and apprentice training regulations; and to pass H.R. 8580 as introduced by Congressman John Anderson (R-IL). This bill would have corrected a ridiculous loophole in the Hobbs (Anti-Extortion) Act as construed by the Supreme Court when it refused to allow violence in a labor dispute to be subjected to federal prosecution.[5]

In 1973, Callas hosted a legislative conference in Washington that was attended by more than 275 ABC members. They were armed with position papers on problems such as economic stabilization, the Davis-Bacon and Hobbs Acts, and union violence at construction jobsites. These ABCers covered the capital's famous "Hill" for two days of personal meetings with their respective senators and congressmen. The conference concluded with an ABC reception attended by eight hundred elected legislators and their aides.

Trade Union Coercion and Violence Run Rampant

The most serious challenge facing Mike Callas as ABC's sixteenth national president in 1973 was the building trades assaults directed at non-union contractors everywhere that ABC members were working. On a regular basis at some construction site somewhere in the nation, pickets blocked ingress and egress at a merit shop job. The arrival of ABC member employees for work would require a police escort. Company personnel at all levels would be slapped, punched, kicked, spat upon, pelted with rocks, and even held captive inside the premises by mass pickets. There would be racial and ethnic slurs. Family members of employees received threatening anonymous phone calls at their homes. Construction site property and materials were torched and destroyed.

Neutral carriers would be forced to leave the jobsite without making pickups or deliveries. Nails and knife cuts were driven into their truck tires. Vehicle

Nothing great was ever achieved without enthusiasm.

RALPH WALDO EMERSON
PHILOSOPHER AND
WRITER

radiators were smashed by iron bars. Pickets would jump onto a neutral's car or truck, ripping off side-view mirrors and breaking windows. The drivers would be threatened with violence if they tried to make another delivery.

With attacks like these going on constantly, ABCers were seeking desperately to protect their constitutional right to work but local law enforcement officials, labor relations agencies, and the courts continued to procrastinate or ignore complaints.[6]

While government at all levels was ignoring this union terrorism, a few conservative national weekly news publications and some influential private sector construction users were exposing the truth about trade union policies and practices. Trundell Blake, director of construction for an industrial giant, the DuPont Company, was one of the first business leaders to describe the financial plight of his firm resulting from construction union excesses. As featured speaker at a national conference sponsored by the Business Roundtable, Blake announced that although DuPont had developed "a strong relationship" with many trade unions over the years, his company was changing to open shop construction as "the only feasible alternative when union building costs escalated." He said

ABC CONTRACTOR

ABC National President Mike Callas (seated fifth from left) represented ABC at a White House meeting where he recommended changes to strengthen the construction industry.

DuPont "had to weigh all of the cost factors together and choose the contractor who could build the highest quality plant at the most reasonable price."[7]

Blake also told his Fortune 100 corporate audience that ABC contractors provided "a new bench mark to measure productivity" by allowing greater flexibility in assigning work according to the abilities of the personnel involved rather than "merely showing up with a union membership card." He added that "50 percent of his company's $700 million construction program already was being done open shop."[8] And a veteran labor relations reporter, Peter Cockshaw, wrote that "Trundell Blake's bombshell was amazing when you realize that DuPont's first experience with the open shop was only two-and-a-half years ago."[9]

DuPont's decision was typical of major construction users in the 1970s. The AFL-CIO building trades share of industrial, commercial, and institutional construction in the United States at that time had shrunk over 45 percent in twenty years. Even Eric Miller, president of the unionized National Constructors Association, publicly warned his members that "major incursions of the open shop into our territory exist because it performs nearly one-third more effectively than we can." Miller concluded that "this alarming growth has turned the tide because the open shop can deliver a completed industrial plant faster, for less labor cost, and more efficiently within time and budget requirements than can a union competitor."[10]

The results of a widely-read survey conducted by *Engineering News-Record* (*ENR*) gave further credence to the fact that low output "due mainly to restrictive union practices" was a major cause of the inflationary wage spiral in the construction industry. This survey showed that poor productivity wasted from 15 percent to 40 percent of every construction dollar or $12 to $16 billion in annual construction volume. And *ENR* hopefully but futilely recommended an obvious solution to the trade union bugaboo: "Return the management functions of the [unionized sector of the] construction industry to management." The *ENR* study concluded that "even union members are fed up, experiencing increased layoffs and looking to non-union projects for work. They can cross craft lines and find these jobs more diversified, more interesting, and steadier."[11]

Victor Riesel, the nationally syndicated labor columnist who was blinded from acid thrown in his face by an underworld hoodlum, pinpointed the trade union dilemma in an article dated April 18, 1972. He called it "Labor Chiefs

Crime is contagious. If a government becomes a lawbreaker, it breeds contempt for the law; it invites every man to become a law unto himself.

Supreme Court Justice Louis D. Brandeis

507

When you are driving your car down the road of life, do you ever look in the rearview mirror?

ANONYMOUS

Worried: Non-Union Construction Work Sweeping the Nation." Here are some excerpts:

> WASHINGTON—Operating on the compelling philosophy that you can't import a low-cost highway, a dam or a skyscraper from Japan, the heavy construction companies have been paying solid gold-carat rates to condescending union craftsmen, including coverage for coffee breaks, slowdowns, featherbedding, bloody jurisdictional warfare, inept work, and walking time for a skilled hand to get around to the site of a nail and hammer it at leisure while the whole costly job waited . . .
>
> The outcome has been that, in the past two years or so, unionized contractors have lost more than $8 billion to open shop companies. This move to non-union construction now virtually is the only conversation piece when the general presidents of the 17 nationwide AFL-CIO building unions get together. Their department president, Frank Bonadio, spends much of his time traveling, trying to convince the rank-and-file around the nation that this is a new era, a new economy, and that they've lost hundreds of millions of dollars annually in wages. . . .
>
> It's been tough for such men as Bonadio and his secretary-treasurer, Robert Georgine. So serious is the non-union invasion that Georgine said recently: "Right now, this is probably the most critical time the building trades has had since their inception, since 1908."

A *Washington Post* bylined report by Haynes Johnson and Nick Katz entitled "Building Trades Fueling Inflation," echoed that same year:

> Today the construction industry is beset by grave internal illnesses that threaten to poison the entire economy. It is crippled by antiquated building codes, bloated by labor union featherbedding, torn by disputes over job jurisdiction, constricted by union hiring hall monopolies, ripped apart by violent union-versus-non-union struggles, and caught in a pervasive, inflationary web of greed.

The Building Trades Vow to "Exterminate" ABC

This economic truth, the adverse publicity about it, and the resulting loss of customers because of it infuriated the building trades unions. Even so, they continued to ignore recommendations that they become competitive by releasing their managerial control of construction labor, holding the line on wages, and streamlining ancient craft traditions. Instead, by way of retaliation, they continued to expand their labor war across the country wherever ABC members were thriving. This crime wave took many forms and the general public was becoming aroused.

Engineering News-Record wrote prophetically that union leaders needed to realize "they are in a sorry state when violence is the only thing they can think of to win back work. It is a disgrace to the construction industry and bound to force ABC to muscle up its legal defense fund."[12] And roving Editor Charles Stevenson of the *Reader's Digest* startled the magazine's millions of readers with even more menacing news: "Word has been spread among the trade unionists that this year, 1973, will bring *extermination* of the enemy."

Then Stevenson posed a question: "Why does a free society permit such storm troopers tactics?" He concluded this award-winning report on "Terrorism in the Construction Trades" by answering his own query:

> The price of [open shop] independence is unrelenting, unchecked terror and sabotage. Obviously, there is an urgent need for new federal legislation. Yet most of our politicians in Washington dare not move against the enormous power of the labor lobby and its millions of dollars in potential campaign contributions. The story of this shameful acquiescence in the face of union terror should arouse every law-abiding American.[13]

Stevenson seemed to be "preaching to the ABC choir." A resolution released by ABC's board of directors declared that "breakdowns in law and order undermine the entire fabric of the nation, discourage free competitive enterprise, set up brutal power as a standard of conduct against civilized order and progress, and bring disgrace upon hundreds of decent building trades

Nothing in all the world is more dangerous than sincere ignorance and conscientious stupidity.

REVEREND MARTIN LUTHER KING, JR.
CIVIL RIGHTS LEADER

509

Force rules the world—not opinion; but it is opinion that makes use of force.

BLAIRE PASCAL
AUTHOR-POET

unionists." Then this resolution urged all law enforcement officials from the President of the United States to the Congress and the courts on down to local sheriffs and policemen on the street beat "to do everything in their power to assure that peace is maintained at construction job sites."[14]

The ABC resolution also called on Congress to amend the aforementioned Hobbs Act so that it would outlaw job site violence and property damage by making such conduct a federal felony, with prosecutorial assistance available from the Federal Bureau of Investigation.[15] An advocate of this positive action, Senator Peter Domenici (R-CO) of the Senate's Labor Committee, told Charles Stevenson of the *Reader's Digest*:

> The fact is that it will be a rugged, uphill fight to enact any labor reform legislation so long as union chiefs are permitted to use their members' money for so-called 'campaign contributions' to buy Congressmen and dictate what bills will be passed or killed. [For example, Senator Harrison Williams (D-N.J.), a member of the Senate Labor Committee, received $150,966 from Big Labor for his 1970 election campaign]...
>
> Our struggle to bring about any legislation can succeed, but only if all Americans who rebel at tyranny will join in a campaign to bring the full weight of public opinion to bear on Congress. This means not just every contractor. It means every open shop worker, union or non-union, who lives in fear of being mauled for trying to work as his own man. It means every honest labor leader whose effort to have the unions serve their members and the public is being besmirched by the plunderers.
>
> If everyone will bring local abuses to the attention of the press and make plain to our legislators that they'd better get with it or lose their jobs come next election, their loyalty to union subsidizers will evaporate; we'll be able to work for a public investigation and a resulting legislative package that will at last give every American, union and non-union, an opportunity to rejoice.[16]

This patriotic plea by Senator Dominici fell on deaf ears. Union political power and economic muscle easily stifled effective congressional and executive branch response to the national construction crisis. Even liberal Senator Russell Long (D-LA) admitted publicly that his Senate Labor Committee "was oriented toward organized labor"—and the judicial arm of government was no more receptive.[17]

Callas Pledges End to Union Terrorism

ABCers became more and more impatient and frustrated. They were caught in a widening web of union violence as they fought each local uprising on a job-site-by-job-site basis in city after city, county after county, state after state, week in-week out. It was becoming unbearable and they wanted some kind of immediate national action.

In February of 1973, Mike Callas wrote all of the Association's members this historic "President's Letter":

> The steady and challenging growth of the merit shop movement throughout the country has not come without major problems. The mere mention that a construction user is planning to invite merit shop contractors to bid a project starts a chain reaction of personal threats and violence as well as property damage on the constructions sites. But arrests and convictions of those responsible for this lawlessness have been few and far between—with government support leaving a lot to be desired.
>
> This virtually unchecked coercion and sabotage on our projects led me to commission a professional security study and analysis of the grave situation. I can now report to you that a representative sampling of open shoppers doing business in the eastern half of our nation indicates that within the past three years about *80 percent* of them have been threatened with labor union violence and *60 percent* actually have been victimized in varying degrees. Their average value in property damages inflicted is *$80,000*.
>
> It has become obvious that these illegal union activities threaten the businesses and very livelihoods of our members, their families, their employees and their customers, and are part of a pattern that is spreading nationwide. If we wait any longer and allow this brutality

The combination of economic and political power in the same hands is a sure recipe for tyranny.

MILTON AND ROSE FRIEDMAN IN *FREE TO CHOOSE*

There are two ways of meeting adversity: You alter the crisis or you alter yourself to meet it.

PHYLLIS BOTTOME
WRITER

to proceed without attempting coordinated legal sanctions, the situation could become a national crisis in a relatively short period of time.

Callas concluded this letter to all ABCers with a bold promise:

To this end, your National ABC Legal Rights and Strategy Committee has met with our general counsel, Samuel Cook, and created a

HAGERSTOWN HERALD MAIL

Michael Callas, Mr. Merit Shop. "Mike loved 'his people.' He cared for and about them. They were in so many ways his responsibility, his family, his reason for winning that bid, his reason for their freedom of association." –Dr. Stuart Dunnan, Headmaster of St. James School near Hagerstown, Maryland.

plan of action. Our goal is to neutralize nationwide union assaults on the jobsites of all ABC members and stop the intimidation of our employees, their families, and their construction users.

We are not yet at liberty to disclose the details of this plan to protect ourselves from these lawless acts being carried out by union goon squads. But we can assure you that through our multi-pronged approach—carefully organized, ably directed, and well financed—every effort will be made to punish all persons and labor organizations that are responsible for these dastardly deeds across America.

I hereby pledge to you that all of our merit shop construction sites throughout the country will return to the peace and harmony expected in a free enterprise society dedicated to law and order!

ABC's heroic leader was ready, willing, and able to counter-attack Big Labor's national conspiracy of terrorism against freedom in the merit shop workplace.

Liberty, when it begins to take root, is a plant of rapid growth.

GEORGE WASHINGTON
1ST PRESIDENNT

CHAPTER 42

PREPARING THE LABOR BOARD'S BIGGEST CASE

AS ABC'S GENERAL COUNSEL, I had been given a challenging assignment by Mike Callas. It did not come as a surprise. He knew I had reviewed all of the legal options and that I was planning a novel and risky course of action on a nationwide basis.

With a prayer and two fingers crossed for good luck, I advised Mike that I was "prepared to pull out all the stops." A massive unfair labor practice charge would be filed. It would request the National Labor Relations Board to restrain the collusive coercion and violence of the entire building trades hierarchy that was plaguing the merit shop throughout much of the United States. The evidence was available; my legal theories were sound; the union-inflation-racked times were ideal; the political climate had become more favorable. And the judicial stage was set.

In facing this never-ending building trades evil, one of the first actions I had taken upon my appointment as ABC's general counsel in 1970 was drafting a Construction Job Site Security Manual for publication and distribution to all ABC chapters and their members. It began by urging all contractors to contact their chapter's executive director for defensive preparation *before* any labor union crisis arose. It also reminded the contractors of their right to a free consultation with the chapter's local labor attorney or my office to review the situation and advise them what to do.

The Manual further noted that ABC National maintained a Legal Rights and Strategy Committee (chaired by ABC's First Vice-President Philip Abrams) to assist ABCers and their local counsel (with advice and monetary

The greatest undeveloped territory in the world lies under your hat.

ANONYMOUS

515

I kept six honest
serving men,
They taught me
all I knew;
The names are
What and Why
And When and
How and Where
and Who.

RUDYARD KIPLING
BRITISH NOVELIST-POET

support) in preparing their attack on illegal union activities that occurred in precedent-setting cases affecting the entire merit shop movement.

A main thrust of my Security Manual was a detailed checklist of how contractors should defend against and respond to these illegal union activities that occurred on their job sites. First, they were told to obtain answers to these six questions: *who, what, why, when, how, where, and who?* A helpful checklist included:

Is your project well-patrolled and well-lighted at night? Is it completely fenced? Do you have security guards? Would canine protection be advisable? Can alarm devices be used? Are trailers, vehicles, equipment and materials securely locked at night? Are fire extinguishers on the site? Can telephone lines be protected? Are separate entrance gates available and reserved for "neutral" firms and their personnel? Can you establish good relations with the local police?

I also stressed the importance of recording these facts in a detailed daily log at each jobsite:

Your project superintendent should maintain an accurate record as to the time, date and substance of every labor-related incident such as the appearance of pickets, what they said, exactly who said it, and what they did. Get written and signed statements from witnesses and take photos of the picket signs and their location. A videotape recorder and/or movie camera should be ready for use if mass picketing, physical violence or property destruction erupts (but not for "surveillance" of any peaceful union activities). Also notify your ABC chapter and the local police at once. All of these facts may become critical evidence for ABC legal action.

I emphasized that as soon as any violence or sabotage was threatened or actually occurred, the targeted contractor should immediately send a telegram to both the local union involved and its affiliated international organization. This parent union would be advised that it should use all necessary means at its disposal to prevent the continuation of the specified illegal activities by its local union. The international also was warned that it would be held *jointly responsible* for any injury to persons or damages to property due to the activities of its local union representatives and members. (That notice always received their undivided attention.)

Sound advice on job-site safety planning beforehand was added by Martin Herman, president of the Baltimore-based and nationally operated Special Response Corporation. He frequently assisted my clients in confronting Big Labor's terrorism and told them:

> Advance planning before a critical need arises is the key to security. You must anticipate the unexpected. Preventive protection includes an audit and assessment of overall safety measures and identification of points of vulnerability. If workplace trouble erupts, we have well-equipped and well-trained protection specialists with law enforcement or military experience who are available anywhere in the country on less than 24 hours notice.[1]

A separate "Anti-Intimidation Manual" also was drafted and distributed to all ABC members. Its preamble began this way:

> Merit shop contractors must respond vigorously to all trade union threats and pressure tactics or else there is a real danger that all of our competitive gains of the past could be lost. The purpose of this Manual is to suggest a variety of measures for *member contractors, chapter attorneys and chapter executive directors* to use in countering union schemes to destroy competition.
>
> Because the building trades attack is multi-faceted, ABC believes that there is no single preferred response which should be expected to prevent a construction owner from succumbing to union coercion and violence. Instead, merit shoppers must respond aggressively by adopting an equally broad-based counter-attack which combines economic, public relations, political and other legally permissible strategies.

God promises us a safe landing, not a calm passage.

A SIGN OUTSIDE ST. PAUL'S BY THE SEA OCEAN CITY, MARYLAND

Even if you're on
the right track,
you'll get run over
if you just sit
there.

WILL ROGERS
HUMORIST-WRITER

ABC's Legal Defense Fund

Returning now to my preparation for our legal attack on the entire building trades union hierarchy, there was an immediate problem: how to pay the mounting legal fees and expenses that were being incurred by my law firm and local chapter counsel throughout the United States in preparing to litigate the huge case. All of the local regional ABC lawyers involved were dedicated to the entrepreneurial cause; they worked with me as a nationally coordinated team; and they frequently kept their remuneration below standard client rates. Some of us donated ("pro bono") a substantial amount of our professional time. Even so, the combined billable legal services for the ABC case was reaching six figures.

To meet this heavy expense, First Vice President Phil Abrams created and supervised a Merit Shop Legal Defense Fund. The Fund's broad purposes were set forth in its articles of incorporation, as follows:

1. To operate exclusively for charitable, scientific, literary and educational purposes within the meaning of Section 501(c)(3) of the Internal Revenue Code and regulations issued thereafter.

2. To render legal aid and financial assistance gratuitously for the benefit of workers and employers who are suffering legal injustice as a result of violence and destruction of property and to assist such workers and employers in protecting rights guaranteed to them under the laws and Constitution of the United States.

3. To prepare educational materials dealing with the problems of violence and destruction of property and the resulting effects upon the civil rights of minority groups and individual employees and employers.

4. To undertake studies and research and to collect, compile and publish full and fair presentations of facts, information and statistics concerning the problem of violence and destruction of property and the effects of such conduct upon the workplace, plus the social and political freedoms of employees and employers as well as its overall effect on the national safety and welfare.

5. To seek out and promote employment opportunities for workers deprived of their jobs or otherwise damaged as a result of union violence and destruction of property.[2]

The initial response from two fund solicitation pledge letters sent to all ABC members by Phil Abrams brought contributions of $190,000. Non-union construction giants like Brown & Root, BE&K, and Daniel Construction Company donated generously, as did hundreds of smaller ABC members. Abrams called this "a truly remarkable expression of desire by contractors to stop illegal union acts of terrorism across the nation and a willingness to put their money behind their beliefs."[3]

> **I don't want to know what the law is. I want to know who the judge is.**
>
> ROY M. COHN, ESQ.
> TRIAL LAWYER

The Labor Board's Critical Political Climate

As to my basic strategy in our case, it was common knowledge in legal circles that the General Counsel of the National Labor Relations Board (hereafter "Labor Board" or "Board"), based in Washington, D.C., wielded tremendous power. He was charged with enforcement of the national labor policy governing America's private sector work life as expressed in the Taft-Hartley Act.

In performing this vital function, the General Counsel commanded a sizable staff of lawyers both at his headquarters in the national capital and in thirty-one regional offices located throughout the United States. His exclusive and final responsibility was to determine when and when not to "indict" either a union or an employer for its *unfair labor practices*. In other words, the general counsel had, and still has, sole discretion in determining whether or not to prosecute unfair labor practice charges for activity in violation of the Taft-Hartley Act. There is no appeal to the courts from his rulings.

The good news was that my prayer for a miracle to overcome Big Labor's political privileges and legal immunities[4] seemed to be answered when Republican President Richard Nixon appointed a new General Counsel to the Labor Board in 1971. His name was Peter Nash and he had a reputation for a balanced interpretation of labor law. His work experience, political background, and published actions at the Labor Board bore no resemblance to the union-slanted ideology of his predecessor in that job for eight years, namely leftist Arnold Ordman—an appointee by Democratic President Lyndon Johnson.

More good news involved the philosophical composition of the five-person Labor Board itself before whom General Counsel Nash would prosecute our case. The interpretation of labor relations law by these presidential appointees (like the Board's general counsel) traditionally changed with the political winds.

Don't kindle a fire you can't put out.

ANONYMOUS

That meant two different sets of legal ground rules evolved under the Taft-Hartley Act over a period of time, depending on which political party controlled the White House and appointed the Board members.

Professor Herbert Northrup of the University of Pennsylvania's Wharton School summarized the political truth this way: "Policies of the Labor Board have always varied from one administration to another as each president has appointed persons conforming to his philosophy for the administration of the National Labor Relations [Taft-Hartley] Act."[5] And a federal court admitted publicly what every practitioner in the labor relations field already knew: "It is a fact of Labor Board lore that certain substantive provisions of the National Labor Relations Act invariably fluctuate with the changing composition of the Board."[6] To state it bluntly, under this tradition, the president of the United States always appoints a three-to-two Board majority favoring his own party's labor-management ideology: A Democrat favors unions and unionized workers. A Republican leans toward management and its non-union employees.

It so happened that luck and/or prayer was on our side again. A majority of the Labor Board members who might ultimately rule on our unfair labor prac-

FROM THE AUTHOR'S PERSONAL COLLECTION

The author (left) and Peter Nash, general counsel to the National Labor Relations Board, at a Federal Bar Association labor relations conference in 1972 in Washington, D.C.

tice charge (Chairman Edward Miller, Ralph Kennedy, and Howard Jenkins) were Republicans while the minority members (John Fanning and John "Doe" Penello) were Democrats. This favorable news of a more "balanced" judicial alignment for our case was confirmed by Nello L. Teer, Jr., president of the Associated General Contractors, in an interview by the *Engineering News-Record*:

> Easing the role of the non-union contractor has been a changing government posture. The Labor Board has shown a decided improvement recently in reestablishing a fair balance between labor and management. For many years, under Democratic administrations, the Board was so dominated by pro-labor and anti-management appointees that open shop contractors were discriminated against, which is not the condition today.[7]

Although fortunate timing placed control of both the Labor Board and its General Counsel located in Washington, D.C., in the hands of government officials whom it appeared were not union-biased, there also was bad news for ABC. The "grunt work" investigation of the tremendous body of evidence that we intended to present in support of our unfair labor practice charge would be culled and prepared for trial by long-service lower-level bureaucrats located in the agency's regional offices throughout the country. Most of them were dedicated liberals who had been sanctified in their jobs by a combination of civil service status and their membership in government labor unions that protected their "permanent" job security.

Working for the federal government was like going to one's eternal rest. Long on seniority and short on impartiality, these underlings were imbued with the Labor Board's historic support of the socialistic goals and policies of the labor union movement dating back to the days of two Marxists—Board Member Edwin Smith and Personnel Director Nathan Witt—in the 1930s.[8] The problem for us was that these subordinates could faithfully carry forward the union "torch" because they worked in a secluded bureaucratic maze within the Board's regional offices, hidden from the scrutiny of less prejudiced superiors based in Washington, D.C. That meant that relevant evidence of union foul play could be omitted or distorted against our case without the knowledge of

Depend not on fortune but on conduct.

PUBLILIUS SYRUS
ROMAN HISTORIAN

521

the new Republican General Counsel and the new Republican members of the Labor Board.

How to Process an "ULP" Charge

The legal ground rules—and the obvious importance of the roles of the liberal regional office staffers described above—in processing a typical unfair labor practice ("ULP") before the Labor Board against a labor organization can be summarized as follows:

1. A ULP charge is filed by the attorney of the aggrieved employer or employee [or union] at the regional office of the Labor Board in the locality in which the ULP took place.

2. The regional office's investigation of the evidence "pro and con" as to the validity of the ULP charge is carried out by one of the aforementioned imbedded staffers. If, after review of the staffer's summary of the evidence and legal arguments submitted by the parties in the case, the regional director and the regional attorney are satisfied that a ULP has in fact occurred, *a complaint will be issued.*

3. At this point, the regional office discards its investigatory mode and becomes the prosecutor of the ULP charge. A formal hearing on the complaint is held by an administrative law judge (formerly called a trial examiner), and a regional attorney from the office of the Board's General Counsel represents the charging party who filed the ULP charge. (The charging party's personal attorney can "assist" to a limited degree.) The judge submits a report of his/her findings and recommended decision to the Labor Board in Washington, D.C.

4. If there is no timely appeal by either party, the recommended decision of the administrative law judge becomes final.

5. If there is an appeal, the Labor Board in Washington will review the case and either affirm, overrule, or modify the administrative law judge's recommendation.

6. The Labor Board may order a "guilty" union or employer "to cease and desist from such unfair labor practice and take such affirmative action as will effectuate the policies of the Act."

7. The Labor Board's order is not self-enforcing, however. If the guilty party declines to obey it, the order must be reviewed, approved, and enforced by an appropriate federal court.

Frequently the Labor Board was reluctant to exercise its mandatory duty to petition a federal court for a Section 10(l) temporary restraining order against the allegedly illegal acts of a union pending final disposition of the unfair labor practice case. Litigation could thus drag on while substantial and irreparable injury to employees and their employer continued to occur. My objective was to make certain that General Counsel Peter Nash was aware of the global magnitude and criticality of our case and the need for *immediate* injunctive relief from its inception. I also wanted to ensure that Nash understood the legal theories behind the extraordinary unfair labor practice charge that we were submitting to him.

Legal Basis of ABC's "ULP" Charge

Our litigation relied on an important 1947 Taft-Hartley Act amendment to the Wagner Act of 1935 (also called the "National Labor Relations Act"). Under it, for the first time, Congress subjected labor organizations (like employers under the original Wagner Act) to certain unfair labor practices (ULPs).[9] In doing so, this newly elected and Republican-controlled legislative body expressed its concern over union bullying and terrorism directed against *non-union employees and their employers* that had increased after passage of the Wagner Act:

> For the last 12 years, as a result of labor laws ill conceived and disastrously executed, the American workingman has been deprived of his dignity as an individual. He has been cajoled, coerced, intimidated, and on many occasions beaten up, in the name of the splendid aims set forth in [the "union rights" section] of the National Labor Relations Act. The employer's plight has likewise not been happy. He has had to stand helplessly by while employees desiring to enter his property to work have been obstructed by violence, mass picketing and general rowdyism.[10]

Congress responded to this flagrant discrimination by amending Section 7 of the Wagner Act so that it balanced every employee's existing right to *join* a

Fairness is what justice really is.

SUPREME COURT
JUSTICE POTTER
STEWART

The execution of the laws is just as important as the making of them.

THOMAS JEFFERSON
3RD PRESIDENT

labor union with a newly expressed right for employees to *refrain* from joining or assisting a union. By way of reinforcing this new policy, the legislators added *Section 8(b)(1)(A)*. It created an unfair labor practice for any labor organization "to restrain or coerce employees in the exercise of the [above stated] rights guaranteed in Section 7."

The U.S. Supreme Court reviewed the legislative history of this Section 8(b)(1)(A) and called it a grant of power in the Labor Board to protect individual workers from union organizational tactics involving "violence, intimidation and reprisals or threats thereof."[11] Coercive union activity, threats of bodily harm or actual bodily harm inflicted by unions on non-union employees to try to make them "go union" thus constituted a new unfair labor practice.

Stated another way, this new Section 8(b)(1)A meant that any type of labor union intimidation to force membership in its ranks upon the employees of a non-unionized employer became illegal activity that the Labor Board's General Counsel—Peter Nash—was required to prosecute and prevent its reoccurrence.

That was the basis for our litigation.

Of further legal assistance in our case, we presumed, was Section 2(13) of the amendatory Taft-Hartley Act. As discussed previously, this provision of the law confirmed the long-settled common law of agency that "in determining whether any person is acting as an 'agent' of another person so as to make such other person responsible for his acts, the question of whether the specific acts performed were actually authorized or subsequently ratified shall *not* be controlling." And the word "person" in this Section 2(13) was construed to include a "labor organization."[12]

Over the years a series of conservative Labor Board and federal court decisions had developed to the effect that Section 8(b)(1)(A) would be violated under the broad Section 2(13) agency test by circumstances such as: (1) coercive acts of union agents performed in furtherance of union objectives even though the illegal acts may *not* have been specifically authorized or ratified and may even have been expressly forbidden;[13] (2) a union's mass picketing and other mob action;[14] or (3) a union's "passivity that amounts to silent approbation" of flagrant misconduct by rank-and-file union members which the union had an affirmative obligation to disavow.[15]

Violent union conduct also was held illegal under Section 8(b)(1)(A) when directed towards *non* rank-and-file employees (such as their company's supervisors and executives) or the *general public* (including police officers) in the presence of open shop (non-union) employees or under circumstances where they were likely to hear about it.[16] A union could even be held responsible for coercive "organizational" activities by *unidentified persons* on the union's behalf when it took no action to control, repudiate or disavow such illegal conduct.[17]

The Labor Board and some federal courts (in this conservative mode) also had ruled that the destruction of a non-union employer's *property* by a union could constitute a Section 8(b)(1)(A) unfair labor practice against that company's non-union employees. Such damage "was calculated to constitute a threat to them that they would have to risk physical violence if they tried to go to work."[18] This sabotage also illegally "threatened their jobs by creating a general atmosphere of fear and violence."[19] And "these destructive acts need not be done in the actual presence of employees since they ultimately would learn of them."[20]

> **Justice, though due to the accused, is due to the accuser, too.**
>
> Supreme Court Justice Benjamin Cardozo

From the author's personal collection

The author (left), as chairman of the D.C. Labor Bar Association, introduces the new chairperson of the National Labor Relations Board—Betty Murphy (appointed by President Gerald Ford)—as guest speaker, and George Meany, president of the AFL-CIO.

Lastly, where there was a continuing pattern of union terrorism such as occurred in areas where ABC employers were doing business regularly (rather than a few isolated or sporadic minor incidents), *circumstantial evidence* was held to be sufficient proof upon which to impute responsibility for the illegal conduct to the labor organization involved. This was particularly true where a trade union's presence on the scene was evident but "the carefully planned suddenness and brutality of the confrontation precluded any chance of identification of individuals." As the Labor Board caustically added in the *Grundy Mining Company* case: "Members of mobs do not normally call for silence and announce their names before committing violent and disorderly acts."[21]

We presumed that General Counsel Peter Nash and the comparatively conservative Republican Labor Board majority would respect and apply these cases as precedent for their interpretation of the Taft-Hartley labor law under the irrefutable evidence we were about to present to them.

ABC Sues the Entire Building Trades Hierarchy

While our contemplated unfair labor practice charge would be processed under the standard legal guidelines summarized above, it differed from typical Labor Board charges in both its judicatory and geographical scope. My strategy was to link the building and construction trades union hierarchy from its headquarters in Washington, D.C., to its seventeen internationals (in the U.S.A. and Canada) to their thousands of affiliated regional councils and local unions in the hinterlands throughout the United States *in one massive civil conspiracy and joint venture against ABC employees and their employers*. We would contend that such violent collusive activity violated Section 8(b)(1)(A) on "union coercion" and Section 2(13) on "union agency" as provided in the Taft-Hartley Act. (A "conspiracy" is simply an unlawful agreement between two or more persons. It may be an agreement to accomplish an unlawful purpose or an agreement to accomplish a lawful purpose by an unlawful means.)

The line of authority in the organizational chart of the AFL-CIO trade union hierarchy that ABC contended was jointly responsible for the illegal activities looked like this:

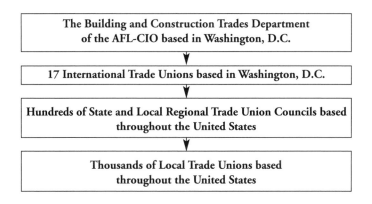

I would also contend that the gravity of the nationwide terrorism merited both speedy injunctive relief and punitive action by the Labor Board under Sections 10(e), (j), and (l) "to effectuate the orderly and peaceful labor policies of the Act" whenever and wherever there was trade union proclivity towards coercion and violence against the employees of ABC member firms anywhere in the United States.

Evidence and Law Linking BCTD to Its Affiliated Unions

Our legal brief would provide the Labor Board with substantial evidence to prove our hierarchical unfair labor practice charge at the senior level of union responsibility. The starting point would be introduction into the case of the Constitution of the "parent" AFL-CIO's Building & Construction Trades Department (hereinafter sometimes "Trades Department") listed at the top of the above-noted trade union organizational chart. It contained these relevant "agency" provisions:

> Art. I, Sec. 2: This organization shall be composed of national and international building and construction trades unions...

> Art. II: The object and principles of this body are: (1) To coordinate and harmonize the activities, functions and interests of the affiliated national and international unions in the building and construction trades industry; (2) To promote the growth and development of all building and construction trades unions and to foster and develop the

If it has webbed feet, feathers, and quacks, it must be a duck.

ANONYMOUS

organization of building and construction tradesmen on traditional trade or craft lines . . .

(7) To encourage the formation or establishment of local building and construction trades councils in order to aid and assist in the organization and development and to coordinate the activities of local building and construction unions; and (8) *To aid and assist all of these affiliated national or international unions in securing improved wages, hours and working conditions through the process of collective bargaining.* [emphasis added]

Article 3, Section 1 of this Constitution confirmed that "the national convention shall be the supreme governing body of the Building and Construction Trades Department." And, as has been mentioned, some of the most devastating evidence in support of our case related to policy decisions and actions adopted at its national conventions held in 1967 and 1971.[22]

The 1967 convention began, for instance, with ABC being described in hostile and inflammatory terms by trade union chieftains from Maryland, Washington, D.C., New York, Pennsylvania, New Jersey, Delaware, Ohio, Michigan, Florida, and Tennessee, where ABC chapters and contractor members were making major advances. Words used included a "union-busting outfit," an "evil force," a "major menace to the very existence of our local building trades unions," and "determined to destroy the Building Trades Department and its affiliated International Unions."

Then, by a unanimously adopted resolution, the 1967 convention delegates, representing all seventeen international craft unions and their state, regional and local unions throughout the United States, were urged to appoint a "special committee." It would "formulate an affiliated organizing campaign to combat ABC" and submit it to "the Executive Committee of the Building Trades Department" because "ABC is a challenge to our livelihood which must be met head on."

Four years later, during floor debate at the 1971 national convention of this same national Building Trades Department, the Baltimore Building Trades Council delegates proposed another conspiratorial resolution. It began by calling ABC a "viciously anti-labor association of open shop contractors dedicated to the destruction of building trades unions as effective bargaining agencies." Then it referred to the similar resolution adopted at the 1967 Department convention and condemned ABC's tremendous growth. Finally, the resolution called on the Trades Department and all of its affiliated International Unions "to initiate an immediate and effective program to combat the ABC," including financing the initiative through an increase in per capita membership dues. This nationwide action, the convention delegates claimed, "would defend the building trades unions from ABC's union-busting attacks while reclaiming the historic jurisdictions which have been lost to the ABC by local trade unions in many areas."

The 1971 resolution was adopted unanimously by the national convention and referred to the central office of the Building Trades Department in Washington, D.C. There its Committee on Organizations confirmed that "the affiliated International Unions fully support the need of affiliation with their local building trades councils by their respective local union members; that such affiliation should be on a full membership basis in the local council's jurisdiction; and that the affiliates should cooperate on an organizational basis to strengthen their membership in every building trades council jurisdiction and otherwise support and cooperate with their local building trades council."[23]

Many officials (i.e., statutory "agents") of the international trade unions, including Peter Fosco, president of the Operating Engineers, William Sidell, president of the Carpenters, vice president Flynn of the Electrical Workers, and Martin Ward, president of the Plumbers & Pipefitters, also instructed their own local unions' members that there was an "all-out war against the evil ABC."

A Six Months Limitation on Evidence

We believed this powerful background evidence of the conspiratorial 1967 and 1971 convention resolutions of the Building Trades Department (called "supreme governing body" of the trade union movement) would be admissible in the presentation of our unfair labor practice charge that would be filed two years later, in 1973. As a precedent for offering these undeniable facts, we relied on the U.S. Supreme Court's ruling that "critical events occurring prior to the Taft-Hartley Act's Section 10(b) six months limitation on charges to be filed may be utilized to shed light on the true character of matters occurring within that time limitations period."[24]

> **If you can't answer a man's argument, all is not lost; you can still call him vile names.**
>
> ELBERT HUBBARD
> WRITER

Law never made men a whit more just.

HENRY DAVID THOREAU
PHILOSPHER-POET

On the other hand, strict compliance with this unusually short statutory time allowance obviously was critical in producing all of our actual Section 8(b)(1)(A) evidence of coercion and violence. We urged ABC members who had been harmed within that period by vicious trade union activities to immediately fill out incident reports based on ABC's Job Site Security Manual.

Three of my most capable and dedicated law partners at Venable, Baetjer and Howard—Joseph Kaplan, Thomas Kenney, and Peter Lareau—plus several of our best legal assistants—teamed up with a senior ABC staff member, Vice President Woodrow Moats. They led the gigantic, time-pressured, fact-finding mission wherever illegal union activities had occurred within the preceding six-month period. The team traveled from chapter to chapter throughout the eastern and midwestern half of the nation, preparing a huge portfolio of exhibits for our case. Many local chapter attorneys assisted too.

This evidence that we would present to the Labor Board with our unfair labor practice charge consisted more specifically of personal interviews and supporting affidavits of witnesses, records of inflammatory speeches and incidents of coercion that were frequently acquiesced in by union officials at all levels of their labor hierarchy. We would also offer the Board court records, photographs of rioting union mobs, sabotage and arson, police and medical reports, newspaper clippings, and any other physical or documentary evidence that helped to prove the national pattern of conspiratorial terrorism by the building trades movement.

The assignment was especially difficult for our attorneys. Many actual incidents were not reported due to witnesses' fear of union reprisals or the documentary records were lost or there was not sufficient time (within the six-month statutory deadline) to make a thorough investigation of all the facts involved.

Our legal team also assisted me in preparing a brief to support this evidence.[25]

A "Culpable" Building Trades Department

Although the parent Building Trades Department in Washington, D.C., never before had been charged with a Section 8(b)(1)(A) unfair labor practice, the evidence we developed proved that it was a "bona fide labor organization" within the meaning of Section 2(5) of the Taft-Hartley Act. Operating under the authority of Article II (8) of the Trades Department's

Constitution (quoted before), the Department's Administrative Committee bargained collectively on a regular basis with unionized employer members of the Associated General Contractors and the National Constructors Association. Issues negotiated included "problems" relating to the wages and working conditions of AFL-CIO building tradesmen. That activity met the Section 2(5) test of a bona fide labor union.

There also was a close analogy between the agency oversight authority of the Trades Department and its regional councils of craft unions located geographically across the nation. Like the Trades Department, these statewide, area-wide, or municipal councils were composed of delegates elected by their affiliated local unions. (See the before-cited building trades organizational chart.) And in *Smith Plumbing Company*, the Labor Board held that "a trade council is [not only] a labor organization under Section 2(5) of the Act" but also, like the Trades Department, is "an organization through which the affiliated crafts function as a unit."[26]

Coupling International Unions with Local Union Terrorism

Having established that the Trades Department was the ringleader of the conspiracy, we also found legal authority for the following points of agency law which would hold the international building trades unions liable (under the above-cited Section 2(13) of the Act) for misdeeds of their local councils and unions in ABC's hierarchical unfair labor practice charge:

1. An international union's constitution could be sufficient evidence to establish control over its local unions and show that they were "alter egos" rather than autonomous bodies.[27]

2. Responsibility of an international union could be predicated on the theory that the local union which actually committed the violence was the agent of the international.[28]

3. International union responsibility was proven if an agent of the international, operating generally within the scope of his assigned authority, participated or acquiesced in local union acts of violence.[29]

4. An international union could be held liable for violent acts committed by its local unions and their members "if the international

> O judge not a law book by its cover. Or else you'll for sure come to grief, For the lengthiest things, you'll discover, Are contained in what's known as a "Brief."
>
> J.P.C. 116
> JUST. 640

No individual raindrop ever considers itself responsible for the flood.

Anonymous

knew that such illegal activities occurred and took no action under circumstances as would make it the duty of the international to repudiate the lawless acts."[30]

5. An international union could be held responsible for forbidden acts of its locals if the misdeeds were committed (as in our case) in the general course of procuring compliance with a stated objective of the international.[31]

We discovered further legal authority for the proposition that different international or local unions that pursue a mutual objective were engaging in a "joint venture that is closely akin to the doctrine of civil conspiracy." Therefore each of such international unions could be held responsible for the illegal collusive activity of the other unions because they were acting as each other's agents.[32] And it was well settled under general agency law that a "civil conspiracy" exists when (1) the evidence shows "a course of conduct from which a tacit agreement to act in concert may be implied," and (2) that the co-conspirators are responsible for the illegal acts of their fellow conspirators even if the ultimate objective of the conspiracy is lawful.[33]

In support of this case law, we prepared evidence to show that high-ranked officials of the Building Trades Department and its building trades internationals based in Washington, D.C., traveled around the country to incite their affiliated trades councils and local union members against "the open shop menace" wherever ABC members were active. These dramatic visits frequently were followed by vandalism and violence on the jobsites of ABC members while neighboring unionized construction projects remain unharmed.

It was also noteworthy that AFL-CIO President George Meany and Building Trades Department President Frank Bonadio were featured speakers at a "get ABC" rally in Philadelphia at about the time of the violent local building trades battle against Leon Altemose at Valley Forge in 1972.[34] And an officer of the International Association of Operating Engineers showed up at that same infamous rally and ranted against ABC in militant terms. He called Altemose "a pimp for ABC" whom the building trades would make "economically extinct."[35]

Parental Union Duty to Remedy Local Violence

Based on this irrefutable evidence, we would contend that the coercion, brutality, and sabotage against ABC by building trades councils and/or their affiliated local unions imposed upon the parent Building Trades Department and all of its international trade union affiliates an immediate and affirmative duty to take *remedial action*. Authority was vested in them by their interlocked constitutions to ensure that this nationwide breach of "the public health, safety and interest"—in defiance of the Taft-Hartley Act's preamble mandate of the peaceful resolution of labor disputes—ceased at once.

Technically known as "acquiescence," "ratification," or "condonation," this doctrine of principal-agent responsibility is premised on the legal theory that one affiliated entity cannot benefit willingly and knowingly from the illegal acts of another affiliated entity and still avoid responsibility for those acts which it did not repudiate. Put another way, we would contend that a legal and binding "principal-agent relationship" as well as a "joint venture and conspiracy" existed throughout the entire trade union hierarchy as one united entity because it accepted, condoned, and benefited from coercion and violence used to destroy the ABC open shop movement.

We would tell the Labor Board that this web of intimidation and terrorism was masterminded and coordinated at the highest departmental and international trade union levels, with its root authority in the convention resolutions of their "supreme governing body"—the Building Trades Department. There was additional proof that information about successful non-union contractors seemed to be collected at a national center and passed from union to union in different localities. As soon as a new ABC Chapter formed, union sabotage and violence erupted.

Top union hierarchy executives made no effort to disavow or repudiate any of this regional or local union wrongdoing. Nor did they make any attempt to take affirmative action to preclude the recurrence of such outrageous conduct through public or even private rebuke of local officers and members who committed the foul deals. And they failed to issue any disciplinary reprimands or fines on individual agents or to impose trusteeships on the offending local unions.

My dear General
McClellan: If you
don't want to use
the Army, I should
like to borrow it
for a while.

ABRAHAM LINCOLN
16TH PRESIDENT

We would remind the Labor Board of the historic and relevant Texas Appellate Court case that upheld Brown & Root's lawsuit in 1952 that the entire AFL building trades hierarchy acted in what amounted to an unlawful civil conspiracy:

> The affiliates of these local unions—the Trades Councils of those respective areas, the State Federation of Labor, the Internationals, and the AF of L—were carrying on a fight against B&R to force it to enter into [illegal] closed shop contracts and agreements. In the furtherance of this common purpose and design, the various affiliates furnished encouragement and aid to the locals, and the acts done by the one in an effort to accomplish a common purpose became the acts of all.[36]

Big Labor Deserves Severe Punishment

We would also remind the Labor Board of the U.S. Supreme Court's view that congressional emphasis on legislating in the sensitive labor relations arena had changed over the years. No longer was there need for protection of a young and weak labor movement. Instead, we contended, there was a modern-day statutory duty on the Board to impose increasing responsibility on the mature and powerful building trades labor organizations for the peaceful resolution of labor disputes. In *United Construction Workers v. Laburnum Construction Corporation*, construing the Taft-Hartley Act, the Supreme Court explained:

> The 1947 [Taft-Hartley] Act has increased, rather than decreased the legal responsibilities of labor organizations. That Act ... sought primarily to empower a federal regulatory body [i.e., the Labor Board], through administrative procedure, to forestall unfair labor practices by anyone in circumstances affecting interstate commerce. The fact that it prescribed new preventive procedure against unfair labor practices on the part of *labor organizations* was an additional recognition of congressional disapproval of such practices. Such an express recognition is consistent with an increased insistence upon the liability of such organizations for tortious conduct and inconsistent with their immunization from liability for damages caused by their tortious practices.[37]

Finally, we would summarize and conclude our legal brief that accompanied ABC's massive unfair labor charge this way:

> This master charge does not pretend to be an exhaustive summary of all that has happened. Practical problems of expense and the six months statute of limitations have restricted our investigative effort. Evidence of coercion by violence and property destruction—like the proverbial iceberg—lies largely below the surface. However, when one considers the severe time and discovery restrictions in our investigative effort, the volume and level of restraint and coercion by the violent activity that we have uncovered is shocking.
>
> A large number of these disorders must be characterized as major civil disturbances or riots. They involve plain and simple mob violence, criminal in nature, carried out in an organized manner in broad daylight by hundreds of men, often under the noses of police who are outmanned or otherwise unable or unwilling to act. Any one of these kinds of disorders, because of its size and the publicity surrounding it, would be significant to intimidate literally hundreds of open shop workers, contractors and prospective users of open shop contractors.
>
> These disorders have been so blatant that it has been necessary in some cases to call out the National Guard and to mobilize large contingents of riot-trained policemen. They sometimes have been attacked and even held hostage until the mob has had its way. There also have been criminal convictions and temporary injunctions issued by state and federal courts and proceedings before the Labor Board. A number of additional indictments recently have been handed down and grand jury investigations are in progress in various areas of the country. Notwithstanding the obvious lawlessness of this conduct, the violence and threats of violence by the building trades against persons and property will continue.
>
> This evidence establishes a joint venture under the applicable law of agency—a national policy and civil conspiracy to destroy the open shop. Made and reaffirmed in the context of the widespread violence, which has occurred, it constitutes incitement, condonation

The promise for the future, rooted in a new birth of spiritual, political and economic freedon, can and must be kept. If we fail, we will be held accountable by those who are yet to come.

CAL THOMAS
SYNDICATED COLUMNIST
AND AUTHOR OF *THINGS THAT MATTER MOST*

and ratification of these illegal acts engaged in by building trades-men. The reactions of union officials, at all levels of the trade union hierarchy, in silently or vocally carrying out the nationwide build-ing trades policy to fight and destroy the open shop on a no-holds-barred-basis, are highly inflammatory, and the resulting coercion and violence is predictable and must be stopped at once.

Peter Cockshaw's *Construction Labor News & Opinion* scooped the national news media by a prediction of ABC's pending legal action. He also noted the fiduciary duty of the entire trade union movement to act responsibly and stop the terrorism:

> What has been most disturbing, ABC sources disclose, is the failure by the internationals and parent AFL-CIO Building Trades Depart-ment to take action and prevent their locals from establishing a nationwide pattern of violent and destructive behavior. The inter-nationals, ABC maintains, have taken the lead in portraying ABC as the enemy of the union tradesman, a threat to his livelihood. And, in this way, internationals have virtually put a club in his hands, then they sit back and watch silently when he goes out and hits someone with it.[38]

Three months earlier, the "President's Letter" to 5,500 fellow ABC members and their 475,000 employees located across half of America had been written by Mike Callas. In it he announced the preparation of a counterattack through the auspices of the National Labor Relations Board against conspiratorial coer-cion and violence by the AFL-CIO Building and Construction Trades Depart-ment and its entire union hierarchy.[39]

On May 10, 1973, Callas gave me the "go" signal and called this litigation "a first in the history of United States labor law."[40] The time for decisive action against nationwide building trades terrorism in the workplace had arrived at last.[41]

A CRUCIAL REPRIEVE ON UNION MAYHEM

ON THE MORNING OF **MAY 16, 1973,** I felt like I was climbing Mt. Everest barefooted. Actually I was walking up a few steps to the office of William Humphrey, director of the National Labor Relations Board's 5th Region, based in Baltimore. That memorable occasion involved the filing of ABC's novel unfair labor practice charge against all of Big Labor's Building and Construction Trade Unions.

It consisted of a thirty-five-page memorandum of law supported by 5,000 pages of witness affidavits, police reports, court records, photographs, and other documentary evidence of union coercion, brutality, and sabotage against the freedom of the merit shop movement.

This master charge was simply labeled *Case No. 5-CB-1381.*

Defendants in the massive litigation (called "respondents" in Labor Board parlance) were: **THE BUILDING AND CONSTRUCTION TRADES DEPARTMENT, AFL-CIO, ITS SEVENTEEN AFFILIATED INTERNATIONAL LABOR ORGANIZATIONS, AND ALL DIRECTLY AND INDIRECTLY AFFILIATED STATE, REGIONAL, AND LOCAL LABOR ORGANIZATIONS.**

More specifically, the seventeen International Trade Unions that we designated as Co-Defendants in this master charge, along with their International Presidents, were: **(1) Asbestos Workers (Andrew Haas); (2) Boilermakers (Harold Buoy); (3) Bricklayers (Thomas Murphy); (4) Carpenters (William Sidell); (5) Electrical Workers (Charles Pillard); (6) Elevator Constructors (Wayne Williams); (7) Granite Cutters (Joseph Ricciarelli);**

> **Talk does not cook rice.**
>
> OLD CHINESE PROVERB

(8) Iron Workers (John Lyons); (9) Laborers (Peter Fosco); (10) Lathers (Kenneth Edwards); (11) Marble Workers (Wylie Lawhead); (12) Operating Engineers (Hunter Wharton); (13) Painters (Frank Raftery); (14) Plasterers and Cement Masons (Joseph Power); (15) Plumbers and Pipe Fitters (Martin Ward); (16) Roofers (Charles Aquadro); and (17) Sheet Metal Workers (Edward Carlough).

Companion unfair labor practice charges directly related to our master charge also were filed that day by several of my law partners against some of these union defendants at other Labor Board regional offices in Boston, Newark, Pittsburgh, Detroit, Cleveland, Cincinnati, and Tampa. The illegal threats and brutality alleged in all of the charges had occurred within the required six-month statutory limitation period preceding May 16, 1973—the filing date of our complaint.

A Summary of ABC's Master ULP Charge

The legalese (unavoidable here) in ABC's master unfair labor practice charge as submitted that May 16, 1973, to William Humphrey, the director of Region 5, read like this:

> Charging Party "ABC," on behalf of its members as a class and all open (merit) shop contractors as a class and their employees as a class, alleges that since on or about November 16, 1972, and continuing to this date, the previously named defendant labor organizations, their officers, agents, representatives and members, jointly and severally, as agents of each other, as co-conspirators, as joint-venturers, as allies and as fiduciaries charged by Congress with a public trust, have interfered with, restrained and coerced *employees* of the aforesaid contractors in the exercise of their rights guaranteed in Sections 7 and 8(b)(1)(A) of the Taft-Hartley Act to *refrain* from concerted activities for the purpose of collective bargaining.

> This illegal conduct has been initiated, engaged in, encouraged, ratified, acquiesced in and/or condoned pursuant to an overt, coordinated plan of action, joint venture and/or conspiracy against Charg-

ing Party ABC and the employees and employers described in the previous paragraph.

Because of the magnitude, geographical scope, frequency and severity of the alleged illegal interference, restraint, coercion, intimidation, violence and property damage that has been initiated, engaged in, encouraged, ratified, acquiesced in and/or condoned by the said defendant labor organizations throughout the United States, Charging Party ABC seeks *extraordinary relief* which the General Counsel and the Labor Board have the power and affirmative public duty to grant under all the circumstances in order to effectuate the policies of the Act.

Since there is reasonable cause to believe that the said unfair labor practices will continue unless restrained and will deprive these construction workers of their very livelihood as well as cause substantial and irreparable personal injury and property damage, Charging Party ABC urges the General Counsel of the Labor Board to seek *immediate nationwide injunctive relief* under Sections 10(e), (j) and (l) of the Act pending final determination of the validity of these charges in order to protect the public interest as well as to prevent a frustration of the basic, remedial purpose of the Act.

Special Remedies Requested

At the conclusion of this master charge (in addition to my request noted above for prompt injunctive relief against all illegal trade union activities across the nation), we asked the Labor Board *to award our contractor "families" compensatory and punitive damages*. These types of relief had never been granted to any non-union employees or employers in a Section 8(b)(1)(A) unfair labor practice case although the Labor Board had statutory authority to grant "extraordinary" remedial requests.[1] It consistently took a spineless pro-union position regardless of the political make-up and philosophy of the five Labor Board members.

Sidestepping this critical enforcement issue, the Board's "standard policy" was that federal, state, and local courts were the only forums with "the necessary

He that goes to law has a wolf by the ears.

ROBERT BURTON
WRITER

539

The impossible
is what can't
be done until
someone does it.

ANONYMOUS

expertise" to award such "make whole" remedies for employees and employers injured by the tortuous (i.e., wrongful) conduct of labor organizations stemming from their use of force and violence in labor disputes.[2]

We hoped that the enormity of the trade union conspiracy that ABC faced and its disastrous affect on labor peace in interstate trade and commerce would embolden the current Labor Board's conservative tilt to recognize an urgent need to level the legal playing field by ordering the following precedential injunctive and punitive relief:

1. Issue a nationwide "Cease and Desist Order" against the defendant trade unions from engaging in future illegal activities against ABC members and their employees.
2. Award back pay to employees of ABC members involved for time lost from work because of trade union restraint, coercion, and violence.
3. Award ABC employees for loss of other compensation, including violence-caused reductions in bonuses and profit sharing.
4. Require all trade unions to publicize this National Labor Relations Board Order in their official union newspapers, journals, and elsewhere; publicly state that such coercion and violence are illegal and must cease; and hereafter confine unionization activities to orderly and peaceful representation election procedures.
5. Order trade union governing bodies at all levels to exercise their authorized disciplinary power (by rescinding local union charters, imposing trusteeships, suspension or fines) whenever their affiliated local councils or unions and/or their members violate any legal rights of open shop employees.
6. Decertify or rescind the employee representation rights of any trade union that violates any term of this Labor Board Order.
7. Order the guilty trade unions to pay ABC's legal fees in connection with this action.[3]

We also requested Peter Nash, as general counsel of the Labor Board, to order the consolidation into our master charge of all of our current and any future supplemental unfair labor practice charges (including those filed separately in

Labor Board Regions 1, 4, 6, 7, 8, 12, and 22) for coordination and speedy enforcement.

News Media Accounts of ABC's Case

On the same day that I was filing the master charge at the Labor Board's Region 5 office in Baltimore, ABC's President Mike Callas, First Vice President Phil Abrams, and Executive Vice President John Trimmer were holding a packed news media briefing at the National Press Club in Washington, D.C. They began the session with a formal statement to typically skeptical reporters and their barrage of network microphones, television cameras, and flash bulbs.

Callas spoke first:

> The time has come to stop mincing words. A "hard hat" has been shot to death on a construction site in Michigan. A Pennsylvania contractor has been beaten up and his life threatened repeatedly. A Philadelphia judge says a job site scene looks like a military attack in a war zone. In New Jersey, policemen have been attacked and even held hostage until the mob had its way. In Michigan, building tradesmen swarm over an open shop project with red arm bands so they don't clobber their own kind. Henry Landau, President of the Sheet Metal Workers International Union, warns: "We don't plan to give up easy [and] we may get a little bloody." Arson is also a favorite tactic. The record of illegal activities goes on and on.
>
> Why? The building and construction trade unions are in a bind. They have priced themselves right out of the competitive marketplace and their unemployment lines range from 15 percent to 50 percent of their membership. The democratic representation election process of the National Labor Relations Board is ignored. Instead, with unprecedented arrogance and disregard for the rights of the open shop sector of the construction industry, these trade unions perpetrate open and violent attacks on both persons and property.
>
> This labor coercion and violence has generally occurred in such locations and in such size and ferocity that local, county, township and state police officials have been unable or unwilling to cope with

Always remember that a soldier's pack is lighter than a slave's chains.

DAVID O. MCKAY
WRITER

it. Tiers of law enforcement "buckpassing" and "bias" has usually resulted in non-enforcement of applicable criminal law.

In a national counter-attack to remedy this critical situation, ABC has gone to the National Labor Relations Board and charged the AFL-CIO Building and Construction Trades Department, its 17 affiliated international building trades unions and all state and local affiliates labor organizations with conspiring to coordinate and condone coercion and violence aimed at driving open shop workers and contractors out of the construction business, in violation of federal labor law. Each and every individual episode of intimidation, physical assault or property damage on an open shop construction job site submitted in our case is one more sign of a social stigma which has assumed national proportions in the labor movement and cannot be allowed to continue to jeopardize the public safety and free enterprise.

ABC will continue its investigation and supply further timely evidence to the Labor Board encompassing other states and other Labor Board regions. Additional unfair labor practice charges will be filed wherever these trade union wrongdoings continue until there is labor peace throughout the construction industry.[4]

After concluding this formal statement, ABC leaders opened the news conference for questions. They also distributed to the assembled journalists a copy of ABC's master charge plus a public relations brochure entitled "*The National Press Reports on Violence in Construction*." It contained photographs, newspaper editorials, and news stories portraying dozens of "trade union construction assault incidents" throughout much of the eastern half of the United States. The brochure's "Foreword" explained its contents:

The violent episodes described in this booklet are not isolated incidents. They are, rather, the continuation of a national conspiracy by the construction arm of the AFL-CIO against open shop construction firms. With unprecedented arrogance and utter disregard for the rights of others, the building trade unions have perpetrated open and violent attacks on both person and property. They attempt to justify their assaults with the specious reasoning that all construction work is inherently theirs through some divine providence.

Do not read the enclosed documentary as a mere conflict of ideologies. Broken bones, torn bodies, death threats and the destruction of property are not philosophic. They are real. They create pain and hardship. ABC pledges every legal effort to assure that Big Labor's collusion against free enterprise and voluntary unionism is stopped.

Over the next few days, a surprising number of elite national newspapers and weekly news magazines featured front-page headlines like these:

SUIT BY OPEN SHOP GROUP AIMS AT BUILDING TRADES UNIONS (*Associated Press*)

BUILDERS CHARGE PLOT BY 17 INTERNATIONAL UNIONS (*New York Times*)

CONTRACTORS SEEK RESTRAINT ON UNION VIOLENCE (*Washington Post*)

NON-UNION BUILDERS FILE COMPLAINT AGAINST UNION VIOLENCE (*Business Week*)

A two-page feature article by *U.S. News & World Report* entitled **NEW MOVE TO CURB VIOLENCE IN BUILDING INDUSTRY** included a photograph of the trade union blitz on Altemose Construction Company at Valley Forge.[5] Here are some excerpts from the magazine's lead story on our groundbreaking Labor Board action:

A far-reaching legal attack on 17 international construction unions—charging widespread destruction and violence—is the latest phase of a nationwide battle between open shop contractors and organized labor. On May 16, one of the largest cases ever to come before the National Labor Relations Board was filed by an association representing 5,500 firms, mainly non-union building contractors.

The employers complain that union attacks on open-shop construction projects and employees are costing more than 5 million

Gompers [AFL
Bldg. Trades
President, 1881–
1924] realized
that if workers did
not use freedom
and its opportuni-
ties for corrective
policies, their
alternatives were
force, violence,
and revolution.

FLORENCE THORNE IN
SAMUEL GOMPERS
AMERICAN STATESMAN

dollars annually in damages to the non-union operations. John Trimmer, executive vice president of the Associated Builders and Contractors, which filed the case, reports that there were fires, dynamiting,
vandalism, assaults and mass picketing. . . .

The ABC said it had filed about 5,000 pages of documentary evidence to support its Labor Board complaint. Examples were cited in
15 states in the eastern side of the country where ABC has seen its
membership more than double in the past four years. Many open
shop contractors have moved into the big commercial construction
field that was once almost exclusively unionized.

The lawsuit requests a permanent restraining order against union
violence on a nationwide basis plus damages for wages lost by employees
of open shop contractors who were prevented by 'illegal activities' from
going to work . . . . [6]

A feature article in *Engineering News-Record* headlined **OPEN SHOP LAW-
SUIT SEEKS LABOR BOARD CURB ON UNION VIOLENCE** included
these comments:

In one of the largest suits ever filed with the National Labor Relations
Board, the open shop Associated Builders and Contractors has begun
a nationwide legal attack on union violence, presently considered one
of the construction industry's biggest problems.

Last week, in a series of formal complaints, ABC charged the AFL-
CIO building trades unions at the national, state and local levels of
conducting a national conspiracy of violence and coercion aimed at
driving open shop workers and contractors out of the construction
business . . .

Filing of the Labor Board charges was announced at a Washington, D.C., press conference last week by ABC president Michael G.
Callas and executive vice president John P. Trimmer. They cited the
inadequacy of local enforcement agencies and local courts in dealing
with the problem as one of their reasons for taking the issue to the
Labor Board . . . [7]

The *Baltimore Sun* newspaper, in the city where ABC was founded, editorialized its concern that trade union violence was widespread and concluded: "Literal enforcement of the amended labor relations law is what the ABC is asking for in its nationwide suit and the Labor Board may well give close attention."

Editor Charles Stevenson added in his award-winning *Reader's Digest* report on trade union sabotage and brutality:

It is clear that thought is not free if the profession of certain opinions make it impossible to earn a living.

BERTRAM RUSSELL
WRITER

Last May, the 5500-member Associated Builders and Contractors—who employ a quarter of a million workers, union and non-union alike, on an open-shop basis—filed suit with the National Labor Relations Board. Their charge: that the building-trades unions have conspired to force them out of business and intimidate their employees. If the Labor Board finds the charge justified, then the nation's major craft unions could be held liable for acts of violence by their locals. *This might be the element needed to bring the terrorism under control.* [emphasis added] [8]

Other favorable accounts of ABC's case appeared in the *Wall Street Journal*, the *Industrial Contractor*, the *Christian Science Monitor*, and *Fortune* magazine. There also were supportive articles by nationally syndicated columnists such as Victor Riesel, Fulton Lewis, Jr., and radio commentator Paul Harvey.

John Trimmer described our litigation as "a great antibiotic for the infection of job site violence." He also noted that "almost overnight ABC was catapulted into the national spotlight and became known as the Voice of Merit Shop Construction."[9]

Win, lose, or draw, we had achieved one of our main objectives: Big Labor, Big Government, the national news media, and some of the general public now knew about ABC's unyielding demand that union terrorism must end and that free enterprise and voluntary unionism in the construction industry workplace must be given legal respect.

The NLRB's General Counsel Procrastinates

The next move in the gigantic case was up to the Labor Board's general counsel, Peter Nash. He felt tremendous political pressure from the Left; the business and political communities were watching him; the Associated Press and other news media were hounding him for comments. And Frank Bonadio, President of the AFL-CIO's Building Trades Department, was quoted in defense of his charged unions: "Any allegation that we are, or have been, involved in a conspiracy of any type is utterly absurd."[10]

We suspected that other AFL-CIO chieftains and Secretary of Labor Brennan (a former union leader) might be urging Nash "off the record" to "protect the labor movement and its unassailable legal right to unionize the unorganized."[11]

Under all the circumstances, General Counsel Nash found himself holding the proverbial tiger by the tail. And so he sat on the case for over a year, avoiding a decision. At first we were disappointed by this inexcusable delay. I met twice with Nash at his Washington office to find out what he would tell me about the status of our charge, but he remained noncommittal.

Eventually we began to realize that after filing our master charge on May 16, 1973, as John Trimmer put it, "there was a noticeable ebbing of union assaults and sabotage." Ironically, Nash's political procrastination had the same positive practical effect as the nationwide cease-and-desist order and injunction against illegal trade union activities that we were requesting from the Labor Board. High-ranking officials within the building trades hierarchy had decided to restrain the strong-arm tactics of their local affiliates. They were afraid of further repercussions from ABC's introduction of more evidence of violence into the pending Labor Board cases against them.

Meanwhile, in an introductory message to the annual meeting of the AFL-CIO's Building Trades Department held in Bal Harbor, Florida, in November of 1973, Department President Bonadio ignored the traditional ceremonial rituals and bluntly warned the hundreds of international, district, and local craft union representatives in attendance to be careful because they were in "stormy seas." And "ABC," he said, is the villain "rocking the boat." These "extremists" have filed "a giant lawsuit with the NLRB charging nationwide collusion by us all to deprive [non-union] workers of their right to work."[12]

Although Bonadio denied that the ABC charges were "factual," he did concede that "the seas were even going to get a lot stormier." He apparently was referring to both our Labor Board prosecutory action against the building trades and ABC-endorsed legislation introduced by Congressman John Anderson (R-IL) in conjunction with our Labor Board case. This bill would have made strike violence subject to the anti-racketeering provisions of the federal Hobbs Act.[13]

As the AFL-CIO Department's annual meeting closed, it adopted unanimously two resolutions: *first*, to continue to vigorously defend against the

Revolt and terror pay a price. Order and law have a cost.

CARL SANDBURG
WRITER-POET

ABC's unfair labor practice charges, and *second*, to oppose passage of the Anderson anti-violence bill. (Big Labor eventually won its resolution number two from Congress.)

Peter Nash Finally Acts

On June 18, 1974, thirteen months after we filed ABC's master charge with the Labor Board, General Counsel Nash released his decision in our case. The negative news for ABC was that he bowed to Big Labor's pressure by rejecting the first legal theory in our master charge. He simply ignored our contention that there was "a nationwide joint venture and conspiracy led by the parent Building Trades Department to engage in coercion and violence against open shop employers and their employees."

Nash knew that the Taft-Hartley Act forbad us to appeal for judicial review of this vital issue because he was given the final "say." He avoided any discussion of the powerful legal arguments and uncontradicted evidence that we had offered to prove our claim, and instead, merely wrote this single insipid and untrue sentence: *"The applicable law and facts do not support ABC's view of the relationships within the AFL-CIO structure."*[14]

Positive news for ABC, however, was that Nash did have the political fortitude to accept a modified version of our "agency" theory. He declared that "some of the international unions ratified the violent conduct of their local affiliates and therefore were jointly responsible for such illegal activity."

Nash thereby agreed with us to the extent that he issued broad "cease-and-desist" complaints against hierarchal and conspiratorial union coercion and violence in Massachusetts (Region 1), New Jersey (Regions 4 and 22), Pennsylvania (Region 6), Michigan (Region 7), and Ohio-Kentucky (Region 8). The defendants he named were *four* international unions (Ironworkers, Roofers, Carpenters, and Laborers), *one* statewide trade council (in Michigan), *one* regional trade council (in New Jersey), and *five* local craft unions (Ironworkers, Roofers, Operating Engineers, Plumbers, and Laborers located in the above-designated Regions).[15]

Related charges filed by ABC against trade unions in two other Labor Board regions were settled informally in ABC's favor by the Office of the General Counsel without the necessity of issuing a complaint.

Here is the Labor Board's terse press release on Peter Nash's decision:

> The General Counsel of the National Labor Relations Board has, after extensive investigation and evaluation of many unfair labor practice charges filed in eight different Regional Offices, made disposition of these charges filed by employers associated with the Associated Builders & Contractors (ABC) and by the ABC itself. These charges, involving alleged acts of violence by various construction unions, have been the subject of extensive publicity over the last year.
>
> In these cases, the particular right involved is the right of employees to *refrain* from joining or assisting labor organizations. The central issue in each case was *not* whether violence occurred (it being clear in each case that it did), *not* whether the Act prohibits such violence by unions (it clearly does), *nor* whether the NLRB desired to act to remedy that activity (it being clear in these and many other cases each year that the Labor Board abhors such activity and moves to remedy it where union responsibility is established).
>
> The central issue was, and is, whether it could be established by fact and law that a labor organization was *responsible* for the violence (an essential element in proving a violation of Section 8(b)(1)(A) and what labor organizations were so responsible.[16] [emphasis added]

Callas and News Media Review Nash's Decision

At an overflowing Washington press conference called by ABC officials a few days later, Mike Callas began by expressing his disappointment that General Counsel Nash failed to link the parent AFL-CIO Building Trades Department to our unchallenged proof of an illegal national joint venture and conspiracy with its affiliated unions. Then Callas praised the eight separate unfair labor practice complaints that Nash did issue. "Linking international trade unions to their locals on a multi-regional basis," is "a great step forward in the cause of industrial peace." And Callas concluded: "The prosecuting arm of the Labor Board finally has placed the responsibility for construction

> **Trust is an admirable trait, but always cut the cards.**
>
> ANONYMOUS

union violence and property damage squarely on the shoulders of some of the international entities in the union hierarchy which can effectively prevent the recurrence of such illegal activity."[17]

About three weeks after this ABC press conference, on July 13, 1974, *Business Week* magazine featured an article entitled **HALTING UNION VIOLENCE AT BUILDING SITES.** It included photographs of Mike Callas and Peter Nash. Here are some passages from it:

> Outbreaks of violence at construction sites have become so commonplace that open-shop employers have taken their case to the courts. Their aim is to try to pin responsibility for the violence on the AFL-CIO and its affiliated international unions...
>
> ABC complained that "the type of violence that has been going on for the last six or seven years has caused millions of dollars worth of damage" and... the Labor Board's general counsel authorized complaints against four international building trades unions and 15 regional and local union groups to determine whether federal laws were violated in outbreaks of violence...
>
> ABC's president, Michael Callas, a non-union contractor from Hagerstown, Maryland, said that "a key factor in the complaints which were issued was that the Labor Board's general counsel is finally prepared to prosecute international labor unions because they knew of illegal activities and failed to take affirmative steps to halt that illegal activity."
>
> The ABC expects to carry its fight [against the trade union hierarchy] through the Labor Board and appellate courts, if necessary. "We will continue this legal process to stop the violence, and in the end we will win," insists ABC general counsel Samuel Cook of Baltimore: "We have gotten to the source of the problem—the 'home office' as they say in the business world."

This *Business Week* article concluded with a notable prediction: *"For organized labor, the case represents the threat of a tough precedent for broader union liabilities in illegal local strikes."*

Statewide Legal Protection in Michigan

One of the most satisfying results of our litigation was a settlement agreement signed by the AFL-CIO's notorious Michigan State Building Trades Council. This labor organization presumably wanted to avoid bad publicity and punitive government action from a months-long trial exposing terroristic activity in one of the unfair labor practice complaints authorized by Peter Nash.

Under the terms of this capitulation agreement as approved by the Labor Board, the statewide Trades Council, its officials, and certain of its local trade union affiliates, agreed to *cease-and-desist* from "directing, authorizing, ratifying or condoning mass picketing, physical violence, vandalism, the destruction of property, and other coercive conduct against ABC employers and their employees in violation of Section 8(b)(1)(A) of the Taft-Hartley Act." Any breach of this agreement was automatically punishable by federal contempt of court proceedings. That ended the bloodshed and sabotage which Michigan's Governor Milliken had termed "guerilla warfare" and which had plagued the construction sites of ABCers for 10 years throughout that state.[18]

The hard work and emotional strain—even fear—that went into gathering evidence for this Michigan case was awesome. The individual ABC contractors involved and their employees endured physical assaults as well as threats on the lives of their families. Some of them were besieged by masses of union pickets for days and even weeks. All of them also witnessed extensive property damage to their job sites.

The pressure on the Michigan contractors was so severe at times that capitulation to the trade unions seemed appealing, even tantalizing. Yet the ABCers persevered in their conviction to do what was necessary to avoid compulsory unionism. These courageous men and women stayed at the scene of union confrontations, recorded eyewitness events, and took photographs detailing the violence. They risked personal injury while doing all those things that were needed to gather evidence for us to support our Labor Board charges.

ABC's Victory Covers Eight NLRB Regions

In due course the international, statewide, and local trade union defendants involved in some of the other unfair labor practice charges processed by

> Victory at all costs, victory in spite of all terror, victory however long and hard the road may be; for without victory there is no survival.
>
> WINSTON CHURCHILL
> BRITISH
> PRIME MINISTER

General Counsel Peter Nash's office (with our assistance as permitted) in eight of the Labor Board's geographical regions also capitulated and signed similar "cease-and-desist" settlement agreements approved by the Labor Board and enforceable in the federal courts. Other union defendants who would not settle their cases were held responsible for their illegal behavior in successful litigation before the Labor Board's administrative law judges and the Board itself.

In the end, all of these guilty unions were ordered to take certain affirmative action: (1) post copies of the Labor Board's restraining order against coercion and violence at conspicuous places in union offices and meeting halls; (2) reproduce and publish the Labor Board's cease-and-desist order in union newsletters mailed to all members; and (3) notify the appropriate Regional Director of the Labor Board as to what steps they had taken to comply with the Board's orders.

They all complied, reluctantly.

The "plaintiff" ABC contractors involved in the charges also were ordered to notify their own employees about the Labor Board's order that would protect them from further illegal union activities. Some of the language in the decision in one of these litigated regional cases—which the Labor Board actually called a "sordid drama"—involved the notorious Philadelphia Roofers Local 30, which continues to appear throughout this history of evil trade union activities. The "bloody back to basics" acts that occurred bear repeating:

> It is difficult to conceive of anything more coercive than the union activities that we have herein examined. Physical assault on both employees and supervisors in the presence of employees; threats directed to employees and to their supervisors of bodily harm to their wives and children and of property damage to their automobiles and homes; the infliction of property damage on the automobiles, trucks, equipment, supplies and buildings of both the employers and their customers; the threat of injury implicit in the high-speed automobile chases of employees and supervisors; and the actual assaults on employees and supervisors all reveal a design of unbridled violence that cannot help but be ultimately coercive to employees... We find

John Trimmer, ABC National's executive vice president (left), and the author celebrate the Association's victory in 1973–1974 at the National Labor Relations Board over the terrorism of the trades unions.

the activities involved here to be ultimately coercive and, committed by or under the direction of the Defendant Union, violative of Section 8(b)(1)(A).[19]

A New Labor Board Policy

Following these ABC victories, General Counsel Peter Nash issued a precedential policy memorandum to all Labor Board Regional Directors throughout the

**It can't be done.
It can't be done.
It can't be done.
It *will* be done.**

ANONYMOUS

United States. It ordered them "to seek immediate injunctive relief in the federal courts to control any coercion and devastation of property by labor organizations whenever local and state government authorities were ineffective."[20] This decision established a new nationwide Labor Board guideline that helped to deter trade union terrorism and obviously was beneficial to the ABC cause.[21]

John Trimmer summarized the results of this interstate legal battle with Big Labor in the '70s as follows in his treatise, *ABC—Profile of a Philosophy*:

> Our national lawsuit was the key to the Association's remarkable success in weathering the union storm and substantially reducing violence and sabotage wherever ABC chapters flourished throughout the nation. This achievement was due chiefly to the courage and ingenuity of ABC leadership. As president, Mike Callas spearheaded the attack and Sam Cook was the legal architect. They enjoyed the assistance of such ardent ABC leaders as Phil Abrams, Joe Rodgers, Fred Schnabel, Jerry Oliver, Joe Burton and Joe LaMonaca—a brave group of past and future ABC presidents hard to match in Association history.
>
> Gene Higgins, who had been named ABC's assistant executive vice president, kept the Association's regular business moving forward with the help of such able staffers as Woody Moats, Scott Robertson, "Butch" Randall and Bob Hepner. They also pitched in where needed on the Labor Board proceedings during this most perilous and spectacular period in ABC's life.

In 1974 *Engineering News-Record* reported "conclusive proof" of the attainment of ABC's primary objective in suing the AFL-CIO building trades hierarchy: "Labor violence that has been a thorn in the side of open shop contractors for many years is no longer the central issue facing the Associated Builders and Contractors. The number of incidents of violence, arson, and vandalism at their construction sites fell from an estimated *$5 million* worth of property damages in 1973 to less than *$150,000* in 1974"—about a 97 percent decrease.

Thanks to the leadership of Mike Callas and his ABC team, the merit shop crusade was healthy and expanding on a comparatively peaceful basis in the construction industry workplace in America in 1974.

One might even suspect that a second miracle had occurred as a latter-day "David" beat another "Goliath."

CHAPTER 44

LANDMARK ANTITRUST AND RICO VICTORIES

DURING THE DAUNTING DAYS OF **1973** while ABC was suppressing trade union savagery across the country with grudging assistance from the National Labor Relations Board, one martyred ABCer—Leon Altemose—was engrossed in a local attack on another legal front. It was his firm's own federal case against the Philadelphia Building & Construction Trades Council ("Trades Council") that he hoped would end its obsession to destroy his business.

The lawsuit centered on the Trades Council's subcontracting agreement which had been executed by 850 unionized general contractors and 4,000 unionized subcontractors in the metropolitan Philadelphia area. Under it, they agreed to do business under trade union conditions exclusively and never to work with open shop contractors who were recorded on the Trades Council's "unfair list." The refusal of Leon Altemose to sign this compulsory unionism agreement led to his epic battle with the local Trades Council at Valley Forge Plaza.[1]

The ultimate overall result of this monopolistic labor contract was that 85 percent of the nonresidential construction work within the City of Philadelphia and 50 to 75 percent in the surrounding suburbs was being performed by builders who pledged to use union craftsmen exclusively. In attempting to force all local open shop general contractors like Altemose to execute the terms of this agreement, the Trades Council and its member craft unions frequently resorted to coercive and violent tactics.

A potential legal precedent for a business firm's protection in this type of situation was the landmark case of *United Mine Workers v. Pennington*. In this 1965 decision, the Supreme Court of the United States ruled that "a labor organization forfeits its exemption from the [Sherman] antitrust law when it is clearly shown that it has agreed with one set of employers to impose a certain wage scale on other employers."[2] Altemose and his attorney, John Pelino, believed that the objective behind the Trades Council attacks in the 1960s and 1970s to force Altemose Construction Company and other open shop firms to sign the agreement or go out of business violated this *Pennington* case. ABC and the Chamber of Commerce of the United States agreed. All parties realized, however, that the conflicting intersection between labor and antitrust laws was one of the most difficult areas of federal jurisprudence in which an employer could litigate, bankroll, and win.

Altemose Sues Big Labor for Anti-Trust Violations

After extensive legal research and substantial financial sacrifice by all concerned, in March of 1973 Altemose Construction Company's attorney, John Pelino, filed a civil antitrust lawsuit under the Sherman Act in the U.S. District Court for the Eastern District of Pennsylvania. The goal was to break up the existing area-wide trade union monopoly over the construction industry and protect free enterprise in the workplace throughout the Philadelphia community. In full support of this action, ABC (represented by me and my law firm, Venable, Baetjer and Howard) and the Chamber of Commerce of the United States (represented by attorney Gerard Smetana) joined Altemose Construction Company as Plaintiffs. The co-defendants that we named were the Philadelphia Building Trades Council and its fifty-six local trade union members, including the infamous Roofers Local 30.

Our complaint alleged that this Trades Council and its member craft unions were using their construction agreement to engage in an illegal combination and conspiracy with all 850 employer-members of the General Building Contractors Association of Philadelphia plus their thousands of subcontractors, suppliers, and lending institutions. We sought permanent injunctive relief from that syndicated scheme, which we claimed restrained interstate commerce and eliminated non-union competition in the industrial and commercial construction industry within a five-county area. We also asked the federal court for punitive relief in the form of the Sherman (Anti-Trust) Act's provision for treble damages and the reimbursement of legal fees to compensate Altemose Construction Company for the Trades Council's illegal activities.

ABC's John Trimmer released a press statement which included these words:

> The building trades unions' reign of terror has existed too long in the Philadelphia area. There is no excuse for these lawless attacks by build-ing trades unions when labor law provides them with the power to hold secret ballot elections and organize wherever construction work-ers so choose. Here is an excellent opportunity for the judicial system of the United States to take off its blinders with respect to the devas-tation by unions. The long history of violent instances brought against open shop firms have caused injury to construction workers and losses in wages, time and materials that run into hundreds of thousands of dollars. They have hounded some open shop contractors out of busi-ness by arson, direct destruction and mayhem.
>
> We trust that the Federal District Court will permit this antitrust case to go to full hearing and put an end to the destruction of human rights that has been wrought by the unionized sector of the construc-tion industry. Justice must be done![3]

Unfortunately for our cause, this lawsuit dragged on and on, year after year, with no prosecution and ever-mounting litigation expenses. There were pre-trial motions, depositions, counter-motions, even a counter-lawsuit and other evasive union tactics that kept postponing a full trial and ruling on the mer-its of the case. It was regarded as a political "hot potato" to be avoided and had to be reassigned as judges withdrew unexplainably during the lengthy legal machinations.

Altemose Wins Round One

On May 13, 1977—four years after our lawsuit was filed—some progress began to be made. At that stage we were required to defend against the

Speak softly and carry a big stick.

THEODORE ROOSEVELT
26TH PRESIDENT

Trades Council's own antitrust counter-claim (by a motion for "summary judgment") that our entire case should be dismissed immediately without a trial.

The Trades Council argued that ABC and the U.S. Chamber of Commerce "conspired to conduct a public relations campaign maliciously designed to make the Council appear to be involved in a conspiracy to destroy Altemose and other open shop contractors." This alleged "publicity effort" by our clients was claimed by the Council "to restrain trade and eliminate competition in the construction industry in the pertinent geographic area."[4]

The Trades Council also claimed that Altemose and ABC attempted to set local wage rates by using these three illegal tactics:

1. Altemose and ABC members combined and conspired to violate federal and state prevailing wage laws and such activity constituted a violation of the Sherman Act.

2. ABC adopted a multi-employer Insurance Trust Fund, otherwise known as the "Security Plan," and a Retirement Plan, both of which were allegedly designed to fix and regulate fringe benefit rates paid to journeymen and laborers employed by open shop contractors. The result was that contractors using union members were foreclosed from successfully bidding against the open shop multi-employer group.

3. Open shop members of ABC combined and conspired to set uniform wage rates among themselves.[5]

We won that first round as Federal District Court Judge Higginbotham denied both of these Trades Council counter-charges and its motion for summary judgment. The judge held that nothing Altemose, ABC, or its members did appeared to be in violation of the Sherman Act. He pointed out that any publicity disseminated by Altemose as to acts of violence directed against his company's construction projects, his workers, and his person "amounted to truthful statements of public record, were not actionable, and our antitrust case should proceed to trial."[6]

Altemose Loses the Second Round

More than six years later, *round two* of the Altemose antitrust case resulted during 1983 in a much different conclusion by a new judge. One count of our original complaint alleged an illegal combination of the unions with the unionized contractors, suppliers, and lending institutions. Our other count alleged an illegal conspiracy solely among the unions. We asked the federal court (on our own motion for summary judgment) to rule for us on both counts and thereby avoid the necessity for a full-blown trial of the case.

On July 5, 1983, District Court Judge Norma Shapiro listened to oral arguments by both sides based on what she called "a voluminous record" of evidence, and wrote a lengthy opinion *against* our motion for summary judgment. She cited almost every significant ruling ever decided under antitrust laws and described the history of the development and application of those statutes. Then she ruled that the law and facts were not applicable to our case in what appeared to us to be a flagrant example of "judicial legislation." In other words, the liberal judge decided the case on what she "felt" the law should be rather than what it actually "was" judicially under the terms of the statute and evidence in question.[7]

More specifically, on our first count, Judge Shapiro found that the "agreements" exacted by the Trades Council from union contractors and subcontractors were lawful "prehire agreements" under Section 8 of the Taft-Hartley Act. She erroneously construed the Supreme Court's *Connell Construction Co.* case and actually exempted the Council from antitrust law.[8] Judge Shapiro also dismissed our second count (erroneously ignoring the clear evidence of a labor-management conspiracy) because "labor unions, when acting alone, enjoy a statutory exemption from the antitrust laws—at least where, as in the instant case, their activities were confined to seeking traditional labor objectives such as organizational activity through a subcontracting agreement."[9]

Altemose Defeats the Trades Council

In *round three*, we appealed Judge Shapiro's inexplicable decision. About twenty months later, on February 15, 1985, we received exciting news. Leon Altemose's firm was awarded a *unanimous preliminary victory* by the federal Third Circuit

> **The best law leaves the least discretion to the judge.**
>
> Latin Proverb

Hypocrit:
"The smyler with
the knyf under
the cloak."

CHAUCER
THE KNIGHT'S TALE

Court of Appeals, sitting "en banc" (i.e., all of the judges). The court's decision (written by Chief Circuit Judge Gibbons) reversed Judge Shapiro's ruling against us and remanded the case for trial on the merits of both of our counts.

Here is some of the federal appellate court's positive reasoning which was given the silent treatment in liberal labor relations circles:

> The defendants [unions] have picketed job sites where non-union tradesmen were working. They have resorted to threats of violence and actual violence at various job sites. They have employed economic pressure not only upon contractors, but also upon developers, owners, and financial institutions, to force contractors to employ union labor and union subcontractors exclusively... The [Trades] Council insisted that unless Altemose signed a building trades agreement, there would be picketing on the job site. On June 5, 1972, approximately 1,000 persons, including some principals of the Council, committed what was described by a Pennsylvania trial judge as a "virtual military assault" on the Valley Forge Plaza jobsite, inflicting physical damage estimated at $300,000...
>
> We hold that the trial court erred in granting summary judgment on *Count I* for lack of evidence from which concert of action between labor and non-labor entities could be inferred. The record contains circumstantial evidence that the unions maintained a "fair contractor" list; that the Council exerted primary and secondary pressure which had the inevitable effect of benefiting contractors on the list; that firms not on the list were almost totally excluded from the market; that the General Building Contractors Association policed its members to prevent use of non-union contractors although the contractors' economic interest would suggest, *prima facie*, use of the lowest responsible bidders without regard to unionization; and that an officer of the Council offered to obtain bids from firms on the "fair contractors" list if Altemose would sign a Building Trades Agreement. A finder of fact evaluating this evidence could reasonably infer that the Council and the General Building Contractors Association acted in concert to exclude non-union firms from the market...

Count II alleges, and the summary judgment record would permit a finding, that the open shop contractors have been injured in their business and property by the exclusion of subcontractors from the construction market in the Philadelphia area, and by the inability of general contractors to obtain bids from union subcontractors. The record is clear that the Council has obtained Building Trades Agreements from hundreds of signatories. It is true that in the *Connell* case the Court made reference to the fact that the plaintiff had signed a contract, implying that this satisfied the *Bradley-Pennington* requirement of participation in the combination of a non-labor party. 421 U.S. at 620,

"Learned counsel should use shorter words. Learned counsel is forgetting that this Court was not an 'A' student."

622. The opinion cannot be read as suggesting, however, that contractors who do not sign a contract but are affected by agreements between a union and non-labor parties are unprotected by the antitrust laws. Clearly the Council did not act unilaterally when it obtained hundreds of agreements from contractors the intent and effect of which was to exclude non-union contractors from the market...

Thus it is clear that contractual provisions prohibiting contracts with non-union firms, entered into outside the collective bargaining context, and coercive concerted activities aimed at obtaining such agreements, remain subject to anti-trust scrutiny under the Sherman Act.[10]

In desperation because of this unanticipated turn of events, the Building Trades Council brought on *round four* by appealing the federal circuit court's decision to the Supreme Court of the United States. Exercising its own discretionary ("certiorari") jurisdiction, a year later the Supreme Court (without comment) decided not to hear the case and let stand our victorious decision from the Third Circuit Court of Appeals. That silence by the Supreme Court in 1986 left the Circuit Court's opinion intact. It also gave Leon Altemose the right to proceed to trial against the Trades Council and its members for violation of the Sherman Anti-Trust Act by conspiring with unionized contractors who were attempting to drive his company out of business.[11]

The Trades Council Gives Up

Round five resulted in a knockout punch by Altemose Construction Company. On December 17, 1987, while we were preparing to litigate the case on its merits, the Philadelphia Building Trades Council surrendered. Under a settlement agreement approved (ironically and reluctantly) by District Court Judge Norma Shapiro four years after she nonsensically denied our case, the Trades Council agreed to pay Leon Altemose's merit shop construction firm the sum of *$1.25 million in damages*. The Trades Council also accepted a *broad court injunction* that banned any picketing by its union members within two hundred yards of every Altemose Company job site or property.[12]

Officials of the U.S. Chamber of Commerce called the settlement "one of the most important labor decisions of the 1980s." And Dan Bennet, ABC's executive vice president, added: "Justice has finally been served in this major victory for the merit shop and business in general."[13]

At a packed press conference following this fortuitous capitulation by Big Labor, Patrick Gillespie, secretary-treasurer of the Building Trades Council, mumbled blandly that local union leaders were faced with "the dilemma of going to trial to prove that we are not guilty of what was alleged." That "gamble," he estimated, "could have cost the Trades Council in excess of $2 million in court expenses and attorneys fees plus the risk of an adverse decision awarding Altemose Construction Company treble damages of about $3 million." Gillespie concluded that the Council's settlement was "one of prudence."[14]

A Precedential RICO Act Victory

Final vindication for Leon Altemose came two years later against his notorious nemesis, Roofers Local Union No. 30 and its corrupt officials. This triumph resulted from a novel (at that time) civil lawsuit.[15] It was filed by President Ronald Reagan's Department of Justice on December 2, 1987, in the federal Eastern District Court of Pennsylvania under the Racketeer Influenced and Corrupt Organizations Act (RICO). Congress supplemented the statute's far-reaching criminal penalties with a private right of action which allows any person who has been economically injured by a "pattern of racketeering activity" to recover *treble damages and attorneys' fees.*

The government's motion to the court requested a preliminary injunction against the illegal activities of the Roofers Union and thirteen of its officers. It also requested the appointment of a neutral trustee to oversee, monitor, audit, and eliminate the Roofers' "barbaric practices."[16]

This RICO statute (as noted in Chapter 39) had been enacted seventeen years earlier (1970) to eliminate the infiltration of organized crime into legitimate businesses. The *Roofers* case involving Altemose Construction Company was one of the first actions brought by the federal government to rely on RICO to enjoin a labor union's pattern of terrorism used to organize the employees of an open shop contractor.[17] The great news for us was that the federal district court upheld a new interpretation of RICO to the effect that it should be read "broadly" and "liberally construed."[18] The court added that RICO suits were not preempted by the jurisdiction of the National Labor Relations Board or

> **If there were no bad people, there would be no good lawyers.**
>
> CHARLES DICKENS
> NOVELIST

Corruption is nothing new to mankind but seldom loses its power to astonish.

ANONYMOUS

the Supreme Court's previously discussed *Enmons* case.[19] Therefore the Roofers Union was held to be an "enterprise" and its individual representatives were considered "persons" subject to prosecution under RICO.[20]

Well-publicized facts about this evil union (which represented 2,000 craftsmen) disclosed that in 1968 it had conceived a plan to govern and exploit the commercial roofing industry in the Philadelphia area. The union tried to force all roofing firms—including subcontractors working with Leon Altemose—to sign a "master" collective bargaining agreement. This scheme "included the use of physical coercion, violence, threats of violence, arson, and terrorism to drive out of business any contractor who refused to submit to Roofers Union control."[21]

More Terrorism: Trade Union Style

Dozens of non-union contractors besides Leon Altemose had felt the economic wrath and physical mayhem of Roofers Local 30 over the years. They included Kitson Brothers, Inc., Keller Roofing Co., D&D Roofing, Alper Company, and many smaller contractors. And rank-and-file members of Local 30 who had bona fide workplace grievances as well as unionized contractors and subcontractors who were required to do business with Local 30 were afraid to mention or resolve their legitimate disputes at the union hall. If they attempted to do so, they would be "outnumbered, intimidated, threatened with physical violence, or physically beaten." It was not uncommon for these "visitors" to suffer injuries at the hands of hired goons and trained boxers.[22]

Bolstering the Justice Department's case, on November 23, 1987 (just a week before this RICO charge was filed), a federal district court jury in the *Traitz* case from the same judicial district agreed that leaders of this corrupt union were guilty of 152 separate criminal acts. They included racketeering, conspiracy, mail fraud, solicitation of kick-backs, bribery of federal, state, and local public officials, extortion, and embezzlement from the union members' benefit plan.[23] Local 30's business manager, John McCulloch, was convicted of collecting unlawful debts for an organized crime ring and resolving disputes between unions and contractors for the Nicodemo Scarfo family arm of La Cosa Nostra in the Philadelphia area. McCulloch eventually was murdered in an organized crime "hit."[24]

On May 23, 1988, six months after the civil RICO lawsuit was instituted by President Reagan's Justice Department, federal judge Louis Bechtel granted the government's request and imposed an unprecedented court-supervised "decreeship" on Roofers Local 30 for its "pattern of racketeering activity" in violation of RICO.

Without a doubt, said Judge Bechtel, "Roofers Local 30 played a leading role in the unlawful intrusion and physical destruction of the Altemose Construction Company job site at Valley Forge, Pennsylvania, in 1972." He noted that many union members had been convicted of violent crimes and were serving prison terms in connection with that attack. Local 30 also was ruled "to have breached its fiduciary obligation to its members" by using union membership dues to pay thousands of dollars for the hoodlums' legal defense. That caused Local 30 to stage a mass protest march at the federal courthouse when the bullies' sentencing occurred. The union even installed a plaque at its meeting hall "listing and honoring" these convicts for their role in the Altemose Company terrorism.[25]

Because of the Roofers' corrupt activities, all labor contract bargaining was suspended temporarily, the court itself took over operation of the Union's affairs indefinitely, and thirteen members of the Union gang who had been convicted of violent crimes were barred from the roofing industry after service of their sentences.[26]

An unusual observation by Judge Bechtel related to a finding of fact by the jury in *United States v. Traitz*, the companion criminal case mentioned above: "Roofers Local 30, through the policies and practices employed by its leaders, engaged in *terrorism*." The judge then added more unsettling words:

> The criminal trial [in the *Traitz* case] dealt with violence but not to the extremes held in this civil case. Accordingly, the racketeering activity here is both longer in duration and broader in variety since it covers more crimes committed by more Union officials and more Union agents . . .
>
> To use the metaphor of one national expert on terrorism, "*terrorism is theater*." [citing Brian Jenkins, *International Terrorism: A New Kind of Warfare*, Rand Paper No. 5261 at p. 4, 1974]. *It is not what terrorists do so much as it is the perception they create. By physically beating*

Laws and institutions are constantly tending to gravitate. Like clocks, they must be cleansed, wound up, and set to true time.

HENRY WARD BEECHER
WRITER

567

It is of great con-
sequence to dis-
guise your
inclination and to
play the hypocrite
well.

MACHIAVELLI
THE PRINCE XI

*one person, a group practicing terrorism can scare and influence a thou-
sand.*[27] [Emphasis added]

Here are more pertinent excerpts from District Judge Bechtel's decision on
how his court coped with this dangerous labor organization:

> The evidence presented to this court in the preliminary injunction
> hearing establishes in a convincing and persuasive form that the rack-
> eteering activity of the individual defendants over the past twenty
> years extends far beyond that for which they have been charged, con-
> victed and sentenced. Furthermore, the evidence establishes the
> involvement of many more officers, agents, members and accomplices
> of the Roofers Union than have been convicted thus far. Indeed, the
> names of many of the perpetrators of many of the threatened violent
> acts and crimes of extortion testified to are not known to the victims,
> although their affiliation with the Union is clear...
>
> Abuses of the past are not likely to stop with the removal of the
> thirteen individual defendants from their positions. The systematic
> practice of functioning on a basis where violence and blatant viola-
> tions of law were official Union policy over the last twenty years cre-
> ates a substantial likelihood of continued violations and the
> perception by people in the industry as well as members of the
> Roofers Union itself that such violations will continue.

Judge Bechtel continued his stern lecture:

> This Union has been dominated by a creed of violence, unlawfulness
> and defiance of authority. The imposition of the creed by force, fear and
> intimidation upon the roofing industry and much of the Union mem-
> bership prevents the Union from quickly restoring itself to the role that
> its current and future membership expects and the law demands...
>
> Under its past leadership, the Union was reduced to a mere shell
> that lost sight of its legitimate goals and allowed the improper means
> it utilized to consume it. Through the injunctive relief outlined herein

the court seeks to restore or maybe create for the first time honest pride in the Union. This labor organization is not capable of curing its problems without the intervention of one or more outside authorities in a form, and for such duration as will provide it with the best chance, if it has one at all, of avoiding dissolution...

We must not make a scarecrow of the law.

WILLIAM SHAKESPEARE
MEASURE FOR MEASURE, ACT II

And Judge Bechtel concluded, in no uncertain terms:

> The court... rejects the Plaintiff's request for a trusteeship and the Union's suggestion of a monitorship. Instead, the court will impose what shall be deemed a "Decreeship." This will simply state that the Union will continue to function in the manner hereafter more carefully described, with its democratic processes in place, its leadership in place, but subject to the authority of a Decree of Court. The Decree will have a number of specific requirements that will result in the replacement of certain improper Union practices of the past, the prohibition of some others, and participation by the court with the Union in others.[28]

After District Court Judge Bechtel converted his preliminary injunction in this precedent-setting RICO case to a final "Decreeship" on July 22, 1988, Roofers Local 30 filed a notice of appeal. On March 23, 1989, the federal Third Circuit Court of Appeals dismissed that review and affirmed the permanent order of the District Court against Roofers Local 30.[29] Thanks in no small part to Judge Bechtel's trail-blazing decision, "RICO became a strategic weapon in the legal arsenal of employers against union corruption and terrorism in labor disputes."[30]

The ordeal of Leon Altemose was over at last. This eighteen-year-long, three-million-dollar battle to defeat compulsory trade unionism in the workplace left him drained physically, mentally, and financially—but unbowed and unbeaten. On June 2, 2000, at ABC's 50th anniversary convention held in Baltimore City, the valiant contractor was named one of ABC's "leaders of the twentieth century who significantly influenced and strengthened the merit shop construction industry throughout the nation."

CHAPTER 45

AN OFFER ABC HAD TO REFUSE

HE **ALTEMOSE CONSTRUCTION COMPANY'S** antitrust and RICO victories in 1987 and 1988 were milestone labor relations decisions. After those two rulings and a few similar cases, many federal courts began to recognize the propriety of holding to the same standard all types of "persons" and "organizations" that use murder, arson, extortion, and other kinds of terrorism as business practices in restraint of free enterprise. It became immaterial whether the structure of the group was the traditional Mafia Cosa Nostra or a "brotherhood" of union workers, or a meld between the two. Formerly successful defensive pleadings by unions to dismiss these cases on routine preliminary motions before trial occurred (called a "summary judgment") went out of judicial favor.

The RICO statute in particular became viable in litigation arising out of labor disputes whenever the evidence showed a pattern of criminal activity by any person or organization.[1] This new broad interpretation of RICO created a much-needed resource for the protection of our homeland security because some segments of the American labor movement have had a long history of ties with organized crime and violence, including unions affiliated with the building trades.

In 1958, Professor Philip Taft of the Graduate School of Business at the University of Chicago wrote that "the connection between high union officers and sections of the underworld is a development which gravely threatens both labor and industry."[2] In 1986, federal judge Irving Kaufman, who

> When we neither punish nor reproach evildoers, we are ripping the foundations of justice from future generations.
>
> ALEXANDER SOLZHENITSYN

was Chairman of President Ronald Reagan's Commission on Organized Crime, issued a report that concluded:

> Labor racketeering is a growing national problem in major metropolitan centers. It has influenced a number of markets such as construction...with staggering costs not just borne by union members but by society as a whole.[3]

Three years later, the Mafia-infiltrated International Brotherhood of Teamsters (an affiliate of the AFL-CIO's Building and Construction Trades Department) capitulated and signed a Consent Decree. It was proffered by the courageous and astute U.S. Attorney, Rudy Giuliani, a Republican who subsequently served with distinction as mayor of New York. It all happened on the eve of his crucial lawsuit against the huge labor organization for violation of RICO. The Justice Department had contended that this labor organization was "a wholly owned subsidiary of organized crime."[4]

The Brotherhood of Teamsters also presumably was concerned—along with its other dilemmas—about the Justice Department's precedential application of this statute (and its severe monetary penalties) to the corrupt activities of Roofers Local Union No. 30 in Philadelphia in the *Altemose* case. That victory could be one of the reasons why the Teamsters made this seldom-quoted settlement admission in its Consent Decree to the federal court: *"There have been allegations, sworn testimony and judicial findings of past problems [of our Union] with La Cosa Nostra corruption and such illegal activities should cease."*[5]

This Court Decree put Prosecutor Rudy Giuliani's RICO trial in abeyance and replaced it with a trusteeship monitored by the previously mentioned Judge David Edelson of the U.S. District Court for the Southern District of New York. In more of Judge Kaufman's blunt words:

> The aim of the Consent Decree is to guarantee free elections and to rid the Teamsters of the hideous influence of organized crime...Cleansing this union will continue to require the strongest, most unified, concentrated, concerned effort. Perpetual vigilance and heroic effort is the cost of democracy.[6]

Defendants named by the U.S. Department of Justice in subsequent RICO Consent Decree enforcement litigation over the years have included Teamsters International President Jackie Presser, other Teamsters officers, its General Executive Board, and the Commission of La Cosa Nostra as well as many Teamsters bosses and enforcers such as: Anthony "Fat Tony" Salerno, Matthew "Matty the Horse" Ianiello, Nunzio "Nunzi Pro" Provenzano, Salvatore "Sammy Pro" Provenzano, Carmine "The Snake" Persico, Angelo "The Nutcracker" LaPietra, John Phillip "Jackie the Lackie" Cerone, Anthony "Figgy" Ficarotta, John "Peanuts" Trolone, Joseph "Joey the Clown" Lombardo, Anthony Thomas "Tony Ripe" Civella, Salvatore "Tom Mix" Santoro, Nicholas "Nicky Glasses" Marangello, and Carl Angelo "Toughy" De Luna.[7]

> **You can get much farther with a kind word and a gun than you can with a kind word alone.**
>
> AL CAPONE
> MAFIA DON

The Story of "The Lip"

One of my memorable experiences with a sinister and powerful Baltimore boss of this Teamster's Union occurred in 1975. He was a foul-mouthed ruffian named Leo "The Lip" DaLesio, and he made a daring proposal to me.

It would have destroyed ABC as a merit shop contractors association.

This stocky, muscular Sicilian who chain-smoked expensive Cuban cigars was the powerful president of Maryland Teamsters' Joint Council 62 (some fourteen local unions) and secretary-treasurer of its Local 311 in Baltimore. DaLesio employed two ex-prizefighters (with rumored underworld connections) as "enforcers." Like Baltimore building trades chieftain Guido Iozzi, DaLesio made a practice of intimidating employers with terroristic tactics. His own eight thousand union members, in a combination of homage and fear, "donated" a special package of personal benefits to him from their compulsory membership dues.

These "perks" that "The Lip" convinced Local Union No. 311 to provide included his own personal "severance fund"—a nest egg for his retirement that grew to $250,000. He also was covered by three other union pension plans: the Teamsters Allied Pension Fund of Maryland, the Teamsters Joint Council No. 62 Pension Fund, and the Teamsters Affiliates Pension Fund.

At DaLesio's disposal were a luxuriously appointed Cadillac and its daily operating expenses, season professional football tickets, an athletic club membership, and a daily dining allowance. Then there was year-round use of a seashore condominium—maintenance free—at Ocean City, Maryland. He also had gratis enjoyment of luxurious suites at the Sheraton Johns Hopkins Inn, the Pikesville Hilton, and two swank high-rise apartments at 2 Charles Center in Baltimore City.

For some inexplicable reason, a federal grand jury and the Federal Bureau of Investigation suddenly dropped their criminal investigation of DaLesio's illegal activities without comment. Almost immediately, a civil lawsuit was filed by two brave Teamsters Union members named Donald Brink and John Kline. It resulted two-and-a-half years later in a ruling by Maryland District Court Judge Joseph Young. He held that under the federal Labor-Management Reporting and Disclosure Act of 1959 "The Lip" was personally liable "for engaging in flagrant breeches of his fiduciary duty to the union membership." Eventually a federal appellate court confirmed Judge Young's decision and ordered DaLesio to reimburse thousands of dollars that he "extorted" from both his Local 311 members and their maladministered pension and welfare funds.[8]

In his prime, DaLesio's standard tactic at a bargaining table opposite a company's negotiators began with a flat refusal to change a single word in his autocratic one-sided "master labor agreement." Every employer signed it or faced a strike. At the same time he would demand huge wage and employee benefits increases for his union members. This inflexible position would be defended with a barrage of earthy four-letter Anglo-Saxon derivations (or their Italian equivalents). He used them interchangeably as adjectives, nouns, and verbs. The tirades were delivered in a contemptuous manner, punctuated by a malevolent sneer behind an odorous cigar-created smoke screen.

And he detested all "mutha fuckin' management lawyers."

On one occasion "The Lip" ranted and raged for two hours against a soft-drink distributor whom I represented. We were officially at a so-called "bargaining impasse," closeted in a Holiday Inn conference room night and day just before a Fourth of July weekend. Nerves were frayed. The pressure was on everybody, but DaLesio even refused the voluntary assistance of an experienced federal government mediator.

The spark that set Leo on one of his rampages was my proposal to remove one comma in a sentence affecting the meaning of a potentially expensive overtime pay penalty from his "sacred" labor contract. He finally consented grudgingly after his own attorney, Cosimo Abato, admitted that he agreed with my interpretation of the intent of the sentence. "The Lip"'s parting shot at me (in front of my client) when we settled the dispute and kept my client's soft drinks on customers' store counters during the summer holiday was: "I bet youse'll get a fat fuckin' fee outta dis goddamn mess."

DaLesio Makes ABC an Offer

This notorious Teamster boss was well aware of (and sometimes participated in) the efforts of his brother union affiliates in the building and construction trades to organize ABC's member construction firms. He also knew that I represented ABC in labor relations matters. An independent maverick at heart, he not only tried to unionize trucking companies and warehouses (his union's traditional jurisdiction) but also manufacturers, retailers, restaurants, hotels, beverage distributors, and, as the saying goes in labor circles, "anything else that wasn't nailed down."

One summer day in 1975, DaLesio telephoned me to ask if I would meet him at the office of his attorney, Cosimo Abato, "abouta importanta matta uva moochul intrest." I accepted and was ushered into a conference room where Leo was sitting alone, puffing on a big cigar. The door was shut behind me by a secretary. Then The Lip handed me a cup of coffee, which I ignored. He followed that gesture with a sinister grin.

"I gotta deal ta maka yousa a biga hero wit da ABC," he began. "Dis deal will solva alla youses damma non-aunion clients' laba problms. Capisce?"

I smiled back at Leo and said: "Tell me more."

He took a deep breath and rasped out: "Heresa deal. Mya union willa sign uh fiva yeah area-wida contract wid all of youses ABC membas—botha generals anna subs. Jus give alla da workers a first year wage dats fiva pacenta below da Bawlmer Buildin' Trades contract plus atree pacenta costalivin raise per yeah derafta. And giva me a fulla union shoppa. Ya can keepa youses owna holidays anna vacation pay and youses shita-poor fringe abenefits—except dat I wanta ma Teamsteah's pension anna health-un-welafara plans."

I didn't move or even blink an eye so DaLesio continued: "And heresa da big enchilada: dere will be noa union hirin' halls. Yousa canna hire anybody yousa wants ta work fer youse. And youse cana worka da men acrossa crafta lines alla da time. Yousa can usa da labors anna prentices anna helprs anna

A verbal contract isn't worth the paper it's written on.

SAMUEL GOLDWYN
MOVIE MOGUL

multa-skillda mechanics any way yousa wanta train an assign 'em. An in whatevera goddamn ratios yousa wants."

I still remained motionless and The Lip went on: "I gotta butiful jobba descriptions righta heah in ma pocket dat saysa so. Plus yousa can even hava dat motha-fuckin' managmnt-rights aclause youse gets apaid an xtra fatta fee fer puttin into da contract."

Leo riveted his beady eyes on me, grinned again, and held out his right hand. I was stunned.

"Has your International Teamsters boss in Washington authorized this deal?" I finally asked, without accepting the handshake.

"Datsa none ova youses goddamma business," came the reply, with a knowing wink of the eye. DaLesio might have had authority from his superiors in the International Brotherhood of Teamsters for this amazing "sweetheart" proposal. On the other hand, he could have been ignoring them to make a deal on the unionization of ABCers that would double-cross both his parent organization and the traditional craft jurisdictional practices of the building and construction trades union movement throughout the entire United States.

I knew what ABC's decision would be, but I excused myself from the law office and made a confirming telephone call outside from a nearby public pay telephone booth. Then I returned to the room, shook my head negatively and said: "Sorry, Leo, our answer is 'no.'"

The verbal bombardment that echoed in my ears as I walked out of that room isn't fit to print.

The Lip's "Radical" Work Concept Gains Support

Over a quarter-century later, in March of 2003, a professional union organizer (who asked not to be identified by name) made an obvious but rarely mentioned (by his peers) public prediction. He told the *Bureau of National Affairs* that "until trade unions adjust their structure to match current work patterns in the construction industry" there is little hope that "bottom up" employee organizational drives under the Labor Board–supervised representation election procedures will succeed. "Current data from the U.S. Bureau of Labor Statistics supports this position," he added, and posed this question:

When 70 percent of the workforce that is non-union is performing multiple tasks to get the job done and the 30 percent that is union is performing a single task to get part of the job done, how can [unions] compete?

Answering his own query, the anonymous trade union representative offered more frank and common-sense observations:

> "Wall-to-wall" [union membership] or a union that represents multi-skilled workers is a more appealing option to construction employers than a union that limits its members to the performance of one task. On a non-union concrete project, for instance, one lower-paid worker can build and strike forms, tie reinforcing rod, and pour as well as finish concrete. On a union concrete job, five different higher-paid crafts may be required to do the same work.[9]

An example of what some unionized contractors are doing to overcome this age-old disadvantage, the union agent explained to *The Bureau of National Affairs*, "occurs in downtown Philadelphia." In that location," he said, "190 million dollars in construction contracts during two months of the year 2003 was awarded to firms signatory to agreements with District 50." (This is a typical "wall-to-wall" labor organization normally representing industrial production and maintenance workers and affiliated with the United Steelworkers of America, AFL-CIO.) But then the secretive union organizer added ominously: "District 50's multiskilled members compete directly with craft unions for construction work throughout Pennsylvania and New Jersey."[10]

It is also true that the Philadelphia Convention Center Authority has made a similar "radical" choice. On July 16, 2003, it signed a "customer satisfaction agreement" with locals of the International Electrical Workers, the Ironworkers, and the Teamsters who handle all of the theatrical and sports "show time" labor in the building. This unusual labor contract eliminates craft jurisdictional lines among the three unions. Individual workers are assigned based on their skills across crafts, and they can perform their own set-up work. According to Michael Nutter, chairman of the convention center's board of directors,

Labor is the divine law of our existence; sloth and repose are desertion and suicide.

GIUSEPPE MAZZINI
HISTORIAN

"The way our customers can do business has been streamlined and will make the convention center user-friendly, cost-effective, and bring customers back."[11]

Another recent competitive problem for some of the building trades is the increasing "infringement" of the United Steelworkers of America (USWA) on heavy/highway construction work. Statistics show that from one-third to one-half of the unionized share of their work in many states has been awarded to USWA members.[12]

In 1975, Leo "The Lip" DaLesio made ABC an offer it had to refuse. But his multi-skilled "wall-to-wall" union representation proposal to contractors was ahead of its time in the archaic building trades labor movement. Today a few sophisticated unionized contractors—along with their "maverick" unions and smart clientele—are beginning to get the message.

Caveat emptor!

CHAPTER 46

PHIL ABRAMS LEADS ABC'S 25th BANNER YEAR

THE PRESIDENT OF **ABC** during its 25th silver anniversary year of 1975—Philip Abrams—was not only a visionary and energetic leader like his predecessor, Mike Callas, but also a stickler for operational efficiency. The Association's phenomenal growth was making its diversified activities difficult to administer and its multi-million-dollar budget had become formidable to underwrite.

Although Abrams was only thirty-five years old when he took over the presidential duties, he had proven his executive and administrative skills in his local ABC chapter in Boston while serving officerships there. He was the right national leader for the times.

The construction industry as a whole was in the doldrums. Overall building activity was down 17 percent and one out of every four unionized construction workers was unemployed. Union wage rates rose 16 percent after escaping from President Richard Nixon's federal controls, thereby aggravating the economic recovery. And the building trades were still furious over the fallout from ABC's unfair labor practice charges at the National Labor Relations Board that exposed and curbed their conspiracy of mayhem to destroy open shop competition throughout the nation.

Abrams's Professional Career

Phil Abrams, a smart and aggressive Yankee who could be a tough taskmaster, grew up in Brookline, Massachusetts. He received a B.A. degree from Williams College and launched his business career by working for his father's unionized general construction firm. He then served for three years as a deck officer aboard the aircraft carrier U.S.S. *Enterprise* during the Cuban blockade and in the Mediterranean arena. After that contribution to his country, Abrams took graduate courses in engineering management at Northeastern University. The following year, 1966, he became co-founder of Abreen Corporation, an open shop general contractor. Under his guidance until 1981, the firm expanded its building of commercial and multi-family residential buildings throughout the northeastern United States.

In 1981, Abrams was appointed by President Ronald Reagan to serve in the U.S. Department of Housing and Urban Development in Washington. Over the next three years he rose to under secretary, attended many presidential cabinet meetings, and streamlined, deregulated, and privatized HUD's policies and practices for the benefit of the agency's customers and the taxpaying public. In 1990 he took the time to obtain a degree from the University of Denver College of Law. From 1982 to 2002 he was a real estate developer-manager and currently he is "of counsel" with the Boston law firm of Hinckley, Allen & Snyder.

Abrams's civic and professional service over the years, in addition to the presidency of ABC in 1975, has included chairmanship of the National Construction Industry Council (1976–1978), a directorship of the National Center for Neighborhood Enterprise in Washington, D.C. (1986–1993), a presidential appointment to the United States Holocaust Memorial Council where, as a member of its building committee, he convinced the Council to build its museum with charitable contributions on a merit shop basis (1987–1992), and membership on the advisory board of Landmark Legal Foundation, also in Washington, D.C. (1991 to the present time).

A Hotel and a Hospital Built "Merit Shop"

In the late 1970's, a local affiliate of the Laborers International Union protested to Nicky Hilton, owner of the famous hotel chain, that a non-union contractor called Abreen Corporation was building one of these hotel and shopping center complexes in Natick, Massachusetts. Hilton's response to the union representative was that he "sold rooms, booze, and meals, not labor organizing." In spite of a mob of 1,500 union pickets at the jobsite on one occasion and subsequent union threats to cancel all future AFL-CIO conventions at Hilton's hotels, he never capitulated to the Laborers' compulsory unionism demands.

Phil Abrams set up the required separate gate for "neutrals" in the labor dispute who were working at or delivering materials to the Natick Hilton jobsite. This gate was picketed and therefore illegally "contaminated" as a secondary boycott by the predatory Laborers Union.[1] Other illegal actions of the Laborers included a threat made by Arthur Coia, its international vice president at the time, to a unionized concrete manufacturer that "there would be a big problem" if concrete planks were delivered to the project. There also was a "warning" by a field representative of the Laborers District Council to Phil Abrams that the project "would never be finished non-union."

In spite of this illegal secondary activity, Abreen Corporation completed construction of the Natick Hilton on time and within budget. Phil Abrams's company also was victorious in a lengthy federal lawsuit alleging monetary damages as a result of the unfair labor practices by the Laborers Union. Its local, district, and international affiliates were all held to be actively involved and therefore jointly responsible, following the precedent of ABC's nationwide Labor Board litigation against the building trades hierarchy. On appeal by the unions, over $100,000 in damages eventually was awarded to Abreen Corporation—and the U.S. Supreme Court denied a union request that it review the decision.[2]

In another precarious labor situation, Phil Abrams was taking an evidentiary photo of improper picketing on his jobsite at the Doctor's Hospital in Worcester, Massachusetts, when several of the unionists pushed him up against a wall and pummeled him severely. More pickets rushed into the project, vandalized equipment, chased open shop workers, and assaulted one of them. Soon after, with ABC's support, the local building trades council signed a "no picketing" agreement rather than face criminal and Labor Board charges of roughing up an executive in front of his employees.

Abrams Assumes ABC Leadership

As soon as Phil Abrams was elected president of ABC for the year 1975, he led a thorough internal audit which modernized its accounting procedures.

> As I grow older, I pay less attention to what men say. I just watch what they do.
>
> ANDREW CARNEGIE
> INDUSTRIALIST-
> PHILANTHROPIST

Hold onto the banister when going up stairs.

Dr. Thomas Turner

Next he moved most of the national association's service departments from the Baltimore-Washington International Airport site to the capital of the United States for enhancement of ABC's stature and speedy access to members of Congress and federal government agencies. Then he increased the Merit Shop Legal Defense Fund, with the help of its other trustees—Mike Callas, Joe Rodgers, Leon Altemose, Donald Ball, Jim Godbe, and Jack Veneklasen—to finance ABC's huge nationwide Labor Board litigation against the above-mentioned nationwide building trades and to help defend ABCers involved in other precedential legal issues.[3]

The first phase of this fund-raising effort required the trustees to canvass large construction users and suppliers who dealt with merit shop builders on a regular basis. The second stage called on each ABC chapter to enlist volunteers for solicitation of users in their local areas. Thirdly, direct mail inquiries were used to reach users not contacted personally by chapter volunteers. This three-pronged campaign raised $300,000 within two years' time. Solicitation of ABC's national and local officers and boards of directors by the Fund's trustees brought in additional thousands of dollars. The net result ended the negative legal expense figures on the Association's balance sheet.

On another front, national and chapter offices and their staffers were being queried by interested contractors, construction users and the news media for a profile of the Association. Similar information was needed by ABC's long-range planning committee. So Abrams retained the Opinion Research Corporation (ORC) of Princeton, New Jersey, to conduct a survey of ABC's membership characteristics. Some of the facts uncovered were the following:

ABC Contractor

Philip Abrams, ABC's 17th national president in 1975 and CEO of Abreen Corporation; he is currently a construction management attorney.

1. The breakdown in ABC membership indicated that 57 percent were subcontractors and 37 percent were general contractors, with 5 percent operating as both.
2. The great majority of work performed by ABC contractors was in the commercial sector, followed by

institutional and industrial construction, which were nearly even in volume. Residential building accounted for a relatively small proportion of the work. Overall, open shop contractors performed about 50 percent of the nation's construction work, indicating a major shift away from the use of union labor.

3. There was a sustained growth pattern in all three construction categories over the three-year period covered by the survey. Open shop contractors continued to be moderate-sized firms, with 85 percent of the generals doing less than $5 million annually. The largest group of generals (28 percent) were in the $1 million to $2.5 million range, while 76 percent of the subcontractors did less than $1 million annually.

4. About 92 percent of the construction craftsmen employed by ABC firms worked more hours per year than their union counterparts who were referred out of AFL-CIO hiring halls. More than 80 percent of ABC workers were employed the equivalent of a 40-hour workweek for 52 weeks a year and by one contractor. Ten percent worked 2,200 to 2,400 hours a year. This statistic compared with only 1,200 man-hours per year for the average union construction worker, according to testimony by building trades representatives before the Joint Economic Committee of Congress.

Facts drawn from the ORC survey also showed that (1) the construction industry overall was more stable than it was originally thought to be; (2) the seasonality of employment in open shop construction was greatly exaggerated; (3) open shop construction workers performed over 50 percent of the nation's building projects while enjoying the same sustained employment and skill levels as any typical industrial worker who averaged two thousand hours of work each year. In a "President's Letter" to all ABC members on the subject, Phil Abrams concluded this way: "The marketplace is forcing changes even as it has redistributed the quantity of work. When operating freely, it favors productivity and performance. That is what the merit shop has to offer."[4]

On the unionized side of the industry, two years later the U.S. Bureau of Labor Statistics released a negative report showing that organized labor was

The road to success is not to be run in seven-league boots. Step by step, little by little, bit by bit, that is the way...

CHARLES BUXTON
WRITER

There can be
no security for
any employee in
any business that
doesn't succeed.
There can be no
growth for that
business. There
can be no oppor-
tunity for the
individual to
achieve his
personal ambi-
tions unless
his organization
is a winner.

DUNCAN C. MENZIES
INDUSTRIALIST

responsible for one-fifth of all strikes throughout the nation and the 19 percent of the total workforce that was idled as a result of these work stoppages
during the previous ten-year period.[5]

ABC Continues to Expand

According to John Trimmer, in the year 1975 ABC "chalked up major progress
in all phases of its Association activities, beginning with an 18 percent increase
in member firms." And existing ABC building areas were expanding from
coast to coast as chapters subdivided and spin-offs occurred. "These affiliates
could have been selfish and built up their strength locally but instead they
elected to separate into sub-chapters that later become full-fledged chapters"
said Phil Abrams. "The add-divide-and-multiply effect on ABC growth was
dramatic."[6]

Spin-offs were responsible for the establishment of new chapters in Maryland, Ohio, Texas, Pennsylvania, Michigan, Tennessee, New Jersey, and
Florida. The Yankee Chapter (based in Boston, Massachusetts) was in the
process of creating two developing states—Connecticut and New Hampshire—to serve the New England territory. And spin-offs within state boundaries led to the creation of statewide ABC organizations that became
instrumental in addressing legislation, union activity, and other wide-ranging
issues.[7]

Chapters also were chartered in new areas—making a total of fifty-two
ABC affiliates throughout the nation in 1975. These chapters were located in
thirty-one states and the District of Columbus, including Alabama, Arizona,
Arkansas, California, Connecticut, Colorado, Florida, Georgia, Illinois, Indiana, Iowa, Kentucky, Louisiana, Maryland, Massachusetts, Michigan, Mississippi, Missouri, Nebraska, Nevada, New Hampshire, New Jersey, New York,
Ohio, Oklahoma, Oregon, Pennsylvania, Tennessee, Texas, Virginia, and Wisconsin.[8]

California Completes Western ABC Circuit

There even was group activity and individual members-at-large occurring in
other localities that had been considered impregnable union strongholds.
For example, in 1970 the state of California was considered "sacred" union

territory and ABC was almost unknown. Five years later the merit shop movement there had grown from a few members-at-large to four chapters with one thousand members geographically dividing the state. ABC's local offices were situated in or near San Francisco, Visalia, Los Angeles, and San Diego.

Robert Wood, president of the Southern California Chapter bragged: "We are growing so fast that I can go to a meeting and not know 75 percent of the contractors because they have joined within the past few months." And Joseph Pope, president of the Golden Gate Chapter, explained that all he had to do to attract new members was "educate them" and their customers "on the vast amount of information and know-how ABC could bring in the area of contractors' rights." Pope noted that "competition and other free enterprise concepts in construction were almost dead." Soon McGraw-Hill's *Daily Pacific Builder* reported that "ABC has established itself solidly in California because of mounting concern about construction costs.[9]

This solidified western status of ABC did not come without violent opposition by the building trades. One horrifying example involved Joe Koboski and his two sons when they were working as cleanup men on a residential tract in Anaheim, California. A union organizer showed up, demanding that they join his labor organization on the property. Koboski refused and there was a fight. He was badly beaten, taken to the hospital in a coma, and died the following morning after a four-hour brain operation. The coroner's report listed it as a death from natural causes: "a non-traumatic brain hemorrhage." And the police investigation was dropped.[10]

ABC Member No. 10,000

Total ABC membership stood at five thousand in 1973—and doubled in three years.[11] It was fitting that the ten thousandth member, John Kalva, joined California's Golden Gate Chapter in 1975. This thirty-nine-year-old inventor, engineer, metal fabricator, and builder began his career in construction at the age of twenty-one. He told ABC's *Merit Shop Contractor* magazine how he "learned the business the hard way, shadowing his employer for twelve years, studying everything he could about metal construction, design, water-air hydraulics, and general engineering problem-solving."

Hard work is a better horse to ride than genius.

WALTER LIPPMANN
AMERICAN JOURNALIST

585

In 1971 Kalva formed a partnership with his employer, and K&K Contractors was created. It set up headquarters in St. Helena, the heart of the famous wine-growing country of Napa Valley. Kalva soon became sole owner of the firm and developed the business at a 30 percent per year volume increase rate, "supplying Napa Valley's wine industry with all the merit shop construction it could use."[12] For K&K Contractors and John Kalva, the solution to uninvited problems was the support and know-how he received from ABC: "I was awarded a contract to build part of a new facility in Sebastapol for the Hospital Corporation of America and I was 'sold' when I found out I wasn't the only contractor operating my business the way I thought it should be run without some labor union telling me what I could and couldn't do." And Kalva contended that it was the users who made the merit shop a dynamic force sweeping California construction. For the first time, he confided, "customers were offered quality work delivered within budget and on time by contractors who believed in open lowest-qualified-bidder competition, the unrestricted use of natural talents, and flexible work practices for the benefit of employees, employers, and users."[13]

To service new ABC members like John Kalva and meet the demand to provide competent local chapter staffs in California and throughout the northwest, Phil Abrams set up a special training program for executive directors. ABC veterans were enlisted in a mentoring program for the newcomers and an updated chapter operations manual was distributed.

More ABC Benefits and National Interfacing

In the area of employee benefits, ABC also scored high marks in 1975. The Association's Security Plan, with group health, accident, and life insurance benefits administered on a national basis, was in its nineteenth year and covered over fifty thousand individuals. It had grown from twenty-three thousand participants in the previous year and provided $20 million in benefits to merit shop families. The individually designed ABC pension program continued to increase its membership and give merit shop contractors the opportunity to participate in multi-employer profit sharing and retirement plans with advantageous pooling of investments and cost-effective centralized administration plus leadership in industry-wide standards.

An ABC credit and savings program, chartered by the Federal Credit Union Administration, began operation as a pilot program with the opening of the first office to serve a chapter in the state of Maryland. A run on a savings & loan association in Newark, Ohio, was averted when ABC members rallied in support of a merit shop firm constructing the facility. Unions urged depositors to withdraw their money from the faltering financial institution but ABCers responded with $400,000 in new deposits—twice the amount withdrawn.

In the realm of business development, Abrams activated substantial networking among ABC contractors and their communities. The new program offered an opportunity for users to obtain accurate information about firms at the local location where they chose to build. It brought millions of dollars' worth of new work to member contractors.

ABC's news magazine for merit shop contractors, created by John Trimmer in 1958 as *The ABC Contractor*, was renamed *The Merit Shop Contractor* and its news coverage, length, format, and circulation were greatly enhanced. It began to receive awards for excellence in its field of publication.

On the national scene, Phil Abrams moved ABC into an even larger role in the industry. He helped to organize the National Construction Industry Council (NCIC), the American Institute of Constructors (AIC), and its subsidiary, the American Council for Construction Education (ACCE). The groundwork was developed in ACCE for accrediting schools of construction technology (which had lacked a centralizing influence) to standardize curricula and bring more professional recognition to the industry.

Abrams was elected the chairman of NCIC (with a goal of providing a single voice in projecting future manpower needs of the industry) and he was featured on the cover of *Building Design and Construction* magazine above this quotation: "We believe that the merit shop construction industry is a key element in the private free market economy and that free market economy is an important underpinning of the preservation of the freedoms that have made this nation great."[14]

All of these initiatives helped to create more national recognition for ABC as the "standard bearer for the merit shop" from publications such as *The Wall Street Journal, Business Week, U.S. News and World Report, Fortune,* and *Engineering News-Record.*

Leadership is the initiation and direction of endeavor in the pursuit of consequence.

ROYAL ALCOTT
WRITER

587

The Building Trades Demand Labor Law Changes

In addition to expanding ABC's national prominence, developing more chapters and members, broadening services and benefits programs while improving internal operational efficiency, a crucial contribution to the merit shop movement by Phil Abrams was in the sensitive field of labor legislation.

It was a time when the nation was recovering from the shock of Richard Nixon's resignation as president on August 9, 1974, as well as the line of White House succession in the person of Vice President Gerald Ford. What concerned Abrams was the news that this new president—a Republican who had been endorsed by ABC while serving as a Michigan Congressman for many years—began to show pro-union leanings.

Ford appointed two liberals to key offices: Nelson Rockefeller as vice president, and Harvard University economics professor John Dunlop as secretary of labor. Rockefeller, although a Republican, was a longtime supporter of compulsory unionism. And Dunlop, a Democrat, was "tainted" from his ineffective experience as Chairman of the Construction Industry Stabilization Committee and his lack-luster membership on the National Commission on Productivity. In making both of these appointments, Ford ignored the role of the ever-expanding merit shop sector and its free marketplace. He also named an AFL-CIO official to a sensitive post in the Central Intelligence Agency.

Those biased actions encouraged the AFL-CIO's Building Trades Department to exert more pressure on President Jerry Ford and on left-wing politicians whom the Trades Department helped to install in Congress during the 1974 elections. So Big Labor announced two major legislative demands: protection and expansion of the farcical Davis-Bacon "prevailing wage" law[15] and removal of the Taft-Hartley Act ban on union secondary boycotts.[16]

With more than $40 billion in federal government construction projects available and private sector building still sluggish, Abrams and ABC led the merit shop's counter-attack against the AFL-CIO on both of these critical lawmaking fronts. First, thousands of "Davis-Bacon Fact Files" were distributed to legislators, the media, and construction-related organizations as part of an education program to dramatize the negative impact of the Davis-Bacon Act on the American economy.[17] Next, Abrams testified before several congressional committees to urge outright repeal of the antiquated wage law. He claimed that "this anachronism of the 1930s has led to inflated union-scale wage rates on public construction through sloppy, negligent, and distorted administration of a statute that has increased the cost of public construction by 15 to 30 percent."

More specifically, Abrams told the Public Works Subcommittee, the Labor-Management Relations Subcommittee, and the Economic Development Subcommittee of the House of Representatives, that

> ...at a time of one of the biggest budget deficits in the country's history, construction wage rates are in no need of artificial government support. The Davis-Bacon Act should be abolished because it has outlived its usefulness, greatly increased the cost of public work paid for by taxpayers and resulted in unemployment, low productivity, and discrimination against minorities. This unfair law gives monopolistic power to the construction unions, the freedom of choice of both employees and employers is destroyed, and the national defense is adversely affected.[18]

Alternatively, at the request of several concerned Congressmen who thought they could not muster enough votes for outright repeal of the Davis-Bacon Act, Abrams outlined several potential amendments to reform this statute, including the following:

- Narrow the Act's coverage.
- Redefine "prevailing" wages to do away with the "30 percent rule" and use a realistic "local average" wage scale.
- Permit open shop contractors to perform their normal work practices, including multi-skilled job assignments and methods that increase productivity.
- Broaden Davis-Bacon Act regulations pertaining to apprentices, helpers and trainees so that there were no craft limitations on their use.
- Eliminate the contractors' weekly submission of certified payrolls.[19]

This ABC counter-offense neutralized the attempt of the AFL-CIO Building Trades Department to make Congress increase labor union control

When in a political war, always keep an eye to the rear.

WESS ROBERTS
AUTHOR,
IN *ATTILA THE HUN*

over administration of the Davis-Bacon Act. The law remained unchanged except that the Abrams testimony influenced the Department of Labor's Wage Appeals Board to hand down a few rational prevailing wage determinations.

In his ABC memoirs, John Trimmer added these observations on the Davis-Bacon Act farce:

> The appearance of Phil Abrams before Congress signified the increasing attention the Association was getting in the legislative forum. And ABC's annual legislative conference brought out more than 300 ABC members that year. Some 700 guests, including 115 congressmen and 11 senators, attended a reception held during the conference.
>
> Academic circles also were developing a keen interest in the Davis-Bacon Act and the great majority of economists were opposed to it. To capitalize on this commitment, the Merit Shop Foundation engaged Armand Thieblot, a professor at the University of Maryland, to undertake a study of prevailing wage legislation in the various states. It proved to be an important educational and lobbying tool over the ensuing years.[20]

The Common Situs Secondary Boycott Battle

Another formidable political fight developed in 1975 over the AFL-CIO Building Trades Department's attempt to legalize secondary boycotts at construction projects through introduction in Congress of a so-called "common situs picketing bill." The origin of this issue (as discussed in Chapter 7) dated back to the Supreme Court's *Denver Building Trades* decision and its confirmation in ABC's subsequent *Stover Steel* case victory at the National Labor Relations Board.

The Supreme Court held in *Denver* that Section 8(b)(4)(A)—the secondary boycott provision of the Taft-Hartley Act at issue—"was in conformity with the dual Congressional objectives of preserving the right of labor organizations to bring pressure on offending employers in primary labor disputes and of shielding unoffending employers and others from pressures in controversies not their own."[21] Indiscriminate picketing of all entrances of an entire construction jobsite which enmeshed "neutral" contractors (separate legal entities) in a labor dispute involving a targeted contractor thus was held to be a violation of Section 8(b)(4)(A).

This hard won statutory edict that restricted common situs picketing was—and still is—vital to the survival of ABC and freedom in the merit shop construction workplace throughout the nation.

An editorial in *Business Week* magazine dated June 9, 1975, and entitled "A Longer Picket Line," supported ABC's position in the political fray and set the stage for a massive legislative battle that ended in the White House:

> During the past decade, high wages and restrictive work practices dictated by the building trades unions have produced the reaction that classic economists would have predicted. Non-union contractors have been gaining rapidly in strength and the so-called merit shop, where union and non-union contractors work side by side on the same job, has been spreading. The Associated Builders & Contractors, a trade association of merit shop employers, claims that 50 percent of all industrial and commercial construction is now handled this way.
>
> The unions, however, are no admirers of Adam Smith [the famous 18th century English economist who emphasized "free competition"]. They are pushing hard for legislation to reinforce their attack on the merit shop. In hearings beginning on June 5 before the House Labor-Management Relations Subcommittee, they will lobby hard for an amendment to the Taft-Hartley Act to permit "common situs" picketing of construction jobs.
>
> Under present law this means that a union may picket a non-union contractor in an effort to make him sign a contract, but it cannot picket other contractors on the same job site. *If Congress authorizes common situs picketing, the picket lines could be extended to all contractors working there. This could close down the whole job, putting extra pressure on the non-union contractor. With this power, the unions could probably wipe out the merit shop.*
>
> Construction admittedly does present some particular problems to union organizers. But Congress should not, under any circumstances,

put this weapon in the hands of unions that have shown no disposition to be moderate in their demands or farsighted in their appraisal of the economic consequences. The growth of non-union contractors has been a healthy development in an industry where the building trades have ruthlessly exploited their monopoly power.

The merit shop deserves encouragement, not a death sentence. Similar moves to amend Taft-Hartley died in committee in 1965 and 1969. Congress should show the same good judgment this time.[22] [emphasis added]

During the same month, Phil Abrams cautioned all ABC members through the *Contractor* magazine about this threat to their businesses from passage of the union-sponsored bill labeled H.R. 5900–S.1479:

1. To you and me as merit shop contractors, passage of this "common situs" bill means that the currently legal use of "reserved" or "separate" gates during informational or organizational picketing would be futile.

2. Our employees' legal freedom to refrain from joining a union would be undermined as labor coercion against other employers at the site would be used to compel unionization of our workers.

3. If we were building an addition to an existing building, we would no longer be able to determine the location of picket activity so that it wouldn't interfere with use of the existing facility.

4. If we were working on a predominantly union job site as a non-union subcontractor, we would no longer be able to prevent the project from being shut down because unions could picket with impunity whenever union craftsmen were working there. We would have to avoid those situations, thereby depriving union general contractors of the competitive opportunities they now make available to our non-union members.

5. Open shop general contractors would no longer be able to shield union subcontractors from picketing, thereby making the utilization of union subcontractors on merit shop job sites a dubious alternative.[23]

Abrams forewarned his readers that "these last two consequences threaten the heart and soul of the merit shop philosophy—the belief that union and non-union contractors and workers should work together in harmony on a building project." And he predicted: "Passage of common situs legislation will force the polarization of our industry as construction jobs become either totally union or totally non-union. The freedom of choice of both employers and employees will be destroyed and national defense will be adversely affected."[24]

ABC was not alone in perceiving the crisis that this common situs bill posed to the entire building industry. Many unionized general contractors and subcontractors had benefited from their job site association with open shop generals and subs. Every major construction association soon united in opposition to the bill. And in his renowned 1975 study on the building industry in the United States, Professor Herbert Northrup of the Industrial Research Unit of the University of Pennsylvania's Wharton School predicted: "It seems likely that open shop construction will continue to expand unless inhibited by the possible change in the Taft-Hartley Act's secondary boycott restrictions."[25]

President Ford and Congress Cater to Big Labor

The bad news for ABC was that President Ford bowed to organized labor's pressure by letting it be known that he would sign the union-sponsored common situs picketing bill "under certain circumstances." But it had to be accompanied, he said, by legislation that (in a non sequitur of spun political weasel words) "would result in substantive reforms of the collective bargaining process in the construction industry."

That fuzzy message gave Big Labor new hope—and the proposed Construction Industry Collective Bargaining Act of 1975 emerged. It soon became known as the "Dunlop bill" because it evolved from several weeks of secretive machinations between Labor Secretary John Dunlop, AFL-CIO Building Trades leaders, and a few large unionized contractors in collaboration with their congressional pets. This Dunlop bill (H.R. 9500–S.2305) was ballyhooed in the left-wing national press as the salvation of the construction industry and the answer to President Ford's request to "reform" the Taft-Hartley Act's collective bargaining ground rules.

Salesmanship consists of transferring a conviction by a seller to a buyer.

PAUL G. HOFFMAN
INDUSTRIALIST

It seemed as though the country's legislative process, at least as it related to construction labor law under the Taft-Hartley Act, had been pre-empted by the AFL/CIO Building Trades Department and Labor Secretary Dunlop. Subsequent "rubber stamp" hearings on the common situs bill before the House and Senate Labor Committees confirmed that suspicion. Particularly noxious was the fact that Congress had been told by the building trades unions that the Dunlop collective bargaining "reform" bill was a take-it-or-leave-it statute that needed to become law as drafted without any change during the legislative process.

The truth was that this Dunlop bill turned out to be a phony political shell game that legalized secondary boycotts and provided two innocuous "reforms": a thirty-day cooling-off period in the collective bargaining negotiations before a strike could occur, and a requirement for international union approval of all locally negotiated labor contracts.

The bill avoided mention of any of the real problems of collective bargaining in the construction industry that needed reformation, such as an economic imbalance in leverage at the negotiating table between powerful unions and weak unionized management. Contract negotiations frequently were held at the peak of the building season and employers who refused to sign a contract risked strikes and customer penalties for failure to complete construction projects on time. Under these conditions, unionized contractors regularly succumbed and passed the inflated labor costs on to their clientele and the public. These "sweetheart" deals helped to cause the nation's economic crisis and cried out for anti-labor "reform."

Phil Abrams summed up ABC's legislative dilemma in these words:

> The whole matter would be laughable if President Ford's veto of common situs legislation didn't hinge on passage of the Dunlop bill. For the sake of this pitifully weak effort to reform collective bargaining, we are faced with the possibility of the President signing the disastrous common situs secondary boycott legislation. Other construction employers' trade associations, while acknowledging the political linkage between the two bills, are prepared to sell out for a pittance and have either endorsed the Dunlop bill or taken a neutral position on it.[26]

In the October 1975 edition of ABC's *Contractor* magazine, Phil Abrams wrote an editorial entitled "At the Crossroads." Some of his concerned comments were:

> Vote-hungry politicians in Washington have conjured up the belief that it is good politics to favor the common situs picketing bill and also give international unions the control of local collective bargaining agreements under the Dunlop bill. It is unbelievable to hear these politicos say that opposition to the legalization of secondary boycotts is something they cannot afford to show in public, no matter how they feel privately.
>
> At this point, ABC's prospects look dim for defeating common situs picketing and Big Labor's prospects look bright for imposing national controls on local collective bargaining contracts.
>
> As for the future of the merit shop, we know one thing: members of ABC who espouse its principles did not get where they are today by cringing at every threat or difficulty that confronted them. On the contrary, they got where they are by facing up to problems and standing up for constitutional and entrepreneurial principles. Our fight against compulsory unionism and for the uncoerced right to work have been and continue to be immutable.

Abrams and ABC Go on the Offense

Returning to the political counterattack, Abrams testified before several congressional committees and labeled the Dunlop collective bargaining reform bill nothing but a "hoax." He said that "it is being used as a smoke screen and sold as a trade-off for passage of a secondary boycott bill which would cause labor chaos by legalizing the means for construction unions to shut down all craft trades at the same time throughout the peak season of the building industry."[27]

Abrams (who was well-grounded in labor law) added that union attempts to link the Dunlop collective bargaining bill with the common situs bill provided no legitimate basis for acceptability by Congress or President Ford. The Dunlop bill, he said, "was not only poorly drafted and ambiguous but, more to the point, it didn't do anything that could be labeled 'a reform that

Liberalism had been supposed to advocate liberty but what the parties that still call themselves "liberal" now advocate is control.

GEORGE SANTAYANA
PHILOSOPHER

595

Valor grows by daring; fear by holding back.

PUBLILIUS SYRUS
ROMAN HISTORIAN

improved labor-management relations.'" He also explained that the Dunlop bill (which passed the House by a vote of 302 to 95) purported to create "a thirty-day cooling-off period" before a union would be allowed to strike during a contract negotiation period. That ploy was "futile and unnecessary," he said, "because it would only duplicate the existing authority of the Federal Mediation Service to do the same thing." And he pointed out that nothing in the bill or any law prevented a strike from occurring thirty-one days later.

With respect to the Dunlop bill's proposed "international union control" over local collective bargaining contracts, Abrams asked:

> Do we really expect that senior union leaders in Washington will assert
> some statesmanship by ordering their local members to withhold slow-

ABC CONTRACTOR

ABC's National President Philip Abrams (far left) testified before the House Subcommittee on Labor-Management Relations as to the controversial labor law reform bill. Joining Abrams on ABC testimony was the author (second from left). Others testifying include: David N. Connor (center) of the National Association of Home Builders; James Pizzagalli (second from right), testifying for Associated General Contractors; and William E. Naumann, also testifying for AGC.

downs and strike pressure in favor of the public interest and the pro-motion of productivity and reasonable wage demands? The history of the labor movement begs issue with that premise. These international unions, which have encouraged or condoned violence, sabotage and other illegal activity over the years to gain their objective, should not be expected to reform and police their local unions' collective bar-gaining agreements for the common good.

On the contrary, the AFL-CIO Building Trades Department would use the Dunlop bill's new power to oversee all local labor con-tracts as a wedge to force their own national political and economic programs on their local unions. The labor problem within the con-struction industry that needs reform is an economic imbalance at the bargaining table. An uneven playing field has emasculated manage-ment's negotiating power. That is the root cause, that is the malaise—and the Dunlop bill only increases that inequity.[28]

Abrams also condemned the AFL-CIO's effort to rush both the Dunlop col-lective bargaining bill and the common situs picketing bill through Con-gress so that opponents of the bills had only three days to prepare themselves before being called on to testify about the issues. And he concluded: "We cannot in good faith support an economic scheme that would have the end effect of selling out free enterprise to satisfy the demands of a special inter-est group."[29]

ABC brought all of its communications skills and political contacts to the forefront in this grim battle for survival. With a Democratic majority in Con-gress and its union-controlled internal committees, the only hope of defeat-ing the nefarious legislation was to obtain a veto of it by President Ford. Towards that goal, Phil Abrams created a network involving not only ABC contractors but also their employees, construction users, business organiza-tions, civic and minority groups, and private citizens. In response to a pub-licly released union "blue sheet" praising the two bills, ABC's public relations team created a "red, white, and blue memo" which detailed the faults of the two bills—and distributed 250,000 copies of it.

I think that American salesmanship can be a weapon more powerful than the atomic bomb.

HENRY J. KAISER
INDUSTRIALIST

Intentionally marked "confidential," these pamphlets were left at every congressional office on Capitol Hill, thus assuring wide reading of ABC's message the next day. Similar background material was sent by ABC to the news media throughout the country. ABC chapters swung into action in their areas. Also fighting alongside ABC on this vital issue were the National Association of Manufacturers, the Business Roundtable, and the U.S. Chamber of Commerce. As a result the business community and general public opposition against the legislation was rising.

In the heat of this conflict—with the looming possibility of an effective filibuster against passage of these two pro-labor bills in the Senate—Congress "compromised" by drafting them into a single "blended" bill. It still allowed *unrestricted* common situs picketing and its proponents believed that President Ford would sign it. The final vote endorsing the amended bill in the House of Representatives was 229 to 189 and the Senate approved the conference report on it by a vote of 52 to 43.

The AFL-CIO headquarters staff in Washington was jubilant.

While all this was taking place, Abrams established an emergency request to ABC members. He urged them to register their protest against the "blended bill" to President Ford and their elected representatives in both houses of Congress. ABC also targeted Republican Party committee members throughout the nation. Most of them were conservative and appalled at the prospect of a Republican president signing such anti–free enterprise legislation. Senator Paul Fannin (R-AZ) and the National Right To Work Committee also recruited thousands of key GOP contributors to flood the White House with telegrams, letters, and postcards imploring President Ford to reject the bill.

As a result of these efforts, Abrams and a large contingent of Republican state party chairmen were able to attend several high-level meetings at the White House. They saw President Ford personally and urged him to veto the proposed legislation. Ford's Council of Economic Advisers agreed and only one Cabinet member—Labor Secretary Dunlop—opposed a presidential veto.

Ford Finally Blocks Labor "Reform"

On January 2, 1976, Jerry Ford announced that "vigorous controversy" had caused him to change his mind and he officially rejected all of Big Labor's "reform amendments" to the Taft-Hartley Act as passed by Congress. The AFL-CIO was stunned, and a chagrined Labor Secretary John Dunlop resigned from government service in protest.

As a follow-up to this awesome legislative achievement, Phil Abrams called for immediate action by all ABC members in the upcoming congressional election campaigns by devoting money and manpower for the election of candidates who would not be subservient to Big Labor. "Unless ABC is willing to make that pledge," he said, "we deserve to get politicians in Congress who respond like Pavlov's dogs to the ringing of the union bell."[30]

John Trimmer wrote a "special comment" for the *Merit Shop Contractor* entitled "Common Situs Veto: A Victory For All." He said: "President Ford's decision to veto the common situs picketing bill was a tremendous win for not only management in the construction industry but also for individual employees who would rather work than engage in job site disruption and loss of wages." Trimmer added these memorable words:

> Rejection of this bill, which would have legalized secondary boycotts in the construction industry, was the result of a vigorous campaign in which ABC was at all times in the forefront and totally committed to its defeat. But it was also a coalition victory. Some 30 national trade associations played varying roles in the fight against it.
>
> There will, no doubt, be many explanations as to how the victory was achieved and many claims among individual groups for having played the stellar role. But the key turn in the struggle appeared to come when ABC's President, Philip Abrams, termed the so-called Dunlop collective bargaining bill a "hoax" after it suddenly appeared as the Siamese twin of the common situs bill . . .
>
> The entire construction industry was united against it and political sugar from Labor Secretary Dunlop did not help the bitter situs picketing medicine go down.
>
> We in ABC who fought the combined bills can be proud of the efforts of Phil Abrams and the rest of our officers, staff and members who rolled up a strong opposition tide against tremendous political

We must remain true to our principles and keep fighting for what we know is right: a less intrusive federal government.

EDWIN FEULNER
PRESIDENT
HERITAGE FOUNDATION

If all men were just, there would be no need for courage.

PLUTARCH'S
LIFE OF AGESILAUS,
XXXII.v

odds. We also remember with gratitude the large number of Representatives and Senators who stood up to intense lobbying pressure from the building trades.[31]

ABC's quarter-century celebration was held in Houston, Texas, in that banner year of 1975. Over 1,500 members attended. Its keynote speaker was the former Governor of California, Ronald Reagan, who was contemplating a campaign for the presidency of the United States. He endorsed enthusiastically the philosophy of the "merit shop"—which he compared to the "Spirit of 1776"—and he received a standing ovation for his remarks.

"Tell me, sir, is there any such thing as just a plain Republican, or are they all staunch?"

The Association, at age twenty-five, had ten thousand active members in forty-two chapters located in thirty-one states, from coast to coast. ABC was the voice of more than half of the country's industrial, commercial, and institutional construction industry. No other employers' organization in America could compare to this remarkable growth.[32]

Under the aggressive and fearless leadership of Phil Abrams, defeat of the building trades common situs picketing bill which would have legalized secondary boycotts (and its companion pro-union collective bargaining "reform" bill) was a major milestone for ABC. It proved once again that aroused public opinion can overcome a powerful special interest group, even if it is Big Labor.

The "Spirit of 1876" in 1975 culminated in continued growth of the Association, both externally and internally, plus a legislative victory of everlasting importance to the continued success of ABC and its merit shop crusade for freedom in the construction workplace.

CHAPTER 47

A UNION DEFEAT NEAR GETTYSBURG

O NE SCORE AND SEVERAL YEARS AGO, I received a mysterious telephone call at my Baltimore law office. The conversation featured a terse male voice on the other end of the line. It proceeded something like this:

"Cook, I represent a company that's non-union and wants its employees to stay that way. Are you interested in helping us in a Labor Board election to keep within the legal ground rules and win?"

"Yes, sir, that's my business. We call it positive employee relations," I answered.

"Good. Meet me at the Apple and Stag Bar of the Fairfield Inn on Route 116 just a bit west of Gettysburg. Be there at 4:00 p.m. next Thursday. I'll be wearing a red necktie."

And he hung up.

My curiosity was aroused about the location that was chosen for this confab, and I discovered that the inn was originally a plantation home of Squire William Miller. He settled there in 1755. In olden days the highway through the town of Fairfield became known as the "Great Road" from York, Pennsylvania, to Hagerstown, Maryland. The inn was a stagecoach stop as well as a drover's tavern. It had been in continuous operation since 1823, including a week in 1863 as mandatory host to the colorful Confederate General, Jeb Stuart, his cavalrymen, and their entourage.

Over a hundred years later, I entered the Fairfield Inn's oak-paneled barroom at the appointed hour. Alone at a table in the far corner sat Mr. Red Tie. He was a medium-sized man with a curt midwestern accent, dressed in

Show me a hero and I will write you a tragedy.

F. SCOTT FITZGERALD
NOVELIST

a conservative business suit. I introduced myself but received no identifying response from him. We nursed a couple of draft beers from pewter mugs while he cross-examined me on my professional career and my personal life. He seemed well briefed in advance on most of the pertinent facts.

Eventually my incognito host stood up, paid the bar tab, shook my hand firmly, and said: "You'll be hearing from me soon."

Culp's Hill Remembered

Driving back to Baltimore, my thoughts were racing between what prominent business firm in the area had a labor relations problem and the personal irony of the locale selected for this covert meeting. I didn't guess the name of the potential client but the nearby town of Gettysburg, Pennsylvania, was—and will always be—near and dear to my heart. The locale made me reminisce about family history…

My mother, Helen Earnshaw Cook (a Culp family descendant) grew up there. My father, Albert Samuel Cook, Sr. (who began his professional career as a one-room-school teacher and eventually became Maryland's state superintendent of schools) was raised on a farm "across the mountain" in Greencastle.

My dear parents are buried just a few hundred yards from the site of President Abraham Lincoln's historic address of November 23, 1863, in which he dedicated part of the battlefield as a cemetery for all the brave soldiers who died there. And the morning of the third and final day of that bloodiest battle in American history—which marked the turning point of the Civil War—was fought across the property of my great-grandfather, Henry Culp, and his wife, Elizabeth.

Two young family cousins who had played on the Culp farmland as boys served with the combined 172,000 troops of General Robert E. Lee's Army of Northern Virginia and General George G. Meade's Union Army of the Potomac who engaged in that horrendous head-to-head confrontation. It resulted in over fifty thousand casualties in three days. In an area encompassing twenty-five square miles, more men fought and more men died than in any battle before or since on North American soil.

Cousin Wesley Culp had been working for a carriage maker in Shepherdstown, West Virginia, when, at age twenty-one, he enlisted as a private in the 2nd

Virginia Regiment of the Confederate Army. Cousin William Culp, Wesley's older brother by eight years, became a lieutenant in Pennsylvania's 87th Regiment of the Union Army.

Wesley was shot at point-blank range and died on July 3, 1863. He had been assaulting the summit of the once thickly wooded "Culp's Hill" on the family farm, in sight of the brick farmhouse that still stands in the valley below. Artillery fire swept away the great oak forest and turned that beautiful hillside into "a precipice of death."[1]

Grove Versus the UAW

Leaving those stirring personal memories and returning to my professional mission, exciting news came by telephone a few days after my meeting at the Fairfield Inn. Mr. Red Tie advised me that Grove Manufacturing Company—the world's largest builder of hydraulic cranes—was ready to retain me as corporate labor counsel as soon as I made contact. My assignment would be to help the company defeat an organizational campaign by the powerful United Autoworkers Union, AFL-CIO (hereinafter "UAW").

I never saw or heard from Mr. Red Tie again.

The UAW's secret ballot election procedure was already in motion under the supervision of the National Labor Relations Board when I entered the case. At stake was union representation of 2,500 workers in a state-of-the-art crane manufacturing plant located in the hamlet of Shady Grove, Pennsylvania. It was just fifteen miles north of the Maryland border and about twenty-five miles west of Gettysburg. The giant facility was surrounded by farmland, grazing beef cattle, a couple of small houses, and a country store.

Grove sold its cranes through a worldwide network of licensed distributors to both unionized and non-union contractors, using precedent-setting techniques of marketing and servicing. The firm owned four jet airplanes to help service its many national and international customers.

To my delight, I learned that Grove also was a member and strong supporter of my client, the tri-state Cumberland Valley Chapter of ABC. It was (and still is) headquartered in nearby Hagerstown, Maryland, representing merit shoppers in Western Maryland, Southwestern Pennsylvania, and West Virginia.

As soon as two or more people work together, they create people problems—and sometimes labor unions.

AUTHOR SAM COOK'S CAVEAT

A leader has two important characteristics. First, he is going somewhere; second, he is able to persuade other people to go with him.

MAXIMILIEN
ROBESPIERRE
FRENCH STATESMAN

As I read a sales brochure on the history of the famous Grove firm, pieces of the puzzle began to fit together. The unusual story began in January of 1947 when two Grove family brothers (John, an engineer, and Dwight, a businessman) plus Wayne Nicarry (a businessman and also an ordained minister of the Church of the Brethren) began producing rubber-tired farm wagons in a two-car garage at Shady Grove. They needed a small yard-type mechanism that they could purchase to lift and transport steel I-beams used as axles in the construction of their wagons. Failing to find one, in 1949 the three men decided to build their own mobile crane. Though crude, it worked well. After major refinements, they introduced their novel hydraulic and ambulatory two-ton lifting machine to the commercial and industrial construction marketplace in 1952.

From that humble beginning, Grove Manufacturing Company grew to a position of worldwide leadership in its field. By 1976, dozens of different crane models were being produced. They all were hydraulic, mobile, self-propelled, operable by one person driving to any jobsite, and capable of being set up in all types of terrain. These models ranged from small stevedore size to giants mounted on a truck chassis, with telescoping, trapezoidal-style booms and a lift capacity of one hundred tons. They simplified and reduced both production and operational cost, thereby revolutionizing the construction business.

The company is known today as "Grove Worldwide."

J. Martin Benchoff: A Born Leader

The man primarily responsible for this success at the time that I became Grove's labor counsel in 1976 was J. Martin Benchoff, the company's president and chief executive officer. He grew up on a horse and beef cattle farm ten miles from Shady Grove in the Blue Ridge Mountains that surround the Cumberland Valley.

As a youngster, Benchoff was fond of horses and became an expert rider. In his twenties, he competed on the standardbred saddlehorse "A Circuit" for a living, handling three, four and five-gaited steeds plus harness rigs. When he won grand championships at Devon, Pennsylvania, and Lexington, Kentucky,

J. Martin Benchoff, president and CEO, Grove Manufacturing Co. in 1976.

Large rough terrain Grove crane, model RT 855, in 1998.
REPRINTED WITH PERMISSION OF GROVE WORLDWIDE

Aerial view photo of the Shady Grove Works of Grove Manufacturing Company.
REPRINTED WITH PERMISSION OF GROVE WORLDWIDE

Who works achieves and who sows reaps.

OLD CHINESE PROVERB

he considered a career as a professional horseman. In a twist of fate, after graduating from the University of Pennsylvania, he turned to the business world and was hired by Wayne Nicarry in 1954 as a farm wagon salesman on a commission basis.

Ten years later, Martin Benchoff became the president and chief executive officer of Grove Manufacturing Company. To know this man was to never forget him. A natural leader, he had a tall, sturdy physique, piercing eyes, and a booming voice. He could be an attentive listener but there was no mistaking who was the boss when a decision needed to be made. He was charismatic, fearless, clever, innovative, and a master student of human nature. He was also a great motivator and communicator with a sense of humor, a super-salesman of Grove cranes and for Grove employees, greatly respected by all (and at times even feared).

I still remember an emergency situation when Martin's personal jet plane picked me up on short notice early one morning at Friendship International Airport in Baltimore. He offered me some coffee as soon as I came aboard while he showed me an anonymous letter threatening to take his life: "You'll get yours in three days..." Then he began to pepper me with tough questions about the legal status of recent union activities at Grove.

Surprised, I hesitated to answer for a few moments, trying to clear my still-sleepy thinking apparatus. Then I hedged (with appropriate gestures) that *on the one hand* there were (here unnamed) facts "A, B, and C" to be considered, and *on the other hand* there also were cases "X, Y, and Z" to be weighed. Martin gave me a stern look, but with a twinkle in his eye, and said: "Damn it, Sam, I don't pay you for that kind of weasel answer. I may have to fire you and get me a one-armed lawyer."

I've never forgotten that client relations lesson.

Benchoff entertained his customers in regal style, conducting business with tycoons of industry and heads of government on a global level. But he regarded the general welfare of his employees as equally important. He frequently strolled along the assembly lines of the huge manufacturing plant at Shady Grove to maintain a friendly relationship with the workforce. He would stop by and chat with many employees whom he knew on a first-name basis. They all understood that the door to his office was always open to them if necessary to solve a workplace problem. They also had proof that he kept his word.

The Union Avoidance Campaign Begins

I began my legal representation of Grove in this union representation election case at a conference with Martin Benchoff in which he outlined his employee relations goals and Grove's managerial structure. Then I met the rest of the top management team to discuss our objective: defeating the UAW in a fair, aggressive, and legal "political" campaign urging the eligible employees to vote "NO UNION." In addition to master strategist Benchoff, there was Arthur Hamilton (the shrewd, conservative vice president in charge of what is now called "human resources" and a former commander in the U.S. Navy); Gary Spickler (the handsome, velvet-voiced, people-oriented manager of production); Rodney Benchoff (a smart young vice president and aide-de-camp to his cousin, "JMB"); and Roger Hockenberry (the energetic, popular, hands-on assistant director of human resources). It was Grove's first serious union organizational attack—and I told these executives both the good and bad news that could be ahead for them.

In July of 1976, a formal hearing was conducted in Shady Grove by the Labor Board to determine which specific coworkers were eligible to vote in the election. It involved the company's 2,500 non-supervisory production and maintenance employees at the main Shady Grove works. I also succeeded in obtaining a ruling that included the company's "loyal" blue-collar employees working at two small auxiliary facilities of Grove (in Greencastle and Chambersburg) within the "appropriate bargaining unit." Then I persuaded the Labor Board to allow the company six weeks' time for "campaigning" before the secret ballot election would take place.

The next step was to review with our management team the lawful rights of the employees and the union, along with the legal "dos and don'ts" for Grove management under the national Taft-Hartley Act. The UAW knew these ground rules and counted on the fact that they would be posted officially throughout the plant (under a Labor Board order) for Grove employees to read before voting took place. Here are some pertinent passages:

An employer generally gets the employees he deserves.

WALTER BILBEY
HUMANIST

609

RIGHTS OF EMPLOYEES:

- To self-organization
- To form, join, or assist labor organizations
- To bargain collectively through representatives of their own choosing
- To act together for the purposes of collective bargaining or other mutual aid or protection
- *To refuse to do any or all of these things unless the Union and Employer, in a State [like Pennsylvania] where such agreements are permitted, enter into a lawful union security clause requiring employees to join the union* [emphasis added]

CONDUCT WHICH INTERFERES WITH THE RIGHTS OF EMPLOYEES AND MAY RESULT IN SETTING ASIDE THE ELECTION:

- Threatening loss of jobs or benefits by an Employer or a Union
- Misstating important facts by a Union or an Employer where the other party does not have a fair chance to reply
- Promising or granting promotions, pay raises, or other benefits, to influence an employee's vote by a party capable of carrying out such promises
- An Employer firing employees to discourage or encourage union activity or a Union causing them to be fired to encourage union activity
- Making campaign speeches to assembled groups of employees on company time within the 24-hour period before the election
- Incitement by either an Employer or a Union of racial or religious prejudice by inflammatory appeals
- Threatening physical force or violence to employees by a Union or an Employer to influence their votes

An Employee Relations Audit

Although it was obvious to me that Grove management had installed a generous employee relations program before the UAW began its organizational drive, the Union still was able to gain substantial support within the Grove workforce. As proof, the UAW submitted confidentially to the Labor Board what it claimed were the personally signed union authorization cards from at least 30 percent of the eligible bargaining unit voters—750 or more cards. This evidence (which the legal ground rules would not permit Grove to inspect and verify) was required by the Board for its own judgment on whether an election should be held.

Humanists Maslow and Layden Are Respected

The Board's affirmative administrative ruling for the UAW also caused me to conduct my own speedy employee relations audit, from recruitment to retirement. I looked for poor morale, insecurity, and job stress that cause sub-par productivity, excessive absenteeism, industrial accidents, time and material waste, and job turnover. My own "guru," Professor Abraham Maslow of Brandeis University, described this natural phenomenon in his renowned "hierarchy of human needs" that range (in the workplace) from basic and bodily wants to the complex and psychological. He listed five progressive stages: personal survival, job security, self-esteem, peer respect, and at the top of the attainment ladder, a goal of self-fulfillment.

Another great humanist, Dr. Milton Layden—a practicing psychiatrist at the Johns Hopkins Hospital in Baltimore—confirmed these truths in his arresting book on *Escaping The Hostility Trap*. He wrote that the decline in a person's security, compatibility, or self-esteem leads to feelings of inferiority and anxiety, followed by outright hostility.[2]

These human characteristics described by Layden and Maslow also frequently make the frustrated, angry workers vulnerable to a union organizational campaign. In the situation at Grove, there was an added incentive. Someone had offered a $100,000 bounty to any labor organization that could unionize Grove's employees.

Summarizing and blending the teachings of Maslow and Layden, I gave Grove my same workplace "golden rule" test that I used with my clients in the building and construction industry: *All employees must be treated as honorable individuals; justly rewarded; offered a friendly, safe, and healthy workplace; given equal employment opportunity; properly trained and fairly assigned; sincerely motivated; encouraged to advance; openly heard; fully informed; and evenly disciplined.*

Grove passed my audit with high marks.

I was especially impressed by the company's longtime program that substituted a valuable non-union counterpart to shop stewards that the UAW assigned along the production assembly lines of the auto and truck manufacturers whose employees it represented. None of these union stewards ever performed any work on building the vehicles; their wages were paid by auto company management, and they were allowed to spend all of their time "policing" the daily enforcement of these UAW contracts. They griped, accosted company supervisors, filed formal workplace grievances, and demanded other "protection" of their union members—at the employers' expense.

Instead of shop stewards, employees known as "ombudsmen" were assigned by Grove in small private offices conveniently near production and maintenance work areas, twenty-four hours a day, seven days a week. The ombudsmen were trained and paid by Grove's human resources department as *fiduciaries* or *trustees* to assist rank-and-file employees in solving their individual problems on a non-adversarial and confidential basis. No aggrieved employee's identification could be disclosed to Grove management unless plant safety or security was involved. The ombudsmen were respected and used frequently by the workers, with excellent results for all concerned.

Six Weeks to Go Before Victory or Defeat

As soon as Grove management received the Labor Board's order setting September 15, 1976, as the date of the UAW election, our "vote no-union" campaign moved into high gear. First we made certain that all eligible voters knew when, where, and how to vote. The Labor Board's official instructions, which were posted in the plant, read like this:

REPRESENTATION ELECTION

The election will be by SECRET ballot under the supervision of the Regional Director of the National Labor Relations Board. Voters will be allowed to vote without interference, restraint, or coercion. Electioneering will not be permitted at or near the polling place. Violations of these rules should be reported immediately to the Regional Director or his agent in charge of the election.

An agent of the Board will hand a ballot to each eligible voter at the voting place. Mark your ballot in secret in the voting booth provided. DO NOT SIGN YOUR BALLOT. Fold the ballot before leaving the voting booth, then personally deposit it in a ballot box under the supervision of an agent of the Board.

A sample of the official ballot is shown here:

Do you wish to be represented
for purposes of collective bargaining by:

INTERNATIONAL UNION, UNITED AUTOMOBILE, AEROSPACE AND AGRICULTURAL IMPLEMENT WORKERS OF AMERICA (UAW)
MARK AN "X" IN THE SQUARE OF YOUR CHOICE

❑ YES

❑ NO

AUTHORIZED ELECTION OBSERVERS

Each of the interested parties may designate an equal number of observers; this number to be determined by the Regional Director or his agent in charge of the election. These observers (a) act as checkers at the voting place and at the counting of ballots, (b) assist in the identification of voters, (c) challenge voters and ballots, and (d) otherwise assist the Regional Director or his agent.

VOTING UNIT

Those ELIGIBLE to vote are all production and maintenance employees, including truck drivers and leadmen, employed at the Grove Manufacturing Company, A Division of Walter Kidde & Company, Inc., facilities in Shady Grove, Chambersburg, Quincy and Greencastle, Pennsylvania, who were employed during the payroll period ending August 15, 1976.

**Tell me, and
I'll forget;
Show me
and I may not
remember;
Involve me and
I'll understand.**

CHINESE PROVERB

Those NOT ELIGIBLE to vote are all office clerical employees, plant clerical employees, graphic art service employees, expediters, schedulers, technicians, research and development employees, sales employees, engineers, draftsmen, confidential employees and guards, professional employees and supervisors as defined in the Act.

DATE OF ELECTION: WEDNESDAY, SEPTEMBER 15, 1976

LOCATION	TIME	POLLING PLACE
Shady Grove, Pa	6:00 a.m. to 12 Noon and 1:00 p.m. to 4:30 p.m. and 5:30 p.m. to 10:00 p.m.	New Training Room
Greencastle, Pa.	6:00 a.m. to 7:00 a.m. and 12 Noon to 6:30 p.m.	Conference Room in Old Farm Building
Chambersburg, Pa.	3:00 p.m. to 5:00 p.m	Carpenters Shop in the Yard

ALL BALLOTS WILL BE TALLIED ON SEPTEMBER 15, 1976,
AT 10 P.M. AT EMPLOYER'S SHADY GROVE,
PENNSYLVANIA, LOCATION

Thus ended the Labor Board's official "Representation Election Notice." As can be seen, the voting procedure was similar to any political election for a government office. Our strategy was to build **"VOTE NO UNION"** momentum gradually so as to reach a peak on the day the election took place. We timed assorted verbal and written communications for every day preceding the voting date of September 15th.

Many of the documents used were enlivened by the company's skilled artists and every action was coordinated with Grove's human resources department and me. There were big, colorful posters attached weekly to all plant bulletin boards, small "buck slip" messages placed in each employee's paycheck envelope, personal letters sent to workers' homes, a weekend bull roast, and informal one-on-one chats between employees and their supervisors during workdays.

Selected topics emphasized the "plusses" of Grove's excellent employee benefits, fair work rules, family atmosphere, and job security versus the "negatives" of union membership. We told voters what UAW control over them would bring into the Grove workforce such disadvantages as: (1) compulsory union dues and special assessments to be paid or be fired by Grove; (2) loss of individualism to bureaucratic collectivism and strict union regulations with fines for disobeying; (3) hostile, lengthy contract bargaining negotiations causing a strike that could result in violence and loss of jobs; (4) internal and external union politics, favoritism, and hypocrisy; (5) shady union financial dealings involving members' dues dollars; and (6) the UAW's negative public image.

The major theme that Martin Benchoff and his staff drummed on for six weeks was the loss of personal freedom that occurs under mandatory union representation. Their repeated message to workers was: **WE DON'T NEED OUTSIDERS HERE. THINK! STAY INDEPENDENT! BE YOUR OWN MAN! VOTE "NO UNION!"**

On a lighter note, lapel buttons about the size of a half-dollar were pinned on all production supervisors. The buttons pictured a regal bull moose encircled by these letters: **W N A U L A M N A H R !** Employees soon became curious and asked what this strange alphabetical message meant. No one knew the answer, not even the supervisors who were wearing the buttons.

Grove offered a cash prize of $350 (equal to a year's membership dues in the UAW) to any employee who could decipher the mysterious message. There were lots of amusing guesses, but after waiting four weeks in vain for a winner, Grove made an announcement. Amidst great fanfare, the button's message was revealed: *We Need A Union Like A Moose Needs A Hat Rack!* ... It infuriated the UAW but Grove management was encouraged by the number of rank-and-file employees who requested and were given permission to wear one of the moose buttons.

The response of professional Auto Workers organizers to the company's "vote no-union" campaign was a continuous flood of anti-company literature and anti-company sales pitches to employees and their families during visits to their homes. (The Labor Board required Grove to give the UAW the names

A typical management campaign "flyer" mailed to employees' homes during a union representation election campaign.

and home addresses of all eligible voters so that it could communicate with them, but the Board would not allow company representatives to visit these residences.)

Another campaign barometer was the three-foot-by-five-foot poster of a fearsome beast created by a Grove artist. The thing's name was "The Rumor Monger." It symbolized management's warning that employees should beware of UAW promises of new employee benefits that the union would "negotiate" for workers and exaggerations about the company's people-problems that the union would "correct."

As part of the company's counter-attack, a new poster of The Rumor Monger appeared on all bulletin boards every week. Its teeth kept growing longer and sharper and its mouth became broader and wider as it spouted forth more and more union "venom." By the last week of the campaign, The Rumor Monger's poster likeness was 90 percent mouth and sharp molars. It was a hideous sight to behold. Below it was this company message: **THINK FOR YOURSELF! BE YOUR OWN MAN! BEWARE OF THE RUMOR MONGER! VOTE "NO UNION"!**

Union Bikinis Backfire

In an attempt to counteract Grove's campaign, one balmy Indian Summer afternoon a bevy of curvaceous young women in bikini bathing attire and spike-heeled shoes sashayed around the Grove plant's main entrance. They wore pert UAW caps as they tantalizingly handed out **"Vote Yes"** union literature to attentive male workers who were leaving their jobs to go home.

I naturally considered it my duty as the company's labor counsel to investigate the "inflammatory" appeal of this risqué type of electioneering under the previously noted Labor Board ground rules. (I had hinted to my client that the young ladies seemed to be "lewdly flaunting constitutional freedom of communications.)"

Luckily for Grove, the tactic backfired on the UAW. Its strategists forgot that many of the employees were devoutly moral, religiously fervent, rigidly conservative Mennonites and members of the Church of the Brethren. They are known as "Plain People" or "Dunkards" and follow literally the same devout and pristine teachings that their immigrant ancestors presented to

Nothing makes a person as mad as the truth.

Mark Twain
HUMORIST-WRITER

617

Governor William Penn in the year 1718.[3] Most of them shocked the *femme fatales* by tearing up their free literature in disgust.

A Fifty-Hour Parley

Probably the greatest influence on the outcome of the Grove election was a monumental task undertaken by company president Martin Benchoff and production manager Gary Spickler. A few days before the voting date, they chose a small office with a plain table located in the midst of the plant production area. There they sat around the clock for two and a half days—with rolled-up shirtsleeves and in work clothes—holding friendly rap sessions with non-supervisory "blue collar" workers.

The two Grove leaders survived this ordeal on high-test coffee and sandwiches, with only a few short rest breaks. During the sedentary marathon they met with every one of the 2,500 eligible Grove voters for about a half hour, in groups of not more than fifteen workers at a time. Benchoff and Spickler answered all questions frankly and asked the employees "to use their prudent and independent judgment after hearing all the pros and cons about the company and the UAW." Then Benchoff ended each session by shaking their hands and reminding them: *"I've never told you wrong!"*

Final Day Campaigning

One of the Labor Board's rules that must be obeyed (or risk defeat in a second re-run election) was that during the last 24-hour period before the voting occurs, an employer was forbidden to have any mandatory mass assemblage of eligible voters. The Labor Board disapprovingly calls this maneuver "an unfair and illegal captive audience to gain the last most telling word."[4] In the Grove case, that meant the period from 6 a.m. on September 15th to the close of all polling places at 10 p.m. that same day.

To avoid this misstep yet still communicate Grove's **"Vote No"** message legally one more time on the eve of the election, Martin Benchoff made three creative decisions. His first ploy was instructing a company artist to post a final picture of The Rumor Monger on plant bulletin boards. Its mouth was bigger than ever but the vicious teeth were gone and it was crying like a baby. It had swallowed humbly all of its anti-Grove "lies."

As a second scoring punch, Benchoff mailed to each voting employee's home a copy of a 33-1/3 rpm record that he had personally cut in a local disc jockey's studio. It was labeled: **A Year of Decision: 1776 and 1976: Be Your Own Man—Think!** In a sincere, calm, and persuasive voice, Grove's Chief Executive Officer told his 2500 voting employees and their families the advantages of a "merit shop" operation over compulsory unionism:

> My name is J. Martin Benchoff and I am the president and chief executive officer of Grove Manufacturing Company. I want to thank you for allowing me to come into your home in this manner to talk to you and your family about a crucial decision which all of us at Grove are facing. You will soon be going to the polls, supervised by the Federal Labor Board, to cast your vote to decide whether Grove will remain union-free or whether we will be forced to deal with each other through third-party outsiders. No one will know how you vote. You do not sign your name. Your vote remains a secret.
>
> As an employee of Grove with 22 years of service, I would like you and your family members to understand how your Company feels about labor unions. Grove is a non-union organization. It always has been and, with the best interest of our employees at heart, it is our sincere desire that it will always be that. We prefer to deal with people directly rather than through a third-party. This does not mean that from time to time we do not have problems. However, we have always been able to work out these difficulties among ourselves without the intervention of outsiders. We have policies and practices to resolve problems rather than fight with each other about them.
>
> While you have the legal right to join and belong to a union, you also have an equal legal right not to join or belong to a union. In today's world there are many pressures. We want to keep our organization free from tensions that can be brought on by the intervention of outsiders such as a labor union. In our opinion, statistics show that it could hurt the business on which we all depend for our livelihood.
>
> We have accepted our responsibility to provide you the best working conditions, pay and benefits that are possible. It is not necessary

Few sinners are saved after the first 30 minutes of a sermon.

MARK TWAIN
HUMORIST-WRITER

> There is no more fascinating business in this world than selling. It is behind every successful enterprise of whatever kind. Character, courage, truthfulness, enthusiasm, patience and courtesy are essential equipment.
>
> George Matthew Adams
> WRITER

for you to pay union membership dues to receive fair treatment in this Company. Each and every Grove employee is an individual and you have the right to speak for yourself and for your family's interest. In making this important decision, I ask only that you examine carefully our record of proven performance at Grove and compare it with the wild promises of these union outsiders.

Do you know where your union dues money would go? Do you really believe that these outsiders are truly interested in you and your family? Or perhaps they are more interested in the many hundreds of thousands of dollars in compulsory union membership dues which they would take from Grove employees each year? Have you thought about the strike record of the UAW? Did you realize that the UAW organizers would continue to get their pay from your union dues while you are out of work on a UAW strike and picket line?

We have a proud tradition in this Cumberland Valley and at Grove of being independent. Inviting a union into your family's life is no experiment. The results can be very final. In the past several weeks we have answered, in our written communications and in our personal meetings with you, all of the questions and rumors that have been raised by these outsiders. I ask you to consider our answers carefully and vote according to your own prudent judgment.

Thank you for allowing me this visit with you and your family, and please remember, *I've never told you wrong!*

The third novel action by Martin Benchoff was a result of the coincidental fact that the national press was publishing headlines almost every day during that September of '76 about a threatened work stoppage by the same United Auto Workers Union against all of Ford Motor Company's manufacturing plants throughout the country. Gambling that this major strike would occur on the day of Grove's representation election, Benchoff sent one of his corporate jets to Detroit to purchase a special advance order of 2,500 copies of the September 15 issue of the *Detroit Free Press*. The newspapers were to be flown back to Shady Grove in time for distribution to all voters as they came to work on Election Day.

Benchoff's hunch was correct, the UAW obliged, and front-page headlines of the *Detroit Free Press* on September 15th blared out: **FORD WORKERS START STRIKE AFTER NEGOTIATIONS DEADLOCK**. The sub-title added: **Bargaining Talks Called A Charade**. Here are some excerpts from that frank article that the Grove workers read:

> United Auto Workers members struck Ford Motor Co. at midnight Tuesday [September 14th], six hours after Union President Leonard Woodcock had declared bargaining covering 170,000 workers was deadlocked and ordered the walkout. "Ford has been unresponsive and unwilling to engage in serious bargaining," Woodcock told reporters at a news conference. "It is our sincere and fervent hope that for the economic and social good of all affected, we can resolve our differences in a minimum of time..."
>
> The thread of hope for a peaceful settlement of the dispute snapped earlier Tuesday when the Union's International Executive Board unanimously authorized the strike. Woodcock and UAW Vice-President Ken Bannon, head of the Union's Ford Department, at that time both flatly ruled out any chance for a strike-free agreement. They said a brief Tuesday morning meeting between Ford and the UAW had made no progress. "It's not just one piece or two pieces or three pieces [that separate the two sides]," Bannon said. "It's a very big ball of wax..."
>
> There was the feeling by some workers that the UAW had failed to keep them properly informed about bargaining issues and failed to push hard enough for local plant concerns such as health standards. "I'd rather not see a strike," said James Suttles, 58, a veteran of the Rouge assembly line who says he has lived through at least four UAW strikes at Ford. "It's pretty difficult to catch up after a strike, no matter what happens at the settlement..."

Attached to a copy of the front page of this Detroit newspaper that all Grove workers picked up voluntarily as they entered the plant to report for work before voting on September 15 was a small yellow handbill. It said:

They can run but they can't hide.

JOE LOUIS
CHAMPION
PRIZEFIGHTER

There is a Divinity that shapes our ends, but we can help by our prayers.

Amish saying

Nobody wins in a strike ...
THINK
Be Your Own Man!

Unbeknownst to Grove management, on the eve of the election all eligible voters received their fourth surprise. And it made me uneasy, knowing the Labor Board's pro-union bias as compared to legitimate "free speech," but the Auto Workers Union never challenged it. This surprise to one and all originated with a respected minister of the local Church of The Brethren. On his own volition, he distributed to many Grove employees off the Company's premises a prayer containing these impassioned passages:

Our Father in Heaven from whom all blessings flow, we come to Thee on this day that can decide important issues that will affect the community, the County, and the lives of many individuals and those who are near and dear to them. You have been our help in ages past and our hope in years to come. To Thee we bring our petitions and ask that you hear our prayer.

We earnestly ask You, in Your infinite love and mercy, to be with all employees who tomorrow cast their vote in this Union Representation Election. Guide Thou their hand, and may it please Thee to guide them to the "No" block on the ballot that will insure the decisive defeat of those men who seek their own at the expense of others.

We ask Thee that the employees of Grove Manufacturing Company may remain free from union domination: from the self-seeking materialism, class consciousness, and hatred that Unionism promotes. Save the Company and its employees from becoming involved in any way with the promotion of Godless Socialism that Organized Labor consciously or unconsciously advocates.

Save the Company and its employees from assisting those individuals, organizations, and ideology that would tear down the principles of honest toil, thrift, respect for the rights of our fellowmen, respect for the Declaration of Independence and the Constitution that this nation was founded upon, and respect for You. May our enemies be confounded this day by Your power working through those who this day mark their ballot, and may those who are promoting turmoil and unrest among us come to see the error of their ways and repenting, turn away from them.

Amen!

A converted cow pasture just a few 45-pound cannonball shots from Gettysburg—where 50,000 brave Americans were maimed or killed within three days during a crucial turning point for their young Republic in 1863—became the site where the local minister's prayer came true. A tallied vote of, by, and for the people of Grove Manufacturing Company in 1976 was 1,599 to 723 against representation by the United Auto Workers Union, AFL-CIO.

Another major ABC member had defeated the compulsory unionization of its workforce and protected freedom in the merit shop workplace.

CHAPTER 48

PROFESSOR NORTHRUP EXAMINES ABC

HERBERT R. NORTHRUP, PROFESSOR EMERITUS of Management at the celebrated Wharton School of the University of Pennsylvania, has had an illustrious career. Along the way it greatly benefited ABC and the merit shop crusade.

Dr. Northrup was born in New Jersey in 1918, received his B.A. degree from Duke University in 1939, a master's degree from Harvard in 1941, and a Ph.D. in economics from Harvard in 1942. During his early professional years, he taught economics at Cornell, industrial relations at Columbia University, and also served as a senior hearing officer at the National War Labor Board (1942–1949).

Over the next twelve years, Northrup worked in the private sector industrial relations field, first as a labor economist for the National Industrial Conference Board and then as a corporate consultant for Ebasco Services, Inc. and an executive with Penn-Texas Corporation (now merged into Goodrich) and General Electric Company. At GE he had the responsibility for all aspects of employee relations, covering seventy-one plants that employed one hundred thousand workers. He also was a member of GE's national collective bargaining committee and handled third-stage grievances under national labor contracts with unions representing certain GE personnel.

In 1961, Herb Northrup decided to return to academia and accepted an offer as a tenured professor on the faculty of the University of Pennsylvania's Wharton School. From 1964 to 1969, he was Chairman of its Department of Management. Thereafter, until his retirement in 1988, he served as Director

My specialty is being right when other people are wrong.

GEORGE BERNARD SHAW
BRITISH PLAYWRIGHT

of the Wharton School's Industrial Research Unit and Chairman of its Labor Relations Council. During those years—and continuing today—he is recognized as one of the nation's foremost authorities on labor relations. Not only is he a prolific writer in this field but he also acts as a consultant and expert witness in litigation involving Fortune 500 companies.

"No Spin" Recognition of the Open Shop

Dr. Northrup's career has been both pioneering and unpopular with politically correct academia plus the elite national news media in a number of respects. For example, he trailblazed as the first eminent economist who gave serious attention to racial discrimination against African-Americans by the organized labor movement.[1] More undeniable proof that Northrup has never allowed bias or hypocrisy to override the truth is his monumental work called *Open Shop Construction*. Written in 1975 with co-author Professor Howard Foster of New York State University at Buffalo, this book was the first scholarly and carefully documented analysis of the phenomenal success of the non-union side of the building and construction industry.

In the foreword to this book on the "open shop," Northrup explained the need for his study—*and startled both Big Labor and Big Business with his irrefutable findings and conclusions*:

For some years it has been apparent that the open shop sector of construction has been expanding at the expense of the unionized one. This has been indicated by the growth of open shop contractor associations, the comments of union and contractor association officials, and in some cases, the violent reactions of unionists to the activities of non-union builders. Moreover, it has also been clear from casual observation that open shop construction firms recruit, train, utilize, and compensate labor quite differently than do their unionized counterparts.

Despite the fact that open shop construction firms undoubtedly perform a majority of the construction work

Dr. Herbert R. Northrup, professor emeritus of management at the Wharton School, University of Pennsylvania, and distinguished author, lecturer, and consultant to management in the construction field.

in this country, no study exists which deals extensively with this sector... For the most part, books dealing with manpower or labor relations in construction have dealt with the unionized sector and ignored the rest of the industry...

The open shop group presents a different pattern even though the growth of open shop associations and the formalization of some hiring and training programs have provided the beginnings of centralized information. For the most part, almost each open shop contractor performs somewhat differently and utilizes labor according to his own needs.

To learn about open shop contractor practices one must do extensive field work, interview numerous persons throughout the country, and collect information bit by bit wherever it exists. To attempt to determine how the highly individualized open shop contractors operate and man their jobs is a costly, time consuming process, but a fascinating one.[2]

Later on in this historic book on the open shop movement in 1975, Dr. Northrup described ABC's structure and growth. Here is another passage:

The most dramatic feature of the ABC has been its recent growth. Its membership has nearly tripled in the past five years. Furthermore, and perhaps as significant, much ABC activity has been concentrated in areas where open shops have not traditionally been conspicuous... This Association has led the fight against illegal picketing, construction violence, and has been playing an increasing role in congressional and state legislative relations. Its staff operates and advises on [labor relations and] benefit and apprentice programs. Its home office in Glen Burnie, Maryland, is considered by friend and foe alike as the central headquarters of open shop interests.[3]

The demand for this landmark publication caused Herb Northrup to update it in 1984 and confirm the seldom-mentioned truth that "the non-union segment of construction has undergone a spectacular expansion and increased its

In the advance of civilization, it is new knowledge which paves the way, and the pavement is eternal.

W. R. WHITNEY
HISTORIAN

capacity to handle larger and larger jobs."[4] These two precedential studies of the building and construction industry gave national recognition and prestige to ABC when it was most needed. The second edition explained that:

> Since 1975, when the first edition of *Open Shop Construction* was published, a tremendous change has occurred in the construction industry's unionized pattern. The trend towards open shop, or non-union construction, has accelerated. Whereas ten years ago it accounted for an estimated 55 percent of construction volume, today [1984] it accounts for close to 70 percent....
>
> Prior to our first volume, this open shop sector was the neglected stepchild of the industry and, to a large extent, still is today. Not only are unions seen as coincident with the industry, but even when union behavior is itself the subject of analysis, it is seldom explicitly approached in terms of response to non-union competition.... This book addresses the employee relations situation applicable to the substantial majority of the industry.[5]

Dr. Northrup reemphasized that the best evidence of the ever-increasing penetration of non-union construction into the previously unchallenged domain of the building trades unions was its greater flexibility and empathy in managing its workforce. ABCers, he said, replaced outmoded craft traditions plus other union inhibitions on productivity with freedom in their workplace:

> Open shop contractors have significant advantages in the deployment of personnel on the job. Unrestricted by union rules, they can pay employees according to skill and productivity while assigning them according to need. Free of worry over [inter-union] jurisdictional disputes, free to determine the skill content of each job, and free to determine the extent of job manning needed, the open shop contractor can, and indeed does, utilize labor more efficiently.... Now, after success, the challenge is still greater, and the future is more than ever in the hands of open shop builders and their organizations.[6]

One caustic literary critic wrote a review of *Open Shop Construction Revisited* in which he complained that Northrup "rejoiced too much" when he showed that "economics wins out over unions" to the extent that non-union building "controls about 80 percent of the construction dollar." Northrup responded that he was not rejoicing but rather thinking "how extraordinary it was that unions were able as long as they did to defy the laws of economics through political and power means."[7]

Over the past fifty years, Dr. Northrup has contributed many other important books, monographs, treatises, and lectures in his field. In the summer of 1995, his article for the *Journal of Research* placed "the open shop share of the construction dollar at a stabilized 70 percent to 80 percent of the total market." He also continues to give expert testimony before Congress and state legislatures, administrative agencies, and the courts in construction employee relations matters.

This expertise is coupled with a professional standard of "spin free" reporting and the courage to challenge a politically sensitive arena where pro-union bias is rampant and where few academicians desire or dare to tread.[8] At its fiftieth anniversary celebration in the year 2000, ABC named Dr. Herbert R. Northrup as one of its nine "Leaders of the 20th century who significantly influenced and strengthened the merit shop construction industry throughout the United States."

We don't believe that bias is when someone presents his point of view. We feel bias is when someone's point of view is eliminated.

ROGER AILES
CEO OF FOX NEWS

629

CHAPTER 49

BE&K'S KENNEDY DEFEATS
A "CORPORATE CAMPAIGN"

BUILDING TRADES TERRORISM across the United States reached a pinnacle by the 1970s and—as described previously—ABC counterattacked victoriously in 1973 through the reluctant legal auspices of the National Labor Relations Board.[1] Big Labor was deflated by this major merit shop defeat of mandatory trade unionism in the eastern and midwestern sections of the nation, and began to target ABC contractors and their construction projects more selectively and more creatively during the 1980s and 1990s.

The rapid westward expansion of ABC members caused the United Brotherhood of Carpenters (UBC) to commission a study that would identify a major contractor in the area which was dominant in one special field of construction. This "victim" would epitomize ABC's merit shop movement that UBC held responsible for the huge reduction of its ranks. Once the target firm was chosen, UBC would use the ultimate weapon in Big Labor's arsenal—called a "corporate campaign."[2]

This "top-down" strategy expanded the combat zone to "a company's board room" where, according to the unions, "the corporate bosses profit from human misery."[3] There would be no attempt to organize the selected corporation's employees through the use of a legal, democratic, and peaceful "bottom-up" secret ballot election procedure supervised by the Labor Board.[4]

> **Recollection of the past is useful by way of provision for the future.**
>
> SAMUEL JOHNSON
> WRITER-PUNDIT-PHILOSOPHER

Anatomy of a Corporate Campaign

The Carpenters' parent organization—the AFL-CIO—prepared a manual that defined a corporate campaign as one which "applies coordinated pressure to perceived points of vulnerability in all of the targeted company's political and economic relationships to achieve union goals." This maneuver "is designed," continued the AFL-CIO manual, "to swarm over the company from every angle and precipitate a crisis in worker, customer, and public confidence while injuring profitability, public image, and reputation." The AFL-CIO "how to" manual stressed that the message to the targeted firm is always the same: "Wherever your company turns, our union will be in your face,"[5] and "the militancy created becomes the death of a thousand cuts rather than a single blow."[6]

In his *Troublemaker's Handbook*, Dan La Botz also described the "upscaling" of a labor dispute through use of a corporate campaign "that inflicts costly consequences on the target company or its allies." Some of the tactics that he and the above-described AFL-CIO manual recommend "to ruin management's public image, cause costly delays in operations and loss of customers, induce corporate fines or other legal penalties, and undermine employee relations" include:

- Contacting individual executives and board of directors members who might be vulnerable to pressure because of other business relationships.
- Communicating with employees to malign their employer.
- Picketing, boycotts, and other publicity initiatives that pressure customers, vendors, and creditors to make them cease doing business with the targeted company.
- Demonstrations outside the offices or homes of targeted company executives.
- Using "loyal" politicians and other community leaders to pressure the company to agree to union demands.
- Disrupting the company's shareholders meeting and pressing for adoption of hostile resolutions or support of inimical candidates for the firm's board of directors.
- Reducing the victim company's stock price by agitation on Wall Street such as exaggerated claims that the company is experiencing production, sales, or other financial problems.

- "Strategic social investing" of millions of dollars in the employer's pension funds that "coincidentally" happen to be influenced or controlled by union "trustees."[7]

There is nothing to be learned from the second kick of a mule.

DICK ARMEY'S
AXIOMS

A corporate campaign also takes advantage of the fact that in America's over-regulated society it is impossible for any employer to achieve 100 percent compliance with all of the thousands of existing federal, state, and local workplace laws and regulations. Sympathetic government agencies at all levels that enforce these statutory policies are induced to assist in union "whistleblowing" harassment.[8] Dan La Botz amplified:

> Both public institutions and private companies are subject to all sorts of laws and regulations, from the Securities and Exchange Commission to the Occupational Safety and Health Act, from the Civil Rights Act to local fire codes [and from the National Labor Relations Board and the Department of Labor to the Environmental Protection Agency and the Securities and Exchange Commission]. Every law or regulation is a potential net in which management can be snared and entangled. A complaint to a regulatory agency can cause the [targeted] company lost managerial time, public embarrassment, potential fines, and the costs of compliance. One well-placed phone call can do a lot of damage.[9]

Use of emotional public appeals from influential union-friendly dignitaries and left-wing private organizations "to torment the targeted employer" is another feature of corporate campaigns, according to La Botz:

> Management's kind of power requires that it be the ultimate authority in the workplace. But the union can challenge that authority by pointing out that there are other authorities. A local priest, minister, or rabbi can ask to talk to management with regard to the congregation's concerns about the company. The NAACP or NOW [or "the Reverend" Jesse Jackson] may want to talk to the company about its equal employment policy. "Greenpeace" may be concerned about toxic dumping, or

Our free enterprise system has supplied the incentive that has challenged every person to give his best in production and creation. Because the incentive has been attractive, we have become the greatest-producing nation on earth. To any degree that the incentive to create and produce is restricted, we will be retarded in our progress to a better America.

RALPH HAYWARD
WRITER

the local block club may want to stop the firm's trucks from driving down side streets at night. A Congressperson may visit an agency to find out how the taxpayers' dollars are being spent, or an alderperson may want to know if the company has kept the promises it made when it got a tax abatement. When other authorities are brought in, management's weight is diminished and the union's weight is relatively greater.[10]

And a corporate campaign, according to Professor Jarol Manheim of George Washington University, is "an organized assault on the reputation of a company" and is "centered around the media, where protagonists attempt to redefine the image of the target company."[11]

The Carpenters' Union believed that these insidious schemes would make the selected employer vulnerable to a "Hobson's choice" of forcing unionization on its employees or becoming a business failure and going bankrupt. The corporate campaign's multi-dimensional strategy would combine frivolous complaints and potential vulnerability in all of the company's internal and external human and business relationships. There would be mass demonstrations, production slowdowns, sickouts, and the filing of expensive lawsuits. This agenda would be blended with attempts to spin the national news media (already sympathetic) and the public at large (totally naïve on this issue) with distorted facts to damage the firm's reputation.[12]

If these comparatively peaceful tactics failed, Big Labor could always revert to its brutal roots of terrorism.

Fortunately for non-union contractors, some judicial bodies are beginning to show concern for the destructive nature of these Machiavellian attacks on free enterprise. The Court of Appeals for the District of Columbia Circuit has defined "corporate campaigns" as:

> . . . a wide and indefinite range of legal and potentially illegal tactics used by unions to exert pressure on an employer. These tactics may include but are not limited to litigation, political appeals, requests that regulatory agencies investigate and pursue employer violations of state or federal law, and negative publicity campaigns aimed at reducing the employer's goodwill with employees, investors or the general public.[13]

634

A recent article by my former law partner, Maurice Baskin, and the afore-mentioned Professor Emeritus Herbert Northrup of The Wharton School at the University of Pennsylvania on this subject lists the following "legal theories" used by employers in defense against these union corporate campaigns but only "with mixed results": the secondary boycott provisions of the Labor Management Relations Act (i.e., Taft-Hartley Act), common law defamation or trespass, abuse of process, tortious interference with contractual relations, RICO, and the antitrust laws.[14]

> "Men," said the Devil, "are good to their brothers; they don't want to mend their ways, but each other's."
>
> PAT HEIN
> MINISTER

From Ironworker's Son to Corporate CEO

In 1986, the United Brotherhood of Carpenters selected BE&K, Inc.—a high-profile general contractor founded by Ted C. Kennedy and two colleagues—for its "corporate target." That decision eventually turned out to be a huge mistake by Big Labor.

Born in Pittsburgh, Kennedy is the son of a union ironworker. No relation to the controversial Massachusetts senator with the same name, he graduated from Duke University with honors in civil engineering. Then he entered the construction business and worked his way up to project superintendent. Over the next fifteen years he helped to build paper and chemical processing plants throughout the United States.

During the early 1970s, as a vice president of Rust Engineering Company based in Birmingham, Alabama, Ted Kennedy was asked to assess the viability of establishing a "double-breasted" open shop subsidiary that was distinct from Rust's unionized operations.[15] After many months of investigation, he became convinced of the desirability of such a plan because customers, as Kennedy put it, were tired of union "cold water tortures," but he was unsuccessful in persuading the board of directors of Rust to go ahead.

Ted C. Kennedy, chairman of BE&K, Inc., and 22nd national president of ABC in 1980; cited by ABC as one of its "Leaders of the 20th Century;" and cited by *Engineering News-Record* as "one of the world's construction leaders."

A successful life is not an easy life. It's built upon strong qualities, sacrifice, endeavor, loyalty, integrity.

GRANT D. BRANDON
WRITER

Discouraged but undaunted, in 1972, at the age of thirty-seven, Kennedy joined with two of his fellow Rust executives, Peter Bolvig and Bill Edmonds, to form BE&K, Inc., an "open shop" union construction company located in Birmingham and bearing the initials of its founders. It concentrated on the pulp, paper, chemical, and metallurgical fields of work. Within just three years, *Engineering News-Record* ranked BE&K one of the fifty largest design and construction companies in the United States.

Today BE&K provides engineering, procurement, construction, and maintenance services to the process, manufacturing, industrial, automotive, and telecommunications industries in addition to its original specialty of constructing and maintaining pulp and paper facilities. (For a recent construction project, see the end of Chapter 52.)

BE&K Practices Positive Human Relations

From its inception, BE&K recognized the advantages of meritorious treatment of multi-skilled workers, quality performance, and interactive management. The company capitalized on these strengths by completing state-of-the-art construction projects on schedule and within budget while providing excellent work opportunities and benefits for its employees, including minority and female recruitment and training.

BE&K not only educates employees on the job but also holds formal evening classes taught by company supervisors and equipment suppliers. The firm arranged for workers to attend courses at local vocational institutions and sponsored correspondence courses. "If employees are not involved, the good ones will leave," says Kennedy. "Productivity challenges have been handed to us on a silver platter from the building trades."[16]

This human relations formula has worked wonders and the company soon became one of the nation's construction powerhouses serving the pulp and paper industry. Seven years after it was founded, BE&K was featured in an article in *Fortune* magazine as "a member of construction's big league." The magazine also mentioned that the company was focusing on the northwestern United States, "which was ripe for the merit shop."[17]

Ted Kennedy, as BE&K's president and subsequently its chairman, has been recognized not only for his innovative management techniques (with a workforce today in excess of ten thousand employees) but also for his contributions of time and financial support to the merit shop cause. He served successively as president of ABC's Alabama Chapter, on its national board of directors, the national executive committee, and as its twenty-second national president. On June 2, 2000, at the fiftieth anniversary convention, ABC chose Kennedy as one of its nine "Leaders of the 20th Century who significantly influenced and strengthened the merit shop construction industry."

When *Engineering News-Record* recently listed BE&K in its select group of the top construction firms in America, it also named Kennedy as one of its outstanding construction executives of the previous 125 years:

> He combined the flexibility of the merit shop philosophy with the worker-oriented focus of a missionary to give the industry a cost-effective way to deal with escalating construction costs in the 1970s. As president of ABC in 1980, moreover, he led the establishment of a national open shop craft training program [originally named "Wheels of Learning" to keep the movement's growth sustainable.[18]

In 2004, Kennedy served again as chairman of this nationally standardized, portable, competency-based, task-oriented and career-directed program in its current state-of-the-art status, now known as NCCER-CONTRENS.[19] Kennedy also has served as advisor to the construction committee of the Business Roundtable, on the Board of Visitors of the School of Engineering of Duke University, on the North Carolina State Pulp & Paper Foundation Trustees, and as Chairman of Inroads, Inc., a national minority youth intern program.

BE&K itself recently has been recognized by *Fortune* magazine as one of "The 100 Best Companies to Work for in America" and by *Working Women* magazine as one of "The 50 Best Companies for Working Mothers." BE&K's Employee Dispute Resolution Program has been hailed by the Equal Employment Opportunity Commission as a model for corporate America. And the company consistently has received safety awards from federal and state agencies, including three "STAR" project sites recognized by the Occupational Safety and Health Administration.

If you want productivity and the financial reward that goes with it, you must treat your workers as your most important asset.

THOMAS PETERS AND ROBERT WATERMAN *In Search of Excellence*

Never let your face show how bad they are kicking your rear.

DICK ARMEY'S
AXIOMS

The Carpenters Union Targets BE&K

It was no wonder that the United Brotherhood of Carpenters chose BE&K as its "public enemy No. 1" and solicited the assistance of the United Paperworkers International Union (UPIU) in getting revenge. A "solidarity committee" was established between the two unions and they began a national corporate campaign against the firm.

Here is company president Ted Kennedy's description of some of the initial union tactics:

> In California, the Carpenters picketed a golf course that I was scheduled to play on. In Atlanta, the hotel where I stayed. In Texas, a conference I addressed. In Chicago and New York City they picketed stockholders meetings of companies we do business with. In Alabama they picketed a bank that my partner happens to be a director of. In Delaware they threatened to sell half a million shares of stock from a company that gives us business. In Tennessee, Maine and California they brought in Jesse Jackson to lead a parade against us on the picket line. Sometimes, when that went on, I felt like the only fireplug on a street full of dogs.[20]

Following this executive harassment, an all-out attack was put into motion. In 1988, a $350 million steel mill modernization project for USS-Posco Industries—involving eight hundred jobs—was the recipient of prolonged acts of intimidation and violence. The unions fought BE&K at every turn, challenging environmental and zoning permits, hand-billing the public, while also lobbying local government agencies for ordinances and land use requirements that would impede the project, initiating other trumped-up litigation, and finally, engaging in unlawful picketing and violence.

The USS-Posco Industries project was located in Pittsburg, Contra Costa County, California, forty miles from San Francisco. Unionists involved in the illegal activities went to extreme lengths to conceal their identities. After initial refusals by the local judiciary to act against severe breaches of the peace, BE&K finally obtained state court injunctions against the illegal destructive activities of the local building trades unions involved.

BE&K and its customer, USS-Posco Industries, also sued California's Contra Costa Building Trades Council in a federal district court in September of 1987. The companies charged that union complaints about construction permits, lobbying for local ordinances, frivolous lawsuits, and collusive union-contractor activities were impeding the project's completion in violation of federal anti-trust laws. BE&K lost the first round of this California case in 1987, but completed the project successfully and appealed the federal judge's decision. The litigation dragged on and on through the appellate process until BE&K's loss finally was affirmed by a federal circuit court seven years later in 1994.[21]

Eternal vigilance is the price of liberty.

WENDELL PHILLIPS
ABOLITIONIST

The Boise Cascade Paper Company Battle

Meanwhile union activists continued their "corporate campaign" against BE&K's construction projects in other locations. It all culminated in 1989 with a scheme to destroy a $500 million pulp and paper mill expansion for Boise Cascade Paper Company in the town of International Falls, Minnesota, a heavily unionized area close to the Canadian border. The region was one of high unemployment, and the Minnesota Building Trades Council had gained political support from the state of Minnesota. This cooperation with Big Labor came from Governor Rudy Perpich, State Attorney General Hubert H. ("Skip") Humphrey, III, and many of the state licensing agencies. They consistently awarded construction work to local unionized firms, ignoring open and competitive bidding.

It was irrelevant to the Minnesota Building Trades Council or the Governor that BE&K made a general practice of subcontracting work in true merit shop fashion to the lowest qualified bidders, regardless of their labor policy for or against unionization. In this situation BE&K went even further. A dozen or more unionized subs (although not low bidders) actually were awarded some of the initial contracts. When the trade unions refused to man these jobs (saying "we go all union or nothin"), they were replaced by BE&K with local non-union workers. BE&K's own non-union employees also were imported from outside the small town of International Falls and furnished temporary housing facilities while they supplemented the striking workforce. (This loss of awarded jobs cost the union subs and their tradesmen $100 million in their paychecks.)

What followed was an unprecedented onslaught of state government agency actions designed to cripple the multi-million-dollar paper mill expansion

The more corrupt the state, the more numerous the laws.

TACITUS

project awarded to BE&K. The Highway Patrol began this perversion of the regulatory processes by setting up weigh stations around the International Falls site and checking all delivery trucks entering the Boise Cascade project. Then the Minnesota Occupational Safety and Health Agency got into the act by conducting "wall-to-wall" inspections throughout the huge project's life. Air pollution and other environmental controls were audited. Electrical and mechanical inspectors made weekly site visits, checking licenses and journeyman/apprenticeship ratio requirements. State agencies governing electrical and high-pressure piping work created obstacles for BE&K workers seeking journeyman licenses. Phony tests included vague essay questions graded on a subjective basis that resulted in virtually no licenses being granted.

The local *Star Tribune*'s political columnist, Dick Youngblood, summed up the governor's inexcusable conduct this way:

> When Minnesota's misguided voters re-elected Rudolph Perpich, I assumed naively that he was elected governor of all the people. It's now become apparent in the Boise-Cascade-union clash that he actually considers himself mostly the duly elected political mouthpiece of the AFL-CIO. Consider: When Boise-Cascade snubbed his grandstanding efforts to mediate a wildcat strike over use of non-union labor, Perpich promptly threatened to jettison $16 million worth of promised tax benefits [for BE&K].
>
> Then the governor-of-some-of-the-people instructed his political operatives to scour the statute books in search of law and permit violations—violations that might be used to bludgeon Boise-Cascade into a more agreeable stance. According to recent reports, his obliging minions seized the assignment with gusto.[22]

Not to be outdone by the governor's subversive activities, Minnesota Attorney General Hubert Humphrey, III, entered the fray. This son of the former vice president of the United States "guaranteed" that "the people of International Falls don't have to work next to non-union scabs."[23]

BE&K's legal action against the biased regulatory practices of these agencies and the executives who supervised them resulted at one point in the

Minnesota Attorney General's Office being held in contempt of court. Eventually BE&K obtained injunctions against the state of Minnesota and halted the bigoted practices.

When these "corporate campaign" efforts to stop BE&K through state government agency harassment proved unsuccessful, the trade unionists once again resorted to their classic strong-arm tactics of mass picketing, violence, and terrorism. BE&K employees were threatened, shadowed, and photos of them were taken. Female workers were harassed sexually. Minority employees were subjected to racial slurs and even threats of lynching. Car tires were slashed. A residence and two automobiles were firebombed. An arsonist's fire caused $250,000 in equipment damage.

More Terrorism at the Boise Cascade Project

A few days later—on September 9, 1989—the labor dispute at the Boise Cascade construction project escalated into a full-scale riot against BE&K that sent shock waves through the entire paper industry. Many out-of-state carpenters and ironworkers chartered buses from Marquette, Michigan, to participate in the brawl. Protective metal fences were cut, trailers overturned, arson-set fires were started, materials and equipment destroyed. Rocks and clubs were used by the rioters to inflict serious personal injuries and property damage. Newly built employee housing facilities for non-area workers on the project were attacked and firebombed. All of this bedlam caused more than $3,000,000 in damages and a number of security guards who were attempting to protect the property were injured.

According to University of Minnesota historian Hyman Berman, the onslaught on September 9th by a mob of 700 demonstrators ranked as one of the state's most severe labor confrontations since the union organizing drives of the 1930's. Jack Murray, the mayor of International Falls, pleaded on the radio that citizens stay at home during the rampage. Motel owners warned tourists not to go downtown and the police ordered that stores be closed.

Characterizing the carnage, former U.S. Secret Service veteran Chuck Vance, who headed Vance International Security at the time, added: "It was as bad as any violence we've encountered at over 100 strike sites during the past five years—including the Pittston coal strikes in Appalachia." Neither

Without victory there is no survival.

WINSTON CHURCHILL
BRITISH PRIME
MINISTER

Vance's security force nor a vastly outnumbered contingent of police officers and sheriff's deputies were able to stop the onslaught.[25]

Another reaction to the anarchy came from ABC of Minnesota's president, Larry White. He charged: "This terroristic attack was clearly an orchestrated event. Unionists from Michigan, North Dakota and various cities in Minnesota participated. All arrived at the same time, dispersed to pre-assigned locations and, as if on signal, invaded private property." White and ABC's national executive vice president, Dan Bennet, offered a $10,000 reward for information leading to the arrest of the riot "coordinators."[26]

For their part, Boise Cascade and BE&K officials promised "vigorous pursuit of both civil and criminal actions against the mobsters." Dozens of interviews with contractors and owner-users echoed this message. Even a few wiser labor leaders conceded that the disastrous fallout for the entire unionized sector of the construction industry greatly outweighed any trade union "benefit" from a fearsome Teamster-like reputation for criminal activities. Typical of off-the-record comments was this assessment by an international building trades union official:

> Here we are busting our tails to create a positive image to help convince owners to give us more jobs. Then these guys (in Minnesota) go after BE&K, a Business Roundtable member! This episode reminds me of the ill-advised AFL-CIO mass demonstration at ABC's San Francisco convention last year. Such highly visible violence plays right into the hands of union-busters who want to tar all of us as a bunch of thugs.[27]

A fair-minded construction user who had been deeply involved in the unionized side of the business for thirty years added:

> Labor's Boise Cascade misadventure is a great disappointment to those of us who champion organized construction as a viable alternative to the merit shop. The unions have thrown away millions of dollars in wages that would otherwise have gone to their membership. A union minority wanted it all or nothing. And they got *nothing.*

By refusing to work "mixed"—alongside non-union workers—a small union minority (less than 20 percent) intimidated, threatened and coerced the majority of hard-working union men and women on the Boise project. They made it totally impossible for them to perform their work. This mindless act is the most serious setback to the building trades since the Philadelphia-area clash at Leon Altemose's project in 1973.[28]

In times of war, the first casualty is truth.

BOAKE CARTER
WRITER

Notwithstanding these conspiratorial tactics of union adherents and state government officials, BE&K was able to complete the Boise-Cascade project ahead of schedule and within budget. And local police eventually gained control of the battlefield. Over fifty-five arrests were made for assault and arson—and prosecuted successfully. Sentences ranged from several days to ten months in jail with fines up to $2,000, community service, or probation.[29]

Additionally, BE&K filed a charge with the National Labor Relations Board to the effect that the unions involved had violated the Taft-Hartley Act "for threatening, coercing and restraining its employees by (1) trespassing and disrupting operations; (2) physical assault and battery; (3) destruction of property; and (4) arson." The Labor Board's general counsel issued a complaint against the unions but the administrative law judge who heard the case exonerated them and the Board concurred with his opinion.[30] BE&K appealed the decision to the U.S. Court of Appeals for the Eighth Circuit, which overturned the Labor Board's ruling five years after the illegal activities begin.[31]

Potlatch Corporation Caves in to Big Labor

Shortly after this phase of the corporate campaign, BE&K was awarded a project for a new client in Arkansas. Potlatch Corporation was installing papermaking machinery at its Pine Bluff mill, and BE&K was looking forward to expanding its client base with the addition of Potlatch to its customer list. In what was thought to be a routine meeting between Potlatch management and United Paperworkers International Union (UPIU) officials representing Potlatch's mill production employees, a UPIU Vice President warned Potlatch of impending trouble if BE&K was not removed from the Arkansas project. He stated that "the Carpenters would come, there would be trouble, UIPU would get involved, and Potlatch wouldn't like it."[32]

Thoughts of International Falls and Boise Cascade were fresh in the mind of Potlatch's management. Believing that "trouble" could mean "strikes, riots and arson," they succumbed to the union threats and BE&K was forced to give up the Arkansas mill job. The UPIU bragged about this loss of the Potlatch work but BE&K responded by bringing a lawsuit against the Carpenters and UPIU. It alleged tortious interference with contract relations involving coercion and violence. A federal jury agreed, awarding BE&K $125,000 in actual damages and $20,000,000 in punitive damages. Ultimately the unions obtained a reversal of this Arkansas verdict and the case was remanded for a new trial against UPIU.

BE&K Defeats Big Labor's Corporate Campaign

Next BE&K filed an action against the senior hierarchy of both UPIU and the Carpenters Union for damages resulting from the Boise Cascade rioting and terrorism. The case was docketed in an Alabama state court in the company's hometown of Birmingham. BE&K claimed there was a civil conspiracy of parent international union involvement and/or ratification of the illegal activities to prevent completion of the Boise Cascade project in International Falls.

The Birmingham litigation stalled due to dubious legal maneuvers before the Alabama Supreme Court as the unions involved continued to deny responsibility for any illegal activity against BE&K. This internal "solidarity" between the Carpenters and UPIU eventually ended and neither case made it back to trial. Instead, in 1999 separate settlement agreements negotiated by BE&K's able general counsel, Fred Garrick, were reached with the International Brotherhood of Carpenters and the United Paperworkers International Union. That capitulation terminated the building trades' ten-year-long corporate campaign to organize the company's workforce.[33]

But it didn't end BE&K's counter-attack on Big Labor.

Back in 1987 when BE&K was targeted for "annihilation" by these trade unions, the company (as previously noted) counter-sued the Contra Costa Building and Construction Trades Council. BE&K lost this case when the trial court ruled that none of the Trades Council's affiliated unions had violated the Sherman Anti-Trust Act by conspiring to delay the $350 million steel mill project for USS-Posco Industries in Northern California. Six years later, in 1994, the federal Ninth Circuit Appellate Court finally got around to reviewing BE&K's appeal of this adverse decision. The appellate judges said they were "troubled" by some of the union actions but found no antitrust law violation.[34]

The National Labor Relations Board immediately upheld an unfair labor practice counter-charge filed by the Trades Council against BE&K under the Taft-Hartley Act. In doing so, the Labor Board agreed with the Trades Council that the company's anti-trust lawsuit was "retaliatory" against the unions in violation of the Taft-Hartley Act. "BE&K," ruled the Labor Board, "was only interested in harassing the unions, not in obtaining justice."[35]

In 2001, the federal Sixth Circuit Appellate Court agreed to enforce the Labor Board's decision to punish BE&K.[36] As a remedy in the case, the Labor Board ordered BE&K to pay all union attorneys fees and other litigation expenses accrued in defending against the unsuccessful anti-trust lawsuit.[37] Union lawyers estimated that their costs in the case could total "millions of dollars" plus more thousands of dollars in interest assessments.[38]

Fifteen years after BE&K and USS-Posco Industries originally filed their antitrust case against the building trades—on June 24, 2002—the U.S. Supreme Court *unanimously reversed* both this decision of the Sixth Circuit Court of Appeals and the Labor Board's order relying on allegedly illegal "company retaliation" against the unions. Justice Sandra Day O'Connor wrote the Supreme Court's decision that relieved BE&K from paying any litigation expenses incurred by the building trades unions and their attorneys. Justice O'Connor emphasized that the Constitution's First Amendment right to petition the government for assistance in the "redress of grievances" is "one of the most precious of the liberties safeguarded by the Bill of Rights." This right is implied by "the very idea of a government, republican in form," she added, and held:

> Because there is nothing in the statutory [Taft-Hartley Act] text indicating that Section 8(a)(1) must be read to reach all reasonably based but unsuccessful suits filed with a retaliatory purpose, we decline to do so. Because the [Labor] Board's standard for imposing liability

A timid person is frightened before a danger, a coward during the time, and a courageous person afterwards.

JEAN PAUL RICHTER
HISTORIAN

The law's final justification is in the good it does to the society of a given place and time.

ALBERT CAMUS
PUNDIT

[against BE&K] under the NLRA [Taft-Hartley Act] allows it to penalize such suits, its standard is thus invalid.[39]

According to the unanimous court, it is insufficient for the Labor Board to find retaliatory motive even though the employer's suit:

- was directed at protected conduct,
- necessarily tended to discourage similar protected activity,
- was admittedly brought to stop conduct the employer thought was unprotected,
- involved unions other than those parties to certain suits against the company,
- was unmeritorious, and
- was supported by anti-union animus.

ABC's General Counsel, Maurice Baskin of Venable, Baetjer and Howard (and my longtime law partner), represented BE&K and USS-Posco Industries in this unanimous victory before the Supreme Court. The ABC Construction Legal Rights Foundation assisted him in support of the precedential ruling. Baskin later told the news media:

> This is a very important decision for employers. It recognizes that their right of access to the courts in the labor context must be protected. The Labor Board had adopted a policy that was unfairly punishing employers for filing reasonable suits against unions whenever such suits were not 100 percent successful. The Supreme Court decision declares that policy invalid. Employers faced with such unfair union tactics in the future will now have greater freedom to respond in court without fear of violating the Taft-Hartley Act.[40]

ABC National Chairman (formerly called "President") Ken Adams ('02) agreed with Baskin: "This decision is of vital importance to construction companies that are being targeted by labor unions. It will ensure that the

National Labor Relations Board respects the constitutionally protected right of any firm to proactively defend itself in court against labor union attacks."[41]

Sound Advice for ABCers

During one of many special ceremonies honoring Kennedy for his outstanding service to ABC over the years and his company's fearless stand and victory over the vicious Carpenters-UPIU corporate campaign, he responded to attending ABC members with the following remarks. They bear repeating—and remembering:

> The past is often prologue to the future. Don't ever become complacent about Big Labor's goal to destroy the merit shop by whatever means it takes. And remember that no contractor can withstand that pressure alone. Our employees had to fight their way through hostile picket lines to get to work every day, day in and day out. Not for just a week. Not for a month, but year after year. Sometimes they needed a police escort to cross safely. And their families were harassed too.

> After a while you begin to wonder if your employees, your subs, your clients and your owners will stick with you or say "the hell with it—you aren't worth the effort." That's why, if you are chosen as a union target, you must have a strong support system. ABC is the network leader that supports BE&K whenever we take on a new project—*and it never fails us.*

> So I will leave you with this thought: sometimes you can tire of paying ABC membership dues. Sometimes you may become tired of serving on ABC committees, writing support letters, visiting Congress or your state legislature...*Don't!*

> Your future depends on remaining vigilant. Your future depends on going back to the politicians again and again. It depends on donating your time and digging into your pocket for ABC. Sometimes you want to relax and think "we've worked awfully hard for ABC so I'll sit back awhile and rest..." *But you can't.*

When you win, nothing hurts.

JOE NAMATH
N.Y. JETS
QUARTERBACK

Maurice Baskin, ABC's general councel from 1987 to the present

Man's destiny lies half within himself and half without. To advance in either half at the expense of the other is literally ridiculous.

PHILIP WYLIE
HUMANIST

Don't disappoint ABC. Don't disappoint your industry. Don't disappoint free enterprise. Don't disappoint yourself. Go out, get into action and be what you have always been—the spirit of the merit shop. *There is always another battle to fight!*[43]

Ted Kennedy's advice was 100 percent correct!

CHAPTER 50

CHICANERY BETWEEN TWO BUSHES

WHILE ON THE CAMPAIGN TRAIL IN **1992**, presidential candidate Bill Clinton converted many voters through his evangelical speeches that promised "a great new day" for our nation. This magical dawn, he eulogized, would feature "more jobs, smaller government, and the most ethical administration in the history of the United States."[1] Unfortunately for the cause of free enterprise, subsequent pronouncements by President William Jefferson Clinton from the White House turned abruptly (and quietly) toward political paybacks of the far Left. His actions on most economic issues became controlled by a special interest group which had delivered many of the crucial votes needed to elect him: Big Labor.

This bias became evident even as the inaugural proceedings were being planned. It was described by ABC's executive vice president, Dan Bennet, in the *Wall Street Journal*. After being told during the presidential campaign that Clinton would have "an inclusive administration that would embrace all Americans," Bennet wrote:

> During the past couple of weeks, caterers have been fired, vendors and contractors have been replaced, and invitations have been rescinded to participate in the inaugural festivities. Why? Because the employees of these companies are not represented by a labor union. In one

> I may not have been the best president, but I've had the most fun eight years.

> BILL CLINTON
> 42ND PRESIDENT,
> IN *NEWSWEEK*,
> DECEMBER 11, 2001

If you retreat, you give up and there's no use of being alive.

CHARLES W. COLE, JR.
BALTIMORE BANKER

incident, an entire printing job was thrown out after the inaugural committee discovery that the union "bug," or seal, which accompanies every union printing job, was missing.

In the case of the Associated Builders & Contractors, the trade group for which I work, no contracts were made, but we were invited to participate in the inaugural parade by supplying several construction workers to ride a float symbolizing the building of America. We told the inaugural committee that we would be honored to participate. Everything, it appeared, was set.

After making a couple of calls and lining up the participants—whom, by the way, we would have paid for missing a day's work—we were again contacted by Mr. Clinton's people. This time they wanted to know if we were a union or non-union organization. When we explained that our members represented the open or merit shop, there was a long pause on the other end of the line. The inaugural staffer then asked us "to hold up on everything." He said "he would get back to us."

Three days later, not to our surprise, we were told, somewhat sheepishly, that "Mr. Clinton wouldn't need our workers after all." Since then, several reports have been published relating other, similar incidents. A pattern is taking shape.[2]

Clinton's seldom (if ever) recorded (before or since) true philosophy on labor-management relations was printed on the dust-cover of a father-and-son book authored by Irving and Barry Bluestone in 1992. It's called *Negotiating the Future*. As a part of Clinton's endorsement of this tome, he boasted that "the Bluestones' thoughtful book will help spread the word on how America is to regain its competitive edge." And here is an excerpted summary of the Bluestones' labor relations policy recommended by Clinton to "improve" workplace productivity in our capitalistic society:

...We believe that the next giant step in labor-management relations—one that is already beginning to be taken in a handful of enterprises—will involve expanding employee participation to this upper

650

level of decision making within the firm. Workers themselves and their union representatives need to be 'brought into the loop' in all of these strategic areas of management. Ultimately, labor must begin to participate and take responsibility with management for decisions at all levels of the firm, from the shop floor to the boardroom.

Economic success today requires that everyone from the janitor and the machinist to the secretary and the senior engineer have a role in the strategic decisions that affect the company's well-being. This even includes input in the pricing of the company's products, in the design of customer relations, and in the very investment decisions that determine the expansion or demise of the enterprise. [3]

Washington is a much more bitter, ugly place, dominated by special interests, than I ever envisioned.

GEORGE W. BUSH
43RD PRESIDENT

Karl Marx could not have said it better.

In stark contrast, during the previous administration President George Herbert Walker Bush ("Bush 1st") issued Executive Order No. 12818 to promote and ensure open and competitive bidding (by non-union and unionized contractors alike) on all federally funded building and construction projects. In the preamble to this order, Bush listed five sound entrepreneurial reasons for his merit shop policy:

1. To increase competition in federal construction contracts.
2. To uphold the rights of workers freely to select, or refrain from selecting, bargaining representatives, and to decide whether or not to be union members, so as to provide access to employment opportunities on federal and federally funded construction projects for all workers.
3. To reduce construction costs.
4. To expand job opportunities, especially for small businesses.
5. To promote the economical and efficient administration and completion of federally funded construction projects.

After Clinton took the oath of presidential office in 1993, he revoked what he called Bush Sr.'s "anti-union" executive order and issued his own pro-union version. The White House staff admitted that the new president's order forced

Clinton's flawed character—his dishonesty, his egotism and his moral cowardice—suffused everything he did and primed him for failure as president.

Rich Lowry
in *Legacy, Paying the Price for the Clinton Years*

"union-only" construction project labor agreements ("PLAs") on all federal building projects. The justification given was that "unionized labor sets better work standards, reduces more cost overruns, provides more timely completion dates by skilled craftsmen, promotes safer working conditions and thereby well-serves American taxpayers and the federal government." This dubious explanation was applauded by Clinton's old college buddy whom he appointed as Secretary of Labor, Robert Reich. He dutifully (and erroneously) agreed that "PLAs restore a level playing field in labor-management relations."[4]

ABC's 35th national president in 1993 and the CEO of Ivey Mechanical, Inc., Joe Ivey, immediately issued an opposition statement to Clinton's executive order on PLAs that received approval in the *Wall Street Journal*.

It included these facts:

REPRINTED WITH PERMISSION, KAL, CARTOON ARTS INTERNATIONAL/CWS FROM THE *BALTIMORE SUN*.

At a time when the Administration is claiming that new taxes will be needed in order to reduce the budget deficit, President Clinton's action [on PLAs] will only increase the government's cost of construction. It will inflate job costs and decrease competition among qualified bidders. A statement released by Clinton, however, said that the Bush ["Sr."] order "prohibited contractors who have entered into project agreements with unions from bidding on federal construction contracts."

Nothing could be further from the truth. There is not one word in the Bush order that discourages union contractors from working on federal projects. It merely assures that open shop contractors will not be arbitrarily excluded from such work.[5]

The GAO and ENR Oppose Discriminatory PLAs

No economic studies or public hearings were offered by the Clinton administration to justify its spurious claim that savings to taxpayers would result from this pro-union PLA executive order. On the contrary, a General Accounting Office report revealed that wage-and-benefit packages paid under these compulsory union-only agreements could run 17 percent to 21 percent higher than the applicable "prevailing wage law" standards set periodically by the Department of Labor for federally funded construction projects. Critical words from the construction industry's non-partisan *Engineering News-Record* magazine on Clinton's political shenanigans added:

> Competitive bidding laws are designed to avoid political favoritism in public bidding. But PLAs favor union contractors and, by extension, unions. Thus, public officials adopting a PLA are currying favor with, and possibly political campaign contributions from, unions. This is just the kind of cronyism the competitive bidding laws seek to avoid.
>
> We believe that all bidders should be treated equally when bidding on public works projects. Where a union contractor is the lowest qualified bidder, it should be awarded the contract. The same should go for the non-union contractor. There should be no artificial, govern-

If there had not been a Candidate Ross Perot, there would never have been a President Bill Clinton.

FOX NEWS
JULY 4, 2003

President William Jefferson Clinton. What a ridiculous waste! Full of promise, intelligence and charisma, this man will go down in history alongside Warren Harding and Richard Nixon as the three most corrupt presidents of the 20th Century.

BILL O'REILLY
THE O'REILLY FACTOR

ment-imposed barrier, like a PLA, to either side. With a level playing field, all workers will have equal cause to celebrate on Labor Day.[6]

This "union-only" PLA sample of Clintonomics reflected the extent to which the "great-new-day" Democrat administration allowed a political covenant with Big Labor to override a campaign commitment to American taxpayers for the "highest integrity in government." The real impact of Clinton's partisan and monopolistic executive order was a policy that pressured all government agencies to adopt unionized PLAs for their construction work, *regardless of the cost.* That meant that hundreds of otherwise qualified open shop contractors and their thousands of versatile non-union employees—who comprise over 80 percent of the country's building industry—were compelled to "go union" or lose the opportunity to compete and bid for lucrative government construction projects.

As this large pool of qualified open shop bidders became eliminated under Clinton's presidential watch, the number of federal construction projects decreased and the cost of federal construction increased. Taxpayers contributed billions of additional dollars to finance inflationary union-only PLAs throughout the United States.[7]

Clinton was undaunted by these economic facts and brushed aside grave legal questions as to his constitutional breach of freedom of association, non-discriminatory competitive bidding, and evasion of civil liberties by fostering mandatory PLAs. Instead, the Artful Dodger issued a memorandum explaining why he rescinded George Bush the 1st's executive order that had required open and competitive bidding on all federal construction, regardless of union or non-union affiliation.

Clinton's directive promised that union-only PLAs "would achieve economy and efficiency in federal construction projects" and "advance the government's procurement interest in cost efficiency and quality."[8] He spun additional justification for unionized PLAs to the effect that they would (in some inexplicable way) "reduce unnecessary government intrusion into workplace relations, promote the shared goals of American workers and management, restore a needed balance in the workplace, and strengthen the ability of the nation's businesses and industry to compete in the world economy."[9]

Without any apparent pangs of conscience, Bill Clinton was duping American taxpayers, fanning the flames of forced unionism, and encouraging the Marxist labor-management relations philosophy of the aforementioned Bluestone brothers.

Archbishop Keehler Defends Capitalism

Motivated by this guaranteed federal work bonanza from their political Santa Claus, local AFL-CIO officials in Maryland demanded that Archbishop William H. Keehler institute a similar obligatory union scale PLA policy in awarding all church-related construction contracts within the Archdiocese of Baltimore. When His Holiness refused to do so, the leader of the Baltimore Building and Construction Trades Council, William Kaczorowski, went on a public attack.

At stake in the confrontation, according to Baltimore's *Daily Record* newspaper, were millions of dollars in construction projects for new buildings and the maintenance of eight hundred existing archdiocesan-owned facilities. They included churches, parochial schools, rectories, convents, parish centers, and multipurpose structures paid for by voluntary private contributions from the Archbishop's loyal flock.

Kaczorowski openly charged His Holiness with violating the Catholic Church's own precepts as stated in its papal encyclicals and other religious writings. The local trades union leader contended that by using non-union contractors who pay "substandard wages and offer no health and welfare benefits to their non-craft-trained employees," the Archdiocese was ignoring unionized workers' "natural human right to form private associations." An allegedly relevant Encyclical Letter of Pope John Paul II cited by Kaczorowski was said to

Get your facts first . . . then you can distort 'em as much as you wish.

MARK TWAIN
HUMORIST-WRITER

CARTOONIST "KAL," BALTIMORE SUN, JANUARY 25, 1998. REPRINTED WITH PERMISSION, CARTOONISTS & WRITERS SYNDICATE AND CARTOON ARTS INTERNATIONAL/CWS

A state, to prosper, must be built on foundations of a moral character. Character is the principal element of its strength and the only guaranty of its permanence and prosperity.

JABEZ L. M. CURRY
HISTORIAN

prove that the use of organized labor amounts to "an indispensable element of social life." But he predicted that "due to heavy financial backing of the Archbishop by non-union contractors, greed would prevail over Encyclicals of the Popes."[10]

In rebuttal to this factually incorrect and encyclically misinterpreted union charge—as well as in clarification of the Church's economically sound and legally non-discriminatory business policy of hiring the lowest qualified and responsible bidder for each building project—Archbishop Keehler released his own "official guidelines."

The Church's "level playing field" required interested construction firms (both non-union and union) to disclose whether they provided "reasonable employee benefits," including health care, sick leave, short-term disability, retirement, and vacation benefits. And a pre-qualification questionnaire, which every contractor was required to complete for the Archdiocese, asked whether the bidding company had a proven record of employing minorities and women.

The Archbishop also required all bidders to supply data about safety and training programs that they offered to their employees. Lastly, they had to comply with the Archdiocese's longtime practice of pre-screening bidders for competence, work experience, financial stability, and fair treatment of workers.

By denying any exclusive preferential status to those contractors who required their employees to be represented by AFL-CIO building trades unions, Archbishop Keehler made it clear that the Church's "open and fair bidding process allows for expanded competition and helps assure that we are receiving quality work at a fair market price."[11] He also told an agitated local press corps (all of whom were compelled to pay dues to their newspaper union) about his entrepreneurial policy:

> To automatically exclude more than 80 percent of the State's contractors from consideration would significantly reduce competition. Such a policy would be a disservice to our parishioners, who rightfully expect the Archdiocese and the parishes and organizations under its supervision to manage their funds prudently.[12]

Clinton's Unionized PLAs Are Exorcized

Good news for ABC and the economy of the United States soon followed. Upon succeeding Clinton as president, George W. Bush ("2nd") cancelled the foxy Democrat's union-mandated federal construction policy and revived the merit shop "lowest qualified bidder" policy of his father, Bush ("1st"). It took the form of new Executive Order No. 13202.

Incensed at this capitalistic turn of events, the Building and Construction Trades Department of the AFL-CIO took the battle over project labor agreements (PLAs) into government procurement agencies and courts throughout the United States. ABC, either as an actual party to these legal proceedings or as an *amicus curiae* (friend of the court), has constantly challenged Big Labor's stance on the issue.

In August of 2001, Big Labor located a liberal federal district court judge in Washington, D.C. who readily approved a "cease and desist order" blocking the Bush executive decree. In this *Albaugh* case filed by the AFL-CIO's Building and Construction Trades Department, the judge ruled that Clinton's "project labor agreements are expressly allowed by the National Labor Relations [Taft-Hartley] Act."[13]

About a year later, on July 12, 2002, a great ABC victory was achieved in the *Albaugh* case. The U.S. Court of Appeals for the District of Columbia Circuit *reversed* the decision of the left-wing district court judge and vacated his injunction against use of Bush's new "merit shop" PLA executive order. The case was prosecuted successfully by Attorney General John Ashcroft's U.S. Justice Department. Maury Baskin (ABC's general counsel and a partner in my law firm of Venable, Baetjer and Howard) represented both ABC and the U.S. Chamber of Commerce as they joined a coalition of business organizations in filing an *amicus curiae* brief supporting the Justice Department's position and opposing the Plaintiff Building Trades' lawsuit.

This *unanimous* decision of the federal appellate court held that "President [George W. Bush] acted within his authority under Article II of the Constitution in issuing Order No. 13202." His Executive Order, continued the appellate court, "expressed a proprietary policy which is not subject to pre-emption by the National Labor Relations [Taft-Hartley] Act." Therefore, the

The great story here for anybody willing to find it and write about it and explain it is this vast right-wing conspiracy against my husband since the day he announced for president.

Hillary Clinton while "First Lady" of the U.S.

If an actor
can become
a president,
a president
can become
an actor.

BILL CLINTON
42ND PRESIDENT

appellate court reasoned, a compulsory Clinton-style unionized PLA could not be "required" on any federally funded construction project covered by Executive Order.[14]

Counselor Maury Baskin told the downcast elite national press:

The *Albaugh* decision is a victory for the Bush administration, a victory for ABC, and a victory for open competition. Now contractors will be free from any union-only requirements on literally billions of dollars worth of construction work across the country. If states are going to accept federal government money, they are going to have to accept the principles of open competition.[15]

CARTOONIST "KAL," BALTIMORE SUN, AUGUST 18, 1998. REPRINTED WITH PERMISSION, CARTOONISTS & WRITERS SYNDICATE AND CARTOON ARTS INTERNATIONAL/CWS

Ken Adams, the National Board Chairman of ABC in 2002 and CEO of Pace Electric Company based in Wilmington, Delaware, predicted to *Engineering News-Record* that the appellate court's ruling "will restore full and open competition in the federal contracting process."[16]

When the U.S. Supreme Court concluded its 2002–03 session on January 27, 2003, the biggest case affecting the construction industry was the one that the justices *declined* to hear. The high court silently exercised its discretionary right of refusal to review (and possibly overturn) the *Albaugh* appellate court decision on project labor agreements. It meant that Bush's executive order barring these discriminatory union PLAs on federally funded projects remained legal and enforceable under the Constitution of the United States.

That negative legal action by the highest court in the United States (called "denying certiorari") made ABC's victory final and complete.[17] It was a major blow to the AFL-CIO and Clinton's Democrat Party, but the politically nonpartisan *Engineering News-Record* reported the good news it provided to the economy and ABC:

> Eddie Rispone, chairman of the Associated Builders and Contractors, was pleased by the court's ruling: "President Bush's common-sense executive order helps to ensure open competition. The Supreme Court's decision is a major victory for U.S. taxpayers and for the construction industry."[18]

To sum up this legal battle over PLAs, upon his election in 1993, President William Jefferson Clinton faced a multi-billion-dollar choice on how federal building and construction work would be awarded. He could take the "right" road by living up to the "job-producing, efficient and ethical standards of government" that Candidate Bill Clinton promised to the American electorate while seeking votes for his election as President. But that would have meant endorsing President George Bush 1st's executive order on PLAs which encouraged competitive bidding, produced efficiency through lower building costs for American taxpayers to fund, and thus frequently caused the building trades unions to lose out. Instead, the newly elected President Clinton broke his cam-

Individual character involves honoring and embracing certain core values: honesty, respect, responsibility. And we must all do our part.

FROM PRESIDENT CLINTON'S PROCLAMATION DURING NATIONAL CHARACTER WEEK

paign promise to the citizenry and took the "left" road by handing Big Labor a pricey, partisan, political plum.

This compulsory unionism directive covering the building of all federal government construction projects is just one of many examples of Clintonian chicanery that flourished in the Oval Office between two Bushes.[19]

CHAPTER 51

BOMBS, BRIEFCASES, AND THE CYCLE OF LIBERTY

B Y THE 1980s, most of the assaults on ABC members and their construction projects by the AFL-CIO's building trades unions had become focused at the Association's annual national convention sites and statewide or local chapter gatherings. On a balmy day in 1984, for instance, more than one thousand pickets, led by AFL-CIO President Lane Kirkland personally, massed and demonstrated in a comparatively controlled fashion outside ABC's annual national convention site in Miami, Florida.

Even this type of hit-and-run thrust seemed to reach its zenith at ABC's 38th annual convention held in California four years later. Attending contractors and their families were greeted at San Francisco's huge Moscone Convention Center by five thousand enraged union tradesmen shouting: "The rats are coming," "go home scabs," and worse obscenities. Some of the rowdies used two-by-four wooden studs to break the windows of contractors' approaching cars and rented buses in order to pitch rocks, rotten eggs, tomatoes, and other garbage on ABC passengers.

At the Center's entrance, conventioneers were forced to dash through narrow corridors between moving vehicles while using newspapers, briefcases, and handbags as protective shields. Soon the main roadway and pavements to the facility became completely blocked and San Francisco police were forced to call out their anti-riot squad. Life-threatening situations erupted, but there were no serious injuries.

> **Truth is history, history is truth; these two domains should not be separated.**
>
> JEAN GUITTON
> PUNDIT

ABC Contractor

Lane Kirkland, president of the AFL-CIO (1979–1995), carries the lead picket sign protesting against ABC at its annual convention in 1984 in Miami, Florida.

We are born angry. Some remain so.

Samuel Beckett
Irish-French
Playwright

"Our members refused to abandon the convention in spite of harassment and physical assaults," said Mike Perkins, a Dayton, Ohio, general contractor who was ABC National's thirtieth president in that year of 1988. He told San Francisco officials: "Keep the buses rolling—we're holding our convention here today." And he added: "This inexcusable confrontation is a perfect venue for us to get the word out across the country that it's what happens when ABCers are just trying to meet and compete peacefully within America's free-enterprise system."[1] He also used the opportunity to accept interviews not only by local network affiliates but also by the *Los Angeles Times*, CBS, ABC, NBC, CNN, the Associated Press, United Press International, the *San Francisco Examiner*, and the *San Francisco Chronicle* during the convention pandemonium.

The March 17, 1988, edition of *Engineering News-Record* contained a negative editorial reaction to that trade union intimidation in the beautiful city by the bay. It included these words:

> The union message was delivered to [property and construction] owners, but it was also broadcast to the ABC membership and the general public in a rather distasteful way—eggs and other biodegradable missiles. Union pickets were not very discriminating about their targets, either: They also plastered hapless members of the American Home Sewing Association, who were meeting in the same convention center.
>
> From a public relations standpoint, the view of a woman slipping on broken eggs and being bombarded by an additional fusillade is

WARNING

The RATS are coming

to San Francisco. The anti-union, The Associated Builders and Contractors (ABC) are going to hold their convention at the Moscone Center, Howard Street between 3rd and 4th Streets.

The Bay Area Building Trade Councils are going to welcome them in a good union way.

JOIN THE RALLY
AT THE MOSCONE CENTER:

MARCH 7	MARCH 8	MARCH 9
MONDAY	TUESDAY	WEDNESDAY
	7:30 A.M. to ?	

Your Wages, Hours and Benefits
ARE ON THE LINE!

For Details Call Your Local Union or

The San Francisco Building Trades Council	415-467-3330
The San Mateo Building Trades Council	415-343-3775
The Alameda Building Trades Council	415-430-8664
The Contra Costa Building Trades Council	415-228-0900
The Santa Clara Building Trades Council	408-265-7643

> **What a difference there is between the barbarian that precedes culture and the barbarian that follows it.**
>
> FREDERICK HEBBEL
> HISTORIAN

> **A conservative is a liberal who got mugged.**
>
> ANONYMOUS

not a very good one—especially when it is broadcast on network television along with views of 150 riot police. Nor is the view of a contractor being pelted while unloading a wheelchair from a car for an associate, who was also hit.

Everyone comes away from such an incident more thoughtful. Owners think more about the way they will build projects, ABC members about their role as individuals and members of a trade association, union members about the role they have to play to protect their jobs, and the public about what limits should be drawn around freedoms of expression. We hope the result is stand-up competition with no violence. Then we'll all be winners.

Lawyers representing ABC's Golden Gate Chapter eventually obtained an injunction against this barbarism from a local court (after union attorneys contended unsuccessfully that throwing garbage at contractors was a constitutionally protected form of free speech). The "cease and desist" order limited the number of "protestors" around the Convention Center to two for each union affiliate within the several building trades councils that were involved. And twenty-five "demonstrators" were arrested.

An ABCer "Conquers" New York City

On a sweltering summer day ten years later, in July of 1998, forty thousand hostile construction workers reverted to terrorism of another kind. Led by the Building Trades Council of Greater New York, they abandoned their own jobs to shut down Manhattan traffic on several blocks of Madison Avenue for seven hours. The object of their anger this time was not an ABC convention site but Roy Kay, Inc., a non-union general contractor from Freehold, New Jersey. As the lowest qualified and responsible bidder, this ABC-member firm had been awarded the contract to build a $36.2 million facility for the New York City Metropolitan Transit Authority on a merit shop basis.[2]

An editorial in the *New York Times* concluded that this public demonstration by building trades unions to remove Roy Kay, Inc., from its communications center project "turned a lawful rally into an illegal assault on civic life." The *Times* also voiced the fact that "no union or its members should be allowed to take the constitutional right to protest and turn it into a license to paralyze the city and rough up civilians and police officers."[3]

The real issue in this donnybrook, according to the *Times*, was "...who will get jobs on publicly financed projects. In a rebounding city economy,[4] unions want as many projects as possible to go to companies that use union crews. Public agencies, most of which already rely heavily on union contractors, want to hold down construction costs. Awarding contracts to the lowest responsible bidders, some of whom may be non-union contractors, is a means to that end."[5]

Several of the publicly scorned union leaders involved in the mob action issued grudging apologies. A few others even offered restitution for injuries and property damage, but the *Times* believed "they all were really winking at the misconduct."[6] That suspicion seemed confirmed when the building trades had the audacity to file labor complaints against Roy Kay, Inc. in courts and government agencies. ABC's Construction Legal Rights Foundation immediately supported the builder in opposing these hypocritical union attacks. It all culminated in a successful merit shop countercharge at the National Labor Relations Board against the unions for engaging in illegal secondary boycott picketing.

The greater triumph, however, was worldwide proof that high-quality, reasonable-cost, non-union construction work can be performed successfully on a major project located in midtown Manhattan at the heart of America's number-one union-controlled city—in spite of Big Labor's creation of a "war zone."[7]

Trade Union Demonstrations Decrease in Vigor

Returning again to the building trades' current-day pattern of shorter and more moderate protest at formal ABC membership meetings, just such an unsuccessful hit-and-run effort to derail an ABC statewide regional conference occurred in Toledo, Ohio, two years later—during May of 2000. At that event, the Northwest Ohio Building Trades Council enlisted 1,500 hostile union protestors for one day, to no avail.

The following month, Baltimore's Building Trades Council toned down much further Big Labor's public demonstrations of hostility towards public ABC gatherings. That occasion was the Association's gala fiftieth anniversary celebration held on May 31 through June 3, 2000, in Baltimore's beautiful convention center. This historic birthday party was called to order by ABC's heroic first pres-

> One ought never to turn one's back on a threatened danger and try to run away from it. If you do that, you will double the danger. But if you meet it promptly and without flinching, you will reduce the danger.
>
> WINSTON CHURCHILL
> BRITISH PRIME MINISTER

PHOTO COURTESY OF CHARLES MULLAN

Founder and first ABC president, Charles Mullan (right) with the featured guest speaker, retired General Colin Powell, at ABC's 50th anniversary celebration in Baltimore, the city of ABC's birth, in June 2000.

ABC CONTRACTOR

ABC's past national presidents and executive committee members lead convention attendees in singing "happy birthday" at the Association's 50th year celebration in Baltimore.

ident, Charlie Mullan ('50), and emceed by Bob Heffner, ABC's able executive vice president for many years who succeeded John Trimmer in that important post.

There was a display of fireworks over the city's famed Inner Harbor, followed by an inspiring address from Colin Powell, former four-star general and chief-of-staff who was appointed secretary of state in 2002 by President George W. Bush. Next the conventioneers received a special anniversary report by Thomas Musser, ABC's national president and chairman of Tri-M Corporation. After that message, the two thousand attendees representing ABC's forty-four chapters located throughout the nation attended workshops, viewed construction displays, and were entertained at social functions.

In feeble opposition to this merit shop semi-centennial celebration, the trade unions hired two tiny airplanes to circle briefly over the surrounding downtown Baltimore neighborhood. The planes carried streamers that read **BUILD UNION**. One amused ABC official told the press: "This is a first. We've never before been picketed from the sky." And two lonely union protesters walked dejectedly in front of the convention center for an hour or so, hand-billing a similar communication. It was apparent that Big Labor knew Baltimore's police riot squad (after being duly forewarned by ABC's labor counsel) was on hand and armed, surrounding the convention structure, ready to maintain law and order.[8]

There was a similar absence of massive union protest at ABC's annual national conventions held in Hawaii during '01, at New Orleans in '02, and San Diego in '03. No union picketing at all occurred in Hawaii in '04 or Orlando in '05.

"Always Keep Your Powder Dry!"

In spite of this relaxation of overt trade union hostilities against the merit shop in recent years, BE&K's chief executive and ABC's twenty-second national president ('80), Ted Kennedy, wisely reminded ABCers that they should never become complacent about the possibility of more union coercion and violence affecting workplace productivity, safety, and security anywhere at any moment.[9] A prime example of what Kennedy had in mind can be illustrated by a recent three-year-long violent (but unsuccessful) strike. The corrupt International Brotherhood of Teamsters[10] (affiliated with the AFL-CIO Building and Construction Trades) attempted to force unionization on the thirteen thousand truck drivers of a major carrier which frequently hauls materials and equipment for merit shop employees, namely, Overnite Transportation Corporation. Over 90 percent of the drivers decided to defy the bloody attack and courageously kept on working. The Teamsters sought and received $500,000 from parental AFL-CIO union membership dues to help fund their campaign of intimidation and terrorism at its cruelist.

Since labor union brutality is overlooked or spun downward by the politically correct liberal news media, here are some excerpts from the shocking unfair labor practices "settlement agreement" reached by Overnite with the Teamsters to end the strike in September of 2003. It was "mediated" under the direction of President George W. Bush's conservative, reconstituted National Labor Relations Board. All of these words are included in the signed agreement that was posted for the guilty Teamsters' local unions and their members to read and obey:

> WE WILL NOT use or threaten to use a weapon of any kind, including but not limited to guns, knives, slingshots, rocks, ball bearings, liquid-filled balloons or other projectiles, picket signs, sticks, sledge hammers, bricks, hot coffee, bottles, two by fours, lit cigarettes, eggs, or bags or balloons filled with excrement against any non-striking Overnite employee or security guard in the presence of any Overnite employee . . .
>
> WE WILL NOT endanger or impede the progress of or harass any non-striking employee or any employee of a neutral person doing

If we keep silent about evil, we are implanting it and it will rise up a thousand fold in the future.

ALEXANDER SOLZHENITSYN PRISONER OF THE SOVIET UNION AND HISTORIAN

> **The usual choice is not between the good and the bad but between the bad and the worse.**
>
> GERMAN PROVERB

business with Overnite, while he or she is operating a company vehicle or his or her own personal vehicle, by forcing or attempting to force him or her off the road, blocking, delaying or limiting his or her access to or passage on any road, swerving toward, driving recklessly near, tailgating or braking abruptly in front of him or her...

WE WILL NOT batter, assault, spit on, blow whistles loudly near a person's ear, throw any liquid or solid object at, or attempt to assault any non-striking employee of Overnite or any member of his or her family...

WE WILL NOT threaten to kill or inflict bodily harm, make throat slashing motions, make gun pointing motions, challenge or threaten to fight or assault employees, threaten to sexually assault non-striking employees or their family members, threaten to follow non-striking employees to their homes, use racial epithets or obscene gestures at non-striking employees or otherwise threaten unspecified reprisals...[11]

Modern-Day Trade Union Pressure Tactics

Despite this recent ferocity by the same labor organization that is trying to persuade a federal court to remove it from trusteeship control due to underworld corruption within its own leadership ranks,[12] the building trades seem to be deferring most of their conventional terror tactics. Today, "white-collar" shysterism and partisan political pressure are featured as Big Labor attempts to regain its historic construction market monopoly and wipe out the merit shop movement.

Instead, the building trades are relying on the "cooperation" of all three branches of government—legislative, executive, and judicial—to fight their battles for them. By "an exchange of firebombs for briefcases," both legal leverage and monetary influence over bureaucrats have become the cornerstones of building trades strategy to force ABC members into submission to unionization from the "top down"—without gaining the support of a majority of the employees involved.

This trade union scheme attempts to defy competitive market standards, dominate government regulatory bodies, and distort judicial and legislative processes. David Bush, ABC's 41st national president ('99) and chief executive officer of Adena Corporation (a general contractor based in Mansfield, Ohio) publicly rebuked this latest building trades subterfuge:

> ABC has never proposed deals or policies or legislation that would exclude unionized contractors from bidding or working on any project in either the private or public sector. Unlike the AFL-CIO building trades, we don't instruct ABC members to harass, coerce, politicize or litigate to drive unionized contractors or their employees out of business. We've never tried to stack the deck against free and open competition. Such tactics are discriminatory, inefficient, and costly to construction users and the taxpaying public.[13]

The prestigious Business Roundtable (a previously mentioned association of "Fortune 200" corporate executives) foresaw the negative impact of this latest trade union ruse on America's construction users and consumers and issued a special report to warn them. It's aptly called *The Growing Threat to Competitiveness: Union Pressure Tactics Target U.S. Construction Owners*. Here are some quotations from the Roundtable report's introductory "overview":

> Every U.S. company that budgets substantial sums of capital for new construction or major maintenance must recognize that the cost of construction is a critical factor in controlling the bottom line—and remaining competitive. It is a mistake to think that construction costs are only the concern of construction firms... Some building trades unions—which once dominated the construction industry—are aggressively trying to pressure owners into abandoning the competitive selection process and instead to use only contractors which employ union labor...
>
> Owners need to become familiar with this threat to construction industry cost effectiveness and be prepared to deal with these tactics in order to ensure that they do not succeed and become even more widespread in the future. This paper reviews pressure tactics which The Business Roundtable has documented and suggests steps owners can take to

A lawyer with a briefcase can steal more than a hundred men with guns.

Don Corleone in Mario Puzo's *The Godfather*

Those in power want only to perpetuate it.

SUPREME COURT JUSTICE
WILLIAM DOUGLAS

ensure they can continue to choose the best available suppliers of low-cost, efficient construction.[14]

The Business Roundtable's report to construction users and owners alerted them about what it called a "Union Tool Box of Major Pressure Tactics" that has been adopted by the building trades to force the unionization of all major construction projects throughout the nation. The following seventeen dubious legal contrivances include, expand, and update the "Union Tool Box" that was reported originally by the Roundtable:

1. **Union-only pre-hire project labor agreements (PLAs)** signed by construction users that eliminate competitive non-union contractor bidding and establish wasteful, discriminatory, and non-competitive use of funds through economic or political coercion achieved by friendly bureaucrats and judges and/or by thinly veiled threats of work stoppages. These PLAs require a construction project to be awarded (rather than to the lowest qualified bidder) only to contractors and subcontractors who agree in advance to abide by a master collective bargaining agreement that recognizes trade unions as the exclusive representatives of all employees working on that project; to pay union membership dues, inflated union-scale wage and benefits rates; to use a union hiring hall to obtain workers; and to obey antiquated union work rules. There is no practical protection against job featherbedding, work slowdowns, or stoppages which result in projects plagued by labor union disputes, cost overruns, job delays, safety problems, and discrimination against minorities and women.[15]

2. A potentially legal scam called "*salting*."[16] It means either the undisclosed or open infiltration by union organizers into employment by non-union construction firms that cannot legally refuse to hire them solely because of their union affiliation. Once hired, the unionists either covertly or overtly (using different tactics) keep their union advised on the employer's anti-union activities, harass and disrupt the firm's operations, impair productivity, apply economic pressure,

create financial hardship, and foment frivolous but costly and time-consuming complaints and litigation, while attempting to motivate the targeted contractor's submission to unionization and its employees to "sign up" or lose their jobs.

3. Using political contacts, websites, the latest communications technology, and the Freedom of Information Act to create false and frivolous **"whistleblowing"** charges filed with solicitous government regulatory agencies that lead to unnecessary job site inspections, delays and costly litigation of unfounded claims of violations of laws and regulations. Phony union charges relate to issues such as workplace safety and health, the environment, zoning and building permits, civil rights, apprenticeship training, prevailing wages and job classifications, hours of work and overtime pay, labor relations, employee benefits, and independent contractor status.

4. Blocking—by litigation, legislation, executive order, or violent job site retaliation—the merit shop's legitimate supplementary cost-saving use of versatile **"temporary workers"** supplied by qualified independent personnel staffing agencies.

5. Expansion of the coverage and monitoring of biased enforcement against non-union contractors of the arcane and maladministered **Davis-Bacon Act** and similar state and local **"prevailing wage laws."** These farcical statutes artificially inflate the cost of public construction projects by discriminatorily adopting trade union wage and benefit scales, compulsory membership dues, restrictive job classifications and antiquated work rules for such projects.[17]

6. Union-slanted **government apprenticeship training regulations and union-dominated training councils** which undermine and oppose the recognition and certification of state-of-the-art ABC programs to qualify non-union mechanics, apprentices, and helpers for public construction work, and which also discriminate against minorities and women.

7. A multi-dimensional, all-out, coordinated attack called a **"corporate campaign."** Here the labor organization uses every conceivable economic, legal, political, public relations, psychological, and

671

corporeal weapon against a major user of non-union labor in its relationships with: its own executives, board of directors, stockholders, employees, subcontractors, customers, government regulatory agencies, competitors, suppliers, investors, financiers, creditors, civic, religious and civil rights organizations, the news media, and the public at large. The union goal is to ruin the image, undermine the operations, and destroy the profits of the targeted employer through constant and unyielding pressure against every aspect of its business.[18]

8. Undue building trades union influence and discrimination against a fair result in National Labor Relations Board-supervised union representation elections by "offering" non-union employees who are voting **a union qualification card**. It allows them to work as skilled mechanics without traditional training or actual experience in the particular craft involved as officially required by union and government certification procedures.[19]

9. **Secondary boycott picketing** at all entrances of a construction site aimed at destroying a non-union contractor on a multi-craft project where unionized contractors also are working, thus causing an illegal work slowdown or strike.

10. Calling on biased government agencies to **"blacklist" open shop contractors** who bid on government contracts if they do not have a so-called "satisfactory" record of "integrity, business ethics, and judgment-free compliance" with a host of nonprocurement-related laws and regulations, including labor and employment practices, safety and health, the environment, and consumer protection.

11. Legislative, judicial, or economic attack on a merit shop contractor's right to operate separate and independent **dual union and non-union "double breasted" construction firms**.

12. Control of a union-owned insurance or investment consortium or control of a collectively-bargained pension fund for union members by its union co-trustees who abuse their fiduciary responsibility to the members, including confiscation of employer contributions to the fund by engaging in **"social investing"** of the fund assets in

high cost or otherwise risky union-only construction projects for personal profit; or by threatening **withdrawal of fund investments** from financial institutions that continue to do business with non-union contractors and their customers; or through influence on **employee stock ownership plans (ESOPs)** and threatened corporate harassment or takeovers.

13. Establishing **union-front organizations** that pretend to be "neutral guardians" of the public interest but whose primary purpose is to provide an information "pipeline" which discredits ABC firms through data-based on-line investigation and public distortion of their compliance records at safety, environmental and other regulatory agencies.

14. Forcing contractors to agree to unwanted union representation through so-called **"neutrality or sweetheart agreements"** made with union organizers not to actively oppose them and/or to accept union recognition based on unreliable proof of union membership through **workers' signed union authorization cards.**

15. Under a **union's potentially illegal job targeting program**, contractors that have bargaining agreements with that union request a subsidy (sometimes called "market recovery funds") to help compete against non-union contractors for a particular construction project. The union collects job-targeting funds from its members as dues. If the union approves the contractor's request for a subsidy, the contractor submits a bid that takes the subsidy into account. If the contractor wins the project, it pays the union workers according to the rates in the bargaining agreement and the union reimburses the contractor for the difference between the actual wages paid and the lower wage rates cited in the bid.[20]

16. **Techno-terrorism organizations** that hold themselves out as "public interest" researchers while using the Internet and other telecommunication devices to obtain and distort the records of merit shop contractors by postings on web sites or sending false and abusive "information" to their current and potential construction clients

as well as to prominent members of local communities and government officials to damage the good reputation of merit shop firms.

17. **A new form of protest called "bannering."** The unions attempt
    to avoid legal grounds rules on picketing by claiming that a raised
    "banner" (such as a casket held up in front of a non-union hopsital
    or a sign saying "there are rats in this [non-union] building") con-
    stitutes free speech rather than an illegal secondary boycott.

The above so-called Union Pressure Tactics Tool Box as described by the Business Roundtable (with my own comments and supplemental union schemes
added) is deployed by Big Labor and its lawyers to organize or demolish all
ABC members and their customers. The whole conspiracy is funded by billions of dollars from mandatory union membership dues and special assessments paid by union members.

Bankrolling Union "Fat Cats"

Ironically, this vast *tax-exempt* union income allows many labor chieftains
to enjoy *sub rosa* their own elite personal life style. It frequently features six-
figure salaries,[21] generous bonuses, lucrative expense accounts for entertainment and travel, swank office facilities, and bloated support staffs. Some of
the "big b'hoys" also give themselves chauffeured limousines, stately residences, Las Vegas casino jaunts, jet airplanes, conventions in exotic settings,
huge personal retirement benefits, and other unreported "perks" of office.[22]

These same high-living trade union officials condemn as "greedy,"
"obscene," or "illegal," the legitimate corporate profits that provide the justifi-
able salaries and personal benefits awarded to senior management executives
who are responsible for the success or failure of their firms. Ignored or forgotten are the creation and maintenance of hundreds or thousands of jobs by these
high-paid executives for their employees and profitable dividends to their stockholders, many of whom are union members. Meanwhile the same hypocritical
labor leaders are extracting work-restrictive and inflationary labor contracts at
the bargaining table from the very business managers they harass and insult.

Such duplicity often backfires and causes corporate deficits. Before long,
red ink on the balance sheet results in the layoff of union members, or work

stoppages and permanent loss of jobs due to strikes and strike replacements, or company shutdowns and bankruptcies. In spite of union unemployment lines created, the salaries, personal "perks," and job security of Big Labor's head-honchos continue unabated—bankrolled by membership dues dollars from the pockets of their own out-of-work members.

An example of this opulent lifestyle was reported by the Associated Press on March 15, 2003:

> The luxury hotel in Florida where labor leaders hold an AFL-CIO executive council meeting this week is at the center of a federal [ERISA] lawsuit [by the Secretary of Labor for 'lack of due diligence'] against its union owners and the pension fund used to buy and renovate it. Approved in 1997 [by the Clinton administration] as a $100 million investment by officials of the Plumbers and Pipe Fitters Union, the 998-room Diplomat Resort and Spa in Hollywood, Fla., opened five years later at a cost of $800 million . . .
>
> This 39-story structure at the edge of the Atlantic Ocean has art deco features, a full-service spa, an 18-hole golf course and a tennis center with 10 clay courts. An outdoor pool has a see-through bottom and waterfalls that flow into a 240-foot lagoon pool. The lobby features a 60-foot glass atrium.
>
> AFL-CIO spokeswoman Lane Windham said the Federation would have lost close to $100,000 had the 2003 meeting not been held at the Diplomat."[23]

Marty Maddaloni, the general president of the 325,000 member Plumbers and Pipefitters Union, and some of his cohorts eventually were ousted from the pension fund board of directors and ordered to pay nearly $11 million in restitution and civil penalties in connection with their "imprudent" management of the fund's massive investment in the Diplomat Resort. The trustees consented to the decree, which awaits a judge's approval, without admitting or denying guilt, according to the National Right to Work Committee.

A more sinister event occurred on October 13, 2004, when a reputed "soldier in the Genovese organized crime family" pleaded guilty to charges that

Callous greed grows pious very fast.

LILLIAN HELLMAN
WRITER

675

he used his influence over Plasterers & Cement Masons Local Union 530 and the New York District Council of the Carpenters Union to gain preferential or no-show jobs for mobsters and allowed favored contractors to "forget" payments to union members' pension funds. This illegal scheme cost the unions involved millions of dollars in members' lost wages and employee benefits.[24]

New Union Financial Accountability

There appears to be hope on the horizon for substantial public disclosure of exactly how and for what purposes these AFL-CIO building trades chiefs spend their union dues treasure chest. In 2003, President Bush's Department of Labor, under its able secretary, Elaine Chao (R-KY), issued a revised "Report Form LM-2." Her justification for the changes included these facts:

> The annual financial forms (LM-2) that unions are required to file under the Labor Management Reporting and Disclosure Act are virtually meaningless. Union members have almost no access to detailed information about their unions' finances. Not only does the Labor Department have a difficult time getting this information, but it lacks the resources to carefully audit all the reports that unions must file. All of that has got to change. Union members need to know their rights and have the ability to exercise them.[25]

Labor Secretary Chao's amended LM-2 specifically requires major labor unions (including the building trades) to provide in electronic detail to their members, the Labor Department, and the public, the dollars they spend on political activities and lobbying, internal union administration, new member organizing, collective bargaining, and other employee representational activities."[26] ABC supported Secretary Chao's amendment, urging that "greater transparency is needed among building trades unions on their job targeting, industry advancement, and market recovery funds."[27]

The AFL-CIO immediately challenged the amendment as "illegally exceeding Chao's authority."[28]

This revised LM-2, according to the *Washington Times*, "promises to be one of the biggest shake-ups to organized labor since the governing legislation, the

Landrum-Griffin Act, was first passed in 1959."[29] That act, continued the *Times*, "has woefully inadequate financial reporting requirements and over the years union dues have been easily diverted to enrich corrupt union bosses." As one such sample, the *Times* noted:

> Federal prosecutors continue to bag Ironworkers Union officials involved in a scam to conceal $1.5 million in food, booze and golf outings... For 40 years, labor bosses and Democratic politicians have ensured that corruption is not found. Now that both houses of Congress have slipped from their grasp, that sorry era may be drawing finally to a close."[30]

Leveling the Financial Disclosure Field

In another recent labor scandal, my old nemesis, the former Building Trades Department President, Robert Georgine, and other building trades union leaders cashed in on a "sweetheart" deal by buying shares of their privately held union insurance company ("ULLICO") at a guaranteed low price. Then they quickly sold the stock back to their company at a guaranteed higher price, even as ULLICO's underlying value plummeted.[31] These "windfall profits" were "repeated through self-dealing at the expense of, and in violation of their fiduciary and contractual duties to ULLICO and its [union] shareholders."[32]

The revelations led to an investigation by former Illinois Governor Jim Thompson and to the dismissal of Allico President Robert Georgine plus other Allico directors. In addition to a $650,000 salary, Georgine claimed $20 million in stock profits, bonuses, and benefits between 1998 and 2001. But the *Wall Street Journal* said that was "just the tip of the garbage heap."[33]

An article written for ABC's *Construction Executive* magazine by ABC's current general counsel (and my longtime law partner), Maurice Baskin, added as follows about this union ignominy:

> The "Enron" type scandal involving a union-owned insurance company known as ULLICO has expanded dramatically during the past year. It appears that leaders of the same building trades unions who have been critical of merit shop construction contractors now face

> **Fraud and falsehood only dread examination. Truth invites it.**
>
> THOMAS COOPER
> HISTORIAN

677

criminal investigations and civil fraud litigation for their own alleged insider trading on a massive scale.[34]

The unspun truth is that Labor Secretary Chao's amended Form LM-2 to some extent would equalize and complement the employer-oriented Sarbanes-Oxley Act of 2002. That statute was hastily overdrafted because of an emotional flurry of liberal distrust of Big Business and Corporate America as a nefarious "capitalistic" class. The meager evidence of executive corruption was widely publicized and denounced by Big Labor and the mainstream news media. (It only appeared in the form of insider trading and accounting scandals by a few devious senior officials in companies such as Enron and some shady bankers on Wall Street.)

Under the leftist leadership of Senator Paul Sarbanes (D-MD), federal law now requires detailed disclosure of all the financial activities of corporate America, including oversight of financial books by an independent auditor for the protection of investors. The 99 percent of honest businessmen and women throughout the country, along with a few would-be swindlers, are forced to comply with another costly maze of nonproductive statistics.

Big Labor Opposes Equal Treatment

Chao's revised LM-2 labor regulation, on the other hand, is justified through undisputed evidence of thousands of abuses of millions of union dues dollars by crooked labor bosses in their Washington home offices and in affiliated local unions all over the country. According to the *Wall Street Journal*, "union corruption is rampant" and "the ULLICO saga [cited above] looks like a symptom of failed union governance, or worse. The compulsory dues-paying rank-and-file deserve to know that their own union leaders will be held accountable every bit as much as Enron executives are."[35]

DEPARTMENT OF LABOR
U.S. Secretary of Labor Elaine Chao.

In April of 2004, the National Institute for Labor Relations Research downloaded LM-2 and LM-3 financial disclosure forms filed with the U.S.

Labor Department by every major labor organization. The Institute found that unions filing these forms had total annual receipts of **$19.4 billion**. It also found that 44 percent of all federally disclosed union receipts, or **$8.5 billion** a year, came directly in the form of union membership dues plus various "fees" and "assessments" imposed on workers.[36]

Not surprisingly, Labor Secretary Chao was criticized by the AFL-CIO because she had the integrity and courage to do her job of fair and impartial representation of America's total workforce of mega-millions, not just the meager unionized minority of it.[37] Two *Wall Street Journal* editorials came to her defense:

> Union leaders have been especially critical of corporate wrong-doing in the last year, and rightly so [but] unions have an obligation to be at least as forthcoming, especially because the union dues they take from workers aren't voluntary.
>
> Ms. Chao, in short, is taking heat from Big Labor precisely because she [is] standing up for rank-and-file union members who deserve to know how their hard-earned dues money is being used—or, far too often, abused...."[38]
>
> AFL-CIO chief John Sweeney has led the posse calling for greater corporate transparency in recent years, yet he and other labor chieftains are working double-time to exempt unions from similar standards. Their lawsuit [against the secretary of labor] labels the [LM-2] rules "arbitrary" and "capricious" and demands an injunction."[39]

Michael Crowley, a regular columnist for *Reader's Digest* and an associate editor of the *New Republic* magazine wrote recently that "there is always something happening somewhere in the country where a union official is treating union dues like his own piggy bank." Though "the government requires unions to submit [LM-2] financial reports," he continued, "fully a third are filed late or not at all—and the unions are rarely audited. Workers who ask for details about their union's finances often get nowhere and there's a climate where union officials aren't accountable to anyone."

Crowley concludes:

You can't stand on principle with feet of clay.

DICK ARMEY (R-TX)
FORMER HOUSE
MAJORITY LEADER IN
ARMEY'S AXIOMS

Politics has got so expensive that it takes a lot of money even to get beat with.

WILL ROGERS
COMEDIAN-WRITER

No wonder that corruption runs rampant. Take the leadership of the 125,000-member International Ironworkers Union. Last year the union's former president, Jake West, was imprisoned for stealing union funds. According to prosecutors, West and other union officials embezzled over $400,000 and spent it on vacations and country club memberships. They also ate well on the union's tab: nearly $500,000 over six years at one Washington, D.C., steakhouse.... America's union workers will only get justice when all the corrupt union bosses get theirs.[40]

The House of Labor Flexes Political Muscles

Huge expenditures from AFL-CIO cash and bank accounts are used—in addition to subsidizing union luminaries—to reward Big Labor's Democratic friends who endorse the aforementioned Union Pressure Tactics Tool Box and to punish Republican enemies who oppose use of the Tool Box against ABC contractors. In the 1999–2000 federal election cycle, for instance, organized labor supported financially several hundred left-wing candidates for public office. That bankroll included more than $90 million that unions funneled into national and local Democratic political party campaigns for so-called "issue advertising and party building activities." Additional union contributions to Democrats in manpower, publications, and communications equaled their cash contributions in importance.[41]

In that same '99–'00 campaign, the AFL-CIO also spent $46 million on television, radio, and other news media while distributing fourteen million propaganda leaflets, including literature drops, bumper stickers, street-side billboards, and campaign buttons. Professional union leaders and "volunteer" rank-and-file members also teamed up to handle publicity, advertising, direct mail, the registration of carefully culled voters, absentee ballots, phone banks, and door-to-door "get out the vote" drives.

As a part of the political blitz, organized labor fielded an army of 100,000 union staffers and members who registered two million "pliable" new voters and worked for the election of 150 radical left-wing candidates for Congress. Journalists Michelle Malkin and Jeff Jacoby of the *Weekly Standard* wrote that "during this federal election cycle, unions funneled an estimated **$800 million** into campaign activities and virtually every cent came out of employees' pockets."[42]

In the same 2000 elections, the AFL-CIO also spearheaded a new program that emphasized both "grassroots" and "checkbook" politics. It represented much more than an attempt to influence elections. Political action dedicated to a so-called "Working Families Agenda" became the strategy of choice to elect Democrat candidates, persuade liberal lawmakers, mobilize union members, and recruit more workers into the organized labor movement. According to a subsequent AFL-CIO's Executive Council Report on this venture:

> Through the coordinated mobilization of union activists, massive education and get-out-the-vote efforts among working family voters, and support of union members running for public office, the AFL-CIO and its member unions have created and sustained strategies for year-round political action.[43]

These huge but rarely reported and usually understated AFL-CIO expenditures on electioneering exceeded the combined political resources of the Democrat and Republican Parties.[44] It is also a well-kept news media secret that six of the top ten political campaign contributors throughout the United States from 1989 through 2002 were labor organizations, according to a recent study released by the Center for Responsible Politics. The study took into account both "hard" and "soft" money contributed over that period of time and 94 percent of Big Labor's contributions went to Democrat candidates. The "top 10" contributors' list included these unions:

- Int'l Brotherhood of Teamsters ($18.9 million)
- Carpenters & Joiners Int'l Union ($18.9 million)
- Int'l Brotherhood of Electrical Workers ($18.8 million)
- Communication Workers of America ($18.7 million)
- American Federation of State, County and Municipal Employees ($32.7 million)
- National Education Association ($22.1 million)[45]

AFL-CIO unions spent even more money from their membership dues treasuries to elect Democrat Senator John Kerry of Massachusetts to the

Power is the great aphrodisiac.

HENRY KISSINGER
FORMER SECRETARY
OF STATE

U.S. presidency in 2005, according to the federation's political director, Karen Ackerman, and its president, Tom Sweeney.[46] Estimated politicking donations by Big Labor amounted to mega-millions of dollars in 2002–2003. And the once highly-touted Bipartisan Campaign Reform Act of '03, cosponsored by maverick Senator John McCain (R-AZ) to prevent the use of "soft money," has proven to be an ineffectual legal morass encouraging new spending loopholes.[47] The act's "main effect is to channel the cash through different political hands and with less accountability," such as the partisan "527s."[48]

Minority Civil Rights Violated by Big Labor

Deplorably, in the interest of fair voter representation, none of the millions of rank-and-file union members who finance these partisan political activities have any voice in the AFL-CIO's political agenda or the selection of its candidates for public office. Yet a substantial minority of them—at least 30 percent to 40 percent—disagree with the socialistic political choices of their professional union leadership, according to Voter News Service of the Center For Responsive Politics,[49] the *Washington Times*,[50] and the *Wall Street Journal*.[51]

Democratic presidential nominee, Massachusetts Senator John Kerry, left (as usual) attends a rally in Washington, D.C., at which the AFL-CIO Building Trades endorsed his bid. Beside him is AFL-CIO President John Sweeney.

PHOTO BY LUKE FRAZZA: AGENCE FRANCE-PRESSE. REPRINTED WITH PERMISSION, DANIEL_SILVERSTEIN@GETTYIMAGES.COM

A 1999 survey of union-represented workers who were interviewed by a national pollster, John Zogby, reported the number of dissenters against official union political positions to be as high as 72 percent.[52]

Few of these conscientious objectors can do anything about their dilemma. One reason is that most dissident union members are not able to summon the internal courage or raise the financial support needed to exercise their constitutional civil rights in opposition to the AFL-CIO leadership's "railroaded" far-left political policies and choices. This problem was explained by a distinguished authority in the labor-management field, Professor Sumner Slichter of Harvard University:

> Leadership of the trade union movement is largely in the hands of full-time professional officers of national unions...The "town meeting" ideal of trade unionism, which envisaged wide-spread participation from the rank-and-file in making decisions of policy, gets farther from realization every day.
>
> This rise of professional labor leaders has led a number of unions to be dominated by individuals or small groups of individuals. Their government is best described as a "dictatorship" or "oligarchy." The rank-and-file have little to say in selecting the policies. Furthermore, in these unions any competition for office at the national level is ruthlessly suppressed."[53]

Admittedly, under the U.S. Supreme Court's seldom used *Communication Workers v. Beck* decision in 1988, these minority union members do have a technical legal right to sue the labor organization which represents them for its "objectionable activities" in the political arena. It also is true that disgruntled unionists may try, under the authority of this *Beck* case, to recover that portion of their mandatory dues money which was used by the union, over their protest, "to support political causes which they oppose" rather than for "legitimate collective bargaining activities."[54] They may even have theoretical causes of action against union discrimination under the aforementioned Labor-Management Reporting and Disclosure Act.[55]

The practical predicament is that the long, lonely, and expensive road to a successful legal protest by these conservative nonconformists becomes mired in years of intentional union harassment and stalling. Contractual, administrative, and judicial procedures plus other costly defensive tactics are used against them by the very labor organization they are forced to subsidize—and which has a binding fiduciary obligation to represent them fairly and openly.

Rather than face an evasive, hostile, and legally expensive reception for fighting the "home office" political machine of Big Labor (with its horde of lawyers), disgruntled members find themselves forced to give up their own

Law: in its nature the noblest and most beneficial to mankind; in its abuse and debasement the most sordid and pernicious.

LORD BOLINGBROKE IN *THE STUDY AND USE OF HISTORY* (LETTER 5, 1739)

Compelling persons to furnish contributions for the propagation of opinions which they disbelieve is sinful and tyrannical.

THOMAS JEFFERSON
FOUNDER AND
3RD PRESIDENT

political beliefs. In the end they become unwilling financial supporters of the AFL-CIO's left-wing agenda that they personally abhor.

Organized Labor's Unique Status

No other private association of Americans is permitted to deny such a fundamental right of citizenship in order that its members hold their jobs. The constitutional right to assemble and associate includes the equal right to disassociate. But labor organizations have become a protected special interest group within our society, and the discrimination is ignored in liberal circles. This disenfranchisement of minority union members was recognized and opposed by Supreme Court Justice Hugo Black in his dissenting opinion in the landmark *Machinists v. Street* case over forty years ago:

> There can be no doubt that the federally sanctioned "union shop contract" as it actually works takes a part of the earnings of some and turns it over to others who spend a substantial part of the funds so received in efforts to thwart the political, economic and ideological hopes of those whose money has been forced from them under authority of law. This injects federal compulsion into a result which I supposed everyone would agree the First Amendment was particularly intended to prevent . . . The stark fact is that this Act of Congress is being used as a means to extract money from these employees to help get votes to win elections for parties and candidates and to support doctrines they are against.

Justice Black also predicted organized labor's current-day ability to confuse, delay, defuse, and defy this fundamental voting franchise of its minority members:

> It may be that courts and lawyers with sufficient skill in accounting, algebra, geometry, trigonometry and calculus will be able to extract the proper microscopic answer from the voluminous and complex accounting records of the local, national and international unions involved [to determine the proper percentage of the "political" dues rebate]. It seems

to me, however, that . . . this formula with its attendant trial burdens promises little hope for financial recompense to the individual workers whose First Amendment freedoms have been flagrantly violated.[56]

A remarkable victory over this unconstitutional treatment of dissenting minority union members occurred recently. With free legal aid from the National Right To Work Legal Foundation, more than one hundred thousand unionized Los Angeles County, California, home care providers received formal notice of a favorable settlement of their anti-union lawsuit. Under it, Local 434-B of the Service Employees International Union (SEIU) must refund to all workers the membership dues it forced them to pay "for union politics and other activities unrelated to collective bargaining." Total rebates due are estimated to be as much as $10 million.[57]

Sweeney Expands Leftist Union Goals

The election on October 26, 1995, of John Sweeney of the Service Employees International Union as president of the AFL-CIO did not bode well for voluntary unionism and a free and competitive marketplace. He succeeded the placid Lane Kirkland and made compulsory union shop pledges to the delegates from seventy-eight affiliated international unions (including the building trades) in his acceptance speech at the annual convention that year.

The deciding vote for Sweeney's election was cast by his friend, Arthur Coia, head of the International Laborers Union—a Building Trades Department affiliate. Coia has been a multi-million-dollar Democrat Party fundraiser, the confidant of First Lady (now a Senator and presidential aspirant) Hillary Clinton (D-NY), called a "mob puppet" by the U.S. Justice Department, and eventually a convicted felon.[58]

In President Sweeney's acceptance speech to the AFL-CIO delegates, he proposed the use of a combination of what amounted to the aforementioned new Union Pressure Tactics Tool Box coupled with old-fashioned coercion and violence to regain certain workers' rights "to speak for themselves in strong unions":

> I'm here to tell you that the most important thing we can do—starting right now today—is to organize every working woman and man

Greater love hath no man than this, that he lay down his friends for his political life.

JEREMY THORPE
WRITER

685

who needs a better deal and a new voice. As long as we speak for scarcely one-sixth of the work force, we will never be able to win what we deserve at the bargaining table or in the legislative process. That is why we're going to pour resources into organizing at a pace and scale that is unprecedented and offer our hands and open our ranks to workers from the rustbelt to the sunbelt . . .

If anyone denies American workers their constitutional right to freedom of association,[59] we will use old-fashioned mass demonstrations as well as sophisticated corporate campaigns to make worker rights the civil rights issue of the times. We're going to spend whatever it takes, work as hard as it takes, and stick with it as long as it takes to help American workers win the right to speak for themselves in strong unions![60]

At Big Labor's annual convention six years later in Las Vegas, Nevada, Sweeney added another "Union Pressure Tool Box" tactic to attain his goals: "We expect to change the face of American politics by electing 2,500 union members to office and changing the course of government with the biggest legislative and political counterattack in our history." He also denounced President George W. Bush "for waging a vicious war on working families" and charged that AFL-CIO "faces the most anti-worker and anti-union administration in every possible way." Richard Michalski, political director of the International Association of Machinists added frankly: "We're at war."[61]

High-profile, ultra-liberal politicians who were honored and cheered for their presence at Sweeney's national convention that year of 2001 included Senator Hillary Clinton (D-NY),[62] House Minority Whip Representative Nancy Pelosi (D-CA), House Minority Leader Richard Gephardt (D-MO), Senate Majority Leader Tom Daschle (D-SD), and the "Reverend" Jesse Jackson.[63]

Sweeney's Militant Socialistic Agenda

Tom Sweeney reconfirmed, to the joy of these powerful guests, that under his leadership the giant labor federation would use 30 percent of its tremendous union dues treasury "to run the most ambitious grass-roots people-powered effort that we have ever had and oust Republicans from public office." A "victory," he vowed, "will send a signal to all public officials that the AFL-CIO holds them to the standards it has established."[64] Fortunately for ABCers and free enterprise, most of Big Labor's favorite Democrats lost in an "off-year" political upset in that year '02 which produced a narrowly controlled Republican Congress.

It is seldom publicized, moreover, but Sweeney is reported to be a card-carrying member of the Democratic Socialists of America ("DSA") which is dedicated, naturally, to "placing socialist values into the mainstream American agenda." The DSA rejects any "economic order sustained by private profit." It is also ignored but equally true that almost every economic plank of the 1928 presidential platform of the U.S. Socialist Party's candidate, Norman Thomas, has been enacted into law in the United States, even though his party has never received more than 6 percent of the popular vote.[65]

Even more hush-hush is the fact that when the Communist Party USA reviewed Sweeney's political platform for the national elections of members of Congress and the Presidency of the United States, it announced that "we are in complete accord with AFL-CIO's policies and plans." *Political Affairs*, one of the USA Communist Party's journals, editorialized that Sweeney's election to the AFL-CIO presidency was "nothing less than historic [and] the most dramatic expression of the fact that a turning point in the class struggle is now taking place."[66]

Edward Sullivan, today's president of the AFL-CIO's nationally affiliated Building and Construction Trades Department, confirmed that he too is "determined to help the Democrats win and keep control of Congress and the White House." Spotlighting what he called "ABC's phony job training programs and anti-union agenda," Sullivan believes

First Lady Hillary Clinton accepts the invitation of the president of the Laborers International Union, Arthur Coia, to address his membership's winter conference at Miami's Fontainebleau Hotel.

PHOTO BY JEFFREY SALTER, MIAMI HERALD, JUNE 24, 1996, REPRINTED WITH PERMISSION

No cause in the history of all mankind has produced more cold-blooded tyrants, more slaughtered innocents, and more orphans than socialism with power. Socialism in action created Lenin, Stalin, Mao Tse-tung, Kim-Il Sung, Ho Chi Minh, and Fidel Castro, to name a few.

DR. ALAN KORS
PROFESSOR OF HISTORY,
UNIVERSITY OF
PENNSYLVANIA

I would trust
big government
over big business
any time.

SENATOR
HILLARY CLINTON
(D-NY)

that labor's response must be "an all-out offensive in organizing and political action." He concludes that "the enemy" are ABC's merit shop contractors and vows that "it is time to take them on and take them out."[67]

Sweeney and Sullivan are humiliated and furious that membership in their labor organizations which represent private sector employees have been in decline for over half a century. Union enrollment as a percentage of the nation's total private sector workforce, as has been noted, peaked back in the 1950's at about **40 percent** and has dropped to **7.9 percent** today.[68] The construction market share of the building trades unions as a semi-autonomous affiliate within the AFL-CIO hierarchy also went down from **87 percent** in the early 1950s to **14.7 percent** today.[69]

Big Labor, the Democratic Party, and Big Government Form a Partnership

A serious predicament facing our capitalistic system of government and the merit shop crusade is that the organized labor movement exercises substantial political and economic clout—far out of proportion to its hemorrhaging private sector membership count.

A recent Federal Elections Committee report concluded that the AFL-CIO's power within the Democratic Party is so great today that, like a shadow government, it "enjoys authority to approve or disapprove plans, projects and needs of the Democratic National Committee and its state parties."[70] Reed Larson, chairman emeritus of the National Right to Work Committee, confirms this unholy alliance:

> The billions of dollars collected through government-authorized compulsory unionism provide the fuel that drives the liberal political machine. Without the disproportionate political muscle of union officials gained through government-granted coercive power, all of our battles against the flood tide of tax-and-spend big government schemes would be won hands down.[71]

Veteran journalist Carl Horowitz adds in a chilling monograph entitled *Union Corruption in America: Still a Growth Industry*, that union crooks—although similar in many regards to other criminals—are unique in that "for decades [they] have had an unwitting assist from government."[72]

Linda Chavez was President George W. Bush's original choice for secretary of labor in 2000 and a former union official. Today she is a syndicated columnist and FOX TV political analyst who, in association with Daniel Gray, has written an explosive book dissecting organized labor. It's entitled *Betrayal: How Union Bosses Shake Down Their Members and Corrupt American Politics.*[73] Chavez reports that while many Americans bemoan the "special interests politics" in Washington, D.C., "somehow the extraordinary power of America's labor bosses has escaped notice." The "fact is," she continues, "unions have a stranglehold on the Democratic Party and now operate essentially as they wish." Big Labor uses this power, concludes Chavez:

> . . . to call the shots in Democratic campaigns and on party policy; for extraordinary influence at all levels of government; billions of dollars in taxpayer-funded federal grants; and special legal privileges that leave them free to act as they please, no matter the consequences for the American people. The cycle of corruption is endless."[74]

Public Sector Unionization Flourishes

Also given the silent treatment by mainstream news media and academia is the *reverse-trend evidence* that tens of thousands of federal, state, and local government workers throughout the nation today are represented by labor organizations and the number is expanding steadily.

For many years public sector unionism was opposed by leaders of the AFL-CIO such as its president, George Meany, and by union-friendly U.S.A. presidents such as Franklin D. Roosevelt and Harry S. Truman.[75] The turning point came in 1958 when the Democratic mayor of New York, Robert Wagner, granted exclusive bargaining privileges to unions of his city workers. The following year, Wisconsin became the first state to enact a compulsory public sector collective bargaining law. And the floodgates were opened wide in 1962 when Democrat President John F. Kennedy—with ardent support from the national press—issued Executive Order No. 10988. It allowed unionization and collective bargaining in the federal civil service. Within the next few

All I need to know is that a man is a human being—that's enough for me; he can't be much worse.

MARK TWAIN
HUMORIST-WRITER

If we could learn
from history,
what lessons it
might teach us!
But passion and
party-politics
blind our eyes.

SAMUEL TAYLOR
COLERIDGE
ENGLISH POET
AND CRITIC

months' time, the U.S. Civil Service herded 85,000 federal bureaucrats into hundreds of separate labor union bargaining units.

Eighteen years later, in 1978, the Civil Service Reform Act was passed by Congress. It was signed into law by one of modern America's most naïve political pawns, Jimmy Carter (D-GA), the peanut farmer who became a one-term president and eventually found his niche in retirement as a globe-trotting pacifist and non-union carpenter.[76] Under this civil rights statute, government unions now are granted exclusive power to negotiate (out of the earnings of taxpayers) the union membership dues, wages, employee benefits, and working conditions of the nation's largest employer: *the United States Government*.

A "New Unionism" Threatens ABC's Workplace Freedom

"Without any doubt, government employment has become the growth industry for organized labor," says David Denholm, noted authority on public sector unionism and President of the Public Service Research Foundation. "When union membership as a percentage of the nation's total work force began to decline and the number of people employed by government began to grow, labor officials saw the public sector as the solution to the membership dues dollars and political clout they were losing in the private sector," Denholm concludes.[77]

In her aforementioned hard-hitting book, *Betrayal*, Linda Chavez discusses "the incredible shrinking labor movement" and how a new organizing strategy today "is putting the public at risk":

> The decision to organize the public sector was a fateful one for the labor movement. It altered not just the face of American labor but the future of American politics as well. In barely 40 years, public employee unions went from being the stepchildren of the labor movement to the head of the labor family."[78]

Today labor unions control **37.2 percent** of America's public sector workforce as contrasted to only an **7.9 percent** unionization of the private sector.[79]

According to Dr. Leo Troy, the Distinguished Professor of Economics at Rutgers University, this phenomenon has created a new form of "creeping socialism" through a different strategy: organized labor is negotiating control of an ever-increasing amount of the national government's income through collectively bargaining with it for its employees' wages and working conditions.

Professor Troy also calls this trend "the New Unionism." One-third of its members have college or post-graduate professional degrees in the huge public workforce that is composed primarily of "white collar" personnel.[80] And Troy believes this New Unionism is in a much stronger position to shape and influence socialistic ideas and goals than unions representing industrial "blue collar" production and maintenance assembly line workers who are the backbone of the "Old (private sector) Unionism." Big Labor's increasing objective, he emphasizes, is a "transfer of income from one group of the population [the capitalistic rich] to another [the proletariat masses] through the economic and social functions of government's domestic programs."[81]

Every Liberal Politician's Smorgasbord

This Marxist-style class warfare is successful because public sector unions obtain "sweetheart" labor agreements from friendly government executives who willingly pass along the cost of inflated and non-productive government workplace entitlements to their customers—*the American taxpayers.*[82] An incentive for left-wing public office holders to entice their government agencies to "go union" is Big Labor's promise to give these politicians who "cooperate" with it vast sums of tax-free money to finance their election campaigns. Partisan special interest politicos also stand to gain thousands of union-controlled "grass roots" campaign helpers who are "allowed" to ignore Hatch Act restraints on such activities during their work time, and more thousands of potentially favorable votes at the ballot box, as noted previously.[83]

Under such favorable circumstances, liberal government officeholders rush to endorse a labor union co-partner in their decision-making process of welfare-state empire-building. They ignore the fact that they are emasculating the U.S. government's exclusive sovereign right and duty—and their own fiduciary oath of office—to administer the nation's business independently while serving the citizenry honestly within their limited constitutional authority.[84] They unethically (and probably illegally) welcome Big Labor's presence with

Government is a trust, and officers of the government are trustees. Both the trust and the trustees are created for the benefit of the people.

HENRY CLAY
SECRETARY OF STATE

691

In general, presidents and congressmen have very limited power to do good for the economy and awesome power to do bad. The best good thing that politicians can do for the economy is to stop doing bad. In part, this can be achieved through reducing economic regulation and staying out of our lives.

Dr. Walter Williams
syndicated pundit
and chairman of the
economics depart-
ment at George
Mason University

open arms (and open pocketbooks) while thousands of dissident rank-and-file union members and the general public are excluded from their constitutional rights in the undemocratic process and pay dearly for the socialistic results.

The Public Sector Union "Quid Pro Quo"

Big Labor, in turn, requires at least five reciprocal commitments that must be executed by all union-targeted bureaucrats in order to receive political and monetary support: (1) Expand government by creating more agencies and by hiring more dues-paying union members; (2) Raise taxes to pay for government union members' wage increases and more new hires; (3) Introduce and adopt more laws, regulations, and policies that inhibit legitimate public and private sector managerial rights, with the goal of a planned leftist economy; (4) Endorse the previously described Union Tool Box of Major Pressure Tactics to unionize more private sector workers; and (5) Endorse final and binding "interest" arbitration of bargaining impasses over *new* wages and working conditions of government employees by an "outsider" third party who is not accountable to the public which shoulders the costs of these economic dispute settlements.[85]

Dr. Troy's thought-provoking book, *The New Unionism in the New Society*, concludes that "creeping socialism" by the giant American Federation of State, County and Municipal Employees (AFSCME) and other labor organizations representing government workers "has already wrought radical, if yet largely unnoticed, changes in the economy and society." They have done so, Troy believes, "through increasing government intervention, through an ever-larger role in the formation of public policy and through a correspondingly diminished role of government sovereignty." He warns that "the unchallenged strategy of these unions is aided by collaboration with other social and political forces, principally in the Democratic party."[86]

More concerned words come from a *Wall Street Journal* editorial on this "New Unionism":

> It is hard to exaggerate just how removed John Sweeney's AFL-CIO is from labor unions of yore. Today four in 10 union members work for government; indeed, the AFL-CIO's largest member is AFSCME [the American Federation of State, County and Municipal Employees], the

1.4 million-strong union of federal, state and local workers. Given this constituency, instead of focusing on an economic growth that would create jobs for more union workers, organized labor needs a growing level of taxation that supports bigger government and their membership rolls.[87]

Clinton Embraced the "New Unionism"

On October 1, 1993, President Bill Clinton issued Executive Order No. 12871. It was intended to emasculate the sovereign right of the federal government to direct its huge workforce for independent service to America's taxpayers without any third party influence or control. The order—entitled *Labor-Management Partnerships*—endorsed the aforementioned Bluestone brothers' socialistic labor relations philosophy.[88] It decreed that the collective

The leaders of government unions know full well that they can hold all of us hostage if they deny us essential services. Big Labor, in short, has a dangerous weapon at its disposal: power over our very lives and well-being.

Linda Chavez
in *Betrayal*

Percentage of Union Members
U.S.A. (1950 - 2004)

Sources:
U.S. Bureau of Labor Statistics
Bureau of National Affairs, Inc.,
Public Service Research Council
Union Sourcebook (Leo Troy and Neil Sheffin)
Government Union Review (Herbert R. Northrup)
Journal of Labor Research (A.J. Thieblot)

693

bargaining travesty quoted below should take place in a "honeymoon" atmosphere between the United States government and Big Labor over the mission, wages, and working conditions of federal employees:

Only by changing the nature of the Federal labor-management relations so that managers, employees, and employees' elected union representatives serve as *partners* will it be possible to design and implement comprehensive changes necessary to reform Government. Labor-management partnerships will champion change in Federal Government agencies to transform them into organizations capable of delivering the highest quality services to the American people...

Sec. 1. There is established the National Partnership Council. The Council shall comprise the following members appointed by the President: (1) Director of the Office of Personnel Management ("OPM"); (2) Deputy Secretary of Labor; (3) Deputy Director for Management, Office of Management and Budget; (4) Chair, Federal Labor Relations Authority; (5) Federal Mediation and Conciliation Director; (6) President, American Federation of Government Employees, AFL-CIO; (7) President, National Federation of Federal Employees; (8) President, National Treasury Employees Union; (9) Secretary-Treasurer of the Public Employees Department, AFL-CIO; (10) A deputy Secretary or other officer with department or agency-wide authority from two executive departments or agencies not otherwise represented on the Council...

Sec. 2. The head of each agency shall involve employees and their union representatives as full partners with management representatives to identify problems and solutions to better serve the agency's customers and mission." [emphasis added]

Fortunately, in the interest of efficient public services, reduction of the cost of government, and protection of the sovereignty of our capitalistic Republic, soon after being sworn in as the 43rd President of the United States, George W. Bush revoked this Marxist-style co-determination of inherent management functions on February 17, 2001.

"Maryland, My Maryland"

In stark contrast to the action of President Bush and in full cooperation with Big Labor's "New Unionism" goals, the Democrat governor of my own state of Maryland from 1995 to 2002—Parris Glendening—voluntarily created a dubious procedure for the unionization of 75,000 state government employees. He simply bypassed the Legislature and used a few strokes of his executive order pen to do the deed. That multi-million-dollar union membership dues payback to AFSCME for helping to elect him in successive four-year terms was subsequently legalized unanimously (while disregarding labor law precedent) by the governor's own(ed) leftist Court of Appeals.[89]

A year or so later, Governor Glendening's equally cooperative liberal state legislature legitimized the executive order by codifying it into an even more pro-union public sector collective bargaining statute. My opposition statement to the Maryland House of Delegates at a public hearing before this labor bill passed was either rudely ridiculed or ignored by the state's biased politicians. They had no idea—and cared less—what an administrative quagmire they were creating for future operation of the state government and the massive monetary cost to Maryland taxpayers, although I warned them:

> Labor unions are drastically changing the way governments are administered and the entire public employment relationship, from recruitment to retirement. Their influence is imprinted on hiring, wages, merit incentives, promotion, discipline, grievances, job descriptions, qualifications, evaluation and classification, health insurance, pensions and many other employee benefits.
>
> They also restrict government's work rules, downsizing, privatization and overall fiscal policy through private third-party impasse dispute resolution of the State's sovereign personnel functions and responsibilities by final and binding arbitration. Experience has demonstrated that once a collective bargaining statute is enacted, there is no turning back from union collectivism—with its inevitable adverse impact on the State's budget, its productivity, its essential public services, its taxpayers and its business climate.

Marxism has not only failed to promote human freedom. It has failed to produce food.

JOHN DOS PASSOS
PHILOSPHER-WRITER

695

As Casey Stengel, the crafty old manager of the world champion New York Yankees Baseball Club would tell skeptics: "It's the truth: You can look it up." Glendening was oblivious to this labor-management relations nightmare he created for succeeding bureaucrats and the financial disaster for taxpayers so he proceeded to cause a multi-billion-dollar state operating deficit for his successor in office, conservative Bob Ehrlich, to confront. (In becoming Maryland's first Republican governor in thirty-six years, Bob had promised the voters that he would not raise taxes. And the state is required legally to have a balanced budget.)

Dangerous Implications of Unionized Government over ABCers

As long ago as 1971, ABC's fifteenth president, Joe LaMonaca, voiced concern about the mandated unionization of government employees. He visualized its disastrous effect on ABC contractors who are compelled to obey the laws and regulations these biased politicians promulgate:

> During the past two years, the largest growth of unionism has taken place in the public sector. Federal, state and local employees are joining unions in large numbers. The AFL-CIO has called for creating a nationwide system of collective bargaining between the federal government and unions representing federal employees, similar to that for postal workers . . . It is also worth noting that there are now ten million public employees at state and local levels and union control over these employees is moving fast.
>
> As for ABC contractors, our dealings with government personnel from the lowest permit clerk to the police to the middle level agency administrators (all belonging to labor unions) who make important decisions affecting their business—how can we possibly get a fair shake? And in the area of enforcement—Wage and Hour Law people, Labor Board agents, safety inspectors, IRS enforcers—think of us being constantly subjected to union propaganda and union boss pressure.
>
> This is no figment of my imagination. It has frequently happened that no sooner is there a picket line than there is also a sudden and

unexplained appearance of Wage and Hour Department inspectors and other government deputies. They were presumably contacted by trades union representatives to harass and coerce ABCers about frivolous charges of violations. Meanwhile, the general public is asleep and elected politicians pretend to ignore it all.[90]

The author (left) with Maryland's Governor Robert Erhlich.

Every year this problem becomes more serious. Among the hordes of unionized government workers across the United States today (some twelve million in the federal workforce alone)[91] are thousands of leftist attorneys and other liberal administrative staff personnel who have long government service records. Many of them are assigned to the Washington, D.C. headquarters of agencies that have a negative impact on the entrepreneurial productivity of the construction industry, such as the National Labor Relations Board, the U.S. Department of Labor, and the Occupational Safety and Health Administration. Others work in their regional offices throughout the nation.

Like the 90 percent of an iceberg hidden under water, these lower-level, permanently embedded liberals sabotage any conservative policy changes attempted by the heads of their government agencies. Instead, from one administration to the next—regardless of the philosophy of the political party in the White House—entrenched civil servants spin, twist, and expand the costly private sector workplace laws that they enforce to favor organized labor's desire. Vanishing in this socialist entitlement scam are the inherent profit-making rights of private sector employers and their employees, including ABC member contractors and their workplace teams.

A typical example of this enigma involves the subject of "flex time." The principle at issue is whether workers and their employers should be able to enter into individual job schedules that benefit everyone concerned. One such solution would allow non-exempt employees to work under existing federal law for eighty hours at straight time wage rates in any combination over a two-week period. In today's complex social world where both men and women are providers, such flexibility could do much to improve family life, advance educational studies, and assist many other personal goals and responsibilities.

In an editorial entitled "9 to 5, R.I.P.," on September 9, 2004, the *Wall Street Journal* reported the bad news on flex time:

> As it happens, a sizable minority of Americans have been using flex time since 1978: *federal employees.* Currently, some 47 percent of full-time, hourly federal employees work a 'compressed' schedule, in which shorter hours in one week can be made up the next. The Employment Policy Foundation estimates that 13 million to 20 million *private-sector employees* would take advantage of this type of arrangement.
>
> Unfortunately, certain politicians have decided that what's good enough for public employees is *too* good for the private work force. Senate Democrats, bowing to unions that are militant about preserving only overtime, have blocked every attempt at making the Fair Labor Standards Act more flexible. In 1997, then-Senator John Ashcroft offered legislation known as the Family Friendly Workplace Act that would have allowed flexible biweekly schedules or flexible hours [in the private sector workforce]. Ted Kennedy, the supposed patron saint of single moms, led the fight to kill it. And the AFL-CIO has since made flex time a litmus test issue in deciding which candidates to support.

A Ray Of Hope

To the surprise and shock of Big Labor and Big Government's liberal underbelly, in February 2005, the Bush administration unveiled new regulations for thousands of Pentagon workers that it said would promote higher performance—but union leaders decried them as "the first step toward diminished rights for the government's entire work force."

Under the proposed rules, raises would be based on annual performance evaluations from managers rather than seniority, and workers could face greater competition from outside applicants for promotions.

According to Melissa Harris of the *Baltimore Sun* staff:

Federal government workers in Washington, D.C., protest the Bush administration's new, flexible rules for overtime pay qualification.

The regulations represent one of the most sweeping overhauls of federal personnel regulations in a generation, affecting virtually every aspect of how the government hires, fires and pays its employees. Though limited initially to 750,000 workers at the Defense Department, administration officials made it clear they intend to eventually extend the changes if Congress approves...

Paul Light, a senior fellow at the Brookings Institution, added: "The fact that the Feds are doing it lends support to those that believe that government employees at all levels should be managed in the tradition of private business."

The National Education Association (NEA) is a glorified political lobby forever advocating politics that have little to do with education and everything to do with the liberal political agenda.

SEAN HANNITY
IN *LET FREEDOM RING*

The Seditious NEA and AFT

Two more major public employee unions that require special mention are America's largest labor organization, the National Education Association (NEA), with 2.7 million members in 13,000 American communities, and the somewhat smaller American Federation of Teachers (AFT). The emergence of these ultra-liberal teachers unions as a powerful force at all levels of government has been called "one of the most significant political developments in the United States since the 1960s."[92]

They have overridden school boards, school administrators, and parent-teacher associations to take radical left-wing control of the educational policies, political ideology, economic principles, anti Judeo-Christian secularism, and teaching practices (including course and textbook selection) of their millions of union-trapped teacher members. Salaries and promotions based on individual instructional merit and student performance are opposed.[93] The right of low-income students from the state's poorest-performing schools to seek tuition assistance for enrollment in superior schools through privately funded corporate scholarships or government vouchers is forbidden.[94] (At the same time, these same teachers union bosses and the politicians they manipulate—like the Clintons and Democrat Senator Paul Sarbanes of Maryland—stealthily paid substantial tuitions to send their own children to the best private schools available.)

Disillusioned and/or naïve public school teachers caught in this web are molding the drug-dulled minds and uninspired lives of our nation's youth during their formative years.[95] One courageous youngster trying to beat the politically correct system was told: "If you are a conservative, you might as well leave this class because your viewpoint is not welcome here."[96] And a *Wall Street Journal* editorial warns that "the failure of America's urban public schools is a national scandal, compounded by politicians who are rarely willing to take on the unions that have created the wreckage."[97]

NEA's Power over the Democratic Party

William McGurn, chief editorial writer for the *Wall Street Journal*, made a sobering observation with regard to the NEA that is related to the critical companion subject of partisan politics:

> Those of us who have long dismissed the National Education Association as a tool of the Democrat Party have been badly mistaken. Apparently it's just the opposite. As documents now sealed under a judge's order indicate, it's the Democrat Party that is the tool of the NEA."[98]

And more rarely publicized facts were uncovered by the *Washington Times*:

> Throughout the past decade, the National Education Association, the nation's largest teachers' union, has spent tens of millions of dollars from members' tax-exempt dues fighting the Democratic Party's political battles and promoting the election of Democrats . . .[99]

At their 2004 convention, nearly 10,000 NEA teacher delegates voted 7,390 to 1,153 to endorse Senator John Kerry for President. Their tax-exempt political action committee contributed many of these dues dollars to the Kerry campaign in spite of the fact that Congress has determined organizations engaging in political conduct should not receive such exemptions. Both the NEA and the AFT also sent hundreds of their paid staffs and assigned "volunteers to the most closely contested states. And more millions of forced dues dollars were set aside "for member education in support of 2004 election efforts."[100]

Rutgers University's aforementioned unique (i.e., conservative) professor and author, Leo Troy, challenged NEA's alleged political "bipartisanship in this effort" and predicts that "The NEA and the AFT will provide the leadership of labor's central body, the AFL-CIO...and can be expected to move organized labor further toward the Left politically."[101]

Dr. Terry Moe, a senior fellow at the Hoover Institution, a member of the Koret Task Force on K-12 Education, a professor of political science at Stanford University, and the winner of the 2004 Thomas Fordham prize for distinguished scholarship in education, adds:

> The teachers unions have more influence over the public schools than any other group in American society. They influence schools from the bottom up, through collective bargaining activities that shape virtually every aspect of school organization. And they influence schools from the top down, through political activities that shape government policy. They are the 800-pound gorillas of public education. Yet the American public is largely unaware of how influential they are—and how much they impeded efforts to improve public schools.

ABC Members Urged to Challenge Academia

As early as 1977, ABC's National Board of Directors became concerned about academia's biased political activity in the student classroom that was mocking, spinning, or ignoring the true history of America's unsurpassed entrepreneurial Republic, its heroic Founders, and the remarkable Constitution they drafted while treasonously risking their own lives. In rebuttal, the ABC Board issued a resolution under the title "Free Enterprise: Essential To

The fact is that in some instances we have used power to protect the narrow interests of our members and not to advance the interests of our schools.

BOB CHASE
PRESIDENT OF
THE NEA IN
TIME MAGAZINE,
JULY 20, 1998

Our schools now focus on dumbing everything down so students can "feel good" about themselves and don't need to deal with competition.

G. GORDON LIDDY
IN *WHEN I WAS A KID, THIS WAS A FREE COUNTRY*

Political Liberty." This prescient declaration—and the ABC Board's positive action recommended to correct the disgrace—is even more relevant when related to the subversive activities of the NEA, AFT, and most secondary school and university faculties today:[102]

WHEREAS various studies of opinions of high school and college students have shown shocking ignorance of the facts regarding our free enterprise economic system;

AND WHEREAS ignorance is particularly reported about such matters as the level of profits; the necessity of a constant flow of capital to sustain a prosperous economy and provide jobs for our millions of citizens; the favorable economic status of our people compared to that under authoritarian regimes; and the great need to preserve the right to go into business and operate with only socially justified restraints by government agencies;

NOW THEREFORE we propose that all of our ABC members contribute their time and effort to participate in some of the many worthy efforts that seek to publicly inform Americans of all ages as to the vital need to maintain our free enterprise system and basic rights granted us by the Founding Fathers under the U.S. Constitution.[103]

That 1977 resolution still needs fulfillment.

Two More Union End Runs Threaten Merit Shop Safety

In 2002, a huge potential political payback to Big Labor's "New Unionism" featured Senator Teddy Kennedy (D-MA), a dominant left-wing force on the Senate's Labor Committee, and Senate Minority Leader Tom Daschle (D-SD). They used the secretive "riding amendment" trick to try to sneak through the Senate a bill that could increase the

"We're All for You, Miss Feeny!"

unionization of government personnel by another million or more workers while endangering national security, including the construction industry workplace.

It all began just two days after the horrendous "9-11" terrorist attack in New York, Washington, D.C., and Pennsylvania, while the nation was in a state of shock. Kennedy and Daschle saw to it that their pro-union bill (S. 952) had a closed-door birth in committee without a single word of testimony. It was ignored typically by the nation's news media liberal nobility and consequently unknown to the American public. Deceptively labeled "The Public Safety Employer-Employee Cooperation Act," the bill was hidden within a "must pass" budget appropriation bill covering legitimate funds to operate the Department of Labor.

Luckily, the phony bill was spotted and opposed by the National Governors Association and the National League of Cities, causing its defeat after a filibuster and a cloture vote that failed, 56 to 44.[104] Few, if any, of the subservient senators who voted "yes" to appease these two Democrat Party bosses had any clue as to the potential negative impact of the bill on our nation's defenses against coercion, violence—and even terrorism.

This devious power grab would have authorized the federal government to compel every state and local government to fund a procedure under which all policemen, firemen, emergency medics, and other similar public safety or law enforcement employees in every public agency in the United States could be coerced to accept exclusive labor union representation. The Daschle-Kennedy bill's original "declaration of purpose and policy" claimed that the unionization of all of America's state and local law enforcement agencies is a panacea for "the health and safety of the Nation" and the "best protection of public sector employers and employees." (They never explained why.)

This bill—reintroduced annually—becomes more ominous when it is realized that the nefarious International Brotherhood of Teamsters, affiliated with the AFL-CIO's Building and Construction Trades Department, has already become the exclusive bargaining representative of many of these government law enforcement personnel throughout the nation—and at the same time is one of America's most corrupt labor organizations.[105] The giant union is never reluctant to cause a violent work stoppage "if needed,"[106] and has been "under

The measure of a man's real character is what he would do if he thought he would never be found out.

THOMAS B. MACAULAY
ENGLISH POLITICAL
LEADER-AUTHOR

703

the hideous influence of organized crime" for many years.[107] And it has already taken advantage of its menacing reputation to organize an estimated ninety thousand police, deputy sheriffs, and correctional officers in 950 state and local government agencies throughout the United States today.[108]

If this labor bill (renumbered S.1765 and H.R. 391 in 2004) is ever enacted, professional unions (such as the tainted Teamsters) will be authorized to administer the same *impartial* criminal law enforcement criteria to their own "brother and sister" AFL-CIO union members who disobey the law as they do to delinquent non-union citizens in both the public and private sectors.

Bill Defies Existing Labor Law

The Kennedy bill creates an obvious conflict of workplace loyalties that Congress actually *forbad* under analogous private sector security guard law by Section 9(b)(3) of the Taft-Hartley Act.[109] This section prevents the National Labor Relations Board from certifying any labor organization as the exclusive representative of a security guard bargaining unit "if such organization admits to membership, or is affiliated directly or indirectly with an organization which admits to membership, employees other than guards." In other words, only independent guards' unions can represent private sector security personnel throughout America today—and the corrupt Teamsters are not eligible to do so. AFSCME also would be ineligible.

Passage of the Kennedy political payoff into law would endanger the fair and even enforcement of safety and property protection at ABC merit shop construction jobsites as well as jeopardize the general welfare of the country's citizenry and workplaces.

The Bogus Union "Card-Check" Bill

An even newer "sleeper" bill, also sponsored by Big Labor's slippery Senator Teddy Kennedy (D-MA) but with Representative George Miller (D-CA) as his partner in 2004, is cynically labeled the "Employee Free Choice Act" (S. 1925/H.R. 3619). Nothing could be further from the truth. The unpublicized bill would force an employer to recognize a labor union as the exclusive bargaining representative of its employees without any Labor Board–conducted secret ballot election choice of the employees. Some 205 House members (just thirteen votes short of a majority) have obediently endorsed this one-sided and coercive legislation.[110]

All militant union organizers would have to do under their Kennedy-Miller "card check" bill (as in pro-labor Canada today) is "encourage" a majority of the workers involved to personally sign a union membership pledge card. From "friendly persuasion" over a few bottles of beer in the union hall to a "personal visit" at the intimidated employee's home to his loss of a ride to work in a "pro-union" car pool to a "guaranteed" wage increase in the first labor contract to every other type of peer and fear pressure imaginable, this personal coercion is notorious. It destroys all proof of the sincere and voluntary intent of a worker to join a union[111]—without allowing his employer to explain the negative side of compulsory union membership.

Even the AFL-CIO's own *Guidebook for Union Organizers* has cautioned its staff as follows on the unreliability of such card-checks:

> NLRB pledge cards are at best a signifying of intention at a given moment. Sometimes they are signed to "get the union off my back." In other cases, workers sign to scare the boss into a raise. Whatever the reason, there is no guarantee of anything in a signed pledge card except that it will count toward obtaining a petition for a Labor Board secret ballot election.[112]

Few politicians have voiced concern about these bills as Congress and the news media ignore the labor-management chaos they would create in the workplace.[113]

A Socialistic Triumvirate

In summary, the national alliance between Big Labor, the Democrat Party, and Big Government has created *a vast left-wing conspiracy* that threatens the productivity and security of the merit shop building and construction industry. During the last half of the twentieth century, this iron triangle frequently reduced politics to a farce of ultra-liberal special interests masquerading as a drama of lofty humanistic principles. Yet political ideologies mold the laws of the land and the future of our great nation.[114]

The press, like fire, can be an excellent servant or a terrible master.

JAMES FENIMORE COOPER
NOVELIST

Someone has tabulated that we have 45 million laws on the books to enforce the Ten Commandments.

BERT MASTERSON
WRITER

There can be no disagreement on the fact that today an avalanche of local, state, and federal statutes, regulations, interpretive bulletins, executive orders, and court rulings control the nation's workplace paternalistically from the womb to the tomb.[115] Syndicated columnist James Kilpatrick described this nightmare as "hundreds and thousands of civil servants engaged in the interminable process of drafting, publishing, enacting, enforcing, amending, rewriting, and re-promulgating incoherent workplace entitlement rules."[116]

In 1986, President Ronald Reagan—never one to lose his Irish sense of humor under any conditions—described the philosophy of this three-headed colossus in these memorable words: "If it moves, regulate it. If it keeps moving, tax it. If it stops moving, subsidize it."[117]

Tip O'Neill, the gruff old Massachusetts Democrat who served as far-left Speaker of the House of Representatives from 1977 to 1986, sponsored many of the political handouts to Big Labor and succinctly summed up his own socio-political goal: "I've always believed in our responsibility as a nation to pay for the health and welfare of the American people."[117] And William Winpisinger, the militant socialistic president of the International Association of Machinists (a building trades union), was even more frank. He bluntly told the *Washington Post*: "I'm convinced that the only way we can repel the armies of right wing radicalism is by fighting for redistribution of the nation's income and wealth."[119]

Sam Gompers Twists in the Hereafter

There is no resemblance between this welfare state sought by most of today's professional AFL-CIO leaders and their political fellow travelers when compared to "the model Republic of the United States of America" as envisioned by Samuel Gompers, the aforementioned founding father of the AFL building and construction trades unions.[120] Writing in the *American Federationist*, he rejected government ownership and control as an alternative to private sector economic order and free enterprise:

> As a matter of fact, governmental ownership and control solve nothing. They simply transfer industrial problems to the political field, restate them in political terms, and then try to solve them by political methods... The industrial injustice resultant from the evils in mod-

ern industry as well as the result of the inherent weakness and characteristics of human nature has not been bettered but made infinitely worse by government ownership and control.[121]

Gompers denounced "political favoritism" when he told his craft union annual convention in 1908:

> The American labor movement is not partisan to a political party; it is partisan to a principle, the principle of equal rights and human freedom...We come to you not as political partisans, whether Republicans, Democrats or other, but as representatives of the wage-workers of our country.[122]

Like Professor Leo Troy of Rutgers University in modern times, Sam Gompers was clairvoyant in sensing the development in the United States of a creeping workplace despotism which he labeled "dictatorship by bureaucrats." He lamented that "government ownership and controls instituted for one phase of industrial relations gradually but inevitably reach out to other connected relations until the whole is under the domination not of the people but of an oligarchy."[123]

Gompers also blocked the socialist infiltration of his own craft union brotherhoods. This summary of his views on the subject was taken from an address at the close of the 1903 AFL Convention:

> I want to tell you Socialists that I have studied your philosophy [and]...kept close watch upon your doctrines for thirty years. I have been closely associated with many of you and know how you think and what you propose. I know, too, what you have up your sleeve. And I declare to you: *economically, you are unsound; socially, you are wrong; industrially, you are an impossibility.* [emphasis added][124]

Of equal importance, throughout Sam Gompers's long and distinguished career as the national leader of America's organized labor movement, he

---

Liberals have dedicated themselves to mainstreaming Marxist ideals at home. They aim to destroy America from the inside.

Ann Coulter
SYNDICATED COLUMNIST
AND AUTHOR OF
TREASON

opposed any recognition of a "counter-revolution" by Bolshevists or their ilk. In 1919 he said that "there is no group of men on earth fit to dictate to the rest of the world" and pointed to evils of the Communist Party that were forced on the people of Russia:

> Russia stands before our gaze like a flaming torch of warning. A thing called Bolshevism has reared its ugly head in that sad and sorry land. Bolshevism is a theory, the chief tenet of which is the *dictatorship of the proletariat*. Leaving out of consideration for the moment the story of murder and devastation that has marched with this theory into practice, we must set down the theory itself as abhorrent to a world that loves democracy.[125]

To his final days on earth, Gompers stated repeatedly that his craft-oriented American Federation of Labor must "revere institutions rooted in voluntarism, personal freedom and individual responsibility for one's own sustenance." He urged the AFL to be a "progressive influence" within the "ideal" country that he loved and respected—but never to be "revolutionary":

> The American labor movement is not at war with society. It seeks to overthrow nothing. It is as loyal and devoted to the ideals of our Republic as any group or individual in all America can be. And it is not fair to the men and the women in the American labor movement to attempt now to place them in the position of disloyalty or failure to appreciate and to give service to this ideal of the world's government, *the Republic of the United States of America*.[126]

Florence Thorne, Gompers's biographer, capsulated his remarkable life work as a labor leader in these words:

> He served the Federation and the United States by adhering strictly to conservative principles; maintenance of individual rights and freedom; the right to membership in private associations for promotion of personal welfare; ownership of private property as the

When shallow critics denounce the profit motive inherent in our system of private enterprise, they ignore the fact that it is an economic support of every human right we possess and without it, all rights would disappear.

Dwight D. Eisenhower, 34th president

708

basis of individual freedom; responsibility for the exercise of rights and the use of opportunities under established law as guided by moral principles."[127]

Relentless Cycles of Liberty

The inalienable right to earn one's livelihood at any lawful calling that was revered by the AFL's Sam Gompers also forms the basic creed upon which the ABC merit shop movement was founded in 1950. This uncoerced freedom to work is one of the pillars of the Constitution that made America the greatest nation the world has ever seen. But national liberty is cyclical and that unparalleled document has become distorted by many powerful individuals, agencies, organizations, and institutions in both the private and public sectors. It has been ignored by others and judicially expanded beyond recognition in some of the nation's highest courtrooms.[128]

To note just one unnerving sign of the times, hard-left Supreme Court Justice Ruth Bader Ginsberg, a Democrat, said in a recent speech to the American Constitution Society: "Our Justices are becoming more open to international law perspectives."[129] Three months later, her more moderate sister Justice, Republican Sandra Day O'Connor, Republican, drew further attention to this disturbing judicial trend when she addressed the Southern Center for International Studies in Atlanta: "I suspect that over time we will rely increasingly, or take notice at least increasingly, of international and foreign courts in examining domestic issues." The two justices seem to be suggesting that a one-world super government and its global legal rules should influence or even control the fiercely independent spirit of our Founding Fathers and the majority of America's citizens today.[130]

A *Wall Street Journal* editorial on March 25, 2004, entitled "Rule of (International) Law" called this trend "one of the most dangerous fads in Supreme Court jurisprudence of late." That's because "American laws are measured not just against the Constitution but against the laws of foreign countries" in a "global context." And Mark Levin, president of the Landmark Legal Foundation and chief of staff to Attorney General Edwin Meese in the Reagan administration, has written a major book on this subject. It documents the ways in which the Supreme Court is "restructuring" our

George Washington could have been king for life, but he refused. The founder of our nation knew that if he accepted the role of Supreme Monarch, the American experiment in a free republic would die. His decision can be summed up by one word: "character."

General John Eisenhower (son of 34th U.S. president)

nation and its workplace, law-by-law while turning it all into a "government-knows-best" society in a barrage of liberal social activism ... [131]

Never-Changing Human Nature

Two-and-a-quarter centuries ago, in 1779, when our great nation was being formed, John Adams[132] set about a momentous task that would affect the lives of all Americans. He drafted a constitution for the Commonwealth of Massachusetts which eventually became the model for the United States Constitution. Adams strongly advocated national "republicanism" as a way to preserve the type of balance he observed within the tripartite-style English government of the Crown with the Houses of Lords and Commons. He insisted on a legal separation of powers among the executive, legislative and judicial branches of government of his new country, emphasizing that "a Republic is a government of laws, not of men." The great fear that he shared with his astute wife, Abigail,[133] was that human nature is forever tempted to abuse raw authority:

> I am more & more convinced that Man is a dangerous creature. The great fish swallow up the small & he who is the most strenuous for the Rights of the people, when visited with power, becomes as eager for the prerogatives of Government.[134]

Thomas Jefferson, coauthor of the Constitution who succeeded John Adams to become the third President of the United States, added prophetically: "When all government, domestic and foreign, in little as in great things, shall be drawn to Washington as the centre of all power, it will render powerless the checks provided of one government on another, and will become as venal and oppressive as the government from which we separated in 1776."[135]

On September 17, 1787, as the Constitutional Convention of the thirteen United States drew to a close, Benjamin Franklin was asked to explain what form of government he and the other Founding Fathers had crafted. He responded: *"A Republic—if you can keep it."* Then he warned:

I believe that the [new government under this Constitution] is likely to be administered for a course of years and can only end in despotism as other forms have done before it when the people become so corrupted as to need despotic government, being incapable of any other.[136]

Consider also the writings of Alexander Fraser Tyler, a noted professor of history at Edinburgh University in Scotland, who lived during the time of the American Revolution and wrote in 1787:

The average age of the world's great civilizations from the beginning of history has been about 200 years. They all progressed through the following sequence: from bondage to spiritual faith; from spiritual faith to great courage; from courage to liberty; from liberty to abundance; from abundance to selfishness; from selfishness to complacency; from

Cartoonist "KAL," Baltimore Sun, October 23, 1997.
REPRINTED WITH PERMISSION, CARTOONISTS & WRITERS SYNDICATE AND CARTOON ARTS INTERNATIONAL/CWS

Day by day, case by case, the Court is busy designing a Constitution for a country I do not recognize.

SUPREME COURT JUSTICE ANTONIN SCALIA

There is the moral of all human tales; 'tis but the rehearsal of the past, first freedom, and then glory—when that fails, wealth, vice, corruption—barbarism at last.

LORD GEORGE GORDON BYRON IN *CHILDE HEROLD* IV, CVIII

The Constitution
of the United
States was made
not merely for
the generation
that then existed,
but for posterity
—unlimited,
undefined, end-
less, perpetual
posterity.

HENRY CLAY
SECRETARY OF STATE

complacency to apathy; from apathy to dependence; from dependence back again to bondage.[137]

British writer/philosopher Paul Johnson concurred with his fatalistic predecessors in these frank words on human nature:

> One of the lessons of history that we have to learn, although it is very
> unpleasant, is that no civilization can be taken for granted. Its per-
> manency can never be assumed; there is always a dark age waiting for
> you around the corner, if you play your cards badly and you make suf-
> ficient mistakes.[138]

The hottest
places in hell are
reserved for
those who in time
of moral crises
maintain their
neutrality.

DANTE ALIGHIERI
PHILOSOPHER

Ludwig von Mises, an Austrian who lived from 1881 to 1973, is an internationally recognized authority on the habitual laws of "human action." This
social philosopher and scholar served for twenty-five years as Professor of Economics at the University of Vienna, and, from 1934 to 1940, he was Distinguished Professor of International Economic Relations at the Graduate
Institute of International Studies in Geneva. He also lectured at British,
French, Dutch, Italian, German, and Mexican universities and the Graduate
School of Business Administration at New York University. Later on, he acted
as an advisor to the National Association of Manufacturers.

Von Mises wrote that "the middle of the road leads to socialism." He
believed that "only a free marketplace, free enterprise, and individual freedom
of all the workers can combine to produce the goods and services so necessary
to safeguard against unlimited government power and collectivistic tyranny."
And he emphasized:

> Liberty and freedom are the conditions of man within a contractual
> society. Social cooperation under a system of private ownership of the
> factors of production means that, within the range of the market, the
> individual is not bound to obey and to serve an overlord. As far as he
> gives and serves other people, he does so of his own accord in order

712

to be rewarded and served by the receivers. He exchanges goods and services, he does not do compulsory labor and does not pay tribute.[139]

Then there are the thoughts on this vital subject of Aleksandr Solzhenitsyn, the world-renowned Russian author and 1970 Nobel Prize winner. He agonized as a political prisoner in Stalinist labor camps for eleven years because he exposed some truths about Marxism and Communism. After he was finally liberated, he came to America and, as the featured speaker, shocked liberal academic intelligentsia assembled at a Harvard University graduation ceremony in 1978.

The furor arose over Solzhenitsyn's frank appraisal that statesmanship in America has been reduced to "mediocrity" because of a "pervasive decline in civic courage and an erosion of ethical ideals." "Politicians," he charged, "use their self-serving rationales as to how realistic, reasonable, intellectually and even morally justified it is to base state policies on weakness and cowardice." Thus "mediocrity triumphs under the guise of democratic restraints." And he asked, rhetorically: "Must one point out that from ancient times a decline in courage has been considered the first symptom of the end?"[140]

Dr. Ravi Batra, a modern-day prognosticator and professor of economics at Southern Methodist University, likewise believes that man is the architect of his own fate, within the bounds of nature. "Humanity," the professor writes, "has evolved in terms of the law of social cycles" which span generations or sometimes centuries:

> Each era moves through five stages—infancy, youth, maturity, senility, and death . . . frequently by violent upheaval.[141]

A major treatise on the value of past precedent as a guide to future action was written by Dr. Warren Carroll. He called it *Cycles of Liberty* and charted the courses of many primary civilizations, beginning with the Middle Eastern and Cretan-Mycenaean eras (2500 B.C. to 1100 B.C.). Professor Carroll showed that they all culminated in these three successively disastrous steps:

It is seldom that liberty of any kind is lost all at once. Slavery has so frightful an aspect to men accustomed to freedom that it must steal in upon them by degrees and must disguise itself in a thousand shapes in order to be received.

DAVID HUME
ENGLISH PHILOSOPHER

The trick in
riding a tiger is
finding a way
to dismount.

CHINESE PROVERB

Step X—Increased government domination, causing the stifling of individual enterprise as human incentive gives way to a corrupt welfare state.

Step Y—A bold government assault on wealth in private hands, necessitated by the continued expansion of government dole and control.

Step Z—Culmination in the economic collapse that comes when government has grown so gigantic and the producer [private sector] has become so overburdened that no possible enforcement measures can any longer collect enough revenue to support the government.[142]

The warnings of these learned scholars should provide a wake-up call for the United States!

Imagine, in vivid contrast, a nation where bureaucrats actually *solve* workplace problems rather than committing economic suicide. Then picture an over-regulated country that privatizes inefficient government services, thus relegating one-third of its public servants to the private sector while saving billions of tax dollars. And dream of an over-taxed society that slashes its progressive income tax rates by 50 percent and eliminates capital gains taxes, excise taxes, sales taxes, death taxes, and tariffs.

Is this hard to believe? It all happened in New Zealand from 1983 to 1994.[143] Another encouraging historical reminder is the positive fact that, in the year 1994, mainstream America voters tossed out of office those government officials whom they perceived to be ignoring the time-honored values of our Founding Fathers.

Two weeks after these 1994 election results were tabulated, the editor of *U.S. News & World Report*, Mortimer Zuckerman, interpreted what he called "The Voters' Message":

> The election results are not a panacea but a cry of pain. Political leaders who have survived, Republican and Democrat, will not find an easy answer to the complex and disturbing trends of economic hard-

ship, the dissolution of family life and family values, crime, and the erosion of the American dream. If our political leaders unite, there may be some hope, since America is a resilient, inventive society. But if partisan politics continue to prevail, the rot will continue eating away at the soul of the country.[144]

Liberal Bias Distorting the News

In November of 2003, the veteran Senator Zell Miller, a plainspoken southerner who represented the state of Georgia for many years, shocked his political party and its ever-leftward undermining of traditional values in a book he authored. It's called *A National Party No More: The Conscience of a Conservative Democrat.* "Regular Americans see through it all," he concluded: "The day has passed when you can piss on them and convince them it's raining."[145]

Maybe yes, maybe no...Only time will tell!

President Bill Clinton's former chief political advisor and now both a commentator for Fox TV News and a syndicated columnist, Dick Morris, agreed with Senator Miller:

> The reason people aren't watching network news and are canceling their subscriptions to establishment press organs is that they are fed up with the manipulation and deliberate juggling of the news they see and read each day. An increasingly educated electorate can spot bias with greater acumen than ever before.[146]

Bernard Goldberg is the winner of seven Emmy awards, having served successively for over thirty years in the prestigious Columbia Broadcasting System as a reporter, a producer, and a talk show host. His two best-selling books, *Bias* and *Arrogance*, shocked the national press establishment by describing how our mainstream communications services such as CBS, ABC, and NBC distort the news. Goldberg began his revelations with this blockbuster statement:

> The old argument that the networks and other "media elites" have a liberal bias is so blatantly true that it's hardly worth discussing anymore.

Our job is to give people not what they want, but what we decide they ought to have.

Richard Salant
FORMER PRESIDENT OF CBS NEWS

No, we don't sit around in dark corners and plan strategies on how we're going to slant the news. We don't have to. It comes naturally to most reporters.[147]

Publisher-financier Malcolm Forbes added an ominous warning that "the very first step taken by every dictatorship since history has been recorded is the prohibition of free speech, the curbing and elimination of a free press."[148]

Economic Facts of Life

Under all the circumstances, one truth is self-evident. Historical cycles of liberty have proven that no free society has ever existed indefinitely. America's workplace independence will be destroyed if its citizens allow omnipotent government to join forces with a leftist political party like the Democrat National Committee and a socialistic private organization such as Tom Sweeney's AFL-CIO—in liaison with its militant building trades affiliates—to suffocate the cycle of liberty by denying:

> **Posterity: You will never know how much it has cost my generation to preserve your freedom. I hope you will make good use of it!**
>
> JOHN QUINCY ADAMS
> 6TH PRESIDENT

"Sorry, Mr. President. We had to discontinue the bridge to the 21st century. The unions went on strike, we can't fill out quota of minority contractors, and the environmentalists have declared this a wetland."

THE CONSERVATIVE CHRONICLE, SEPTEMBER 11, 1996,
REPRINTED WITH PERMISSION, SCRIPPS HOWARD, UNITED MEDIA, CARTOON BY H. PAYNE

(**1ˢᵗ**) The inalienable right of employees to voluntarily and peacefully choose either union membership or individual self-reliance in their workplace;

(**2ⁿᵈ**) The constitutional command that a Republic rules according to the limited sovereign voice of its founding charter, without any private sector third-party partnership and co-determination of its functions;

(**3ʳᵈ**) The general public's inherent right to the procurement of goods and services at reasonable prices in a free and competitive marketplace; and

(**4ᵗʰ**) Private management's entrepreneurial right to own and operate its business efficiently, fairly, and independently, while earning a reasonable profit in a capitalistic society.

The Human Choices

Is our peerless nation witnessing the twilight days of a Marxist-style labor union movement? Or, on the contrary, will hard-left politicians combine with organized labor and big-time bureaucracy to defeat conservative bipartisanship and swing the workplace pendulum further towards control by the "New Unionism?" Will America's unique system of merit shop construction become consumed by the AFL-CIO building trades' firebombs or briefcases...or both? How will future generations of our children and grandchildren be affected by today's increasing erosion of freedom in the workplace? What stage has America reached in its inevitable cycle of liberty?[149]

About fifty years ago, William Z. Foster, the leader of American communists, predicted: "American society is headed to communism through an intermediary state of socialism which will be operated on the basis of a planned economy."[150] In modern-day rebuttal, a scholar of Nobel Laureate stature in the field of economics, a winner of the Presidential Medal of Freedom and the National Medal of Science, the Distinguished Service Professor Emeritus of Economics at the University of Chicago, and a presidential advisor—Milton Friedman—reminds that "our society is what we make it" and urges "free enterprise" as the only choice:

> We can shape our institutions...and build a society that relies primarily on voluntary cooperation to organize both economic and other activity, a society that preserves and expands human freedom, that

---

It has been said that history is the patter of silken slippers descending the stairs and the thunder of hobnail boots coming back up. Back through the years we have seen people fleeing the thunder of those boots to seek refuge in this land. Now, too many of them have seen the signs that were ignored in their homeland before the end came are appearing here. They wonder if they will have to flee again. But they know there is no place to run to.

George Gilder
chairman,
Gilder Publishing

717

The fundamental fact about American conservatism is that it is "American." [It] has survived because it went with the grain of American culture, tapping into many of the deepest sentiments in American life: religiosity, capitalism, patriotism, individualism, optimism.

MICKLETHWAIT AND WOOLDRIDGE OP. ED., *WALL STREET JOURNAL,* JUNE 8, 2004

keeps government in its place, making it our servant and not letting it become our master.[151]

In the widely acclaimed book, *Free To Choose*, Dr. Friedman and his wife, Rose, also a renowned economist, explain, more specifically:

> When labor unions get higher wages for their members by restricting entry into an occupation, those higher wages are at the expense of other workers who find their opportunities reduced. When government pays its employees higher wages, those higher wages are at the expense of the taxpayer. But when workers get higher wages and better working conditions through the free market, when they get raises by firms competing with one another for the best workers, by workers competing with each other for the best jobs, those higher wages are at nobody's expense. They can only come from higher productivity, greater capital investment, more widely diffused skills.
>
> The whole pie is bigger—there's more for the worker, but there's also more for the employer, the investor, the consumer, and even the tax collector. That's the way a free market system distributes the fruits of economic progress among all the people. That's the secret of the enormous improvement in the conditions of the working person in the United States over the past two centuries.[152]

As if in affirmative response to the Friedmans, independent polls in 2003 conducted by the American Enterprise Institute and by the Gallup organization found that a vast majority of Americans are "deeply patriotic" and "extremely proud" of their country. "Whatever its faults," they said, "the United States still has the best system of government in the world."[153]

At the other end of the socio-eco-political spectrum is the foreboding but undeniable fact that the final result of the natural cycle of liberty of every primary civilization throughout the history of the world has been self-destruction—from the Roman Empire to Italy, Germany, Japan, and the Soviet Union.

Now fanatical Islamics preach and practice a new brand of homeless, borderless, global terrorism to decapitate "all infidels" (i.e., everybody in the world who opposes their religious and political insanity). It is a hideous worldwide conflict with no foreseeable end and with enemies as evil as they are invisible. Some of them are embedded covertly in the United States.

Prophetically, Founding Father Samuel Adams wrote, "there never was a society that did not commit suicide." Lord Acton's signature proverb has proven time and time again that "power tends to corrupt and absolute power corrupts absolutely." The famous philosopher, George Santayana, minced few words in warning that "those who cannot remember the past are condemned to repeat it." And one of America's greatest patriots, President Ronald Reagan, cautioned that "freedom is a fragile thing and is never more than one generation from extinction."

21st Century America Speaks

On November 2, 2004, Americans spoke again as a nation. They reelected Republican President George W. Bush, a leader of proven courage and integrity. And his popularity also helped to increase the Republican majority in Congress while defrocking the House's minority leader, Democrat Tom Daschle of South Dakota. Bush believes in—and supports—traditional values, a compassionate free ownership society, voluntary unionism, and proactive protection of his fellow citizens from all types of terrorism. "Freedom," he says "is on the march and the trumpet of freedom never calls retreat." The positive effect on the workplace of enslaved people throughout the tyrannical Middle East has been remarkable.

Americans on that same November 2 rejected a presidential nominee who would accommodate massive governmental control over private enterprise by the redistribution and confiscation of wealth (except his wife's Heinz catsup fortune) plus a co-partnership with Big Labor and its compulsory unionism. The candidate Americans turned down also condones international cowardice by the United States as a subservient member of the corrupt United Nations and its Marxist goal to control the entire global workplace. This devious Democrat, John Kerry, is the U.S. Senate's most extreme left-wing politician.

Big Labor threw billions of its members' hard earned union dues dollars down the drain in another lost political cause—*and ABC scored again*!

A month or so after Bush's reelection, economist Milton Friedman wrote about the changing political philosophy in the United States:

> To summarize: After World War II, opinion was socialist while practice was free market. Currently, opinion is free market while practice is heavily socialist. We have largely won the battle of ideas (though no such battle is ever won permanently); we have succeeded in stalling the progress of socialism, but we have not succeeded in reversing its course. We are still far from bringing practice into conformity with opinion.

The age-old human conflict between individual freedom and collective coercion in the workplace reflects in capsule the dangerous world of today. This collision threatens ABC's Merit Shop Crusade and festers at the heart of America's Cycle of Liberty.

CARTOONIST "KAL," BALTIMORE SUN, JANUARY 25, 1998. REPRINTED WITH PERMISSION, CARTOONISTS & WRITERS SYNDICATE AND CARTOON ARTS INTERNATIONAL/CWS

CHAPTER 52

AGAINST ALL THE ODDS: ABC TODAY

AS THE **A**SSOCIATED **B**UILDERS AND **C**ONTRACTORS defends our Republic's workplace freedom and harmony from the absolutism and brutality of the AFL-CIO's building and construction trades unions and their political friends, a new millennium challenges ABC private enterprisers to continue to prove that their "merit shop builds best."

National headquarters of this great organization are located close to Washington, D.C., in Arlington, Virginia. A half-century after ABC was created—against all economic, political, financial, and legal odds—it has won many professional awards. And it is the only major institution that represents the entire construction industry. That coalition includes general contractors in all disciplines, specialty contractors, material and equipment suppliers and distributors, surety firms, architects and engineers, accounting firms, law firms, and other businesses that serve this field.

Today ABC is the major voice of the construction industry and this is its contemporary mission statement:

> To provide the best educational and entrepreneurial activities and ensure all of its members the right to work in a free and competitive business climate, regardless of union or non-union affiliation; to add efficiency and quality to the construction industry's services and products; to enhance the success of the industry's customers; and to improve the workplace skills and lives of its employees.

ABC is one organization I can count on to stand up for free enterprise in the state of Maryland. Few organizations enjoy the reputation that ABC does. It may not always take the most popular stands, but it does take the courageous ones.

GOVERNOR ROBERT EHRLICH (R-MD)

This concept has transformed and revitalized the American construction industry. As documented in this history, over **80 percent** of the nation's private sector edifices of all kinds, shapes, and sizes are now built on a merit shop basis.[1]

All ABC members are equal, have one vote, and can hold any Association office to which they are appointed or elected at the chapter and national levels. This unique Association speaks for and operates on behalf of twenty-three thousand construction and construction-related firms through a network of eighty affiliated chapters spread across the entire United States from Maine to Florida and from Texas to California, Hawaii, and Guam. These affiliates are chartered by the national organization but are operated locally, subject to certain uniform central policies and practices.

The Association is governed by an unpaid "chairman of the board" (formerly called "president") and a two-hundred-member board of directors composed of unpaid volunteer ABC members elected from its affiliated chapters located throughout America. The national professional staff is headed by Kirk Pickerel, formerly designated as executive vice president. On January 1, 2001, he was given the new job title of president and chief executive officer.[2]

Kirk has been employed by the Association since 1985. He served first as membership director for the Virginia Chapter and then as executive director of the Southeast Pennsylvania Chapter before coming to ABC National. The unan-

Kirk Pickerel, president and chief executive officer of ABC

imous recommendation of a prestigious search committee that Kirk Pickerel was "the best candidate for the top staff job" has proven correct. He succeeded Robert P. Hepner who retired (amid equally high praise) at the end of the year 2000.

Associated with Pickerel in operating the national office are Mike Dunbar, the capable, long-service vice president in charge of "special-projects-that-nobody-else-wants-to-do" (as he describes his job) and seven other vice presidents. These senior ABC executives are responsible for overseeing and administering the many activities and services provided by the Association for its members.[3] Some sixty national staff associates report to them, working in every area of member assistance. Combined with the eighty local chapters grouped in seven regions, total ABC staff personnel number over seven hundred professionals.

ABC National's Services to Members

In response to ever-increasing needs, ABC National offers a comprehensive list of services for its members and their local chapters to help assist them, their customers, and the public with competitively bid, high-quality, safe, on-time, and within-budget merit shop construction. They include:

- A direct telephone "hot line" and a fax "Action Alert" communications system to help members solve business and personnel problems, including labor union harassment and sabotage.

- A Labor Relations Fact File that has become the industry "bible" for doing business as an open shop contractor. This publication outlines the responsibilities and what can and cannot be done to stay "union free" yet be certain that labor practices adhere to current law.

- A World Wide Web site (*www.abc.org*) on line that provides members with instant information on every facet of ABC and the construction industry.

- A nationwide government affairs and legislative vigilance and political action network which encourages the involvement of every ABC member in protecting and defending merit shop principles, policies, and free enterprise at the federal, state, and local government levels. Top priorities include labor/workplace issues.

- Legal assistance through the ABC Lawyers Network, the National Legal Rights and Strategy Committee, and the Construction Legal Rights Foundation which helps to fund legal expenses to protect the rights of members, their employees, and customers in precedent-setting cases approved by a Legal Rights and Strategy Committee.

- A Political Action Committee governed by federal election laws that works within the political process to further goals of ABC members and the merit shop philosophy.

It is the willingness of people to give of themselves over and above the demands of the job that distinguishes the great from the merely adequate organization.

PETER DRUCKER
HUMANIST-WRITER

Speaker of the House Dennis Hastert (R-IL) addresses an ABC National Legislative Conference.

Speaker of the House Newt Gingrich (R-GA)—and currently a politicial analyst for FOX TV and author of "Winning the Future"—receives a "Champion of the Merit Shop" award from ABC President Ben Houston ('98) during an ABC National Legislative Conference.

Former Congressman J.C. Watts (R-OK) addresses a Legislative Conference breakfast.

Senator Orrin Hatch (R-UT) addresses an ABC National Legislative Conference.

Senate Majority Leader Bob Dole (R-KS) with ABC President Gary Vos at the National Legislative Conference in Washington, D.C. Dole urged ABC members to get involved in the political process, saying, "Politics is not a spectator sport."

Major General Pat Stevens IV, deputy chief of engineers, U.S. Army Corps of Engineers, addresses ABC's board of directors in Phoenix.

ABC President Gary Hess ('96) speaks at a news conference sponsored by the Dole-Kemp presidential campaign.

Senator Tim Hutchinson (R-AR), left, speaks with ABC President John Jennings ('97) about legislation opposing union-only project labor agreements.

725

American free enterprise is the just, generous and prosperous system which opens the way to all, gives hope to all, and energy, progress and improvements of conditions to all.

ABRAHAM LINCOLN
16TH PRESIDENT

- Nationally recognized, standardized, and portable apprenticeship training courses in every recognized craft, using ABC's original state-of-the-art "Wheels of Learning" program as directed by the National Center for Construction Education and Research and approved by the Bureau of Apprenticeship Training of the U.S. Department of Labor.

- An annual ABC National Craft Olympics and a nationwide "Schools to Career" program to bring high school and junior college students into the construction industry.

- ABC's "Merit Choice Insurance Program" consisting of group life, health, medical, dental, vision, disability, and other employee benefits plans and special business insurance plans provided for members, their employees, and dependents at competitive prices, sold and serviced through the ABC Insurance Trust.

- The ABC-endorsed "Prime Years Program" featuring flexible 401(K) profit sharing and executive retirement plans.

- A National Diversity Committee which reaches out to minorities and women to join the ABC merit shop workforce, in cooperation with the National Association of Minority Contractors, the National Association of Women in Construction, and other similar organizations.

- An outstanding communications system, beginning with preparation and distribution of the *Construction Executive*, successor magazine in 2003 to the award-winning *ABC News* magazine, and other publications and news alerts that keep members informed promptly on important economic, labor, technical, legal, regulatory, commercial, and government legislation and developments directly affecting ABC and the construction industry.

- A Construction Education Foundation which operates as a 501(c)(3) organization to support ABC's education, training, and workforce development program, provide scholarships and grants to young men and women to begin careers in construction, and link with academia in the area of construction science and management.

- Award-winning safety programs, including increased education, training, employee accountability, substance abuse prevention, and a self-assessment audit to improve jobsite safety and health and comply with OSHA and other government laws and regulations.

- An annual "Awards of Excellence" program that honors ABC members for outstanding contributions to the construction industry and the nation as well as for outstanding construction projects, and an "Accredited Quality Contractor" program that recognizes member contractors for their commitment to safety, employee benefits, job training, equal employment opportunity, and community service.

- Business team-building opportunities through the Contractors Referral Service that matches the specific needs of construction users with the unique expertise of ABC members.

- An annual 800-page national membership directory and construction users guide.

- Regular national meetings, including annual conventions, legislative, safety and legal conferences, leadership institutes, and educational workshops that feature recognized dignitaries and experts as speakers and also provide important business contacts and social entertainment.

- Special purchase discounts to ABC members for office and construction-related services, equipment, and supplies from leading national vendors.

- Networking opportunities in ABC councils for contractors employing various specialty trades.

- Joint programs with the American Institute of Architects, the U.S. Chamber of Commerce, the National Federation of Independent Businesses, and allied trade, civic, and charitable organizations.

- Opportunities to demonstrate group leadership, political activism, civic responsibility and community service inside ABC and throughout the country.[4]

ABC members are able to meet fellow contractors and exchange information and ideas during chapter meetings, local professional development seminars, and social gatherings. And all construction users have access to an experienced source of merit shop contractors through ABC's international

Our immediate future as Americans may depend upon the living we make, but the future of America depends upon the life we live and the services we render.

WILLIAM J. H. BOETCKER
HUMANIST

People who stay in the middle of the road get run over.

Aneurin Bevan
AMERICAN POLITICIAN

Web site noted above and through extensive regional chapter arteries. The national Contractors Referral Service keeps ABC members and customers in touch with specialty and general contractors that meet construction specifications and qualifications in all fifty states. ABC also provides business and networking opportunities to its members and construction users on a worldwide basis.

ABC Publications

The Association's regular monthly newsmagazine for members over the years has had various names such as *ABC Contractor* and later on, *ABC Today*. It eventually reached a circulation of thirty thousand copies and many more "pass along" readers. Its articles provided insight into political, labor, and industry trends, offered valuable business advice, highlighted outstanding construction projects, and shared newsworthy national, local chapter, and individual member activities.

The talented editor and associate editor duo of *ABC Today* were Lisa Nardone and Amy Ingram, ably assisted by Pam Hunter. Recent publication honors included: winner of the American Society of Association Executives Gold Circle Award (1992, 1996); the SNAP Silver Award for general excellence (2000); an Association Trends special citation (2000); and an APEX Award of Excellence (2000, 2001).

For more construction information on a weekly basis, ABC National offers *Newsline*, an online report of the latest legislative, regulatory, labor, safety, and other timely news events affecting its members. To sign up, members visit ***www.abc.org/getnewsline*** or email **newsline@abc.org**.

PHOTO BY ABC

ABC National President Henry Kelly (right) in 2001 with Vice President Dick Cheney during a special White House briefing.

On January 1, 2003, a major new monthly publication called *Construction Executive* took the place of *ABC Today*. It is edited by ABC's vice president of public affairs, Gail Raiman, and the aforementioned Lisa Nardone, assisted by staff writers Jennifer Spilane and Lauren Pinch. In the inaugural issue of this state-of-the-art magazine, a foreword entitled "2003 Industry Forecast" by its publisher (and president/CEO of ABC), Kirk Pickerel, explained the broadened goals as follows:

> ABC is charting a bright new course with the publication of this monthly business magazine to provide construction executives with news and information on the wide variety of issues facing contractors today. *Construction Executive* will be 'the place' where all contractors— owners, presidents, CEOs, CFOs, project managers, safety directors and other construction professionals—go to learn about the latest news, projects, programs and services to improve their efficiency and bottom line. Decision-makers in companies of all sizes will benefit from the magazine's easy-to-read format that offers real 'take-home' value in every issue.
>
> Each month, *Construction Executive* will cover hot-button issues such as business and workforce development; project management; safety and liability; technology; accounting and tax reform; the impact of legislation and regulations; new construction procurement methodologies, and more. In addition, industry leaders will be featured in the magazine's executive roundtable discussions, sharing their thoughts on current issues that impact the construction industry.

In October of its first year of publication, this magazine won a silver Ozzie Award in the prestigious Folio Prize Competition for best-designed national association magazine. And overall substantive reviews are in too: it's "a real hit," with an official circulation of 44,000 copies in 2004 and growing.

At the local level, a typically outstanding ABC chapter that represents the metropolitan Baltimore, Maryland area, and is led jointly by its Chapter Board Chairman Eric Regelin ('04) of the Atlantic Builders Group and

If you wish in the world to advance, Your merits you're bound to enhance, You must stir it and stump it, And blow your own trumpet, Or, trust me, you haven't a chance!

Sir William S. Gilbert
Ruddigore, Act I

729

> Coming together is a beginning; keeping together is progress; working together is success.
>
> HENRY FORD, II
> INDUSTRIALIST

Chapter President Mike Henderson, has used this additional membership solicitation literature:

THE TOP 11 REASONS FOR JOINING ABC

1. **ABC Trains Your Work Force:**

   ABC Baltimore is now the largest provider of craft training in the state of Maryland. Through its state-of-the-art school-to-work training programs in Baltimore City, Baltimore County and Harford County, ABC is reaching out to the junior and senior high schools to promote construction as a career to our young people. ABC members save nearly 50 percent on tuition.

2. **ABC Saves Your Business Lots of Money:**

   ABC CompAdvantage, the chapter's worker compensation discount program, offers members the highest premium discount in Maryland. Members are also discovering that they can save literally thousands of dollars because of their chapter membership on such services as F.W. Dodge New Services; Primavera Software; mobile office leasing and much, much more.

3. **ABC Helps Keep the Government Off Your Back:**

   ABC Baltimore works hard on its members' behalf in the state capital of Annapolis, Maryland, and on Capitol Hill in Washington, D.C. We keep members apprised of new legislation or regulations at both the state and national level that can affect their ability to compete. ABC's national office near Washington is the watchdog of the industry and has proven to be extremely effective over the years in protecting contractors against harmful legislation.

4. **ABC Helps to Handle Your Labor Problems:**

   Management and labor issues have long plagued business owners. How do you protect your company's interest when hiring? When firing? ABC members have available to them a wide array of human resources and legal services designed to help them effectively practice positive and productive employee relations. ABC members receive information on everything from "fool-proof" employee applications to how to cope legally with a union organizing campaign. ABC members also receive free initial legal consultation on these subjects.

5. **ABC Helps You Build More Safely:**

ABC Baltimore has a full-time safety director to provide you with a full range of information, training, services and safety devices.

6. **ABC Educates Your Front-Line Managers:**

ABC offers seminars on everything you need to help your project so that your project managers, supervisors and safety directors perform their jobs faster, smarter and more cost effectively. There are course offerings on project management, safety and health, financial management and specialized instruction for electrical and mechanical contractors. Through our partnership with the Community Colleges of Baltimore County, ABC members can receive college credit for many of these classes.

7. **ABC Keeps You Informed:**

The chapter's award-winning newsletter and legislative infomercial update keep you informed about important industry developments locally as well as what is happening in our state capitol at Annapolis and in Washington, D.C. Nationally, ABC's new monthly magazine, *Construction Executive*, keeps you abreast of change in the industry and provides you with valuable information on labor, management and financial issues that affect your business.

8. **ABC Helps You to Network:**

Each month the chapter offers an opportunity for you to meet fellow ABC members. From our Awards Program in the spring to our Network at Night at the Bay Café in August to the black tie Winter Gala, the chapter provides your company a variety of opportunities to make that important contact with general contractors, subcontractors, architects, engineers and material suppliers.

9. **ABC Reaches Out to Your Clients:**

ABC has formal partnerships with the American Institute of Architects and the Engineering Society of Baltimore. Annual and semi-annual symposiums on timely construction industry issues provide

There must be something so very right about Americanism. It brought us from thirteen undeveloped colonies to the world's greatest-ever nation and brought Americans to new highs in life, liberty and well-being.

J. KENSER KAHN
COLUMNIST

your firm with an opportunity to network with existing and potential clients and to affect positive changes in our industry.

10. **ABC Recognizes Your Superior Work:**

ABC offers a variety of programs that promote your company to your most important audience: your clients. Our "Awards of Excellence" program every spring is one of the most popular events of the year. Your excellent work also is showcased in the Baltimore Construction Magazine. There is also a Safety Award Program which recognizes members who have outstanding workplace safety records.

11. **ABC Gets You New Business:**

Our Construction Referrals Service is the best single source for construction buyers all over the country. It helps them identify the right contractor for their project. The CRS refers literally thousands of ABC contractors to construction buyers every year.

This publication helped the Metropolitan Baltimore ABC Chapter to increase its membership from 350 in 1998 to 550 in the year 2000.

ABC Members Lead a World-Wide Marketplace

National census figures track over a million self-employed artisans and tiny "ma and pa" handy-crafters in the construction industry. The average ABC contractor employs from 15 to 30 people but many of America's construction giants—with thousands of employees and gross volumes of business in the billions of dollars—are members too. The Bureau of National Affairs reports that between 1992 and 2002, the number of non-union construction jobs in the country increased from 3.9 million to 5.8 million.[5]

ABCers of all sizes team up to lead their industry in constructing and rehabilitating the offices where Americans work, the highways we traverse, the edifices where we worship, the schools where we send our children, the hospitals that care for our sick, and much more: shopping malls, public utilities, research laboratories, high-tech facilities, oil refineries, manufacturing plants, government buildings, historical renovations, airports, zoos, air, rail, and seaport facilities, sports stadiums, banks, hotels and motels, museums, military bases, libraries, bridges, dams, ski resorts, and convention centers.

Among the top fifty contractors in the United States, ranked on revenue and in approximate order of size, according to the October 2004 issue of *Engineering News-Record*, are twenty ABC members. And seven of the first ten also are ABCers: 1st- Bechtel (CA); 2nd- Centex (TX); 3rd- Kellogg, Brown & Root (TX); 4th- Fluor Corp. (CA); 5th- The Turner Corp. (TX); 8th- Bovis Lend Lease (NY); 9th- Foster Wheeler, Ltd. (NJ); 11th- Clark Construction Group, Inc. (MD); 13th- Washington Group Int'l, Inc. (ID); 14th- Gilbane Building Co. (RI); 15th- PCL Construction Enterprises, Inc. (CO); 19th- Hensel Phelps Construction Co. (CO); 22nd- Granite Construction, Inc. (CA); 28th- TIC Holdings, Inc. (CO); 32nd- Austin Industries (TX); 36th- Brasfield & Gorrie LLC (AL); 38th- Zachry Construction Corp. (TX); 44th- BE&K, Inc. (AL); and 46th- ABB Lumus Global (NJ).

Many of these giant firms operate on an international basis. The geographical boundaries of ABC builders have become vast in scope. Canada, Mexico, South America, Europe, Africa, the Middle East (including the rebuilding of Iraq), and Asia are some of the global arenas that have been penetrated. While competing successfully in this worldwide marketplace, ABC members provide employment for hundreds of thousands of people.

ABC in the Hub of the Planet

ABC PHOTO

Neil Coakley, chairman of Coakley & Williams and second president (1960) of ABC's Metro-Washington, D.C., Chapter.

Washington, D.C., is the most influential city in the free world. It is also the home base of the AFL-CIO, yet many multi-million-dollar edifices have been built by ABCers in the nation's capital over the years. The merit shop today is credited with 75 percent of the major construction projects inside the city and its outlying Virginia and Maryland metropolitan areas.[7] Here are a few of them:

- Rebuilding the *Pentagon* for the Department of Defense. This largest renovation ever undertaken in the United States is managed by a consortium called PEN-REN/C, along with its many individual firms, some of which are: Hensel Phelps Construction, Facchina Construction, Shirley Pentagon Contractors, Modern Continental Construction, Electronic

**Belief in a
thing can
make
it happen.**

FRANK LLOYD WRIGHT
ARCHITECT

Data Systems, General Dynamics Network Systems, and Coakley &
Williams Construction Co.[8]

- The *U.S. Holocaust Memorial Museum*, built by Blake Construction
  Company.
- *FedEx Field* (Redskins Football Stadium).
- *The Women In Military Service Memorial*, built by Clark Construction
  Company.
- *The Woodrow Wilson Bridge*.
- The *National World War II Memorial*, built by the Tompkins/Grunley-Walsh Joint Venture.

Lauren Pinch of ABC's *Construction Executive* magazine described the historic monument in these words:

> It is built of bronze, granite and memories. Throughout its construction, veterans, their families, tourists and passersby stopped to peek through security barriers while workers labored at the jobsite. Every person you met had a different story. "Some veterans even threw their dog tags in and wanted them put in the concrete," says James Walsh, president of Walsh Construction and project executive for the memorial. "It was an emotional experience. It colored everything."

Grunley-Walsh Construction and Tompkins Builders previous combined project experience included the Washington Monument, the Jefferson Memorial, the FDR Memorial, the National Air and Space Museum, the White House, the Capitol Building, and many other federal buildings in the Washington area.

The World War II Memorial honors sixteen million people who served in the U.S. armed forces, the four hundred thousand who died, and the millions who supported the war effort from home. It is located on 7.4 acres of the National Mall between the Lincoln Memorial and Washington Monument. Two forty-three-foot arched pavilions stand at the north and south ends of the site to symbolize the Atlantic and Pacific theaters. Fifty-six seventeen-foot wreathed pillars represent the U.S. states and territories at the time of the war. Workers excavated thousands of cubic yards of soil and installed a concrete foundation of more than ten thousand cubic yards. The structure includes a vast array of tunnels and equipment rooms that sustain fountains and lighting.

Once workers finished the difficult groundwork phase, stone setting began. Designers selected Kershaw granite from South Carolina for the vertical design elements and Green County granite from Georgia for the main plaza. Academy Black and Mount Airy were used to reconstruct the Rainbow Pool. New England Stone Company, a subcontractor based in North Kingstown, R.I., precisely pre-cut granite slabs so that each of the pieces would fit in the foundation puzzle.

The World War II Memorial came in under budget cap and celebrated a massive opening-day ceremony in 2004. Veterans and visitors continue to frequent the site—to sit, contemplate, pay their respects, or make new friends. The memorial offers this linking experience. "You'll see total strangers sitting there talking. You'll see a myriad of people connecting—it's very special," says Jim Walsh.[9]

> Symbolic of the defining event of the 20th Century, the memorial will be a monument to the spirit, sacrifice and commitment of the American people to the common defense of the nation and to the broader causes of peace and freedom from tyranny throughout the world.
>
> AMERICAN BATTLE MONUMENTS COMMISSION

A Bleak Future for Compulsory Craft Unionism?

On the other side of the construction industry—despite huge political power and deep union dues pockets—the building trades' decreasing share of the national construction market and its dwindling membership ranks are signs that it may be losing some of its clout.[11] More than twenty-five years ago, *Engineering News-Record* recognized this trend and published a dramatic article proclaiming **OPEN SHOP CONSTRUCTION KEEPS GROWING BIGGER, GETTING STRONGER.**

> "The open shop is continuing to spread across the country, gaining new capabilities and making major inroads into construction markets and geographical areas that had been union strongholds. "No job is too big for them," Plumbers Union General President Martin Ward told a building trades group...Many union companies are going either double-breasted or entirely open shop.[12]

Moving forward to current times, in 1998 the equally non-partisan Construction Industry Institute (CII) prepared an "Analysis of Multiskilled Labor Strategies in Construction." It expressed concern about labor union productivity, strict craft training, and the declining number of entrants into the construction field. It recommended that "alternative labor utilization strategies and modified labor practices are needed if the [unionized side of the] industry is to address these growing concerns effectively." And the CII report voiced its apprehension that

> . . . currently used craft delineations in practically all [unionized] sectors of the industry have changed very little in their organization by the same craft groupings. As a result, little experimentation with alternative strategies has been tried. These old craft/trade paradigms have proven to be resistant to change.

Next the CII report defined and praised the long-established versatility of the non-union sector of the construction industry. Its findings were significant but came as no surprise to ABC members and their customers. The conclusion of the report included an analysis of a non-union industrial construction project and the exploration of its multiskilling applications to construction. The benefits of such flexible labor utilization were demonstrated with regard to project labor cost, employment opportunities for construction craft workers, and related labor issues. The proven advantages included total dollar savings, a reduction in the required project work force, an increase in the average employment duration of each worker, and an increase in earning potential for multiskilled construction workers.[13]

Three years later, in 2001, Professor Armand J. Thieblot, Jr., published the definitive treatise on *The Fall and Future of Unionism in Construction*. It was no coincidence that Dr. Thieblot received his doctorate degree at the University of Pennsylvania and its Wharton School, followed by work there as a Senior Research Associate under Professor Herbert R. Northrup.[14] After that service under the master, Thieblot became an adjunct professor of management at the University of Baltimore as well as a recognized authority, consultant, and expert witness in his own right in the field of construction labor-management relations.

Through research based primarily on U.S. Department of Labor statistics, Thieblot proved that the total component cost of labor in construction (that is, "the sum of its proportions of labor, management, materials, and capital") averages 15 percent to 18 percent higher for a unionized contractor than for a non-union builder. This historic disparity is still existent at the beginning of the twenty-first century, as described in the Thieblot treatise:

> Construction unions have failed to adapt to the changing needs of the industry created by developing new technologies and have failed to allow their employers to compensate for high wages through efficient labor deployment or the use of semi-skilled, subjourneymen workers. Constructive change in these areas also has been impeded by prevailing wage laws and pro-union government procurement decisions as well as the unions' own proclivities to perpetuate their craft-journeyman orientations... When unionized contractors find themselves thrown into competition against cheaper and increasingly competent non-union or open shop contractors, they win a shrinking portion of work and therefore can offer few job slots or annual hours to building trades unionists.[15]

Today (as has been noted) the outmoded building trades unions only control about one-sixth (14.7 percent) of the total commercial, industrial, institutional, and public construction market throughout the United States. Dr. Thieblot adds: "It is increasingly difficult for individual unions to provide demonstrable incentives to new recruits or even to maintain critical mass among their existing members."[16]

More Bad News for Craft Unionism

Building trades solidarity has been shattered further because of a temporary if not permanent withdrawal of the International Carpenters Union and its half-a-million members from the parent AFL-CIO in March of 2001. "Philosophical differences with AFL-CIO leader Tom Sweeney" were cited as a primary cause.[17]

The maverick Carpenters International Union's President, Douglas McCarron, lamented the fact that the AFL-CIO "dotes on social engineering"

> There is nothing to be learned from the second kick of a mule.
>
> DICK ARMEY (R-TX)
> FORMER HOUSE
> MAJORITY LEADER, IN
> *ARMEY'S AXIOMS*

737

The search for someone to blame is always successful.

ROBERT HALF
PUNDIT

financed by "special per capita taxes" on its members while de-emphasizing the more conservative and practical "bread and butter" issues (championed by the AFL founder Sam Gompers) that still are important to rank-and-file workers. McCarron commented further that "too many unions continue to endorse candidates, almost exclusively Democrats, and make their decisions based on what works in Washington—or at least what they tell each other works in Washington—regardless of what their members tell them."[18]

The AFL-CIO's Building Trades Department also was stunned by the failure to negotiate a compulsory "union only" project labor agreement (PLA) in a sensitive political situation. It involved construction work performed on the privately funded $150,000,000 presidential library in Little Rock, Arkansas, that ex-President Bill Clinton is building as a sanitized tribute to his eight debased years in the White House. Incredible as it seems, a non-union construction firm called CDI Contractors, located in Little Rock, has been a general manager on the massive library project.

In protest against this "disloyalty," on April 17, 2002, the AFL-CIO Building Trades voted at their annual convention to cut off contributions to the Democratic National Committee until Clinton relented on his library project's merit shop construction contract and began to comply with his own presidential policy of mandatory unionism for all construction work at all times.[19]

"The embarrassing part about this outrageous agreement," said Edward Sullivan, president of the Building Trades Department, "is that it sends a terrible message to our politically active rank-and-file members who worked so hard across America to elect President Clinton, and our affiliated unions are furious."[20] One conservative journalist and television pundit—Robert Novak—observed that "the Clinton Library did an imitation of the Associated Builders and Contractors in fighting any project labor agreement (PLA)."[21]

All of these distressing facts caused sixty-six international unions to schedule an emergency powwow and vote for a mandatory four-cents-per-member increase each month in the per capita tax that all affiliated local unions pay to their parent AFL-CIO. The fund was supposed to generate an additional $7 million for the political war chest.[22] The money was also to be used to encourage union members to run for public office under the auspices of a select AFL-CIO political action committee and provide expert training on how to win a "strategically targeted election."[23]

In Michigan—a state where Big Labor and the Democrat Party traditionally dominate government, commerce and industry—a lament by the Mid-Michigan Construction Alliance mirrored the concern of unionized builders throughout the nation: "The end result is that, broadly speaking, the organized sector is being slowly but surely marginalized."[24] Even more to the point was the honest admonition of David Kusnet, a former speech writer for President Clinton and thereafter a staff member of the powerful American Federation of State, County, and Municipal Employees: *The labor movement is in danger of becoming history.*"[25]

Reacting to these dire warnings, leaders of the AFL-CIO convened again in Washington, D.C., on January 10 and 11, 2003, for the first "organizing summit" held in more than forty years. They acknowledged that "the labor movement will not survive unless it finds new, more successful strategies for organizing more members." Led by President Tom Sweeney, they agreed that they should become "much more aggressive" in developing and implementing organizational tactics.[26]

During August of the same year, the AFL-CIO, in further desperation, announced that it was creating an organizational anomaly for *non-union* workers "who agree with the labor movement on many issues and want to campaign alongside labor on those issues." It's called "Working America."[27]

In December 2003 further bad news came from a five-year-long survey by the NEA-Association of Union

Quality is never an accident; it is always the result of high intention, sincere effort, intelligent direction and skillful execution; it represents the wise choice of many alternatives.

WILLIAM A. FOSTER
MANAGEMENT
CONSULTANT

Contractors and the National Maintenance Agreements Policy Committee. The results were compiled and analyzed by the Construction Labor Research Council. It found a lack of career opportunities "due to union restrictions on available workers" and low productivity due to "poor craft worker attitude."[28]

A New Labor Trades Solution?

Evidence that the entire unionized labor-management side of the construction industry may finally be looking for mutual ways to solve its competitive problems also was disclosed recently by the Bureau of National Affairs:

> Leaders of building trade unions, contractor associations, and major corporate owners met in Hollywood, Fla., on January 16, 2003, to launch a tripartite initiative to seek "attainable, measurable, and meaningful" ways to improve construction cost effectiveness, the parties announced in a joint statement.
>
> One industry official described the gathering as a "breakthrough meeting," among the parties. The representatives talked about ways "to improve the construction industry through meaningful dialogue, collaboration, and mutual commitment to positive change by owners, contractors, and building trades unions," according to a statement from the parties . . .
>
> The meeting marked the first time that owners, contractors, and union presidents have come together nationally to address construction cost effectiveness. BCTD [Building & Construction Trades Dept.] President Edward Sullivan said the industry "historically has been compartmentalized into different interest groups, with different agendas for success." Sullivan added "there is little doubt we have taken the first positive step toward real tripartite collaboration in our industry. I'm excited about where this can lead."[29]

A year later the Bureau of National Affairs announced that unionized contractors meeting during the Associated General Contractors convention in Orlando on March 10–13, 2004, were "upbeat" about a vote by trade unions to address work stoppages arising from jurisdictional disputes and other jobsite issues. It seems that the governing board of presidents of the Building and Construction Trades Department voted unanimously to approve the "union responsibilities" section of a tripartite report prepared under the auspices of the Construction Users Roundtable to eliminate work disruptions in the construction industry. "This section relates to work disruptions of any kind," Ralph Johnson, senior vice president of Turner Construction and a past AGC president, told the group.

Johnson was referring to the preamble of the final draft of CURT's work stoppages report which provides that "jurisdictional disputes contribute to only a portion of the disruptions in the industry. Many more work disruptions are caused by a general lack of respect for the interests of other parties involved in a project." The CURT preamble further states that "a culture must be developed" on construction jobsites that "work disruptions are not acceptable, except when there is an imminent danger to the safety and health of those at the site."[30] (That caveat still allows the huge loophole for a traditional union excuse to strike.)

Shifting Union Voices

Meanwhile, in Chicago on July 10, 2004, members of a new labor organization known as UNITE HERE closed their merger convention by listening to leaders of the so-called New Unity Partnership (NUP) lambaste the AFL-CIO as a "fortress of ineffectiveness and self-interested unions." NUP leaders Bruce Raynor and John Wilhelm of the hospital industry were appointed as UNITE HERE's general president and president along with three more co-leaders who are presidents of the Service Employees International Union, the Laborers' International Union of North America (LIUNA) and the United Carpenters Union. They formed NUP "to push for major changes in the structures of all unions, including advocating the merger of existing unions into larger, more powerful organizations."

Terrence O'Sullivan, president of LIUNA, told the convention delegates: "I hope you will be the spark that lights the fire that returns the labor movement to its activist roots." All five of these labor leaders stressed the importance of helping Senator John Kerry (D-MA) win the presidential election in November 2004. And O'Sullivan proposed a mechanism to consolidate the federation's financial units. He envisages a single, powerful financial entity that will generate enough revenue to subsidize labor union growth and offer workers a variety of financial and insurance services and products.

More proof of work loss by the building trades occurred at a first-ever Sheet Metal Industry Week Partnership Conference held in Las Vegas, Nevada, at about the same time. "Job growth" was the focus on an address by the Sheet Metal Workers International Association's Secretary-Treasurer, Tom Kelly. He claimed that "residential work accounts for 60 percent of the construction market," and concluded that "if contractors want more work and unions want to increase membership, residential is the market they must go after.[31]

The 317,000 member United Association of Plumbers and Pipefitters ("UA") has done something unheard of in the history of its traditional "fathers-and-sons club." Public relations advertising was instituted and allied with academia to lure applicants who want a college degree as well as a union card. This is part of a marketing campaign costing $2 million annually. UA President Martin Maddaloni explained: "We're trying to take a different approach to show who we are."

Other AFL-CIO member unions also "are in the midst of soul-searching" to come up with new ways to revitalize the labor movement, according to the Bureau of National Affairs. Getting into the cable news business and creating "labor centers" to promote cooperative organizing among unions are among many proposals that have been submitted to the AFL-CIO for consideration by its executive committee.

Another "shifting voice" with immediate effect on the construction industry is the United Steelworkers of America's "invasion" of traditional building trades union territory in Pennsylvania and New Jersey. As noted in Chapter 45, the USA is out-bidding construction union competitors through the use of "wall-to-wall" multi-skilled mechanics to replace antiquated single craft journeymen and apprentices.

Last but far from least, "personal values, faith, and moral character" are unusual subjects being recommended for adoption by one of the smaller but also one of the most sophisticated and human-relations-oriented labor organizations affiliated with the AFL-CIO. It is the brave International Association of Firefighters of "9-11" fame. Its veteran president, Harold Schaitberger, and his able young executive assistant, Kevin O'Connor, admit that the labor movement is "at a crossroad" and must broaden its message well beyond "voter turnout" by its members. Here are excerpts from the IAF's remarkable policy changes recommended to its parent AFL-CIO in 2005:

> Today the Federation [AFL] has lost its efficacy, voice and edge at the national level. As a result, the Labor Movement no longer has a prominent place in our national debate and is viewed by many as irrelevant and ineffective. If this is not changed soon, it will lead to the demise of the American Labor Movement... At the time of the merger of the American Federation of Labor and the Congress of Industrial Organizations in 1955, there were 13.5 million union members, which represented 34 percent of the nation's workforce. Fifty years later, the AFL-CIO's membership remains essentially the same at 13.5 million members, but now represents only 13 percent of the nation's workforce and only 9 percent in the private sector...
>
> There are a variety of factors that have contributed to new job opportunities and shifts in the type of employment. The U.S. population continues to grow and suburban/ex-urban areas are expanding. Technology is changing the way people work, methods of production and the location of worksites... The current wave of globalization is making North America a service, retail and knowledge economy with a corresponding workforce. Many corporations, producers and industry sectors continue to merge into fewer and fewer enterprises with ever-greater economic strength. More people work in environments characterized as part-time, independent contractor, or with little or no traditional benefits...
>
> The Federation needs to appeal [on an "emotional level"] to the personal needs of members and not just their economic interests. Workers are concerned with many cultural, moral, and religious issues... And the issues of security, a strong nation, and national defense need to be woven together with the federation's core message of economics, worker safety, and health care, among others...

Lots of folks confuse bad management with destiny.

KIN HUBBARD HUMAN-
IST-WRITER

The Federation should retain a nonpartisan pollster to conduct an "objective" survey of the attitudes and priorities of union members. Based on the results, the AFL-CIO needs to "develop a theme" that embraces faith and moral character, while also ensuring that we stand for a strong national defense, securing our homeland, and protecting our citizens and families...The Federation also must end its practice of being subservient to just one political party—the Democrats—and instead engage in meaningful outreach to Republicans or its political and legislative influence will continue to decline.

Being organized must not just be an option—we must show workers it is a necessity. While we preserve the existing union model where it works, we must be willing to create newer models for emerging work cultures.[32]

This farsighted and sophisticated but long-discarded and politically incorrect union ideology sounds more like AFL Founder Sam Gompers than today's AFL-CIO President Tom Sweeney.

No one can predict exactly where the private sector trade union movement is headed but one fact is apparent: the traditional Big Government–Democrat Party–Big Labor political machine is beginning to sputter.[34]

ABC Supported President Bush—and Vice Versa

A timely twist of fate for ABC in 2001 found its officials working with the newly elected administration of Republican President George W. Bush. They assisted his White House team during the transition period as it prepared to reverse eight previous years of Clintonian domestic welfarism, international cowardice, personal immorality, and obstruction of justice. *Engineering News-Record* reported that, although ABCers weren't claiming to have actually put George W. Bush in the White House, at the Association's annual convention in March of 2002, they did announce that they believed "they helped him reach his goal." ABC's PAC (political action committee) also endorsed 206 conservative candidates for various government offices throughout the country and 168 won election—an 82 percent success rate.[35]

ABC representatives soon became welcome in the office of America's Chief Executive and met with high-ranking officials on a number of economic issues. Vice President Dick Cheney gave briefings for ABC members during the Association's legislative conferences in Washington, and senior ABC officials occasionally attended special White House meetings with President Bush himself.

These summit sessions must have made some impact. Not long after Bush was sworn into office, he pledged that he would "work with Congress to ensure that no

CARTOONIST "KAL," BALTIMORE SUN, NOVEMBER 4, 2004. REPRINTED WITH PERMISSION, CARTOONISTS & WRITERS SYNDICATE AND CARTOON ARTS INTERNATIONAL/CWS

worker is forced to join or support a union unless he or she freely chooses to do so." True to the new president's word, union-slanted executive orders signed furtively by Clinton during the final days (and hours) of his administration were overturned.[36]

Pronouncements (such as Secretary Chao's amended LM-2 report) and a marginal Republican-led Congress helped to influence a new political mindset in Washington.[37] More politicians began to have respect for legitimate managerial prerogatives and a co-existing obligation for everyone to accept personal responsibility for his or her own welfare rather than rely on government subsidies, entitlements, and welfare.

This Bush administration workplace philosophy of "compassionate conservatism" enabled ABC to make progress in achieving some of its merit shop goals. In 2003, to give an example, all of the newly appointed "Bush" National Labor Relations Board members were finally confirmed by the Senate. It will be "significantly more management-leaning than the Clinton-era Labor Board that overruled longstanding precedent in several areas," predicted Commerce Clearing House's *Labor Law Journal*. And here are some of the government-induced

Our reliance against tyranny is the love of liberty which God has planted in us. Our defense is in the spirit which prized liberty as the heritage of all men, in all lands everywhere. Destroy this spirit and you have planted the seeds of despotism at your own doors.

ABRAHAM LINCOLN
16TH PRESIDENT

pro-union controls over legitimate management operations that the reconstituted Labor Board presumably will "correct and reverse":

> ...use of mail ballot elections, union videotaping of employees; "mixed" bargaining units of jointly employed and solely employed workers; *Weingarten* [union-type representation] rights for non-union employees; a successor employer's obligation to bargain without a challenge to the union's majority status; the "employee" status of graduate assistants and medical interns; and supervisory status for utility dispatchers."[38]

The Republican-controlled Labor Board is also likely to swing the legal ground rules back towards the protection of reasonable management rights in these "less-publicized areas," according to the *Labor Law Journal*:

> ... expanding the findings of supervisory status; expanding findings that an employer has rebutted the presumptive appropriateness of a petitioned-for single location unit; finding more employee committees lawful; limiting the use of mandatory bargaining orders; expanding findings of the existence of an impasse in bargaining and expanding what proposals can be lawfully implemented when an impasse exists; expanding findings of waivers of bargaining rights; limiting an employer's obligation to bargain over work relocation decisions; and expanding a successor employer's right to set initial terms and conditions of employment.

Bob Gorrell, editorial cartoonist, in the *Washington Times*, November 14, 2004.

With President Bush triumphantly serving another term (through 2008), other pro-union Clinton-era Labor Board cases will be amended or reversed. One, for example, allows temporary workers from outsider agencies such as Manpower, Inc. to join previously established bargaining units and another one permits use of an employer's email system to disseminate union information.[39]

The general public has no knowledge or appreciation of these positive workplace changes that the Bush administration is creating. Opposed by Democrats, the "blue ribbon" national media, and academia, the Republican White House is helping to return the inherent right to manage to employers where it belongs. The previous eight-year-long emasculation of many legitimate business prerogatives by the Clinton Labor Board's leftist "Bluestone brothers" model presumably is over, at least until 2008.[40]

ABC Leads the Merit Shop Way

There is an obvious economic truth that the engine of growth in any successful society is its income-producing private enterprise sector, not its deficit-spending–tax increasing–union-dominated government sector. With only about a sixth of the construction workforce in the United States under the control of Big Labor today, the merit shop crusade has become a major factor in creating the world's preeminent economy. And its conservative contractor's Association—ABC—has been named by *Fortune* magazine for two consecutive years (along with such entrepreneurial luminaries as the U.S. Chamber of Commerce, the National Association of Manufacturers, and The Business Roundtable) as "one of the most influential organizations in terms of public policy influence" in the nation's capital. It is also one of the country's largest employer federations.[41]

The impact of this merit shop crusade on the construction industry by encouraging and adopting ever-advancing technology and multi-skilling practices has finally begun to cause the building trades' reluctant modification of obsolete craft union tools and job featherbedding to some extent. Professor A. J. Thieblot, in his aforementioned treatise published during the year 2002, explains:

> Certain common themes are detectable in the reaction of the construction industry to technological changes that transcend sector boundaries. They fall into two broad categories, each of which has impact on the traditional organizational pattern of a limited number of discrete crafts having a very small number of vertical skill divisions.

The Constitution creates a limited government that respects the God-given rights of each individual, not a massive, centralized bureaucracy that oversees virtually all private sector activity, manages entitlement programs, confiscates property, and redistributes wealth. In other words, the Constitution does not support the establishment of a massive welfare state with few if any limits on its power.

SEAN HANNITY
TV-RADIO COMMENTATOR, IN *LET FREEDOM RING*

First, there has been a leveling of the skill requirements in many of the journeyman trades. Some artisan secrets and skills of the craftsman... have been replaced by standardized factory-made sub-assemblies, materials, and fasteners, by specialized tools and techniques, and by other engineering solutions. Less needs to be known now by a journeyman than previously and his command of the tools of his trade can be lower...

Furthermore, one fully skilled craftsman can frequently set up a job for execution or completion by semiskilled followers, so all workers on a job need not be equally skilled journeymen. On the other hand, most laborers—doing work more significant than flagging, truck unloading or cleanup—now handle much broader ranges of tools and need to have higher skills than once were expected of the unskilled. So, at both ends of the spectrum, new technologies have resulted in a flattening of the skill differentials between journeymen and laborers, and in the development of multiple places for semi-skilled workers to fit between them.

Second, the explosion in the number of specialty trades needed by each sector of the industry, noted above, created demands for sprinkler fitters, sound proofers, dry-wall tapers, pile drivers, metal building erectors, concrete block setters, carpet layers, spray painters, heli-arc welders, and a profusion of others who had no pre-existing home among the organized trades. Both of these outcomes have not only affected job ownership by specified craftsmen, but have also called into question what sort of preparation and training is appropriate for them and how individuals' competency can be ascertained by potential employers. Current [union] apprenticeship programs, lasting from three to five years (about how long it takes to turn a baccalaureate degree into a doctorate), are unnecessarily protracted for most trades and are unavailable for others. [42]

This far-reaching study by Professor Thieblot concludes with proof of the remarkable positive influence of ABC's policies and practices on today's building and construction in America:

BOVINE ECONOMICS

Communism: **You have two cows. The government takes both and shoots you.**

Fascism: **You have two cows. The government takes both and sells you the milk.**

Socialism: **You have two cows. The government takes both and gives you the milk.**

New Dealism: **You have two cows. The government takes one, milks it, and then throws the milk away.**

Leftwingism: **You have two cows. The government promulgates an executive order unionizing them both and adding a 50 percent milk tax.**

Capitalism: **You have two cows. You sell one and buy a bull.**

By the 1990s, the *non-union* domain had become the dominant one and had developed its own pattern of job designations and pay administration. Also by that time, the impacts of technology in the fractioning of jobs into different specialties and new levels of skill demand were well established. It is clear that a great array of new job titles and a profusion of semiskilled categories of construction work have developed which were not represented by unions when the unions established the labor structure that dominated the industry for many years...

Unquestionably, the old union-based paradigm for labor relations is broken. The idea that (with minor exception) all construction work should be done by fully trained journeymen (paid the same rate by craft) assisted only by common laborers using no tools and by a limited number of registered apprentices in training for a handful of specialties is increasingly impossible to sustain.[43]

In its January, 2004, issue, ABC's new *Construction Executive* magazine posed a question and offered a prediction:

Want a sneak peek into the future of construction? Picture nanotechnology, carbon-fiber materials, intelligent walls and glass, white lighting and LEDs, and pre-assembled whole buildings ready to drop onto a foundation. Imagine a single master builder, no more disparate

To face tomorrow with the thought of using the methods of yesterday is to envision life at a standstill. To keep ahead each one of us, no matter what our task, must search for new and better methods—for even that which we now do well must be done better tomorrow.

JAMES F. BELL
CONSULTANT

functions and services working independently of each other. In the future, members of the A/E/C community work as equal partners, all utilizing the latest and greatest, most environmentally efficient materials.

ABC's Mullan and the AFL's Gompers: Two Great Patriots

When one reflects on the unprecedented construction workplace achievements that were trail-blazed by ABC and its members over half a century, despite the savage opposition of Big Labor and the historical pro-union bias of Big Government, *memories of the year 1950 return.* That was the time when the building trades unions and the contractors they represented controlled over 85 percent of all industrial, commercial, institutional, and government construction performed in the United States.

That was also the time when a non-union general contractor named Charlie Mullan made a bold decision which eventually turned out to have national and even global impact. In the year 1950—one-on-one and eyeball-to-eyeball—he told "Kingfish" Ellis, the powerful boss of the Baltimore Building Trades Council:

> You know damn well I choose qualified union subcontractors to work on my projects from time to time as needed. But your threats against me, my family and my business will never make me force my own employees to join your union against their will.[44]

Mullan never broke that promise and the Associated Builders and Contractors, Inc., was born in his house in Baltimore. He and six other courageous businessmen meeting there vowed to fight for the freedom to work together in harmony, without any coerced union affiliation of their firms and employees.

These seven contractors were the first warriors in the merit shop crusade. They were fighting for labor relations "voluntarism" over any form of "union compulsion." That meant the ABCers also were fighting (coincidentally and ironically) to defend a life-long conviction of Sam Gompers, the immigrant cigar maker's apprentice who rose to found and lead the AFL Building and

Construction Trades Unions for forty-three years.[45] Gompers proclaimed in an address to his members in 1916:

> The workers of America adhere to voluntary institutions in preference to compulsory systems which are held to be not only impractical but a menace to their rights, their welfare and their liberty.[46]

The Reverend Edward Keller of the University of Notre Dame, in his book entitled *The Case for Right to Work Laws, a Defense of Voluntary Unionism*, referred to the great success of the Samuel Gompers creed of "voluntarism" even in the days "when unionism was relatively weak," and concluded:

> It ill befits the United States, as the one place in the world where the personal worth, dignity and liberty of the individual is a cherished tradition, to set the example of compulsion where voluntarism is not merely possible but practical and effective. Experience proves that union leaders can 'sell' good unionism on a voluntary basis.

ABC's Many Heroes

As this history of the merit shop crusade comes to a close, special tribute is paid to ABC's membership roles that have been filled for more than fifty years with self-reliant, honorable, courageous, patriotic men and women. They all have believed in traditional American core values of liberty and a free choice to work competitively and peacefully, with a minimum of outside influence or control by any person or entity.

Defying malevolent opposition and in the face of dangerous attacks, many of these ABC leaders moved up through construction company ranks from helper, apprentice, and mechanic to supervisor, estimator, project manager, or senior executive. Others defied the odds even further, with just a few dollars in their pockets, by establishing their own construction firms. And, as this history can attest, they all have remained dedicated to the merit shop philosophy of ABC—the contractor's association that stood by them and helped them along the way.

One person with passion is better than forty who are merely interested.

Thomas K. Connellan
BUSINESS SPEAKER AND WRITER

A few more of the countless success stories that could be written about these American freedom fighters are repeated here.

Si and Bob Fluor, Charlie Daniel, and Buck Mickel

The world's largest general construction firm—and a flagship ABC member—was founded over a century ago. When Si Fluor, an immigrant from Switzerland, established Fluor Brothers Construction in Oshkosh, Wisconsin, in the year 1880, he had $200 to capitalize it. In 1912, Fluor moved his family to Santa Ana, California, and changed the name of the firm to Fluor Construction Co. One of the little firm's first significant contracts was a project to build meter shops and an office building for Southern Counties Gas Co.

Twelve years thereafter, Si Fluor incorporated. At that time he employed one hundred people. California's oil boom soon led him out of the general contracting business and into major industrial construction. The firm's first gas plant project was for Sandoma Gas Co. in Santa Fe Springs, California. By the 1940s and 1950s Fluor Corporation had taken giant strides and expanded its projects and revenue both inside and outside the United States, while defeating AFL-CIO building trades attempts to force unionization on its workers.

John Robert "Bob" Fluor took over the company's reins in due course and subsequently was singled out by the editors of *Engineering News-Record* as one of the construction industry's world leaders:

> In his trademark bow tie, Fluor was as comfortable with the Shah of Iran as he was with the football coach of his beloved University of Southern California Trojans. But his relationships with world leaders helped boost Fluor Corp. into a global megabuilder, with a $3-billion Indonesian refinery and a $5-billion South African coal gasification project among his prize ventures. Few others would take on the logistical challenges. In South Africa, Fluor trained 20,000 workers as welders, pipefitters and electricians.[47]

During that same period, Daniel Construction Co. was founded by Charlie Daniel in North Carolina. This contractor worked almost exclusively on federal and state jobs. Over the years, while it expanded as an ABC member,

Daniel won many violent clashes with the AFL-CIO building trades over exclusive union membership. Some years after Buck Mickel (1925–1998) became the chief executive officer of Daniel International Company, he joined Bob Fluor as one of *Engineering News-Record's* selected world leaders of the construction industry. The magazine said:

> What friends and employees like most about Mickel are his "Buck Bullets," personal notes of congratulations and praise in his trademark red ink. Formidably dynamic as president of Daniel International Co., with a keen sense for spotting a trend, he took the Company from a regional player to a global construction giant. To support the growing open-shop movement, he developed one of the best craft-training programs in the U.S., and worked with South Carolina to develop a network of technical schools as the state moved away from its agricultural roots.[48]

Daniel International merged with Fluor Corporation, creating the world's number one engineering, procurement, construction, and maintenance services company. To accommodate the amazing growth of this ABC member, the century-old firm is based on a 105-acre site in Irvine, California. Today Fluor-Daniel's combined annual revenues are over $13.5 billion. It has thousands of employees in more than eighty regional offices around the world. And it still operates on a merit-shop basis. [49]

Carole Bionda: ABC's 46th CEO

Moving to the present, ABC's national chairperson for the year 2004 is a remarkable executive in the midst of an outstanding career, including her selection as the second woman to lead ABC.[50] Carole L. Bionda—in her professional life—is vice president and general counsel for Nova Group, Inc., a general engineering company based in Napa, California, and founded in 1976. The firm spans the globe, installs hydrant-fueling systems, constructs wharves and piers, and operates a state-of-the-art hydraulic dredging fleet to complement its waterfront operations. Nova employs about three hundred people both inside and outside the United States, with annual revenue of

Duty, honor, country: Those three hallowed words reverently dictate what you ought to be, what you can be, what you will be. They are your rallying point to build courage when courage seems to fail, to regain faith when there seems to be little cause for faith, to create hope when hope becomes forlorn.

General Douglas MacArthur's farewell address to West Point cadets

If an American wants to preserve his dignity and his equality as a human being, he must not bow his head to any dictatorial organization or government.

DWIGHT EISENHOWER
FROM ADDRESS
AS PRESIDENT OF
COLUMBIA
UNIVERSITY, 1949

approximately $75 million. The U.S. Department of Defense is one of its major clients. (See Nova photo at end of this chapter.)

Ms. Bionda received a law degree at Stanford University and a bachelor's degree from the University of California, Berkeley. She is also a member of the faculty at Sonoma State University, where she teaches construction law as well as personnel management and labor relations and onsite management.

Carole Bionda joined the Nova Group in 1986 and her extensive experience in the construction industry dates back to her labor relations clients as a lawyer. Once employed inside Nova, she soon became interested in ABC. At the chapter level, she began in 1987 as a member of the ABC Golden Gate Chapter government affairs advisory committee. She also acted as Chapter president (1995), spent seven years as a member of the ABC Golden Gate Chapter board of directors, as Chapter legislative committee chair and member, and as Chapter membership committee chair, as well as serving on the Chapter political action committee.

On the national level, Carole Bionda has been a member of the ABC National Board of Directors for eight years and served two terms as Region One vice chair, representing ABC members across the states of California, Colorado, Alaska, Arizona, Hawaii, Nevada, New Mexico, Oregon, Utah, and Washington as well as Guam. She also has acted as chair of ABC's national Minority/Women Task Force and Design-Build Task Force, and as a member of the Membership Diversity Committee, the Bylaws Committee, the Legislative Team, the Government Contracts Committee, the Labor Committee, the ABC Political Action Committee, and the Construction Legal Rights Foundation.

In answer to the question, "How did you first get involved with ABC?" she explains:

Si Fluor, founder in 1880 and chief executive officer.

For Nova as a company, it was in 1979. We had a project in Elk Hills, California, near Bakersfield. This was a federal government pipeline, oil patch project. When we bid on it, we didn't realize that the Boilermakers, the Plumbers and the Steamfitters Unions thought that this was their work and off limits to a merit shop contractor. There was violence, there were pickets, and the only group out there that helped us was ABC, with its dual gate [restrictive picketing] signs and belief that merit shop contractors had the right to perform that work.[51]

A model example of ABCers' commitment to "pro bono" professional, civic, and community service,[52] Carole is a past national president of Women Construction Owners and Executives, a member of Associated General Contractors, and the small business committee of the Society of American Military Engineers. She also is a past board member of the Family Support Network, a non-profit organization providing counseling to children and families at risk, as well as a volunteer in the Redwood Gospel Mission.

With this record of achievement, it is understandable that Carole Bionda has received many awards. To name just one, she was the USA Women Construction Owners & Executives "Executive of the Year" in 1992. Even more impressive, however, is her conservative philosophy in guiding ABC as its newest national leader. On February 26, 2004, she gave a stirring address at the 2004 annual ABC convention in Hawaii. Here are some pertinent excerpts from it:

> Thank you so much for the tremendous honor you have bestowed on me. ABC is an incredible group, with incredible people. We're special because the glue that holds us together isn't what we do, it's what we believe. I like to think of it as "super glue."
>
> For many of our members, especially those who joined in the early days of ABC, becoming part of this Association was much more than writing a dues check. It was drawing a bulls-eye on your back. Joining ABC wasn't a decision of convenience; it was a decision of conviction, of conscience, of bravery. Many of you know exactly what I'm talking about. Our own company, Nova Group, kept an old pick-up truck in a back lot as a reminder. The side panels were full of bullet holes.

And Carole Bionda concluded:

All we ask for is an even playing field. We respect the freedom of choice of all workers. This is not the unions' industry or the government's industry. It is our industry and ABC is the voice of merit shop construction.

KEN ADAMS
OF PACE ELECTRIC AND
ABC's '02 CHAIRMAN

PHOTO BY ABC

Carol Bionda, ABC's national president, in 2004.

I believe that leadership is a means to an end. It is a process by which a person influences others to accomplish a shared mission and directs the organization to become more cohesive. I see myself as a team leader, leading by example and fostering an environment in which people reach their highest potential as team members and individuals.

Carole Bionda
ABC Chair
[Nova Group]

By becoming an ABC member, you put your personal and professional lives on the line. By being an ABC member, your job sites have been destroyed, your family threatened, and the future of your business put in jeopardy. Why? Because you dared to believe that every American has a right to participate in this nation's free enterprise system.

If you look back at our history—how we got to where we are today—the answer is "a lot." Just seven contractors founded ABC. They were zealots for free enterprise. They were also considered fools by many of their peers. All were successful Baltimore businessmen back in 1950. Why would they ever risk their professional and personal success by taking on organized labor? Simple. It was the right thing to do.

While the world was turning left, ABC's founders were willing to take the chance to turn right. And because they did, *ABC changed an industry and a nation.* A few members with vision made a difference, even though, at the time, it may have seemed so small and the task so overwhelming. And that's why your involvement is so important to our continued success. I challenge each one of you. Always be willing to take those right turns…

You do make a difference!

Gary D. Roden: ABC's 47th CEO

It has been said that ABC's national chairman for the year 2005 is "engineered for success" in today's ever-changing electronic age. That is beyond debate, but it didn't happen overnight. The second generation ABCer graduated from Texas A&M University with a B.S. degree in mechanical engineering in 1983. That four-year stint was followed by extensive graduate work in business administration at the University of North Texas. Soon after, he took advantage of a unique opportunity to work for Trane Air Conditioning just as it was going into the controls and telecommunications businesses.

Roden picks up the story of his ABC career at that point:

With Trane, I had a great mentor, Jerry Gray, who was a local ABC chapter chairman and ran the local Trade office. I worked for him for twelve years. Jerry inspired me to get involved in ABC…

Ben Houston of T.D. Industries, ABC's 1998 national chairman, also has been an important mentor…And seeing last year's chair Carole Bionda at work has been terrific. It has been great to see her enthusiasm and passion.

Roden's career with ABC, like all its national stars, began with a leadership role in a local (North Texas) chapter, from 1990 to 2001. His national ABC activities followed, including Region 3 vice chair; (representing the states of Texas, Oklahoma, Arkansas, and Louisiana); a Trimmer Education Foundation trustee; a Governance Task Force member, 2002-2003; and an ABC executive committee member from 2002 to 2005.

Gary also serves many local, civic, community, charitable, and industrial organizations while still finding time to be actively involved in his church, his school district, and as a coach of four sports.

In the merit shop construction world today, Roden has risen to become the executive vice president and chief operating officer of AGUIRREcorporation, a fifty-five-person team including architects, engineers of many types, program managers, and general contracting professionals. With annual revenue of more than $25 million, his Dallas-based corporation specializes in the development, design, and management of programs, construction, and facilities. He is proud of his firm's employees who "work in a very open environment." Operational, financial, and sales information is shared throughout the staff and "merit is the key to advancement," (See color photo of an AGUIRRE-designed project at the end of this book.)

Gary Roden's vision for ABC in 2005 includes "leveraging the outstanding free enterprise gains that the organization has made in the past." In addition, he intends to "increase the membership and expand the management education offerings being made to members." And he hopes to "utilize the presence of ABC across the nation to better communicate with facility owners regarding the inherent value of merit shop construction." Finally, he believes that the construction industry must stay involved in the political process through ABC "to ensure that frivolous lawsuits, restrictive government regulations, and illegal workplace activities are brought to an end, and that the merit shop philosophy will continue to flourish in the years ahead."

The new generation in our industry wants more technology and more online education. Today more than four out of five construction workers choose the merit shop way. We must continue to protect their hard-won freedom by advancing the merit shop philosophy in Washington, D.C., and in the state and local legislatures.

HENRY KELLY
ABC's 43RD CHAIRMAN
(AUSTIN INDUSTRIAL, INC.)

Mullan, Reagan, and Trimmer "Say It All"

At ABC's golden anniversary celebration during the year 2000 in Baltimore, Maryland, Charles Mullan was honored as a founder and senior among ABC's nine "Leaders of the 20th Century who significantly influenced and strengthened the merit shop construction industry." Charlie used the historic occasion to summarize his great pride in—and amazement at—ABC's phenomenal success. And he recalled some inspiring words spoken by Ronald Reagan, the keynote speaker at ABC's silver birthday party held in Houston, Texas, in 1975:

> In this year of ABC's 25th anniversary, there are also many celebrations for our precious Republic. The United States of America is about to become 200 years old and we are reminded of the courage of our Founding Fathers. They were eager to establish a Republic, although some leaders of that time questioned whether it could long endure.
>
> Today we honor the determination and bravery of your own Founders, who laid the base for the merit shop. It was a product of the times, an expression of economic determinants and the rights of individuals in the true American tradition. It has surely proven its endurance.
>
> We also know that ABC's struggle for workplace freedom is being challenged by those who favor constraints and compulsion. But the Spirit of 1776 remains a beacon in the struggle toward liberty, whose price is eternal vigilance.[53]

REPRINTED WITH PERMISSION OF *CONSTRUCTION EXECUTIVE*; PHOTO BY JOHN W. DAVIS/VISUAL DESIGN

Gary Rodin, 2005 National Chairman of ABC

This history ends where it began, with the wise words from John Trimmer—revered senior staff executive known as "Mr. ABC"—who served his beloved Association valiantly from 1952 until his death in 2002.[54] He worked beside more of ABC's national pacesetters than any other person and he was an honored attendee at ABC's silver and golden anniversary jubilees in 1975 and 2000. On many occasions John described the American construction industry's dramatic transformation from union domination and terrorism to free market capitalism. His valuable treatise called *ABC—Profile of a Philosophy* condensed a half-century history of blood, sweat, and tears into these unforgettable words:

In the beginning, most contractors considered each other as natural enemies. Tensions between generals, subs and trade unions were inherent in the nature of the business. Eventually, however, it was the mutuality in defending the right to work together voluntarily and competitively—but united—that became the strength of ABC. As we grew, the mistrust among rival contractors diminished through membership in a singular organization which continues to create services and programs for the betterment of the entire construction industry.

Those of us who pioneered to make the merit shop a reality were inspired by the truly American idea of free enterprise: the award of building and construction projects on the basis of merit to the lowest qualified bidders, working voluntarily in harmony, regardless of nonunion or union affiliation.

The remarkable pattern of growth that the merit shop has established promises to continue. Many in the industry never realized its extent until well after it had captured the smaller commercial and industrial markets and began moving in on larger and larger industrial work.

This all happened because the merit shop is ideally suited to accommodate those types of changes that have altered the face of the entire industry and parts of the economy and society as well. This unique movement also has offered its workers more opportunities to practice non-discriminatorily a variety of trades and skills while simultaneously increasing the productivity of merit shop firms.

Our member contractors who have given their time and money for this cause over the years, exercising wit and showing great courage in many dangerous situations, are

Charlie Mullan, right, Association founding father, receives his "Leader of the Century" award from ABC Chairman Tom Musser during ABC's 50th anniversary national convention in 2000.

in the thousands—*and they revolutionized the way this great nation builds.* Like the signers of the Declaration of Independence, ABCers pledged their lives, their fortunes and their sacred honor to the cause of freedom. As one of these patriarchs told me: "We can't choose our martyrs but we surely provided the opportunity for our heroes."

The curtain has closed on ABC's momentous twentieth century performance—against all the odds. Yesterday is the prologue to tomorrow and the Merit Shop Crusade must continue to protect America's Cycle of Liberty in a free workplace by prospering and expanding in the twenty-first century.

Let us salute all of ABC's heroes—past, present, and future!

THE END

ENDNOTES

Prologue

1. *Webster's New World Dictionary of the American Language* (New York: Simon & Schuster, 1980).

2. A. J. Thieblot, "The Fall and Future of Unionism in Construction," *Journal of Labor Research* (Spring 2001): 288; see also A. J. Thieblot, "Technology and Labor Relations in the Construction Industry," *Journal of Labor Research* (Fall 2002): 559; Amy Ingram, "Construction Employment," *Construction Executive* (January 2003): 28–29.

3. *Engineering News-Record, Sourcebook,* (September 29, 2002): 4.

4. *Construction Executive* (June 2004): 22.

5. "Career Guide to [Construction] Industries," *U.S. Department of Labor, Bureau of Labor Statistics* (August 2002).

6. *Construction Executive* (June 2004): 22.

7. "What's Ahead For 2004?" *Special Kiplinger Letter* (January 2004): 19.

8. *Construction Executive* (February 2003): 32.

9. *Construction Executive* (January 2003): 32 and (April 2003): 9; "Unions Reach Everywhere for Members as Ranks Decline," *Baltimore Sun* (January 25, 2004); compare *Bureau of National Affairs Construction Labor Report* (January 24, 2001): 1440; Herbert R. Northrup and Linda Alario, "Construction Union Membership Decline," *Government Union Review* (2000): 3–8; A. J. Thieblot, "The Fall and Future of Unionism in Construction," *Journal of Labor Research* (Spring 2001): 287; "Career Guide to [Construction] Industries," *U.S. Department of Labor, Bureau of Statistics* (August 2, 2002); A. J. Thieblot, "Technology and Labor Relations in the Construction Industry," *Journal of Labor Research* (Fall 2002): 569; "Unions," *Engineering News-Record* (March 17, 2003): 18.

10. See Robert Gasperow as cited in *Cockshaw's Construction Labor News and Opinion* (October 2004).

11. *Engineering News-Record* (May 20, 2002): 63–64.

12. F. C. Duke Zeller, *Devil's Pact: Inside the World of the Teamsters* (Secaucus: Birch Lane Press, 1996); Carl Horowitz, "Union Corruption: Why It Happens, How to Combat It," *National Institute for Labor Relations Research*, (1999): 35–64; David Kendrick, "Violence: Organized Labor's Unique Privilege," *National Institute for Labor Relations Research* (1996): 5–6; A. Samuel Cook, "Labor Union Foxes Guarding Police and Fire Hen Houses," *Public Service Research Council* and *Maryland Business for Responsive Government* (1998): 4–6.

Chapter 1

1. Charles Stevenson, "The Tyranny of Terrorism in the Building Trades," *Reader's Digest* (June 1973): 89–90; *Miami News* (November 22, 1972).

2. John Trimmer, *ABC: Profile of a Philosophy* (hereafter cited as *"John Trimmer's ABC"*).

3. Stevenson, "The Tyranny of Terrorism," 81; Thieblot and Haggard, *Union Violence* (Philadelphia: University of Pennsylvania, 1983), 154–155, and 2nd edition with author Herbert Northrup added, *Labor Relations Series,* No. 25 (1999).

4. Florence Calvert Thorne, *Samuel Gompers: American Statesman* (New York: Philosophical Library, 1957), 36–40, 50, 112.

5. Ibid, 60–61.

6. Ibid.

7. Philip Taft, *Corruption and Racketeering in the Labor Movement* (Ithaca, Cornell University, 1970); Carl Horowitz, "Union Corruption," *National Institute for Labor Relations Research* (1999): 5.

8. Harold Seidman, *Labor Czars: A History of Labor Racketeering* (New York: Liveright Publishing, 1938), 147.

9. John Hutchinson, *The Imperfect Union: A History of Corruption in American Trade Unions* (New York: E.P. Dutton & Company, 1970), 27; Lester Velie, *Labor U.S.A. Today* (New York: Harper & Row, 1959), 171–192.

Chapter 2

1. See graphic, Part III, Ch. 51.

Chapter 4

1. According to ABC's corporate minutes, the following ABCers attended: Henry Albert, Jr., William Anthon, Leonard Beam, Daly Byrnes, Philip Cloyes, Ed. P. Colwill, P. Costanza, Ectar Crocetti, Louis Crocetti, John R. Crooker, Theo. H. Diener, Jos. G. DiPaola, Dominic Drecchio, Joseph Falatico, Charles H. Feihe, George B. Gwynn, William H. Holland, Raymond Holland, John Hurska, G. I. Kendrick, Irvin Keyser, Catherine K. Kirby, Fabian Kolker, M. Budd Kolker, Charles A. Knott, John L. Knott, Martin Knott, John Larichiuta, Jack Leitess, F. W. Massey, Arthur J. Miller, John H. Miller, Charles G. Mills, Charles Mullan, Thomas Mullan, Lewis L. Notaro, Jos. G. Phillips, George W. Pohlman, Ira Rosenzwog, N. Stanley Rosenzwog, H. A. Sands, P. E. Schumann, Harold M. Shade, Donald W. Sheeler, E. Ver-

non Stiegler, Joseph Torre, J. W. Wagner, O. R. Wright, Vincent Zaccaria, and Herbert R. O'Conor, Jr., Counsel.

2. *John Trimmer's ABC*, 16.

Chapter 5

1. See Chapter 16 for a detailed discussion of this antiquated Davis-Bacon Act prevailing wage law.

2. *John Trimmer's ABC*.

3. John Funk, chairman, and *Commission on Prevailing Wages v. Mullan Contracting Company* et al., 197 Maryland 192, 194, 202 (1951).

4. On May 14, 1969, over the vigorous protest of ABC, Governor Marvin Mandel (D-MD) signed the state's current prevailing wage law ("Little Davis-Bacon Act") covering public construction projects. See Maryland Ann. Code, "Contracts for Public Works," Art. 100, § 96 et seq. Still later on, the Maryland Court of Special Appeals noted (but ignored the fact) that "significant efforts have been made in Congress to repeal the Davis-Bacon Act [the Maryland statute's federal counterpart] on the grounds that it is inflationary, cumbersome, and has outlived its original purpose." *Barnes v. Commissioner of Labor and Industry*, 45 Maryland App. 396, 404, fn. 8 (1980), cert. denied, 288 Maryland 73 (1980), aff'd 290 Maryland 9 (1981). The AFL-CIO and its building trades union lobby have blocked all subsequent efforts by ABC to convince the leftist Maryland legislature to repeal this farcical statute.

Chapter 6

1. A bound copy of the ABC board of directors' corporate minutes for the years 1950 to 1958 (including the above-listed expenses) is on file at ABC's national office.

2. *John Trimmer's ABC*.

3. See Chapter 12.

4. *Contractor* (December 1955): 23.

5. *John Trimmer's ABC*.

6. "ABC Salutes John Trimmer," *ABC Today* (October 2002): 8.

7. *Engineering News-Record* (September 9, 2003): 72.

8. *John Trimmer's ABC*.

9. Ibid.

10. Liber 7143, Folio 488, Charter Records of Maryland State Tax Committee, Baltimore, Maryland.

11. "ABC Salutes John Trimmer," *ABC Today* (October 2002).

12. Ibid.

13. Ibid.

Chapter 7

1. *Wagon Drivers Union of Chicago, Local 753 v. Meadowmoor Dairies, Inc.*, 312 U.S. 287, 293 (1941); *Senn v. Tile Layers Protective Union*, 301 U.S. 468 (1937).

2. See *Developing Labor Law* (Washington, D.C.: American Bar Association and Bureau of National Affairs, Vol. II, 2001), 1621. A union "loophole" closed in 1959 by the amendatory Landrum-Griffin Act provides in pertinent part, that a union may not "threaten, coerce or restrain any person...where...an object thereof is...forcing or requiring any person...to cease doing business with any other person...."

3. See *Capiletti Brothers, Inc. v. Local 487, International Union of Operating Engineers*, 5th Cir. CA, 514 F.2d 1239 (1975).

4. *Pierce v. Stablemen's Union*, 156 Cal. 70, 103 Pac. 324 (1909).

5. *Atchison, Topeka & Santa Fe Ry. Company v. Gee*, 139 Fed. 582, 584-585 (S.D. Iowa, 1905).

6. Jack London, *War of the Classes* (New York: McMillan Company, 1903): http://sunsite.berkeley.edu/London/Writings/WarOfTheClasses/scab.html.

7. *Old Dominion Branch No. 496 v. National Association of Letter Carriers*, 418 U.S. 264, 268 (1974); *Associated Grocers of New England v. NLRB*, 562 F.2d 1333, 1335 (1st Cir., 1997).

8. *Webster's New World Dictionary* (2nd Edition, Simon & Schuster).

9. H.H. Walker Lewis, Esq., U.S. District Court of Maryland (Maryland Bar Association and Paul Harrod Company, Baltimore, Maryland, 1977) 76.

10. See *Merit Shop Contractor* (February 1976): 11.

11. *Piezonki d/b/a Stover Steel Service v. NLRB*, 219 F.2d 879, 880-881 (4th Cir. 1955).

12. Ibid., 880.

13. Ibid., 883.

14. Ibid., 882–883.

15. Ibid., 883; see also *Sailors' Union of the Pacific* (Moore Dry Dock Company), 92 NRLB 547, 549 (1950) and its progeny.

16. Ibid, see also *New Orleans Building. & Construction Trades Council* (Markwell and Hartz), 155 NLRB 319 (1965), enf'd 387 F.2d 76 (5th Cir., 1967), cert. den. 391 U.S. 914 (1968) on the use of "reserved gates."

17. *Abreen Corp. v. Laborers' International Union*, 709 F.2d 748, 755 (1st Cir., 1983), cert. den. (1984). In this decision, the court awarded Abreen Corporation $120,000 in damages for the Laborers' illegal secondary boycott activity. Philip Abrams, a general contractor and CEO of Abreen, served as national president of ABC in 1975. See Chapter 46.

18. *NLRB v. Denver* Building & Constr. Trades Council, 341 U.S. 675, 689–692 (1951).

19. *John Trimmer's ABC*.

20. Ibid.

Chapter 8

1. The first issue of *Engineering News-Record* was published on April 5, 1917. In an editorial, James McGraw expressed the following goal for his journal: "In sum, the paper must be above personalities, above editors and publishers—it must be an institution. Its principles must be so grounded in truth that they cannot be changed, its policies so well crys-

tallized that they appear unconsciously in every issue"... On January 1st, 1987 the acronym "ENR" was adopted as the title of the magazine. Keeping up with global technological advances, ENR now has a home on the World Wide Web. At http://www.enr.com, the ENR staff makes available information about the current issue and many other items of interest to subscribers. On the Internet site, this editorial mission of the magazine is outlined: "ENR, a Division of McGraw-Hill Publishing Company, provides the business and technical news needed by anyone who makes a living in or from the construction industry... We give readers the weekly news and analysis they need to make decisions in their work, covering all sectors of the industry from buildings to highways to hazardous waste cleanups. We highlight significant events worldwide. Good ideas don't stop at political boundaries nor does the business of construction... We serve about 75,000 subscribers with an additional pass-along readership of 350,000. Subscribers include contractors, engineers, architects, owners, city, state and federal government officials, producers, suppliers, colleges and libraries. Readers cross the spectrum of job classifications from chief executives to equipment operators and represent all sectors of the construction industry."

2. *John Trimmer's ABC.*

3. Ibid.

4. *Bricklayers, Masons and Plasterers International Union of America, AFL-CIO, et al. v. Selby-Battersby & Company and Associated Builders and Contractors of Maryland,* 117 NLRB 366 (1957).

5. Ibid.

6. *Selby-Battersby & Company and ABC of Maryland v. NLRB and Baltimore Building Trades Council,* 259 F.2d 151, 154, 157 (4th Cir. 1958), cert. denied 359 U.S. 952 (March 30, 1959).

7. Ibid.

8. *John Trimmer's ABC.*

Chapter 9

1. Although ignored by local courts and the National Labor Relations Board, a valid legal argument can be made that the state of Maryland does have a long-existing public policy against compulsory unionism. For example, in a concurring opinion in *AFL v. American Sash and Door Company* 335 U.S. 538, 554 (1949), which upheld the constitutionality of Arizona's right to work law, Supreme Court Justice Felix Frankfurter observed that "several states in addition to those at bar now have such laws." One of the states the Justice named was Maryland. See also Stanley Mazaroff, *Maryland Employment Law* (Charlottesville: Michie Company, 1990), 73–74; A. Samuel Cook, "The Case for a Maryland Right-to-Work Law," *Maryland Business for Responsive Government* (1996): 21–24.

2. The recognized right to work states, with date of enactment, are as follows: Alabama (1953); Arizona (1946); Arkansas (1944); Florida (1944); Georgia (1947); Idaho

(1985); Iowa (1947); Kansas (1958); Louisiana (1976); Mississippi (1954); Nebraska (1946); Nevada (1951); North Carolina (1947); North Dakota (1948); Oklahoma (2001); South Carolina (1954); South Dakota (1946); Tennessee (1947); Texas (1947); Utah (1955); Virginia (1947); and Wyoming (1963).

3. 111 U.S. 746, 762 (1884).

4. 239 U.S. 33, 41 (1915).

5. 233 U.S. 63, 636 (1914).

6. 335 U.S. 525, 530 (1949).

7. 347 U.S. 442, 472 (1954).

8. *See Railway Employees' Department v. Hanson*, 351 U.S. 225, 238 (1956). The Supreme Court ruled that a union shop agreement compelling "financial support of the collective bargaining agency by all who receive the benefits of its work is within the power of Congress under the Commerce Clause and does not violate either the First or Fifth Amendments." See also *Abood v. Detroit Board of Education*, 431 U.S. 209, 222 (1977); *Buckley v. Television & Radio Artists*, 496 F.2d 305 (2d Cir.), cert. denied 419 U.S. 1093 (1974).

9. Florence Calvert Thorne, *Samuel Gompers, American Statesman* (New York: Philosophical Library, 1957), 24, 58–62.

10. See George Meany's "Foreword" to *Seventy Years of Life and Labor* by Samuel Gompers (New York: E. P. Dutton, 1957).

11. See *National Right to Work Newsletter* (March 2003): 8.

12. *Local 514, Transport Workers Union of America v. Keating*, 2003 OK 110 (2003). Eastern Oklahoma Building Trades Council v. Pitts, Oklahoma, No. 99792, December 26, 2003.

13. See *ABC Today* (October 2001): 5.

14. *National Right to Work Newsletter* (November–December 2002): 5.

15. Ibid., "Big Labor Furious at Defiant Sooner Employees," (November–December, 2001): 6.

16. *National Right to Work Committee Newsletter* (April 2004): 3.

17. "Report of the Task Force on State Economic Development," *Johns Hopkins University Center for Metropolitan Planning & Research* (March 1978): 14–15.

18. "Jobs Up in Right to Work States," *National Institute for Labor Rel. Research*, (1995); see also graph statistics provided by National Right to Work Committee cited in this chapter.

19. Kathy Chen, "Wooing Companies," *Wall Street Journal* (July 10, 2002).

20. Robert Hunter, "Government Union Review," *Public Service Research Foundation*, Volume 20, Number 3 (September 2002): 27–30.

21. *John Trimmer's ABC.*

22. *Merit Shop Contractor* (March 1976): 10–13.

23. 335 U.S. 538, 551–552 (1949).

24. George Schatzki, "Majority Rule, Exclusive Representation and the Interest of Individual Workers," *University of Pennsylvania Law Review*, Volume 123:897 (1975); Rev-

erend Edward Keller, *The Case for Right to Work Laws, a Defense of Voluntary Unionism* (University of Notre Dame and Heritage Foundation, 1956), 42.

25. *John Trimmer's ABC.*

26. See "Right to Work Bill Defeat Highlights Shameful Situation in Annapolis," *ABC Contractor* (April 1955): 6.

27. Ibid.

28. See Michelle Amber (Bureau of National Affairs, AFL-CIO Conference Report, March 5, 2003), 26; *National Right to Work Newsletter* (March 2003): 8.

39. Stan Greir, "Secret Ballot Elections," *National Institute for Labor Rel. Research*, (October 2003): 9.

30. See "Union Security," Chapter 26, Volume II, 4th Edition, *Bureau of National Affairs* (2002); Jay Shafritz, *Dictionary of Labor Relations* (Oak Park, IL: Moore Publishing Company), 348.

Chapter 10

1. See Chapter 8.

2. See Chapter 7.

3. Compare *Overnight Transportation Company*, 130 NLRB 1007 (1961), enf'd 332 F.2d 693 (5th Cir. 1964), cert. denied nom. 379 U.S. 913 (1964).

4. *John Trimmer's ABC.*

5. Terms of the "open shop project performance clause" include language such as this: "Subcontractor shall at all times supply a sufficient number of skilled workers to perform the work covered by this contract with promptness and diligence. Subcontractor shall not be entitled to any allowances or extensions of time for delays caused by labor disputes. Should any workers performing work covered by this contract engage in a strike or other work stoppage or cease to work due to picketing or a labor dispute of any kind, Contractor may, at its option and without prejudice to any other remedies it may have, after forty-eight (48) hours written notice to Subcontractor, provide any such labor on its own and deduct the cost thereof from any monies then due or thereafter to become due Subcontractor. Further, Contractor may at its option, without prejudice to any other remedies it may have, terminate the employment of Subcontractor for the work under this contract, and shall have the right to enter upon the premises and take possession for the purpose of completing the work hereunder with all Subcontractor's materials, tools and equipment thereon and to finish the work either with Contractor's own employees or other Subcontractors. Subcontractor shall not be entitled to any further payments under this contract but shall remain liable for any damages which Contractor incurs as a result of any such stoppage of work, and Contractor shall have a lien on all of Subcontractor's materials, equipment, tools and other property at the premises to secure the payment of any unpaid balance due Contractor."

Chapter 11

1. *Contractor* (October 1976): 23.

2. See "Labor and Employment Law," Sec. 11-403 et seq., Annotated Code of Maryland.

3. See Garth Mangum, *MDTA: Foundation of Federal Manpower Policy* (Baltimore: Johns Hopkins University Press, 1968), 45–46, in which he noted that BAT's leadership, staff, and policies have all emanated from organized labor, especially from the construction trade unions.

4. *John Trimmer's ABC.*

5. Ibid.

6. Ibid., 3; *Contractor* (October 1976): 23.

7. *Contractor* (1971).

8. Ibid., 19.

9. *Clayton Daugherty et al v. U.S.A. and Secretary of Labor Brennan*, 1974 WL 215 (S.D. Texas) 86 LRRM (BNA) 3075.

10. *Associated Builders and Contractors v. Alexis Herman, Sec'y of Labor*, 166 F.3d 1248, 1254-1256 (CA DC, 1999). ABC was represented in this case by Maurice Baskin, a partner in my firm, Venable, Baetjer and Howard.

11. OAH Case No. 95-DEED-MATC-05-043 (November 19, 1996). ABC was represented in this case by my law partner, Todd Horn, of Venable, Baetjer and Howard.

12. Bureau of National Affairs, *Construction Labor Report* (December 5, 2001): 1140–1141.

13. "Building Trades Call For DOL Probe," Bureau of National Affairs, *Construction Labor Report* (October 19, 2003): 1144–1145.

14. Ibid., an historical discussion of "training and development in the construction industry"; see also Herbert R. Northrup, *Open Shop Construction Revisited* (Wharton School, University of Pennsylvania, 1984), 409–465.

15. Ibid.

Chapter 12

1. Bureau of National Affairs, *Daily Labor Report* (February 28, 2003): AA-1.

2. "The AFL-CIO," Bureau of National Affairs, *Construction Labor Report* (December 12, 2001): 1164. In the author's opinion, the Bureau of National Affairs is one of the foremost publishers of electronic news, analysis, and reference products. It provides intensive, impartial coverage of legal and regulatory developments for professionals in business and government, including labor relations and employment law, and is cited frequently in this book.

3. See Chapter 9.

4. Ibid.

5. *Teamsters Local 357 (Los Angeles-Seattle Motor Express) v. NLRB*, 365 U.S. 667 (1961); see also my former law partner, N. Peter Lareau, "A Review of Bargaining Relationships in the Construction Industry," *Bender's Labor Bulletin* (September 2003): 528–534.

6. *John Trimmer's ABC.*

7. *Contractor* (June 1973): 16.

8. Ibid.

9. "The Hiring Hall in the Construction Industry" *Business Roundtable* (1974): 17.

10. Ibid.

11. Ibid.

12. The National Labor Relations Board recently ruled that a local trade union "breached its duty of fair representation by failing to comply with contractual rules for operating an exclusive hiring hall" in Portland, Oregon. International Brotherhood of Electrical Workers, Local 48, 342 NLRB No. 10 (June 28, 2004).

13. Compare A. J. Thieblot, "Technology and Labor Relations," *Journal of Labor Research* Vol. 23, No. 4 (Fall 2002).

14. Sal Palmeter, "Open Shop Versus Closed Shop Construction," *Merit Shop Contractor* (July 1978): 21, 23.

15. *Developing Labor Law* (American Bar Association, Bureau of National Affairs, Washington D.C., Vol. II, 4th Edition, 2001): 1848.

16. *Contractor* (April 1972): 16–17; see also A. J. Thieblot, "Technology and Labor Relations," 287.

17. *John Trimmer's ABC.*

18. Herbert R. Northrup, *Open Shop Construction Revisited* (Wharton School, University of Pennsylvania, 1984): 407.

19. Ibid.

20. *Compare American Newspaper Publishers Association v. NLRB*, 345 U.S. 100 (1953).

21. *Florida Power & Light Company v. International Brotherhood of Electrical Workers*, 417 U.S. 790, 808–809 (1974).

22. "Exclusive Jurisdiction in Construction," Report C-1, Construction Industry Cost Effectiveness Project, *Business Roundtable* (1982): 1.

23. "Painters Keep Wall Work but Blast 'Raid' Tactics," *Engineering News-Record* (July 26, 2004): 12.

24. *Merit Shop Contractor* (November 1975): 14.

25. *Cockshaw's Construction Labor News* (June 1993): 5.

26. *John Trimmer's ABC.*

27. See Chapters 1 and 9.

28. 335 U.S. 538, 551–552 (1949) and quoted in Chapter 9.

29. A. J. Thieblot, "The Fall and Future of Unionism in Construction," *Journal of Labor Research* (Spring 2001): 294.

30. "Subjourneymen in Union Construction" Construction Industry Cost Effectiveness Project, Report D-1, *Business Roundtable* (1982): 8. See also Herbert R. Northrup, *Open Shop Construction Revisited,* 396 and "The Helper Controversy in the Construction Industry," *Journal of Research,* Wharton School, University of Pennsylvania (Fall 1992): 427; Marc Linder, *Wars of Attrition: Vietnam, the Business Roundtable, and the Decline of Construction Unions* (Fanpihua Press, 1999).

31. "Temp Agencies Have Union Eye," *Engineering News-Record* (April 24, 2000): 12; see also *Engineering News-Record* (September 11, 2000): 14.

32. Nick Phillips, "The Labor Leasing Paradigm," *Construction Executive* (November 2003): 62.

33. Ibid.

34. Jay Bowman in *Construction Executive* (June 2004): 24.

35. *Merit Shop Contractor* (October 1980): 27.

36. "Training Manpower Today for Tomorrow's Use," *Merit Shop Contractor* (September 1980): 3, 24–30.

37. *John Trimmer's Merit Shop.*

38. *Builder & Contractor* (June 1982): 8–9.

39. For an historical discussion of ABC's "Wheels of Learning" program, see Herbert A. Northrup, *Open Shop Construction Revisited*, 427–430.

40. *ABC Today* (January 1998): 11.

41. *Engineering News-Record* (August 20, 2001): 11.

42. "Craft Training: NCCER Raising the Bar," *ABC Contractor* (September 1988): 16; "Owner Demands Craft Training," *Engineering News-Record* (November 23, 1998): 42.

43. *Cockshaw's Construction Labor News* (September 2001): 3.

44. *ABC Today* (January 1998): 11.

45. *Engineering News-Record* (October 21, 2002): 92.

46. Amy Ingram, "ABC's Craft Olympics," *ABC Today* (January 2002): 10.

47. *John Trimmer's ABC.*

48. "Government Limitations on Training Innovation," Business Roundtable Construction Industry Cost Effectiveness Project, Report D-2 (1982): 6.

49. "Work Force Development," *Engineering News-Record* (June 14, 2004): 29–30.

50. See also "Flag House Gets Touch of Glass," *Baltimore Sun* (June 13, 2003): 3B

51. *Construction Executive* (January 2003): 46.

52. See Graphic in Chapter 51; for an overview of "The Fall and Future of Unionism in Construction," see also treatise by A. J. Thieblot, *Journal of Labor Research* (Spring 2001): 287–306.

Chapter 13

1. See *Engineering News-Record* (March 27, 1975): 42 and (October 27, 1977): 24, for facts throughout this chapter.

2. *ABC Contractor* (February 1973): 5.

Chapter 14

1. See Amy Ingram, "Diversity—The Answer to Labor Force Shortages," *ABC Today* (April 1999); "Times Are Changing," *ABC Today* (July 1997).

2. *Engineering News-Record* (March 27, 1975): 42 and (October 30, 2000): 10.

3. *Construction Executive* (November 2003): 8.

4. See A. J. Thieblot, "The Fall and Future of Unionism in Construction," 202; Kirk Pickerel, "Workforce Development: A Top Priority," *Construction Executive* (March 2003): 4.

5. *Contractor* (October 1973): 11–13.

6. "View from the Bottom," *Merit Shop Contractor* (December 1978): 17.

7. Ibid.

8. "Women Breaking Workplace Barriers," *Baltimore Sun* (May 13, 2002).

9. "The Sky is the Limit," *Builder & Contractor* (February 1986): 8–12.

10. *John Trimmer's ABC.*

11. See Lisa Nardone, editor, *ABC Today* (September 2000): 14; *Building & Construction* (February 1986): 10–12.

12. Ibid.

13. Ibid.

14. Ibid.

15. *Engineering News-Record* (March 5, 2001): 12.

16. Ibid.

17. Bureau of National Affairs, *Construction Labor Report* (March 21, 2001): 74.

18. See Melanie Hinkle, "A Monumental Success," *ABC Today* (January 2000): 8–9.

19. The remainder of this Chapter 15 involving women in construction is summarized from a feature article by Jennifer Spillane that appeared in the July 2004 issue of *Construction Executive*.

20. See Charles Youric, "In Defense of Lieutenant Bush," *Washington Times* (October 11, 2004).

21. *Kiplinger Newsletter* (2002); *Construction Executive* (January 2003).

22. In a press interview Thurgood Marshall, the first member of his race to serve on the U.S. Supreme Court, told the *Baltimore Sun* that he never became accustomed to the word "black," preferring to use the word "Negro" long after it had been abandoned. Eventually, he said, he decided to use "Afro-American" in his court opinions because it has a long history in the culture of his race. See Lyle Denniston, "Thurgood Marshall Drops 'Negro' for 'Afro-American,'" *Baltimore Sun* (October 17, 1989). Today, the preferred designation is "African-American" or "black."

23. *Contractor* (June 1968): 6.

24. Ibid.

25. *Contractor* (May 1968): 29.

26. Ibid., (January 1974): 13.

27. Ibid., (December 1973): 20–21.

28. Ibid.

29. See *ABC Today* (1995).

30. *ABC Contractor* (1999).

31. Ibid.

32. See Chapter 41 on Mike Callas.

33. Melanie Hinkle, "ABC Chapters Reach Out To Hispanic Workforce," *ABC Today* (January 2002): 5.

34. *ABC Today* (June 1995): 7.

35. *Linda Eldrige v. Carpenters Local 46*, Northern California Counties Joint Apprenticeship and Training Committee, 94 F.3d 1366, 1372 (9th Cir. 1996).

36. *Contractor* (July 1971): 20.

37. Ibid., (January 1974): 12.

38. *Merit Shop Contractor* (February 1978): 6.

39. *Alexander v. Local 496, Laborers' International Union of North America*, 177 F.3d 394, 405, 410 (6th Cir., 1999).

40. Bureau of National Affairs, *Construction Labor Report* (July 28, 1999): 567.

41. See Bureau of National Affairs, *Construction Labor Report*. (August 2, 2000): 632.

42. *John Trimmer's ABC*.

43. *ABC Today* (July 2000).

Chapter 15

1. Over the past several years, the trend among employer associations has been to designate the top staff person "president and chief executive officer" and the chief elected officer "chairman of the board." The primary reason given by ABC for this change in title effective January 1, 2001, was that the "chairman" or "chairperson"—an active contractor elected by the board of directors—donates his or her services for one or two years and sets policies and goals (with approval of the board of directors). The paid senior professional appointed by the board of directors is the "president and chief executive officer" who reports to the chairman and implements these policies and administers the daily operations of the Association. To avoid confusion, the old titles will be used herein until the story line reaches January 1, 2001, the date on which the titles officially changed.

2. *Construction Executive* (April 2003): 4.

3. *ABC Today* (November 1997): 1.

4. Rachel Cohen, "Disaster Remediation," *ABC Today* (March 1999).

5. Lisa Nardone, "Oklahoma Disaster," *ABC Today* (June 1, 1995): 10.

6. See Melanie Hinkel, "ABC Members Help America Rebuild," *ABC Today* (August 2001); Amy Ingram and Pam Hunter, "Special One-Year Anniversary Memorial Edition," *ABC Today* (September 2002).

7. Ibid.

8. Ibid.

9. A new job title. See second endnote at beginning of this chapter.

Chapter 16

1. See *Building Trades Department v. Raymond Donovan, Secretary of Labor*, 712 F.2d 611, 613 (DC Cir., 1983), cert. denied, 464 U.S. 1069 (January 17, 1984).

2. See Richard Vedder and Lowell Galloway, "Cracked Foundation, Repealing the Davis-Bacon Act," Center for the Study of American Business Policy Brief 159 (October 1995); Armand J. Thieblot, Jr., "Prevailing Wage Legislation," Wharton School Industrial Research Unit, Labor Relations Series No. 27 (1986): 29–30.

3. "Outrageous Government Programs," *Human Events* (March 10, 2003): 4.

4. Frank Gamrat, "Prevailing Wages: Costly to Taxpayers," *Government Union Review* Vol. 20, No. 2 (2001): 1–17.

5. Ibid., two footnotes directly above by Frank Gamrat and *Human Events*.

6. See Lowell Galloway and Richard Vedder, "Prevailing Wages," *Government Union Review*, Vol. 20, No. 3 (September 2002): 3.

7. See Prologue endnote 10.

8. See *Contractor* (July 1964): 5.

9. Ibid., *Building. Trades Department v. Donovan*, 616.

10. For a more detailed exposure of this government maladministration of prevailing wage laws, see Armand J. Thieblot, Jr., "Prevailing Wage Legislation" and his "New Evaluation of Impacts of Prevailing Wage Law Repeal"; see also Herbert R. Northrup, "The Helper Controversy in the Construction Industry," *Journal of Labor Research*, Vol. XIII, No. 4 (Fall 1992): 421–435.

11. Ibid.

12. Ibid., 616, in which an amicus curiae brief was filed on behalf of ABC by the author's law firm. See also Thieblot on Prevailing Wage Legislation: 84–87.

13. *Contractor* (October 1964): 19 and (February 1965): 16.

14. Ibid.

15. *Contractor* (January 1968): 13.

16. See Prologue and graphic in Chapter 51.

17. Ibid., Thieblot on Prevailing Wage Legislation, 58–62.

18. See Davis-Bacon Legislation: Hearing before Subcommittee on Housing of the Committee on Banking, 96th Cong., 1st Sess. (May 2, 1979); Thieblot on Prevailing Wage Legislation, 60.

19. Milton Friedman and Rose Friedman, *Free to Choose* (New York: Harcourt Brace Jovanovich, 1980), 235–237.

20. *Associated Builders and Contractors v. Michigan*, 869 F. Supp. 1239 (1995).

21. *Associated Builders and Contractors v. Perry*, 115 F.3d 386 (1997).

22. Bureau of National Affairs, *Construction Labor Report*, Vol. 45, No. 2245 (September 22, 1999).

23. Ibid., *Galloway and Vedder*, 3.

24. Armand J. Thieblot, Jr., "The Fall and Future of Unionism in Construction," *Journal of Labor Research* Vol. 22, No. 1 (Spring 2001): 300, and Thieblot's "Prevailing Wage Laws and Market Recovery Strategies of Construction Unions," *Journal of Economic Research*, George Mason University, Vol. XVIII, No. 1 (Winter 1997): 31.

25. Ibid., Thieblot on Prevailing Wage Legislation, 59; Bureau of National Affairs, *Construction Labor Report* Vol. 45, No. 2238 (July 28, 1999): 567–568.

26. Ibid., Northrup on The Helper Controversy, 422; Northrup's *Open Shop Construction Revisited* at 391–394.

27. Ibid., *Building Trades Department v. Ray Donovan, Sec. of Labor*, 622.

28. Ibid., 623, 629.

29. Ibid., 623.

30. Ibid., 623.

31. *Merit Shop Scoop* (July 18, 1983) 1.

32. Ibid., Northrup on The Helper Controversy, 430–432.

33. *Building Trades Department v. Lynn Martin, Secretary of Labor*, 961 F.2d 269, 273–274 (D.C. Cir., 1992).

34. See Bureau of National Affairs, *Construction Labor Report* (September 16, 1998) 720-721.

35. *Associated Builders and Contractors v. Alexis Herman, Secretary of Labor*, 976 F. Supp. 1, 8 (D.D.C. 1997).

36. Bureau of National Affairs, *Construction Labor Report* (September 9, 1999): 799.

37. See *ABC Today* (January 2001).

38. Ibid.

39. *U.S. Potash Company and International Association of Machinists*, 100 NLRB 1518, 1519 (1952).

40. Bureau of National Affairs, *Construction Labor Report* Vol. 46, No. 2307 (December 20, 2000): 1257.

41. Ibid., Frank Gamrat: 5 and Chapter 14.

42. Richard Vedder and Lowell Galloway, "Cracked Foundation, Repealing the Davis-Bacon Act," Center for Study of American Business, Washington University, Policy Study No. 127 (November 1995).

43. *Journal of Labor Research* Vol. 24, No. 2 (Spring 2003): 271.

44. See Bureau of National Affairs, *Construction Labor Report* Vol. 45, No. 2238 (July 28, 1999): 567.

45. Ibid., Galloway and Vedder, 22.

46. Ibid., Thieblot on Prevailing Wage Legislation, 55.

47. Bureau of National Affairs, *Daily Labor Report* (June 3, 1996) AA-1. See also Thieblot on Prevailing Wage Legislation, 52–57, 77–84.

48. Ibid., Vol. 45, No. 2220 (March 17, 1999): 81; Vol. 44, No. 2212 (January 20, 1999): 1167.

49. *ABC Today* Vol. 6, No. 5 (March 24, 1997).

50. Congressional Budget Office, Budget Options for 2001 (February 2001): Sec. 920-05-B, 8; see also A. J. Thieblot, Jr., "A New Evaluation of Impacts of Prevailing Wage Laws", *Journal of Labor Research*, George Mason University, Vol. 17, No. 20 (Spring 1996): 297–298, 313–314.

51. Ibid., Frank Gamrat, 6–17.

52. "Davis Bacon Act Repeal" (October 8, 2003): 19.

53. "Maximized Wages," *Wall Street Journal* (April 28, 1996).

54. Ibid.

55. For the dates of passage or elimination of individual state prevailing wage laws, see Armand J. Thieblot, *State Prevailing Wage Law, An Assessment*, a study prepared for ABC in 1995.

56. Aaron John Loeb, ed., *The Wit & Wisdom of Mark Twain* (New York: Barnes & Noble Books, 1996), 57.

Chapter 17

1. *ABC Today* (June 1996): 6, 12.

2. Ibid., (July 1995): 5; Herbert R. Northrup and Linda Alario, "Gov't Mandated Project Labor Agreements," *Government Union Review* Vol. 19, No. 3 (2000): 31.

3. *Contractor* (April 1964): 10.

4. *Merit Shop Contractor* (October 1975): 27.

5. *John Trimmer's ABC.*

6. *Contractor* (September 1972): 24.

7. *ABC Today* (January 1996): 12–13.

8. Bureau of National Affairs, *Daily Labor Report* "Highlights" (June 14, 2002): 1 and AA-1.

9. See *Construction Executive* (April 2004): 8.

10. Ibid.

11. Jerry Goldstein, "Workplace Violence v. Employee Rights," *Maryland Bar Journal* (January-February 2002): 46–49; see also "National Crime Victims Survey," U.S. Department of Justice, 1993–1999.

12. Ibid.

13. ABC Rocky Mountain Chapter's "Safety Lines," reported in *ABC Today* (June 2000): 11.

14. See *Suburban Hospital v. Kirson*, 362 Maryland 140, 170 (2000).

15. CA 4, No. 03-1033 (January 23, 2004).

16. See Walter Olson, *The Excuse Factory* (Kessler Books, The Free Press, 1997).

17. Frank Murray, *Washington Times* (September 11, 2002).

18. "Building for a Secure Future," a special report by *Engineering News-Record*; and Architectural Record, *Engineering News-Record* (March 25, 2002).

19. "Commemorating 9/11/01," *Engineering News-Record* (September 9, 2002): 4.

20. Compare Tom Sawyer, "Researchers Challenged to Improve Construction," *Engineering News-Record* (June 30, 2002): 50.

21. R. Alonso-Zaldwas, "Administration Forbids Airport Screeners Union," *Baltimore Sun* (January 10, 2003).

22. Excerpts from *Engineering News-Record* report in *ABC Today* (September 2002): 13.

23. Ibid.

Chapter 18

1. See Chapter 7.

2. "Union Organization in the Construction Industry," *Journeyman Edition*, IBEW Special Products Dept. (1990): 16–19.

3. *NLRB v. River City Elevator Company*, No. 01-2887 (7th Cir., May 13, 2002), citing Nestle Ice Cream Company, 46 F.3d at 584.

4. See Steamfitters Local 342 Contra Costa Electric, Inc., Bureau of National Affairs, *Constr. Labor Rep.*, Vol. 45, No. 7248 (October 13, 1999): 877.

5. Mark Erlich, "Up Against the Open Shop," Midwest Center for Labor Research (1988): 4, 15–16, 18.

6. See Chapter 7.

Chapter 19

1. See Chapter 12.

2. See Oversight Hearings before the Subcommittee on Labor-Management Relations of the Committee on Education and Labor, U.S. House of Representatives, Ninety-Sixth Congress, First Session, Vol. I, 436–438, 441 (Superintendent of Documents, U.S. Government Printing Office, Washington, DC).

3. "Labor Relations Consultants: Issues, Trends, and Controversies" (Bureau Natl. Affairs, Inc.).

4. Section 8(c) of the Taft-Hartley Act provides that "The expressing of any views, argument, or opinion, or the dissemination thereof, whether in written, printed, graphic, or visual form, shall not constitute or be evidence of an unfair labor practice under any of the provisions of this Act if such expression contains no threat of reprisal or force or promise of benefit."

5. See A. Samuel Cook, "The Glass House of Labor," Venable, Baetjer and Howard's *Workplace Labor Update*.

6. AFL-CIO and Field Representatives Federation, 120 NLRB 969, 970 (1958). As recently as June 14, 1994, moreover, J. J. Barry, President of the International Brotherhood of Electrical Workers, similarly wrote the international staff representatives of his own union that "I strongly believe it is not in the best interests of the IBEW or its international representatives to establish an organization to negotiate your terms and conditions of employment." For many other examples of this union hypocrisy, see note directly above, "The Glass House of Labor" by the author, and also the *Baltimore Sun* (February 11, 1990).

7. *The Record*, Northern New Jersey (March 17, 1985).

Chapter 22

1. *Contractor* (January 1968): 25; John Wheeler, Jr. and Melissa Kinsey, "Magnificent Failure: The Maryland Constitutional Convention of 1967–1968," National Municipal League (1970): 181–189.

Chapter 23

1. Gerace Construction, Inc., 193 NLRB 645 (1971).
2. *Radio & Television Broadcast Technicians Local Union 1264 v. Broadcast Service of Mobile*, 380 U.S. 255, 256 (1965).
3. Twenty-first Annual Report of NLRB (1956) 14-15; Gerace Construction Company, endnote above.
4. Peter Kiewit Sons' Company and International Union of Operating Engineers, 231 NLRB 76, 77 (1977) and its progeny, including 206 NLRB 562 (1973) and its journey to the Supreme Court as *South Prairie Construction Company v. Local 627, International Union of Operating Engineers*, 425 U.S. 806 (1976).
5. In a split decision clearly designed to overturn long-established policy, President Bill Clinton's Labor Board (with a dissent by Republican Board Member Cohen) eroded the traditional legal protections granted to doublebreasting operations and opened the possibility of giving unions control over non-union dual shop firm employees. See Painter & Allied Trades District Council No. 51 (Manganaro Corp.), 321 NLRB 158 (1996); District Council of New York City United Bd. of Carpenters & Joiners, 326 NLRB No. 31 (August 26, 1998); Daniel V. Yager, NLRB Agency In Crisis (1996) 98. Essentially the Manganaro decision permits a union to demand at the bargaining table a work preservation clause which would give it control over conditions at a non-union shop company with the same ownership as a unionized one, thus potentially forcing the non-union company out of business. Previously, this would have been outlawed as an illegal secondary boycott. But see also Labor Board decisions in Alessio Construction, 310 NLRB 1023 (1993) and South Western Materials, Bureau of National Affairs, *Daily Labor Report* (August 11, 1999), which are more favorable rulings toward protection of the legality of a dual shop. The currently reconstituted President George W. Bush's Labor Board may revisit and overrule this hypocrisy.
6. A. Samuel Cook, "The Pros and Cons of Operating Union and Non-union Dual Shops," *McGraw-Hill Construction Business Handbook*, 2nd Edition (New York: McGraw-Hill, 1984), and republished in the *Merit Shop Contractor* (August-September 1977); Herbert Northrup's *Open Shop Construction Revisited*, cited frequently above, Appendix C, 607–641. See also Northrup, "Double-breasted Operations and the Decline of Construction Unionism," *Journal of Labor Research*, Vol. XVI, No. 3 (Summer 1995).

Chapter 24

1. See Chapter 7.
2. *NLRB v. Denver Building & Construction Trades Council, et al.*, 341 U.S. 675, 692 (1951).
3. *Merit Shop Contractor* (August 1976): 25.
4. *John Trimmer's ABC*.
5. Ibid.
6. See Chapter 51.

7. "President's Report," *Contractor* (January 1962): 11.
8. "President's Corner," *Contractor* (March 1963): 17 and (August 1963): 4.
9. *Contractor* (March 1964): 4.
10. See Chapter 9.
11. *Contractor* (December 1966): 6.
12. "Unions, Open Shop Clash Over Jobs," *Engineering News-Record* (May 27, 1982): 10; see also Northrup's *Open Shop Construction Revisited* at 358–359.
13. *Contractor* (December 1966): 15.
14. *Contractor* (May 1968): 4.
15. *Contractor* (June 1969): 1.
16. *Builder and Contractor* (August 1990): 43.

Chapter 25

1. *John Trimmer's ABC.*
2. *Contractor* (1970).
3. Ibid.
4. See Chapter 12.
5. See Chapter 11 quote by Blough's Roundtable "Project"; see also *Contractor* (November 1970): 15 and (January 1972): 25.
6. Ibid.
7. *Contractor* (November 1970): 1.
8. Ibid., (March 1968).
9. *Contractor* (November 1963): 2.
10. *John Trimmer's ABC.*

Chapter 26

1. See ABC brochure, *Unions Go Back to Basics*; see also Chapter 37 herein.
2. *Webster's New World Dictionary of the American Language* (Simon & Schuster).
3. See Chapter 39; see also David Kendrick, "Violence: Organized Labor's Unique Privilege," National Institute for Labor Rel. Res. (1996).
4. Thieblot, Haggard and Northrup, *Union Violence: The Record and the Response by Courts, Legislatures and the NLRB* (2nd edit., Olin Instit. of George Mason University, Labor Rel. Series 25, 1999), 221.
5. *John Trimmer's ABC.*
6. Ibid.
7. Ibid.
8. Ibid.

Chapter 27

1. *Baltimore Sun* (April 26, 1964 and April 3, 1966).
2. Ibid
3. *John Trimmer's ABC.*
4. *Contractor* (January 1968): 6–7.

5. *John Trimmer's ABC.*

6. Ibid., *Contractor.*

7. Ibid.

8. *Contractor* (January 1968): 8.

Chapter 28

1. *Baltimore News-American* (September 30, 1965).

2. *Baltimore Evening Sun* (September 29, 1965).

3. *Contractor* (October 1965): 7; see also *Baltimore Sun* (December 15–17, 1965 and December 21, 1967); *News-American* (September 29 and 30, 1965).

4. For a detailed report of this case, see local press coverage by the *Baltimore Sun, Baltimore Evening Sun,* and *Baltimore News-American* (October 1965 through January 1966). See also *Contractor* (October 1965).

5. *Keller v. State, 2 Maryland App.* 623 (1967). See also the *Baltimore Sun* (December 16-18, 1965 and December 21, 1967).

6. *Baltimore Sun* (April 22 and 27, 1966).

7. For a more detailed report of this case, see local press coverage by the *Baltimore Sun,* the *Evening Sun,* and the *News-American.*

8. *Baltimore Sun* (February 12–13, 1969).

9. *Baltimore Sun* (March 28, December 15, 16, 19, 1969); *Contractor* (April 1969): 8.

10. Ibid., December 23, 1968.

11. Ibid., January 3, 1969.

12. Ibid., March 26, 1969.

13. Ibid., May 6, 1969.

14. Ibid., May 23, 1969.

15. Ibid., February 18, 1969.

16. *United States v. Guido Iozzi, Jr.,* 420 F.2d, 512, 514 (4th Cir., 1970).

Chapter 29

1. *Contractor* (October 1996): 4.

2. Ibid.

3. Ibid.

4. Ibid.

5. For more detailed reports on the Baltimore Building Trades Council's war against ABC merit shoppers during the 1960s and 1970s, see the *Baltimore Sun.*

6. Ibid.

7. *Baltimore Sun* (February 1, 1972)

8. *John Trimmer's ABC.*

9. Compare recent U.S. Supreme Court case allowing to stand a state appeals court ruling that a union "defamed" a construction subcontractor by falsely stating on picket signs that the company was not paying its workers "prevailing wages and benefits."

International Union of Operating Engineers v. Lowe Excavating Company, U.S., No. 02-346, cert. denied, November 18, 2002.

10. *Contractor* (February, 1972): 18-20; *Baltimore Sun* (February 1, 1972).

11. Ibid.

12. *John Trimmer's ABC.*

13. See "Sabotage And Arson Hurting State's Non-Union Builders" (*Baltimore Sun*, May 22, 1973): C-28.

14. *Contractor* (March 1973)

15. Ibid (April 1973): 14.

16. *Baltimore Sun* (May 22, 1973).

17. *Baltimore Evening Sun* (May 24, 1973).

Chapter 30

1. *John Trimmer's ABC.*

2. Ibid.

3. *John Trimmer's ABC.*

4. Ibid.

5. Building Trades Council of Philadelphia and Fisher Construction Company, 149 NLRB 1629 (1964).

6. *NLRB v. Building Trades Council of Philadelphia*, 359 F2d 62 (3rd Cir., 1966).

Chapter 31

1. Network ABC's TV News Program *60 Minutes* (Mike Wallace, commentator).

2. *Contractor*

3. Ibid.

4. Ibid; see also ABC's TV News Program *60 Minutes* (March 1975).

5. Charles Stevenson, "The Construction Unions Declare War," *Reader's Digest* (July 1973): 81-82.

Chapter 32

1. *John Trimmer's ABC.*

2. *Altemose Construction Company v. Building Trades Council of Philadelphia and Local 30, United Roofers Association*, Supreme Ct. Pa., 296 A.2d 504 (1972), cert. denied, 411 U.S. 932 (1973). *See also Altemose Construction Company v. NLRB*, 514 F.2d 8 (3rd Cir., 1975).

3. *Philadelphia Bulletin* (June 6, 1972); *Philadelphia Inquirer* (June 6, 1972); ABC publication, "The National Press Reports on Violence in Construction" (1973).

4. Ibid., *Altemose* case in Sup. Ct. Pa., 507.

5. Ibid; see also Herbert Northrup, *Open Shop Construction Revisited*, 354-358; Charles Stevenson, "The Construction Unions Declare War," *Reader's Digest* (July 1973): 81–83.

6. Ibid., *Altemose* case in Sup. Ct. Pa.

7. Ibid., *Altemose* case in Sup. Ct. Pa., 509.

8. Ibid., *Altemose* case in Sup. Ct. Pa., 509; Victor Riesel, *Inside Labor* (November 22, 1972).

9. Ibid., Stevenson on "Construction Union War" (July 1973): 82–83.

10. Ibid., *60 Minutes* interview.

11. Ibid., *Altemose* case, Sup. Ct. Pa. (1972), 514; see also *Altemose Construction Company v. Building Trades Council of Philadelphia*, Supreme Court of Pennsylvania, 337 A.2d 277 (1975), denying the Building Trades Council motion to dissolve the preliminary injunction.

12. Ibid., 1st *Altemose* case, Sup. Ct. Pa. (1972).

13. Ibid., Stevenson, *Construction Union War* (July 1973): 82–83.

14. See Chapter 51 under "union tool boxes."

15. Altemose Construction Company (Young and Zaleski), 210 NLRB 138 (1974).

16. *Altemose Construction Company v. NLRB*, 514 F.2d 8, 17 (3rd Cir. 1975)

17. *Hirsch v. Building Trades Council of Philadelphia*, 530 F.2d 298 (3rd Cir., 1976).

18. For further reference to detailed Philadelphia newspaper accounts of the Altemose ordeal, see above-cited Thieblot's "Union Violence" (1st edition): 153.

19. See Herbert Northrup, *Open Shop Revisited*, 357–358. See also J. Riggio, "The Hardhat's Holy War LXII," *Philadelphia Magazine* (August 1972): 55–61, 126–138; Series of articles by L. Ditzen, *Philadelphia Evening Bulletin* (July 15–18, 1974); *Philadelphia Evening Bulletin* (April 10, 1975): 6; *Thieblot on Violence*, 1st edit., 155.

20. *Commonwealth of Pennsylvania v. Reeves, et al., Pennsylvania Superior Ct.*, 387 A.2d 877, 880, 889 (1978).

21. Ibid., 880, 889.

22. Ibid.

23. See national network ABC's *60 Minutes* (March 1975) cited above.

24. *John Trimmer's ABC*.

25. See *Contractor* (March 1973): 8.

Chapter 33

1. Ibid. (June 1972): 22.

2. See *Engineering News-Record* (August 21, 1975): 18.

3. Sources for this chapter, in addition to Joe M. Rodgers personally, include *Contractor* (June 1972): 22–25 and (April 1973): 23–24; *Engineering News-Record* (April 21, 1975): 18–23; and *Advantage, the National Business Magazine* Vol. I, No. 12 (April 1979): 49-63.

4. *John Trimmer's ABC*.

Chapter 34

1. Ibid., below.

2. *Texas State Federation of Labor v. Brown & Root*, 246 S.W. 2nd 938, 943-944, Ct. Civil App., Texas (1952).

3. Ibid., 941, 947.

4. Ibid., 948.

5. *John Trimmer's ABC*

6. *Contractor* (January 1975): 18–19.

7. See Chapter 12.

8. NCCER News Publication, 1999.

9. The author acknowledges with appreciation the valuable assistance of Emil Zerr, Don Griswold, Rebecca Johansson, and William Bedman, Esq., of Kellogg Brown & Root, in writing this chapter.

Chapter 35

1. For an explanation of the right-to-work law movement, see Chapter 9.

Chapter 36

1. *Contractor* (February 1969): 22.

2. *John Trimmer's ABC.*

3. *Contractor* (May 1970): 1 and (November 1970): 1, 14.

4. Ibid., (March 1971): 21.

5. For a discussion of the farcical Davis-Bacon Act, see Chapter 16.

6. John Trimmer, "The Day Davis-Bacon Was Suspended," *ABC Today* (April 2000): 7–8.

7. Ibid.

8. "The Freeze Highlights," *Contractor* (January 1972): 14–16.

9. Ibid.

10. *Contractor* (January 1971).

11. *Contractor* (1971).

12. Ibid.

13. *John Trimmer's ABC.*

14. *Contractor* (1972).

15. *Contractor* (1972).

Chapter 37

1. Thieblot, Haggard, and Northrup, *Union Violence: The Record and the Response by Courts, Legislatures and the NLRB*, (George Mason University, Labor Rel. Series, 2nd edit., 1999), 149–150 and 201–206 for a "sampling of violence incidents by the building trades."

2. See Chapters 27 and 29.

3. See Haynes Johnson and Nick Kotz, *The Unions* (New York: Washington Post National Reports, Pocketbooks, 1972), 21; ABC brochure, *Back to Basics*.

4. See ABC publication: "The National Press Reports on Union Violence" (1973).

5. Ibid.

6. Herbert R. Northrup, *Open Shop Construction Revisited* (Wharton School, University of Pennsylvania, Industrial Rel. Research Unit No. 62, 1984), 351–371.

7. Charles Stevenson, "Building Trades Terrorism, The Construction Unions Declare War," *Reader's Digest* (July 1973): 79.

8. See Chapter 9 on this subject.

9. *Contractor* (September 1971): 5 and (June 1972): 5; *Reader's Digest* (June 1973): 91.

10. *Reader's Digest* (June 1973): 90.

11. Ibid.

12. See *Contractor* (1973).

13. Ibid.

14. For an explanation of right-to-work laws, see Chapter 9.

15. *Contractor* (November 1969): 1.

16. Charles Stevenson, "Terrorism In The Building Trades," *Reader's Digest* (June 1973): 92.

17. Ibid.

18. *Contractor* (December 1965): 5–8.

19. Thieblot and Haggard, *Union Violence*, 158.

20. *Detroit Free Press* (February 19 and 20, 1973).

21. Ibid.

22. Ibid., Thieblot note, 159.

23. See Herbert R. Northrup, *Open Shop Construction Revisited*, 363-365.

24. *Contractor* (March 1968): 6–7.

25. *Contractor* (1970).

26. *Contractor* (January 1973): 16; see also Stevenson on "Terrorism," *Reader's Digest* (December 1973): 90.

27. See Cockshaw's *Construction Labor News* (May 1973): 1 Opinion.

28. See *Providence Journal* (February 1 and 15, 1973); *Contractor* (March 1973): 6.

29. See Chapter 51.

30. Ibid., *Providence Journal*.

31. Ibid.

32. *Contractor* (1973). See also Chapter 33.

33. Charles Stevenson, "Arson-to-Order in the Building Trades," *Reader's Digest* (March 1976): 85–90. See also Sylvester Petro, *Power Unlimited, the Corruption of Union Leadership* (New York: Ronald Press Company); Thieblot and Haggard, *Union Violence: The Record and the Response by Courts, Legislatures, and the NLRB* (Philadelphia: Wharton School, 1983); Thieblot, Haggard, and Northrup, *Violence*, rev. edit. (Virginia: John Olin Institute, 1999): 151.

34. Ibid., Charles Stevenson, "Arson to Order": 85.

35. See Thieblot and Haggard, *Union Violence*,151; Northrup on Open Shop Construction Revisited, 353–354.

36. Ibid (Stevenson on Arson).

37. Ibid., 85–90.

38. Charles Stevenson, "The Tyranny of Terrorism in the Building Trades," *Reader's Digest* (June 1973): 89–93 and (July 1973): 79).

39. Ibid.

Chapter 38

1. Donald R. Richberg, *Labor Union Monopoly Power* (Chicago: Henry Regnery Company, 1957): vi.

2. See *National Right to Work Foundation Newsletter* (September 1977); see also David Denholm, "Why Unions Are Still Powerful," *Gov't Union Review* (December 2003) 39–51.

3. For an overview of this subject, see Charles W. Baird, "Freedom and American Labor Relations Law," *The Freeman* (May 1966): 299–309; Armand J. Thieblot, Jr. and Thomas R. Haggard, *Union Violence, the Record and the Response by Courts, Legislatures and the NLRB* (Philadelphia: Industrial Res. Unit, Labor Rel. Series, No. 25, 1983) and 2nd edit. (1999), co-authored by Herbert R. Northrup.

4. See 56 Corpus Juris Secundum 33, Sec. 211; 35 American Jurisprudence, 445–446, Secs. 2–3. See also "The Right to Manage," by the author, *CCH Labor Law Journal* (March 1958): 187–217.

5. *Payne v. Western & ARR Company.*

6. *Adair v. United States*, 20 U.S. 161, 174-5 (1908).

7. In re Debs, 158 U.S. 564 (1895).

8. 79 Cong. Rec. 7565 (1935). See also American Bar Association, *The Developing Labor Law*, Vol. I, 4th Edition (Washington, DC: Bureau of National Affairs), 27.

9. *Vaca v. Sipes*, 386 U.S. 171, 182 (1967); *NLRB v. Allis-Chalmers Manufacturing Company*, 388 U.S. 175, 180 (1967).

10. Compare *Abood v. Detroit Bd. Of Education*, 431 U.S. 209 (1977); see also Charles Baird, "Labor Relations Law," *Gov't Union Review* (December 2003): 9–28.

11. 78 F. Supp. 146, 155–56 (D.D.C. 1946), aff'd., 334 U.S. 854 (1948).

12. Charles Baird, "Freedom and American Labor Relations Law, 1946-1996," *The Freeman*: 301.

13. See Charles Baird, *Labor Relations Law* (Gov't Union Review, December 2003), 9–29.

14. See Fred A. Hartley, Jr., *Our New National Labor Policy* (New York: Funk & Wagnalls Company, 1948), 16.

15. See Chapter 7.

16. See Chapter 9.

17. Ibid.

18. Legislative History of the Labor-Management Relations Act, Vol. I., 409–410 (1947); Senate Report 105, 80th Congress, 1st Session.

19. See *Life* magazine (January 1953).

20. *Fibreboard Paper Products Corp. v. NLRB*, 379 U.S. 203, 225–226 (1964).

21. *Milk Wagon Drivers Local 753 v. Lake Valley Farm Products, Inc.*, 311 U.S. 91, 102 (1940).

22. *International Association of Bridge Workers v. Pauly Jail Building Company*, 118 F.2d 615, 617 (8th Cir., 1941), cert. den. 314 U.S. 639. See also Frank Stewart and Robert

Notes

Townsend, "Strike Violence: The Need for Federal Injunctions" (Vol. 114, No. 4, February 1966, University of Pennsylvania Law Review): 459.

23. *National Union of Hospital Employees, District 1199-E v. Lafayette Square Nursing Center*, 34 Maryland App. 619, 631 (1977).

24. See Jeffrey Ayres and Kathleen Gavin, "Maryland's Outdated Statute Restricting Labor Injunctions," Vol. 18, *University of Baltimore L. Rev.*, 528–543 (1989). See also Thieblot and Haggard, *Union Violence*, 1st edition,197–244.

25. Susan Schivochau, "The Labor Exemption To Antitrust Law: An Overview," *Journal of Labor Research*, Vol. XXI, No. 4 (Fall 2000): 535.

26. *U.S. v. Hutcheson*, 312 U.S. 219, 232 (1941). See also *Allen Bradley Company v. Local Union No. 3, International Bro. of Electrical Workers*, 325 U.S. 797 (1945).

27. Ibid., Hutcheson, 232.

28. *Hunt v. Crumboch*, 325 U.S. 821, 829–831, (1945). See also A*llen-Bradley Company v. Local Union No. 3, International Brotherhood of Electrical Workers*, 325 U.S. 797 (1945).

29. *United States v. Enmons*, 410 U.S. 396, 400 (1973), affirming 335 F. Supp. 641 (ED La. 1971). See also Thieblot and Haggard, *Union Violence*, 1st edition, 245–300.

30. Ibid., 413, 418.

31. *National Right to Work Newsletter* (December 1999).

32. Thieblot and Haggard, *Union Violence*, 2nd edition, 355; see also Chapter 44.

33. *Sedima v. Imrex Company*, 473 U.S. 479, 481 (1985).

34. Hardin and Higgins, *Developing Labor Law* (Washington, DC: American Bar Association and Bureau of National Affairs, 2001), 2327.

35. "Rico In Labor Disputes," American Bar Association, Tele-Conference Series (October 2003).

36. A "tort" may be defined as a private or civil (rather than criminal) wrong—not arising out of contract—for which a remedy may be obtained, usually in the form of damages. A "tortious act" is the commission or omission of an act by one [person], without right, whereby another receives an injury, directly or indirectly to his person, property or reputation. See Am. Juris., 2d edit. (Vol. 74, West Group, 2001) 604–605; *Black's Law Dictionary* 4th edit. (1951).

37. Roscoe Pound, "Labor Unions and Public Policy," American Enterprise Association (1958): 146, 168; and "Legal Immunities of Labor Unions," *Journal of Labor Research*, George Mason University: 70, 92.

38. Compare David Kendrick, "Violence: Organized Labor's Unique Privilege," National Instit. For Lab. Rel. Res. (1998): 6–7.

39. *United Mine Workers v. Gibbs*, 383 U.S. 715, 736 (1966).

40. *Carbon Fuel Company v. United Mine Workers*, 444 U.S. 212, 216–222 (1979).

41. Aladdin Industries, 147 NLRB 1392, 1396–1400 (1964).

42. Sylvester Petro, *Power Unlimited—The Corruption of Union Leadership* (New York: Ronald Press, 1959), vi.

43. Ibid., and Kendrick on Violence, 21, above.

44. Frank Stewart and Robert Townsend, "Strike Violence: The Need for Federal Injunctions," 114 *University Penn. Law Rev.* (February 1966): 459–460.

45. Milton and Rose Friedman, *Free to Choose* (New York: Harcourt Brace Jovanovich, 1980), 237.

46. *United Brotherhood of Carpenters v. Humphreys*, 127 SE 2d 98, 103 (Va. 1962), cert. denied, 371 U.S. 954 (1963).

47. Carl Horowitz, "Union Corruption: Why It Happens, How to Combat It," National Inst. For Labor Rel. Research (1999).

48. Roscoe Pound, "Legal Immunities of Labor Unions," *Journal of Labor Research* at George Mason University (1958): 69; "Labor Unions and Public Policy," American Enterprise Association (1958): 145.

49. Voluntary unionism does prevail (when enforced properly) in the 22 right-to-work states—see Chapter 9.

Chapter 40

1. For a summary of the history of the Taft-Hartley Act, see Chapter 39.

2. See James A. Gross, *The Reshaping of the National Relations Board* (Albany: State University of New York Press, 1981). See also Harvey Klehr, *The Secret World of American Communism* (New Haven: Yale University Press, 1995), 98–106.

3. Ibid.

4. *NLRB v. McGough Bakeries Corporation*, 153 F.2d 420, 421–422 (5th Cir. 1946).

5. *Indiana Metal Products Corporation v. NLRB*, 202 F.2d 613, 616 (7th Cir. 1953).

6. *NLRB v. Sidran*, 181 F.2d 671, 674 (5th Cir. 1950).

7. *NLRB v. Globe Automatic Sprinkler Company*, 199 F.2d 64, 70 (3rd Cir. 1952).

8. *NLRB v. Mac Smith Garment Company, Inc.*, 203 F.2d 868, 871 (5th Cir. 1953).

9. *NLRB v. Dorsey Trailers, Inc.*, 179 F.2d 589, 592 (5th Cir. 1950).

10. *NLRB v. Rockaway News Supply Company*, 345 U.S. 71, 75 (1953).

11. Section 9(h) was later removed from the Taft-Hartley Act by Congress.

12. *National Maritime Union of America v. Herzog*, 78 F.Supp. 146, 181 (DDC) aff'd 334 U.S. 854 (1948). See also Thomas E. Woods, Jr., *A Politically Incorrect Guide to American History* (Washington, DC: Regnery Publishing, 2004): 160.

13. Ibid.

14. Ibid.

15. See *U.S. News & World Report* (September 14, 1992): 54.

16. I eventually discovered that in the politically correct elite national news media, the words "conservative" or "Republican" usually are preceded by a negative or hostile adjective such as extreme right-wing, radical, ideologue, unyielding, belligerent, mean-spirited, contentious, hard-line, firebrand, rock-ribbed, antagonistic, cantankerous, hard-core, or highly partisan. But the word "liberal" or "Democrat" is spliced or replaced entirely by a flattering noun or adjective like moderate, progressive, realist, humane, fair-minded, sensitive, centrist, statesmanlike, mainstream, middle-of-the-

roader, professorial, judicious, intellectual, articulate, dedicated, bipartisan or highly respected. See David Brady and Jonathan Ma, "Spot the Difference," *Wall Street Journal* (November 12, 2003) op. ed.

17. J.Peter Grace, Chairman of President Reagan's Committee on Government cost Control, *War on Waste* (New York: Macmillan Publishing Co., 1985).

18. *ABC Contractor* (March 1966).

19. See enf. denied, *NLRB v. W.C. McQuaide, Inc.*, 552 F.2d 519, 526–528 (3rd Cir. 1977).

20. 255 NLRB No. 180 (1981), enf. den. *Chevron USA v. NLRB*, 672 F.2d 359 (3rd Cir. 1982).

21. See enf. denied, *Associated Grocers of New England v. NLRB*, 562 F.2d 1333, 1337 (1st Cir. 1977).

22. *NLRB v. Duie Pyle, Inc.* 115 LRRM 3428 (3rd Cir. 1984).

23. Redwing Carriers, Inc., 130 NLRB 1208, 1214 (1961); Central Mass. Joint Board, Textile Workers Union (Weinstein Company), 123 NLRB 590, 606 (1959).

24. Ibid., Thieblot on Violence, 2nd edit, 414.

25. Milk Wagon Drivers Local 753 v. Meadowmoor Dairies, Inc., 312 U.S. 287, 293 (1941). See also Thieblot and Haggard, *Union Violence*, 1st edition, 228.

26. *Chevron USA v. NLRB*, 762 F.2d 359 (3rd. Cir. 1982), den. enf. 255 NLRB No. 180 (1980).

27. Chamberlain, Bradley, Reilly, and Pound, *Labor Unions and Public Policy* (Washington, DC: American Enterprise Association, 1958), 145–146, 148–155, 168.

28. See Chapter 39.

29. Graces Trucking Company, 246 NLRB 344 (1979), enf. as mod. 111 LRRM (7th Cir. 1982).

30. 313 U.S. 177 (1941).

31. Taxicab Drivers Union Local 777, 145 NLRB 197, 205 (1963), enf'd. 340 F.2d 905 (7th Cir. 1965).

32. Roofers Union Local 30 and ABC, 227 NLRB 1444 (1977). See also International Union of Operating Engineers (Long Construction Company), 145 NLRB 554 (1963), Locke Point Pipe & Company, 202 NLRB 399 (1973); Thieblot and Haggard, *Union Violence* (1999), 445–449.

33. Kenneth C. McGuiness, *The New Frontier NLRB* (Washington, DC: Labor Policy Association, Inc., 1963), 78, 83, 198–199.

34. See David Kendrick, *Violence: Organized Labor's Unique Privilege* (Virginia: National Institute For Labor Rel. Research).

35. Thieblot and Haggard, *Union Violence*, 17; and Thomas R. Haggard, "Labor Violence," *Nebraska Law Rev.*, Vol. 59, No. 4 (1980).

Chapter 41

1. *ABC Contractor* (February 1975): 18.

2. *ABC Contractor* (January 1973).

3. *John Trimmer's ABC.*

4. Ibid.

5. See Chapter 39.

6. See Chapter 40.

7. *Contractor* (1972).

8. Ibid.

9. *Cockshaw's Construction Capsules* (1972).

10. *Contractor* (September 1972): 4.

11. Ibid., (April 1972): 16–17; Chapter 12.

12. See ABC brochure *Back to Basics.*

13. Charles Stevenson, "The Construction Unions Declare War," *Reader's Digest* (July 1973): 83.

14. *Contractor* (1973).

15. See Chapter 37.

16. Charles Stevenson, "Labor Violence—A National Scandal," *Reader's Digest* (August 1973): 155–158.

17. Ibid.

Chapter 42

1. Special Response Corp.'s Security Manual.

2. *ABC Contractor* (May 1973).

3. Ibid., (June 1973).

4. See Chapter 3.

5. Herbert R. Northrup, *Ronald Reagan's America* (Connecticut: Greenwood Press, 1997), 315.

6. Epilepsy Foundation of Northeast Ohio, aff'd D.C. Ct.

7. *Engineering News-Record* (November 2, 1972): 21.

8. See Chapter 40.

9. See Chapter 39.

10. Subcomm. on Labor of the Senate Comm. on Labor and Public Welfare, H.R. Rep. No. 245, 80th Cong., 2d Sess.

11. See *NLRB v. Drivers Local Union No. 639* (Curtis Brothers), 362 U.S. 274, 290 (1960); NLRB v. Local 639, International Brotherhood of Teamsters, 362 U.S. 274, 286 (1960).

12. See Chapter 39.

13. Sunset Line and Twine Company, 79 NLRB 1487 (1948); Tennessee Wheel & Rubber Company, 160 NLRB 165 (1967); NLRB v. Local 3, IBEW, 467 F.2d 1158 (2nd Cir. 1972) enforcing 193 NLRB No. 111 (1971); E. J. Lavino & Company, 157 NLRB 1637 (1966).

14. Ibid., Sunset Line and Twine; Cory Corp., 84 NLRB 972 (1949).

15. *NLRB v. Bulletin Company*, 443 F.2d 863, 867 (3rd Cir. 1971), cert. denied 404 U.S. 1018 (1972); V&D Machine Embroidery Company, 134 NLRB 879 (1961).

16. Eureka Chemical Company, 164 NLRB 1158 (1967); Brooklyn Spring Corp., 113 NLRB 815 (1955) enf'd 233 F.2d 539 (2nd Cir. 1956); Carrier Corp., 132 NLRB (1961); B. Brown Associates, 157 NLRB 615 (1966) enf'd 375 F.2d 745 (2nd Cir. 1967).

17. General Electric Company, 189 NLRB No. 10 (1971); Coca Cola Bottling Company of Louisville, 160 NLRB 1776 (1966); Glover Steel Building Sales, Inc., 186 NLRB 732 (1970); Grundy Mining Company, 146 NLRB 176 (1964); Local 612, International Brotherhood of Teamsters (Deaton Truck Lines), 146 NLRB 498, 503 (1964).

18. North Electric Mfg. Company, 84 NLRB 136 (1949).

19. P&L Services, Inc., 144 NLRB 1089 (1963), enf'd 340 F.2d 71, 72 (2nd Cir. 1965).

20. *NLRB v. United Mine Workers*, 429 F.2d 141, 147-8 (3rd Cir. 1970); Brooklyn Spring Corp., 113 NLRB 815, enf'd 233 F.2d 539 (2nd Cir. 1956).

21. Grundy Mining Company, 146 NLRB 176, 182 (1964).

22. See Chapters 27 and 29.

23. See Chapter 29.

24. *Machinists Local Lodge No. 1424 v. NLRB* (Bryant Manufacturing Company), 362 U.S. 411, 416 (1960).

25. See "Charging Party's Memorandum of Law" filed by the author and Venable, Baetjer and Howard in *Associated Builders and Contractors v. Building and Construction Trades Department, AFL-CIO, et al.*, NLRB Case No. 5-CB-1381 and related charges (June 20, 1973).

26. Smith Plumbing Company, 164 NLRB 313 (1967).

27. Burt Manufacturing Company, 127 NLRB (1629) 1960), enf'd 232 F.2d 141 (D.C. Cir. 1961), cert. denied 368 U.S. 896 (1961); *International Brotherhood of Teamsters v. United States*, 275 F.2d 610 (4th Cir. 1960); United Furniture Workers Local 472 (Colonial Hardwood Flooring Company), 84 NLRB 563 (1949) (close relationship between local and the international, under the latter's constitution, was relied on in part by the Labor Board in finding both units to be jointly responsible for acts of violence); Franklin Electric Construction Company, 121 NLRB 143, 151–152 (1958); Riley-Stoker Construction Company, 197 NLRB 738, 743 (1972); George Rose, "The Relationship of the Local Union to the International Organization," 4 *CCH Labor Law Journal* 334 (1953).

28. United Mine Workers (Blue Diamond Coal Company), 143 NLRB 795, 797 (1963).

29. United Furniture Workers, Local 472 (Colonial Hardwood Flooring Company), 84 NLRB 563, 583-85 (1949); United Furniture Workers, Local 309 (Smith Cabinet Mfg. Company), 81 NLRB 886, 889–91 (1949).

30. *Great Coastal Express v. Teamsters*, 350 F. Supp. 1377 (ED Va., 1972), aff'd, 511 F.2d 839, reh'g denied, 532 F.2d 956 (CA 4, 1975), cert. denied, 425 US 975 (1976).

31. Ibid., Burt Manufacturing Company

32. Overnite Transportation Company, 130 NLRB 1007 (1961), enf'd 332 F.2d 693 (5th Cir. 1964), cert. denied 379 U.S. 913 (1964); Vulcan Materials Company v. United Steelworkers, 430 F.2d 446 (5th Cir. 1970).

33. See "Conspiracy," § 50, 16 Am. Jur. 2nd, 277 (West Group, 1998); "Conspiracy," § 4, 15-A C.J.S.

34. See Chapters 31 and 32.

35. *ABC Contractor* (1973).

36. *Texas State Federation of Labor v. Brown & Root*, 246 S.W.2nd 938, 948, Ct. Civil App., Texas (1952); See also Chapter 34.

37. *United Construction Workers v. Laburnum Construction Corp.*, 347 U.S. 656, 666 (1954).

38. *Cockshaw's Construction Labor News* (1973).

39. See end of Chapter 41.

40. *Contractor* (July 1973): 2.

41. Compare Charles Stevenson, "Yes, Union Construction Terrorism Is Real," *Reader's Digest* (December 1973): 90.

Chapter 43

1. *Phelps Dodge Corp. v. NLRB*, 313 U.S. 177 ('41).

2. International Union of Operating Engineers, Local 513 (Long Construction Company), 145 NLRB 554 (1963); Local 30, United Roofers Association and Associated Builders and Contractors, 227 NLRB 1444 (1977).

3. *Contractor* (May 1973): 20–22.

4. *John Trimmer's ABC.*

5. See Chapters 31 and 32.

6. *U.S. News & World Report* (May 28, 1973).

7. *Eng. News-Record* (May 24, 1973): 8–9.

8. Charles Stevenson, "Yes, Construction Union Terrorism Is Real," *Reader's Digest* (December 1973): 90.

9. *John Trimmer's ABC.*

10. See "New Move to Curb Violence in Building Industry," *U.S. News & World Report* (May 28, 1973): 101.

11. *John Trimmer's ABC.*

12. *Contractor* (1973).

13. See Chapter 39.

14. See NLRB press release; see also *Contractor* (July 1974).

15. Case No. 1-CB-2316. A Section 8(b)(1)(A) complaint was authorized against Local 357 of the Iron Workers and the Iron Workers International Union based on threats of violence and property damage in March, 1973, at a site in Westfield, Massachusetts, where C. J. & Sons was engaged in construction work. Case No. 4-CB-2127. A Section 8(b)(1)(A) complaint was authorized against Roofers Local 30 and the International Union of Roofers based on extensive property damage, mass picketing, and threats of violence in March, 1973, at a site in Mount Laurel Township, New Jersey, where William Hargrove Roofing Company and the Prince Company were engaged in construction. (See also 227 NLRB 1444.) Case No. 6-CB-2683. A Section

8(b)(1)(A) complaint was authorized against Operating Engineers Local No. 66, based upon mass picketing, threats of violence, and rock throwing at a site in State College, Pennsylvania, where Glenn O. Hawbaker Company, was engaged in construction work in March, 1973. Case No. 7-CB-2834. A Section 8(b)(1)(A) complaint was authorized against the Michigan State Building and Construction Trades Council, certain of its named agents, certain affiliated Regional Labor Councils, Plumbers Local 388, Operating Engineers Local 324, and Ironworkers Local 340, based upon mass picketing, property damage, and threats of violence between January and March, 1973, where J.D. Parish Company, Inc., Tri-Cities Construction, Inc., and Shierbeck Construction Company were engaged in construction work at sites in Lansing, Hastings, Roscommon, and Kalkaska, Michigan. Case No. 7-CB-3030. A Section 8(b)(1)(A) complaint was authorized against Michigan State Building and Construction Trades Council, certain of its named agents, and the Carpenters International Union, based upon mass picketing, property damage, threats of violence, and physical assault in February 1974, at a site in Lansing, Michigan, where Long Development, Inc. was engaged in construction. Case Nos. 8-CB-2102, 2112. A Section 8(b)(1)(A) complaint was authorized against Operating Engineers Locals 18, 18A, 18B, the Laborers International Union, and Laborers Local 245, based upon threats of violence and property damage between March and May, 1973, at a site along Interstate I-90 in Ohio where Apex Contracting, Inc. was engaged in construction work. Case No. 22-CB-2437. A Section 8(b)(1)(A) complaint was authorized against the Building and Construction Trades Council of Middlesex County, New Jersey, based upon threatened assaults, threats of violence and mass picketing between April and May, 1973, at a site where Donald B. Ludwig Company was engaged in construction work in Woodbridge, New Jersey. Case No. 22-CB-2598. A Section 8(b)(1)(A) complaint was authorized against Operating Engineers Local 825, based upon mass picketing, threats of violence, property damage, rock throwing, and assault on an employee in December, 1973, at a site in Morristown, New Jersey, where Disch Construction, Inc. was engaged in construction work. See also *Contractor*, July 1974) 5; See also Northrup, Open Shop Construction Revisited, 352; Thieblot and Haggard, *Union Violence* (1983), 150.

16. *Contractor* (July 1974): 4.
17. Ibid.
18. Ibid.
19. Roofers Association and its Local 30 and Associated Builders and Contractors, 227 NLRB 1444, 1450 (1975).
20. *ABC Contractor* (March, 1, 4 and May, 15, 1975).
21. Ibid.

Chapter 44

1. See Chapters 31 and 32.
2. *United Mine Workers v. Pennington*, 381 U.S. 657, 665 (1965).
3. *ABC Contractor* (April 1973): 3–4.

4. *Altemose Construction Company v. Building & Const. Trades Council*, 433 F. Supp. 492, 495–496, 508 (ED Pa. 1977).

5. Ibid.

6. Ibid.

7. *Altemose Construction Company v. Constr. Trades Council*, No. 73-773, Slip op., 1983 U.S. Dist. LEXIS 15697 (ED Pa. 1983).

8. See *Connell Construction Company v. Plumbers & Steamfitters Local 100*, 421 U.S. 616 (1975). In this case, a union picketed a unionized general contractor to compel it to do business exclusively with subcontractors who had signed contracts between the union and the general contractor. Reasoning that the union's "top down" activity would prevent more efficient non-union subcontractors from effectively competing, the Supreme Court in Connell held, directly contrary to Judge Shapiro's opinion, that the union in such a situation (involving an employer co-conspirator) was not exempt from antitrust liability.

9. Ibid., *Altemose* case.

10. *Altemose Construction Company, Associated Builders and Contractors, and Chamber of Commerce of U.S. v. Building & Constr. Trades of Phila.*, 751 F.2d 653, 656–661 (3rd Cir. 1985).

11. *Altemose Construction Company et al., v. Building & Constr. Trades Council of Phila.*, cert. denied, 475 U.S. 1107 (1986).

12. Bureau of National Affairs, *Daily Labor Report* (December 28, 1987): A-1.

13. *ABC Contractor* (January 1988)

14. Endnote above, Bureau of National Affairs, *Daily Labor Report*; see also ABC Newsline, Vol. II, No. 4 (January 6, 1988).

15. A 1985 American Bar Association study found that only 9 percent of all civil RICO cases involved organized crime or alleged offenses normally associated with professional criminals; 40 percent involved securities fraud, and 37 percent involved garden variety business fraud and contract disputes.

16. *United States v. Local 30, Slate, Tile and Composition Roofers, etc.*, 686 F. Supp. 1139, 1149–1168 (E.D. PA, 1988).

17. Compare Chapter 45, which comments on then-U.S. Prosecutor Rudy Giuliani's RICO lawsuit against the International Brotherhood of Teamsters litigated at about the same time.

18. Ibid., Roofers Local 30 and Chapter 39.

19. Ibid., Roofers Local 30 and Chapter 39.

20. Ibid., Roofers Local 30, Roofers Local 30 at 1143–1144, 1164–1165; see also Hardin and Higgins, *Developing Labor Law* (American Bar Association and Bureau National Affairs, 4th edit., Vol. II, 2324–2441 covering "RICO and Labor Law; Thieblot on Violence (2nd edit, 353–355); Herbert R. Northrup and Charles H. Stern, "Union Corporate Campaigns as Blackmail"; "The RICO Battle At Bayou Steel," *Harvard Journal of Public Policy*, Vol. 22, No. 3 (Summer 1999).

21. Ibid., Roofers Local 30 at 1144.

22. Ibid., Roofers Local 30, at 1147–1154, 1162.

23. *United States v. Traitz, et al.* (Criminal No. 86–451).

24. Ibid., Roofers Local 30 at 1141, 1157; see also Herbert Northrup on Open Shop Revisited, 357-358 (cited).

25. Ibid., Roofers Local 30 at 1144.

26. Ibid., Roofers Local 30 at 1139–1141; see also *United States v. Local 30, United Slate, Tile and Composition Roofers, etc.*, 824 F. Supp. 559 (ED Pa., 1993).

27. Ibid., Roofers Local 30, et al. 1163, 1145, 1166–1167.

28. Ibid., Roofers Local 30, 1162–1163, 1168.

29. *United States v. Local 30, United Slate, Tile and Composition Roofers, etc.*, 871 F. 2d 401 (3rd Cir. 1989).

30. See "RICO in Labor Disputes: The Thermonuclear Litigation Device," American Bar Assn's Teleconference Series (October 1, 2003); see also Chapters 39 and 45.

Chapter 45

1. Ibid. See also *The Developing Labor Law*, Vol. II, 2324–2441, covering "RICO and Labor Law"; Thieblot and Haggard, *Union Violence*, 2nd edition (1999): 374.

2. Philip Taft, "Corruption and Racketeering in the Labor Movement," New York State School of Industrial and Labor Relations, Cornell University, Bulletin 38, 2nd ed. (1970): 12.

3. *Daily Labor Report,* Bureau of National Affairs (January 15, 1986): D-1 and D-2; David Kendrick, "Violence: Organized Labor's Unique Privilege," National Institute for Labor Relations Research (1996): 5-6; Carl Horowitz, "Union Corruption: Why It Happens, How to Combat It," National Institute for Labor Relations Research (1996); A. Samuel Cook, "Union Foxes Guarding Police And Fire Hen Houses," Maryland Business for Responsive Government (1998).

4. Jennifer Hickey, "Hoffa Has a Plan," *Insight* magazine (September 6, 1999): 11.

5. *United States v. International Brotherhood of Teamsters et al.*, 905 F.2d 610, 613 (2nd Cir. 1990).

6. *United States v. International Brotherhood of Teamsters et al.*, 725 F. Supp. 162, 169 (SD NY, 1989), aff'd 905 F.2d 610 (2nd Cir. 1990); United State v. International Brotherhood of Teamsters et al., 1997 U.S. Dist. LEXIS 20216 at *20 (SD NY, 1997).

7. See *United States v. International Brotherhood of Teamsters et al.*, 948 F.2d 98 (2nd Cir. 1991); *United States v. International Brotherhood of Teamsters et al.*, 964 F.2d 1308 (2nd Cir. 1992); *United States v. International Brotherhood of Teamsters et al.*, 697 F. Supp. 710, USDC SDNY (1988); *United States v. International Brotherhood of Teamsters, et al.*, 948 F.2d 98 (2nd Cir. 1992); F.C. Duke Zeller, *Devils Pact: Inside the World of the Teamsters Union* (Birch Lane Press, Carol Publ. Group, 1996); "International Longshoremen's' Union Cesspool of Corruption," *National Right to Work Newsletter* (September 2003).

8. *Brink et al. v. DaLesio et al.*, 667 F.2d 420, 423, 429 (4th Cir. 1982), affirming in part 496 F. Supp. 1350 (DC Maryland 1980). See also Allegra Bennett, "DeLasio Ordered To Pay Back Funds," *Baltimore Sun* (1979).

9. See lead article by Brian Lockett in *Constr. Labor Rep.*, Vol. 49, No. 2415 (March 3, 2003): 6.

10. Ibid.

11. "Construction," Bureau of National Affairs, *Daily Labor Report* (July 22, 2003): A-5.

12. See Cockshaw's *Construction Labor News and Opinion* newsletter (September 2004).

Chapter 46

1. See Chapter 7.

2. *Abreen Corp. v. Laborers' International Union et al.*, 709 F.2d 748, 1st Cir. Ct. App., 1983, cert. denied, 464 U.S. 1040 (1984).

3. See Chapters 41, 42 and 43.

4. *Merit Shop Contractor* (November 1975): 1

5. Ibid., (November 1975): 5. and (November 1977): 20

6. Ibid., (July 1976).

7. Ibid.

8. Ibid., (January 1976).

9. Ibid., (September 1976): 16–17.

10. Charles Stevenson, "Yes, Construction Union Terrorism Is Real," *Reader's Digest* (December 1973): 86.

11. "ABC's 5,000th Member," *Contractor* (February 1973): 16.

12. Ibid., (September 1976): 14–15.

13. Ibid.

14. *Merit Shop Contractor* (1975).

15. See Chapter 5.

16. See Chapter 7.

17. See Chapter 16.

18. *Contractor* (June, 12 and 26, and November 6, 1975).

19. Ibid.

20. *ABC Today* (July 1993): 6.

21. *NLRB v. Denver Building & Construction Trades Council, et al.*, 341 U.S. 675, 692 (1951); see also *Piezonki d/b/a Stover Steel Service v. NLRB*, 219 F.2d 879, 880-881 (4th Cir. 1955).

22. See *Contractor* (June 1975): 12.

23. Ibid.

24. Ibid.

25. See Chapter 48 and *Contractor* (1975).

26. *Merit Shop Contractor* (October 1975): 1–2.

27. Ibid.

28. Ibid.

29. Ibid.

30. *John Trimmer's ABC.*

31. *Merit Shop Contractor* (January 1976): 13.

32. See Herbert R. Northrup, *The Decline of Construction Unions* (*Journal of Labor Research*, Summer 1995), 379.

Chapter 47

1. See records of the Gettysburg National Military Park Library; the Adams County Historical Society; General Edward Stackpole and Colonel Wilbur Nye, The Battle of Gettysburg (Stackpole Books, Harrisburg, Pa., 1963) 71–73.

2. Milton Layden, *Escaping the Hostility Trap* (New Jersey: Prentice-Hall, 1977).

3. See Henry Kulp Ober, *The Plain People of Lancaster County* (http: www.horseshoe.cc/pennadutch): 2.

4. Peerless Plywood Company, 107 NLRB 427 (1953).

Chapter 48

1. Herbert R. Northrup, Organized Labor and the Negro (Harper & Bros., '44). See also Bruce Kaufman, An Interview with Herbert R. Northrup (19 *Journal of Labor Research* 669, 1998).

2. Herbert R. Northrup and Howard Foster, *Open Shop Construction* (Industrial Research Unit, Wharton School, University of Pennsylvania, 1975), iii.

3. Ibid., 18–19.

4. Northrup, *Open Shop Construction Revisited* (Industrial Research Unit, Wharton School, University of Pennsylvania, 1984) iii.

5. Northrup, *Open Shop Revisited*, 2nd edit. 3.

6. Ibid., Northrup on Open Shop Revisited (31, 407, 581).

7. Kaufman interview, above, 678.

8. Diversity of opinion is rare in America's left-wing academia. A poll by Luntz Research Companies found that only 3 percent of the professors among Ivy League university faculties were Republicans, over 80 percent of them voted for Al Gore for president over George W. Bush in 2000, and Bill Clinton was the Ivy League faculties pick for "best president of the past 40 years." See Robert Stacy McCain, "Ivy League Profs" (The *Washington Times*, Weekly Edition, January 21–27, 2002).

Chapter 49

1. See Chapters 41, 42 and 43.

2. Patty Parsons and Albert Palewitz, "Union Corporate Campaigns" (Maryland Bar Journal, March–April 1993, Vol. 26, No. 2) 35.

3. Ibid., 38.

4. See Chapters 18, 19, and 47.

5. Industrial Union Dept., AFL-CIO, "Developing New Tactics: Winning with Corporate Campaigns" (1985).

6. "Union Officials Stress International Scope of Organizing, Bargaining Campaigns" (Bureau of National Affairs, *Daily Labor Report*, November 16, 1992) A-5; see also Charles R. Perry, Union Corporate Campaigns 2-3 (1987).

7. Dan La Botz, A Troublemaker's Handbook: How to Fight Back Where You Work and Win (A Labor Notes Book, Detroit, MI, 1991).

8. See Chapter 21.

9. Ibid., Dan La Botz, 127. See also Herbert R. Northrup, "Corporate Campaigns: The Perversion of the Regulatory Process" (*Journal of Labor Research*, Vol. 17, No. 3, Summer, 1996), 345–358; Herbert R. Northrup and Charles Steen, "Union 'Corporate Campaigns' as Blackmail" (Harvard Journal of Law & Public Policy, Vol. 22, No. 1, Summer, 1999).

10. Ibid., La Botz above, 127–128. See also Herbert R. Northrup, "Union Corporate Campaigns and Inside Games as a Strike Form," *Employee Relations Labor Journal* (Vol. 19, No. 4, Spring 1994): 510.

11. Jarol Manheim, *The Death of a Thousand Cuts* (New Jersey: Lawrence Erlbaum Associates, 2004).

12. For a more detailed discussion of this union tactic, see "Symposium: Corporate Campaigns," *Journal of Labor Research*, Vol. 27, No. 3 (Summer 1996): 327–424.

13. *Food Lion, Inc. v. United Food & Commercial Workers*, 103 F.3d 1007, 1014 n. 9 (D.C. Cir. 1997).

14. See *The Labor Lawyer* (American Bar Association, Fall 2003), 217.

15. See Chapter 23.

16. *John Trimmer's ABC.*

17. "A Time Of Reckoning for the Building Unions," *Fortune* (June 4, 1979).

18. *Engineering News-Record* (August 30, 1999): 28; *ABC Today* (September 10, 1999); *Engineering News-Record*'s "Top People," World Construction Leaders (Construction Facts, 2003): 64.

19. See Chapter 12.

20. *John Trimmer's ABC.*

21. *See USS-Posco Industries v. Contra Costa City Building Trades Council*, 31 F.3d 800, 804 (9th Cir. 1994).

22. *Cockshaw's Construction Labor News 1* Opinion (September 1989).

23. Ibid.

25. Ibid., Cockshaw.

26. *John Trimmer's ABC.*

27. Ibid., Cockshaw.

28. Ibid.

29. "Minnesota Pardons Board Refuses Riot Conviction Clemency Requests," 36 *Construction Labor Report* (BNA) 1121 (January 16, 1991).

30. Iron Workers 783 (BE&K Construction Company), 311 NLRB 734 (1993).

31. *BE&K v. NLRB*, 23 F.3d 1459 (8th Cir. 1994); cert. denied, Local No. 783, Bridge, Structural & Ornamental Workers v. BE&K Constr. Company, 513 U.S. 1076 (1995). See also Thieblot and Haggard, *Union Violence*, 2nd edition, 212.

32. Ibid., Cockshaw.

33. See Bureau of National Affairs, *Daily Labor Report* (April 13, 1999, No. 70): A-8 and A-9.

34. Ibid., *USS-Posco Ind. v. Contra Costa, etc.*; see also Thieblot and Haggard, *Union Violence*, 2nd edition, 210-214.

35. BE&K Construction Company, 329 NLRB 717, 723 (1999).

36. *BE&K Construction Company v. NLRB*, 246 F.3d 619, 628 (6th Cir. 2001).

37. This doctrine was contrary to the general rule of American law that each party in a lawsuit pays its own legal fees and costs, regardless of the decision in the case.

38. *204 Daily Labor Reporter* (BNA): A-11 and 12 (October 22, 1999).

39. *BE&K Construction Company v. NLRB*, 536 U.S. 516 (2002). Justices O'Connor, Rehnquist, Scalia, Kennedy, and Thomas joined in the opinion of the Court on all issues, and Justices Breyer, Stevens, Souter, and Ginsberg concurred in the result in total but dissented as to the secondary issue of what the court's standard on "retaliation" should be in future cases.

40. "ABC Hails Major U.S. Supreme Court Victory," *ABC Today* (June 2002): Vol. 11, No. 6, 1; see also "High Court Curbs NLRB Legal Power," *ENR* (July 1, 2002): 12; Maurice Baskin and Herbert Northrup, "The Impact of BE&K Construction Company v. NLRB on Employer Responses to Union Corporate Campaigns and Related Tactics," *The Labor Lawyer* (Fall 2003): 215–246; see also Bureau of National Affairs, *Construction Labor Report* (September 8, 2004): 1, vol. 50.

41. Ibid.

43. *John Trimmer's ABC.*

Chapter 50

1. *Washington Times* (1992).

2. Dan Bennet (with Mike Henderson): "No Union Card, No Inauguration," *Wall Street Journal* (January 18, 1993): A-10.

3. Barry Bluestone and Irving Bluestone, *Negotiating the Future: A Labor Perspective on American Business* (Basic Books Div. of Harper Collins Pub., 1992), 23.

4. Bureau of National Affairs, *Daily Labor Report* (1993).

5. *ABC Today* (February 8, 1993).

6. *Engineering News-Record* (September 6, 1999).

7. Compare Maurice Baskin, "The Case Against Union-Only Project Labor Agreements," *Journal of Labor Research*, Vol. 19, No. 1 (Winter 1998): 115–123; Herbert R. Northrup and Linda E. Alario, "Harbor-Type Project Labor Agreements in Construction," *Journal of Labor Research*, Vol. 19, No. 1 (Winter, 1998): 48; Max Lyons, "The Estimated Cost of Project Labor Agreements on Federal Construction," *Journal of*

Labor Research, Vol. 19, No. 1 (Winter 1998): 74; Linda Chavez and Daniel Gray, *Betrayal* (Crown Forum, Div. of Random House, 2004), 98–100.

8. Ibid., Max Lyons, 74.

9. Ibid.

10. *Daily Record* (May 3, 1993) and correspondence from Mr. Kaczorowski received by the author.

11. Ibid.

12. Ibid.

13. *Building and Constr. Trades Department v. Joe Albaugh*, 172 F. Supp. 2nd 138 (D.D.C. DATE, 2001).

14. *Building and Constr. Trades Department v. Joe Albaugh*, 295 F.3rd 28 (D.C. Cir., July 16, 2002) (get cites)

15. "Appeals Court Upholds Bush PLA Order," *ABC Today* (July 2002).

16. "Appeals Court Upholds PLA Ban," *Engineering News-Record* (July 22, 2002): 12.

17. *Building & Constr. Trades v. Joe Albaugh*, U.S. No. 02-527 (January 27, 2003) cert. denied.

18. *Engineering News-Record* (February 3, 2003): 13; see also ABC's *Construction Executive* (February 2003): 4–5.

19. See *Historic Record of Clinton Crimes* (Washington, DC: Judicial Watch, 2003); Linda Chavez and Daniel Gray, *Betrayal* (Crown Pub. Company, Div. of Random House, 2004) 68–72; "A Case for Impeachment?" *Human Events* (1997); Christopher Hitchens, *No One Left to Lie To* (R.R. Donnelly & Sons, 1999); Gary Aldrich, *Thunder on the Left* (Washington, DC: Regnery Publ. Company, 2004); Bill Gertz, *How The Clinton Administration Undermined American Security* (Washington, DC: Regnery Publ. Company, 1999); Ledeen and Moroney, "The White House Joins the Teamsters," *American Spectator* (November 1998): 38–88; Richard Miniter, *Losing Bin Laden: How Bill Clinton's Failure Unleashed Global Terror* (Washington, DC: Regnery Publ. Company, 2004).

Chapter 51

1. *Baltimore Metro ABC Report* (Summer 1998): 9; *ABC News Release* (March 1988); *San Francisco Chronicle* (March 8, 1988).

2. "A Year In Review," ABC News (July 1998).

3. Ibid., see also ABC's News Program *60 Minutes*.

4. Ibid.

5. Ibid.

6. Ibid.

7. Ibid., Mike Wallace TV documentary.

8. Rona Kobell, "Open Shop Association Marks 50th Anniversary," *Baltimore Sun* (June 2, 2000); Sherie Winston, "ABC Launches New Programs as Few Protestors Show Up," *Engineering News-Record* (June 12, 2000): 15.

9. See also end of Chapter 49.

10. As recently as May, 2004, a Hoffa, Jr. appointee—Ed Stier—to the Teamsters' so-called "Respect, Integrity, Strength and Ethics" program resigned in protest. He claimed that Hoffa "has permitted anti-corruption investigations to be undermined to a degree that honest Teamsters who came forward with information, believing that the union would protect them, now feel abandoned . . . I have become convinced that continued efforts to create an anti-corruption program in the Teamsters Union would be futile." See "Forced Union Abuses Exposed," National Right to Work Comm. (May 2004).

11. "The Teamsters Promise," *Wall Street Journal* (September 30, 2003). See also "legal issues" at www.teamster.org/divisions/freight/freight.asp; *Overnight Transportation Company v. International Brotherhood of Teamsters, USDC,* West. Dist. Tenn., July 19, 2002; note above, Chavez and Gray on Betrayal, 143–145.

12. See A. Samuel Cook, *Labor Union Foxes Guarding Police Hen Houses* (Public Serv. Res. Council and Maryland Bus. For Responsive Gov't., 1998), 4-6.

13. "David Bush, ABC's 1999 President," *ABC Today* (January 1999): 5.

14. See *ABC Today* (February 8, 1993) and *An Anti-Intimidation Manual for Merit Shop Contractors* (an ABC publication).

15. See Chapter 50; "Project Labor Agreements Increase Costs, Reduce Competition, ABC Study Finds," *Constr. Labor Report,* Vol. 46, No. 2311 (January 24, 2001): 1449; "Symposium on Government Mandated Labor Agreements in the Construction Industry," *Journal of Labor Research,* Vol. XIX, No. 1 (Winter 1998); "Union-Only Project Labor Agreements: The Public Record of Poor Performance," (Associated Builders and Contractors, 2000).

16. A typical trade union "salting" ploy begins with a letter like this to the non-union contractor: "Attention Electrical Contractor: This letter is in response to your classified ad seeking manpower. As you are aware, it is getting harder and harder to find qualified help in today's market. With a local manpower pool in excess of 1750 qualified journeymen electricians and apprentices, we can help you solve your manpower problems. Our apprentices attend an apprenticeship program approved by the state of Maryland which enables you to use them on certified payroll jobs. When you become a signatory contractor with our Union this highly skilled pool of electricians will be just a phone call away. We currently have an organizing drive to organize all electricians in the Baltimore area, including your employees. With this in mind we have arranged for several members of our union to come to your office and fill out the necessary paperwork to gain employment to help you solve your manpower needs. This will also give you the opportunity to see how skilled our electricians are. Looking forward to hearing from you in the near future." (signed by organizers of the International Brotherhood of Electrical Workers, Local Union 24)

17. See Chapter 16.

18. See Chapter 49.

19. See *NLRB v. River City Elevator Company,* No. 01-2887 (7th Cir., May 13, 2002).

20. See Maurice Baskin, "Is Union Job Targeting an Unfair Labor Practice?" *Construction Executive* (December 2003): 10.

21. The average salary for the international presidents of five major building trades unions in 2002 was $223,691, according to the LM-2 financial disclosure forms filed with the Labor Department; See Bureau of National Affairs, *Constr. Labor Rep.* (December 31, 2003): 1399.

22. Compare "Online Database Reveals Top Pay," *Engineering News-Record* (July 1, 2002): 10; "Special Report on Union Corruption," *U.S. News & World Report* (September 8, 1980): 33–36.

23. See "Feds Sue over Hotel Investment," describing *Chao v. Maddaloni*, an ERISA lawsuit alleging that "five union trustees of the Plumbers and Pipefitters National Pension Fund purchased and developed the [Westin Diplomat Resort & Spa in Florida] property without the slightest due diligence to determine the financial viability of the project...and also failed to maintain adequate controls over construction costs and paid excessive fees to service providers." *Engineering News-Record* (September 23, 2002): 10.

24. See Bureau of National Affairs, *Constr. Labor Report* (October 20, 2004): 1065 and *United States v. Moscatiello*, S.D.N.Y., No. 04-CR-343; *Engineering News-Record* (February 5, 2001): 56; *Engineering News-Record* (November 8, 2004): 1D.

25. "Labor Law," Bureau of National Affairs, *Construction Labor Rep.* (February 5, 2003): 1463.

26. Bureau of National Affairs, *Daily Labor Rep.* (October 6 2003); "Union Leaders See Politics Behind New Regulation," *Baltimore Sun* (October 5, 2003): 15A; "Union Doozy," *Wall Street Journal* (October 8, 2003): edit. A24.

27. Bureau of National Affairs, *Constr. Labor Rep.* (October 15, 2003): 1086.

28. Bureau of National Affairs, *Daily Labor Report* (July 1, 2004): 1; see also Chavey and Gray, *Betrayal*, 181–184.

29. See Chapter 39.

30. "Forty Years Of Corruption," *Washington Times*, edit. (January 1, 2003); Bureau of National Affairs, *Constr. Labor Report* (December 1, 2003): 1289; "Sweeney's Swindlers," *Washington Times* (November 4, 2002); "Former Iron Workers Union President Pleads Guilty to Embezzlement," Bureau of National Affairs, *Constr. Labor Rep.*, Vol. 48, No. 2398 (October 30, 2002): 1021; "Compulsory Unionism Facilitates Big Labor Abuse of Worker Pension Funds," *Exposed*, National Right to Work Comm., Vol. 1, No. 6: 1.

31. "The Lessons of ULLICO," *Wall Street Journal* (June 17, 2003): edit. A16; Kimberley Stassel, "Sam Waksal [of Tyco International] Meet, Robert Georgine [of the building trades]," *Wall Street Journal* (June 17, 2003): editorial page. Other building trades bosses involved included Jacob West (International Iron Workers), Joseph Maloney (Building Trades Dept.) and Doug McCarron (Carpenters International).

32. Bureau of National Affairs, *Constr. Labor Rep.* (November 5, 2003): 1169; and *Carabillo v. ULLICO*, D.C. No. 03-1556 (November 3, 2003).

33. "Dear Uncle Bob," *Wall Street Journal* (June 3, 2004): editorial page.

34. Compare "Big Labor's Enron." *Washington Times* (November 17, 2002): edit.

35. "Union Don'ts-And Dues," *Wall Street Journal* (January 21, 2003): editorial page A17; *Wall Street Journal* (April 16, 2003): editorial page

36. See Chavez and Gray, *Betrayal*: 1–15, 26, 34–41 and *National Right to Work Newsletter* (June 2004): 7

37. See graphics infra, this chapter; Bureau of National Affairs, *Daily Labor Report* (January 22, 2004): 1; *Baltimore Sun* (January 25, 2004): 8D.

38. *Wall Street Journal* (March 3, 2003): A-16.

39. Ibid., (December 3, 2003): edit.

40. Michael Crowley, "Brotherhood of Thieves," *Reader's Digest* (June 2004): 34–35; see also www.nlpc.org for a weekly report of labor corruption on a union-by-union basis.

41. "Labor's Loot," *Wall Street Journal* (September 11, 2001): A26; Taylor Dark, "Labor and the Democratic Party," *Journal of Labor Research*, George Mason University (Fall 2000): 627–640; Linda Chavez, "Union-Made Power Grab," *Human Events* (March 22, 2004): 5.

42. See *National Right to Work Newsletter* (April 2002 and January 2003); see also Chavez and Gray, *Betrayal*, 3.

43. Bureau of National Affairs, *Daily Labor Report* (2003).

44. *Human Events* (March 5, 2001): 8; Chavez and Gray, *Betrayal*, 11–15.

45. ABC's *Construction Executive* (February 2003): 7.

46. Bureau of National Affairs, *Daily Labor Report* (August 11, 2004): 2.

47. See *The Union Political Machine in 2004* (National Institute for Labor Relations Research at its www.nilrr.org website); *National Right to Work Newsletter* (October 2004): 5.

48. "The Billionaire's Boom," *Wall Street Journal* (November 3, 2004): edit.

49. "Democrats to Rely on Big Labor Dollars," *Wall Street Journal* (October 13, 2002): A-16; "Exposing the Forced-Dues Base of Big Labor's Political Machine," National Inst. for Labor Rel. Res. (October 27, 2000).

50. "Will Sweeney Be 0-5?" *Washington Times* (November 27, 2002): edit.

51. "Big Labor Pains," *Wall Street Journal* (September 6, 2004): editorial page

52. *National Right to Work Newsletter* (January 2003): 2.

53. Quoted in *Merit Shop Contractor* (February 1977): 25.

54. *Communications Workers of America v. Beck*, 487 U.S. 735, 1988.

55. See Chapter 9.

56. *International Association of Machinists v. Street*, 367 U.S. 740, 789–790, 796 (1961).

57. National Right to Work Foundation, News Release (January 29, 2004).

58. See "Mrs. Clinton's Union Dues," *Washington Times* (July 1996): edit.; "The Clintons and the Boss," *Reader's Digest* (April 1996): 93; Chavez and Gray, *Betrayal*, 68, 72–76; "Fruits of their Labor," *Time* (June 24, 1996): 37; David Kendrick, "Violence: Organized Labor's Unique Privilege," National Inst. for Labor Rel. (1996): 19; "The

Trumpa Card," *Wall Street Journal* (November 12, 1999): edit.; "LUNA, Justice Department Meet," Bureau of National Affairs, *Constr. Labor Rep.* (October 14, 1998): 833; Jerry Seper, "Labor Boss Likely to Plead, Then Quit," *Washington Times* (October 2, 1999); Bureau of National Affairs, *Daily Labor Rep.* (September 2 1999): A-11; "A Corrupt Union Escapes Justice," *Wall Street Journal* (July 27, 1998); "Another Convict for Clinton," *Washington Times* (February 8, 2000).

59. Author's note: Sweeney presumably meant "anyone other than his own AFL-CIO and its compulsory union shop membership requirement."

60. Bureau of National Affairs, 1995 *Daily Labor Report*, 208 d28 (Westlaw). See also "Sweeney On Mission to Revitalize Labor," *Baltimore Sun* (September 2, 1996).

61. Mark Murray, "On the Ropes," *National Journal* (March 8, 2003): 726; See also note directly below.

62. See Barbara Olson, *Hell to Pay: The Story of Hillary Clinton* (Washington, DC: Regnery Publ., 2001); R. Emmett Tyrrell, Jr., *Madame Hillary: The Dark Road to the White House* (Washington, DC: Regnery Publ., 2004); Dick Morris, *Rewriting History* (Regan Books Publ., 2004); Peggy Noonan, *The Case Against Hillary Clinton* (New York: Harper Collins Publ., 2002); Chavez and Gray, *Betrayal*: Chapter 2.

63. See *Washington Times* (December 12, 2001); *Wall Street Journal* (December 10, 2001): A-18; BNA *Daily Labor Report* No. 233, December 6, 2001: C1-C3 and No. 39 (February 27, 2002): A-11.

64. Ibid.; see also *Baltimore Sun* (November 1, 2000 and January 25, 2004): 8D; Bureau of National Affairs, *Construction Labor Report* (Vol. 46, No. 2283): 475–476; *National Right to Work Newsletter* (September 2000).

65. Milton and Rose Friedman, *Free to Choose*, 287 and Appendix A; Kenneth Weinstein, "Mr. Sweeney's Avowed Socialism," *Washington Times* (May 3, 1996): A21; *Human Events* (March 5, 2001): 8; Chavez and Gray, *Betrayal*, 15, 19–21, cited above.

66. Ibid.

67. Ibid (*Sun* and *Times*)

68. U.S. Bureau of Labor Statistics and Bureau of National Affairs.

69. Bureau of National Affairs, *Constr. Labor Rep.* Vol. 46, No. 2311 (January 2001): 1440; Seymour Martin Lipset and Ivan Katchanvoski, "The Future Of Private Sector Unions in the U.S.," *Journal of Labor Research* Vol. 22, No. 2, Part I (Spring 2001): 229; A. J. Thieblot, "The Fall and Future of Unionism in Construction," *Journal of Labor Research* Vol. 22, No. 2 (Spring 2001): 287–288; Chavez and Gray, *Betrayal*, 15, 96.

70. "Labor's Loot," *Wall Street Journal* (September 11, 2001): A-26; Taylor E. Dark, III, "Labor and the Democratic Party," *Journal of Labor Research*, George Mason University (Fall 2000).

71. Reed Larson, "Government-Granted Coercive Power: How Big Labor Blocks the Freedom Agenda," an address at Hillsdale College (September 15, 1999).

72. *National Right to Work Newsletter* (May 2004): 5.

73. BNA's *Construction Labor Report* (February 2, 2005).

74. Ibid., cover jacket and Chapter 1, 26.

75. This chapter, Chavez and Gray, *Betrayal*, 17, 92.

76. See James Taranto, "What Makes a President Great," ranking Carter "below average" in 30th place among his peers. (*Wall Street Journal*, June 10, 2004) op. ed.

77. David Denholm, "Why Unions Are Still Powerful," *Government Union Review* (December 2003): 39–51.

78. Ibid., Chavez and Gray, *Betrayal*, 96.

79. Bureau of National Affairs, *Daily Labor Report* (January 22, 2004) AA-1; "The Union Label," *Wall Street Journal* (October 2 2003): edit.; Charles Baird, "Government Sector Unionism," *Government Union Review*, Public Service Research Fnd'n. (May 2002): 25–34; Chavez and Gray, *Betrayal*, 96.

80. Gary Andres, "Creeping Disunion," *Washington Times* (November 20, 2003): op. ed. P. A-23.

81. Leo Troy, *The New Unionism in the New Society* (Virginia: George Mason University Press, 1994), 1–17, 134–135, 157–158; Dan Seligman, "Driving the AFL-CIO Crazy," *Forbes* (November 1, 1999); Lipset and Katchanvoski, note above: 229–230; Charles W. Baird, *Freedom and American Labor Relations Law*, note above, 161 of Part Two.

82. Karl Marx and Frederick Engels, *Manifesto of the Communist Party* (Part II on Proletarians and Communists, 1848): 5; Socialist Party Platform of 1928. See also "The Non-Taxpaying Class," *Wall Street Journal* (November 20, 2002); Kiplinger Letter (November 8, 2002). Walter Williams, "The Legitimate Role of Government in a Free Society," *Imprimis*, Hillsdale College, Vol. 29, No. 8 (August 2001); Tony Snow, "American Journal and the Constitution," *Imprimis*, Hillsdale College, Vol. 30, No. 12 (December 2001).

83. Ibid., below, Baird on "Gov't Sector Unionism."

84. Charles Baird, "Government Sector Unionism," *Gov't Union Review*, Pub. Serv. Res. Fnd'n, Vienna, VA, Vol. 20, No. 2: 25–28; Leo Troy, note directly below, Chapter III.

85. Ibid., Chavez and Gray, *Betrayal*, this chapter.

86. Ibid., Troy, 2 (*The New Unionism*).

87. "Al Gore's Labor Pains," *Wall Street Journal* (March 16, 2000).

88. See Chapter 50, 2nd paragraph et seq.

89. *McCulloch and Maryland Chamber of Commerce v. Glendening*, 347 Maryland 272. See also Appellant McCulloch-Maryland Chamber of Commerce's legal brief to the Court of Appeals in this case, drafted by the author and my law firm.

90. *Contractor* (February 1971): 1.

91. Steve Chapman, "Losing the Fight Against Big Government," *Baltimore Sun* (September 30, 2003): edit.

92. Charles Haar, "The PTA, the NEA and Education," *Gov't Union Rev.* (December 2002): 18; "NEA Plays Democratic Role," *Baltimore Sun* (July 24, 2004): 2B.

93. Chavez and Gray, *Betrayal*, 109–138.

94. William McGurn, "Yes, There Is a Voucher," *Wall Street Journal* (February 2, 2004): op ed.; Milton and Rose Friedman, "The Voucher Challenge," *The School Choice Advocate* (January 2004): 1–3; Linda Chavez, note. above in this chapter; Robert Enlow, *Grading Vouchers: Ranking America's School Choice Programs* (Friedman Foundation, May 2004).

95. Compare David Horowitz, "Pro-Monopoly Laws Gag Dissenting Teachers," *National Right to Work Newsletter* (September 2003): 6; "The Probers and the NEA," *Wall Street Journal* (March 14, 2004): editorial page.

96. See letter from Congressman Tom DeLay, House Majority Leader (October 8, 2004).

97. "Witness Protection for Teachers," *Wall Street Journal* (November 24, 2003): A-14; "NEA Audited for Political Spending," *Baltimore Sun* (November 26, 2003); see also "Teacher Liberation," *Wall Street Journal* (January 27, 2004): editorial page.

98. William McGurn, "Are the Democrats Teachers' Pets?" *Wall Street Journal* (August 2, 2001): editorial page; "NEA: Lawbreaker," *Washington Times* (April 25, 2002): editorial page; "A Lesson This Labor Day," *Washington Times* (September 2, 2002): editorial page; *Washington Times* (November 14, 2002).

99. "The NEA's Dubious Expenditures," *Washington Times* (September 10, 2003): edit.; "The Probers and the NEA," *Washington Times* (March 31, 2004): edit.

100. "Insiders Report," Concerned Teachers Against Forced Unionism (Fall 2004): 6.

101. Leo Troy, "Twilight for Organized Labor," *Journal of Labor Res.*, George Mason University, Vol. 22, No. 2 (Spring 2001): 257.

102. See Ruth Wisse, "John Kerry U," *Wall Street Journal* (October 25, 2004): editorial page. Exposed the paucity of the political diversity at the University of California, Harvard, Cornell, Dartmouth, Yale, and Brown, where over 90 percent of the faculty members contributed their dollars to the "John Kerry for President Campaign" in 2004.

103. *Merit Shop Contractor* (November 1977).

104. Linda Chavez, "Union-Made Post-September 11 Power Grab," *Human Events* (March 22, 2004): 5; Chavez and Gray, *Betrayal*, 101-102.

105. Prologue; A. Samuel Cook, "Labor Union Foxes Guarding Police And Fire Hen Houses," Public Serv. Res. Council, Vienna, VA (1998) and Maryland Business for Responsive Gov't, Baltimore, MD (1999); "Teamsters Anti-Corruption Chief Resigns, Accuses Union of Obstruction," Bureau of National Affairs, *Daily Labor Report* (May 3, 2004): 1.

106. "The Teamsters Promise," *Wall Street Journal* (September 30, 2003): editorial page.

107. *United States v. International Brotherhood of Teamsters, et al.*, 725 F. Supp. 162, 169 (SD NY, 1989), aff'd 905 F.2d 610 (2nd Cir. 1990).

108. Ibid.

109. Ibid.; "More Power for Union Bosses," *National Right to Work Comm. Newsletter* (May and June 2002); Clark and Powers, "Constitutional and Practical Pitfalls," *Journal of Labor Research*, George Mason University (Fall 2003): 621; David Denholm, "Organized Labor's Special Agenda," Public Serv. Res. Council (October 2000).

110. See "Union Bosses Browbeat Friends into Taking Unpopular Positions in 2004 Elections," *National Right to Work Newsletter* (November–December 2004).

111. See Chapter 18.

112. AFL-CIO Publication #42, 10.

113. Contact the Public Service Research Foundation in Vienna, Virginia, for further information on this subject.

114. Compare Chavez and Gray, *Betrayal* (Chapter 1 entitled "For Sale: The Democratic Party, the American Worker and the United States Government").

115. James Bennett and James Taylor, "Labor Unions: Victims of Their Political Success?" *Journal of Labor Research*, Vol. 22, No. 2, Part 2 (Spring 2001): 270–271; Walter Olson, *The Excuse Factory: How Employment Law Is Paralyzing the American Workplace* (New York: Kessler Books, Free Press, 1997).

116. See *John Trimmer's ABC*.

117. Robert Pollock, "A Socialist Third Way," *Wall Street Journal* (June 17, 1998).

118. Tip O'Neill, *Man of the House* (New York: Random House, 1987), epilogue.

119. *John Trimmer's ABC*.

120. See Chapter 1.

121. Florence Calvert Thorne, *Samuel Gompers—American Statesman* (New York: Philosophical Library, 1957): 53; Chapters 1 and 9.

122. Ibid., 120, 122.

123. Ibid., 53, 106.

124. Ibid., 91.

125. Ibid., 40 and Chapter 1.

126. Ibid., 122.

127. Ibid., 122.

128. Robert Bork, *Coercing Virtue: The World-Wide Rule of Judges* (Washington, DC: AEI Press, 2003) and *The Tempting of America: Political Seduction of the Law* (New York: Free Press, 1990).

129. Compare Policy Memorandum, *The Federalist Society* (December 1, 2003).

130. "Danger from Foreign Legal Precedent," *Wall Street Journal* (March 25, 2004): edit. pg.

131. Mark Levin, *Men in Black, How the Supreme Court Is Destroying America* (Washington, DC: Regnery Publishing, 2005).

132. See Cokie Roberts, *Founding Mothers, The Women Who Raised Our Nation,* (New York: Harper Collins, 2004): xvi-xvii. "It's safe to say that most of the men who wrote the Declaration of Independence and the Constitution, fought the Revolution, and formed the government couldn't have done it without the women. And it was the women who … helped to keep the fragile new country from falling into partisan discord."

133. Ibid.

134. "The Constitution," Adams National Historic Site; see also *The Political Writings of John Adams*, edited by George W. Carey.

135. Ibid.

136. Ibid.

137. Quoted in David Jeremiah, *Before It's Too Late* (Thomas Nelson Publishers, 1982): 167.

138. A quotation from Paul Johnson's best-seller, *Modern Civilization*.

139. Ludwig von Mises, *Human Action* (Chicago: Contemporary Books): 282; see also William Simon, *A Time for Truth* (McGraw Hill Book Company, 1978).

140. *A World Apart*, Solzhenitsyn's commencement address at Harvard University on June 8, 1978 (Harper & Row): 9–10.

141. Ravi Batra, *The Great Depression of 1990* (New York: Simon & Schuster, 1985): 51.

142. Warren Carroll, "Cycles of Liberty: Will History Repeat?" *Freedom* magazine (October 1968).

143. See Professor Maurice McTigue's open letter of October 15, 2004, from the Mercatus Center at George Mason University in Virginia.

144. Mortimer Zuckerman, "Behind the Voters' Message," *U.S. News & World Report* (November 21, 1994): 100.

145. Publisher: Stroud and Hall, 2003; see also *Human Events* book review (November 17, 2003): 12.

146. Dick Morris, *The Hill* (August 13, 2003).

147. Bernard Goldberg, *Bias: A CBS Insider Exposes How the Media Distorts the News* (Washington, DC: Regnery Publishing, 2002), 13, and *Arrogance: Rescuing America From the Media Elite* (New Yotk: Warner Books, 2003). See also Prologue, note 2; "A Rather False Story," *Washington Times* (September 14, 2004): editorial page; Kohn, *Journalistic Fraud: How The New York Times Distorts the News* (October 2004); Bernard Goldberg, "60 Minutes of Fame," *Wall Street Journal* (September 17, 2004): editorial page; John Leo, "Self-Inflected Wounds," *U.S. News & World Report* (October 11, 2004): editorial page 64; Michael Hill, "Media Circus," *Baltimore Sun* (October 3, 2004).

148. *Forbes Book of Business Quotations*, edited by Ted Goodman (1997).

149. Compare Bill O'Reilly, *Who's Looking Out For You?* (New York: Broadway Books, 2003); Sean Hannity, *Let Freedom Ring* (New York: Regan Books, 2002) and *Deliver Us From Evil* (New York: Regan Books, 2004); Peggy Noonan, *A Heart, A Cross and a Flag* (New York: Free Press, 2003); and Dinesh D'Souza, *What's So Great About America* (Washington, DC: Regnery Publishing, 2002).

150. Donald Richberg, *Labor Union Monopoly* (Chicago: Regnery Company, 1957): vii.

151. Milton and Rose Friedman, *Free to Choose* (New York: Harcourt Brace Jovanovich, 1980): 37.

152. Ibid., 247.

153. See *Wall Street Journal* (July 8, 2004): editorial page.

Chapter 52

1. See graphs and citations in Chapter 51.

2. Over the past several years, the trend among employer associations has been to designate the chief elected officer "chairman of the board" and the top staff person "president and chief executive officer." The primary reason given by ABC for this change in

The Flag House and Star Spangled Banner Museum in Baltimore, Maryland. General Contractor Henry H. Lewis, LLC.

Country Music Hall of Fame, General Contractor JMR Group, Nashville, Tennessee, May 2003.

City of Murphy Municipal Complex in Murphy, Texas. Designed by AGUIRRECorporation.

500MW Co-Gen Power Plant in Georgia. General Contractor, BE&K, Inc., Birmingham, Alabama.

Fluor built this ExxonMobil low sulfur mogas project.

A design-build project that involved a pier and dolphin structure for the U.S. Navy on San Nicolas Island, southwest of Los Angeles. Prime Contractor: Nova Group, Inc., Napa, California.

San Fernando Cathedral Restoration, San Antonio, Texas. SpawGlass Contractors, Inc.

Oklahoma State Capitol Dome, Oklahoma City, Oklahoma. Capital Dome Builders, a Joint Venture Manhattan Construction Company & Flintco, Inc.

The future Schermerhorn Symphony Center which will open in 2006 as home to the Nashville Symphony. Ground was broken in December 2003, and construction continues. General Contractor JMR Group, Inc.

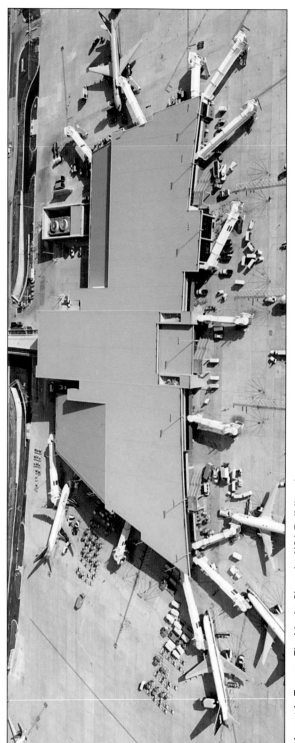

Airport in Tampa, Florida, by Skanska USA Building, Inc.

title effective January 1, 2001, was that the "chairman" or "chairperson"—a practicing contractor elected by the board of directors—donates his or her services for one or two years and sets policies and goals (with the board of directors) while the "president" is the senior staff professional appointed and paid by the board of directors as the "chief executive officer" who implements these policies and administers the daily operations of the Association.

3. Currently these vice-presidents are Kathie Berry (Finance and Administration), Bill Spencer (Governmental Affairs), Mary Schroer (Information Technology), Gail Raimon (Public Affairs), Bob Piper (Workforce Development), Joseph Rossmann (Insurance) and Timothy Welsh (Member Services).

4. For a more comprehensive summary of ABC's recent accomplishments, see "2001: The Beginning of a New Era," *ABC Today* Supplement (February 2002).

6. "Forced-Unionism Abuses Exposed," *National Right to Work Comm. Newsletter* (September, 2003): 2.

7. *John Trimmer's ABC.*

8. See Lauren Pinch, "Renovating the Pentagon," *Construction Executive* (September 2004): 13–18; see also Chapters 15 and 17.

9. Lauren Pinch, "World War Memorial Evokes Emotion, before and after Completion," *Construction Executive* (September 2004): 20–21.

11. Mark Murray, "On the Ropes," *National Journal* (March 8, 2003): 726; A. J. Thieblot, "Technology and Labor Relations in the Construction Trades," infra, this chapter.

12. *Engineering News-Record* (October 27, 1977): 20; see also Herbert R. Northrup, "Double Breasted Operations and the Decline of Construction Unionism," *Journal of Labor Research*, Vol. 16, No. 3 (Summer 1995): 380-381.

13. Armand J. Thieblot, Jr., "An Analysis of Multiskilled Labor Strategies in Construction," Construction Industry Institute 137-1, Research Summary (April 1998): v, 1.

14. See Chapter 48.

15. A.J. Thieblot, Jr., "The Fall and Future of Unionism in Construction," *Journal of Labor Research*, George Mason University, Vol. 22, No. 2 (Spring 2001): 296, 303; see also *Contractor* (April 1972): 16–17; *Merit Shop Contractor* (July 1978): 23; A. J. Thieblot Jr., "An Analysis of Multiskilled Labor Strategies in Construction," Construction Industry Institute, Research Summary 137-1 (April 1993): v, 1; and his "Technology and Labor Relations in the Construction Industry," *Journal of Labor Research*, George Mason University, Vol. 23, No. 4 (Fall 2003); Chapter 12 of this book.

16. Ibid., Thieblot's Fall of Unions, 291.

17. *Engineering News-Record* (March 4, 2002): 14; "Carpenters Quit AFL-CIO," *Engineering News-Record* (April 9, 2001): 10.

18. "McCarron Stresses Bipartisan Approach," Bureau of National Affairs, *Construction Labor Report*, Vol. 48, No. 2381 (June 19, 2002): 463; Donald Lambro, "Change of Heart for Labor's Affection?" *Washington Times* (March 11, 2002): editorial page; "Sweeney Orders BCTD to Drop Carpenters," Bureau of National Affairs, *Constr. Labor Rep.* (August 6, 2003): 775.

19. See Chapter 50.

20. Bureau of National Affairs, *Construction Labor Report* Vol. 48, No. 2380 (June 12, 2002): 436 and Vol. 48, No. 2379 (June 5, 2002): 413.

21. Robert Novak, "Labor's Clinton Problem," 2002 Creators Syndicate, TownHall.com Columnists (May 29, 2002): 1; *Washington Post* (May 30, 2002): editorial page; see also Chapter 50.

22. Ibid., Lambro, *Washington Times*; *Wall Street Journal* (February 19, 2002); see also *Washington Times* (February 26, 2002); Bureau of National Affairs, *Construction Labor Report* Vol. 48, No. 2378 (May 29, 2002): 390.

23. "AFL-CIO Unveils Expanded Political Program," Bureau of National Affairs, *Daily Labor Rep.* (December 6, 2001): C-1.

24. Peter Cockshaw, "The Union Sector's Challenges," *Cockshaw's Construction Labor News* (September 2002): 3.

25. David Kusnet, "Troubled, the Labor Movement Must Face Real Human Needs," *Baltimore Sun* (June 2, 2002): 10E.

26. Bureau of National Affairs, *Daily Labor Report* (January 14, 2003):. C-1.

27. *Construction Executive* (November 2003): 9.

28. Bureau of National Affairs, *Construction Labor Report* (December 10, 2003): 1339–1340; see also *Engineering News-Record* (June 28, 2004): 10.

29. Ibid., (January 22, 2003): 1384.

30. Ibid., (March 17, 2004):. 94.

31. AFL-CIO, *The AFL-CIO Changing For The Future*, Int'l Ass'n of Firefighters (Jan. 3, 2005).

32. Ibid.

33. Stefan Gleason, "Dance with Who Brung You to the Party," *Washington Times* (October 30, 2002): editorial page.

34. Ibid., Leo Troy; Stefan Gleason, "Confrontation, Not Concession," *Washington Times* (November 14, 2002): editorial page; *National Right to Work Newsletter* (October 2002): 8.

35. "Open Shop Flexes Politically," *Engineering News-Record* (March 11, 2002): 11; see also "Free Enterprise Majority," *ABC Today* (November 2002): 1.

36. See Chapter 50.

37. "The Beginning of a New Era," *ABC Today* (February 2002): 1; "Clinton's Anti-Business Legacy," *ABC Today* (February 2001): 9.

38. Labor Law Journal, Commerce Clearing House (2004).

39. The Kiplinger Letter (January 23, 2004) 4.

40. See Chapter 50.

41. *ABC Today* (2002).

42. A. J. Thieblot, "Technology and Labor Relations in the Construction Trades," *Journal of Labor Res.*, George Mason University, Vol. 23, No. 4 (Fall 2002): 569, 571.

43. See also "Career Guide To [Construction] Industries," Department of Labor, Bureau of Labor Statistics (August 2, 2002): 10: "These estimates are calculated with data collected from employers in all industry divisions in metropolitan and non-metropolitan areas in every State and the District of Columbia: Construction Occupations. First-Line Supervisors/Managers of Construction Trades Workers; Boilermakers; Brickmasons and Blockmasons; Stonemasons; Carpenters; Carpet, Floor and Tile Installers and Finishers; Tile and Marble Setters; Cement Masons and Concrete Finishers; Terrazzo Workers and Finishers; Construction and Building Inspectors; Construction Laborers; Paving, Surfacing, and Tamping Equipment Operators; Pile-Driver Operators; Operating Engineers and Other Construction Equipment Operators; Drywall and Ceiling Tile Installers; Tapers; Electricians; Glaziers; Insulation Workers; Painters and Paperhangers; Pipelayers; Plumbers, Pipefitters and Steamfitters; Plasterers and Stucco Masons; Reinforcing Iron and Rebar Workers; Roofers; Sheet Metal Workers; Structural Iron and Metal Workers; Elevator Installers and Repairers; Fence Erectors; Hazardous Materials Removal Workers; Highway Maintenance Workers; Septic Tank Servicers and Sewer Pipe Cleaners; Segmental Pavers; Derrick Operators; Rotary Drill Operators; Service Unit Operators, Oil and Gas; Earth Drillers; Explosives Workers; Ordnance Handling Experts and Blasters; Rock Splitters, Quarry; Roof Bolters; and Helpers in many of these job classifications."
44. See Chapter 3.
45. See Chapter 4.
46. Florence Thorne, *Samuel Gompers—American Statesman* (New York: Philosophical Library, 1957): 97. See also Gompers "voluntarism" creed quotations in Chapters 1, 4, and 9.
47. "World Construction Leaders," *Engineering News-Record* (November 2003): 64.
48. Ibid.
49. See "From Tadpole to Construction Rex," ABC National Directory (2000): 18.
50. Ibid., "Carole Bionda: ABC's 2004 Leader," ABC's *Construction Executive* (January 2004): 10–15.
51. Ibid.
52. See Chapter 15.
53. *Merit Shop Contractor* (January 1976): 13.
54. See Chapter 6.

INDEX